# GLOBAL ECONOM

# GLOBAL ECONOMIC HISTORY

*Edited by Tirthankar Roy and Giorgio Riello*

BLOOMSBURY ACADEMIC

LONDON • NEW YORK • OXFORD • NEW DELHI • SYDNEY

BLOOMSBURY ACADEMIC
Bloomsbury Publishing Plc
50 Bedford Square, London, WC1B 3DP, UK
1385 Broadway, New York, NY 10018, USA

BLOOMSBURY, BLOOMSBURY ACADEMIC and the Diana logo are trademarks
of Bloomsbury Publishing Plc

First published in Great Britain 2019

Cover design by Rawshock Design
Cover image: Passengers crowd the subway at People's square underground station
on January 7, 2009 in Shanghai, China. (© Lucas Schifres/Getty Images)

A catalogue record for this book is available from the British Library.

A catalog record for this book is available from the Library of Congress.

ISBN: HB: 978-1-4725-8842-5
PB: 978-1-4725-8843-2
ePDF: 978-1-4725-8844-9
eBook: 978-1-4725-8845-6

Typeset by Deanta Global Publishing Services, Chennai, India
Printed and bound in Great Britain

To find out more about our authors and books visit www.bloomsbury.com
and sign up for our newsletters.

*This book is dedicated to Patrick O'Brien without whom the field of global economic history would not exist.*

# CONTENTS

Contents

# LIST OF TABLES

# LIST OF FIGURES

# CONTRIBUTORS

**Gareth Austin** is Professor of Economic History at Cambridge University.

**Maxine Berg** is Professor in the History Department of the University of Warwick.

**Trevor Burnard** is a professor of American History and Head of School in the School of Historical and Philosophical Studies at the University of Melbourne.

**Youssef Cassis** is Professor of Economic History at the European University Institute in Florence.

**Karel Davids** is Professor of Economic and Social History at the Vrije Universiteit Amsterdam.

**Jack A. Goldstone** is Virginia E. and John T. Hazel, Jr. Professor of Public Policy at George Mason University.

**Regina Grafe** is Professor of Early Modern History at the European University Institute in Florence.

**Bernd-Stefan Grewe** is Professor of History Didactics and Public History at the University of Tübingen.

**Bishnupriya Gupta** is Professor of Economics at the University of Warwick.

**Karolina Hutková** is Postdoctoral Fellow at the London School of Economics.

**Alejandra Irigoin** is Associate Professor in Economic History at the London School of Economics.

**J. Thomas Lindblad** retired from his position as Professor at Leiden University.

**Debin Ma** is Associate Professor in Economic History at the London School of Economics.

**John R. McNeill** is Professor of History at Georgetown University.

**Patrick O'Brien** is Professor of Global Economic History at the London School of Economics.

**Prasannan Parthasarathi** is Professor of History at Boston College.

**Kenneth Pomeranz** is Professor of History at the University of Chicago.

**Maarten Prak** is Professor of Social and Economic History at the University of Utrecht.

**Giorgio Riello** is Professor of Global History at the University of Warwick.

# Contributors

**Tirthankar Roy** is Professor of Economic History at the London School of Economics.

**Alessandro Stanziani** is a professor of Global History at the École des Hautes Études en Sciences Sociales in Paris.

**Kaoru Sugihara** is Senior Professor at the National Graduate Institute for Policy Studies in Tokyo.

**Peer Vries** is Honorary Fellow at the International Institute of Social History in Amsterdam and was previously Professor of Global Economic History at the University of Vienna.

# PREFACE

Why does a global perspective matter in the study of economic history? Which are the problems addressed by a new field called Global Economic History? Which are its debates and methodologies? As this book shows, there is a variety of answers to these questions. Because there are a range of answers, instead of imposing our own definition of the field, we (the editors) collected a set of illustrations on why a global perspective matters to economic history.

This book is timely as the field of economic history has seen major developments in the past two decades. Since 2001, the 'divergence debate' led to path-breaking new research on Asia, Africa, and Latin America, and pushed the boundaries of comparative economic history much further back from the nineteenth century. It also fostered the adoption of new methodologies such as the use of reciprocal comparison and the engagement with new interpretive works on comparative politics and society. We see the positive effects of more detailed research on key questions on regions and localities where we once knew little, though the negative effects of a new fragmentation and retreat to internalist disputes are now equally evident.

We invited nineteen contributions exploring specific aspects of the question: Why a global perspective matters. The chapters included in this volume are thus an attempt to contextualize the economic history of the world by providing entries and insights into large and small debates. We do not aim for completeness of information, or treatment, or chronologies. But we hope that by breaking up the big question into manageable parts, the book will show why global interconnections and comparisons matter to economic history, and why they matter so much that economic history and global history need serious and continuous dialogue. Let us call that dialogue global economic history.

For students of global economic history, the chapters will show why certain economic concepts, problems, and keywords make a difference; why historians and economists debate them; and why they may disagree about them. Ultimately this book should help to make sense of the shape of today's economic world by studying its past transformations, mutations, crises, and not infrequent disasters.

We are grateful for the financial support provided by the London School of Economics and the University of Warwick. Our thanks also to the anonymous referees who provided much-needed advice at different stages of this project and to Dr Helen Clifford who has helped us with the editing of this volume. Professors Kent Deng (London School of Economics), Pat Hudson (Cardiff University), and Masayuki Tanimoto (Tokyo University) acted as commentators at the workshop held at the London School of Economics in May 2016 when papers were originally discussed. Their comments have been particularly valuable in shaping the editors' introduction. We also thank several colleagues and the anonymous referees for their comments and feedback.

## Preface

This book draws on the pioneering discussions carried out by groups of scholars gathered together at the London School of Economics and the University of Warwick over the past twenty years. The Leverhulme-funded Global Economic History Network active between 2003 and 2007 and coordinated by Patrick O'Brien was instrumental in shaping the discipline of global economic history by focusing on issues of divergence and the global integration of markets through commodity exchange.

Giorgio Riello and Tirthankar Roy
July 2018

# INTRODUCTION: GLOBAL ECONOMIC HISTORY, 1500–2000

*Giorgio Riello and Tirthankar Roy*

## Economic history and its global turn

Economic history utilizes historical and quantitative methods to study economic change over long chronologies. Trajectories of economic change vary across space because of local conditions such as the quality of natural resources, local institutions, and a number of other factors including labour markets, and the availability of labour, capital, and technologies. Economic change is shaped also by patterns of interaction that occur between localities, nations, and wider world regions. Global economic history operates in these realms of variations and interactions between world regions sometimes adopting the world as a unit of analysis.

From the nineteenth century, when the Western Europe industrialized, inequality between nations started rising rapidly, and world trade also grew at an unprecedented speed. Intellectuals, economists, social reformers, and philosophers became interested in understanding the history of economic change at a global level. One might say that Karl Marx and Max Weber were both global economic historians in this sense. Despite their legacies, however, economic history emerged as a discipline in the first half of the twentieth century and evolved over the following fifty years with a more national than international orientation. In publications of economic historians, the most common mode of analysis was that undertaken at the level of the nation state.

From the 1980s at least, if not earlier, environmental history and the world systems school made a credible case for changing the unit of analysis from the nation to the world. Varieties of Marxist historiography continued to produce books that were global in scope. The movement that later became known as new institutional economic history started as a reinterpretation of economic change in Europe, but its arguments had obvious implications for the rest of the world. Imperial history was, by its nature, global in scope. These were neither exceptional, nor outside the mainstream. However, their impact on the shape of the subject of economic history was, until the 1990s, limited to the 'schools' that they propagated. By and large, these works were more at home on Europe and America than the rest of the world.

From about 2000, history has witnessed an emphatic global turn, in the wake of the recent phase of globalization and rapid spread of connections between parts of the world.[1] Economic history too began to be transformed by a somewhat distinct set of factors. The availability of cross-country historical income data, the popularity of institutionalism in top economics departments of North America, and new developments in the theory of growth rekindled interest in an old and half-forgotten question: Why do some countries grow rich and others remain poor? In the 2000s, historians criticized institutionalism. The exchange that followed became known as the divergence debate. In the last twenty years, the divergence debate has formed the stem of the economic history field. The economic emergence of countries like China or India – long regarded as textbook examples of 'why nations stay poor' – questioned Eurocentric world history.

Interest in the inequality question was only one part of the global turn within economic history. The global turn added to economic history other insights, questions, and methods. There was a renewed sensitivity to time, especially long chronologies stretching back over millennia. New modes of enquiry emerged. One example is 'historical economics', which tests causal models of economic growth with long-range data sets. Connections across oceans, geographies, and frontiers began to be investigated with an interest in economic change. There was a return of the 'grand narrative', which post-modernism had briefly expelled from history. Social and cultural historians reassessed the relevance of economic change to their own fields of study.

In the backdrop of what one might call the 'rediscovery of the world' by economic historians, we may be closer than ever before to a definition of global economic history as a field. This book is an attempt to contribute to that programme, and to think about global economic history as a field.


## Global economic history: Debates and questions

This book divides up the subject of global economic history into three types of enquiries. The three-part structure of the book reflects the three types of stories that global economic history often tells. The first part of the book entitled 'Divergence in Global History' considers the economic trajectories of different world areas and reflects on recent debates about 'wealth and poverty' in relation to economic divergence and inequality. Part II, entitled 'The Emergence of a World Economy', explores the ways in which global economic connectivity changed especially in the nineteenth and twentieth centuries and reflects on the integration and emergence of a world economy. Part III, 'Regional Perspectives to Global Economic Change', considers a set of macro-regions and reflects comparatively on simultaneous processes of change in various economies. These chapters also show that the study of the integration between a regional economy and the world economy can offer a useful perspective on the region itself; in other words, global history can be a method to study regions. The three-part structure was adopted because the discussions and debates in global economic history form overlapping but distinct clusters; the three parts try to retain that distinction while the book as a whole represents a shared agenda between these.

Let us follow these themes a little further. The 'Great Divergence' as conceptualized by Kenneth Pomeranz in a book with the eponymous title is a natural starting point for an enterprise of this kind.[2] Divergence in experience of economic growth and development has provoked new investigation of why the world became richer and specifically why certain parts of the world industrialized first. This well-known debate also encompasses a discussion of the origins of world inequality. Explaining why the world became more unequal in modern times requires comparisons of regions regarding their endowments and attributes, an enterprise that has attracted a great deal of fresh work in the last twenty years, drawn economists and historians together into conversations, and supplied a strong motive for studying global history.[3]

The question of the origins of inequality and its connection with the origins of 'modern economic growth' has been around for a long time, but recent scholarship has made it less Eurocentric and truly worldwide in reach. While there is no agreement as to the causes and chronologies of divergence, debate has developed to consider a series of old and new topics, ranging from institutions to the role of science and technology and the impact of transnational consumption in a comparative global perspective. It has made economic history less insular and more concerned to address the origin and emergence of inequality. The latter topic has generated a great deal of debate not just in relation to global inequality (between nations especially across the classic divides between developed, developing, and the underdeveloped world) but also within nations as exemplified by Piketty's successful work.[4]

The second part of the book considers at least two other reasons why global economic history matters. First, whether or not it explains inequality and growth, interconnectedness is important in itself. The slave trade transformed human societies; population growth and the adoption of fossil fuels changed the relationship between societies and the natural environment, and trade produced world empires. The world has been interconnected for centuries through trade, migration, investment, state formation, environmental change, and knowledge exchange. These cross-border connections are growing so rapidly in the present times that now more than ever we need to understand, with tools of history, why they grow and what they mean. A further set of contributions in Part II of the book focuses on integrative processes, led directly or indirectly by the prospect of material gain.

The study of connections links up with two defining features of what Chris Bayly called 'the birth of the modern world': transcontinental empires and economic globalization.[5] Connections also include possibilities of sharing knowledge and information between sets of people who were not in the same network – 'weak ties' that are sometimes created as externalities of economic exchange like trade and, of course, migration of capital and labour.[6] Yet, connectivity cannot fully explain the functioning of a global economy. Economic historians have to address also 'integration', referring to the process by which regions are drawn into pre-existing networks of economic exchanges – for example, the way the Slave Coast of West Africa was integrated in the Atlantic trade of the seventeenth and eighteenth centuries, or how the textile-producing areas of India were integrated in a similar set of worldwide exchanges that shaped the future of these regions and the future shape of the world economy at the same time.

Connections can be real, or inferred, for example, through the simultaneous emergence of similar institutions in locations that are not necessarily connected in an obvious way. As considered in the final part of this book, the causal link between these processes, which we can call parallel developments, remains open to interpretation.[7]

From the seventeenth century to the nineteenth century, most manual labour took place under bondage and other legal restrictions imposed on the labourers. These restraints began to weaken, to be replaced by a different set of laws, and were also resisted more easily from the end of the nineteenth century. Was this change – which one contributor in the book calls 'the great transformation of labour' – an outcome of ideology, politics, or markets, or a strange set of interrelated but worldwide processes that we do not yet understand?[8]

At the end of the day, regions have their own distinctive features, nation states play a powerful role on the economies that they manage, and sources needed for historical research are typically produced by states. In short, a global perspective must be consistent with region- and nation-bound histories. If the first two broad themes considered in this book – the comparative history of growth and connectedness – place the 'world' at the centre of the discourse with regions forming building blocks in arguments about economic change in the whole world, there is a counterpart theme, where the 'local' or the regional forms the centre, and the world economy acts as a building block in, for example, arguments about why India, China, or West Africa evolved in the way they did. Global history should not ignore differing perspectives, especially those deriving from 'area studies' such as the Americas; Africa; East, South, and Southeast Asia; and, perhaps more surprisingly, Europe. Nor should global history submerge the distinctness of regions that derives from geography, culture, or forms of governance. And the third set of chapters in this book pursues a region-focused agenda.

The studies in this volume often use the term 'world economy' and refer to 'global approaches'.[9] Yet, they do so for different reasons and in different ways. At the same time, historians of all kinds use these terms with increasing frequency. Why? In the next section, we consider how the global turn in economic history came into being, and what was distinctive about it from earlier versions of global economic history.

## World economy: The history of a concept

A search for the term 'world economy' in Google Books turns up a surprisingly large number of books with 'world economy' in their titles, many published in the last twenty years. Apparently, half of them deal with history. These books do not use the term in similar contexts or for similar purposes. The significance of world economy in historical scholarship has tended to shift. These shifts may give global economic history the image of a literature without a centre. Although, as a taught subject, global history is becoming popular, the impression of disjointedness does not help teachers of the subject. A quick tour through the history of the term, however, shows that there is a deeper unity of purpose and method in the literature than it may at first seem.

Historians who have studied societies that have access to the seaboard have long been aware of the significance of cross-border economic exchanges in shaping the course of history. The sea as a distinct economic geography, one that helps long-distance transactions and gives these a certain shape, is a concept akin to the world economy, and perhaps the most profound and convincing way in which interconnections on a big scale have been considered by historians. Fernand Braudel's classic *The Mediterranean and the Mediterranean World in the Age of Philip II* started a new historiography by placing the sea at the centre of a chronological narrative, thus looking at history through the lens of comparisons, connections, and diffusion.[10] Braudel inspired a generation of European historians who globalized the programme. Starting from the premise that the growth of European overseas trade in the sixteenth century was a landmark in world history, they explored intercontinental trade, long-distance merchant networks, and 'the rise of merchant empires'.[11] In the 1970s and the 1980s, K. N. Chaudhuri, Kenneth McPherson, Ashin Das Gupta, Om Prakash, Sinnapah Arasaratnam, and Anthony Reid, to name only a few of the leading contributors, pursued the same agenda from the perspective of regions bordering the Indian Ocean.[12] Since the 1990s, the Atlantic has also been placed within a similar 'global' perspective, particularly in relation to merchant networks and communities.[13]

The idea that connected geographical spaces could be arranged in a hierarchy became popular in the 1970s, through the influential work of Immanuel Wallerstein. World economy, or the capitalist world economy, became a *world system* in Wallerstein's work. European overseas trade was a pivotal force because it allowed for European hegemony to be established over world trade and politics. The world systems school that followed Wallerstein's early work joined the idea of connections with the economic concepts of division of labour, surplus appropriation, and redistribution of gains from trade, to suggest why Europe gained substantially from the sixteenth-century world system and came to dominate the world.[14]

The world systems approach has been criticized for being Eurocentric. In 1998, Andre Gunder Frank's *ReOrient* made a passionate attack on the concept of European hegemony, suggesting that the world economy was dominated by China for much longer than we think, an idea that resonated well with China's domination of world trade in the early twenty-first century.[15] In the 2000s, further revisions of the concept of world systems were offered, significantly, differentiating world system history from the theory of the 'modern' world system.[16] The scholarship on world systems borrowed from other contemporary strands in global history. The building blocks in both were the international division of labour and the transfer of surpluses through the system mostly from the periphery to the metropole. The significance of specialization and the meaning of surplus are subject to dispute, but the combined emphasis on market exchange on a world scale popularized the ideas that capitalism became global since the 1600s and that capitalism was formed from a series of interconnected market exchanges, an altogether more flexible and easy definition of capitalism than the orthodox Marxist one based on patterns of ownership of assets. Global history should be able to tell us why goods acquired more value as they moved from market to market. And by doing so, we should know not only how capitalism worked in practice, but also why it became global, even if that story does not necessarily enlighten us about the origin of growth and inequality.[17]

The notion that modern economic growth and inequality had developed from forms of interconnectedness that emerged since the seventeenth century faced a strong challenge from institutional economic history in the 1980s. Douglass North and others argued that the modern West discovered secure property rights and contractual law in the seventeenth and eighteenth centuries, thanks to attributes and processes that were uniquely European.[18] If such was the origin of modern economic growth, one would need to explain the origin of world inequality by showing that the non-West had remained trapped in an economic world that was unsafe and unpredictable. Early institutional economic history implicitly assumed that this was the case, and in the process overlooked huge diversity within the non-Western experience. Nor did early institutional economic history offer interconnectedness a definite role in the explanatory framework.

In the 2000s, two more influential ideas were proposed, again linking growth, inequality, and interconnectedness. One of these was Kenneth Pomeranz's proposition that European expansion changed the course of human history by giving Europeans access to plentiful land and minerals.[19] Pomeranz said little about technologies, trade, or colonialism as such, but the proposition did suggest that settler colonies in the New World were better off because they were more resource-rich than many Old World societies.[20] The fact that the settlers appropriated these resources by means of labour servitude and land-grab institutions does however give a very different spin on the intrinsic superiority of European institutions.

Pomeranz's book gave the flood of publications on global history to occur since 2000 a collective name, the 'divergence debate'. Some of these works were statistical, and measured when and to what extent regions forged ahead or fell behind.[21] Some were comparative. Others were done in the narrative history mode, and focused on regions.[22] Some deconstructed Europe and distinguished between 'great' and 'little' divergences.[23] Others re-established the importance of trade in the economic emergence of Western Europe.[24] Explaining world inequality was the common purpose, though not all of their authors felt equally driven by that purpose.

A further idea has re-established the importance of trade both for the early modern and the post-1800 periods. The work by Flynn and Giráldez, and von Glahn, argued for the creation of a world economy in the seventeenth century emanating from the discovery and trade by Europeans of vast reserves of silver in the Americas.[25] Although this does not change the structure or chronologies for Wallersteinian interpretations, it provides for a renewed emphasis on trade, in particular trade in those Asian commodities exchanged for silver. Thus the so-called silverization of the Chinese economy (as a 'silver sink') lubricated world trade in Southeast Asian spices and manufactured commodities such as Chinese silks and porcelain, Indian cottons, and later on tea from China and India and other produce such as sugar, coffee, and cocoa.[26] Jan de Vries has concluded that while both the Indian and Atlantic Oceans were key to the reshaping and growth of European economies, it was the Atlantic trade (of slaves, cotton, and goods manufactured in Europe) that was quantitatively more important for the creation of a world economy.[27]

Notwithstanding the now substantial literature on world trade in the early modern period, suggesting the creation both of an integrated world economy and of a process of 'globalization' through trade, supporters of 'hard globalization' argue that a world economy characterized by both commodity and factor-price convergence emerged only in the nineteenth century.[28] Kevin O'Rourke and Jeffery Williamson in *Globalization and History: The Evolution of a Nineteenth-Century Atlantic Economy* (2001) showed that increasing trade led to specialization and factor-price convergence on both sides of the Atlantic in the late-1800s.[29] Trade was not only an engine of economic growth but also aided transmission of growth until a 'backlash' began to form in the interwar period. In a follow-up work *Trade and Poverty* (2001), Williamson extended the framework, controversially, to explain why the Third World did not experience convergence in the same way, mainly because it suffered de-industrialization as a result of overconcentration upon the export of primary products.[30]

Global interconnectedness, as said before, mattered in itself, as a feature of modern capitalism, as a factor that shaped regional histories, and as a process that progressively added value to capital, labour, and goods, or destroyed values that they commanded in earlier centuries. One did not have to bat for a theory of the Great Divergence to study the world economy. Several new publications were written from this perspective, usually studying a commodity, a time, or a region, and in each case contributing to the narrative of globalization and the emergence of global capitalism.[31] At the minimum, this was a Wallersteinian programme, minus the baggage of surplus extraction and appropriation. Some of these works, however, went further and made use of globalization to rethink the rise of the West. Several chapters in the two-volume *Cambridge History of Capitalism* shared the same aim: to explain global capitalism. But contributors were free to smuggle in afterthoughts about the Great Divergence.[32]

A large part of the pre-2000 scholarship discussed in this section interacted with economic history occasionally; the dialogue became more serious and systematic since then. Their overlap deserves a closer look.

## The tools of global economic history

A field should be defined by the questions that it seeks to answer. From before the divergence debate took off, historians have reflected on the methodology of global history. In an influential article published in 1997, Sanjay Subrahmanyam suggested ways to think about connectedness in early modern history.[33] In a now classic statement, Patrick O'Brien wrote an overview of the field and asked why a craft such as history that in antiquity frequently engaged with the world, lost interest in the global since the nineteenth century, and why the global was now making a return. O'Brien contrasted two ways of doing global history, comparisons and connections, and predicted that the rationale of the field in the future would depend on the global historians' ability to construct 'new cosmopolitan meta-narratives' that challenged the 'teleological chronicles designed to reinforce people's very own set of values enshrined in canonical Christian, Muslim, Hindu, Confucian and other sacred texts'.[34]

Varied methodologies have been adopted by the different social sciences in their approach to global (economic) history. Much work has been done on connections, establishing in particular what we might mean by connections and connectivity. But while economists and economic historians preferred to concentrate on integration (possibly an outcome of connections), cultural historians explored concepts such as entanglements, *histoire croisée*, and hybridity among the many.[35] Many historians took O'Brien's call for challenging 'teleological chronicles' seriously, though many shied away from adopting metanarratives (even if cosmopolitan in nature). Global history in the past decade has definitively moved towards more 'micro' approaches. This is the case of 'micro-global histories' that raise the issue of agency, of perspective, and of the relationship between the global and the local.[36] At the same time, however, global history has experienced a continuing success of 'macro' approaches, though these have been less interested than in the past in large-scale metanarrative and more concerned with long-term analysis of change. This is the case of' 'Big' and 'Deep' histories stretching back to the pre-historical period if not the Big Bang.[37] They provide sweeping narratives that pull together comparisons, connections, and 'holistic' views of history. They also connect history to the sciences including biology, ecology, and psychology.[38]

Global economic history is, among the different types of global history today, the one that has followed O'Brien's view most closely. Whether macro or micro, global economic history has created sustained debate and discussion around major themes and problems, some of which are of long-standing importance for the discipline of economic history. Many of these debates are referred to in contributions in this book. We wish here to highlight three of them as paradigmatic of how the discipline of global economic history has evolved over the past two decades: first, that of technological change and its relationship with industrialization; second, large-scale projects on inputs, outputs, prices, and wages that have addressed debates such as industrialization and divergence; and finally an emerging concern about the 'age of Anthropocene' as an attempt to bridge economic and environmental histories.

The Industrial Revolution, and more widely the process of industrialization in Europe and elsewhere, remains a key topic in economic history. Several chapters in this book comment on the ways in which the debate about the origin of modern economic growth, of industry, and of a drastic transformation of economies worldwide has been reshaped by the divergence debate. Although science, technology, and knowledge did not play an important role in Pomeranz's original formulation, the work of several economic historians, most prominently Joel Mokyr, has provided new ideas about the role played by technology in economic history.[39] The literature is now vast but one might say that it has attempted to bridge the gap between historians of science and technology on the one hand and economic historians on the other. The focus on useful and reliable knowledge, for instance, has allowed researchers to consider the ways in which both knowledge and information – and their transfer in time and space – were key to both product and process innovation.

Technological innovation is at the centre of one set of explanations concerning the capital-intensive path undertaken by the European (and British in particular) economies in the eighteenth century. Based on a large-scale project comparing silver wages across Eurasia from ancient times to the nineteenth century, Robert Allen explains the recourse to mechanical devices in eighteenth-century British manufacturing as a response to high wages.[40] This explanation is based on a large collective quantitative undertaking measuring not just wages in different cities in Europe and Asia but also prices and estimates of GDP.[41] This project extends analyses that until recently were confined to individual nations. This labour-intensive exercise of data mining, collection, and interpretation has produced an important knowledge base that is conscious of its biases, gaps, and limitations. It provides economic history with a 'global' data set that, as always, needs to be interpreted with care if we wish to make use of it in debates over economic divergence and differentials in living standards or simply in comparative work across cultures.

The projects on inputs, outputs, wages, and prices take GDP as a key measure and economic growth as the metre through which to evaluate economies over time and space. This approach has faced some criticism, on measurement as well as on conceptual grounds.[42] Similarly, recent scholarship on the 'age of Anthropocene' captures the rising criticism towards the toolkit used by economic historians. What is the meaning of GDP when it includes expenditure for armaments (leading to potential and often real destruction) and does not include the damage made to the environment? How do we deal with issues of inequality not just in wealth and income but also in access to education, basic resources such as water, or life expectancy?[43]

These three examples show how global economic history has been in recent years in a 'revisionist' mood. The enlargement of the chronological and especially the geographic spectrum has led to questioning the very foundations of the discipline. While new debates emerge and others evolve into larger and more ambitious enterprises, the toolkit and methodologies of economic history cannot remain unaltered.[44] Furthering that programme requires taking stock of the cosmopolitan narratives the field has produced in the last twenty years. This anthology takes a step in that direction. Others have done it before us. The distinctive feature of this project is its accent on joining economic history with everything that we know now matters to economic history, from politics, to resources, and to culture.[45]

## The structure of this book

This volume gathers together historians and economists who have, in their careers, tried to think big on one of the three dimensions of global economic history – comparisons, connections, and the interaction between the local and the global. The editors gave the contributors an open agenda. The contributors were free to define the questions and the debates that mattered. This people-oriented approach left some obvious gaps in the volume among which a lack of specific chapters dedicated to topics such as 'empire', 'gender', and 'North America'. These are important themes that are to be found across the book, gender being an important dimension in the discussion of labour and institutions; North America in chapters on silver and slavery, and elsewhere in the book.

Seven chapters in the first part of this book are dedicated to the re-examination of the divergence debate. Parthasarathi and Pomeranz present an overview of their positions on divergence and extend the original Sino-European comparison to include also South Asia and underline the ways in which the divergence debate has influenced both Chinese and Indian scholarship. Jack Goldstone continues this critical analysis of divergence by concentrating on the part played by the gathering and interpretation of data and the implication that this has on the chronologies of economic development of Europe and Asia.

Patrick O'Brien and Karel Davids consider respectively useful and reliable knowledge and technology as two of the key factors explaining differing trajectories of global economic change. Responding to a premise of the divergence debate that the world displayed more similarities than differences before the nineteenth century, O'Brien suggests that global historians should engage with a proposition that Europeanists put forward, that a distinct 'regime for the accumulation of useful and reliable knowledge' had emerged in early modern Europe as a result of an interdependent evolution of natural philosophy and institutions of learning. Davids, on the other hand, cautions against the tendency to emphasize sharp breaks or 'divergences' in technological change, and shows how innovations could build on local practices by arguing that big differences could emerge from small variations.

As the debate over divergence matured, new contexts and topics have been added to the discussion. The role of institutions and institutional change in sustaining modern or productivity-driven economic growth is well known to economic historians. Regina Grafe and Maarten Prak offer an analysis on institutional change compatible with 'the slow transition from early modern to modern intensive growth'. They consider changes in family systems, collectives, and the state, and offer a measured conclusion that cautions against drawing causal link between institutions and growth, and between institutional change and European exceptionalism. Trevor Burnard asks what the role of plantation economies was in the Great Divergence, a topic that has found less attention than expected by historians. And finally Maxine Berg, moving away from traditional concerns over production and the economy, connects divergence and global history to the history of consumption and debates over the standards of living.

The second part of this book explores the emergence of a world economy by concentrating on different aspects of what we might call economic globalization. In a joint contribution, the editors of this book charter the importance of trade in structuring global connections over the long period, showing its changing scale especially in the nineteenth and twentieth centuries. If trade is often acknowledged as central to the connectedness and integration of the world economy, John McNeill alerts us that due attention should be given also to the environment. Adopting a multidisciplinary perspective, McNeill argues that the creation of a world economy coincided with a new relationship between man and natural environment, what today is called the 'age of Anthropocene'.

Alessandro Stanziani continues this analysis by concentrating on labour and the mobility of labour as one of the key factors in the creation of global markets and the structuring of a world economy. He challenges established classifications that oppose free versus coerced labour. This line of enquiry is further developed by Kaoru Sugihara in a chapter dedicated to varieties of industrialization. Considering different Asian regions, Sugihara challenges the European industrial paradigm as the template for global economic growth. The final two chapters, by Bernd-Stefan Grewe and Youssef Cassis, consider respectively the role of commodities and finance in structuring global markets. Global commodity chains and global value chains, Grewe argues, provide unique methodological perspectives to the study of the world economy and challenge established notions of core and peripheries. A similar approach is adopted by Cassis who shows the importance of global cities in the shaping of financial transactions worldwide since the mid-nineteenth century.

The six chapters in the third and final part of this book shift our perspective from global connectedness to the contribution of specific world areas. They collectively raise the issue of how beneficial the 'lateral thinking' provided by a 'placed' perspective is to global economic history. They also challenge the idea of a 'natural' unit of analysis by showing how discretionary labels such as Africa, East Asia, South Asia, and even Europe are, and how they subsume a variety of experiences and trajectories of economic change. Gareth Austin considers sub-Saharan Africa and engages with colonial and post-colonial theories of economic development. Alejandra Irigoin's contribution observes how global economic history has concentrated on Eurasia at the expense of the role played by the Americas, especially in the production and trade of enormous quantities of silver that 'oiled' the world economy in the early modern period. Debin Ma shows how a shared culture characterized the economic trajectory of a diverse region defined as East Asia but observes also how modernization and industrialization were accompanied by conflict and warfare.

The acknowledgement of differentiation is also central to a chapter by Peer Vries on the European economy in the past five centuries. Far from constituting a monolithic model of economic development for the rest of the world to follow, Vries presents a continent characterized by deep-rooted economic inequality that has survived to the present. Bishnupriya Gupta and Tirthankar Roy address instead the topic of decline of the South Asian economy especially after 1800. They argue that its loss of status as an exporter of industrial goods should be seen in connection with the development of textile technologies in Europe, thus arguing for an entangled approach to economic history. Finally a chapter by J. Thomas Lindblad on the economy of Southeast Asia argues that we should appreciate both continuities and discontinuities when evaluating the economic trajectory of a world area and its constituting nation states and areas.

Together these chapters aim to be both thought-provoking and informative. They attempt to charter some of the debates that global economic history had developed in the past two decades. This field of enquiry is still novel, ambiguous in its contours and methodologies, and uncertain in its findings. While chartering the uncertain terrain of global economic history, it is our hope that this collection of contributions might provide inspiration for the field's future direction.

## Notes

1. See, for example, Sebastian Conrad (2016), *What Is Global History?* Princeton: Princeton University Press.

2. Kenneth Pomeranz (2000), *The Great Divergence: China, Europe and the Making of the Modern World Economy*. Princeton: Princeton University Press.

3. The literature on divergence is now vast. See the chapter by Pomeranz and Parthasarathi in this volume as well as Parthasarathi's critique of Pomeranz's work. P. Parthasarathi (2002), 'Review article: The Great Divergence', *Past and Present*, 176, 275–93. For an introduction to the debate, see the special issue of *Historically Speaking*, 12 (4), published in 2011 and dedicated to the divergence debate as well as two shorter books: R. B. Marks (2002), *The Origins of the Modern World: A Global and Ecological Narrative*. New York: Rowman & Littlefield Publishers; J. Goldstone (2008), *Why Europe? The Rise of the West in World History, 1500–1850*. New York: McGraw-Hill Higher Education; and J. W. Daly (2014), *Historians Debate the Rise of the West*. London: Routledge.

4. T. Piketty (2014), *Capital in the Twenty-First Century*. Cambridge, MA: Belknap Press. For a recent analysis of how Piketty's book has challenged the discipline of economic history, see P. Hudson and K. Tribe (eds) (2016), *The Contradictions of Capital in the Twenty-First Century: The Piketty Opportunity*. London: Agenda Publishing.

5. C. A. Bayly (2004), *The Birth of the Modern World, 1780–1914*. Oxford: Blackwell. See also S. Subrahmanyam (1997), 'Connected histories: Notes towards a reconfiguration of early modern Eurasia', *Modern Asian Studies*, 31 (3), 735–62; Idem (2004), *Explorations in Connected History: From the Tagus to the Ganges*. Delhi: Oxford University Press; Idem (2004), *Explorations in Connected History: Mughals and Franks*. Delhi: Oxford University Press.

6. On migration, a good book to begin with is Patrick Manning with Tiffany Trimmer (2013), *Migration in World History*, 2nd edn. New York: Routledge. On 'weak ties', Mark Granovetter (1983), 'The strength of weak ties: A network theory revisited', *Sociological Theory*, 1 (6), 201–33.

7. V. Lieberman (2003), *Strange Parallels: Southeast Asia in Global Context, c. 800–1830. Vol. 1. Integration on the Mainland*. Cambridge: Cambridge University Press; Idem (2009), *Strange Parallels: Southeast Asia in Global Context, c. 800–1830. Vol. 2. Mainland Mirrors: Europe, Japan, China, South Asia, and the Islands*. Cambridge: Cambridge University Press.

8. J. Lucassen (ed.) (2008), *Global Labour History: A State of the Art*. Bern and Oxford: Peter Lang. See also L. Lucassen (2016), 'Working together: New directions in global labour history', *Journal of Global History*, 11 (1), 66–87.

9. While there is a distinction between 'world history' (concentrating on large world areas and civilizations) and 'global history' (preferring instead the analysis of connections), we find this distinction not particularly useful when applied to economic history. See B. Mazlish (1998), 'Comparing global history to world history', *Journal of Interdisciplinary History*, 28 (3), 385–95.

10. F. Braudel (1996, 2nd edn), *The Mediterranean and the Mediterranean World in the Age of Philip II*. Berkeley: University of California Press.

11. N. Steensgaard (1973), *Carracks, Caravans and Companies: The Structural Crisis in the European-Asian Trade in the Early 17th Century*. Copenhagen: Studentlitteratur; and J. D. Tracy (ed.) (1990), *The Rise of Merchant Empires: Long-Distance Trade in the Early Modern World*. New York: Cambridge University Press.

12. For an overview of the literature, see P. Parthasarathi and G. Riello (2014), 'The Indian Ocean in the long eighteenth century', *Eighteenth-Century Studies*, 48 (1), 1–19.

13. See for instance, F. Trivellato (2012), *The Familiarity of Strangers: The Sephardic Diaspora, Livorno, and Cross-cultural Trade in the Early Modern Period*. New Haven: Yale University Press.

14. I. Wallerstein (1974–2011), *The Modern World-System*, vols. 1–4. Berkeley: University of California Press; New York: Academic Press.

15. A. Gunder Frank (1998), *ReOrient: Global Economy in the Asian Age*. Berkeley: University of California Press.

16. Robert A. Denemark and Barry K. Gills (2012), 'World-system history: Challenging Eurocentric knowledge', in Salvatore J. Barbones and Christopher Chase-Dunn (eds), *Routledge Handbook of World-Systems Analysis*. London and New York: Routledge, 163–71.

17. On the recent interest in the history of capitalism, see L. Neal and J. G. Williamson (2014), *The Cambridge History of Capitalism*, 2 vols. Cambridge: Cambridge University Pres; J. Kocka (2016), *Capitalism: A Short History*. Princeton and Oxford: Princeton University Press.

18. D. C. North (1981), *Structure and Change in Economic History*. New York: Norton; and D. C. North and R. P. Thomas (1973), *The Rise of the Western World: A New Economic History*. New York: Cambridge University Press.

19. Pomeranz (2000), *The Great Divergence*.

20. See Parthasarathi, 'Review article: The Great Divergence'; P. H. H. Vries (2001), 'Are coal and colonies really crucial? Kenneth Pomeranz and the Great Divergence', *Journal of World History*, 12 (2), 408–46.

21. See for instance, S. Broadberry and B. Gupta (2009), 'Lancashire, India and shifting competitive advantage in cotton textiles, 1700–1850: The neglected role of factor prices', *Economic History Review*, 62 (2), 279–305.

22. J.-L. Rosenthal and R. Bin Wong (2011), *Before and beyond Divergence: The Politics of Economic Change in China and Europe*. Cambridge, MA: Harvard University Press; P. Parthasarathi (2011), *Why Europe Grew Rich and Asia Did Not: Global Economic Divergence, 1600–1850*. Cambridge: Cambridge University Press; P. Vries, *Escaping Poverty: The Origins of Modern Economic Growth*. Vienna: V&R Unipress; Idem (2015), *State, Economy and the Great Divergence*. London: Bloomsbury; R. Studer (2015), *The Great Divergence Reconsidered: Europe, India, and the Rise to Global Economic Power*. Cambridge: Cambridge University Press.

23. J. L van Zanden (2009), *The Long Road to the Industrial Revolution: The European Economy in a Global Perspective, 1000–1800*. Leiden: Brill; K. Davids (2012), *Religion, Technology, and the Great and Little Divergences: China and Europe Compared, c. 700–1800*. Boston and Leiden: Brill.

24. J. E. Inikori (2002), *Africans and the Industrial Revolution in England: A Study in International Trade and Economic Development*. Cambridge: Cambridge University Press.

25. D. O. Flynn and A. Giráldez (eds) (1997), *Metals and Monies in an Emerging Global Economy*. Aldershot: Ashgate; D. O. Flynn, A. Giráldez and R. von Glahn (eds) (2003), *Global Connections and Monetary History, 1470–1800*. Aldershot: Ashgate.

26. M. Berg (2004), 'In pursuit of luxury: Global history and British consumer goods in the eighteenth century', *Past & Present*, 182, 85–142.

27. J. de Vries (2010), 'The limits of globalisation in the early modern world', *Economic History Review*, 63 (1), 710–33.

28. This position is criticized by P. de Zwart (2016), 'Globalization in the early modern era: New evidence from the Dutch-Asiatic trade, c. 1600–1800', *Journal of Economic History*, 76 (2), 520–58 who shows price convergence for some key commodities traded by the Dutch East India Company from Asia to Europe in the course of the eighteenth century.

29. K. H. O'Rourke and J. G. Williamson (2001), *Globalization and History: The Evolution of a Nineteenth-Century Atlantic Economy*. Cambridge, MA: MIT Press.

30. J. G. Williamson (2011), *Trade and Poverty: When the Third World Fell Behind*. Cambridge, MA and London: MIT Press.

31. G. Riello and T. Roy (eds) (2009), *How India Clothed the World: The World of South Asian Textiles, 1500–1850*. Leiden: Brill; Roy, *India in the World Economy*; G. Riello (2013), *Cotton: The Fabric That Made the Modern World*. Cambridge: Cambridge University Press; J. Osterhammel (2014), *The Transformation of the World: A Global History of the Nineteenth Century*. Princeton: Princeton University Press; S. Beckert (2014), *Empire of Cotton: A Global History*. New York: Alfred A. Knopf; M. Berg, et al. (eds) (2015), *Goods from the East, 1600–1800. Trading Eurasia*. Basingstoke: Palgrave. On Atlantic commerce, see R. Findlay and K. H. O'Rourke (2007), *Power and Plenty: Trade, War, and the World Economy in the Second Millennium*. Princeton: Princeton University Press.

32. S. Broadberry and K. O'Rourke (eds) (2010), *The Cambridge Economic History of Modern Europe*. Cambridge: Cambridge University Press.

33. Subrahmanyam, 'Connected histories'.

34. P. K. O'Brien (2006), 'Historical traditions and modern imperatives for the restoration of global history', *Journal of Global History*, 1 (1), 3–39.

35. C. Dean and D. Leibsohn (2003), 'Hybridity and its discontents: Considering visual culture in colonial Spanish America', *Colonial Latin American Review*, 12 (1), 5–35. Gould, 'Entangled histories, entangled worlds'; C. Douki and P. Minard (2007), special issue on 'Histoire globale, histoires connectées', *Revue d'Histoire Moderne et Contemporaine*, 54 (4 bis).

36. J. Brewer (2010), 'Microhistory and the history of everyday life', *Cultural and Social History*, 7 (1), 87–109, and F. Trivellato (2011), 'Is there a future for Italian microhistory in the age of global history?' *California Italian Studies*, 2 (1), 1–24.

37. D. Christian (2005), *Maps of Time: An Introduction to Big History*. Berkeley: California of California Press; C. Stokes Brown (2007), *Big History: From the Big Bang to the Present*. New York: New Press; A. Shryock and D. L. Smail (2012), *Deep History: The Architecture of Past and Present*. Berkeley: University of California Press.

38. On the methodological approaches to global history, see M. Berg (2013), *Writing the History of the Global: Challenges for the Twenty-First Century*. Oxford: Oxford University Press and British Academy; Conrad, *What is Global History?*.

39. J. Mokyr (1990), *The Lever of Riches: Technological Creativity and Economic Progress*. Oxford: Oxford University Press; Idem (2002), *The Gifts of Athena: Historical Origins of the Knowledge Economy*. Princeton: Princeton University Press; Idem (2017), *A Culture of Growth: The Origins of the Modern Economy*. Princeton: Princeton University Press.

40. See among the many, R. C. Allen (2001), 'The great divergence in European wages and prices from the middle ages to the First World War', *Explorations in Economic History*, 38, 411–47; R. C. Allen, J.-P. Bassino, D. Ma, C. Moll-Murata and J. L. van Zanden (2011), 'Wages, prices,

and living standards in China, Japan, and Europe, 1738–1925: in comparison with Europe, Japan, and India', *Economic History Review*, 64 (supplement S1), 8–38; R. C. Allen (2015), 'The high wage economy and the industrial revolution: A restatement', *Economic History Review*, 68 (1), 1–22.

41. Datafiles of Historical Prices and Wages: http://www.iisg.nl/hpw/data.php (accessed 15 April 2017). J. Bolt and J. L. van Zanden (2014). 'The Maddison Project: Collaborative research on historical national accounts', *Economic History Review*, 67 (3), 627–51.

42. P. K. O'Brien and K. Deng (2015), 'Locating a chronology for the great divergence: A critical survey of published data deployed for the measurement of nominal wages for Ming and Qing China', *Economic History Working Paper Series*, 213 (The London School of Economics and Political Science); Idem (2016), 'China's GDP per capita from the Han Dynasty to communist times', *Economic History Working Paper Series*, 229 (The London School of Economics and Political Science).

43. P. Hudson (2017), 'Economic History for the Anthropocene: Reflections on the Scope and Normative Nature of Measurements Currently used by Economists and Historians', Paper prepared for the conference "Rethinking Economic History in the Anthropocene", Boston College, 24–25 March 2017.

44. Boldizzoni and Hudson, 'Introduction'.

45. J. Baten (2016), *A History of the Global Economy: 1500 to the Present*. Cambridge: Cambridge University Press.

# PART I
## DIVERGENCE IN GLOBAL HISTORY

# CHAPTER 1
# THE GREAT DIVERGENCE DEBATE
*Prasannan Parthasarathi and Kenneth Pomeranz*

The question why parts of Europe surged ahead economically from the eighteenth century while much of Asia, Africa, and even the Americas (with the exception of the United States), lagged behind has been debated for more than a century. Great thinkers of the nineteenth and twentieth centuries, ranging from Karl Marx to Max Weber, have addressed this large and important issue, as have a number of leading historians in our own times, including Eric Jones, Douglass North, and David Landes. The 'Great Divergence' as it has come to be known is, therefore, a very old question, but the contours of the present debate were shaped by the publication of Kenneth Pomeranz's book of that title in 2000. While Pomeranz's book focused on China – and more precisely on the Yangzi Delta – it ranged into Japan, India, and Southeast Asia, but the entry of India into the debate more fully would await the publication of Prasannan Parthasarathi's *Why Europe Grew Rich and Asia Did Not* in 2011.

The predilections of the two authors and the different perspectives that China and India bring to the problem have meant that the explanations for divergence differ in the two books. While Pomeranz has a far greater environmental history focus, Parthasarathi devotes more time to questions of technology and the state. Nevertheless, both works devote considerable attention to the economic conditions and institutions in the run-up to divergence. All of the above have been subject to great debate.

In the last fifteen years one can distinguish several overlapping strands of contention and not surprisingly the debate has focused far more on China than on India. In part, this is due to the earlier publication of the Pomeranz work and the long dominance of China–Europe comparisons. Such a debate is also not surprising given the greater number of historians of China than India in the United States and Europe, which has kept the discussion alive and thriving. There has also been more interest in the question of divergence in China and Japan than in India. While economic history is currently a flourishing field in East Asia, in South Asia it has gone into sharp decline since its heyday in the 1960s and 1970s.

This chapter will focus on comparisons between the advanced regions of Europe, China, and India, which have been the areas upon which much of the literature on the question has concentrated. It takes up four sets of issues. The first has to do with methodological questions connected to how we explain divergence. The chapter contrasts the structural approach that characterized an older and conventional approach to the problem with a conjunctural approach that has been introduced in the writings of Pomeranz and Parthasarathi. The structural approach rests upon enduring differences between Europe and Asia, which have been challenged in recent writings. Several important contemporary writings explain divergence as a consequence of conjunctures which led to different paths of economic development in different parts of the world.

The recent arguments for comparability between the advanced regions of Europe, China, and India in the period before divergence at the end of the eighteenth century bring us to the second set of issues considered in this chapter. The Pomeranz and Parthasarathi claims for broad similarity have inspired debates and challenges to their position. The chapter reviews these debates as well as the closely related question of the timing of divergence and concludes that there is still striking disagreement on both these issues as well as on issues related to institutions and scientific knowledge and the role that these played in divergence. This brings the chapter to the third set of issues, which has to do with the problem of how to settle upon the 'truth' in economic history. The writing of history is an interpretive act, and it relies upon the reading of complex and fragmentary evidence. Theoretical biases and questions of value shape how one analyses the evidence. In such a situation is it possible to settle upon an explanation of divergence which receives wide assent? Finally, this chapter considers the ways in which a global and comparative debate, such as that on divergence, has been received and has influenced scholarship in India and China.

## Structure versus conjuncture

The classic writings of Karl Marx and Max Weber argued that the exceptional path of European economic development emerged from exceptional European conditions. Europe, in other words, was fundamentally different in some way from the advanced regions of China and India, and it was this difference that gave Europeans an economic edge and put the continent on a different trajectory. Such explanations are often called 'structural' in that they argue for deep social, political, economic, or cultural differences.

For Marx this difference was capitalism. Europe gave rise to a new economic order which rested on private property and wage labour, which was dynamic, innovative, and ever changing. Capitalism began in the countryside, where it transformed the agrarian order, but it soon spread to the world of manufacturing and its restlessness and dynamism produced the Industrial Revolution in the eighteenth century. However, capitalism as a new mode of production had longer origins, which means that the process of divergence began long before the eighteenth century, a point that the chapter will return to. By contrast, China and India remained static and unchanging, trapped in an Asiatic mode of production. As Marx wrote of India: 'Indian society has no history at all, at least no known history. What we call its history, is but the history of successive intruders who founded their empires on the passive basis of that unresisting and unchanging society.'[1]

While Max Weber took a more cultural tack to understanding capitalism, he shared with Marx an approach which emphasized deep-seated differences between Europe, in particular its Protestant areas, and China and India. For Weber, the critical development in Europe was the affinity between the tenets of Protestantism and a spirit of capitalism, which transformed the approach to economic activity, making it more systematic, calculating, and rational. These changes laid the foundation for the economic transformation of Western Europe from the eighteenth century, but in Weber's view predated that era. Weber argued that the affinity between religious thinking, economic rationality, and a transformative impulse found in Europe, had no counterpart in China or India. Therefore, it was Europe which led the way to a new economic order.[2]

Twentieth-century historians approached the problem of divergence in much the same way as Marx and Weber as they sought to identify what made Europe different from even the economically advanced and thriving regions of Asia. Douglass North and Robert Paul Thomas assert the superiority of the political and economic institutions that emerged in Western Europe during the seventeenth century. For Eric Jones, Europe possessed exceptional environmental conditions and a competitive state system which was not found in Asia. David Landes attributed Europe's success to an advantageous culture. And Joel Mokyr has pinpointed the scientific culture of Europe as exceptional and critical to its economic path.[3]

Parthasarathi and Pomeranz, on the other hand, built on arguments for rough comparability and similarities between the advanced regions of Europe, China, and India and they argued that there is little evidence for European exceptionalism. In their view, divergence was the product of conjunctures between needs and opportunities.[4]

Pomeranz's book emphasized ecological relief which was provided by coal and overseas trade. Pomeranz argued that Britain and the Yangzi Delta – the most advanced regions in Europe and China, respectively – both faced pressures on the land, which provided the food, fuel, and fibre that were needed for survival. Britain was able to overcome its land constraint by substituting wood with coal and by importing foodstuffs and raw cotton from the Americas. In effect, Britain vastly expanded its land area. The Yangzi Delta, by contrast, did not have such ecological windfalls. While China as a whole had plentiful deposits of coal, these were difficult to access because they were located in Northwest China, at some distance from the Yangzi region, which was in the south. The external trade of the Yangzi Delta did not provide the same ecological benefits. (Pomeranz recognizes that a stream of new machines cannot be explained simply by the availability of energy to fuel them, and he has no quarrel with scholars who emphasize the contributions of European science as long as they do not claim that this is a complete explanation.)

For Parthasarathi, ecological relief in the form of coal is certainly part of the explanation and is especially critical for understanding the process of industrial development from the 1820s – 'the railway age', to use the language of an earlier generation – although he notes that the advanced regions of India did not face the ecological pressure of shortages of wood which were found in Britain and the Lower Yangzi. Parthasarathi argues that ecological relief must itself be placed in a larger political and economic context in which state policies were important in shaping the coal revolution as well as technological change more broadly. His approach to science questions its centrality for European economic change in the late eighteenth and early nineteenth centuries. He also challenges the differentiation of science along geographical boundaries and views it as a global enterprise, arguing that in early modern scientific endeavours, India was an important contributor and participant. (Pomeranz also points to non-European contributions to some emerging sciences, such as forestry, but emphasizes this point less than Parthasarathi.)

For Parthasarathi, ecological relief marks a later stage in the onset of divergence and becomes of central importance in the nineteenth century. In the late eighteenth century, however, a dramatic reshaping of global trade in manufactures began to take shape as Britain displaced India as the chief supplier of cotton textiles to the consumers of the world. The key to this shift was technical and organizational innovations, which, Parthasarathi argues, emerged as a response to the competitive pressures placed on Britain, as well as other regions, from Indian cotton manufacturers, combined with state policies of protection. The textile producers of India and China were not subject to these pressures and thus did not face any need to innovate, which pressed upon Western Europe (as well as other parts of the world such as the Ottoman Empire).

As can be seen from these very brief summaries, both *The Great Divergence* and *Why Europe Grew Rich and Asia Did Not* built upon long-standing lines of thinking in British economic history. Pomeranz, for instance, stands on the shoulders of E. A. Wrigley, while Parthasarathi's point of departure includes classic works such as *The Cotton Trade and Industrial Lancashire* by A. P. Wadsworth and Julia de Lacy Mann. However, both scholars take these lines and develop them in new ways as a consequence of the global and comparative frameworks which they develop.[5]

## How much divergence, and when?

The conjunctural approaches of Pomeranz and Parthasarathi rest on arguments on the comparability of living standards, as indicated by various measures (each of them imperfect on its own), well into the eighteenth century. The divergence between Europe and Asia, or more accurately, the advanced regions in those two continents, was in their view a recent phenomenon, dating back to the late eighteenth or early nineteenth century. This position has been hotly contested, and there have been lively debates on the timing and location of divergence as measured by living standards, wages, and so on. These discussions are critically important, but can quickly lead one into a thicket of fine details. Although this is not the place to wade into those details, some sense of the broad contours of the disagreements is essential.

### China

One of Pomeranz's key claims, and confirmed by others, is the strength of the agricultural order in the Lower Yangzi. Robert Allen's reconstructions suggest that, as late as 1820, productivity per labour day in Yangzi Delta farming was 90 per cent of England's and that annual net income for a Delta tenant family (including a wife who made cloth part time, as was quite common) was slightly higher than for a similar English household. Another study puts labour productivity in Yangzi Delta farming c. 1800 as equivalent to that of Holland, which was 94 per cent of English levels.[6] Meanwhile, land productivity was far higher in the Delta than anywhere in the world except parts of Japan and was roughly nine times that of England. Thus, the Delta's total factor productivity was also extremely high and much higher than in various European countries which did industrialize in the nineteenth century. Agricultural labour productivity in Germany, for instance, was about 50 per cent of English levels, and its land productivity was also lower.[7] These and other points challenge 'agrarian fundamentalism', which argues that readiness for industrialization must be a direct function of agricultural efficiency as this makes it possible to free labour and capital for other uses and keeps food prices, and thus wages, low.[8] Agrarian fundamentalism has also been challenged from the Indian perspective, which we will turn to shortly.

A different version of agrarian fundamentalism had also long held sway in Chinese historiography. *The Great Divergence* has generally been well received in China, but there have also been criticisms, many of which have come from scholars convinced that peasant production (as opposed to large farms largely worked by wage labour) cannot have yielded either the surpluses above subsistence or the flexibility necessary to begin sustained per capita growth. This position had long been a given of mainland Chinese historiography, but it cannot be reconciled with labour and total factor productivity figures like those cited earlier, or the impressive twentieth-century economic performances of Japan, Taiwan, and, more recently, Eastern China – all places featuring small-scale farming by families with strong ownership or usufruct rights.

*The Great Divergence*'s larger claim that living standards and per capita incomes were comparable between Europe and China, and between England and the Yangzi Delta has required some revision. Originally, Pomeranz suggested that this was probably still true in 1800, and almost certainly around 1750. The 1750 claim remains plausible, though disputed; the former less so. A recent paper by Stephen Broadberry, Hanhui Guan, and David Daokui Li suggests a divergence in per capita GDP at a date closer to 1700 than 1750. However, this may be a sign that the range of disagreement is narrowing, since Guan and Li had previously claimed that a huge gap already existed in the fifteenth century.[9] Still more recently, Patrick O'Brien and Kent Deng have questioned the feasibility of any GDP or wage comparisons and argued for a focus on consumption, beginning with grain; even here, numbers vary, but they suggest comparability between the Lower Yangzi and England at least until 1750, and maybe beyond.[10]

## India

The debate on standards of living in India is more spatially scattered and at an earlier stage than that on China, for which there are more contributions and which are centred regionally on the Yangzi. The debate may be said to have been launched in 1998 with the publication of Parthasarathi's 'Rethinking wages and competitiveness', which has been challenged by several economic historians but most forcefully in several writings by Broadberry and Gupta.[11]

Broadberry and Gupta have recently summarized their position: Silver wages were substantially lower in India than in England in the seventeenth and eighteenth centuries, which is a point that Parthasarathi made in 1998 and which he argued was the reason for the competitiveness of Indian cotton cloth exports. While Parthasarathi argued that grain wages (a rough measure of the real wage) were comparable in the mid-eighteenth century, Broadberry and Gupta conclude that while they were roughly comparable in the seventeenth century – the Indian figure ranged between 80 and 95 per cent of the English – in the eighteenth century there was a sharp decline and the Indian grain wage was only 33–40 per cent of the English.[12]

Broadberry and Gupta's findings for the eighteenth century have been disputed by not only Parthasarathi but also Sashi Sivramkrishna. The latter has drawn upon the voluminous material contained in Francis Buchanan's account of a journey through South India, mainly Mysore, in the early nineteenth century and has showed a rough comparability of real wages based on a broader basket of consumption goods. Parthasarathi has questioned Broadberry and Gupta's conclusions as they exclude well-known estimates for earnings of outcaste labourers in agriculture, which would have represented a wage floor in South India, and derive earnings for skilled weavers that fall in the same range as those of these degraded labourers.[13]

There are other problems with the Broadberry and Gupta figures: There is no allowance for non-monetary perquisites, which Parthasarathi included in his original calculations; we have no information on how many days per week labourers worked in England and India and the extent of unemployment and underemployment (impressionistic evidence suggests that these labour market conditions favoured workers in India, where there were widespread labour shortages before the nineteenth century). Finally, Broadberry and Gupta do not provide any explanation for their findings, especially given what we know about structures of contracts and the bargaining power of labourers in the two places, which again favoured labourers in India.

Obviously the jury is still out on the question of the comparability of wages and standards of living in India and Europe. However, it is unlikely that quantitative evidence alone will be sufficient to resolve this issue, and broader conditions of work and the position of labourers in the political and economic orders must also be considered. In his original contribution, Parthasarathi brought a broad perspective to the problem, but his critics have tended to be narrowly quantitative. To continue this discussion requires a deep immersion in regional economies and deep familiarity with local conditions and prices. Broadberry and Gupta range widely over the Indian subcontinent as a whole and mix together prices from diverse areas, which can be seen in their most recent summing up of the debate. Finally, the low-estimate earnings that Broadberry and Gupta provide for the eighteenth century raise the question of how labourers survived in that period. We know from other sources such as anthropometric data that South Indian workers, for instance, shrank in size over the course of the nineteenth century. The second half of the nineteenth century was also an extraordinary period of famine in several regions of India. Why did these things not happen in the eighteenth century?[14]

## Discussion

Even if we accept the most pessimistic estimates, which suggest that rough parity in standards of living had vanished by 1750 (in the case of China) or as early as 1700 (for India), this represents a major revision of previously dominant views. Angus Maddison's widely cited per capita GNP estimates, for instance, suggested that both China and India fell behind Europe centuries earlier,[15] and many other scholars claimed that a fundamental divergence had occurred by 1500, year 1000, or even earlier.[16] Fixing a precise date is probably not crucial or even possible. Nevertheless, some rough dating is needed because that will determine the universe of plausible explanations for divergence. For, if there was rough parity between the advanced regions of Eurasia in 1700, then some traditional favourite explanations would be eliminated. For instance, if the cause of divergence was, as David Landes claims, a difference between freedom and despotism that went back to ancient Greece, and gave Europeans a much greater propensity to innovate, it would be very hard to explain why East and South Asia remained so close to Europe more than 2,000 years after Pericles.[17]

Even if economic divergence came later than we once thought, a significant gap appears to have emerged by 1800 between the advanced regions of Europe and China, and perhaps between those of Europe and India as well. Certainly, the gap grew rapidly thereafter. This was largely because non-agricultural workers were generally much more productive than farmers in Europe and England than in China and Japan, and the number of non-farmers was growing at both ends of Eurasia.[18] Again, this suggests that explanations are best sought outside agriculture, and without relying on black-and-white contrasts between entire societies. This still leaves us far from consensus, but it narrows the range of possibilities considerably.

Divergence seems to have come earlier to unskilled wages, both urban and rural, than to living standards. Though the data are poor, especially on the Chinese side, they indicate that by the mid-eighteenth century – when other indicators still suggest close comparability between Jiangnan and advanced regions of Europe – Delta wages had already fallen far behind, resembling those of Milan or even Warsaw more than those of London.[19]

At first these two points seem irreconcilable; but a gap in real wages can be quite consistent with comparable living standards. Wage labourers were probably under 10 per cent of rural adults even in the highly commercialized Lower Yangzi, where one might expect widespread landlessness. By contrast, nearly half of the working population in England and Holland in c. 1700 probably relied on wage earning.[20] Because most tenants in the Delta had strong usufruct rights, they earned much more than unskilled labourers – roughly three times as much, according to the best estimates Pomeranz can put together (smallholders would have netted almost five times what a labourer earned).[21] Thus, a comparison of unskilled real wages is a comparison of the bottom of the income scale in Jiangnan with something close to the middle in Northwest Europe, reconciling significant wage differences with comparable average living standards.


## The role of institutions

Since politics as well as markets structured global trade flows, institutions are also of importance. And institutions, of course, also figure in other explanations of East–West divergence. Indeed, the variety of institutional differences that have been invoked by one scholar or another can seem endless: domestic political arrangements; property rights; contract enforcement; fiscal and financial systems; institutions for encouraging, suppressing, and/or protecting inventions; organizations for trading and building empires overseas; and so on. These debates have been a good deal broader than those about the extent and timing of divergence, and participants have often talked past each other – not only because they have been working on many different subtopics, but also because it has not always been clear how to move from describing differences to assessing their significance. We here highlight a few points that have become relatively well accepted.

Although East Asian property rights and contract enforcement differed from those taking shape in Northwest Europe, Pomeranz argues that they were adequate for the efficient product markets that Smithian growth requires (i.e. growth based on the expansion of the market and the extension of the division of labour).[22] When it comes to factor markets, the previous discussion of agriculture makes it hard to deny the effectiveness of Chinese (and Japanese) systems for allocating access to land. The evidence on capital markets is more mixed. It appears that capital in Japan and China was more expensive than in Europe, but the higher costs did not inhibit typical eighteenth-century kinds of economic activity such as handicraft production, commerce (including long-distance trade), agricultural improvement, or even early factories. East Asian manufacturing techniques tended to be less capital intensive than those in Europe, but not necessarily less efficient.[23]

The biggest differences related to capital markets were in the area of public finance. European states clearly had much more effective systems for raising immediately available funds by pledging future revenues. However, it is not clear that this mattered much to the overall economic growth in early modern times, due to three crucial conditions:

a) The overwhelming majority of European government spending was for warfare, and so was not very constructive in the short run, although long-run linkages were important.

b) China, and especially Japan, faced much lower and more episodic military costs; these could generally be met by temporary exactions which were not large or frequent enough to discourage wealth accumulation.

c) The technologies available did not require either very large-scale fixed investment that took many years to fully repay initial costs (as, for instance, railroads would in the nineteenth century) or really major public investments in physical and human capital (e.g. universal schooling), some of which also took a number of years to begin yielding a return.

In the nineteenth century, all of these conditions changed. Moreover, Europe after 1800 reaped large *delayed* rewards from the overseas colonization it had carried out earlier: an activity that had required large amounts of patient capital, and was tied in various ways to military/fiscal issues. But the relevant institutions here were not simply matters of 'secure property' or 'competitive markets': They represented a much messier, and often far from liberal, set of arrangements. Perhaps the most important point here, which seems to be fairly well established, is about discontinuity. Institutions that were functional (or dysfunctional) for an economy with one set of constraints and possibilities could be much less (or more) facilitative of growth under the very different conditions of a later period.

## The role of science

One of the most contentious areas in the divergence debate continues to be the contribution of science. Three positions may be identified in the literature. The first argues that science was not relevant, at least in the early stages of industrialization, and that it was artisanal knowledge that was important. Allen and Pomeranz are representative of this perspective.[24] The second argues that by the eighteenth century – if not even earlier – European science was critical and that what Europeans brought to the enterprise of production was in global terms a unique approach to knowledge and its application. Margaret Jacob, Joel Mokyr, and Patrick O'Brien may be seen as exemplars of this position.[25] A final position may be seen as a hybrid of the two aforementioned positions and is articulated by Parthasarathi. On the one hand, it argues that the application of knowledge to production was found outside Europe, in this case early modern India; that in important respects early modern science must be seen as transcending national or continental frames and emerged from contact; and finally, this approach agrees with Allen that in the early stages of industrialization artisanal knowledge was more important than scientific and that the creation of knowledge of the natural world often followed technical breakthroughs.[26]

The role that European science and knowledge systems played in divergence will continue to be debated for some time. However, it is striking that economic historians address these issues in radically different ways compared with historians of science. First, historians of science have moved away from an old emphasis on the laboratory or bench top as the main site of scientific activity to include field sciences such as botany, in which there was widespread cooperation across the world. With this shift in approach, historians of science have uncovered the contributions that scientific-minded individuals outside Europe made to the development of modern science. The label 'global science' would be a more accurate descriptions of many things that have been labelled as 'European science'. Second, historians of science have found it very difficult to connect scientific knowledge and technological change at the micro level and therefore have moved away from making blanket statements about the connection between the two. There are many instances well into the nineteenth century of major technological advances emerging in the workshop and the science that lay behind the new technology was understood only afterwards. The steam engine is the quintessential example. The scientific principles, what we know as thermodynamics, were fully worked out long after the steam engine had been put to work for many decades. Finally, the growing evidence of scientific interest in seventeenth- and eighteenth-century South Asia and political and economic interest in knowledge production for its usefulness mean that arguments for the exceptional nature of European science have to be rethought. In sum, the differing approaches of economic historians and historians of science will need to be reconciled if the debate is to advance.[27]

## Telling what's right

Both *The Great Divergence* and *Why Europe Grew Rich and Asia Did Not* drew upon generations of scholarship on the British Industrial Revolution and the industrialization of Europe more broadly. The Industrial Revolution is one of the most intensely debated events in the discipline of history. Its only rival may be the French Revolution, the other event which along with the Industrial Revolution gave rise to the modern world in Eric Hobsbawm's famous and enduring formulation of dual revolutions.[28]

*The Great Divergence* builds upon classic writings on coal and British industrialization. The energy approach may be traced back to the nineteenth century with works such as the *Coal Question* by William Stanley Jevons. In the 1930s, John Nef published a major two-volume study of the rise of the British coal industry. The most important recent exponent of the energy approach is Tony Wrigley, who, in 1988, brought coal back to the centre of the story of Britain's exceptional path of economic development. Pomeranz also draws upon the work of Eric Jones, who introduced the concept of 'ghost acres' in his classic study of divergence, *The European Miracle*, and in a more indirect way on Eric Williams' study of Caribbean slavery and English growth.

*Why Europe Grew Rich and Asia Did Not* picks up on other significant strands of writing on the British Industrial Revolution. The book's focus on cotton has a long lineage and may be traced back to nineteenth-century works such as Edward Baines' *History of the Cotton Manufacture in Great Britain*. In the twentieth century, cotton was central to numerous classic accounts – from that of Paul Mantoux's *The Industrial Revolution in the Eighteenth Century* to David Landes' *Unbound Prometheus* and Eric Hobsbawm's *Industry and Empire*. It was Hobsbawm who declared that 'whoever says industrial revolution says cotton'.[29] *Why Europe Grew Rich and Asia Did Not*'s periodization of British industrialization into stages, cotton followed by coal, is faithful to that offered by John Clapham.

As the overview of the debate on divergence has indicated, the lines of debate and disagreement are many. These revolve around the relative 'levels' of economic development in the advanced areas of Europe and Asia, the nature of the industrialization process, the contribution of institutions, and the contribution of science and knowledge to that process. How are we to judge between competing explanations and settle upon which one is right or true?

In the case of several of these issues, adjudicating between different positions rests on the interpretation of qualitative data.[30] The contribution of institutions to the process of economic development or the level of scientific knowledge is not amenable to quantification; thus, to some extent, the judgement of these factors is subjective and 'in the eye of the beholder'. The interpretation of these sorts of factors is made more difficult by the lack of research on them in the Asian context, and thus places limits on our historical knowledge. The historical scholarship is far thinner on science in the seventeenth and eighteenth centuries for India than for Europe, for example.

A focus on factors that can be quantified is not a solution to this dilemma. If only such factors, such as wages, incomes, and prices, are part of the analysis, important dimensions of social, cultural, economic, and political life, which play a significant role in economic development, could be excluded. Quantification does not eliminate the interpretive and subjective elements that are present in the case of qualitative evidence. Making sense of quantitative evidence is no less 'in the eye of the beholder'.

The creation of quantitative data rests upon hundreds, if not thousands, of judgements, each of which can introduce error into the final figures. This is the case today when economists construct national income and other figures of economic performance. However, these difficulties are compounded when dealing with historical data and are made worse the further back we go. Eric Hobsbawm, who was not averse to quantification but recognized the difficulties, put it well more than fifty years ago when he pointed to the complexities of calculating money wages for even British workers in the nineteenth century: 'We know next to nothing of what people actually earned. How much overtime or short time did they work? How often were they unemployed and for how long? Who knows?'[31] Converting these money wages into real wages introduces further pitfalls and is no easy task even in contemporary times. Hobsbawm writes: 'We know from modern experience how full of pitfalls cost-of-living indices can be even in our own time, when considerable efforts are made to collect statistics specially for their compilation.'[32]

Kent Deng and Patrick O'Brien have pointed to a number of these same issues in a critical review of the wage and price data that are available for China. They urge scholars to 'remain sceptical towards all published comparisons of wage levels and trends for the Chinese and by extension other Asian empires'.[33] While their careful analysis focuses on the sources for a quantitative economic history of China, they conclude that the same limitations apply to those for India and the Middle East.

Even if we were able to assemble quantitative information that was able to accurately represent economic reality, that data would still have to be interpreted, which is neither simple nor straightforward. Stephen Marglin, in his classic comparison of economic paradigms, writes that it is difficult to conclude on the basis of empirical tests whether neoclassical or non-neoclassical frameworks better describe the workings of the economy because even sophisticated statistical analysis yields results that are consistent with both theoretical approaches.[34] Marglin draws this conclusion from the analysis of savings in the US economy, and the difficulty is that the results of even sophisticated statistical analysis are consistent with a number of approaches to why individuals and firms save.

What is one to do? Marglin argues: 'We must either back off from purely empirical means of distinguishing between theories, or despair of sorting out the competing claims. Consistent positivists should prefer agnosticism. The rest of us will prefer to look more closely at the premises of the theories … to examine the extent to which these theories correspond to a plausible conception of the world. In short, if we are to choose between theories of saving at this stage of our knowledge, it must be on the basis of their inherent plausibility.'[35]

Applying Marglin's recommendation to the divergence debate, a plausible explanation must take into account *all* the available evidence, both quantitative and qualitative. At a minimum, such an explanation must acknowledge three important facts about China, India, and the global economy in the period between 1600 and 1900. First, for 200 years, the advanced regions of China and India maintained what might be thought of as export surpluses.[36] These regions shipped large quantities of manufactured goods throughout the world, cotton textiles in the case of India and porcelains and silk cloth (as well as an agricultural product, tea) in the case of China, in exchange for silver, and in the Indian case, to a lesser extent gold. These exports suggest that these regions possessed sophisticated economies and commercial systems which were able to maintain a competitive hegemony for a period of centuries. Second, the military encounters between Europeans and Asians were evenly matched till the early nineteenth century, which indicates that technological capability was comparable and that technological development in places like India was not stagnant.[37] Finally, it is widely acknowledged that the economies of the advanced regions of India and China regressed in the nineteenth century. This regression suggests some degree of prosperity in the eighteenth century from which the economies of these areas fell back.

## The divergence debate in China and India

In the English-speaking-and-reading world, the divergence debate has been dominated by scholars based in the United States and Western Europe. However, a surprising degree of discussion of the question has been taking place in East Asia. South Asia, by contrast, has witnessed very limited interest in the issue, perhaps because of the decline in economic history in what had been major global centres of research in economic history, such as the Delhi School of Economics.

Driven by scholars in China and some Western Sinologists, two pre-existing debates in Chinese historiography have been connected to that on divergence. One debate was about whether the late imperial Chinese economy had contained within it 'sprouts of capitalism', and if so, what had prevented them from blossoming. The second debate ensued as it became clear that the absence of a thorough capitalist transformation in China could not be fully explained by external forces such as the Manchu conquest in the seventeenth century or Western imperialism in the nineteenth as some scholars had suggested, and therefore, had to have explanations rooted in Chinese society.[38] This discussion centred on to what extent rural China in particular could have experienced any sustained per capita growth within the late imperial social system, and what the relationship might be between the limited (or according to some, non-existent) extent of per capita growth and the undoubted growth in population during the late imperial period. Both these debates thus take us back to 'agrarian fundamentalism', but in two rather different guises: one essentially Marxist, the other Malthusian.

The Marxist debate has analogues in Indian history, particularly Mughal, where in the 1960s the 'potentialities of capitalist development' in Mughal India were explored, most extensively by Irfan Habib. Since then, South Asian history has moved away from the applicability of these types of totalizing frameworks that have been derived from the European historical experience, which marked a larger retreat from Marxism. An important moment in this shift was the debate in the *Journal of Peasant Studies* in the early 1980s on the applicability of feudalism to medieval India, which was initiated by Harbans Mukhia. Parthasarathi developed Mukhia's insights to query the utility of the category of capitalism for the study of early modern India in a volume of essays in honour of Mukhia.[39]

In Chinese economic history, one of the central debates in the People's Republic of China – which, not coincidentally, often focused on the *advanced* Yangzi Delta – concerned the so-called 'sprouts of capitalism': whether or not one could find in the sixteenth to eighteenth centuries an emerging Chinese capitalism that was then aborted by the Qing conquest of 1644 (or for some scholars, by the Opium War of 1839–42). The emphasis in this debate was firmly on identifying China's dominant 'mode of production' in a Marxist sense, and development was charted above all based on evidence that wage labour was becoming increasingly prevalent (with a subsidiary effort to track growing markets for land and capital), rather than by looking for changes in per capita income, productivity, or technology.[40] While many scholars were, by the late 1980s, increasingly unsatisfied with this focus, it was not clear what might replace it in Chinese historiography.

More than anyone else, Li Bozhong began to push Chinese economic history towards an emphasis on output, rather than labour relations. He also argued for a long period of slow but generally steady per capita growth based on market-driven organizational and technical change, beginning perhaps as early as the eighth century, but becoming particularly strong between the mid-sixteenth and mid-nineteenth centuries.[41] Some important senior scholars once associated with the 'sprouts' debate, such as Wu Chengming, endorsed Li's approach, though most have not been willing to go as far as he did; the scholars who were impressed by Li's work have been generally receptive to *The Great Divergence*.

The Sinologists who have been most sceptical about *The Great Divergence*, both in China and in the United States, have been those who have combined some influences from the 'sprouts of capitalism' literature with a strong emphasis on the negative consequences of late imperial population growth. Probably the most notable has been the Chinese–American historian Philip Huang (Huang Zongzhi); while based for many years at the University of California, Los Angeles (UCLA), Huang has also been active in scholarly circles in China. Huang reaffirmed the argument of his UCLA colleague Robert Brenner that only capitalist farms based on wage labour (and ruthlessly minimizing costs by driving 'excess' workers off the land) could generate rising labour productivity, capital accumulation, and sustained growth. Much of Brenner's work has been devoted to insisting that these essential dynamics emerged only in England, and to explaining why.[42]

In an influential 1990 book, Huang took China, including the Yangzi Delta, to represent an even more extreme case of the qualitative stagnation that Brenner attributes to continental Europe. As he sees it, most Chinese peasants held on to their land (much like in France, but unlike in Britain). As population grew and plot sizes shrank, they had to maximize per acre yields; this is what enabled them to pay such high rents that landlords had no incentive to replace them with wage labourers. These high yields were achieved by working extraordinary numbers of labour days per acre, and by putting even more days into labour-intensive handicrafts; this labour intensification continued even at the cost of reducing peasants' earnings per labour day to extraordinarily low levels. Households working this hard could sustain large families, but only at bare subsistence levels, and at the cost of further increasing pressure on the land in the next generation. This locked in a process of numerical growth that was the antithesis of true development, and which Huang calls 'involution'.[43]

This is not the place to rehearse all the details of the debate that followed.[44] Suffice it to say that Pomeranz's views have largely prevailed, in part because the debate uncovered a basic error in Huang's work: In estimating the earnings per labour day for Yangzi Delta weavers, he misplaced a decimal point, throwing his calculations of gross earnings off by a factor of 10 (and of net earnings by even more).

Unsurprisingly, it is the sections of *The Great Divergence* that deal with China (as opposed to Europe or other places) that have excited the most interest in China. Most of that discussion has treated the book as part of a larger 'California school' which has become the topic of a number of articles. The members of this 'California school' vary with the person defining it – which is hardly surprising since it has never had a firm institutional identity or a complete consensus on the issues – but R. Bin Wong, James Lee and his collaborators, Li Bozhong, Robert Marks, Richard Von Glahn, Jack Goldstone, and Pomeranz are usually included.

Chinese responses to this 'school' have naturally been varied, but it is fair to say that it has stimulated increased interest in comparative history within China. Moreover, this has been comparative history which, unlike the 'sprouts' and 'involution' literatures, goes beyond comparing China to a 'typical' (i.e. stylized European capitalist) path. In fact, one common feature of 'California school' comparisons has been an insistence that neither society should be treated as defining a norm from which the other society is a deviation.[45] It has helped stimulate new approaches to the Qing era, in which the state is (for better or worse) a less overwhelming presence, and the motors of social change are to be found elsewhere in society. Increased interest has been paid to long-run, slowly developing trends in Chinese society – perhaps going all the way back to the Song dynasty – that continue up into the twentieth century. Such a view, quite forcefully expressed in a conference volume called *The Song-Yuan-Ming Transition*,[46] seems to be replacing older stories in which 'revolutionary' changes in Song and late Ming were followed by equally sharp reversals, frustrating what both Marxism and Western modernization theory thought 'should' have happened next, and defining Chinese history in terms of those alleged blockages.

## Conclusion

As this chapter has shown, the debate on divergence is remarkably broad, touching upon not only prices and incomes, the traditional bread and butter of economic historians, but also ranging far and wide to include science, rationality, the environment, politics, and the state. While the debate has raised difficult empirical questions, it has also brought to the fore equally challenging problems of method. Its sheer scope and complexity make the question an enduring one not only for historians but also for a range of social scientists from sociologists to economists and political scientists. It will continue to remain a central problem for decades to come.

## Notes

1. K. Marx (1978 [1853]), 'The future results of British Rule in India', in R. C. Tucker (ed.), *The Marx-Engels Reader*. New York: Norton, 659.

2. M. Weber (1930), *The Protestant Ethic and the Spirit of Capitalism*, trans. Talcott Parsons. New York: Scribner; Idem (1951), *The Religion of China*, trans. H. H. Gerth. New York: Free Press; Idem (1958), *The Religion of India*, trans. H. H. Gerth and D. Martindale. New York: Free Press.

3. D. C. North and R. P. Thomas (1973), *The Rise of the Western World: A New Economic History*. Cambridge: Cambridge University Press; E. L. Jones (1981), *The European Miracle: Environments, Economies, and Geopolitics in the History of Europe and Asia*. Cambridge: Cambridge University Press; D. Landes (1998), *The Wealth and Poverty of Nations*. New York: W.W. Norton; J. Mokyr (2002), *The Gifts of Athena: Historical Origins of the Knowledge Economy*. Princeton: Princeton University Press.

4. K. Pomeranz (2002), *The Great Divergence: China, Europe, and the Making of the Modern World Economy*. Princeton: Princeton University Press; P. Parthasarathi (2012), *Why Europe Grew Rich and Asia Did Not: Global Economic Divergence, 1600-1850*. Cambridge: Cambridge University Press.

5. E. A. Wrigley (1988), *Continuity, Chance and Change: The Character of the Industrial Revolution in England*. Cambridge: Cambridge University Press; A. P. Wadsworth and J. de Lacy Mann (1931), *The Cotton Trade and Industrial Lancashire*. Manchester: Manchester University Press.

6. B. Li and J. L. van Zanden (2012), 'Before the Great Divergence? Comparing the Yangzi Delta and the Netherlands at the beginning of the nineteenth century', *Journal of Economic History,* 72 (4), 956–89.

7. R. C. Allen (2000), 'Economic structure and agricultural productivity in Europe, 1300–1800', *European Review of Economic History*, 4 (1), 20.

8. See for instance R. Brenner (1985), 'Agrarian class structure and economic development', and 'The agrarian roots of European capitalism', in T. H. Aston and C. H. Philpin (eds), *The Brenner Debate.* Cambridge: Cambridge University Press, 10–63, and 213–327; M. Overton (1996), *Agricultural Revolution in England: The Transformation of the Agrarian Economy 1500–1800.* Cambridge: Cambridge University Press. For the term 'agrarian fundamentalism' see R. C. Allen (1992), *Enclosure and the Yeoman: The Agricultural Development of the South Midlands.* New York: Oxford University Press, 2–3.

9. S. Broadberry, H. Guan and D. Li (2014), 'China, Europe, and the Great Divergence: A study in historical national accounting, 980–1850', http://eh.net/eha/wp-content/uploads/2014/05/Broadberry.pdf. Guan and Li had previously argued that China was far behind by the fifteenth century, if not earlier, and had fallen even further behind over the succeeding centuries. See H. Guan and D. Li (2010), 'Mingdai GDP ji jiegou shitan' [A study of GDP and its structure in China's Ming dynasty], *Zhongguo jingji jikan*, 9 (3), 787–829, http://en.cnki.com.cn/Article_en/CJFDTotal-JJXU201003003.htm

10. P. K. O'Brien and K. Deng (2016), 'Nutritional standards of living in England and the Yangtze Delta (Jiangnan), circa. 1644 – circa 1820: Clarifying data for reciprocal comparisons', *Journal of World History,* 26 (2), 233–67; P. K. O'Brien and K. Deng (2017), 'How well did the facts travel to support protracted debate on the history of the Great Divergence between Western Europe and Imperial China?' February 2017, available at New Economics Papers, http://econpapers.repec.org/paper/pramprapa/77276.htm; K. Pomeranz (2017), 'The data we have vs. the data we want: A comment on the date of the Divergence Debate', Pt. I and Pt II, New Economics Papers (8 June 2017) https://nephist.wordpress.com/2017/06/06/the-data-we-have-vs-the-data-we-need-a-comment-on-the-state-of-the-divergence-debate-part-ii/ (Part 1, immediately below).

11. P. Parthasarathi (1998), 'Rethinking wages and competitiveness in the eighteenth century: Britain and South India', *Past & Present*, 98, 79–109.

12. S. Broadberry and B. Gupta (2006), 'The early modern Great Divergence: Wages, prices and economic development in Europe and Asia, 1500–1800', *Economic History Review,* 59 (1), 2–31.

13. S. Sivaramakrishna (2009), 'Ascertaining living standards in erstwhile Mysore, Southern India, from Francis Buchanan's *Journey* of 1800–01: An empirical contribution to the Great Divergence debate', *Journal of the Economic and Social History of the Orient*, 52 (3), 695–733; Parthasarathi, *Why Europe Grew Rich and Asia Did Not*, 37–46.

14. L. Brennan, J. McDonald, and R. Shlomowitz (1994), 'Trends in the economic well-being of South Indians under British rule: the anthropometric evidence', *Explorations in Economic History*, 31 (2), 225–60; M. Davis (2002), *Late Victorian Holocausts: El Niño Famines and the Making of the Third World.* London: Verso.

15. A. Maddison (2001), *The World Economy: A Millennial Perspective.* Paris: OECD, 42, suggesting that Western Europe overtook China in c. 1300.

16. See D. Lal (1998), *Unintended Consequences: The Impact of Factor Endowments, Culture, and Politics on Long-Run Economic Performance.* Cambridge, MA: MIT Press; London: Eyre

Methuen; E. Jones (1987), *The European Miracle*, 2nd edn. Cambridge: Cambridge University Press; I. Wallerstein (1976), *The Modern World-System, Volume I*. New York: Academic Press.

17. Landes, *The Wealth and Poverty*, 33–5, 59, and *passim*.

18. See Li and van Zanden, 'Before the Great Divergence'.

19. R. C. Allen, J. P. Bassino, D. Ma, C. Moll-Murata and J. L. Van Zanden (2011), 'Wages, prices and living standards in China 1738–1925: In comparison with Europe, Japan, and India', *Economic History Review*, 64 (1), 8–38. This article's estimates of agricultural wages in China are, as the authors note, actually very close to Pomeranz's. R. C. Allen (2009), 'Agricultural productivity and rural incomes in England and the Yangzi Delta, ca. 1620–1820', *Economic History Review*, 62 (3), 544, suggests that Lower Yangzi wages were about the same as English ones in the mid-seventeenth century, and Delta peasants were far more prosperous than English farm labourers at that time. Ibid., 546. And see R. C. Allen (2004), 'Mr. Lockyer meets the index number problem: The standard of living in Canton and London in 1704', available at http://www.iisg.nl/hpw/papers/allen.pdf, for a different (smaller) dataset, suggesting comparable wages in Canton and London in 1704.

20. C. Tilly (1984), 'Demographic origins of the European proletariat', in D. Levine (ed.), *Proletarianization and Family History*. Orlando: Academic Press, 1–85 uses a looser definition, and gets even higher figures: see esp. 36.

21. Calculations in K. Pomeranz (2006), 'Standards of living in rural and urban China: Preliminary estimates for the mid-eighteenth and early twentieth centuries'. Paper for Panel 77, World Economic History Congress, Helsinki.

22. On market integration in China and Europe, see W. Keller and C. Shiue (2007), 'Markets in China and Europe on the eve of the Industrial Revolution', *American Economic Review*, 97 (4), 1189–216.

23. See esp. J. L. Rosenthal and R. B. Wong (2011), *Before and Beyond Divergence: The Politics of Economic Change in China and Europe*. Cambridge, MA: Harvard University Press. See also Pomeranz, *The Great Divergence*, 180–2, on why interest rates per se may not be the best indicators of whether credit markets were obstructing development.

24. R. C. Allen (2009), *The British Industrial Revolution in Global Perspective*. Cambridge: Cambridge University Press; Pomeranz, *Great Divergence*.

25. M. Jacob (2014), *The First Knowledge Economy: Human Capital and the European Economy, 1750–1850*. Cambridge: Cambridge University Press; Mokyr, *Gifts of Athena*; and Patrick O'Brien's chapter in this volume.

26. Parthasarathi, *Why Europe Grew Rich and Asia Did Not*, ch. 7.

27. H. J. Cook (2007), *Matters of Exchange: Commerce, Medicine, and Science in the Dutch Golden Age*. New Haven: Yale University Press; K. Raj (2007), *Relocating Modern Science: Circulation and the Construction of Scientific Knowledge in South Asia and Europe*. Delhi: Permanent Black.

28. E. J. Hobsbawm (1962), *The Age of Revolutions: Europe, 1789–1848*. London: Weidenfield and Nicolson.

29. E. J. Hobsbawm (1969), *Industry and Empire*. London: Penguin, p. 56.

30. See the chapter by Jack A. Goldstone in this volume.

31. E. J. Hobsbawm (1964), *Labouring Men: Studies in the History of Labour*. London: Weidenfield and Nicolson, 107.

32. Hobsbawm, *Labouring Men*.

Global Economic History

33. K. Deng and P. K. O'Brien (2016), 'Establishing statistical foundations of a chronology for the great divergence: A survey and critique of the primary sources for the construction of relative wage levels for Ming–Qing China', *Economic History Review*, 69 (4), 1075. Also see K. Deng and P. K. O'Brien (2016), 'China's GDP per capita from the Han Dynasty to communist times', *World Economics*, 17 (2), 79–123; and Deng and O'Brien (2017), 'How well did the facts travel?'

34. S. A. Marglin (1984), *Growth, Distribution, and Prices*. Cambridge, MA: Harvard University Press, ch. 18.

35. Marglin, *Growth, Distribution, and Prices*, 430.

36. But on the dangers of treating precious metals as equivalent to modern money, as an 'export surplus' reading does, see D. O. Flynn (1995), 'Arbitrage, China, and world trade in the early modern period', *Journal of the Economic and Social History of the Orient*, 38 (4), 429–48; and D. O. Flynn and A. Giráldez (1997), 'Introduction', in D. O. Flynn and A. Giráldez (eds), *Metals and Monies in an Emerging World Economy*. Aldershot: Variorum, xv–xl.

37. It might be objected here that since the battles were fought in Asia, leaving Europeans with very long supply lines, this is a risky inference. But for an argument that the decisive advantage of East India Company forces in India was not technological, see K. Roy (2011), 'The hybrid military establishment of the East India Company in South Asia, 1750–1849', *Journal of Global History*, 6 (2), 195–218.

38. It is worth noting that the earlier preference for externally driven explanations of Chinese 'failure' was convenient both for mainland scholars committed to the universality of a rigid Marxist set of stages of society and for nationalists wishing to emphasize the damage done to China by imperialism.

39. T. J. Byres and H. Mukhia (eds) (1985), *Feudalism and Non-European Societies*. London: Frank Cass; P. Parthasarathi (2008), 'Was there capitalism in early-modern Indian history?' in R. Datta (ed.), *Rethinking a Millennium: Perspectives on Indian History from the Eighth to the Eighteenth Century: Essays for Harbans Mukhia*. New Delhi: Aakar Publications, 342–60.

40. W. Chengming (1985), *Zhongguo zibenzhuyi yu guonei shichang* [Chinese capitalism and the national market]. Beijing: Zhongguo shehui kexue chubanshe; and X. Dixin and W. Chengming (1985), *Zhongguo zibenzhuyi de mengya* [The Sprouts of Capitalism in China]. Beijing: Zhongguo shehui kexue chubanshe, are the most important compendia of this work.

41. B. Li (1998), *Agricultural Development in Jiangnan, 1620–1850*. New York: St. Martin's Press; B. Li (2000), *Jiangnan de zaoqi gongyehua* [Proto-industrialization in Jiangnan]. Beijing: Shehui kexue wenxian chubanshe; B. Li (2003), *Fazhan yu zhiyue: Ming Qing Jiangnan shengchanli yanjiu* [Development and Constraint: Research on Productive Capacity in Ming-Qing Jiangnan]. Taibei: Lianjing; B. Li (2005), 'Farm labour productivity in Jiangnan', in R. C. Allen, T. Bengtsson and M. Dribe (eds), *Living Standards in the Past: New Perspectives on Well-Being in Asia and Europe*. Oxford: Oxford University Press, 55–76; B. Li (2010), *Zhongguo de zaoqi jindai jingji: Huating-Louxian diqu GDP yanjiu* [China's Early Modern Economy: Research in the GDP of the Huating-Louxian Region]. Beijing: Zhonghua shuju.

42. R. Brenner (1985), 'Agrarian class structure and economic development', and 'The agrarian roots of European capitalism'; R. Brenner and C. Isett (2002), 'England's divergence from the Yangzi Delta: property relations, microeconomics, and patterns of development', *Journal of Asian Studies*, 61 (2), 609–62. Pomeranz's complete answer to Brenner is not yet published (it is supposed to appear in a long-delayed volume based on a debate held at UCLA) but some comments are included in K. Pomeranz (2009), *La Force de L'Empire: Révolution industrielle et écologie, ou pourquoi l'angleterre a fait mieux que la Chine*, ed. with an introduction by Philippe Minard. Alfortville: Éditions ère, 77–110.

36

43. P. Huang (1990), *The Peasant Family and Rural Development in the Lower Yangzi Region, 1350-1988*. Stanford: Stanford University Press.

44. P. Huang (2002), 'Development or involution in eighteenth century Britain and China? A Review of Kenneth Pomeranz's *The Great Divergence: China, Europe and the Making of the Modern World Economy*', *Journal of Asian Studies*, 61 (2), 501–38; P. Huang (2002), 'Fazhan haishi neijuan? Shiba shiji Yingguo yu Zhongguo – Ping Peng Mulan 'Da fenliu: Ouzhou, Zhongguo ji xinadai shijie jingji de fazhan', *Lishi yanjiu*, 149–76; P. Huang (2003), 'Further thoughts on eighteenth-century Britain and China: Rejoinder to Pomeranz's response to my critique', *Journal of Asian Studies*, 62 (1), 157–67; K. Pomeranz (2002), 'Beyond the East-West binary: Resituating development paths in the eighteenth century world', *Journal of Asian Studies*, 61 (2), 539–90; K. Pomeranz (2003), 'Facts are stubborn things: A response to Philip Huang', *Journal of Asian Studies*, 62 (1), 167–81; K. Pomeranz (2003), 'Shijie jingji shi zhong de jinshi Jiangnan: bijiao yu zonghe guancha' [Early modern Jiangnan in global economic history: comparative and integrative perspectives], *Lishi yanjiu*, 284, 3–48. See also essays by R. B. Wong (2003), 'Integrating China into world history', *Journal of Asian Studies*, posted at www.aasianst.org/catalog/wong.pdf; J. A. Goldstone (2003), 'Europe vs. Asia: Missing data and misconceptions', *Science and Society*, 67 (2), 184–94; J. Lee, C. Campbell, and F. Wang (2002), 'Positive check or Chinese checks?' *Journal of Asian Studies*, 61 (2), 591–607; S. Cao and Y. Chen (2002), 'Maerasi lilun he Qingdai yilaide de Zhongguo renkou: ping Meiguo xuezhe jinnianlai de xiangguan yanjiu' [Malthusian theory and Chinese population from the Qing dynasty onwards: A critique of recent American scholarship), *Lishi yanjiu*, 275, 41–54; and A. Wolf (2001), 'Is there evidence of birth control in late Imperial China?', *Population and Development Review*, 27 (1), 133–54, among others.

45. R. B. Wong (1997), *China Transformed: Historical Change and the Limits of European Experience*. Ithaca, NY: Cornell University Press; Pomeranz (2000), *The Great Divergence*.

46. P. Smith and R. von Glahn (eds) (2003), *The Song-Yuan-Ming Transition in Chinese History*. Cambridge, MA: Harvard University Press.

# CHAPTER 2
# DATA AND DATING THE GREAT DIVERGENCE
*Jack A. Goldstone*

## The problem of the great divergence

Since the classic works of Karl Marx and Max Weber, a distinction has been drawn between dynamic European economies, which in an early modern period experienced the onset of modern economic growth, and Asian societies, particularly China, which were considered to have remained economically stagnant until they were overwhelmed by Western influences in the nineteenth century.[1] In this view, since at least 1500 (some scholars place the date earlier, in the Italian Renaissance or even medieval times), an accumulation of capital and productive technologies began in Europe that had no equal outside of the continent.[2] By 1800, Europe's industrialization was enabled and propelled by prior economic advances that had already long supported more consumption, more innovation, more consistent income growth, and more production per head than in any other major world economy.

This process was not synchronous across Europe; various countries took the lead at different times. Yet scholars see this as a *single process*. Italy made its contribution in the Renaissance; then the Netherlands made their contribution in the sixteenth and seventeenth centuries; England made its contribution in the eighteenth and early nineteenth centuries, then Germany in the late nineteenth and early twentieth centuries. Cumulatively they put Europe on a steady path of rising income between 1500 and 1900.

Twenty years ago, a small group of scholars, based mainly in California, argued that this view, which had prevailed among researchers for over a hundred years, was profoundly mistaken.[3] What has been defined as the 'California School' has drawn on new scholarship in China's economic and social history[4] as well as that on Japan, India, and the Ottoman Empire, to argue that despite differences in culture and politics, the economic and technological conditions in Europe were not greatly superior to those in the leading Asian empires until the early nineteenth century. The Great Divergence that was apparent by the middle of the nineteenth century, with Europe enjoying clearly superior military and economic technology, and rapid and sustained growth in both population and income per capita, was thus a far more recent phenomenon, starting not much before 1800, or about 300 years later than was previously thought.

Members of the California School did not agree on what caused the Great Divergence. Pomeranz fell back on the established idea of capital accumulation, arguing that Europe's access to convenient coal and to land reserves in overseas colonies provided a key advantage. Andre Gunder Frank argued that Europe surged ahead of China only because of the temporary failure of China's political institutions in the late Qing. Bin Wong and Jack Goldstone put more emphasis on Europe's scientific and engineering advances that began to accumulate over the course of the eighteenth century. Since then, others have argued that labour/capital ratios, or physical geography, better political organization, or still other factors were responsible, on various time scales.[5]

Unfortunately, despite the importance of this dispute to understanding the major patterns of world history for the last millennium, the arguments on both sides were made with data that was, admittedly, fragmentary. Ideally, it would have been desirable to have annual or at least decadal data on GDP and GDP per capita to assess the rates and levels of economic growth in various regions and societies since at least 1500. But, of course, GDP as a concept and measure was only invented in the twentieth century. Scholars have thus had to make do with proxies for living standards, including wills and testaments, tax assessments, estimates of farm income, scattered wage contracts, and estimates of consumption of agricultural and manufactured goods. Estimates of output based on trade data, tax rolls, diaries, gazetteers and handbooks, and census data (where available) have also been used.

To get at levels of economic development, one also has to determine economic output per capita. This requires data on population that is limited before modern censuses. Some pre-modern censuses were compiled, but these are only available at long intervals, sometimes centuries, during which wars and plagues may have greatly altered the population. Such censuses usually focused on households, not individuals, and households varied in size and composition across regions and times. Parish records in Catholic and Anglican countries provide excellent local data, as do lineage records in Asia, with identification of specific individuals by birth, marriage, death, and households. But such information is painstaking and difficult to collect and aggregate.[6]

Things get even more complex when we compare different world regions: What geographical or social unit should be the basis for estimation? Is it fair to compare income levels in Holland, which was the richest, most urban, and most internationally supplied portion of the still-small country of the Netherlands – which was in turn the richest and most urbanized country in Northern Europe for several centuries – with the much larger and more diverse countries of England and Wales, or France, much less China? Pomeranz tried to compare what he called the 'most advanced' regions of Europe and China, but even here how to proceed? Should one take the Yangzi Delta in the seventeenth and eighteenth centuries, as he did, which is still a diverse region of twenty-five million in population, and compare it with regions such as England (six million) or the Netherlands (two million) or even Holland (800,000)? Also when should one make the comparison? Each region had its own economic cycles of prosperity and decay, and comparing one region during a boom with another during a slump could give a very misleading picture of longer-term conditions.

## The challenge of new data

Given the enormous difficulties discussed above, the creation of a comprehensive set of national accounts for Britain and Holland from 1500 to 1800 that are unprecedented in their comprehensiveness and detail is a true achievement.[7] Such datasets survey agriculture, including grain and livestock and other crops; output in manufacturing, including the production of textiles, ceramics, leather goods, mining and metals, soap, beer, books, and so on; and services, analysing trade and transport, finance, housing, and government spending. They attempt to track output in each of these sectors year by year over several centuries, in some cases going all the way back to the early Middle Ages.

These estimates open up new possibilities for evaluating several of the arguments over the Great Divergence. One can scrutinize the national accounts for Britain and Holland to seek internal patterns: By what dates do they seem to have achieved a self-sustaining pattern of growth in income per head? We can compare this data with more fragmentary but still useful estimates of output per capita in other times and places to ask: By what dates do they seem to have achieved a level of income per capita that goes beyond levels previously achieved in pre-modern times? Finally, this income data can be checked against other sources and estimates for consistency, such as data on physical heights or competing estimates of consumption.

As far as the compilers of the new data are concerned, they feel they have now firmly dated the origins of the Great Divergence, and that their data strongly supports the classical view that it began centuries before 1800. They argue that the data shows early and sustained growth in GDP per capita in Northwest Europe, starting from the late Middle Ages. This is a return to the views of scholars such as Fernand Braudel, Immanuel Wallerstein, and Carlo Cipolla, who saw a commercial revolution starting in the thirteenth and fourteenth centuries in Europe with great fairs and growing cities, and trade then expanding through the age of exploration and colonial empires from the sixteenth through the nineteenth centuries.[8] All this created a distinctive growth path in Europe long before the Industrial Revolution. Broadberry thus argues that 'the Great Divergence between Europe and Asia had its origins in the late medieval period and was already well under way in the early modern period, as in the traditional economic history literature'.[9] De Pleijt and van Zanden similarly state that the Industrial Revolution was 'a continuation of trends going back to the late Middle Ages'.[10] Rather than seeing the process as uniform across Europe, the compilers of the new GDP data argue that this process began with a 'Little Divergence' in which first the Netherlands and then Britain launched on the path to higher income per head while other parts of Europe fell behind; at the same time, the great empires of Asia were falling into stagnation or decline from now distant medieval peaks of productivity, leaving only Northwest Europe poised to develop further into industrial nations.

This argument, if accepted, would overturn the claims of the 'California School' that European growth was not exceptional or sustained before the late eighteenth century. The great similarities that California School scholars claim to see between the leading pre-industrial European economies and those of Asia would be outweighed by greater differences. Yet this chapter argues that the authors of these new GDP studies have overstated such differences. Indeed, I claim that on closer scrutiny, there was a sharp break in the pattern of economic growth only *after* 1750, and that there is no evidence of an exceptional pattern of sustained or rapid growth in GDP per capita in Europe before that. First, I show that while Holland had a very impressive efflorescence of growth in real income during its sixteenth century Golden Age; it thereafter returned to a centuries-long stagnation. Next, I demonstrate that before 1750 England did not experience both population growth and significant growth in income per capita. Finally, I compare the levels of income per capita found in Holland and Britain with data on GDP per capita from other times and places. They show that the economic achievements of Holland and Britain before 1800 are notable but not unprecedented. When industrialization arose in Europe, it therefore came without any steady advances in income per capita, or attainment of exceptional pre-industrial incomes, during the early modern period.

## Dutch economic growth, 1510–1800: Efflorescence or modern growth?

In 2002, I introduced the concept of 'efflorescences' in economic history to counter the notion that all nations' economic history was binary – that there was only Malthusian stagnation or modern steady increases in income.[11] I argued that while most pre-modern economies were usually bound by Malthusian constraints, unable to sustain any growth in income per capita if population was growing, there were exceptions to the rule scattered throughout history.

At various times, even pre-modern societies made breakthroughs in productivity through improvements in agricultural tools and practices (in the use of animals, crops, and crop rotations); through improvements in energy and water transport (windmills, watermills, exploiting peat or coal, new designs for boats and canals); the importation or creation of new production techniques and products (e.g. for paper, silk, ceramics, metals, glass, or textiles); or advances in organization and finance (e.g. more extensive and systematic accounting, banking, credit, insurance, and monetary instruments). The added value of these advances encouraged higher levels of urbanization and of trade. More extensive trade, both within the society and without, led to further gains from exploiting comparative advantage, which often involved taking market share from other regions. Such a burst of creativity could augment population increase, leading to a rapid rise in both population and income per capita, thus breaking the Malthusian bounds through 'Schumpeterian' or innovation-led growth. In such periods – often deemed 'Golden Ages' – even pre-modern societies start to look more 'modern', as surging productivity, gains in the service sector and investments in libraries and education, and high levels of cultural production and consumption created a richer and more diversified economy and lifestyles. Whether in Song China (remarkable for its production of iron), or the Caliphate of Baghdad (famed for its libraries as well as its science), Renaissance Italy (renowned for its art), or Golden Age Holland (bustling with trade and manufacturing), such episodes set standards for sophistication that often stood for centuries.

Yet unlike in modern economic growth, where we have seen centuries of steady increases in output per capita, such episodes usually lasted only a few decades. Once the gains of the initial productivity breakthroughs had been absorbed and exhausted, there were no further such 'Schumpeterian' gains. At that point, population growth would again push against the new resource boundary. At best, slowing population growth and much more moderate gains in total output could sustain the prior levels of GDP per capita; but there would be no further marked gains in GDP per capita in succeeding centuries. At worst, a new period of war or revolution, or competition from other societies experiencing a surge of productivity and taking market share away, or simply continued population increase, could lead to a decline in GDP per capita. One might still see income per capita rise in subsequent periods if there is a subsequent decline in population that is greater than the decline in output, or if output grew modestly while population remained constant or depressed. However, total GDP per capita would still remain within the bounds of pre-modern efflorescence peaks, and the vigorous sustained growth in both GDP per capita, and population that is characteristic of modern economic growth does not reappear. Rather, after the efflorescence has peaked, a new Malthusian equilibrium pattern takes over.

Jan Luiten van Zanden and Bas van Leeuwen have painstakingly reconstructed a set of national accounts for Holland going back to the late Middle Ages. I will here focus on their data for the period of 1510–1807. This is the period that encompasses Holland's 'Golden Age', and is a period in which many observers, including van Zanden and van Leeuwen, as well as Jan de Vries and Ad Van den Woude, have claimed to find evidence for the emergence of 'modern' economic growth.[12]

Holland in its Golden Age has many features of a modern economy, including a low fraction of GDP in agriculture; a high level of artistic and educational output and consumption; and a high level of government and economic organization. But some of this is inherent in the selection of the province of Holland in isolation as the unit of analysis. Holland, anchored by Amsterdam and its other coastal cities, was an exceptionally urbanized area: Its 337,000 residents were far more dependent on services and trade than any regions with ten to twenty times that population could be – indeed far more so than even other parts of the United Provinces, of which it was the largest and richest. As early as 1510, 49 per cent of Holland's GDP came from services, with 29 per cent from crafts and manufacturing and only 22 per cent from agriculture and fisheries. Many of those services derived from Holland's role in the international economy, where it was a depot for trade between the Baltic and the North Sea and the Atlantic, and provided financial and warehousing services to merchants from throughout Europe. The economy of Holland would be more like the economy of today's Greater London, or for that matter the cities of Rome, Florence, or Constantinople in their heydays, for apt comparison. It was thus unlike the economy of any other pre-modern European economy, where typically half or more of the population was engaged in agriculture.

The chronological developments for Holland are shown in Figure 2.1. The left scale shows real GDP in constant 1800 prices in Dutch guilders; the right scale shows real GDP per capita in the same measure.[13] GDP started to rise strongly from the 1540s to the 1560s, faltering slightly in the next decade when the Dutch war for independence with Spain began. However, after the 1570s there was rapid and unbroken growth up to the 1640s, when total GDP was four times larger than in the early sixteenth century.

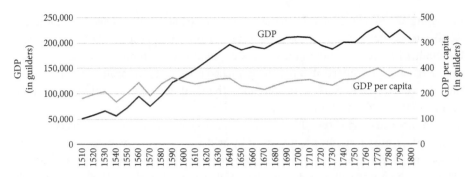

**Figure 2.1** GDP and GDP per capita in Holland, 1510–1800 (Decade Averages in constant 1800 prices).

The trajectory of this growth shows a clear 'efflorescence' pattern. From the 1540s to the 1570s there was a sudden, one-time shift in the composition of GDP, as more efficient services and new energy, transport, and manufacturing processes took hold. In the 1540s, the sectoral distribution of Holland's GDP was still virtually identical to that in 1510, with 48.4 per cent in services, 30.3 per cent in crafts and manufacturing, and 21.3 per cent in agriculture. But by the 1560s, as new techniques spread, there was a dramatic shift, with services leaping to 64.7 per cent of output, while crafts and manufacturing dropped to 21.7 per cent and agriculture to a mere 13.6 per cent. Over the next century, this pattern would be preserved, so that by 1640, services still contributed 62.5 per cent of output, crafts and manufacturing 26.9 per cent, and agriculture 10.6 per cent. Most of Holland's growth in output during this Golden Age was thus in services, and specifically in trade, whose real value increased fivefold to sixfold. Still, these trade gains reflected widespread gains in the economy as every sector grew in absolute terms.

After 1640, however, the picture changed. For over a century after the 1640s, until the 1750s, real GDP was never more than 2 per cent above the 1640s peak. And the sectoral structure of the economy remained unchanged: In the 1750s, services still contributed 59.4 per cent of GDP, crafts and manufacturing 30.1 per cent, and agriculture 10.5 per cent. Indeed, this pattern remains unchanged all the way up to the 1790s.

There was a slight spurt of new growth in the late eighteenth century, with GDP in the 1760s, 1770s, and 1790s up by about 10 per cent from the 1640–1750 level; but this too faltered and by 1800–1807 GDP was back to within 5 per cent of the then 160-year-old peak. According to this new data, real GDP grew by 300 per cent from 1540 to 1640, but by no more than 5 per cent for the next 150 years. That certainly represented, as Simon Schama has written, an 'embarrassment of riches' in the seventeenth century.[14] However, this efflorescence was followed by no further changes in the size or structure of the economy for 150 years after the 1640s.

Further evidence for this conclusion comes from looking at changes in GDP per capita over this period. From 1540 to 1590 GDP per capita grew strongly, gaining roughly 56 per cent in these five decades. This was accompanied by vigorous population growth, increasing 37 per cent from 337,000 in the 1540s to 462,000 in the 1590s. After these five wondrous decades, however, gains in per capita income disappeared. GDP grew strongly for another half-century, but in those years population growth more than kept pace, so that GDP per capita dipped after the 1590s, inched up to that level again in the 1640s, but then fell for the next century, so that not until the 1760s did GDP per capita again reach its level of the 1590s, more than 150 years earlier.

Even more striking is that the rise in GDP per capita in the last few decades of the eighteenth century is hardly accompanied by evidence of vigour in the economy; rather it looks more like a slight Malthusian positive wave. For the GDP per capita level in 1800–07, which was still only 4.5 per cent higher than that of the 1590s, rose mainly because Holland's population declined. Shortly after the 1640s peak in GDP, population also hit a peak in the 1670s, at 876,000. By the 1750s, population had declined by almost 100,000 to 783,000, and then fell yet another 34,000 by the years 1800–07.

All of this can be observed in Table 2.1. The annual GDP growth rates from the 1540s to the 1640s stand out; they are wholly atypical for the period as a whole. GDP growth steadily declined thereafter, virtually disappearing after the 1640s. Even more striking, GDP per capita shows tremendous growth in the five decades from the 1540s to the 1590s, but that is all. After the 1590s, growth in per capita income turned negative for over a century, and even the return of growth in GDP per capita in the eighteenth century was almost risible, reaching 0.08 per cent per year only because the decline in Holland's population over the eighteenth century (−0.11 per cent per annum) was greater than the decline in real GDP (−0.03 per cent per annum).

In sum, the Netherlands illustrate a classic pre-modern economic 'efflorescence': several decades of truly remarkable growth in GDP, GDP per capita, and population, followed by a return in the succeeding two centuries to virtually zero growth. Indeed, for all these quantities, their level in the first decade of the nineteenth century is indistinguishable from their level in 1640s, as is the sectoral composition of the economy. In my view, these facts not only make the late-sixteenth-century Dutch Golden Age even more impressive, but also indisputably distinguish it from being the onset of true modern economic growth. However, several economic historians have argued that although growth faltered in the Netherlands, from the seventeenth century onwards it took off in England. They argue that we should see the joint trajectories of England and the Netherlands as comprising a 'Little Divergence' from the rest of Europe that carried this world region into new frontiers of economic performance.

## British growth, 1270–1800

There is no dispute that after 1800, Great Britain was launched upon a remarkable period of economic growth. Fuelled by vast gains in productivity in agriculture, transport, and especially in textiles, mining, and metallurgy, Britain had so transformed itself by 1850 as to be the wonder of the world. Its railways moved people and freight at previously unimaginable speeds, its steam-powered and iron-clad warships subdued the mightiest

**Table 2.1 Growth in Holland, 1510s–1800s: GDP, population, and GDP per capita**

| | GDP (1510s = 100) | GDP Growth since prior date (% p.a.) | Population (1510s = 100) | Population Growth since prior date (% p.a.) | GDP per capita (1510s = 100) | GDP per capita Growth since prior date (% p. a.) |
|---|---|---|---|---|---|---|
| 1510s | 100 | | 100 | | 100 | |
| 1540s | 111.1 | 0.35 | 121.4 | 0.64 | 91.4 | −0.30 |
| 1590s | 241 | 1.56 | 166.4 | 0.63 | 144.7 | 0.92 |
| 1640s | 389 | 0.96 | 271.4 | 0.98 | 143.3 | −0.02 |
| 1700s | 418.5 | 0.12 | 301.6 | 0.18 | 138.8 | −0.05 |
| 1800s | 407.9 | −0.03 | 269.9 | −0.11 | 151.2 | 0.08 |

*Source:* Jan Luiten van Zanden and Bas van Leeuwen as the 'Reconstruction National Accounts of Holland'; at: http://www.cgeh.nl/reconstruction-national-accounts-holland-1500-1800-0.

empires in the world, and its factories allowed this small island to replace the centuries-old leadership of the vast Indian and Chinese empires and become the world's leading exporter of cotton goods.

What is still a matter of great debate, however, is how far in this direction Britain's economy had moved prior to 1800. Was Britain, already by 1700 or earlier, embarked on a path of economic growth that showed a clear break with past Malthusian patterns? Or was such growth only evident after the onset of industrialization, in the late eighteenth or even only the early nineteenth century?

Table 2.2 shows recent data for growth in real GDP per capita in half-century periods from the 1270s through the 1860s, along with data on population growth. If we exclude two periods – the late fourteenth century and the late seventeenth century – then the average annual growth rate in real GDP per capita for all other periods from the 1270s to the 1700s, a period of over 400 years, was essentially zero. By contrast, in the two growth periods, we see very rapid gains in income per capita, of 0.57 per cent and 0.72 per cent

Table 2.2  Growth rates for population and real GDP per capita in England and Great Britain (% per annum)

|  | Population | Real GDP per capita |
|---|---|---|
| *England* | | |
| 1270s–1300s | 0.23 | −0.02 |
| 1300s–1340s | −0.06 | 0.07 |
| 1340s–1400s | −1.32 | 0.57 |
| 1400s–1450s | −0.14 | −0.07 |
| 1450s–1500s | 0.29 | 0.11 |
| 1500s–1550s | 0.66 | −0.16 |
| 1550s–1600s | 0.64 | 0.18 |
| 1600s–1650s | 0.45 | −0.05 |
| 1650s–1700 | −0.06 | 0.72 |
| *Great Britain* | | |
| 1700s–1750s | 0.31 | 0.18 |
| 1750s–1800s | 0.82 | 0.39 |
| 1800s–1830s | 1.43 | 0.41 |
| 1830s–1860s | 1.17 | 1.15 |

*Source*: Stephen Broadberry; Bruce Campbell, Bruce; Alexander Klein, Mark Overton, and Bas van Leeuwen (2015), *British Economic Growth, 1270–1870*. Cambridge: Cambridge University Press, Appendix 5.3.

per year. These stand out as periods of remarkable pre-modern growth, greater in fact than the growth rates in GDP per capita observed from 1800 to 1830. The new GDP data thus shows that all the growth in English GDP per capita between the Middle Ages and the eighteenth century was due to growth in these two periods.

The late fourteenth century of course was the era of the Black Death, and income gains were largely derived from population decline. But it should not be thought that these gains were automatic. Many other areas, including Egypt, China, and Eastern Europe, suffered equally devastating losses in population. Yet they did not sustain their gains in real GDP per capita as England did. In England, the demographic decline was accompanied by major changes in the organization of the economy. In the fifteenth and sixteenth centuries, serfdom was largely abolished, a flourishing export trade in wool was developed, and the country's legal and judicial system continued to evolve. By contrast, in Eastern Europe peasant labour was enserfed after the Black Death, while in Egypt vast areas fell out of cultivation and in China the plague helped usher in the collapse of the Mongol Yuan Empire.

Nonetheless, in Britain for the first 250 years after the Black Death, slow growth in total GDP just barely kept pace with slow growth in population.[15] If we were to stop the clock in 1650, it would be obvious that England had not yet embarked on anything like modern economic growth. From 1400 to 1650, England floated on a Malthusian equilibrium, with population and GDP both slowly recovering, and two-and-a-half centuries with no gains at all in income per capita. There were also no major shifts in the structure of the economy: Agriculture's share in real GDP was 45.5 per cent in 1381, 39.7 per cent in 1522, and 41.1 per cent in 1600.[16]

After 1650, however, there are clearly signs of change. From 1650 to 1700 income per capita grew more strongly than ever before, although this was accompanied by a slight population decline. From 1700 onwards, Britain was able to combine growth in both population and GDP per capita. Yet growth in both population and income per head were still very weak from the 1700s to the 1750s. Only after 1750 do we see stronger growth in both population and income per head, with the growth rate of GDP per capita moving well above pre-modern levels.

Determining precisely when England's modern economic growth began thus depends greatly on how we view events from 1650 to 1800. When in this period do we clearly see a break from past patterns of pre-modern, Malthusian growth? When does income per capita break free from both population constraints and pre-modern rates of economic growth?

Let us first focus on the half-century from 1650 to 1700 – what happened in these decades? The answer is that a significant structural transformation in the economy coincided with a period of slight population decline, to produce a huge surge in income per capita. The structural transformation was threefold. First, in manufacturing there was a leap in the export production of textiles, driven by the 'new draperies', a blend of wool and other fibres that was lighter than the 'old draperies' of heavy wool. The new draperies were wildly popular, and allowed England to seize market share from

Holland and other European wool producers. This success propelled a large number of workers into spinning for merchants.[17] Second, there was the importation of Dutch agricultural techniques into England, leading to shifts in crop rotations, and use of fodder crops (clover and turnips) that allowed light-soil regions to greatly increase their productivity for wheat, allowing heavy-soil regions to specialize more in livestock raising.[18] And finally, religious shifts in this period were favourable to Britain. Despite the turmoil of the Puritan Revolution, Restoration, and the Glorious Revolution, Britain in the late seventeenth century remained a region open to Protestants. Britain thus attracted Protestant refugees from the continent, especially from France, who brought capital and skills with them, providing a positive shock for production and trade.

Nonetheless, it is clear that these changes were not transformative. Changes in agriculture, for instance, were minimal and real output in agriculture in these decades rose only 0.2 per cent per year. Industrial output rose rapidly by 1.01 per cent per year in this period, as did output in services, at 0.71 per cent per year. The slow growth in agricultural output compared to industry in this period means that industry's fraction of the economy rose and agriculture's fell – but this did not yet reflect a fundamental change in the economy. According to Broadberry and his co-authors' analysis of labour shares, the male workforce in agriculture in 1688 was still 46 per cent, and remained 43 per cent as late as 1759. While this was a significant reduction from the 67 per cent level that had prevailed in the fourteenth to sixteenth centuries, it did not yet presage the modern increases in productivity that would follow.[19]

Even in the period 1700 to 1750, we do not see anything in the GDP figures that looks like modern economic performance. In this half-century population growth was also quite slow, only half the rate of the entire sixteenth century, and only equal to the rate of population growth in the late fifteenth century. Surely with such modest population growth, a modern economy should have been able to produce significant gains in income per head. Yet in fact the momentum of the late seventeenth century petered out, and growth in income per head was no different than that in earlier centuries. Indeed, the growth in income per head in 1700–50, of 0.18 per cent per year, was identical to the growth rate for the period from the 1270s to 1700.

Perhaps most striking is that Broadberry and his co-authors find no continuation of the strong growth in industrial productivity and output that sparked the per capita income growth from 1650–1700. Instead, where industrial output per capita in Britain had risen by 73 per cent from 1650 to 1700, such gains came to an abrupt end by 1700, as in the next half-century it rose only 9 per cent, or just one-eighth as much.[20] This was a much lower rate of growth in industrial output per person than England had seen even in the late sixteenth century, to say nothing of the late seventeenth. In short, there was nothing distinctive about the rate of growth in either British GDP per capita or industrial output per head in the first half of the eighteenth century. Macroeconomic performance in this period, with slow population growth and minimal (0.18 per cent) growth in GDP per capita, is simply typical of what was observed since the Middle Ages.

## Comparing divergence across cases

One could argue that even if the rate of growth in Holland and Britain was neither sustained nor historically exceptional prior to 1750, it was the level of output per capita achieved that was unusual, and so marked a 'Divergence' from prior global patterns. If the Netherlands, or Britain, were precocious in achieving levels of GDP per capita that went significantly beyond the attainments of other pre-modern societies, it could be that achievement which set the stage for their later breakthroughs to modern growth. Drawing on data assembled by Broadberry and others, I argue that this is not the case.

What is remarkable in fact is how rigid the ceiling appears to be on pre-modern peak levels of GDP per capita. Table 2.3 shows estimates of the highest levels of GDP per capita found for a variety of societies, along with the dates at which those levels were achieved, at any time up to 1800.[21] These were generally associated with 'efflorescences' that marked peaks of high culture and economic achievement, along with technical advances that boosted output and trade. They include Song China in the eleventh century, medieval Spain, Renaissance Northern Italy, the Netherlands at the dawn of the nineteenth century (we only have data for Holland earlier, which for reasons noted above is not an apt unit of comparison with much larger countries), and Britain in the mid-eighteenth and beginning of the nineteenth centuries.

It is astonishing that with the exception of medieval Spain, which was low, and Great Britain in 1800, which is exceptionally high, the figures are almost all within 10–15 per cent of each other. Even compared to Song China, almost 800 years earlier, the Netherlands in 1800 had a GDP per capita only 15 per cent higher; and they were only 4 per cent richer than the level Northern Italy had achieved 350 years earlier. Great Britain in 1750 was not yet evidently any better off than any prior successful pre-modern

**Table 2.3  Peak GDP per capita in various societies in history in Geary-Khamis International 1990 dollars**

| Country (Year) | Peak GDP per capita | Ratio: compared to Song China/ to Renaissance Italy |
|---|---|---|
| China (1020) | 1,518 | 1.00/0.90 |
| Spain (1348) | 1,030 | 0.68/0.61 |
| Northern Italy (1450) | 1,688 | 1.11/1.00 |
| The Netherlands (1800) | 1,752 | 1.15/1.04 |
| Great Britain (1750) | 1,710 | 1.13/1.01 |
| Great Britain (1800 – Broadberry et al.) | 2,080 | 1.37/1.23 |

*Source*: Stephen Broadberry; Bruce Campbell, Bruce; Alexander Klein, Mark Overton, and Bas van Leeuwen (2015), *British Economic Growth, 1270–1870*. Cambridge: Cambridge University Press, Table 10.02.

country – GDP per capita was only 13 per cent higher than Song China and only 1 per cent higher than Renaissance Italy. If we exclude the bottom two lines – that is, look at the world's leading economies from 1020 to 1750 (or 1800 for the Netherlands) – the message is one of remarkable uniformity: None of the European countries at any time achieves any meaningful advantage in GDP per capita over any other's peak achievement, nor over the peak achievement of China. At least as regards peak GDP per capita, as late as 1750 there is no divergence of any kind, anywhere.

In sum, if one confines one's view to the years before 1800, there is nothing in either the pattern of growth or the level attained in GDP per capita anywhere in Northwest Europe that is at all indicative of a break with prevailing pre-modern patterns. This is not to deny that crucial things were happening, such as the flurry of inventions in Europe, the advance of parliamentary governments, the rise of learning, the conquest of the seas, the advance of religious pluralism, or dozens of other factors that contributed to subsequent economic achievements. It is only to say that one cannot find, in the available GDP data, evidence of sustained, rapid growth in GDP per capita nor advances to unusual pre-modern levels at any time before the nineteenth century. Both the Netherlands and Britain did have episodes of impressive growth in GDP per capita; but these merely raised them to levels seen earlier by other very successful countries. Once they reached those heights, they were marooned there – the Netherlands had no further growth in GDP per capita from the 1590s to 1790s, and Britain had no return to the growth rates in GDP per capita seen in 1650–1700 until at least 1750 and perhaps not until after 1800.

It is true that other nations suffered a considerable decline in GDP per capita over the centuries since their peak, leaving the Netherlands and Britain in a relatively stronger position as the nineteenth century opened. History makes clear, however, that such an advantage is no automatic guarantee of further progress. Song China and Renaissance Italy in their day held commanding leads in GDP per capita over their neighbours, and did so at a level of income per capita not significantly different (evidently within 10 per cent in real terms) from that of Britain and the Netherlands, without subsequently progressing to take GDP per capita to further heights. For that matter, the Netherlands' great riches relative to other nations achieved in the late sixteenth century appears to have done nothing to boost its GDP per capita in the succeeding two centuries. Relative advantage is nice to have, but it in no way guarantees a better future.

## Conclusion

This chapter has said nothing about the ultimate causes of the 'Great Divergence'. That debate remains open and is considered in other chapters in this book. Still, in order to explain something, it is important to know exactly what is to be explained. The new data makes it indisputable that the onset of a distinctive and new pattern of economic growth was a relatively late phenomenon, only evident in the GDP per capita data from 1750 onwards. Whatever caused the Great Divergence to arise c. 1750, it was not a centuries-long prior record of exceptional growth rates or levels of GDP per capita in Northwest Europe.

This new analysis of the data of Broadberry and co-authors makes it clear why even expert observers of the British economy in the eighteenth century, such as Adam Smith, could not see signs of any economic divergence. There was simply no evidence of any departure from pre-modern growth patterns before 1750.

Explanations for the 'Great Divergence' that claim to find its roots in late medieval or early modern growth patterns are thus mistaken. Certainly there were episodes of prior growth, but such episodes lasted only a few decades and then stalled, and only led the Netherlands and Britain to catch up with levels of GDP per capita attained many centuries earlier in Northern Italy and Song China. To understand the onset of distinctively modern economic growth – with sustained increases in both population and real income at high rates leading to levels of income not seen in prior eras – we need to develop explanations for a relatively late and sudden transition to a new mode of economic growth that appeared only after 1750.

## Notes

1.  Ho-fung Hung (2003), 'Orientalist knowledge and social theories: China and the European conceptions of East-West differences from 1600 to 1900', *Sociological Theory*, 21 (3), 254–79. Adam Smith offered the same view: 'China has been long one of the richest, that is, one of the most fertile, best cultivated, most industrious, and most populous countries in world. It seems, however, to have been long stationary'. A. Smith (1776), *An Inquiry into the Nature and Causes of the Wealth of Nations*, Feedbooks http://en.wikisource.org, 48.

2.  See for instance, P. Hoffman (2015), *Why Did Europe Conquer the World?* Princeton: Princeton University Press; G. Clark (2007), *A Farewell to Alms: A Brief Economic History of the World*. Princeton: Princeton University Press; T. Huff (2003), *The Rise of Early Modern Science: Islam, China and the West*. Cambridge: Cambridge University Press; I. Wallerstein (2011), *The Modern World System*. Berkeley: University of California Press; D. N. McCloskey (2016), *Bourgeois Equality: How Idea, Not Capital or Institutions, Enriched the World*. Chicago: University of Chicago Press; J. Mokyr (2016), *The Culture of Growth: The Origins of the Modern Economy*. Princeton: Princeton University Press; S. R. Epstein (2000), *Freedom and Growth: The Rise of States and Markets in Europe, 1300–1750*. London: Routledge.

3.  K. Pomeranz (2000), *The Great Divergence: China, Europe, and the Making of the Modern World Economy*. Princeton: Princeton University Press; R. B. Wong (1997), *China Transformed: Historical Change and the Limits of European Experience*. Ithaca: Cornell University Press; A. Gunder Frank (1998), *ReOrient: Global Economy in the Asian Age*. Berkeley: University of California Press; Bozhong, *Agricultural Development in Jiangnan*; R. Marks (2006), *Tigers, Rice, Silk and Silt*. New York: Academic Press; J. A. Goldstone (1991), *Revolution and Rebellion in the Early Modern World*. Berkeley: University of California Press; Idem (1998), 'The problem of the "Early Modern" world', *Journal of the Economic and Social History of the Orient*, 41 (3), 249–84; Idem (2000), 'The rise of the West – or not? A revision to socio-economic history', *Sociological Theory*, 18 (2), 157–94; D. O. Flynn and A. Giráldez (2010), *China and the Birth of Globalization in the Sixteenth Century*. Farnham: Ashgate; P. Parthasarathi (2011), *Why Europe Grew Rich and Asia Did Not: Global Economic Divergence, 1600-1850*. Cambridge: Cambridge University Press; P. Vries (2003), *Via Peking Back to Manchester: Britain, the Industrial Revolution and China*. Leiden: Leiden University.

4. Among the most important were W. Skinner (1977), *The City in Late Imperial China*. Stanford: Stanford University Press; W. Rowe (1992), *Hankow: Commerce and Society in a Chinese City, 1796–1889*. Stanford: Stanford University Press; J. Z. Lee and W. Feng (2001), *One Quarter of Humanity: Malthusian Mythology and Chinese Realities*. Cambridge, MA: Harvard University Press; P. Perdue (2005), *China Marches West: The Qing Conquest of Central Eurasia*. Cambridge: Belknap Press; T. Brook (1998), *The Confusions of Pleasure: Commerce and Culture in Ming China*. Berkeley: University of California Press; S. Naquin and E. S. Rawski (1987), *Chinese Society in the Eighteenth Century*. New Haven: Yale University Press.

5. On labour/capital ratios, see R. C. Allen (2009), *The British Industrial Revolution in Global Perspective*. Cambridge: Cambridge University Press; J.-L. Rosenthal and R. Bin Wong (2011), *Before and Beyond Divergence: The Politics of Economic Change in China and Europe*. On physical geography, see I. Morris (2010), *Why the West Rules – For Now*. New York: Strauss and Giroux-Farrar; J. Diamond (1999), *Guns, Germs and Steel*. New York: W.W. Norton. On political organization, see P. Vries (2013), *Escape from Poverty: The Origins of Modern Economic Growth*. Vienna: University of Vienna Press.

6. The classic demonstration of how population data can be extracted from parish records is E. A. Wrigley and R. S. Schofield (1989), *The Population History of England and Wales 1541–1871*. Cambridge: Cambridge University Press. Additional research using data from local registers in Europe and lineage and other records in China can be found in R. C. Allen, T. Bengtsson and M. Dribe (eds) (2005), *Living Standards in the Past: New Perspectives on Well-Being in Asia and Europe*. Oxford: Oxford University Press; T. Bengtsson, C. Campbell and J. Z. Lee (eds) (2009), *Life under Pressure: Mortality and Living Standards in Europe and Asia, 1700–1900*. Cambridge, MA: MIT Press; and N. O. Tsuya, W. Feng, G. Alter, J. Z. Lee, et al. (eds) (2010), *Prudence and Pressure: Reproduction and Human Agency in Europe and Asia, 1700–1900*. Cambridge, MA: MIT Press.

7. The British data have been published in S. N. Broadberry; B. M. S. Campbell; A.Klein, M. Overton and B. van Leeuwen (2015), *British Economic Growth, 1270–1870*. Cambridge: Cambridge University Press. Kindle Edition. The Dutch data have been published online by the Centre for Global Economic History by J. L. van Zanden and B. van Leeuwen as the 'Reconstruction National Accounts of Holland', at: http://www.cgeh.nl/reconstruction-national-accounts-holland-1500-1800-0.

8. F. Braudel (1973), *Capitalism and Material Life 1400–1800*. New York: Harper Collins; I. Wallerstein (1974), *The Modern World System I: Capitalist Agriculture and the Origins of the European World Economy in the Sixteenth Century*. New York: Academic Press; C. M. Cipolla (1976), *Before the Industrial Revolution: European Society and Economy, 1000–1700*. New York: W.W. Norton.

9. S. Broadberry (2013), 'Accounting for the Great Divergence', *LSE Economic History Working Papers*, 814, 3.

10. A. M. de Plijt and J. L. van Zanden (2013), 'Accounting for the "Little Divergence": What drove economic growth in pre-industrial Europe 1300–1800', *Working Papers* 0046, Utrecht University, Centre for Global Economic History.

11. J. A. Goldstone (2002), 'Efflorescences and economic growth in world history: Rethinking the "Rise of the West" and the Industrial Revolution', *Journal of World History*, 13 (2), 323–89.

12. De Plijt and van Zanden, 'Accounting for the "Little Divergence"'; J. de Vries and A. Van der Woude (1997), *The First Modern Economy. Success, Failure and Perseverance of the Dutch Economy*, 1500–1815. Cambridge: Cambridge University Press.

13. The decadal averages shown in Figure 2.1, and the period growth rates in Table 2.1 below, are calculated by the author from the annual data provided in 'Reconstruction National Accounts of Holland'.

14. S. Schama (1988), *The Embarrassment of Riches*. Berkeley: University of California Press.

15. Population and GDP data from Broadberry, et al., *British Economic Growth*, Table 5.06.

16. Broadberry, et al., *British Economic Growth*, Table 5.01.

17. C. Muldrew (2012), '"Th'ancient Distaff" and "Whirling Spindle": Measuring the contribution of spinning to household earnings and the national economy in England, 1550–1770', *Economic History Review*, 65 (2), 498–536. It also helped that England won a series of naval wars with Holland in this half-century, greatly expanding British access to international trade.

18. J. A. Goldstone (1988), 'Regional ecology and agrarian development in early modern England and France', *Politics and Society*, 16 (2–3), 287–334; R. C. Allen (1999), 'Tracking the agricultural revolution in England', *Economic History Review*, 52 (2), 209–35.

19. Productivity data from Broadberry, et al., *British Economic Growth*, Table 5.07; male labour in agriculture from Broadberry, et al., Table 9.08.

20. Computed from Broadberry, et al., *British Economic Growth*, Table Appendix 5.3.

21. The collection of macro-data on national GDP and GDP per capita, and its reduction to comparable real levels through Geary-Khamis constant dollars or other metrics, has been roundly criticized on the basis of difficulties in making meaningful comparisons in terms of highly varied local currencies and the diverse regional economies in any large state, e.g. Deng and O'Brien, 'China's GDP per capita'. Yet this project is seen by many others as valuable and worth perfecting, e.g. Bolt and van Zanden, 'The Maddison Project'.

# CHAPTER 3
## USEFUL AND RELIABLE KNOWLEDGE IN EUROPE AND CHINA
*Patrick O'Brien*

Metanarratives celebrating the economic rise of the West have been challenged in recent times by two theses proposed by the California and World Systems Schools of historical sociology.[1] The first insists that economic divergence between Europe and Asia became apparent much later than what previous generations of historians have suggested. It reconfigures the economic history of the pre-modern era into a world of 'surprising resemblances' to use Kenneth Pomeranz's now famous expression.[2] It also rejects assertions that Europe alone possessed the cultures and institutions for modern economic growth.[3] The second thesis explains more than three centuries of divergence between East and West with reference to Europe's favourable location and natural endowments. These, combined with high and persistent levels of investment in warfare, colonization, and mercantilist policies (by way of coercion and unequal exchange), enabled Europeans to garner most of the gains from trade from the fifteenth to the nineteenth century.[4]

As observed by Jack Goldstone in this book, critiques among European and American historians have concentrated upon the statistical evidence deemed to demonstrate that divergence could be located earlier in time.[5] The Divergence debate cannot be conducted only with reference to macroeconomic statistics. This chapter considers and compares regimes (clusters of connected elites and institutions) engaged with the discovery, development, diffusion, and application of innovations based upon 'useful and reliable knowledge' in China and Europe. It is deemed that such innovations augmented the productivity of labour employed by households, farms, and firms.[6]

Global histories of science and technology suggest that some European cultures became permeated by a cosmography that was conducive to the accumulation of useful and reliable knowledge. Gradually, the embrace of new knowledge by educated and wealthy elites embodied a cultural and a more directly applicable potential for advances in total factor productivities that allowed Western populations to escape from age-old Malthusian threats into modern economic growth before the populations of Asia.[7] This view was supported by a programme of historical research led by Joseph Needham, expanded by Mark Elvin, analysed in a series of conference papers by the Achievement Project in the 1990s, synthesized in three books by Joel Mokyr, and became an accepted theme among scholars engaged in the divergence debate.[8] Assuming that the established consensus which suggests that the locus of scientific discovery and technological innovation shifted from Asia to Europe by, if not sometime before, the end of the fifteenth century, this chapter provides an outline comparing Europe's own trajectory towards the formation and consolidation of a regime for the sustained generation of useful and reliable knowledge with China.

I wish to address the hypothesis posed by Weber, and developed by Butterfield, Needham, and later followers, who suggested that the innovations introduced into early modern European agriculture and industry were connected to changes in conceptions of the natural world held by Europe's educated, wealthy, and political elites. Cultural change led these elites to support networks of proto-scientists, inventors, and artisans and to establish institutions that might conceivably generate and adapt knowledge with potential to generate private profit, support the geopolitical power of states, and secure the health, security, and material welfare of European societies.[9] The thesis that a switch in mentality shaped by science came on stream in the seventeenth and eighteenth centuries became the subject of a debate between two great Sinologist historians of science that is ongoing.[10]

Stimulated by debates on the Great Divergence, challenges to this view have been mounted on two fronts. The first repeats familiar arguments from traditional controversies between science and religion, namely that beliefs espoused and enforced by Christian churches were at best neutral and at worst repressive towards investigations into the natural world.[11] The second and more recent wave of literature from histories of science maintains that knowledge discovered, developed, and utilized for purposes of production was 'socially constructed'.[12] This literature points out that science originated from several parts of the world and that its connections to the beliefs promoted by European elites were at best of tenuous significance for technological change.[13]

Recent histories of science are more inclined to accept that monotheistic Christendom evolved into a culture that *ceteris paribus* embodied elements recognized as significant for the promotion of a functional cosmography for the comprehension of nature.[14] Before the Reformation, European Christianity had consolidated its role as a hegemonic quasi-autonomous, hierarchically organized religion that over time had suppressed all but one system of beliefs about nature and the operations of the natural world in favour of its own revealed truths for which its clergy held a monopoly of interpretation. Nevertheless, as it evolved over the centuries into a supranational organization, the hierarchy of the Roman Church recognized that faith in truths as revealed in the New Testament, the Bible, and other canonical references would not be sufficient for competition with monotheistic Islam, to combat heresies, or to retain its ideological influence over royal power. Thus the papacy and bishops found it expedient to establish, patronize, and control institutions based upon Greek and Roman models for the higher education of clerical and secular elites that included classical modes of conducting 'rational' arguments in law, medicine, natural philosophy, and even theology.[15]

Under strictly regulated conditions, proto-universities spread across the cities of medieval Europe and established faculties and curricula for compulsory introductory courses in natural philosophy based upon texts by Aristotle, Plato, Ptolemy, Galen, Hippocrates, and other pagan authors. These included a corpus of classical speculations about the operations of the celestial, terrestrial, and biological spheres of what the Church resolutely insisted was a divinely created and ordered natural world.[16]

In recent years, scholars working on the medieval origins of modern science have rehabilitated this long tradition of classical and post-classical endeavours to comprehend the natural world.[17] They have researched how far and how deeply European levels of cosmographical comprehension had developed, before they were displaced by Copernicus' seminal work on astronomy in 1543. Thereafter, the introduction of innovative paradigms for an accelerated accumulation of more useful and reliable knowledge marked the onset of what many historians continue to recognize to as the 'Scientific Revolution'.[18]

That plateau in knowledge formation depended upon the diffusion of printed books, which formed the basis for conversations, correspondence, associations, and debate among Europe's growing numbers of natural philosophers and theologians dissatisfied with, or sceptical of, revealed spiritual truths.[19] Scholars belonging to what has been called the 'Republics of Letters' became interested in the workings of God's natural world and in the possibilities for its control and manipulation.[20] They widened agendas for discussion and education to comprehend a range of natural phenomena including the age, size, shape, geography, and limits of planet earth; movements of the sun, moon, and stars; seas and their tides; climates; earthquakes; minerals; chemical substances; soils; plants; animals; fish; and human bodies. They engaged in debates concerned with mathematical and rational methods for the study of medicine, law, and even theology, which coexisted in a hegemonic but uneasy relationship with natural philosophy.

That tension became more fraught during the Renaissance when another cycle of humanist scholarship recovered a series of classical texts, which opened up a wider range of discourse about the nature and operations of God's universe.[21] Thus a wave of classical scholarship not only questioned Aristotelian natural philosophy as expurgated and beatified by the Church, but came dangerously close to challenging the logical and evidential basis of revealed truths about the world contained in the Scriptures and other sacrosanct texts propounded by theologians in the service of the Roman Church.[22] Thereafter irreversible and fundamental changes in a cosmography embodied in the cultures of European elites, in line with developments cautiously anticipated and outlined by a minority of precursors during the Middle Ages, became clear and powerful.[23]

The period also witnessed the European 'discovery' of a new continent, the division of Christendom into Catholic and Protestant countries and communities, horrendous wars of religion, and the consolidation of regular transcontinental commerce. This eventful conjuncture has also been contentiously, but plausibly, configured by historians of Europe to mark a new regime for the accumulation of useful and reliable knowledge that actively promoted and supported sustained economic growth.[24] Its development was neither revolutionary in pace nor linear in trend. Its historically validated connections to an ongoing but gradual process of innovation were for many decades confined to a limited range of technologies that in time became useful and reliable for navigation by sea, the surveying of space, the derivation of energy from water, atmospheric pressure and steam power, drainage, the accuracy of artillery, the bleaching of textiles, and the like.[25]

Debate over their nature and economic significance has been protracted and remains unresolved. Nevertheless, the contention of this chapter is that the significance of this famous conjuncture for narratives concerned with the economic divergence between Asia and Europe resides essentially in an unmeasurable but unmistakable impetus towards the formation of confident conceptions among Europe's educated and wealthy elites that the natural world was in process of becoming more intelligible and manipulable for material gain and human health than their ancestors living in Roman and feudal times had ever imagined.[26] Unfortunately, that impetus in the conceptions and perceptions of Western elites cannot be validated because historical evidence for its emergence consists essentially of books written by famous names in the histories of science, technology, and cosmography, which have been subsequently selected as contributions to the development of a plethora of specialized disciplines which were part of the natural sciences.[27] Attempts to validate this hypothesis statistically have produced some positive but inconclusive results in the form of a dramatic rise in the numbers and discernible decline in the prices of printed books published between 1450 and 1750 in Western Europe following the invention and diffusion of the printing press.[28]

The flow of published knowledge representing a reformed cosmography was almost certainly rising rapidly during a period when the number of students attending universities and taking a compulsory course or two in natural philosophy was also increasing faster than populations at large.[29] Nevertheless, the case for an increasing flow of knowledge about the operations of a natural world remains almost impossible to demonstrate. Thus, an argument for cultural shifts in the cosmographical beliefs of an increasing proportion of educated Europeans can only be made on a priori and probabilistic grounds and with reference to the beliefs that their counterparts held about the natural world and prospects for its control before, say, 1450 or in other parts of the world in early modern times.[30]

One tenet remained hegemonic: It was dangerous to challenge Christianity's foundational belief that the universe had been created by God; that operations of its celestial, terrestrial, and biological spheres were divinely ordained, regulated, and suspendible; and that mankind's primary purpose was to live but a short interlude on earth according to moral principles enunciated in sacred Christian texts as interpreted by God's one and only true Roman Catholic Church. Its hierarchy had, moreover, ordained that if men wished to understand the operations of a divine natural world, they should first seek guidance from the Scriptures. Alternatively, they could consult a rather restricted range of licensed classical authorities: first and foremost Aristotle on anything but particularly on logical ways of comprehending the universe, Ptolemy on the heavens and solar system, Galen on the human body, Hippocrates on medicine, Pliny on plants and animals, Euclid on mathematics, and so on.[31]

Centuries passed before Europe's traditional belief system became 'secularized' by a scientific cosmography. Before the age of Enlightenment, elite culture changed slowly. Progress could certainly have been assisted by appealing to the authority of a wider number of classical authors other than Aristotle – particularly to Plato, Archimedes, Lucretius, and Epicurus.[32] Paradoxically, the worldly and politicized hierarchy of the

Catholic Church advised by Jesuit intellectuals acted from time to time as a buffer against fundamentalist attacks on the diffusion of knowledge that endangered 'truths' about nature as revealed in Christianity's sacred texts.[33]

By 1750 – in contrast to their ancestors – most educated Europeans supported what had matured into a tradition of state and private investment in voyages of 'discovery' and intra-continental exploration. Most believed that the skies and heavens could be mapped and that their own planet earth, displaced from the centre of an infinite universe, rotated daily on its axis and circled the sun along with all other planets. Within an infinitely expanded universe, they recognized their own insignificance.[34] Man and his common sense were no longer the measure of all things. His sensory perceptions and understandings of nature were recognized as limited, but had and would predictably continue to be successfully extended by instruments in the service of speculations, hypotheses, and controlled experiments designed and monitored by 'networks of experts' with credentials and codes of conduct maturing into scientific disciplines.[35]

These men not only had produced maps of the world and its seas and oceans with more mathematically precise coordinates for purposes of trade and navigation, but also were mapping the skies for the same utilitarian purposes. After decades of inconclusive investigations into the powers of flowing water and the pressures and weight of air, they had also discovered new sources of energy with potential to be developed, harnessed, and diffused for production.[36] In the course of a protracted intellectual conflict between 'ancients and moderns' marked by 'battles of the books', the traditional classical authorities such as Aristotle, including Ptolemy, Galen, and Hippocrates, had been effectively degraded by the systematic exposure of their errors, by geographical discoveries, by solar observations, and by the elevation of mathematical logic and experimental methods into hallmarks for new and more productive ways of accumulating reliable and useful knowledge about the natural world.[37]

For economic development, clear and direct links between Europe's reconfigured and extended investigations in natural philosophy and breakthroughs in technologies for agronomy, mechanical engineering, and bodily health have proved difficult to document.[38] Moreover, in recent years, historians of science have argued that many acclaimed natural philosophers including Galileo, Hooke, Boyle, Beekmans, Huygens, and Newton continued to engage seriously with the claims to knowledge by alchemists and astrologers involved with rather unsystematic and unexplained manipulations of materials and natural sources of energy sold to gullible customers and powerful patrons.[39] In any case, the 'experiments' of alchemists and observations of astrologers contributed to debates about scientific ways of knowing and understanding how the natural world really worked.[40]

## Natural philosophy and the transition to science in the West

Over the long run, direct connections between Europe's tradition in natural philosophy, which matured into science allied to technological innovations, remain unmistakable.[41] Global economic history's concerns have, however, been latterly with the economic divergence between Europe and Asia. In the absence of bodies of secondary literatures comparable in volume, scope, and sophistication to recent historical analyses of European science, religions, and cosmography, it may be premature to agree with Joseph Needham's insights and conclusions published two generations ago. As a Christian Marxist of unsurpassed erudition in global histories of science and technology, Needham also remained deeply aware of the significance of the fortuitous but ultimately fortunate religious and classical antecedents and foundations for Europe's peculiar but promotional cosmology for the accumulation of useful and reliable knowledge.[42]

Furthermore, global historians need to be reminded that Butterfield saw Europe's 'scientific, agrarian and industrial revolutions as forming such a system of complex and inter-related changes that in the lack of a microscopic examination, we have to heap them altogether as aspects of a general movement'.[43] Herbert Butterfield's view could never develop into the kind of history that could appeal to economists. To be elevated into a key chapter for narratives of divergence, it could only be tested for plausibility by way of reciprocal comparisons with the cosmographies and regimes for the production, development, and diffusion of useful and reliable knowledge operating within Islamic empires, China, and India in pre-modern times.

Of course, to paraphrase Ben Elman, Asian intellectuals continued to be engaged in endeavours that understood the natural world on their own terms and in their own ways.[44] Nevertheless, the question of how effective their engagement became for the discovery, development, and diffusion of technological, institutional, and biological innovations is the issue. The 'cultural' dispositions towards innovation displayed by the political, economic, and intellectual elites managing early modern Asian societies continue to be represented as embedded in traditions of belief and thought that appear to be indifferent and sometimes even hostile to systematic investigations into nature and technology.[45]

Unfortunately, only a limited literature is currently available for the construction of a comprehensive academic survey of the beliefs of elites and institutions in South, West, and Central Asia.[46] At present, the only prospect for an intellectual engagement in reciprocal comparisons with the evolution of Asian beliefs and institutions that is comparable to and coterminous with the conjuncture in the culture of Western Europe can be read in histories of imperial China.[47]

Thanks to the Needham programme for the history of science and civilization in China, relevant secondary literature that could be plausibly taken to represent East Asian thoughts and beliefs has become extensive, diverse, and sophisticated enough to enable a brief but tentative survey of relevant literatures published in English.[48] A number of scholars still accept Needham's view that developments in the formation of useful and reliable knowledge faltered sometime after if not before 1500.[49] Thereafter Chinese contributions can be plausibly discussed not as stasis but rather as a history of relative retardation. No consensus exists, however, as to when and why a climacteric emerged and persisted during the Ming and Qing dynasties.

Constructivist and cultural narratives have pointed to several theoretically and potentially salient contrasts with the economies of Western Europe.[50] For example, and in order of significance, the share of the empire's population located in towns and cities regarded as hospitable locations for the formation of the human capital and institutions required to engage with scientific and technological innovation declined from a 20 per cent level under the Song dynasty (960–1279 CE) to well below the ratios estimated for the advanced economies of Europe by 1700.[51] Furthermore, a high proportion of the empire's stock and flows of men (with the education, skills, talents, and motivation required for the discovery, development, and diffusion of useful and reliable knowledge) invested time and family money on acquiring the credentials and qualifications prescribed by the Chinese state for entry into and advancement within a bureaucracy recruited on merits as displayed in a competitive and empire-wide examination.

The curricula for this admirably meritocratic system, which persisted dynasty after dynasty, exercised a dominant influence on the mission, form, and content of all types of education undertaken by Chinese males beyond levels of basic literacy. Secondary education was, moreover, regulated by and for the state to serve two other purposes essential for the governance of an extensive and complex empire. The first was to endow its mandarinate of officials with the prestige and authority derived from their status as a meritocracy, implementing the decrees and orders of an emperor whose power to rule over the heterogeneous populations and territories of a vast empire was widely proclaimed as a mandate from heaven.[52]

The second purpose of imperial China's tightly regulated system of secondary education was to clarify, disseminate, and debate how a set of interrelated moral principles enshrined in ancient texts for the governance of an extensive, complex, and agrarian empire could be internalized into personal and social behaviour. China's ancient philosophical texts (as Jesuit missionaries to the empire appreciated) can be plausibly represented as analogous to the canonical texts of Christendom. Over centuries that predated the birth of Christ by way of commentaries, critiques, adaptations, and the selective absorption of elements from rival systems of belief including Buddhism, Daoism, and Monism, the theology cum ideology of Ming and Qing China became consolidated into a code for righteous behaviour framed by the writings of Confucius, which is conventionally referred by intellectual historians as Neo-Confucianism.[53]

Neo-Confucian texts dominated the syllabus for the imperial examination system and curricula for the education of China's elites. These texts were studied, memorized, and analysed using philological methods by the best and brightest young minds in China, and they instilled a quasi-spiritual reverence for ancient classical authorities including Mencius and Laozi and particularly Confucius.[54] This ancient and quasi sanctified 'wisdom' can be understood as providing an education in moral and political philosophy that inculcated the virtues embodied in the cultivation of personal enlightenment through humanistic and didactic forms of scholarship and, above all, through respect for and compliance with hierarchy reposed in patriarchy, within families, and politically in dynasties of emperors mandated from heaven and served by officials exercising paternal and moral rule over the peoples of an agrarian empire.[55]

From an Euro-centred perspective, the content of Chinese education, the forms of teaching adopted by institutions for secondary education, and the absence of a tradition of disputation among masters and their pupils, as well as its enlightened but overwhelming concerns with personal behaviour, social stability and political order seem to be less hospitable and encouraging towards the study of investigations of the natural world than was apparently the case for the cosmography evolving in medieval and early modern Europe.[56] Nevertheless, it would be entirely erroneous to conclude that knowledge that was useful and reliable for the comprehension, control, and manipulation of the celestial, terrestrial, and biological spheres of that world had not accumulated at a more impressive rate in the Chinese empire than in Western Europe before 1500 or that it lapsed into stasis thereafter.[57]

Apart possibly from theories of probability, all approaches to investigations into the natural world operating in Europe between the sixteenth and the eighteenth centuries were also at least present in China.[58] Furthermore, only a minority of the empire's educated elite obtained posts in the bureaucracy and even those privileged scholar officials found it necessary to acquire some practical knowledge of agronomy, meteorology, hydrology, pharmacology, and medicine. Growing numbers of men (literati) educated in Neo-Confucian philosophy and statecraft became experts and wrote treatises, manuals, and entries for encyclopaedia, on the properties, uses, and purposes of 'things' such as birds, coinage, copper, drugs, dyestuffs, lacquerware, porcelain, salt sugar, and textiles. They consorted with craftsmen in order to publish specialized and presumably useful knowledge of many 'things' (*gewu*) as well as speculations about the 'concrete forces' embodied in sound, light, and magnetism.[59]

In China, however, the pursuit of this type of knowledge was neither rewarded with prizes from the state nor protected for purposes of individual material gain by patents for monopoly. Above all, this knowledge was not regarded as anything like as prestigious as classical forms of learning that contributed to harmonious family life, to stability for the social order, and to the benign governance of a huge pre-modern empire.[60] By late Ming times, some scholars began to question the hegemony and utility of classical learning and sought, with limited success, to redefine the social and cultural status of more practical and material forms of knowledge including knowledge imported into China, as artefacts and industrial technologies as well as the new mathematics, astronomical methods, and observations communicated by Jesuit missionaries and European merchants.[61] All proposals for reform were predictably resisted by scholar officials concerned to protect their own status and cultural capital. Under the Qing dynasty, reformers could be persecuted but generally they failed to convince the political establishments of either the more open Ming regime or the alien Manchu dynasty (who conquered the empire between 1636 and 1683) to modify let alone overturn Neo-Confucian ways of thinking about an interconnected and harmonious cosmic and moral order that included the heavens and all things on earth including man and his organic relations with nature. After all, the development and dissemination of that cosmology had for millennia served efficiently as an ideology for the maintenance of centralized rule by a long succession of dynasties.[62]

There may have been, as some revisionist historians have recently claimed, lost moments and promising opportunities for reform to the ways that China's talented and educated elites conceived of ways to explore and interrogate the natural world under late Ming emperors.[63] Greater attention and respect might have been paid to Western knowledge that only became accessible to China's literati through the less than objective conduits of Jesuit missionaries educated in Western natural philosophy and resident at court, as well as self-interested European merchants trading through Canton.[64] Perhaps the takeover of the empire by an alien dynasty anxious to secure legitimacy by suppressing departures from classical Han Chinese traditions as misplaced, degenerate, and potentially destabilizing can be plausibly represented post hoc as an obstacle to the relocation and reconfiguration of ways of investigating the natural world in new and potentially more productive ways?[65]

## Conclusion: China and Europe

Technological advances had appeared in China within the framework of a cosmography that remained virtually intact until the fall of the empire in 1911. The Chinese had certainly discovered and accumulated a great deal of useful and reliable knowledge and observations about the natural world long before Europeans embarked upon a more sustained and innovatory quest to comprehend its operations largely for purposes of material gain and geopolitical power, and which complemented a religious conviction that investigations into nature revealed God's creation to mankind.

For centuries Chinese intellectuals promoted the accumulation of knowledge within parameters of a different cosmology that seems to have been far more flexible and less intolerant towards notions of discovery than Christendom with its theology of revealed truths, conveyed and interpreted by hierarchal religions.[66] Yet, that epistemology provided almost no support for a separable intellectual role with its own autonomous institutional base that embodied social prestige for systematic and sustained interrogations of nature. Investigations (*gewu*) into 'things' of immediate practical and political concern continued to take place in a piecemeal manner. In a recent book, a distinguished Sinologist suggested that these genres in the Ming and Qing era could be represented as 'a scattered landscape of individual reactions, rather than a unified or linear narrative of knowledge in the making'.[67] The study of many things not only occupied a small space and place below the study of texts in Confucian philosophy but also struggled for credibility and attention by presenting evidence, findings, and recommendations in a traditional Confucian style and manner.

For the discovery, development, and diffusion of useful and reliable knowledge, those elements included not merely the social and political status accorded to Chinese intellectuals who allocated time and resources to 'evidential research' into the natural phenomena but also the conceptual frameworks, vocabularies, and mind-sets they brought to the task. 'Things' were studied less for their potential utility and more for their qualities, authenticity, and provenance within a system of thought that remained deferential towards the dominant tendency in Confucian and other classical authorities to conceive of man as part of nature and of nature as one harmonious organic whole in which all things were somehow conducted through the prisms of such philosophical notions as *qi* and *li* and *ying* and *yang* and to be correlated and connected.[68]

Needham recognized that 'the Chinese, wise before their time, had worked out an organic theory of the universe which included nature and man, church and state and all things past, present and to come', and added that the Chinese 'had no confidence that the code of nature could be read'.[69] Poignantly he added that unlike their European counterparts, the Chinese lacked 'confidence that the code of Nature laws could be unveiled and read because there was no assurance that a divine being ever more rational than ourselves had ever formulated a code capable of being read'. Needham's scholarship, insights and questions cannot be evaded.[70] Along with most Western scientists and the educated and wealthy elites of his times, England's great eighteenth-century chemist and theologian, Joseph Priestley, would have agreed with Needham. 'If', Priestley wrote, 'there were no laws of nature … there could be no exercise for the wisdom for the understanding of intelligent beings and no man could lay a scheme with a prospect of accomplishing it.'[71] And as Iliffe has demonstrated, Newton also 'believed that natural philosophy was largely a religious entreprise'. [72]

## Notes

1. J. Daly (2015), *Historians Debate the Rise of the West.* Abingdon: Routledge.

2. K. Pomeranz (2000), *The Great Divergence. China, Europe and the Making of the Modern World Economy.* Princeton: Princeton University Press.

3. R. B. Wong (1997), *China Transformed: Historical Change and the Limits of European Experience.* Ithaca: Cornell University Press.

4. I. Wallerstein (1974, 1980, 1989, 2011), *The Modern Word System.* New York: Academic Press; A. Gunder Frank (1998), *ReOrient: Global Economy in the Asian Age.* Berkeley: University of California Press.

5. A. Maddison (2007), *Chinese Economic Performance in the Long Run, 960–2030.* Paris: OECD Publications; S. B. Broadberry and S. Hindle (eds) (2011), 'Asia in the Great Divergence', *Economic History Review*, 64 (Special Issue).

6. J. Mokyr (2002), *The Gifts of Athena.* Princeton: Princeton University Press.

7. J. Mokyr (2017), *A Culture of Growth: The Origins of the Modern Economy.* Princeton: Princeton University Press.

8. J. Needham (1969), *The Great Titration: Science and Society in East and West.* Toronto: Toronto University Press; M. Elvin (1973), *The Pattern of the Chinese Past.* Stanford: Stanford University Press; P. Gouk (1995), *The Achievement Project 1990–1995* (www.alanmacfarlane.com); Pomeranz, *The Great Divergence*; M. Elvin (2010), 'Overview and introduction', in H. U. Vogel and G. Dux (eds), *Concepts of Nature: A Chinese-European Cross-Cultural Perspective.* Leiden: Brill, 1–55.

9. Vogel and Dux, *Concepts of Nature.*

10. Needham, *The Great Titration*; J. T. Fraser (ed.) (1986), *Time, Science and Society in China and the West*. Amherst: Massachusetts University Press; N. Sivin (1995), *Science in Ancient China and Medicine, Philosophy and Religion in Ancient China. Researches and Reflections*. Aldershot: Variorum and Ashgate; D. Wootton (2015), *The Invention of Science*. London: Penguin.

11. E. Grant (2004), *Science and Religion from Aristotle to Copernicus, 400 BC–AD 1550*. Baltimore: John Hopkins University Press.

12. J. Golinski (1998), *Making Natural Knowledge: Constructivism and the History of Science*. Cambridge: Cambridge University Press.

13. M. Biagioli (ed.) (1998), *The Science Studies Reader*. London: Routledge; and M. Osler (ed.) (2000), *Rethinking the Scientific Revolution*. Cambridge: Cambridge University Press.

14. J. Hannam (2009), *God's Philosophers: How the Medieval World Laid the Foundations for Modern Science*. London: Icon Books.

15. D. C. Lindberg (ed.) (2007), *The Beginnings of Western Science: The European Scientific Tradition in Philosophical, Religious and Institutional Context 600 BC–AD 1450*. Chicago: Chicago University Press.

16. V. L. Bullough (ed.) (2004), *Universities, Medicine and Science in the Medieval West*. Aldershot: Ashgate.

17. Lindberg, *The Beginnings of Western Science*.

18. E. Grant (2007), *A History of Natural Philosophy: From the Ancient World to the Nineteenth Century*. Cambridge: Cambridge University Press.

19. P. Rossi (1970), *Philosophy, Technology and the Arts in the Early Modern Era*. New York: Harper Row.

20. P. Rossi (2001), *The Birth of Modern Science*. Oxford: Blackwell; and J. V. Field and F. A. S. L. James (1993), *Renaissance and Revolution: Humanists, Scholars, Craftsmen and Natural Philosophers in Early Modern Europe*. Cambridge: Cambridge University Press.

21. P. Long (2001), *Openness, Secrecy Authorship, Technical Arts and the Culture of Knowledge from Antiquity to Renaissance*. Baltimore: Johns Hopkins University Press.

22. T. Rabb (2006), *The Last Days of the Renaissance and the March to Modernity*. New York: Basic Books.

23. S. Gaukroger (2006), *The Emergence of Scientific Culture and the Shaping of Modernity. 1210–1685*. Oxford: Oxford University Press.

24. P. Dear (2006), *The Intelligibility of Nature: How Science Makes Sense of the World*. Chicago: Chicago University Press.

25. Mokyr, *The Gifts of Athena*.

26. Dear, *The Intelligibility of Nature*.

27. J. F. Cohen (1994), *The Scientific Revolution: A Historiographical Inquiry*. Chicago: Chicago University Press.

28. J. L. van Zanden and M. Prak (eds) (2013), *Technology, Skills and the Premodern Economy*. Leiden: Brill.

29. De Ridder-Symoens (ed.) (1996), *A History of the University in Early Modern Europe, 1500–1800*. Cambridge: Cambridge University Press.

30. S. Gaukroger (2010), *Science and the Shaping of Modernity, 1660–1760*. Oxford: Oxford University Press; and Wootton, *The Invention of Science*.

31. J. Bona (1995), *The Word of God and the Language of Man: Interpreting Nature in Early Modern Science*. Madison: University of Wisconsin Press.

32. M. A. Gillespie (2008), *The Theological Origins of Modernity*. Chicago: University of Chicago Press.

33. T. Worcester (2008), *Cambridge Companion to the Jesuits*. Cambridge: Cambridge University Press; and M. Feingold (2002), *Jesuit Science and the Republic of Letters*. Cambridge, MA: MIT Press.

34. Wootton, *The Invention of Science*; and Gaukroger, *Science and the Shaping of Modernity*.

35. G. E. R. Lloyd (2009), *Disciplines in the Making*. Oxford: Oxford University Press; and D. Headrick (2000), *When Information Comes of Age*. Oxford: Oxford University Press.

36. I. Inkster, and K. Deng (eds) (2004), *History of Technology*, vol. 25 (Special Issue). London: Institute of Historical Research.

37. J. M. Levine (1991), *The Battle of the Books: History and Literature in the Augustan Age*. Ithaca: Cornell University Press; and P. Smith and B. Schmidt (eds) (2007), *Making Knowledge in Early Modern Europe: Practices, Objects and Texts, 1400–1800*. Chicago: Chicago University Press.

38. This excludes a significant and well-documented history of experiments concerned with the properties of atmospheric pressure, with magnetism, with acids, human anatomy, and navigation.

39. P. Smith (1994), *The Business of Alchemy: Science and Culture in the Holy Roman Empire*. Princeton: Princeton University Press.

40. W. R. Newman and A. Grafton (2001), *Secrets of Nature: Astrology and Alchemy in Early Modern Europe*. Cambridge, MA: MIT Press.

41. D. Noble (1997), *The Religion of Technology: The Divinity of Man and the Spirit of Invention*. London: Penguin.

42. P. K. O'Brien (2009), 'The Needham question updated: A historiographical survey and elaboration', *History of Technology*, 29, 7–28.

43. H. Butterfield (1949), *The Origins of Modern Science, 1300–1800*. London: Bell, 36–8.

44. B. Elman (2005), *On Their Own Terms: Science in China, 1550–1900*. Cambridge MA: Harvard University Press.

45. Sivin, *Science in Ancient China*.

46. J. E. McClellan and H. Dorn (1999), *Science and Technology in World History*. Baltimore: Johns Hopkins University Press.

47. C. A. Ronan (1983), *The Illustrated History of the World's Science*. Cambridge: Cambridge University Press.

48. R. Temple (1998), *The Genius of China*. London: Prism Books.

49. D. Bodde (1991), *Chinese Thought, Society and Science*. Honolulu: Hawaii University Press.

50. J. Lin (1995), 'The Needham puzzle: Why the Industrial Revolution did not originate in China', *Economic Development and Cultural Change*, 43 (2), 269–92.

51. R. von Glahn (2016), *The Economic History of China: From Antiquity to the Nineteenth Century*. Cambridge: Cambridge University Press; and J.-L. Rosenthal and R. Bin Wong (2011), *Before and Beyond Divergence: The Politics of Economic Change in China and Europe*, Cambridge, MA: Harvard University Press.

52. B. Elman (2000), *A Cultural History of Civil Examinations in Late Imperial China*. Berkeley: California University Press.

53. W. T. de Bary (1981), *Neo Confucian Orthodoxy and the Learning of Mind and Heart*. New York: Columbia University Press.

54. B. Elman (1984), *From Philosophy to Philology*. Cambridge: Cambridge University Press.

55. L. M. Jensen (1997), *Confucianism: Chinese Tradition and Universal Civilization*. Durham: Duke University Press; and Y. Xinzhong (2002), *An Introduction to Confucianism*. Cambridge: Cambridge University Press.

56. G. E. R. Lloyd and N. Sivin (2002), *The Way and the Word: Science and Medicine in Early China and Greece*. New Haven: Yale University Press.

57. Sivin, *Science in Ancient China*; and Elman, *A Cultural History of Civil Examinations*.

58. M. Elvin (2004), *The Retreat of the Elephants: An Environmental History of China*. New Haven: Yale University Press.

59. P. S. Ropp (1990), *Heritage of China: Contemporary Perspectives on Chinese Civilization*. Berkeley: University of California Press; and B. Elman, and A. Woodside (eds) (1994), *Education and Society in Late Imperial China, 1600–1900*. Berkeley: University of California Press.

60. J. B. Henderson (1991), *Scripture, Canon and Commentary*. Princeton: Princeton University Press.

61. T. Brook (2010), *The Troubled Empire: China in the Yuan and Ming Dynasties*. Cambridge, MA: Harvard University Press.

62. J. B. Henderson (1984), *The Development and Decline of Chinese Cosmology*. New York: Columbia University Press.

63. H. Zurndorfer (2002), 'Old and new visions of Ming society and culture', *Toung Pao*, 87, 151–69.

64. C. Jami, P. Engelfreit and G. Blue (eds) (2001), *Statecraft and Intellectual Renewal in Late Ming China*. Leiden: Brill.

65. R. J. Smith (1994), *China's Cultural Heritage: The Qing Dynasty, 1644–1912*. Boulder: Westview Press.

66. Vogel and Dux, *Concepts of Nature*.

67. D. Schäfer (2011), *The Crafting of 10,000 Things: Knowledge and Technology in Seventeenth-Century China*. Chicago: Chicago University Press, 19.

68. J. Needham (ed.) (1956), *Science and Civilization in China*, vol. 1. Cambridge: Cambridge University Press, 543–82; J. Needham (ed.) (1961), *Science and Civilization in China*, vol. 2. Cambridge: Cambridge University Press, 1–43; and Y. S. Kim (2010), 'Confucian scholars and technical knowledge in traditional China', *East Asian Science: International Journal*, 4, 207–28.

69. Needham, *The Great Titration*, 120; see also: Mokyr, *A Culture of Growth*.

70. Needham, *The Great Titration*, 120.

71. J. T Rutt (ed.) (1817), *The Theological and Miscellaneous Works of Joseph Priestley*. London: George Smallfield.

72. R. Iliffe (2017), *Priest of Nature: The Religious Worlds of Isaac Newton*. Oxford: Oxford University Press.

# CHAPTER 4
## TOOLKITS, CREATIVITY, AND DIVERGENCES: TECHNOLOGY IN GLOBAL HISTORY
*Karel Davids*

Economic historians agree that technological change after 1800 has been much more rapid and pervasive than in earlier centuries, and since the late nineteenth century, the United States has been the frontrunner in this development. As Robert Gordon claimed, if productivity growth in the United States is now slowing down and the potential for further revolutionary innovations is limited, this could mean that the pace of technological change globally will diminish once the fruits of catching up with the United States have been reaped.[1] But will it? The nature and timing of future innovations remain notoriously hard to predict, even though examples of successful forecasting exist.[2] There is no compelling reason why technological leadership should rest with the United States forever. Historians surely cannot offer a safe guide to the future. What historians, and especially global historians, *can* do is analyse and explain underlying patterns and contexts of long-term technological change. Looking at connections and making comparisons between different parts of the world, global historians can propose answers to big questions such as: To what extent do different societies share the same bodies of knowledge? When, where, and why do innovations take place? When and why do divergences in technological development occur, and why does technological leadership shift from one place to another?

These are the questions that figure prominently in the debate on the Great Divergence. Answers, however, vary wildly. At one extreme are David Landes and Joseph Needham. Landes claimed that from the Middle Ages onwards, Europe saw a continuous flow of inventions and accumulation of technical knowledge, which eventually (also aided by other factors) culminated in the Industrial Revolution in Britain.[3] Joseph Needham, by contrast, insisted that China was far ahead of the West in many areas of technological achievement up to at least 1500.[4] At the other extreme are those who play down differences in technological development between Eurasian societies before the nineteenth century and reject the idea that Europe had any advantage over China, India, or the Middle East. In their view, differences in technology between these societies were far outweighed by broad similarities. Eurasian societies in this period by and large supposedly shared the same 'toolkits' of technical knowledge – to borrow a term coined by prehistorians and archaeologists.[5]

André Gunder Frank denied that there was such a thing as 'European technology' at all, let alone 'European technological superiority', before 1800. The 'very substantial' diffusion of technology and worldwide division of labour implied that technological development was a 'world economic process' rather than a regional or national one. Frank insisted that even the technological advances of the Industrial Revolution, whose importance he acknowledged, should not be seen as purely European achievements.[6] John Hobson and Jack Goody likewise lambasted the idea of a European lead in technological development before the Industrial Revolution.[7] Edmund Burke III argued that the Islamic world, borrowing innovations from a variety of sources, between about 650 CE and 1700 CE played a central role in the formation of standardized 'toolkits' of knowledge on subjects such as water management, writing, information processing, and mathematics, which Europeans later turned to good account. These 'technological complexes', as he prefers to call them, include both specific technologies and 'the culture knowledge' that made this technology possible.[8] More generally, Jared Diamond postulated that for all societies much or most new technology is not invented locally but is instead borrowed from other societies. According to Diamond, diffusion is key to technological development. For the rest, 'technology tends to catalyse itself'.[9] This is a long way from Robert Gordon's techno-pessimism.

Other scholars hold a position somewhere between these extremes. Comparing science and technology in India and Europe in the seventeenth and eighteenth centuries, Prasannan Parthasarathi concluded that 'Europe indeed showed a "scientific and technological verve"' but that the key Revolution did not reside in 'any purported cultural, economic or social exceptionalism' but in 'the specific challenges the Europeans faced'. The technological breakthrough in Britain resulted from a combination of external competitive pressures, ecological shortfalls, and a mercantile state.[10] Kenneth Pomeranz acknowledged that 'a surge in European technological inventiveness certainly [was] a necessary condition of the Industrial revolution', but stressed the crucial role of 'coal and colonies' in removing the constraints for sustained growth of per capita income.[11] Peer Vries, by contrast, argued that coal and colonies could only become relevant factors in the divergence between Europe and China because Western Europe, in contrast with China, had experienced 'a long process of continuing and self-sustaining invention and innovation' and by the eighteenth century had established a 'wide-ranging lead'. The West was leading especially in fields 'that had most potential for increasing productivity', and this lead was not a matter of accident but the outcome of a long-term development.[12] Joel Mokyr, too, emphasized that the divide between the East and the West essentially sprang from prior differences in technology. More specifically, Mokyr related this development to the Scientific Revolution in the seventeenth century, which contributed to the rise of a new and unique environment for the creation of useful forms of knowledge, which he called the 'Industrial Enlightenment'. Useful knowledge was 'knowledge of natural phenomena and regularities that had the potential to affect technology'.[13]

Yet another perspective has been suggested by Jack Goldstone. On the one hand, he underscored the similarities between all societies in world history that experienced a period of economic, political, and cultural 'efflorescence' (such as Song China, Northwestern Europe in the high Middle Ages, Golden Age Holland, or high Qing

China). On the other hand, he pointed to the unique emergence of 'engine science' – a reliance on engines for understanding the world – and its spread into popular culture in eighteenth-century England, which eventually led to the Industrial Revolution. Thus, there was perhaps something special about the development in this part of Europe after all.[14]

This chapter will discuss the three big questions introduced earlier, and the different answers to these, in relation to the debate on the Great Divergence. The first section examines the matter of toolkits. To what extent did different societies in the past share the same bodies of knowledge? Was much or most new technology indeed borrowed from other societies, and if so, how? The second section concerns the issue of technological creativity. How did new technical knowledge come into being and how can its creation be explained? The third section, finally, addresses the question of divergences. When and why did divergences in technological development occur, and why did technological leadership shift from one place to another? If there was a shared body of knowledge between Eurasian societies, why did Europe, and in particular Britain, eventually move into the forefront of technological development?

## Toolkits and travelling knowledge

Although scholars have used the notion of a common human 'toolkit' of technology, implicitly or explicitly, for quite some time, it is actually not firmly established whether such a toolkit has existed at all. André Gunder Frank's confident assertion that technological development was a world economic process and that there was no 'European' technology at all is not substantiated by evidence. Similarly, Jared Diamond does not offer evidence for his far-reaching claim that 'much or most new technology' is borrowed from other societies instead of being invented locally. Edmund Burke III does indeed provide support for his thesis that major technological complexes in the lands of Islam partly rested on innovations that had been developed in various regions in 'Afroeurasia' and subsequently underwent a process of standardization, but he is much more sparing with offering proof that the Islamic world then served as a vital source of knowledge for other parts of the world concerning, for example, water management and the development of universities. Whether there really has been a toolkit on which all societies could draw still remains a moot point.

The notion of 'toolkit' actually conflates several modes and layers of technological development that analytically can be kept apart. It presents an oversimplified answer to questions that in reality are quite complex: the issue of the relation between mobility and rootedness of knowledge and the issue of the relation between diffusion of knowledge and multiple independent inventions or improvements. 'Toolkit' suggests that technical knowledge was transmitted across societies and cultures rather than being developed or discovered locally. Yet, demonstrating that a certain item or process existed at the same time in different places, or that it existed earlier in one region than another, does not imply that there was some underlying common reservoir of knowledge or that knowledge actually travelled. The fact that dikes can be found both in China and in the Low Countries does not necessarily mean that the Chinese borrowed knowledge on dike-building from the North Sea area or vice versa. Coexistence does not imply common origin, nor does precedence entail causation. On the other hand, connections *can* have existed and diffusion *can* have taken place.

Technology could in fact be borrowed or shared in a variety of ways. First of all, it could remain more or less stable in space, yet move between different societies and cultures. The debate on the 'Watson thesis' shows that both phenomena could well go together in historical reality. Andrew Watson claimed that agriculture in the Mediterranean and West Asia was transformed between about 700 CE and 1100 CE under the impact of the rise and expansion of Islam. Once the entire region between Spain and Afghanistan had been unified under Muslim rule, Watson propounded, many 'new' crops and farming techniques were diffused in this area, which mostly 'originated' and had been 'domesticated' in the Indian subcontinent or lands farther to the East. Among these 'new' crops were sorghum, rice, hard wheat, sugar cane, cotton, lemons, limes, bananas, spinach, mango, watermelons, and coconut palms. The diffusion of these plants and the techniques that facilitated their cultivation (especially improvements in irrigation) led to a rise in agricultural productivity, which made possible a growth of trade, an increase in specialization, and a rise in urbanization in the Islamic world.[15]

Historians of technology and specialists on the history of the Mediterranean and West Asia have criticized Watson's thesis at many points, arguing notably that Watson got his chronology of innovation seriously wrong. Evidence showed that several crops on his list were already present in the Mediterranean and Western Asia before the rise of Islam and that irrigation and other techniques had been more advanced than Watson acknowledged. Peregrine Horden and Nicholas Purcell insisted that 'innovation of the utmost importance (was) going on continuously' in antiquity. Michael Decker, too, took issue with the idea of 'rapid and deep changes in Muslim agricultural practices'. In his view, 'Islamic farming structures were built atop earlier Roman and Persian landscapes; these were usurped rather than swept away.'[16] Although, as Paolo Squatriti remarked,[17] such critiques do not invalidate the thesis – because Watson stressed diffusion rather than introduction or invention – they nevertheless make an important point about technological development. Change was multi-layered; innovations were embedded in pre-existing local practices and structures.

Once we view technological development in a given region in a long-term perspective, labels turn out to be crude at best. The fact that an innovation emerged or thrived in a place and time when a particular culture in this region reigned supreme (e.g. during the Roman Empire or the Abbasid Caliphate) does not necessarily mean that this innovation can be labelled as a product of that culture. 'Roman' technology was partly based on technical knowledge developed in the Mediterranean and West Asia under Hellenistic regimes and 'Islamic' technology partly rested on technical knowledge developed in the same region during the Roman, Byzantine, and Sassanid empires.[18] Michael Lewis' case study on the development of windmills between about 800 CE and 1200 CE suggests that key innovations such as the introduction of the horizontal mill, the vertical mill, and the tower mill first appeared on the Iranian plateau and in the Aegean due to successive combinations of ideas of Greeks, Persians, Byzantines, and Seljuk Turks.[19]

A second way in which technology could be borrowed or shared was by the movement of culture groups from one place to another. David Anthony showed that speakers of proto-Indo-European dialects brought revolutionary innovations such as the horseback riding and the use of wheeled vehicles and chariots from the Eurasian steppes to the lower Danube Valley, Iran, and the Indian subcontinent from the fourth millennium BCE. These very innovations in transportation also opened up the steppes as 'a corridor of communication' between China, India, Iran, and the West.[20]

Finally, technology could also move from one place or culture to another via the travelling of people and the circulation of storage devices such as manuscripts, drawings, prints, books, and artefacts. According to Watson, travelling people were essential agents for the diffusion of knowledge about new crops in the lands of Islam. Apart from envoys acting on the authority of rulers, 'thousands of mostly unknown individuals from many levels of society', including soldiers, pilgrims, and traders, must have been instrumental in the movements of plants 'over shorter or longer distances'.[21] Sweet potatoes (and the knowledge of how to grow and to store them) reached China from Central America by way of the Philippines, thanks to Spanish seafarers crossing the Pacific and a Chinese merchant visiting Manila in the 1590s.[22] The 'Silk Road', which connected China and Transoxiana from the second century BCE, functioned as a passageway for refugees, missionaries, craftsmen, traders, and other groups of travellers, who – among other things – transmitted technologies from one side of Eurasia to another. While the art of glass making moved to China from the West, the techniques of weaving silk and making paper travelled from China in the opposite direction. Paper making was probably introduced in Transoxiana by Buddhist monks by the end of the seventh century.[23] The wide availability of paper and the invention of printing, which followed in the eighth century, further helped to enhance the mobility of knowledge, even apart from the physical movement of people. The growth in the production of books, whether copied by hand or printed with woodblocks or movable type, meant that technical knowledge could be stored and circulated on a much larger scale than ever before.[24]

Movements of knowledge between places and cultures were not a neutral process. Circulation of knowledge involved both translation and transformation. Moreover, as Harold Cook and Sven Dupré observed, 'the parties involved, whether speakers or listeners' were changed in the process of translation as well.[25] The massive Graeco-Arabic translation movement under the early Abbasid Caliphate, for example, according to Dimitri Gutas did not only generate 'an Arabic scientific literature with a technical vocabulary for its concepts' but also preserved many non-literary Greek texts in Arabic translation and 'contributed, through the demand it created for secular Greek works, to their preservation … in Greek' by accelerating their transcription in manuscript copies.[26] Knowledge in transit was thus not a ready set of tools packed in a box. Knowledge changed in the very process of movement.

## Technological creativity

How did new technical knowledge come about? Does technology tend to catalyse itself, as Jared Diamond argues? Arguably technological advances often 'depend upon previous mastery of simpler problems' and 'new technologies and materials make it possible to generate still other new technologies'.[27] But this process is far from automatic. Technological development can take unexpected turns. In many areas in Europe during the early Middle Ages, for example, sophisticated water systems from Roman times were neglected or abandoned. Aqueducts fell into disrepair. Fired brick (and concrete) was not used in building north of the Alps for a long time.[28] In North Africa, the Middle East, and Iran, wheeled vehicles were abandoned in favour of the camel as a means of transport for over a thousand years.[29] The extensive use of paper and the proliferation of books in the lands of Islam were not followed by an early adoption of the printing press.[30] Watermills were well known in the Mediterranean and West Asia from Roman times onwards, but it was only in medieval and early modern Europe that water power was harnessed for a wide variety of industrial purposes on a massive scale.[31]

The rate and direction of technological change thus vary considerably in time and space. How can it be explained? A common type of argument holds that factor prices determine when and where inventions are adopted. The lack of more mechanization in the Roman Empire, for example, has been ascribed to the abundance of cheap labour, notably slave labour, relative to other factors of production. Scarcity of labour relative to the abundance of land has been adduced as a crucial stimulus to mechanization in the antebellum era in the United States. High wages relative to cheap energy have been proposed as the single most important factor in explaining why the Industrial Revolution happened in Britain in the eighteenth century.[32]

This approach is illuminating up to a point. Private entrepreneurs doubtless take relative prices of production factors into account when making decisions about whether or not to adopt a particular technique. But the explanatory power of this sort of argument is limited. For one thing, it is not evident that other types of actors who had an impact on technological change in the past, such as governments, princes, religious organizations, and community associations, likewise based their decision making on information about relative factor prices. The fact that until 1719 Muslims in the Ottoman Empire were not allowed to operate a printing press had more to do with the high esteem for the handwritten word in the Islamic world and with the economic and political power of thousands of copyists in Istanbul than with the relative prices of production factors.[33] Secondly, even if decisions about the adoption of inventions partly depended on information on factor prices, this does not mean that the direction of inventive activities themselves was determined by these particular conditions. Christine MacLeod has shown that, contrary to expectations, most applicants for patents in eighteenth-century England did *not* state the saving of labour as the goal of their invention but the saving of capital or the improvement of the quality of products.[34] Thirdly, and most fundamentally, factor prices do not explain where knowledge embodied in technology actually came from. How was knowledge supplied? How were inventions generated? What made the creation of new techniques possible? Relative factor prices, in short, can be proximate causes for the adoption of technologies, but they do not regulate the process of creation of knowledge itself and they are certainly not the ultimate cause of technological creativity.

Like the diffusion of knowledge, the creation of knowledge could occur in a multiplicity of ways. One of them was the creation of what are called 'inventions'. The term 'invention' suggests that the production of new knowledge is a discrete, distinct event, a kind of happening which can be exactly pinpointed in place and time. This is, historically speaking, quite a recent idea. It arose in Italian cities during the high Middle Ages as part of an increasing tendency to consider knowledge as a type of 'property'. These growing proprietary attitudes manifested themselves on the one hand in formal or informal arrangements to reserve specific knowledge to practitioners of a particular craft or trade, and on the other hand in institutional provisions to protect property rights on knowledge in the form of patents for invention. While from the thirteenth century onwards patents for invention of new techniques of mechanical devices were granted on an ad hoc basis, the practice became enshrined in law in many parts of Europe at the end of the fifteenth century. The first law that guaranteed a right to the ownership and commercial exploitation of a new invention was enacted by the Senate of the Republic of Venice in 1474.[35] The chief criterion for granting a patent in this Venetian statute and subsequent regulations by other governments in early modern Europe was not the originality of an invention as such, but its novelty to a particular locality. Apart from providing a reward for the labours of private inventors, patents were equally used as an instrument by cities and states to attract 'new' knowledge from elsewhere to give a boost to their own economies.[36] After the idea of an invention as something 'new', which could be clearly identified, had taken hold in Renaissance Europe, literati began to produce catalogues of inventions or discoveries that had not been known in the ancient world. The most famous one is no doubt the set of three 'inventions' that 'changed the face and state of the world' mentioned in Francis Bacon's *Novum Organum* in 1620: gunpowder, the compass, and the printing press.[37] Following Bacon's example, data on the frequency and significance of inventions in the historiography of technology long remained a yardstick for comparing the technological creativity of societies.[38]

The number of patents for invention granted in European countries increased by leaps and bounds from the sixteenth century onwards. The level of patenting reached in Venice was exceeded in the Dutch Republic after 1590, which was in its turn surpassed by Britain in the eighteenth century. Britain during the nineteenth century ceded place to the United States, which saw the ratio of patents relative to its total population truly explode after the Civil War.[39] Figures on patenting can to some extent be taken as an indicator of technological creativity. However, even after the institution of patenting came into existence, inventive activities continued to take place outside patent systems as well. Prizes, premiums, contracts, tax exemptions, and other sorts of privileges or rewards granted by public authorities or private organizations could in early modern Europe fulfil similar functions for individual inventors as patents.[40] Even in the United States, the patent system was not always the only institution that promoted or protected inventive activities. Robert Gordon observed that patenting in the United States actually declined during part of the twentieth century, when inventive activities came to a large extent to be concentrated in research laboratories of large corporations.[41]

Technological creativity, however, could manifest itself in other ways than through the development or discovery of a distinct new thing or process, which could qualify for a patent for invention or for some other kind of reward. 'Macro-inventions', that is 'inventions in which a radical new idea, without clear precedent, emerges more or less ab nihilo' (as Joel Mokyr defines them), have been quite rare. One of the few inventions that comes close to this ideal type is the steam engine. Throughout much of human history, technological advance, on the contrary, largely proceeded through 'micro-inventions', 'small, incremental steps that improved, adapted, and streamlined existing techniques already in use' (again as defined by Mokyr), or what Eric Jones has called 'technological drift'.[42] Trial and error, random mutations, learning by doing, or learning by using all could help to make this slow change possible.[43] Although such mundane, gradual improvements, adaptations, or refinements often have not been identified as distinct 'inventions' – let alone patented – they nevertheless have made a contribution to the growth of productivity and were sometimes instrumental in realizing major breakthroughs. The successful ventures of European seafarers across the Atlantic and into the Indian Ocean in the 1490s, for example, owed much to slow improvements in shipbuilding and navigation during the Middle Ages as well as to the continuous, painstaking accumulation of knowledge about wind patterns in the northern and southern Atlantic.[44]

However, variations in the rate and direction of technological change must be related to more factors than mere steady, ordinary technological drift or movements of knowledge between places or cultures. These factors in themselves after all cannot explain why creativity *differed*. Historians have sought additional underlying causes of technological creativity in contextual variables such as competition between states, warfare population growth, environmental challenges, cultural climates, and institutional arrangements. On closer inspection, however, many of these factors turn out not to have as much explanatory power as suggested. Sometimes they appear to stimulate innovation, sometimes they appear to inhibit it, and sometimes they do not seem to have much effect on technological creativity at all. Warfare, for example, can work out both ways. Ecological pressures and/or population growth do not invariably lead to technological breakthroughs.[45] Some values and attitudes, such as respect for manual labour, may have provided a more favourable climate for technological creativity than others, such as a submissive attitude to authority, but it is doubtful whether the presence of such cultural characteristics in itself has been a necessary or sufficient condition for innovation.

Still, cultural factors may have affected technology in an indirect way, namely by influencing the development of institutions, which facilitated technological creativity. Apart from arrangements specifically rewarding inventive activities, such as patents, prizes, or privileges, these technology-friendly institutions also include institutions supporting the dissemination, certification, and creation of knowledge more broadly such as craft guilds, schools, academies, libraries, and research laboratories. David Mowery and Nathan Rosenberg even termed the emergence of a R&D system in the United States in the twentieth century as the 'institutionalization of innovation'.[46] At the present state of inquiry, this institutional perspective, with a focus on infrastructures of knowledge, offers the most promising strategy for understanding variations in technological creativity. It may also help explain divergences in technological development between different parts of the world which emerged over time.

## Divergences

In the nineteenth century, global divergences in technological development became patently obvious. While technological change generally was faster and more comprehensive than before, Europe and the United States were clearly ahead of other regions in the world. Technological advantage translated into an edge in productivity as well as into political and military ascendancy. Western imperialism made great strides, thanks to the use of advanced technologies. Innovations such as steamships, telegraphs, rifles, and quinine after 1840 became effective 'tools of empire', as Daniel Headrick called them, and connections between technology and imperialism persisted long into the twentieth century.[47] But when and why did these divergences in technological development come about?

The debate on this issue has mostly concentrated on comparisons between Europe and Asia – in particular China and India – and to a lesser extent on comparisons between regions within Europe between about 700 CE and 1800 CE. Taking the 'Great Divergence' in technology first, we should consider the matter from two sides. On the one hand, there is no convincing evidence that either Europe, China, or India had achieved technological 'superiority' over any other world area by the end of the eighteenth century. Extravagant claims for the supremacy of Europe or China such as those put forward by David Landes or Joseph Needham are not solidly grounded in facts. All the different types of machines and mechanical devices described in Needham's *Science and Civilisation in China*, for example, can equally be found in late medieval and early modern Europe while energy and the use of energy sources before the middle of the eighteenth century did not greatly differ.[48] Like Europe, Qing China still saw gradual technological change, especially in the agricultural sector. A 'relative technological standstill', as Mark Elvin surmised, did not occur.[49] As for India, Prasannan Parthasarathi has made a plausible case for the thesis that the knowledge and skills of eighteenth-century artisans on the subcontinent were not inferior to those of European craftsmen in industries such as textile making, shipbuilding, arms manufacture, and iron smelting.[50] In 1800, the level of technology that was actually used in Europe, China, or India did not yet substantially differ.

On the other hand, we should be careful to be fixated on similarities alone. If there were no differences between these regions of Eurasia before 1800 at all, where did the disparity in the nineteenth century come from? How can the technological lead of European countries and the United States after 1800 be explained? Parthasarathi sought the answer in 'the specific challenges' Europeans faced. In his view, the threat of being outcompeted by Indian textiles on global markets and the increasing scarcity of traditional sources of energy acted as triggers for 'revolutionary technological breakthroughs' in Britain, which laid the foundation for the Industrial Revolution. Maxine Berg in the same vein argued that imports of luxury goods from Asia 'activated' product innovation and invention in Britain.[51] But this kind of explanatory reasoning begs the question why Britain in particular, or Europe more generally, was able to meet these challenges by developing a radical new response. Failures to meet challenges are after all not uncommon in history. Industrial revolutions on the contrary rarely happen. What made this unprecedented leap forward in technological capability possible?

On closer look, differences in technological development between various regions of Eurasia already existed before the end of the eighteenth century. Even though the general level and rate of technological change in China and Europe did not vary greatly before 1800, there were differences in the nature of technological development, the formation of human capital, the circulation of technical knowledge, and processes of technological creativity. The potential of specific innovations was not always realized as fully in China as in Europe. Clocks, cannon, the magnetic compass, and printing by movable type are cases in point. In addition, technological change in early modern Europe had a wider scope: it took place not only in the agricultural sector and in urban industries, but also in various other branches of economic activity, such as the shipping industry. Formation of human capital through specialist, technical education in China developed not as far as in European countries. Schools with a vocational emphasis, for example, remained a relatively rare phenomenon. Moreover, although the output of printed books, including technical writings, in Late Ming and Qing China strongly grew, the extent of circulation of these materials did not increase accordingly; libraries were often only accessible to the selected few. As for processes of creation, Chinese technicians, unlike European artisans, did not use drawings to 'think on paper'.[52]

India and Europe were not similar in every respect either. Parthasarathi argues that modes of transmission for 'useful' knowledge present in early modern Europe, such as 'schools, universities, lecture halls, associations', were not entirely absent in India, but he admits that evidence about their actual importance is hard to discover. Infrastructures of knowledge in India cannot be demonstrated to have been the same as in Europe. Furthermore, while patronage of states may have been 'critical' for the diffusion of knowledge in India, especially through the establishment of libraries and the sponsorship of translations, Europe saw, besides states, also other actors and institutions such as cities, trading companies, and religious organizations playing an important role in the circulation of technical knowledge. Europe probably surpassed India with regard to the circulation of printed books and periodicals.[53] This may have been a relevant factor in the emerging divergence as well. Although much technical knowledge in the past did not find its way into print, this does not mean that all forms of knowledge could equally well circulate and advance through learning by doing or learning by using. Not all knowledge can be subsumed in a broad, hybrid category called 'the mindful hand'.[54] Distinctions between 'tacit' and 'explicit' knowledge or between 'manual abilities' and 'inquiry into nature' *do* matter. 'Prescriptive knowledge'

(knowledge 'how') and 'propositional knowledge' (knowledge 'what'), as Mokyr terms them, *can* be distinguished.[55] And the latter type of knowledge in Europe increasingly circulated in storage devices such as printed texts, which made a significant contribution to technological advance. Prescriptive knowledge alone would not have made it possible for European seamen to sail regularly from Europe to India or China, and back, nor have enabled European inventors to design the steam engine, the railway, the telegraph, and the internal combustion engine.

Divergences between Europe and Asia thus began to arise long before the end of the eighteenth century. Some of the foundations for the spurt in technology capability in Europe after 1800 were put in place as early as the late Middle Ages. But technological change was not equally spread over Europe. Divergences within Europe emerged as well. Some regions advanced earlier and developed more rapidly than others. Technological leadership in Europe first rested with Northern Italy, south Germany, and the Southern Netherlands, then shifted to the Dutch Republic and eventually moved to England. 'Technological leadership' meant that a given country, region, town, or cluster of towns played an initiating role in the development of new technologies in a wide variety of fields for a lengthy period of time.[56]

Life cycles of technological leaders before 1800 showed a more or less fixed pattern. Before starting on a prolonged technological advance, a future leading region, town, or cluster of towns first developed into the hub of a widespread trading network. The scope of the technological advance was at first usually rather narrow, but once the domination over an extended trade network had been firmly established, it broadened in many ways. No centre of leadership started from scratch. Each new centre partly built on the achievements of its precursors, while expanding and transforming the body of knowledge in the process. South Germany borrowed from Northern Italy, Flanders and Brabant borrowed from Italy and South Germany, the Dutch Republic borrowed from all three, and Britain in its turn borrowed from the Dutch and its predecessors. Movements of knowledge and skills via the travelling of people and the circulation of storage devices such as books, manuscripts, drawings, and artefacts thus contributed to the accumulation of know-how from one centre of leadership to another.[57] Although a technological leader often did not succeed in retaining a competitive edge in all those areas where it achieved its initial supremacy, it still could for a while compensate for the loss of the original strongholds by building new ones. Frontrunners explored new routes of technological advance. While initial achievements of technological leaders usually consisted more in improvements in physical productivity than in gains in quality, the order was often reversed later on. Eventually, however, substitutions of old sectors of growth by new ones became ever rarer. Leadership moved to a place that showed a higher rate of innovation.[58]

At the end of the seventeenth century, foreign observers considered the Dutch Republic as a model of technological creativity. A Swedish traveller called Holland in the 1690s an 'officina machinarum'. In his travelogue *The Grand Tour* of 1749, Irish writer Thomas Nugent stated that 'there (was) no nation where the people apply themselves with more diligence to all manners of mechanical arts, than the inhabitants of the United

Provinces'.[59] In the course of the eighteenth century, however, England achieved a still higher rate of technological innovation than the Netherlands by realizing a combination of 'prescriptive knowledge' and 'propositional knowledge' which the Dutch did not achieve. As Goldstone and Mokyr observed, English society and culture offered a uniquely congenial environment for the emergence of 'engine science' or, more broadly, the creation of 'useful knowledge' in the sense of knowledge of natural phenomena and regularities that had the potential to affect technology. This 'Industrial Enlightenment' was a powerful factor in the making of the Industrial Revolution. The technological leadership of the United States, which became manifest from the late nineteenth century onwards, in its turn built on the foundation laid by these revolutionary breakthroughs in industry in Britain.[60]

## Conclusion

Technological change took place more or less continuously throughout history, though at different rates and with different consequences. Sometimes advances occurred with leaps and bounds, and often they were barely noticeable at all. Over time, divergences emerged between technological developments in different parts of the world. This chapter argues that these variations between times and places should neither be magnified nor smoothed over. Neither point of view is very helpful for understanding technological change and its role in global history.

This chapter proposes a more analytical, comparative perspective instead. It suggests the adoption of a differentiated view of the circulation of knowledge and of its relation with local inventions and improvements, rather than to utilize the notion of a common human toolkit of technology. It suggests that we look beyond relative factor prices to explain the rate and direction of technological change and that we examine more closely the varied ways in which new technical knowledge actually could come about and the congenial institutional settings in which creativity could flourish. Finally, the chapter argues that similarities in the level and rate of technological change at a certain point in time may well go together with slowly emerging differences in development, which can eventually build up into major disparities. The Great Divergence in technology between China and India on the one hand and Europe and the United States on the other, which became patently clear in the nineteenth century, had its origins in initially minor differences which began to appear many centuries before.

## Notes

1. R. J. Gordon (2016), *The Rise and Fall of American Economic Growth: The U.S. Standard of Living since the Civil War*. Princeton: Princeton University Press, 1–8.
2. Cf. J. Mokyr (2013), 'Is technological progress a thing of the past?' http://voxeu.org/article/technological-progress-thing-past; and Gordon, *Rise and Fall*, 590–2.

3. D. Landes (1998), *The Wealth and Poverty of Nations*. New York: W.W. Norton, 44–54, 187–93.

4. J. Needham (1965), *Science and Civilisation in China*. Vol. IV, *Physics and Physical Technology* part 2 *Mechanical Engineering*. Cambridge: Cambridge University Press; J. Needham, W. Ling and D. K. de Solla Price (1960), *Heavenly Clockwork: The Great Astronomical Clock of Medieval China*. Cambridge: Cambridge University Press.

5. E. Burke III (2009), 'Islam at the center: Technological complexes and the roots of modernity', *Journal of World History*, 20 (2), 166.

6. A. Gunder Frank (1998), *ReOrient. Global Economy in the Asian Age*. Berkeley: University of California Press, 186, 204, and 285.

7. J. Hobson (2004), *The Eastern Origins of Western Civilization*. Cambridge: Cambridge University Press, 50–61, 190–214; J. Goody (2004), *Capitalism and Modernity: The Great Debate*. Cambridge: Cambridge University Press, 19–20, 25–7.

8. Burke, 'Islam at the center', 167–8.

9. J. Diamond (1997), *Guns, Germs and Steel: A Short History of Everybody for the Last 13,000 Years*. London: W.W. Norton, 254, 258–9.

10. P. Parthasarathi (2002), 'Review Article: the Great Divergence', *Past and Present*, 176, 282; Idem (2011), *Why Europe Grew Rich and Asia Did Not. Global Economic Divergence, 1600-1850*. Cambridge: Cambridge University Press, 222 and 263.

11. K. Pomeranz (2000), *The Great Divergence. Europe, China, and the Making of the Modern World Economy*. Princeton: Princeton University Press, 68.

12. P. Vries (2001), 'Are coal and colonies really crucial? Kenneth Pomeranz and the Great Divergence', *Journal of World History*, 12 (2), 437; Idem (2013), *Escaping Poverty. The Origins of Modern Economic Growth*. Vienna and Göttingen: Vienna University Press and Vandenhoeck und Ruprecht, 307–11.

13. J. Mokyr (1990), *The Lever of Riches. Technological Creativity and Economic Progress*. Oxford: Oxford University Press, 81; Idem (2002), *The Gifts of Athena. Historical Origins of the Knowledge Economy*. Princeton: Princeton University Press, 4–21, 34–42; Idem (2017), *A Culture of Growth. The Origins of the Modern Economy*. Princeton: Princeton University Press, 274.

14. J. Goldstone (2002), 'Efflorescences and economic growth in world history: Rethinking the "rise of the West" and the Industrial Revolution', *Journal of World History*, 13 (2) 323–89; Idem (2008), *Why Europe? The Rise of the West in World History, 1500-1800*. New York: McGraw-Hill Education, ch. 8.

15. A. M. Watson (1974), 'The Arab agricultural revolution and its diffusion', *Journal of Economic History*, 34 (1), 8–35, Idem (1983), *Agricultural Innovation in the Early Islamic World: The Diffusion of Crops and Farming Techniques, 700–1100*. Cambridge: Cambridge University Press, 2–3, 5, 77–8.

16. P. Horden and N. Purcell (2000), *The Corrupting Sea: A Study of Mediterranean History*. Oxford: Wiley, 257–63, esp. 262; M. Decker (2009), 'Plants and progress: Rethinking the Islamic agricultural revolution', *Journal of World History*, 20 (2), 187–206.

17. P. Squatriti (2014), 'Of seeds, seasons, and seas: Andrew Watson's medieval agrarian revolution forty years later', *Journal of Economic History*, 74 (4), 1210–15.

18. K. D. White (1984), *Greek and Roman Technology*. London: Thames and Hudson; A. Y. al-Hassan and D. R. Hill (1986), *Islamic Technology: An Illustrated History*. Cambridge: Cambridge University Press.

19. M. J. T. Lewis (1993), 'The Greeks and the early windmill', *History of Technology*, 15, 141–89; Horden and Purcell, *Corrupting Sea*, 257.

20. D. W. Anthony (2007), *The Horse, the Wheel and Language: How Bronze-Age Riders from the Eurasian Steppes Shaped the Modern World*. Princeton: Princeton University Press, 457–63.

21. Watson, *Agricultural Innovation*, 88–94, esp. 90.

22. C. C. Mann (2011), *1493: How Europe's Discovery of the Americas Revolutionized Trade, Ecology and Life on Earth*. London: Granta, 168–9.

23. V. Hansen, (2012), *The Silk Road: A New History*. Oxford: Oxford University Press, 137–9, 238–9; J. M. Bloom (2001), *Paper before Print: The History and Impact of Paper in the Islamic World*. New Haven: Yale University Press, 43.

24. Cf. Hansen, *Silk Road*, 138; Bloom, *Paper*, 110–23, E. Eisenstein (1979), *The Printing Press as an Agent of Change: Communications and Cultural Transformations in Early-Modern Europe*. Cambridge: Cambridge University Press.

25. K. Raj (2007), *Relocating Modern Science: Circulation and the Construction of Knowledge in South Asia and Europe, 1650–1900*. Basingstoke: Palgrave Macmillan, 20–1; H. J. Cook and S. Dupré (2012), 'Introduction', in H. J. Cook and S. Dupré (eds), *Translating Knowledge in the Early Modern Low Countries*. Zürich and Berlin: LIT Verlag, 10.

26. D. Gutas (1998), *Greek Thought, Arabic Culture: The Graeco-Arabic Translation Movement in Baghdad and Early 'Abbāsid Society (2nd–4th/8th–10th Centuries)*. London: Routledge, 192.

27. Diamond, *Guns, Germs and Steel*, 258–9.

28. A. Wilson (2002), 'Machines, power and the ancient economy', *Journal of Roman Studies*, 92, 32; R. Magnusson (2001), *Water Technology in the Middle Ages: Cities, Monasteries, and Water Works after the Roman Empire*. Baltimore: Johns Hopkins University Press, 4; S. Aiyar, C-J. Dalgaard and O. Moav (2008), 'Technological progress and regress in pre-industrial times', *Journal of Economic Growth*, 13 (2), 127–8.

29. R. W. Bulliet (1975), *The Camel and the Wheel*. Cambridge, MA: Harvard University Press.

30. Bloom, *Paper*, 110–16, 220–4.

31. Ö. Wikander (2000), 'The water-mill' and 'Industrial applications of water-power', in Ö. Wikander (ed.), *Handbook of Ancient Water Technology*. Leiden: Brill, 371–400 and 401–10; White, *Greek and Roman Technology*, 56; al-Hassan and Hill, *Islamic Technology*, 52–4; T. S. Reynolds (2003), *Stronger than a Hundred Men: A History of the Vertical Water Wheel*. Baltimore: Johns Hopkins University Press.

32. White, *Greek and Roman Technology*, 56; Mokyr, *Lever of Riches*, 165, 103–95; J. J. Habakkuk (1962), *American and British Technology in the Nineteenth Century*. Cambridge: Cambridge University Press; Allen, *The British Industrial Revolution*, 2, 142.

33. Bloom, *Paper*, 222.

34. C. MacLeod (1988), *Inventing the Industrial Revolution: The English Patent System, 1660–1800*. Cambridge: Cambridge University Press, 158–81, esp. 159–60; Mokyr, *Lever of Riches*, 165–6.

35. P. O. Long (2001), *Openness, Secrecy, Authorship: Technical Arts and the Culture of Knowledge from Antiquity to the Renaissance*. Baltimore: Johns Hopkins University Press, 89, 93–6, L. Molà (2000), *The Silk Industry of Renaissance Venice*. Baltimore: Johns Hopkins University Press, 186–9.

36. M. Belfanti (2004), 'Guilds, patents, and the circulation of technical knowledge: Northern Italy during the Early Modern Age', *Technology and Culture*, 45 (3), 569–89; MacLeod, *Inventing*, 11.

37. Eisenstein, *Printing Press*, 20–1; M. Popplow (1998), *Neu, Nützlich und Erfindungsreich. Die Idealisierung von Technik in der frühen Neuzeit*. Münster: Waxmann; J. Spedding, R. L. Ellis and D. D. Heath (eds) (1857), *The Works of Francis Bacon*, vol. 1, *Novum Organum*. London: n.a., Aphorism CXXIX.

38. For a recent example, see Vries, *Escaping Poverty*, 305–11.

39. K. Davids (1993), 'Technological change and the economic expansion of the Dutch Republic', in K. Davids and L. Noordegraaf (eds), *The Dutch Economy in the Golden Age: Nine Studies*. Amsterdam, 95–6; MacLeod, *Inventing*, 146, 150; Gordon, *Rise and Fall*, 570–1.

40. MacLeod, *Inventing*, 97–114; L. Hilaire-Pérez (1994), 'Inventions et inventeurs en France et en Angleterre au XVIIIe siècle', 4 vols. Paris: doctoral thesis; K. Davids (2008), *The Rise and Decline of Dutch Technological Leadership: Technology, Economy and Culture in the Netherlands, 1350–1800*. Boston and Leiden: Brill, 410–16, 481–2.

41. B. Zorina Khan (2015), 'Inventing prizes: A historical perspective on innovation awards and technology policy', *Business History Review*, 89 (4), 631–60; Gordon, *Rise and Fall*, 571–2; David C. Mowery (1998), *Paths of Innovation: Technological Change in 20th-Century America*. Cambridge: Cambridge University Press, 11–46.

42. Mokyr, *Lever of Riches*, 12–13; E. Jones (2003), *The European Miracle: Environments, Economies and Geopolitics in the History of Europe and Asia*. Cambridge: Cambridge University Press, 45–69.

43. K. G. Persson (1988), *Pre-industrial Growth: Social Organization and Technological Progress in Europe*. New York: Blackwell, 7–12; G. N. von Tunzelmann (1995), *Technology and Industrial Progress: The Foundations of Economic Growth*. Cheltenham: Edward Elgar Publishing, 7–9, 117–19 and 399, Mokyr, *Lever of Riches*, 13.

44. F. Fernández-Armesto (2000), *Civilizations*. London: Macmillan, 488–500.

45. Jones, *European Miracle*, 45, Mokyr, *Lever of Riches*, 159–92; Diamond, *Guns, Germs and Steel*, 249–51; Landes, *Wealth and Poverty*, 45–59, D. R. Headrick, (2010), *Power over Peoples: Technology, Environments, and Western Imperialism, 1400 to the Present*. Princeton: Princeton University Press, 4; L. White Jr. (1978) 'Cultural climates and technological advance in the Middle ages', in L. White Jr (ed.), *Medieval Religion and Technology: Collected Essays*. Berkeley: University of California Press, 217–53; D. Acemoğlu and J. A. Robinson, (2012), *Why Nations Fail: The Origins of Power, Prosperity and Poverty*. London: Profile, 76–9.

46. Mowery and Rosenberg, *Paths of Innovation*, 11–46.

47. Headrick, *Power over Peoples*, 5–6; Idem (1981), *The Tools of Empire: Technology and European Imperialism in the Nineteenth Century*. New York: Oxford University Press; Mokyr, *Lever of Riches*, 81–148, A. Grübler (1998), *Technology and Global Change*. Cambridge: Cambridge University Press, 117–26.

48. Needham, *Science and Civilisation in China*, vol. IV, part 2, table 56; P. Malanima (2006), 'Energy crisis and growth 1650–1850: The European deviation in a comparative perspective', *Journal of Global History*, 1 (1), 101–12, K. Davids (2013), *Religion, Technology and the Great and Little Divergences. China and Europe Compared, c.700-1800*. Boston and Leiden: Brill 5–8.

49. Cf. M. Elvin (1973), *The Pattern of the Chinese Past*. London: Eyre Methuen, 301, 312–15.

50. Parthasarathi, *Why Europe Grew Rich*, 210–13, 217–19.

51. Ibid., 221–2; M. Berg (2004), 'In Pursuit of Luxury: Global Origins of British Consumer Goods in the Eighteenth Century', *Past and Present*, 87, 91, 97, 99 and 126 and 182.

52. Davids, *Religion*, 9, 13–14, 162, 188–9, 227 and 229; P. J. Golas (2001), 'Technological illustration in China: A post-Needham perspective', in A. Arrault and C. Jami (eds), *Science and Technology in China: A Post-Needham Perspective*. Belgium: Turnhout Brepols, 43–58.

53. On India, Parthasarathi, *Why Europe Grew Rich*, 214–16, 313 footnote 98; on Europe, see Davids, *Religion*, chs. 2, 3 and 4.

54. L. Roberts and S. Schaffer (2007), 'Preface', in L. Roberts, S. Schaffer and P. Dear (eds), *The Mindful Hand: Inquiry and Invention from the Late Renaissance to Early Industrialization*. Amsterdam: Koninklijke Nederlandse Akademie van Wetenschappenpp, xv, xix, xxiv.

55. Mokyr, *Gifts of Athena*, 4–17; Parthasarathi, *Why Europe Grew Rich*, 219–21. See also Patrick O'Brien's essay in this volume.

56. E. Ames and N. Rosenberg (1963), 'Changing technological leadership and industrial growth', *Economic Journal*, 73, 13–31; D. S. L. Cardwell (1972), *Turning Points in Western Technology*. New York: Watson Publishing International, 190, 206; Mokyr, *Lever of Riches*, 207; Davids, *Rise and Decline*, 2–7.

57. K. Davids (1995), 'Shifts of technological leadership in early modern Europe', in K. Davids and J. Lucassen (eds), *A Miracle Mirrored: The Dutch Republic in European Perspective*. Cambridge: Cambridge University Press, 339–41; Idem, *Rise and Decline*, chs. 4 and 5.

58. Davids, 'Shifts', 342.

59. Thomas Nugent (1749), *The Grand Tour*, vol. I. London, 32. See also, Davids, *Rise and Decline*, 48.

60. R. R. Nelson and G. Wright (1992), 'The rise and fall of American technological leadership: The postwar era in historical perspective', *Journal of Economic Literature*, 30 (4), 1931–64; G. Wright (2007) 'Historical foundations of American technology', https://web.stanford.edu/~write/papers/Historical%20FoundationsR.pdf.

# CHAPTER 5
## FAMILIES, FIRMS, AND POLITIES: PRE-MODERN ECONOMIC GROWTH, AND THE GREAT DIVERGENCE
### Regina Grafe and Maarten Prak

Institutions are usually defined as 'the humanly devised constraints that shape human interaction'. They include not only formal rules and organizations, but also informal norms and customs.[1] Since the 1980s, a whole field of studies, New Institutional Economics, has turned them into a core element in the debate about development, economic and otherwise. In its briefest form, the argument is that 'poor' institutions drive up the so-called transaction costs associated with doing business. Economic growth slows when information is hard to find, traders cheat, cartels corner the market, the police want a cut, and the courts do not function.[2] That begs the question we ask in this chapter: Which role, if any, did public and private institutions play in economic growth across the globe in the centuries leading up to the Industrial Revolution, and do such institutions explain at least some of the divergences that eventually emerged between different countries and world regions?

Initially, institutional economics focused mostly on the insecurity of individuals' property rights. Whenever those were threatened, transaction costs rose, and economic growth was stymied. In this story, rulers and elites mostly featured as revenue-maximizing predators of private property.[3] More recently, North, Wallis, and Weingast have recognized that states as organizations were also needed to check uncontrolled violence. Rulers not only created rents by interfering with open markets to line their own pockets, but also used rents as a means of co-opting an elite that served as a check on violence. For North and his co-authors, only the emergence of democratic constraints on political elites in a small number of 'Open Access' societies during the nineteenth century eventually unleashed the productive forces of industrialization.[4]

It is beyond doubt that institutions mattered, but tracing their impact is a challenge. This chapter surveys a broad perspective of institutions, covering rules as well as organizations, both formal and informal, including practices and beliefs.[5] In this way, we can create a historically more flexible set of scales to weigh the varying mixtures of allocation mechanisms available to historical actors and discuss their impact on efficiency.

Following Polanyi, we distinguish between reciprocity (non-market exchange), markets, and redistribution as coordination tools that can produce economic efficiency or inefficiency, and social equality or inequality.[6] Part of the complexity of understanding institutions is that the three allocation mechanisms played varying roles at distinct levels, which we identify as the family, the firm, and the polity. To complicate matters further, choices on one level mattered for those at the others.[7] For example, Greif has argued that family structures tended to impose a logic of collective behaviour in Asia and the Middle East, but favoured individualist behaviour in Western Europe. That turned out to be good for family firms in the former, but placed them in the very long run at an economic disadvantage vis-à-vis the latter.[8] The interactions between institutional and organizational arrangements regarding families, firms, or entire states also imply that the effects of the same institution can be positive (efficient) in one context and negative (inefficient) in another. Institutions come in interrelated sets, which are 'co-evolutionary'.[9]

In this chapter, we will use the comparative method to identify institutional environments that seem to coincide with positive economic outcomes in the short, medium, and long term. We start from the smallest scale of organization, kinship, and move on to the next, at institutions that governed production and trade, firms, trading diasporas, guilds, and mercantile companies. Finally we turn to political governance proper.

## The family and economic development

One influential way in which families as an institution have been connected with economic development is through their choices of how to allocate their labour inputs and the products of their labour. The theory of the 'family economy' held that peasant households tried to minimize their contacts with markets and sustained a situation of economic self-sufficiency, by combining the labour inputs from all family members and redistributing returns within the household. Historians of gender portrayed the family economy as an environment of relative equality between the sexes. With the arrival of capitalism and its labour markets, women were relegated to the poorly paid jobs, and as a result also lost much of their clout within the household, where the male 'breadwinner' used his higher wages to obtain all sorts of privileges.

In the 1970s, the theory of the family economy was extended to the world of 'proto-industry'. European peasant households in regions of poor soils incorporated work for putting-out merchants in their annual schedule in an attempt to save their smallholdings. More recent research on proto-industrial regions and on farming families has undermined the idea of the household as a closed unit of production, and the idea of a 'family economy' stage, preceding capitalism, has therefore been by and large abandoned.[10] Nonetheless, historians have remained sensitive to the household as a place where economic decisions on consumption, production, and reproduction were actively being taken.[11]

A second close connection between families and economic development is through reproduction. Pre-modern societies balanced population and economic capacity through Malthusian checks, that is, reproductive constraints that reduced, or epidemics that wiped out excess population. The theory of the European Marriage Pattern (EMP) argues that, with the help of late marriage and a high degree of celibacy, Europeans were able to actively limit the number of children. While in other regions of the world population growth outstripped economic resources, Europeans managed to free those resources for investments in education and innovation. It was argued that this EMP emerged in the late Middle Ages, especially in Northwest Europe, through a fortuitous confluence of Catholic doctrine sponsoring juveniles' agency in the choice of a partner, inheritance practices that favoured the establishment of separate households (neo-locality), and a strong demand for wage labour after the Black Death.[12] The implication suggested that European population patterns were more growth-friendly.

Yet, the picture of a pre-modern world mired in Malthusian constraints has been equally questioned from the Asian perspective. China's spectacular population growth during the Ming and Qing eras was achieved without a substantial decline in living standards. In Asia generally, where the age of marriage was lower than in Europe, the regulation of fertility worked partially through infanticide. Because it was applied sex-specifically, the percentage of male bachelors in the Chinese population around 1800 was on a par with England and Scandinavian countries. Chinese females, moreover, had lower fertility within marriage than Europeans, suggesting a capacity to proactively regulate family size.[13] Overall, pre-modern societies in both Europe and Asia are now understood to have been more capable of demographic self-regulation than neo-Malthusian theories assumed.

A third approach to the connection between family and economy has been through 'family systems'. It has been proposed that Middle Eastern and Asian social structures favoured a collective mindset, compared to European incipient individualism, an idea that harks back to Max Weber's attempts to similarly frame the distinct trajectories of Europe and Asia. The argument is that the structure of economic organization was shaped by whether responsibility for wrongdoing was collective (i.e. an entire family can be punished for wrongdoing) or individual. Societies organized around collective responsibility would find the size of business organization capped. This was because organizations could rely on internal monitoring mechanisms, which were the very strength of such societies. But such internal mechanisms became less effective as the size of the organization increased. By contrast, systems shaped by more individualist social structures, where organizations could not rely on strong internal monitoring, would have increased the demand for a 'third-party enforcer', an independent political body that enforced rules and punished infractions. In Europe, where family-, lineage-, or clan-based monitoring was deficient, organizations were keener to see the town, or princely authorities control misbehaviour. But this, paradoxically, had the unintended consequence of increasing the optimum size of the organization, and with it the market.[14]

Critics of this view argue that it misrepresents the notion of family or lineage across Eurasia. In China, lineage was, to some extent, a fiction created by adoption. In eighteenth-century Beijing, adoption rates varied between 6 and 10 per cent. And Japan may have actually benefited from its traditional family structure, with three-generation households and emphasis on lineage. Stable family relationships led to lifelong learning and employment that created eventually the conditions for Japan's steep growth trajectory.[15] Family systems were, in other words, flexible, and their economic outcomes not predetermined.

At the same time, new data sets and daring attempts to classify societies according to family systems have produced some intriguing results for the post-1800 period. The first and most significant is that the connection between family and economy runs to an important extent through the channel of female agency. In so far as family systems support the education and labour participation of women, the economy will benefit; when female agency is constrained, the economy tends to suffer. Yet, the size of the effect clearly depends on the interactions with other institutional levels. Cultural restrictions for Chinese women to work outside the household might have been less important since a large share of the population had access to their own land and were thus less involved in waged labour anyway, according to Pomeranz.[16]

In the modern world, positive correlations can be established not only between family systems and economic growth directly, but also between late marriage, educational attainment, and female voting rights, which in turn also have a positive effect on economic development. For the pre-modern period, the evidence for Northwest Europe suggests an economic stimulus emanating from the institution of the family, but for other regions we still lack the evidence to fully understand its economic impact during the pre-modern era.[17] Still, the argument could be made that at this lowest level of institutional structures, belief systems and religious and social norms were of particular importance because they determined gender relations and reproductive behaviour, both of which have been shown to be subject to particular persistence. In turn, they created limits (or not) to productive organization within and outside the household.

## Firms, guilds, and chartered companies

At the meso level, three distinct types of organizations have dominated the debates about efficient institutions: firms, guilds and similar types of collective organizations, and finally chartered and joint-stock companies. All of them faced the main challenges of any economic enterprise of the early modern period: insecurity (the known unknowns) and uncertainty (the unknown unknowns). The unpredictability of the business environment started at the very basic level of bookkeeping: merchants and entrepreneurs used methods to record their transactions that made it practically impossible to keep track of the sources of profit and loss. Epidemics, fires, shipwrecks, piracy, and other natural and human infringements of production and exchange likewise posed external risks. To combat these problems, entrepreneurs would try to shield their activities through collaboration and collusion.[18] Practices that restricted the access of outsiders to markets and protected insiders were ubiquitous. Sometimes such institutional arrangements produced both private and social gains, but at other times the private gains were a social loss.

The early modern firm was an organization of production and trade set up around the family and kin as one way to deal with business risks. By pooling human and physical capital, handling the redistribution of returns partially as a non-market transaction, and guaranteeing succession in business, it introduced elements of stability. At the same time, family firms were also subject to limitations in size. The selection of the most skilled workers and succession in the firm were prone to mere chance. Traditionally, scholars have thus argued that the transition to legally backed organizational forms of business from Italian medieval family firms, via joint-stock trading companies, to the modern corporation was an important element in economic growth. Companies could increase in size, guarantee inter-temporal persistence, and raise larger amounts of capital. The path towards the modern company in Europe was juxtaposed to a supposed continued reliance of businesses centred on kin of religious institutions in Asia and the Middle East as one part of the story of economic divergence.

There are several problems with this attractive but oversimplified story. At the European end of the story, chartered and joint-stock companies were central to the modernization argument. As handmaidens of a 'world economy', the Dutch East India Company (Vereenigde Oostindische Compagnie – VOC) and the English East India Company (EIC) were the first to be financed by shares traded on the stock market. Yet, more recent research has shown that the VOC created its first shares more or less by mistake and used the instrument hardly at all after the company's start-up phase. Moreover, very few other companies were financed through shares. Profits moved from an early high on a downward trend, and by the mid-eighteenth century, the VOC traded at a loss. The EIC was subject to the same trend.[19] That is not to say that the companies were not economically important. The VOC alone was responsible for 13 per cent of the Dutch Republic's foreign trade, and its trading volume was larger than all the imports from Baltic ports into Holland combined. Yet, commercial expansion beyond Europe had arguably as much to do with aggressive state policies as with the particular organizational form of the companies themselves. As Fernand Braudel had already observed, chartered companies, with their state backing and strong-arm tactics, were ill-fitted to act as role models of 'free enterprise'.[20]

At the Asian and Middle Eastern ends, the story of the path towards the modern firm is also more complicated than what was once thought. There is strong evidence that in China the concept of lineage as the basis of business organization and credit networks remained central. It is also likely that the co-evolution of norms and institutions might well have reinforced those initial conditions that favoured clan-based business structures.[21] However, Chinese lineages worked very differently from European families: lineage-based businesses were not organized in a strict genealogical sense; they could rewrite the past if that was useful in the present and for the future. Not surprisingly, evidence of Chinese business practices has been uncovered that looks remarkably akin to those in the West.[22]

A separate argument holds that Middle Eastern development was at a disadvantage vis-à-vis European business because Islamic family and business law made it harder to guarantee the inter-temporal persistence of businesses. At the same time, alternative institutions that were used to pool capital, especially religious foundations known as *waqf*, were allegedly too inflexible to substitute for what some see as the quintessential European credit institution, the bank.[23] Yet, that argument, too, has been criticized. Too little research exists right now for us to understand the application of Islamic law as related to business practices. Moreover, in parts of Europe and its overseas empires, notably the Hispanic world, much of the credit markets were organized in the form of religious institutions, which seems to have sustained commercial expansion and economic development at relatively low costs (i.e. interest rates) well into the eighteenth century.[24]

Just as important as individual firms were organizations that looked after shared interests of trades in most pre-modern societies. Professional associations are still common today and by no means a hallmark of the 'traditional' economy. What distinguished pre-modern trade organizations, guilds, and trading nations was the routinely imposed requirement for everyone in the same trade to become a member. This requirement was usually backed up by legislation that established a 'monopoly' position for the members of the guild as a group. It is important, though, to stress that they would continue to compete with one another inside the association. This set them apart from joint-stock companies such as the VOC or EIC, which held a proper monopoly in the sense understood by modern economists.[25]

Craft guilds in turn should be distinguished from commercial organizations. In Europe, merchant guilds emerged before craft guilds, to reduce the risks related to commitment and enforcement in long-distance trade. They were still active in the sixteenth century. But at least in the more advanced centres of trade, they were gradually losing ground by 1600 as market institutions became sufficiently solid to support transactions without the guild framework as an enforcement mechanism. Locally, shopkeepers' guilds remained active, but with low entrance barriers and as a result broad membership.[26]

Chinese guilds usually recruited their members on the basis of shared geographical backgrounds. As these often also determined the line of trade, economic and regional identities tended to overlap. Most Chinese guilds emerged out of temple organizations and shared their premises with religious buildings. They regulated weights and measures, set prices (usually in conjunction with the local authorities), maintained codes of professional conduct, and lobbied local government to promote the interests of their members. There is, however, no hint of an exclusive access to particular trades for members of a specific guild. Membership was available to anyone who fit the membership profile, that is, originated from the region or was active in the occupation covered by the guild.[27]

Craft and merchant guilds were also common phenomena in Ottoman towns and cities. Ottoman guilds set quality controls and prices for both raw materials and final products. Guilds regularly made their wishes known by petitioning the authorities, and their proposals were usually accepted and absorbed into the body of regulations. Guilds were numerous, as well as popular in the sense that they organized a very substantial part of urban populations in the Ottoman Empire.[28]

European craft guilds took on a number of distinct roles. Economically, they sometimes coordinated the purchase of raw materials and the branding of products. More commonly, they provided training through apprenticeship schemes and tests of acquired skills in the form of master examinations. Some guilds, especially in export trades, branded goods by attaching a seal of approval after the product had been examined by guild officials. Guilds might also provide recourse for dissatisfied customers. Socially, some guilds assisted members in need through mutual support schemes. Guilds could double as civic militias, and guilds everywhere lobbied local authorities, seeking support for their trade.[29]

Strong claims have been made for and against the economic benefits of guilds, especially in the European historiography. Against the guilds, Adam Smith famously argued in *The Wealth of Nations* (1776) that they were a 'conspiracy against the public'. Modern critics of the guilds argue that they used their 'monopoly' rights to exclude newcomers, minorities, and women and to create rents for established masters and their offspring. The question is how widespread this was. In one area, the debate has been settled in favour of the pessimists. With some notable exceptions women were excluded from the corporate world.[30]

The optimists have nonetheless raised a number of counterarguments. One is that guilds were the pre-modern equivalent of the firm. A second is that centres of economic growth, like Antwerp, Amsterdam, and London, also had a strong guild presence.[31] A third, and perhaps the most relevant, claim is that guilds helped organize the training of the workforce or, in other words, the creation and transmission of human capital through skills education.

In its strongest form, this argument claims that apprenticeship contracts, enforced by guilds, helped to iron out the mismatch between the masters' investment in training during the early stages of the process and the temptation for apprentices to move elsewhere once they had gone through those early stages to claim a higher wage. New research has demonstrated that the relationship between master and apprentice was much more fluid than this model assumes. Guilds did not oversee the apprenticeship process, but merely registered its progress. Their role in the training process may therefore have been more limited to the registration of an apprenticeship, and as appeal boards for contracts that broke down.[32]

Perhaps most importantly, research on the geographical background of guild membership has clearly demonstrated that many masters, very often a majority, originated from another town than the one in which they were working. This implies a choice of business location. The same applied to merchants. In the late fifteenth century, many migrated from Bruges to Antwerp. When the Dutch Revolt broke out in the second half of the sixteenth century, a second wave of migration took Antwerp merchants first to London, Hamburg, and Cologne, and ultimately to Amsterdam. In the same vein, Jewish merchants from Iberia who wanted to settle in Holland negotiated with various local governments about the conditions these could offer them. All of this points to the fact that European towns were competing to establish comparative advantages. Institutionally, such advantages consisted of a bundle of arrangements. Like the guilds themselves, they served multiple purposes at the same time. Inter-urban competition also supported the diffusion of institutional innovations.[33]

All these arguments are much more difficult to verify outside the European contexts, where guild documents have not been preserved as abundantly as in European archives.

In India and Japan, there were no formal guilds; it has been argued that Indian castes were their functional equivalents, while Japan had brotherhoods that brought together businessmen in the same trades. Guilds were introduced in the New World by European colonizers, but in differentiated ways. In the Spanish colonies, they were numerous and often admitted people of all ethnic backgrounds and sometimes even slaves. In their North American colonies, British authorities were reluctant to create special interest organizations for industrial producers, which might become a source of protectionism against imports from the metropolis. As far as we know, the regulation of apprenticeship had no equivalent in China or the Middle East.[34] We have no way to test numbers against economic performance.

Nevertheless, certain organizational structures seem to have been almost ubiquitous across cultures and geographies. Such is the case of the clustering of certain crafts people in urban settings. Whether these were imposed by urban institutions on the crafts, or emerged out of the self-organization of the crafts, or responded to a location around a religious shrine, clearly they were an early response to the benefits of external economies of scale, and of agglomeration economies. Examples are the famous porcelain makers of Jingdezhen and the production of cotton in parts of Bengal.[35] The same might be true for the role of the polity in creating enterprises. Several European countries – France and Austria stand out – created state manufactures.[36]

What can we make of this? There certainly were distinctions in the way business was organized across the globe in the pre-modern world. With the wisdom of hindsight, certain institutional forms can be identified that would eventually emerge as being very significant. The importance of shareholding companies in the long run is uncontested, but their precursors were probably more important as the extended military arm of European states than as capital-raising business enterprises or revolutionary management solutions. Producers and trader associations raise similar concerns: Why was urban economic development associated with their presence for centuries? And why did their disappearance not create more growth in all places where this happened? Finally, why did China not reap benefits from being less constrained by 'monopolistic' guild structures?

## States and empires

This takes us to the third level of our analysis, the polity. Early modern political formations were characterized by diversity, not only globally, but also within larger continental spaces. City states, territorial states, and empires coexisted across Asia, Africa, and Europe. Only in the Americas, transatlantic empires prevailed. Such overseas empires existed, however, side by side with land-based empires, like Mughal India or Safavid Persia. Polities also differed strongly in how they were constituted socially, economically, and politically. The question to ask is whether we can observe clear correlations between particular sets of political institutions and societies' potential for long-term economic growth.

Political structures, generally quite loosely described as 'states', have long been central to arguments about the economic benefits of parliamentary versus so-called absolutist regimes in early modern Europe. The underlying problem is that societies face a contradiction: Without enforcement of a set of rules that govern political and economic life, the survival and property of individuals are permanently at risk, damaging their willingness to engage with the market. An independent third-party enforcer is therefore needed to protect subjects/citizens from random violence, and to enforce contracts where necessary. But a political regime strong enough to protect is also strong enough to blackmail and act as predator.[37] So how could the institutions of governance be designed in such a way that power holders would refrain from predating and extortion and thus from raising transaction costs in society?

The answer given by much of the literature was that rulers needed to be constrained by formal rules and parliamentary institutional arrangements that created sufficient checks, such as those in place in England after the Glorious Revolution of 1688. Economic historians have pointed out that the transition from pre-modern to modern intensive growth was initially less about an acceleration of growth rates than about economies no longer going into reverse gear. 'Growth without a reverse gear' was only thought to be possible once political regimes relied on representation within a formal (though not necessarily written) constitution. A related line of research has claimed that particular legal systems were more suited to guaranteeing subjects/citizens property rights, also singling out Anglophone legal origins as particularly growth-friendly.[38]

This returns us to the problem that any polity tasked first to guarantee external defence and second to provide a third-party enforcer service also needs to be financed. The legal capacity of the state depends on the coercive power to defend the state's public property rights to taxation, that is, its fiscal capacity.[39] But all early modern polities were states 'under construction'. Their administrative capabilities were severely constrained by rudimentary administrative systems, limited information, and high costs of administering sometimes far-flung territories. Estimates of the share of GDP that polities could hope to appropriate as tax income, a proxy for state capacity that is often called the state quota, are notoriously hard to come by. Today it ranges in OECD countries from 30 to over 50 per cent. In the sixteenth century, the revenues in terms of share of GDP per capita of the Ottoman Empire and most European polities are estimated at 2 to 5 per cent. By the later eighteenth century, Ottoman revenues still hovered around 6 per cent of GDP and that of China might have been somewhere between 4 and 8 per cent.[40] But in Britain, it had in the meantime reached 12–15 per cent, with other Western European states somewhere between this and Asian or Ottoman levels.[41] Was the divergence in fiscal capacity at the heart of growth divergence?

Several hypotheses have been advanced that link institutional forms of state formation to the likelihood of a more capable state emerging. Underpinning many of them is the idea that there was an optimum size of the state, or more precisely a particular combination of size, degree of centralization, and administrative efficiency. City states did not suffer from the information costs that larger polities faced and might well have benefited from an easier alignment between citizens' interests and the fiscal exigencies of the polity. But in competitive state systems, especially in Eurasia, the internal success of city states might over time be cut off by the external threat from larger neighbours. Local elites that had guaranteed the financial survival of many of the most successful city states for centuries sometimes turned into conservative and exclusionary ruling oligarchies. Princes were not as aligned with commercial interests as urban burghers, but they did quite often explicitly seek to foster economic development. Territorial states, princely or republican, had an advantage when it came to raising the revenue to withstand inter-polity competition. But in order to turn the advantage of more taxpayers into more revenues, they needed to achieve a certain degree of centralization that afforded the state a greater ability to appropriate and redistribute resources.[42]

If city states were considered too small, empires in general, but in particular land-based empires, were considered too large and as lacking the resources necessary to develop state capacity. While early institutionalists blamed excessive centralization for their poor growth performance, now imperial decentralization is stressed as an obstacle for growth. In the Ottoman Empire, an increasing share of fiscal resources remained in the regions, where it attracted a large number of intermediaries that ate into the receipts of the central state. Similarly, China's very large size delayed the organization of effective tax systems when compared to early modern Japan. In the Spanish Americas too, only a very small share of the fiscal resources ever made it to the supposed centre of the empire; most continued to circulate on the western side of the Atlantic.[43]

Caution, however, seems warranted in accepting too close an association between the share of the product appropriated by the polity and state capacity. At very low levels of fiscal capacity, polities clearly struggled to develop legal capacity. In Africa underpopulation in large parts of the continent probably resulted in a high land–labour ratio, which in turn limited the ability of polities to tax. Low population density in turn was initially driven by a combination of sleeping sickness limiting the availability of draught animals and few fertile lands. Where land was abundant, peasants could move on if taxed. That left rulers with a choice of either very coercive means of extraction of rents from labour or taxes that were imposed on major trade routes, which could not be avoided by merchants for reasons of climate and geography as for example in the trans-Saharan trade. This delivered at least four blows to prospects for growth. Labour markets were pushed into forced labour, because slavery and forced labour were forms of population tax. Trade, which already suffered from high costs caused by environmental conditions, was burdened even more, and the consolidation of efficient and effective political power was held back. Low levels of state capacity might have pushed economies off their growth path repeatedly. Finally, fiscally weak polities were also very exposed to external threats to their survival as independent polities that manifested themselves in the nineteenth-century 'scramble for Africa' on the part of European states.[44]

Most Eurasian polities and the American territories attached to them, however, had during the early modern period lean but reasonably stable administrative structures that could tax land and population, as well as trade and consumption. The assumption that empires were too large to achieve efficient degrees of fiscal capacity can also be challenged. Most of the large land-based and overseas empires were by 1800 not the 'dead men walking' that early institutionalists had described them as. They had successfully guaranteed their survival as political units, and a new historiography now sees significant indications of economic dynamism in many of them as late as the eighteenth century.[45]

More important, a focus on the gross revenue as a means to assess state capacity is in danger of confusing two fundamental state functions: that of third-party enforcer and that of coordinating the articulation of the economy domestically and in the growing international economy. The function of third-party enforcer could be achieved by one of two means. A state that was centralized and therefore could exert coercion at relatively low cost could also rely on such coercion to raise the necessary fiscal means. However, high degrees of coercion provoked resistance because they undermined the legitimacy of the state. In such a polity, fiscal capacity and legal capacity could only be aligned through formal constraints that guaranteed some restraint in discretionary coercion and a use of the state's means that met the approval of the represented elites. Historically, the mechanisms to achieve such balance probably emerged by chance. Royal power in England was stronger and the realm more centralized than any other European polity early on. Thus English medieval monarchs could force the nobility to attend parliamentary sessions while their continental neighbours had trouble calling up the nobility for duty. But centuries later, the English Parliament managed to turn its forced meetings into a representative institution in large part because nobles *had to attend*.[46]

A second and more common model, however, was that of the poorly integrated polities. This was the case of most empires, constituted as composite or polycentric states. Coercion was expensive under such circumstances. Polycentric states were also less characterized by the centre–periphery dynamics of nineteenth-century colonialism. Instead they featured a governance regime that allowed for the retention of resources at various locations and sub-centres; co-optation was likely more efficient than coercion in these cases because it supported the state's legitimacy. In these cases, decentralization, rather than a sign of state weakness, was actually promoting the efficient use of resources that bought off opposition and reduced the cost of coercive practices, while still offering strong legal capacity.[47] Local and regional agency converted large parts of local elites into stakeholders of the polity. It generated quasi-voluntary compliance, which reduced inefficiencies in fiscal systems compared to states that had to apply more force as some have argued for the Spanish Americas.[48] Likewise, in the notoriously de-centralized Dutch Republic, the urban heritage may have helped to create trust and cooperation between citizens and their rulers. The state could thus collect high taxes efficiently and provide useful public goods. Quasi-voluntary compliance increased efficiency by reducing coercion costs and left more revenue to be spent on other purposes.[49]

Still, polycentric forms of political institution building might have engendered collateral damage in terms of economic growth. Powerful territorial and/or urban elites in larger polities often created non-market obstacles to the movement of goods, capital, and people in defence of local power. They did not hinder market development because of their tendency to disrespect private property rights. Instead, their political and social aspirations led to smaller and shallower markets, which in turn meant that allocative efficiencies were removed only very slowly.[50] Domestic markets remained poorly integrated. Perhaps the creation of states with strong polycentric features, from China to the Austrian Habsburg Monarchy, was a response to a perceived need to substitute for market forces in the deepening of the market.

Polycentric rule also made it impossible for rulers to develop cohesive external commercial policies at a time when the share of international trade in economic development was strongly increasing. Mercantilist policies of the kinds that Britain or France developed in the eighteenth century presupposed a relatively high degree of political integration. The transfer of sovereign power to the English East India Company and the creation of a company state were possible because sovereignty could be understood as hybrid on the Indian subcontinent. But it was also an expression of a powerful domestic centralized ruler, with real military might and increasingly ill at ease with such hybridity.[51] Where mercantilist policies were used to control market access, as in British competition in the textile sector with India, such policies were able to significantly change the growth path of both economies, upwards in the former case, downwards in the latter. Polycentric states, by contrast, lacked the ability to create functioning mercantilist systems. Giving priority to one territorial interest over another would have entailed very high coercive costs. The Dutch case was an interesting intermediate example that combined strong polycentric structures in the Netherlands with mercantilist policies in its colonies.[52]

This then brings us back to the co-evolution of institutions. Perhaps the debate about states and empires has been wrong-footed from the very beginning. In a very nineteenth-century manner, historians have assumed that states (and empires) are the proper level of analysis to capture the effect of governance structures. However, given the constraints states faced, more attention should probably be paid to the way they connected to other levels of society. The role of towns and their citizens particularly merit our attention.[53] After all, towns acted as hubs in commercial networks and were also the locus of industrial activity. Increasing levels of urbanization always indicated rising economic prosperity, even if specialists in European and Japanese proto-industry insist that non-agricultural production in the country might well have been an alternative source of growth.[54] Urban elites' personal interest in trade and industry and the efficiencies emerging from an overlapping of economic and political elites remain good candidates as growth-fostering institutions.[55]

Nevertheless we should be careful not to impose too simple a causality. Europe's economically most vital regions developed mechanisms to translate urban interests into state policies: the city state in Renaissance Italy, federalism in the Dutch Republic, and parliamentary rule in post-1688 England. At the same time, not all European areas with very strong urban traditions were able to turn this heritage into faster economic development. One notable example is Spain, where strong urban political rights (together with territorial rights) acted as effective constraints of political power – but failed to promote market development. Urban interests sometimes needed to be overridden to let the market grow. In China, it has been argued, cities and towns were not so much suppressed, as left in the cold: poorly regulated, poorly funded, and far removed from state supervision, they were an easy prey for opportunistic officials and corrupt practices.[56]

The co-evolution of political and economic institutions at various levels of social organization produced an almost infinite number of variations. In a world of poor transport and high information costs, that is, one in which using the market could be costly, urban spaces were relatively privileged because here the market could function more easily. Where higher level political institutions left those urban markets at the mercy of greedy lords or officials, their development was hindered just as much as where higher level political institutions left urban elites entirely in charge, allowing them to restrict market size and depth. The role of states in coordinating the market has probably been underestimated, but it was rarely independent of governance at the urban level or at that of the many historical territories or provinces that had been joined up in larger units.

## Conclusion

The notion of a static early modern world, proclaimed by Emmanuel Le Roy Ladurie in 1974, has since been comprehensively overturned.[57] However, we still only partially understand the forces that determined the tension between stasis and change. The slow transition from early modern extensive growth to modern intensive growth was mostly about economies stopping to go into reverse gear. The data, however imperfect, suggest that this was achieved in pockets of Europe earlier than elsewhere. Any explanation for that exceptional surging ahead cannot overlook the Industrial Revolution. However, a growing consensus suggests that some European economies were going through fundamental changes well before 1800, while the impact of modern industry took quite a while to materialize after 1800. If we accept that industrialization was part of a larger process of transformation that took several centuries, can we then argue that institutional change was the driving force that took the reverse gear out of the engine?

At the most basic level, family systems clearly mattered. But for our period it has so far proved difficult to produce convincing evidence that particular family systems were associated with more or less growth, even if gender relations and inheritance systems remained important. The analytical problem might in part be the co-evolution of institutional forms: a particular form of lineage or family evolves in combination with organizational forms of production, say the craft workshop or the agricultural unit of the extended family, and is regulated and sanctioned by urban, religious, or state regulation. For the historian it is difficult to identify which part of that set of institutions helped or hindered growth. Looking at each of them in isolation might in fact be unpromising to start with from a methodological standpoint.

Historians have traditionally paid much attention to the intermediate organizational level. The current state of research highlights the role of guilds, that is, merchants' and producers' associations, as significant, but guilds' ubiquity at the same time reduces their value as an explanation for divergence between civilizations. Business innovations from Italian family firms to joint-stock companies have been seen as being at the heart of European divergence. We are not convinced. As new research emerges on business practices and legal structures underpinning credit and goods markets in Asia and the Middle East, perceived dramatic divergences seem smaller. As for joint-stock companies, much of their impact before the late eighteenth century was limited to overseas trade. On balance we would argue that the large diversity in institutional solutions to commercial challenges and the development of crafts, and the competition between them, might have been more important. Here we do see a link with the more or less autonomous towns and a range of states in Europe that offered such diversity.

Finally, we see the role of the state as that of a coordinator of economy and society. Property rights were a part of that remit, but the Dutch Revolt or the Glorious Revolution were concerned with legitimacy as much as anything else. Given the constraints of distance and limited means of communication, coordination was expensive as well as difficult to achieve effectively in large territorial units. The most successful states tended to be small to medium-sized, even in the European context; the Industrial Revolution itself was a regional, rather than a national, phenomenon. The more successful polities also had institutional mechanisms that enabled the articulation of local concerns at state level. The presence of multiple states, moreover, offered a mixed menu of institutional combinations as well as various routes for 'exit', and therefore 'voice', to economic interest groups, and an escape route for those who had fallen foul of a particular elite or ruler.[58] We do not believe that Europe had many superior institutions. But it might have benefited from more institutional diversity that developed in, and benefited from, the co-evolution at various levels of articulation.

There is thus not one single institutional factor that explains the 'Great Divergence'. In so far as institutions contributed to diverging trajectories of growth and stagnation, we have tried to demonstrate that it was not 'Europe' versus the 'rest'. Both categories are too heterogeneous. The exceptional pockets in Europe were institutionally distinct because of their small family units, strong urban institutions, and small state units. There are indications that, precisely as a result of these features, those same regions managed to create organizations that embraced more people and covered larger distances. Theoretically, there could have been other sets of co-evolved norms, organizations, and institutions that might have eventually led to the same path; historical examples of such alternative trajectories are, however, not available.

## Notes

* Thanks are due to the Social & Economic History Group at Utrecht University and to the helpful suggestions of the audience at the authors' workshop for this volume at the London School of Economics in May 2016.

1. D. C. North (1990), *Institutions, Institutional Change and Economic Performance*. Cambridge: Cambridge University Press.

2. D. C. North (1992), *Transaction Costs, Institutions, and Economic Performance*. San Francisco: International Center for Economic Growth.

3. D. C. North and B. R. Weingast (1989), 'Constitutions and commitment: The evolution of institutions governing public choice in seventeenth-century England', *Journal of Economic History*, 49 (4), 803–32, North, *Institutions*; R. B. Ekelund and R. D. Tollison (1999), *Politicized Economies, Monarchy, Monopoly, and Mercantilism*. Enskede: TPB.

4. D. C. North, J. J. Wallis and B. R. Weingast (2009), *Violence and Social Orders: A Conceptual Framework for Interpreting Recorded Human History*. Cambridge and New York: Cambridge University Press.

5. T. Kuran (2009), 'Explaining the trajectories of civilizations: The systemic approach', *Journal of Economic Behaviour and Organizations*, 71 (3), 593–605.

6. K. Polanyi (2001), *The Great Transformation: The Political and Economic Origins of Our Times*. Boston: Beacon Press.

7. A. Greif (2005), 'Commitment, coercion, and markets: The nature and dynamics of institutions supporting exchange', in C. Menard and M. M. Shirley (eds), *Handbook of New Institutional Economics*. Dordrecht and Netherlands: Springer, 727–86.

8. O. Williamson (2000), 'The New Institutional Economics: Taking stock, looking ahead', *Journal of Economic Literature*, 38 (3), 595–613; A. Greif (1994), 'Cultural beliefs and the organization of society: A historical and theoretical reflection on collectivist and individualist societies', *Journal of Political Economy*, 102 (5), 912–50.

9. E. Ostrom (2005), *Understanding Institutional Diversity*. Princeton: Princeton University Press.

10. L. Tilly (1977), *Women, Work, and Family*. New York: Holt, Rinehart and Winston; P. Kriedte, H. Medick and J. Schlumbohm (1981), *Industrialization before Industrialization: Rural Industry in the Genesis of Capitalism* [or. ed. in German 1978]. Cambridge: Cambridge University Press; A. Knotter (2000), 'Problems of the "family economy": Peasant economy, domestic production and labour markets in pre-industrial households', in M. Prak (ed.), *Early Modern Capitalism: Economic and Social Change in Europe, 1400–1800*. London: Routledge, 135–60.

11. J. de Vries (2013), 'The industrious revolutions in East and West', in G. Austin and K. Sugihara (eds), *Labour-Intensive Industrialization in Global History*. London and New York: Routledge, 65–84; Idem (2008), *The Industrious Revolution: Consumer Behavior and the Household Economy, 1650 to the Present*. Cambridge and New York: Cambridge University Press.

12. J. Hajnal (1965), 'European marriage patterns in perspective', in D. Glass and D. V. Eversley (eds), *Essays in Historical Demography*. London: Arnold, 101–43, J. L. van Zanden, T. De Moor and S. Carmichael (forthcoming), *Girlpower: The European Marriage Pattern: Female Empowerment and Economic Development in Western Europe 1300–1800*; N. Voigtländer and H.-J. Voth (2013), 'How the West "invented" fertility restriction', *American Economic Review*, 103 (6), 2227–64; T. Dennison and S. Ogilvie (2014), 'Does the European Marriage Pattern explain economic growth?', *Journal of Economic History*, 74 (3), 651–93.

13. J. Lee and W. Feng (1999), 'Malthusian models and Chinese realities: The Chinese demographic system 1700–2000', *Population and Development Review*, 25 (1), 33–65.

14. A. Greif (1994), 'On the political foundations of the late medieval commercial revolution: Genoa during the twelfth and thirteenth centuries', *Journal of Economic History*, 54 (2), 271–87.

15. D. Faure (1996), 'The lineage as business company: Patronage versus law in the development of Chinese business', in R. A. Brown (ed.), *Chinese Business Enterprise: Critical Perspectives on Business and Management*. London: Routledge, 82–106; Lee and Feng, 'Malthusian models'; O. Saito (2010), 'The stem family and labour markets: Reflections on households and firms in Japan's economic development', unpublished conference paper presented in Utrecht.

16. K. Pomeranz (2013), 'Labour-intensive industrialization in the rural Yangzi Delta: Late imperial patterns and their modern fates', in Austin and Sugihara (eds), *Labour-Intensive Industrialization*, 122–43; Idem (2005), 'Women's work and the economics of respectability', in B. Goodman and W. Larson (eds), *Gender in Motion*. Lanham, MD: Rowman and Littlefield, 239–63.

17. S. Dilli (2017), 'The deep causes of economic development: Family systems and female agency', in J. L. van Zanden, A. Rijpma and J. Kok (eds), *Agency, Gender, and Economic Development in the World Economy, 1850–2000: Testing the Sen Hypothesis*. London: Routledge, 138–61; R. Maseland (2015), 'The rise of deep determinants', unpublished paper, University of Groningen, consulted at http://papers.sioe.org/paper/1262.html.

18. D. W. Allen (2012), *The Institutional Revolution: Measurement and the Economic Emergence of the Modern World*. Chicago and London: University of Chicago Press; P. Gervais (2014), 'Early modern merchant strategies and the historicization of market practices', *Economic Sociology – The European Electronic Newsletter*, 15, 19–29.

19. G. Dari-Mattiacci, O. Gelderblom, J. Jonker, E. C. Perotti (2017), 'The emergence of the corporate form', *Journal of Law, Economics, and Organization*, 33 (2), 193–236; L. Petram (2014), *The World's First Stock Exchange*. New York: Columbia Business School Publishing; J. de Vries (2003), 'Connecting Europe and Asia: A quantitative analysis of the Cape-route trade, 1497–1795', in D. O. Flynn, A. Giráldez and R. von Glahn (eds), *Global Connections and Monetary History, 1470–1800*. Aldershot: Ashgate, 35–106; J. de Vries, and A. van der Woude (1997), *The First Modern Economy. Success, Failure, and Perseverance of the Dutch Economy, 1500-1815*. Cambridge: Cambridge University Press.

20. P. K. O'Brien (2013), 'The formation of states and transitions to modern economies: England, Europe, and Asia compared', in L. Neal, and J. G. Williamson (eds), *The Cambridge History of Capitalism, Vol. 1. The Rise of Capitalism: From Ancient Origins to 1848*. Cambridge: Cambridge University Press, 357–402; S. Beckert (2014), *Empire of Cotton: A Global History*. New York: Alfred A. Knopf; F. Braudel (1984), *Civilization and Capitalism, 15th-18th Century*. London: Collins, ch. 4.

21. A. Greif and G. Tabellini (2017), 'The clan and the corporation: Sustaining cooperation in China and Europe', *Journal of Comparative Economics*, 45 (1), 1–35.

22. T. W. Guinnane, R. Harris, N. Lamoreaux, et al. (2007), 'Putting the corporation in its place', *Enterprise & Society*, 8 (4), 687–729; M. Zelin (2009), 'The firm in early modern China', *Journal of Economic Behavior and Organizations*, 71 (3), 623–37; K. Pomeranz (1997), '"Traditional" Chinese business forms revisited: Family, firm and financing in the history of the Yutang Company of Jining', *Late Imperial China*, 18 (1), 1–38; Gelderblom, de Jong and Jonker, 'The formative years'.

23. T. Kuran T. (2010), *The Long Divergence: How Islamic Law Held Back the Middle East*. Princeton: Princeton University Press.

24. C. Milhaud (2015), 'Priests or bankers? The ecclesiastical credit in modern Spain'. *Working Paper HAL Archives Ouvertes*, https://hal-pse.archives-ouvertes.fr/hal-01180682; A. Lavrín (1966), 'The role of nunneries in the economy of New Spain in the eighteenth century', *Hispanic American Historical Review*, 46 (4), 371–93; R. Grafe (2012), *Distant Tyranny: Markets, Power and Backwardness in Spain 1650–1800*. Princeton: Princeton University Press.

25. F. van Waarden (1992), 'Emergence and development of business interest associations: An example from the Netherlands', *Organization Studies*, 13 (4), 521–62; G. Richardson (2001), 'A tale of two theories: Monopolies and craft guilds in medieval England and modern imagination', *Journal of the History of Economic Thought*, 23 (2), 217–42.

26. O. Gelderblom and R. Grafe (2010), 'The rise, persistence and decline of merchant guilds: Re-thinking the comparative study of commercial institutions in pre-modern Europe', *Journal of Interdisciplinary History*, 40 (4), 477–511; O. Gelderblom (2013), *Cities of Commerce: The Institutional Foundations of International Trade in the Low Countries, 1250–1650*. Princeton: Princeton University Press; S. Ogilvie (2011), *Institutions and European Trade: Merchant Guilds, 1000–1800*. Cambridge and New York: Cambridge University Press.

27. C. Moll-Murata (2008), 'Chinese guilds from the seventeenth to the twentieth century: An overview', in J. Lucassen, T. De Moor and J. L. van Zanden (eds), *The Return of the Guilds*. Cambridge: Cambridge University Press, 213–48; R. Belsky (2005), *Localities at the Center: Native Place, Space, and Power in Late Imperial Beijing*. Cambridge, MA: Harvard University Asia Center, distributed by Harvard University Press; W. T. Rowe (1984), *Hankow: Commerce and Society in a Chinese City, 1796–1889*. Stanford: Stanford University Press; L. Tan (2013), 'Market-supporting institutions, gild organisations, and the Industrial Revolution: A comparative view', *Australian Economic History Review*, 53 (3), 221–46.

28. S. Faroqhi (2009), *Artisans of Empire: Crafts and Craftspeople under the Ottomans*. London; New York: I. B. Tauris; E. Yi (2004), *Guild Dynamics in Seventeenth-Century Istanbul: Fluidity and Leverage*. Leiden and Boston: Brill; A. Raymond (1973), *Artisans et Commerçants au Caire au XVIIIe Siècle*. Damascus: Institut Français d'Etudes Arabes de Damas.

29. The literature on early modern European craft guilds is huge, and growing, but see A. Guenzi, P. Massa and F. Piola Caselli (eds) (1998), *Guilds, Markets, and Work Regulations in Italy, 16th-19th Centuries*. Aldershot: Ashgate; M. Prak, C. Lis, J. Lucassen, et al. (2006), *Craft Guilds in the Early Modern Low Countries: Work, Power and Representation*. Aldershot: Ashgate; A. Kluge (2007), *Die Zünfte*, Stuttgart: Steiner; S. R. Epstein and M. Prak (eds) (2008), *Guilds, Innovation, and the European Economy, 1400–1800*. Cambridge: Cambridge University Press; Lucassen, De Moor and van Zanden, *The Return of the Guilds*.

30. See S. R. Epstein (2008), 'Craft guilds in the pre-modern economy: A discussion', *Economic History Review*, 61 (1), 155–74 versus S. C. Ogilvie (2008), 'Rehabilitating the guilds: A reply', *Economic History Review*, 61 (1), 175–82; S. C. Ogilvie (1997), *State Corporatism and Proto-industry: The Württemberg Black Forest, 1580–1797*. Cambridge and New York: Cambridge University Press; Idem (2003), *A Bitter Living: Women, Markets, and Social Capital in Early Modern Germany*. Oxford and New York: Oxford University Press; and Idem (2011), *Institutions and European Trade*. Also C. H. Crowston (2008), 'Women, gender and guilds in early modern Europe: An overview of recent literature', in Lucassen, De Moor and van Zanden, *The Return of the Guilds*, 19–44.

31. U. Pfister (2008), 'Craft guilds, the theory of the firm, and early modern proto-industry', in Epstein and Prak, *Guilds, Innovation and the European Economy*, 25–51; G. S. de Krey (1985), *A Fractured Society: The Politics of London in the First Age of Party 1688-1715*. Oxford and New York: Oxford University Press, ch. 10.

32. S. R. Epstein (1998), 'Craft guilds, apprenticeship, and technological change in preindustrial Europe', *Journal of Economic History*, 58 (3), 684–715; P. Wallis (2008), 'Apprenticeship and training in pre-modern England', *Journal of Economic History*, 68 (3), 832–61.

33. M. Prak, C. Crowston, B. De Munck, C. Kissane, C. Minns, R. Schalk and P. Wallis (2018), 'Access to the trade: Citizens, craft guilds and social and geographical mobility in early modern Europe', LSE Economic History Working Papers 282; Gelderblom, *Cities of*

*Commerce*; R.G.Fuks-Mansfeld (1989), *De Sefardim in Amsterdam tot 1795: Aspecten van de Ontwikkeling van een Joodse Minderheid in een Hollandse Stad.* Hilversum: Verloren; Gelderblom and Grafe, 'The rise, persistence and decline of merchant guilds'; R. Grafe (2014), 'Polycentric states: The Spanish reigns and the "failures" of mercantilism', in P. Stern and C. Wennerlind (eds), *Mercantilism Reimagined: Political Economy in Early Modern Britain and Its Empire.* Oxford: Oxford University Press, 241–62.

34. T. Roy (2008), 'The guild in modern South Asia', in Lucassen, De Moor, and van Zanden, *The Return of the Guilds,* 95–120; and M. L. Nagata (2008), 'Brotherhoods and stock societies: Guilds in pre-modern Japan', in ibid, 121–42; L. L. Johnson (1986), 'Artisans', in L. S. Hoberman and S. Socolow (eds), *Cities and Society in Colonial Latin America.* Albuquerque: University of New Mexico Press, 227–50; C. I. Archer (1977), *The Army in Bourbon Mexico, 1760–1810.* Albuquerque, NM: University of New Mexico Press; C. S. Olton (1975), *Artisans for Independence: Philadelphia Mechanics and the American Revolution.* Syracuse: Syracuse University Press.

35. G. Riello and T. Roy (eds) (2009), *How India Clothed the World: The World of South Asian Textiles, 1500-1850,* Leiden: Brill; C. Moll-Murata (2013), 'Guilds and apprenticeship in China and Europe: The case of the Jingdezhen and European ceramics industries', in M. Prak and J. L. van Zanden (eds), *Technology, Skills and the Pre-modern Economy in the East and the West: Essays Dedicated to the Memory of S.R. Epstein.* Leiden: Brill, 225–58.

36. P. Deyon and P. Guignet (1980), 'The royal manufactures and economic progress in France before the Industrial Revolution', *Journal of European Economic History,* 9 (3), 611–32.

37. North and Thomas, *The Rise of the Western World*; M. Levi (1988), *Of Rule and Revenue.* Berkeley: University of California Press.

38. North and Weingast, 'Constitutions and commitment'; R. La Porta, F. Lopez-de-Silanes and A. Shleifer (2008), 'The economic consequences of legal origin', *Journal of Economic Literature,* 46 (2), 285–332.

39. Epstein, *Freedom and Growth*; T. Besley and T. Persson (2009), 'The origins of state capacity: Property rights, taxation, and politics', *American Economic Review,* 99 (4), 1218–44. See also M. Olson (2000), *Power and Prosperity: Outgrowing Communist and Capitalist Dictatorships.* New York: Basic Books.

40. K. K. Karaman and S. Pamuk (2010), 'Ottoman state finances in European perspective, 1500–1914', *Journal of Economic History,* 70 (3), 608–9; P. H. H. Vries (2015), *State, Economy and the Great Divergence: Great Britain and China, 1680s-1850s.* London: Bloomsbury.

41. N. Palma and J. Reis (2016), 'From convergence to divergence: Portuguese demography and economic growth, 1500–1850', *GGDC Research Memorandum,* 161 (Working paper, Groningen Growth and Development Centre).

42. A. Alesina and E. Spolaore (2003), *The Size of Nations.* Cambridge, MA: MIT Press; J. L. van Zanden and M. Prak (2006), 'Towards an economic interpretation of citizenship: The Dutch Republic between medieval communes and modern nation-state', *European Review of Economic History,* 10 (2), 111–45; S. R. Epstein (2006), 'The rise of the West', in J. A. Hall and R. Schroeder (eds), *An Anatomy of Power: The Social Theory of Michael Mann.* Cambridge: Cambridge University Press, 233–62; H. Spruyt (1994), *The Sovereign State and Its Competitors: An Analysis of Systems Change.* Princeton, NJ: Princeton University Press; Epstein, *Freedom and Growth*; D. Stasavage (2011), *States of Credit: Size, Power, and the Development of European Polities.* Princeton and Oxford: Princeton University Press. For a quantitative test of the hypothesis see M. Dincecco (2011), *Political Transformations and Public Finances: Europe, 1650–1913.* Cambridge and New York: Cambridge University Press.

43. Karaman and Pamuk, 'Ottoman state finances'; C. Moriguchi and T. H. Sng (2014), 'Asia's little divergence: State capacity in China and Japan before 1850', *Journal of Economic Growth,*

19 (4), 439–70; R. Grafe and A. Irigoin (2012), 'A stakeholder empire: The political economy of Spanish imperial rule in America', *Economic History Review*, 65 (2), 609–51.

44. J. I. Herbst (2000), *States and Power in Africa: Comparative Lessons in Authority and Control*. Princeton: Princeton University Press; G. Austin (2010), 'African economic development and colonial legacies', *International Development Policy*, 1 (1), 11–32.

45. K. Pomeranz (2000), *The Great Divergence. China, Europe and the Making of the Modern World Economy*. Princeton: Princeton University Press; R. B. Wong (1997), *China Transformed: Historical Change and the Limits of European Experience*. Ithaca, N.Y.: Cornell University Press; P. Parthasarathi (2011), *Why Europe Grew Rich and Asia Did Not: Global Economic Divergence, 1600-1850*. Cambridge: Cambridge University Press.

46. D. A. Boucoyannis (2015), 'No taxation of elites, no representation: State capacity and the origins of representation', *Politics and Society*, 43 (3), 303–32.

47. P. Cardim, T. Herzog, J. J. Ruiz Ibáñez, et al. (2012), *Polycentric Monarchies: How Did Early Modern Spain and Portugal Achieve and Maintain a Global Hegemony?*, Eastbourne and Portland, OR: Sussex Academic Press; Karaman and Pamuk, 'Ottoman state finances'; R. Grafe and A. Irigoin (2013), 'Negotiating power: Fiscal constraints and financial development in early modern Spain and the Spanish Empire', in D. Coffman (ed.), *Questioning Credible Commitment: Perspectives on the Rise of Financial Capitalism*. Cambridge: Cambridge University Press and Winton Centre for Financial History, 188–227.

48. Grafe and Irigoin, 'A stakeholder empire'.

49. Van Zanden and Prak, 'Towards an economic interpretation'; Levi, *Of Rule and Revenue*.

50. Grafe, *Distant Tyranny*.

51. P. J. Stern (2011), *The Company-State: Corporate Sovereignty and the Early Modern Foundations of the British Empire in India*. New York: Oxford University Press.

52. O'Brien, 'The formation of states'; Parthasarathi, *Why Europe Grew Rich and Asia Did Not*.

53. See for instance, P. Clark (ed.) (2013), *The Oxford Handbook of Cities in World History*. Oxford: Oxford University Press, 3, 221, 231, 386, 421, 452, and 584.

54. de Vries, 'The industrious revolutions in East and West'.

55. J. B. De Long, and A. Shleifer (1993), 'Princes or merchants: European city growth before the Industrial Revolution', *Journal of Law and Economics*, 36 (2), 695–6; J. L. van Zanden, E. Buringh and M. Bosker (2012), 'The rise and decline of European parliaments 1188–1789', *Economic History Review*, 65 (3), 835–61.

56. M. Prak (2018), *Citizens without Nations: Urban Citizenship in Europe and the World, 1000-1789*. Cambridge: Cambridge University Press; L. Brandt, D. Ma and T. G. Rawski (2014), 'From divergence to convergence: Re-evaluating the history behind China's economic boom', *Journal of Economic Literature*, 52 (1), 61–80.

57. E. Le Roy Ladurie (1974), 'L'histoire immobile', *Annales ESC*, 29, 673–92.

58. S. Pollard (1981), *Peaceful Conquest: The Industrialization of Europe, 1760–1970*. Oxford and New York: Oxford University Press; also M. Prak (1994), 'Regions in early modern Europe'; and S. Pollard (1994), 'Regional and interregional economic development in Europe in the eighteenth and nineteenth centuries', *Debates and Controversies: Proceedings Eleventh International Economic Congress (A-sessions)*. Milan: Bocconi University, 17–55 and 57–92 respectively; and J. de Vries (2001), 'Economic growth before and after the Industrial Revolution: A modest proposal', in Prak, *Early Modern Capitalism*, 177–94; A. O. Hirschman (1970), *Exit, Voice, and Loyalty: Responses to Decline in Firms, Organizations, and States*. Cambridge, MA: Harvard University Press; J. D. Tracy (ed.) (1991), *The Political Economy of Merchant Empires*. Cambridge: Cambridge University Press; Mokyr, *A Culture of Growth*.

# CHAPTER 6
## PLANTATIONS AND THE GREAT DIVERGENCE
*Trevor Burnard*

Few institutions define world history in the early modern period more than the plantation complex. It has been argued that the plantations in America provided one of two crucial ingredients (along with the presence of large coal deposits allowing for cheap energy) propelling Britain and then Europe to the economic superiority of Europe over China by 1800. Kenneth Pomeranz suggests that 'the extraordinary ecological bounty of the new world' lifted previous limits to the supply of land. Plantations added millions of 'ghost acres' to Britain's supply of agricultural land, providing food for a growing population and freeing up resources for other activities.[1] The plantation system is thus vital for determining the extent to which wealth coming from the Americas in the seventeenth century and, especially, in the eighteenth century can be seen as crucial in the foundations of 'the Great Divergence'. Significantly, the important role that is often attached to plantations in accounts of 'the Great Divergence' suggests an importance for plantations that is sometimes absent in the literature, where the plantation system seems only to have added to the immiseration of humans generally and to the underdevelopment of Africa specifically.[2] In this chapter, I examine the role of plantations in fostering 'the Great Divergence', paying particular attention to Britain which as a major imperial actor in the plantation societies of the Americas and the first industrial nation is especially crucial to arguments connecting the plantations of the Americas to eighteenth-century industrial development.

That the Americas would be crucial to Europe in overtaking China as the driver of the global economy by 1800 would have seemed surprising before the maturation of the plantation system in the eighteenth century. By 1650, the settlement of the Americas was mostly a failure. There were some successes. Spain and Portugal had placed themselves firmly into Central and South America, with the Spanish developing silver mines in Potosí in upper Peru that provided a torrent of bullion to the home country, albeit with decidedly mixed results for economic development.[3] The Portuguese had established the first plantation complex in the Americas, producing sugar for export to Europe from the 1550s, though this innovative use of American land had less positive results for Portugal than might have been expected.[4] Some new foodstuffs, like maize, tobacco, and potatoes, had made their way from the Americas to the rest of the world, as did exotic drugs like tobacco, leading to transformations of parts of the world economy.[5]

The overall effect of the Columbian encounter, however, was mostly catastrophic, especially for the native inhabitants of the Americas. Much of the Americas reverted to wilderness, possibly taking some carbon out of the atmosphere and perhaps contributing to the Little Ice Age of the seventeenth century.[6] Population decline was good news for forests, which grew bigger and taller in the Americas than they had done for millennia. For European settlers, these gigantic forests looked as if they were ancient but in fact they were very new. These huge trees when chopped down provided the nutrients for extensive agricultural cultivation, notably in northeastern Brazil from the 1550s and in the smaller islands of the eastern Caribbean, settled by the British and the French, in the second quarter of the seventeenth century. Once cleared, however, especially in places like Barbados where there was no indigenous population to hamper European colonization efforts, the rich soils of deforested land proved perfect places for the establishment of farms for the production of tropical crops – in the Americas, these included tobacco, cotton, rice, indigo, coffee, and above all sugar.[7]

In English America, these farms were called 'plantations'. The rise of plantation agriculture after 1650 and the nearly coincidental beginnings of the financial and then industrial revolutions in seventeenth- and eighteenth-century England and later Britain is the focus of fierce historiographical attention with less attention paid to similar connections in other European empires. Nevertheless, despite the concentration in this chapter on developments in Britain, if slavery and the slave trade created capitalism and made a major contribution to the Industrial Revolution, then the place where industrialization should also have occurred was France. The French Caribbean, especially the powerhouse of Saint-Domingue, expanded far more rapidly than the British Caribbean after 1714 and particularly after 1763. By 1776, the French Caribbean produced 43 per cent more crops by value than was the case for the British Caribbean. That difference accelerated during the American Revolution and the 1780s. Of course, the French economy was greater by aggregate than the British in the eighteenth century, and international trade was relatively small. Nevertheless, the contribution of the French Caribbean to French prosperity before 1791 was considerable, even if slavery and the slave trade are assigned limited importance in accounts of French industrialization. In addition, a stronger argument for the importance of the slave trade for wider externalities is beginning to be made for the Netherlands.[8]

It is possible that forthcoming work on the French economy in the late eighteenth century might make a strong case for the contribution of the plantation economy to French economic growth. Atlantic history has until recently been marginalized within French historiography and the sudden collapse of Saint-Domingue after slave rebellion in the 1790s and 1800s has tended to hide the dynamic influence of wealthy planters in French commerce before the French Revolution. But wealth from the Antilles helped to fuel important economic changes in the metropolitan economy after the end of the Seven Years' War, notably real estate speculation in the French capital. Some of the money gained in Paris during the period in which the French capital was transformed from an administrative and manufacturing centre into a financial powerhouse was reinvested back into the Antilles. For example, Jean-Joseph Laborde, the wealthiest man in France in the 1770s, invested heavily in Saint-Domingue after retiring as a financier. By 1789, he owned 1,400 enslaved workers. Conversely, Saint-Domingue planters put their money back into the metropolitan economy. Jean-Baptiste Hotten, for example, a plantation owner with 219 slaves, became in the 1780s a Parisian real estate mogul.[9] As we learn more about such cross-fertilization between the French metropole and the colonies, we will appreciate more how events in Saint-Domingue put a halt to the influence of the Atlantic economy on French economic transformation during the Old Regime.[10]

But it was in Britain where the connections between the plantation system and the 'Great Divergence' have been most explored. The term 'plantation' was derived from English settlement in Ireland in the late sixteenth century, initially denoting an overseas colony.[11] By the middle of the seventeenth century, the term had assumed its meaning of a large agricultural enterprise in a tropical region, managed for profit, which produced an export crop for sale in Europe and elsewhere and which had a labour force that was hierarchically stratified. That labour force could be local or imported. Nevertheless, the contingencies of history – which meant that the most important early manifestations of the plantation complex were in the Americas and in places where indigenous labour was unavailable for exploitation – led to the management and ownership of plantations being in the hands of Europeans while the mixed-sex labour force was African or of African descent.

The make-up of the labour force meant that for the majority of the period in which plantations were most important for world economic growth, the plantation complex was intimately linked to another global phenomenon: the forced migration through the Atlantic slave trade of eleven million enslaved persons, mostly from West and Central-West Africa. In the early modern period, that enslaved population tended (except in the American South from the mid-eighteenth century) not to be self-sustaining, as heavy mortality rates necessitated the continual replacement of workers through the slave trade. The plantation was also an inherently colonial form of economic organization, with control over the complex lying in the metropolitan centres of Britain, the Netherlands, France, Portugal, Spain, and Denmark until the nineteenth century. Most important of all, plantations, as they existed from the mid-seventeenth century in British and French America, were large-scale agricultural enterprises requiring anything from fifty to several hundred workers. All facets of production were done within the physical boundaries of the plantation, making these farms capitalist in economic orientation, even if (especially in sixteenth-century Brazil) they retained some elements of feudalism.[12]

## Plantations and economic growth

The development of plantation agriculture was crucial for the success of colonization in the Americas.[13] As Barbara Solow notes, 'It was slavery that made the empty lands of the western hemisphere valuable producers of commodities and valuable markets for Europe and North America. What moved in the Atlantic in these centuries was predominantly slaves, the output of slaves, the inputs of slave societies, and the goods and services purchased with the earnings on slave products.'[14] What planters in

Barbados did in the 1650s was to create a form of labour organization that produced large enough quantities of sugar to bring wealth sufficient for substantial reinvestment. The organization of labour involved ganged labour, with its lockstep discipline and its liberal use of the whip that forced slaves to work as hard as possible. Having gained effective forms of coercion over recalcitrant, demoralized, and traumatized African enslaved people, slave forces increased dramatically in size, reaching well over a hundred slaves per plantation in the West Indies and over fifty per plantation in the American South. These large integrated plantations had significant economies of scale over other agricultural enterprises. Most importantly, planters worked slaves very hard. Slaves on sugar plantations in Jamaica worked on average 3,288 hours per year in the later eighteenth century, which pushed them to the outer edge of work hours in the pre-industrial world.[15] Significantly, these hours included more backbreaking work than was normal for European or African peasants. It was not just the hours that were worked that accounted for the remarkable growth of productivity on plantations; it was the manner of the work that was performed. Planters were relentless in their demands on enslaved people. They worked women as hard as, if not harder than, men (most women worked in the field while some men were trained as tradesmen), and set children to work very young. Planters approached slave welfare with great indifference. A project comparing 12,000 skeletons from various countries since 1000 BCE placed eighteenth-century South Carolina field hands in rice planting near the bottom of all historical populations, in the same range as pre-Columbian populations facing extinction or demographic disaster.[16] Not surprisingly, the victims of such punishing work regimes hated doing what they were forced to do. A slave rebel in seventeenth-century Barbados declared that 'the Devel is in the Englishman; that he makes everything work, he makes the Negro work, the Horse work, the wood work, the Water work and the winde work'.[17]

Over time, these methods of work became refined. Planters paid great attention to enhancing the value of their human capital, using scientific methods of accounting and modern management methods to make sure that enslaved people were placed in jobs that enhanced their rising capital value. In places like Jamaica, such assiduous attention to the developing science of modern management led to remarkable advances in productivity.[18] Barry Higman estimates that per capita output increased from roughly £8 to £29 4s. by 1800. He concludes that in the second half of the eighteenth century, Jamaica 'performed strongly not only by comparison with other plantation economies but also relative to the emerging industrial nations'.[19] It achieved these strong productivity gains mostly through the application of basic concepts of what today we call modern management in the division of labour and specialization of tasks within a large labour force, all deployed in a disciplined and coordinated way. By contrast, the gains in agricultural productivity obtained in late eighteenth-century English agriculture lay in increasing the quantity of work done rather than by improving productivity in any real sense, as can be seen in a dramatic increase in the days worked by the average person from 258 in 1760 to 333 in 1800.[20]

A plantation was in important respects therefore a precursor of the modern factory, based on its scale of capital investment in land, machines, and people, and in regard to its output, technology, processing functions, and large labour force. The success of the late-eighteenth-century plantation system as an example of modern management encouraged planters and merchants to keep investing in plantations well after the emancipation of slavery (which occurred between 1834 and 1888 in various slave holding countries). Indeed, around 1900, the plantation sector followed a wave of new colonization efforts to become important in a range of new locations, notably in different areas of Asia. Its advantages over other forms of agricultural organization lay in its rational and scientifically based form of cultivation and in the ability of plantation owners, normally by this stage resident in Europe with operatives working on their behalf in colonial areas, to extract maximum labour from a generally uneducated and often imported workforce. By 1900, plantations had strong industrial components, notably in the production of rubber in Malaya and Cochin China (Vietnam) where plantations were especially like factories. The main move was towards free enterprise capitalism and away from forced labour. But the state became ever more important, especially in places like Java in Indonesia, where the Dutch government declared all land to be the property of the state. Thus, government control over agrarian development was exercised through control over space, territory, and property rather than through direct control over people's bodies.[21]

Pomeranz's 'Great Divergence' argument makes sense in the nineteenth century when cotton production in the United States meant that, due to the elasticity of raw material supplied from America, the cotton industry could develop at a uniquely rapid rate without substantial real price increases for raw cotton fibres. Even then, if cotton had not existed, one can imagine industrialization happening, albeit probably more slowly and in different forms, perhaps based on woollen textiles sourced from Australia (which had the advantage of being a British possession) or linen from Russia.[22] For the seventeenth and eighteenth centuries, Pomeranz's 'ecological bounty' is less convincing, given that most of the commodities produced by plantations were subtropical groceries and semi-luxuries. Their impact on economic growth was likely to be indirect, rather than direct, creating a demand for commodities that needed to be purchased for cash, thus encouraging specialization in household economies.[23]

We concentrate too much on production rather than consumption when looking at what the plantations provided to Europe. Each of the crops produced could be sold only through an exploitation of demand that had previously not existed: people had to learn how to smoke tobacco, to use sugar in puddings, and to replace woollen clothing with more fashionable cotton clothing. Demand was thus very important. Take sugar, for example. It moved in a century from being an elite commodity to being a product that ordinary people could afford.[24] These new plantation products fed into the rise of capitalist farming and into changes in consumer demand. These changes led people to want to do new things in a society with steadily growing productivity in agriculture, permitting a shift in the structure of demand for necessities, comforts, and even luxuries. It was during the early modern period, for example, that Europeans first acquired a sweet tooth and the nicotine habit, closely tied to new ways of marketing desires for such products.[25]

## The plantations and the fiscal-military state

Plantation agriculture, of course, was important for several European countries besides England/Britain. Before England had established a viable plantation system in Barbados in the mid-seventeenth century, the Portuguese had developed a highly productive plantation system – partly capitalist and partly feudal in nature – that revolved around small farmers growing cane on rented land before taking canes to be harvested in mills owned by *senhores de engenhos*.[26] Yet Portugal was too small, too poor, and too economically underdeveloped to be able to use the considerable plantation wealth it acquired from Brazil and from the Atlantic slave trade with Angola to enhance its own economy. Indeed, during the ministry of the most important eighteenth-century Portuguese statesman, the Marquis of Pombal (1750–77), a strict adherent to classical mercantilism, Portuguese efforts in Atlantic commerce were mainly directed towards stimulating and diversifying Brazil's plantation economy with little effort put into using plantation money to enhance the metropolitan Portuguese economy.[27]

The Dutch were better placed in Europe than the Portuguese to benefit from their involvement in the development of plantations because of the advanced nature of their commercial economy in the early seventeenth century and their aggressive expansion in the 1620s and 1630s into imperial conquest in Africa, Asia, and the Americas. But when the Portuguese retook Brazil in 1654, combined with the end of the seventeenth-century Dutch 'Golden Age', the ability of the Dutch to prosper from their involvement in plantation agriculture was severely dented. The 'Dutch moment' in the Atlantic passed quickly.[28] The Dutch, however, remained important as a nation devoted to plantation agriculture in Southeast Asia, especially in Java, which was the most important plantation sector in nineteenth- and twentieth-century Asia.[29]

In regard to Britain, it is interesting to speculate on the coincidental timing of the start of the large integrated plantation system in Barbados and upon significant changes in the economic history of England.[30] What happened in Barbados in the middle of the War of the Three Kingdoms in the 1650s came at a propitious time in English history. Meticulous research into English and British economic growth over the long durée suggests that sustained positive economic growth only began from this period. Recent estimates show that between 1650 and 1760, GDP in England/Britain grew at 0.61 per cent per annum, increasing to 0.83 per cent per annum from 1780 to 1800 before attaining modern growth rates in the nineteenth century of over 1.6 per cent per annum. Due to rapid population growth in the eighteenth century, growth in GDP per capita was less impressive after 1690, being just 0.23 per cent per annum between 1700 and 1780, before returning nearly to rates of per capita GDP growth attained between 1650 and 1690.[31]

Correlation is not causation but it is worth investigating what role the new-found wealth of the plantation colonies played in stimulating a permanent rise in English wealth.[32] Gregory King estimated that by 1688 England's overseas trade accounted for about 20 per cent of national income.[33] Nuala Zahedieh argues in a detailed exploration of the growth of colonial trade that England's increasing stake in the Atlantic shaped the long build-up of economic change that culminated in the Industrial Revolution. The trade in plantation-produced goods expanded wealth, relieved Malthusian pressures, and encouraged investment in new skills, useful knowledge, and adaptive efficiency. As she states, 'Endogenous responses to the market opportunities created by imperial expansion stimulated adaptive innovations on several main fronts: the accumulation and improvement of manufacturing capacity in the capital and beyond; the extension and enhancement of transport networks to create an increasingly integrated and commercialized national economy; and a major investment in the mathematical and mechanical skills which raised England to technological leadership in Europe.'[34] Zahedieh's study of the copper industry is a specific example of how colonial trade facilitated improvements in England's technological capabilities in the late seventeenth century. She shows that colonial demand for fairly mundane copper vessels helped foster inventive mentalities, uniting interest in natural knowledge with craft skills, providing the means whereby a once-moribund industry was able to attract the human and financial investment necessary for applying major technological breakthroughs in industries like smelting and mining.[35]

The development of the large integrated plantation in Barbados also coincided with the beginning of the fiscal-military state in England – an institutional evolution that distinguished England from every other state in Europe. Patrick O'Brien connects the rise of the fiscal state with conflict in the English Civil War in the mid-seventeenth century. He insists that Britain came to be a high-taxing, fiscally powerful state because wealthy elites were so devastated by the destruction of the Civil War that they were willing to make a government fiscally powerful in order that this government would pass legislation that secured individual property rights. Thus, England was able to develop a fiscal state in which revenue from taxation was much higher than anywhere else in Europe. As O'Brien notes, it was fortunate that this domestic reconstruction of the state occurred 'when England's domestic economy began to generate the kind of accelerated commercialization, colonization, urban concentration, and proto-industrialization that facilitated the collection of duties on domestic production and imports.'[36]

Plantation profits played a crucial role in making the fiscal-military state a success. Pat Hudson notes that the fiscal-military state gave a great stimulus to growth and innovation, with plantation produce, which was liable to consumption taxes, very important in redistributing wealth from taxpayers and government creditors to merchants and manufacturers, especially in emerging industrial regions like Lancashire. Although export dependence at the national level was never more than 35 per cent before the American Revolution, some firms and industrial sectors in Lancashire depended upon exports for 70 to 80 per cent of their markets, with much capital finding its way across the Atlantic or to Africa as a result of the slave trade and the plantation economy. She emphasizes how plantation trade had strong multiplier effects, stimulating process, product, and financial innovations, and generating institutional provisions that affected wide areas of the economy. In short, the effect of the plantation goods coming into Britain from the late seventeenth century led to hothouse conditions conducive to technological and organizational innovations, in response to accelerating demand for exotic crops.[37]

## Imperial benefits

The argument about whether American plantations were valuable to Britain is handicapped by a methodological problem that obscures the true relationship of the American colonies to Britain. Colonies of settlement, which all the American colonies were before the American Revolution, were not like colonies of exploitation, like India, attached to Britain lightly and by ties of economic interest only. By contrast, the American colonies were, as British Americans insisted, an intrinsic part of Britain, full of proud British subjects who considered themselves just as British as any resident of England, Wales, or Scotland and more British than Roman Catholic residents of Ireland. That Britons and Americans were fundamentally the same, tied together by ties of mutual affection and shared inheritances, was a central point in Benjamin Franklin's 'Observations on the Increase of Mankind' (1751), a pioneering essay in the developing field of political economy. Franklin predicted that in a few generations white settlers in British North America would eventually outnumber the number of people in the metropolis, to the mutual benefit, he thought, of both areas, adding to the great glory of the empire. He crowed that rapid population increase in North America meant that there 'in another Century, the greatest Number of *Englishmen* will be on this Side of the Water. What an Accession of Power to the *British* Empire by Sea as well as Land! What Increase of Trade and Navigation! What Numbers of Ships and Seamen!' These new Britons would be firm defenders of the empire, as 'there is not a single native of our country who is not firmly attached to our King by principle and affection'. Britain had to do nothing to maintain that affection. There was no danger, he thought, of America 'uniting against their own nation, which protects and encourages them, with which they have so many connections and ties of blood, interest and affection and which 'tis well known they all love more than they love one another'. Indeed, Franklin continued, 'I will venture to say, an union among them for such a purpose is not merely improbable, it is impossible.'[38]

Some Britons also recognized that the colonies could not be divided from Britain just because they happened to be overseas possessions. For Joshua Gee, writing in 1720, British growth and prosperity was inseparable from its connection to the colonies. 'If we take a view of our own Kingdom,' he wrote, 'we shall find our Trade and Riches came but very slowly till our Plantations began to be settled, and as they throve, our Trade and Riches increased, our Lands rose in value, and our Manufactures increased also.'[39] Malachy Postlethwayt extended the theme: 'Since we have established colonies and plantations our condition … has altered for the better, almost to a degree above credibility. Our manufactures are prodigiously increased, chiefly by the demand for them in the plantations, where they at least take off one and a half and supply us with many valuable commodities for re-exportation, which is as great an emolument to the mother kingdom as to the plantations themselves.'[40] C. Knick Harley insists that while the Atlantic economy made a central contribution to the causes of the Industrial Revolution, the route through which this contribution came was through trade to the non-plantation colonies of British North America. These colonies wanted industrial goods from Britain and financed them by developing the burgeoning provision trade to the West Indies.[41]

The greatest benefit that British North America and the West Indies brought to Britain, however, was not the sugar, tobacco, rice, and cotton that they sent to metropolitan Britain or was not even their importance as a market for British manufactures and a potential reservoir of manpower for any war Britain wanted to embark upon against European rivals. The most important benefit was their overall wealth and the opportunities that such wealth afforded for British migrants. That wealth was extraordinary as early as 1700 and exceptional by 1774. Free white people in the Thirteen Colonies that later became the United States of America had higher levels of income and more importantly much higher standards of living in 1700 than their fellow countrymen in England. Their wealth increased by 1774, although the differential between income levels in Britain and the Thirteen Colonies diminished due to remarkable population growth in America that increased dependency ratios and kept the increase in colonial incomes lower than otherwise.[42]

British movement to the Americas was part of an expansion of the physical space of Britain analogous to how England absorbed Wales in the fourteenth century and to how England joined together with Scotland in the eighteenth century. Consequently, Pomeranz's contention that the colonies provided 'ghost acres' for Britain that allowed it to overcome Malthusian constraints is misplaced. By 'ghost acres', Pomeranz means lands that were not part of the landmass of Britain and thus were additional acres that could be added to British agricultural potential. The problem was that such acres were not 'ghost acres' unless one takes the reductionist belief that only acres in the British Isles counted as part of British possessions and that acres in the British Americas were somehow not owned by the British. Neither Britons nor Americans or West Indians made such a fundamental distinction between 'local' and 'foreign' acres: all belonged to an expansionary British state. These American acres devoted to plantation agriculture were 'real' acres that formed part of the physical and economic expansion of a Greater Britain.[43] They were no more 'ghost acres' than were acres devoted to sheep in Sussex or grain in East Anglia. Moreover, these 'ghost acres' were farmed by real Britons. All acres were part of a growing territorial empire.

The colonies were in particular a reservoir for British migration, especially in the seventeenth century. Jim Horn and Philip Morgan estimate that 303,000 Britons (including Irish) went to the Americas between 1640 and 1700, 289,000 arrived between 1700 and 1760 and a further 615,000 went there between 1760 and 1820. In the seventeenth century, most migrants went to plantation colonies while the Middle Colonies of British North America became the primary destination in the eighteenth century.[44] Extrapolations of what might have happened to English, Scottish, and Irish economic growth if the safety valve of migration to the Americas had not existed are difficult, given the multitudinous variables involved in this sort of counterfactual explanation. Without the large migration to plantation colonies as the plantation system started in the 1640s and 1650s, it is possible that the negative population growth of England between 1650 and 1700 might have been reversed, hindering the steady growth of income per capita. Possibly, England/Britain may have faced more severe Malthusian constraints if its local population rose at the same rate as it did but with the 1.3 million people (including the many who went to Ireland) who migrated to the Americas in the two centuries before 1780 staying put.[45] Between 1640 and 1699, emigration to the New World from England and Wales accounted for as much as 69 per cent of the natural increase of the population. As population increased and emigration slowed in the eighteenth century, that percentage dropped to about 20 per cent – a still not negligible factor in helping Britain avoid a Malthusian crisis.[46]

The wealth that the plantation sector produced for Britons who lived in these regions was remarkable. British American prosperity helps explain its settled political state before the American Revolution and makes clear why many Britons were willing to risk very high mortality, especially in the areas of greatest wealth, like the Carolina Lowcountry and the British West Indies, for the chance to make a decent competency or even a large fortune. Estimations of the total physical wealth of British America compared to that of Britain on the eve of the American Revolution make clear just how much money had been accumulated in plantation America within a century of the large integrated plantation system being established in Barbados. Britain had total physical wealth of £314 million around 1774, of which 87 per cent was in England and Wales and 13 per cent in Scotland. The wealth of British America was over half of this sum, at £162 million, with plantation America accounting for £104 million, or 64.4 per cent of British American wealth or 21.9 per cent of the wealth of Britain and its American colonies combined (excluding Ireland, for which GDP figures are unavailable, but which had probably a GDP of £50 million and per capita GDP of about £12, assuming a population of four million).

To put this in perspective, plantation America was almost three times as economically valuable to Britain as was Scotland and twice as valuable as Ireland. Of course, a large proportion of the wealth of plantation America – perhaps £28 million if we value the 800,000 slaves in the colonies as worth £35 each – was in the form of human capital, which did not exist in Britain. If we exclude this form of capital from our analysis, then plantation America had total physical wealth of £76 million, or more than twice the wealth of Scotland. Almost all the benefits of this wealth accrued to white settlers. British Americans had in general over twice the wealth of people in England or Wales and 3.5 times the wealth of Scots. But real wealth was concentrated among free whites in the plantation colonies, especially in the West Indies. Average per capita white wealth in plantation America was £201 if wealth tied up in slaves is counted and £147 if enslaved people are excluded. In the West Indies, average per capita white wealth was £1,144 if wealth in slaves is included and £826 if the value of enslaved people is excluded. Whatever else can be said about the economic value of the plantations, it is clear that they afforded in the eighteenth century a degree of wealth for white people that made them appreciably richer than any group of white people in Greater Britain.[47]

One way of appreciating the wealth of white West Indians is to note that if the wealth of the 45,401 whites in the British West Indies in 1774 was added to the 6,572,104 residents of England and Wales, average per capita white wealth, excluding wealth in the form of slaves, would have increased by £5.81. If the wealth of the 519,301 white inhabitants of the plantation regions of British America in 1774, excluding wealth in slavery, is added to those of England and Wales, then average white per capita wealth would have increased by £8.46. If slaves are included, then average white per capita wealth would have increased by £11.62. By contrast, much lower wealth in Scotland and especially Ireland substantially reduced average per capita white wealth in the British archipelago. If Scottish and Irish wealth was added to that of England and Wales, then average per capita white wealth drops to £30 – a fall of £12.3. Moreover, the wealth of these plantation regions was advancing at a much greater rate than was wealth in Britain. Whereas the GDP of England and Wales increased by a healthy 426 per cent between 1700 and 1774, total physical wealth grew by an astounding 1,100 per cent in Jamaica in the same years.[48]

## The plantations and industrialization

Our discussion still leaves the question moot about the extent what happened in the colonies contributed to economic growth in other sectors of the British economy, notably in industrial sectors. Most attention has been paid to crops sent from the British plantations to Britain in the eighteenth century. There is little doubt that the amount of such crops sent to Britain was considerable and was the most dynamic part of eighteenth-century overseas trade from the colonies to Britain. Sugar was supplemented and then surpassed by American-grown cotton. Cotton imports were spectacular in size and crucial to the development of the quintessential industry in the Industrial Revolution. Between 1750 and 1810, European cotton consumption increased between sixfold and eightfold.[49] The size of the imports was so large that South Carolina senator, James Henry Hammond, famously declared on the floor of the Senate in 1858 that 'no power on earth dares to make war upon it. COTTON IS KING.' Without southern cotton, he thundered, 'England would topple headlong and carry the whole civilized world with her, save the South.' It was one of the more famously mistaken statements in American history, as Great Britain had no intention of ever supporting the Confederacy against the Union, given how much it had staked its international reputation upon its commitment to antislavery.[50]

There have been some recent attempts to prove that Hammond was right. Historians heavily influenced by Wallerstein world-systems theory have argued that slave-produced cotton was responsible for British and northeastern industrialization.[51] Their polemical intentions are different from Hammond (they argue that slavery was key to the invention of capitalism because they want to associate capitalism with illiberalism) but their arguments are similar. And, like Hammond, they overstate the case for cotton in the development of the British and then the global economy. American cotton arrived on the scene – becoming only important after the invention of the cotton gin in 1793 and dominant only from the 1820s – too late to determine the beginnings of industrialization.[52]

By 1700, England's transoceanic trade was not overwhelmingly large but in its dynamic growth it was essential for new industries, like copper, and for sustaining industries, like shipbuilding, vital for British defense. Moreover, it was central in encouraging the financial innovations vital to the commercial 'revolution'. Many of the advances were hindered by vested interests diverting capital and enterprise into rent-seeking activities but what the British state realized from around 1700 was that the success of the American plantations showed that mercantilism worked. As Nuala Zahedieh concludes, the highly performing plantation trade not only outperformed other sectors, but also stimulated 'adaptive innovations which took the country to a new plateau of possibilities from which Industrial Revolution was not only possible but increasingly likely'.[53] Between the Glorious Revolution of 1688 and the end of the Seven Years' War in 1763, the British state supported planters wholeheartedly. It had reason to do so, as John Gee and Malachy Postlethwayt recognized. The plantations brought great profits, benefited significant economic agents like London and Bristol merchants, and provided desirable consumer goods that added to the happiness of its inhabitants. The plantations were rewarded for their contributions to the greater welfare of Britain by favourable imperial legislation, by support for an increasingly efficient and effective slave trade, and by tacit acceptance of colonial demands that slaves should be thought of as property, not as humans.[54]

Opinion later turned against the planter class, and the system of economic exploitation that sustained them. Here Eric Williams was also right. But, contrary to what Williams believed, the decline of the influence of the planter class was not due to notions that plantations were economically ineffective and could be discarded as soon as industrial capitalism took over. Plantations were efficient means of organizing labour to gain profits and were as capitalist an enterprise as any factory, even if work was organized differently. Fogel and Engerman's controversial *Time on the Cross* (1974) showed conclusively how slavery and capitalism could work together and that nineteenth-century views of plantation agriculture as being inherently backward and thus just a way station between feudalism and industrial capitalism were incorrect.[55]

Plantations did more than just provide 'ghost acres' that provided Britain with an ecological release from Malthusian constraints. They gave the owners and managers of plantations, if never workers, high incomes and notable social prestige. But their economic success was accompanied by pernicious social, and usually racial, consequences in a colonial context that became increasingly disturbing to metropolitan observers. Eventually, the plantation became a place in the European imagination that was so ideologically suspect that its economic benefits needed to be denied. But if ideologically suspect, it was never anything but economically successful.

## Conclusion

Plantations were a principal means whereby Europeans could exploit the Americas, through the agency of West Africa. There is no doubt that plantations brought great wealth to their owners, enormous misery to enslaved people, and considerable economic and geopolitical benefits to European imperial nations with American possessions, including France, the Netherlands, and Britain. Some historians, following in the footsteps of Eric Williams, have argued for an even greater impact of the plantation system – as the impetus towards Britain's precocious late-eighteenth-century industrialization. Such arguments are overstated. We do not need to have the plantations be responsible for British industrialization in order to accept their enormous role in advancing British wealth and power (as also in France, where little emphasis has been customarily put on the role of plantations in fostering French industrialization). Britain's transoceanic trade contributed significantly to various areas of trade and helped cement financial innovations that secured Britain's eighteenth-century commercial revolution. It is in these areas that profits from the plantations were most important. It helps explain Britain's wholehearted support of planters and the plantation system before the Seven Years' War brought into public discourse less positive assessments of the effects of the plantation economy upon the British sense of morality about their overseas empires.

## Notes

1. K. Pomeranz (2000), *The Great Divergence: China, Europe and the Making of the Modern World Economy*. Princeton: Princeton University Press, 275–7. This method of 'ghost acres' was pioneered in E. L. Jones (2003), *The European Miracle: Environments, Economies and Geopolitics in the History of Europe and Asia*, 3rd edn. Cambridge: Cambridge University, ch. 1.

2. D. Eltis (2000), *The Rise of African Slavery in the Americas*. Cambridge: Cambridge University Press; and W. Rodney (1972), *How Europe Underdeveloped Africa*. London: Bogle L'Ouverture Books.

3. B. Yun-Casalilla (1996), 'The American empire and the Spanish economy: An institutional and regional perspective', *Revista de Historia Económica*, 16 (1), 123–56.

4. S. B. Schwartz (1985), *Sugar Plantations in the Formation of Brazilian Society, Bahia, 1550–1835*. Cambridge: Cambridge University Press.

5. N. D. Cook (2015), 'The Columbian exchange', in J. H. Bentley, et al. (eds), *The Cambridge World History*. Vol. VI. *The Construction of a Global World, 1400–1800 CE*. Part 2 *Patterns of Change*. Cambridge: Cambridge University Press, 103–35. See also the chapters by J. R. McNeill and Alejandra Irigoin in this volume.

6. G. Parker (2013), *Global Crisis: War, Climate Change and Catastrophe in the Seventeenth Century*. New Haven: Yale University Press.

7. D. Watts (1987), *The West Indies: Patterns of Development, Culture and Environmental Change since 1492*. Cambridge: Cambridge University Press.

8. D. Eltis and S. W. Engerman (2000), 'The importance of slavery and the slave trade to industrializing Britain', *Journal of Economic History*, 60 (1), 130–31; T. Burnard and J. Garrigus (2016), *The Plantation Machine: Atlantic Capitalism in French Saint-Domingue and British Jamaica*. Philadelphia: University of Pennsylvania Press; J. Horn (2006), *The Path Not Taken; French Industrialization in the Age of Revolution, 1750–1830*. Cambridge, MA: Cambridge University Press; P. C. Emmer, O. Pétré-Grenouilleau and J. V. Roitman (eds) (2006), *A Deus Ex Machina Revisited: Atlantic Colonial Trade and European Economic Development*. Leiden: Brill; and K. Fatah-Black and M. van Rossum (2015), 'Beyond profitability: The Dutch transatlantic slave trade and its economic impact', *Slavery & Abolition*, 36 (1), 63–83.

9. Burnard and Garrigus, *Plantation Machine*, 22–3; A. Potofsky (2011), 'Paris-on-the-Atlantic: From the old regime to the revolution', *French History*, 25 (1), 89–107.

10. K. O'Rourke (2006), 'The worldwide economic impact of the French Revolutionary and Napoleonic Wars, 1793–1815', *Journal of Global History*, 1 (1), 123–49; C. Vidal (2006), 'The reluctance of French historians to address Atlantic history', *Southern Quarterly*, 43 (4), 153–89.

11. N. Canny (1998), 'The origins of empire: An introduction', in N. Canny (ed.), *The Oxford History of the British Empire. Vol. 1. The Origins of Empire*. Oxford: Oxford University Press, 8.

12. P. D. Curtin (1990), *The Rise and Fall of the Plantation Complex: Essays in Atlantic History*. Cambridge: Cambridge University Press, 11–13. See also K. Morgan (2016), *A Brief History of Transatlantic Slavery*. London: I.B. Tauris.

13. T. Burnard (2015), 'Plantation societies', in J. H. Bentley, et al. (eds), *Cambridge World History*, vol. 6, part. Cambridge: Cambridge University Press, 263–82.

14. B. Solow (1991), 'Slavery and colonisation', in B. Solow (ed.), *Slavery and the Rise of the Atlantic System*. Cambridge: Cambridge University Press, 21–42.

15. J. Roberts (2013), *Slavery and the Enlightenment in the British Atlantic, 1750–1807*. New York: Cambridge University Press, 86.

16. T. A. Rathbon and R. H. Steckel (2002), 'The health of slaves and free blacks in the East', in R. H. Steckel and J. C. Rose (eds), *The Backbone of History: Health and Nutrition in the Western Hemisphere*. Cambridge: Cambridge University Press, 208–25.

17. (1676), *Great Newes from the Barbadoes*. London: L. Curtis, 6–7.

18. C. Rosenthal (2016), 'Slavery's scientific management: Accounting for mastery', in S. Beckert and S. Rothman (eds), *Slavery's Capitalism: A New History of American Economic Development*. Philadelphia: University of Pennsylvania Press, 62–82.

19. B. W. Higman (2005), *Plantation Jamaica 1750–1850: Capital and Control in a Colonial Economy*. Kingston: University of the West Indies Press, 2–3, 8–9.

20. G. Clark (1987), 'Productivity growth without technical change in European agriculture before 1850', *Journal of Economic History*, 47 (2), 419–32; H.-J. Voth (2001), 'The longest years: New estimates of labor input in England, 1760–1830', *Journal of Economic History*, 61 (4), 1065–82.

21. J. Breman (1989), *Taming the Coolie Beast: Plantation Society and the Colonial Order in Southeast Asia*. Delhi and New York: Oxford University Press; Idem (2015), *Mobilizing Labour for the Coffee Market: Profits from an Unfree Work Regime in Colonial Java*. Amsterdam: Amsterdam University Press.

22. G. Riello (2013), *Cotton: The Fabric that Made the Modern World*. Cambridge: Cambridge University Press, 240–6.

23. J. de Vries (2008), *The Industrious Revolution: China, Europe and the Making of the Modern World Economy*. New York: Cambridge University Press. See also the chapter by Maxine Berg in this volume.

24. S. Mintz (1985), *Sweetness and Power: The Place of Sugar in Modern History*. New York: Penguin.

25. E. A. Wrigley (2008), *Continuity, Chance and Change: The Character of the Industrial Revolution in England*. Cambridge: Cambridge University Press; C. Shammas (2000), 'The revolutionary impact of European demand for tropical goods', in J. J. McCusker and K. Morgan (eds), *The Early Modern Atlantic Economy*. Cambridge: Cambridge University Press, 163–85.

26. S. B. Schwartz (2004), *Tropical Babylons: Sugar and the Making of the Atlantic World, 1450–1680*. Chapel Hill: University of North Carolina Press.

27. K. Maxwell (1995), *Pombal: Paradox of the Enlightenment*. Cambridge: Cambridge University Press, 119–28, 134–48.

28. W. W. Klooster (2016), *The Dutch Moment: War, Trade, and Settlement in the Seventeenth-Century Atlantic World*. Ithaca: Cornell University Press.

29. A. Reid (1988–93), *Southeast Asia in the Age of Commerce*, 2 vols. New Haven: Yale University Press. See Thomas Lindblad's chapter in this volume.

30. R. R. Menard (2006), *Sweet Negotiations: Sugar, Slavery, and Plantation Agriculture in Early Barbados*. Charlottesville: University of Virginia Press; and S. D. Newman (2013), *Free and Bound Labor in the British Atlantic World: Black and White Workers and the Development of Plantation Slavery*. Philadelphia: University of Pennsylvania Press, 54–9.

31. S. Broadberry et al. (2015), *British Economic Growth, 1270-1870*. Cambridge: Cambridge University Press.

32. D. Acemoglu, S. Johnson and J. Robinson (2005), 'The rise of Europe: Atlantic trade, institutional change, and economic growth', *American Economic Review*, 95 (2), 546–79.

33. P. Laslett (ed.) (1973), *The Earliest Classics: Graunt and King*. Farnborough: Gregg, 207.

34. N. Zahedieh (2010), *The Capital and the Colonies: London and the Atlantic Economy, 1660-1700*. Cambridge: Cambridge University Press, 4, 7, 285. But see P. K. O'Brien (1982), 'European economic development: The contribution of the periphery', *Economic History Review*, 35 (1), 1–18.

35. N. Zahedieh (2013), 'Colonies, copper, and the market for inventive activity in England and Wales, 1680-1730', *Economic History Review*, 66 (3), 805–25.

36. P. K. O'Brien (2011), 'The nature and historical evolution of an exceptional fiscal state', *Economic History Review*, 64 (2), 435–36.

37. P. Hudson (2014), 'Slavery, the slave trade and economic growth: A contribution to the debate', in C. Hall, N. Draper and K. McClelland (eds), *Emancipation and the Making of the British Imperial World*. Manchester: Manchester University Press, 36–59. See also J. E. Inikori (2002), *Africans and the Industrial Revolution in England: A Study in International Trade and Economic Development*. Cambridge: Cambridge University Press.

38. B. Franklin (1959), 'Observations on the increase of mankind', in L. W. Labaree, et al. (eds.), *The Papers of Benjamin Franklin*. New Haven: Yale University Press, IV, 225–34.

39. J. Gee (1720), *A Letter to a Member of Parliament, Concerning the Naval-Stores Bill*. London: n.a., 18.

40. M. Postlethwayt (ed.) (1764), *Universal Dictionary of Trade and Commerce*, 2 vols. 4th edn. London, vol. I: entry under 'Colonies'.

41. C. K. Harley (2015), 'Slavery, the British Atlantic Economy, and the Industrial Revolution', in A. B. Leonard, et al. (eds), *The Caribbean and the Atlantic World Economy*. Basingstoke: Palgrave Macmillan, 182.

42. P. Lindert and J. Williamson (2016), *Unequal Gains: American Growth and Inequality since 1700*. Princeton: Princeton University Press, chs. 2–3.

43. R. R. Davies (2000), *The First English Empire: Power and Identities in the British Isles, 1093-1343*. Oxford: Oxford University Press; D. Armitage (1999), 'Greater Britain: A useful category of historical analysis?', *American Historical Review*, 104 (2), 427–45.

44. J. Horn and P. Morgan (2005), 'Settlers and slaves: European and African migrations to early modern British America', in E. Mancke and C. Shammas (eds), *The Creation of the British Atlantic World*. Baltimore: Johns Hopkins University Press, 20–4, 33–4.

45. Horn and Morgan, 'Settlers and slaves', 23.

46. M. Daunton (2015), 'Afterword: Mercantilism and the Caribbean and the Atlantic World Economy', in A. Leonard and D. Pretel (eds), *The Caribbean and the Atlantic World Economy*. Basingstoke: Palgrave Macmillan, 298.

47. T. Burnard (2015), *Planters, Merchants and Slaves: Plantation Societies in British America, 1650–1820.* Chicago: University of Chicago Press, 9–10. For Scotland's GDP as 13.1 per cent of Britain's, see Maddison, *The World Economy*, 247. He also suggests that Ireland's GDP in 1774 was between 16 and 20 per cent of England Wales, suggesting GDP of around £50 million or £12 per capita. Thus, the average white West Indian, including slave wealth, was over 100 times as rich as the average Irish person. Dependency ratios in the various regions, of course, were very different, with the West Indies having very few children or old people.

48. Burnard, *Planters, Merchants, and Slaves*, 167; Broadberry, et al., *British Economic Growth*.

49. P. Bairoch (1993), *Economic and World History: Myths and Paradoxes.* Hemel Hempstead: Harvester Wheatsheaf, 158.

50. S. Drescher (2002), *The Mighty Experiment: Free Labor versus Slavery in British Emancipation.* New York: Oxford University Press, 202–3, 231–7.

51. See in particular, S. Beckert (2014), *Empire of Cotton: A New History of Global Capitalism.* New York: Alfred A. Knopf, 29–82.

52. Harley, 'Slavery, the British Atlantic economy, and the Industrial Revolution', 182.

53. Zahedieh, *Capital and Colonies*, 292.

54. L. S. Walsh (2010), *Motives of Honor, Pleasure & Profit: Plantation Management in the Colonial Chesapeake, 1607–1763.* Chapel Hill: University of North Carolina Press.

55. R. W. Fogel and S. W. Engerman (1974), *Time on the Cross: The Economics of American Negro Slavery.* Boston, MA: Little Brown; New York: Norton.

# CHAPTER 7
## CONSUMPTION AND GLOBAL HISTORY IN THE EARLY MODERN PERIOD
*Maxine Berg*

## Introduction

There is a large recent historiography on consumption and social and cultural history, yet there is much less on consumption and economic history. Recent textbooks of British economic history have no chapters on consumption. Instead, there is a traditional place for chapters on wages and the standard of living.[1] And yet consumption is a key factor in economic policy formation, for it is currently the source of much British tax revenue. During the eighteenth century, too, a key source of much government revenue was excise taxes and customs duties – that is, taxes on consumer goods. Political debate over these taxes fuelled radical reform movements and contributed to the American Revolution.[2]

Consumption, especially of luxury goods, was the key factor in debates on economic improvement during the Enlightenment; indeed, discourse around consumption stimulated the emergence of political economy as an intellectual subject area. Today, consumer economic theory and other social science theory raise many fascinating subjects, and have moved out in recent years to behavioural psychology.[3] And yet economic historians, apart from a few exceptions, have been reluctant to engage in an analysis of consumption in economic change.

Economists from Jevons to Marshall introduced analysis of consumption in terms of marginal utility.[4] But mainstream economists showed little interest, even at the end of the nineteenth century and the early twentieth century, in the wider aspects of consumption. It was those of heterodox views who took it up: Veblen, Ruskin, and Hobson. Heterodox voices converged between the end of the nineteenth century and the First World War to analyse, deconstruct, and criticize a period of rapid growth of new wealth and luxury expenditure in Europe and America. Luxury goods, excess consumption, and collecting were manifestations of Europe's and America's new superrich bourgeois classes. Banking and industrial families built palatial residences to be filled with all manner of globally sourced luxury goods, and they collected antique objects, pictures, and other art objects. There was a whole fin-de-siècle debate on the decline of capitalism, moral corruption, and social division. Sombart, Simmel, and Veblen all published their critical texts on hedonism during this period.[5]

There was some interest in consumption among economists in the 1960s and 1970s, but the subject remained on the margins of mainstream economics. While product development was advancing rapidly in this period, economists focused on productivity change. There was much discussion of consumer choice, but this was conceived as a choice between price and quantity; tastes, products, and qualities were assumed by most economists to be fixed. Two critical voices from within mainstream microeconomic theory, Kelvin Lancaster and Duncan Ironmonger, pointed out in the 1960s that consumers selected not just a consumer good, but among the many characteristics and qualities contained by such goods, but few took up the analysis of tastes that this implied.[6]

A few years later, Tibor Scitovsky argued the case for the importance of novelty to consumer choice. Habituation in meeting demands needed to be punctuated by novelty and uncertainty; thus he highlighted novelty, variety, complexity, and surprise, which aroused the senses and stimulated pleasure.[7] In recent years, Marina Bianchi has used these ideas to develop her concept of the 'active consumer': one who is not a passive price taker, but who actively engages to form tastes, responds to new goods, and combines these in diverse ways to make an identity. This active consumer might well base her choices on sensual satisfaction over everyday convenience and even necessity.[8]

The use by these economists of 'hedonic indices' and the psychological theories that underpin them has also stimulated the economic historian Avner Offer to use such theories to explain twentieth-century consumer trends. He argues that many economists assume that individuals can rank their different wants consistently, that they want as much as they can get, and that they act on their own preferences. But this is not frequently the case. Wants become less compelling the more they are satisfied; and many people shift their preferences sequentially to more psychologically pressing ones. We live in states of anticipation and consummation, seeking the serial fulfilment of our transient desires.[9] True prosperity in Offer's view is a good balance between short-term arousal and long-term security; the challenge is not to maximize consumption, but to pace it back to a level of optimal satisfaction.[10]

These issues of the factors lying behind consumption – the choices, the stimuli, and the complexities of satisfaction – are central to explaining a history of consumption in the early modern world. What difference has global history made to the history of consumption? What part has consumption played in the factors considered in global economic history?

## The Great Divergence and consumption

In his work dedicated to the concept of the Great Divergence, Kenneth Pomeranz compared consumption and luxury consumption across Europe, China, Japan, and India to argue that these were not significant factors explaining differences between the great regions of the pre-modern world. As he mostly adopted a comparative methodology, he offered little analysis of the global connections in commodity trade as a factor behind the Great Divergence.

Pomeranz's findings suggested that sugar consumption in China in 1750 was higher than in continental Europe, even as late as 1800; but at some point after this, China's per capita consumption of sugar declined, while Europe's grew rapidly especially after

1840.[11] China's tea consumption was also much higher than Europe's at 11 ounces per person as compared to Europe's 2 ounces per person in 1780s.[12] Pomeranz also compared the consumption of textiles and clothing in both regions to argue that Chinese textile consumption compared quite well against that of Europe in the mid- to late eighteenth century.

There was, furthermore, evidence of a moral debate on excess consumption among the popular classes and peasants in the Lower Yangzi region of China and in eighteenth-century Japan. And there was evidence of fashion in clothing and some consumer durables in Ming China and Muromachi and Tokugawa Japan, though not in India or Southeast Asia.[13] Pomeranz found less change in the use of houses and their contents and the generations they contained in Asia than in Europe. But there was nevertheless a market for high-quality purchased goods even in villages in China's remote macro-regions. There were likewise many consumer products in late Tokagawa and early Meiji era villages.[14]

Pomeranz reinforced his support for the case for high standards of living in eighteenth-century China and East Asia more generally. He found higher consumption there of tea and silk than in Europe, widespread consumption of tobacco, and per capita cloth consumption on par with Germany. Expenditure on ritual was high, and though meat and dairy consumption in China was lower than that in Europe, comparable levels of protein intake could be found in these two world regions.[15]

What differed was the role of trade and imports. The Chinese consumed their own domestically produced sugar, tobacco, and tea. These products – so crucial to Europe's changing consumer habits – in China produced only a low profit margin trade among small merchants, no significant revenues for the state, and thus no powerful lobbies to encourage their increased consumption. Europe, by contrast, grew all its sugar, tobacco, and coffee in overseas colonies, and bought tea from China in exchange for silver from the Americas. Europe drew its cotton from colonies or ex-colonies, while China grew much of its own.[16] The regional connections of commodities were thus missing from the divergence debate. As Jan de Vries has pointed out recently, trade was toppled in this new historiography from the central role ascribed to it by Andre Gunder Frank.[17] Instead, Pomeranz focused on the trade that did not emerge in Ming/Qing China. There was no extensive specialization and interregional trade, and the Chinese trading diaspora in Southeast Asia did not give rise to a large trade in tropical goods to the Chinese metropole.

Both Pomeranz and Parthasarathi argued that China and India did not cultivate long-distance trade links because they had no need of them. The need for silver in both places did, however, generate a supply of goods for export sufficient to elicit from Europe an influx of silver capable of, as de Vries observed, 'oiling the wheels of the Chinese economy' and acting as the 'motor' of the Indian subcontinent'.[18] The point made by Pomeranz for China and Parthasarathi for South Asia was that Asia and Europe had at least similar levels of consumption of goods such as sugar, tobacco, tea, and textiles. However, the part played by traded goods in consumption was much higher in Europe, and it escalated in the eighteenth century.

What part, then, did traded consumer goods play in Europe? Jan de Vries compared the levels of East India Company trade between Asia and Europe on the one hand and Atlantic trade on the other. His data showed that Atlantic trade grew more than twice as fast as the Asia–Europe trade, and contributed twice the value to European GDP, and yet the indirect effect of the Asia–Europe trade was disruptive and highly significant in shifting consumer cultures.[19]

Standard explanations for the appeal of Asian commodities in early modern Europe are that they were exotic, unique or superior, and cheap. But more important than their appeal was the information flows they brought in their wake. Merchants brought new knowledge about goods, and participated in developing innovative ways of incorporating these into European lifestyles with new uses and new products.[20] The East India companies were effective in gathering, processing, and analysing large amounts of information about access to goods and ways of developing markets for them. In Europe, most of these imported Eastern goods were sold in the company auctions, but distributing these goods out to wider European markets and re-exporting them beyond Europe were left to private trade. The variety of these goods and gradations of quality brought a new signifier to taste and product development in Europe. Such goods drew more households into the market. In de Vries' words, 'information and industriousness were highly correlated'.[21]

Pomeranz recognized the impact of new goods on shifting social behaviours. He acknowledged Adam Smith's fine analysis of the role of exotic baubles that appealed to the senses in motivating elites to acquire objects in lieu of retainers. Exotic goods, Pomeranz wrote, also stimulated societies with strict sumptuary laws because such goods were previously unknown and thus not yet assigned or forbidden to any specific group. Goods with remote origins were more easily mystified, and acquired greater 'value' than local or known goods with similar uses.[22] Pomeranz accepted Jan de Vries' case for an 'industrious revolution', that is, that the demand for newly available goods helped to create new worker and consumer behaviours, but he did not provide any analysis for what difference this might have made for diverging paths of economic development.

Part of the reason for this lies in the view held by China's historians that external trade was less important for Chinese industry than it was for that of Western economies. As we have seen, sugar and cotton were internally produced in China. Europeans, facing supply constraints and high transactions costs in acquiring these goods externally, were stimulated to seek substitutes in other parts of the world that they controlled as colonies or through their own process and product innovation. Europeans learned to produce to Asian standards, varieties, and qualities.

They key external commodity which stimulated the economies of China and India was silver, but even this was not, in Pomeranz's view, transformative. Since the publication of *The Great Divergence*, there has been much research on various aspects of consumption in many parts of the world, China among these. Zheng Yangwen's work, for instance, investigates the taste for European goods in early modern China. Goods from fragrances and clocks to foodstuffs and architecture were 'indigenized' and contributed to commercial specialization. There may be parallels in the transformation of the

Chinese economy and society by foreign goods to the European experience, but they did not entail the connections that de Vries drew between the 'industrious revolution' and the Industrial Revolution.[23]

Much of the more recent research on the history of consumption in other parts of Asia is focused on the nineteenth and twentieth centuries, and addresses social and cultural history.[24] Similarly, research on the Mughal and princely courts of India reveals rapid changes in fashion, taste, and styles, but these remained confined to the court environment and did not penetrate into urban communities.[25] Bayly depicted this consumer culture as a collecting culture, and a part of what he termed 'archaic globalization'. Rulers amassed goods from distant lands, and there was also a tributary flow of consumption; the nawabs and other rulers controlled flows of goods and services for the rest. The courts also sought unique or highly specialist goods. Whereas modern complexity demands the uniformity of Levis and trainers, the archaic simplicity of everyday life demanded that 'great men prized difference in goods ... In one sense archaic lords ... were collectors, rather than consumers.'[26]

While imported goods, fashion, and extensive product and quality differentiation were significant to consumption in India, they did not reach out to wider urban society, nor embed themselves in the everyday life of large groups of the population. While they existed, they were not the stuff of the kind of 'industrious revolution' of Northern Europe.[27]

## Historiography: Is there an economic history of consumption?

To what extent do we have an economic history of consumption for the early modern world, or even parts of the early modern world apart from Europe? When we look to Europe, that historiography is focused on Jan de Vries' 'industrious revolution'.[28] What debate we have in the historiography generated in the wake of the 'Great Divergence' is not one over consumption, but one over wages and standards of living. Again, this is a debate over comparisons and not connections. It does not tell us about consumer goods, or incentives to produce or to buy these; it does not tell us about the impact of some parts of the world on others, for example, the impact of the Columbian Exchange of foods, plants, and diseases, nor of colonial groceries or the impact of a global trade in resources and materials, nor of that in manufactured goods.

What can we glean from that debate on wages and standards of living? Carole Shammas asks 'When and why did consumption of material goods become the measure of the "standard of living"?'[29] Up to the years immediately following the Second World War, the standard of living was conceived in purely material terms – that is, the goods and services at one's disposal. Thus GDP per capita became the yardstick, but as we know, these indices did not show inequality or investment in human capital. Now most indices of well-being skip over household budgets and real wages, and turn instead to life expectancy, health status, and heights, as well as other indices of well-being such as education.[30]

Shammas summarized a widely accepted position on European living standards to date: earlier estimates of early nineteenth-century income growth were revised downwards, and pre-industrial standards were revised upwards. New products were brought into Western Europe; diets became more varied, cotton fabric entered the clothing market, and textile prices dropped. Brick and stone replaced wood and clay in many cities, glass windows became widespread, and interior furnishings improved. This was not due to lower grain prices, but to higher real incomes, lower costs of durables and semi-durables, or better use of household labour.[31]

Among economic historians of the early modern period, there has been intense debate over levels of wages and living standards; most of this centred on explaining industrialization and divergence. Was there a great divergence in 'wages and prices'? What does this add to an older debate on wages and the standard of living led by Hobsbawm in the 1960s? The purpose of the debate in the 1960s and after, and in more recent configurations in studies of working-class budgets led by Horrell and Humphries, was to discover the impact of industrialization on the poor.[32] The purpose for the current wage divergence debate is different. That purpose for one leading contender, Robert Allen, is to discover high wages in Britain compared with the rest of the world, and thence to argue that this wage premium could explain her prescient and rapid pace of technological change and subsequent industrialization.[33]

These debates over wages do not, however, take us much further into the history of consumption beyond that of basic foodstuffs. Allen's work remains a good example. He refers to an Indian diet of rice, millets, and pulses; in some areas, fish provided the only source of animal protein. He writes of the poverty of 'scanty clothing and barefoot', of mud huts with thatched roofs, of few furnishings beyond bamboo mats, and of cooking done in earthen pots. His sources are Raychaudhuri and Habib from 1982.[34] He finds similar dearth in China, based on an account of Charles Lockyer, an early-eighteenth-century merchant traveller. It seems obvious to him that Northwest Europe with its white bread, meat, dairy products, and beer had the highest standard of living. But is this so clear? The new histories of food and its preparation need to be linked to the wage baskets used by economic historians, as do the data we now have on the consumption of luxuries and novelties: tropical foodstuffs such as tea, sugar, coffee, and chocolate and imported Asian manufactures – cotton, silk, porcelain, and British and European imitations. Economic historians now need to look more deeply into the consumption of specific types of goods – those associated with inequality and those that shifted behaviours.

## Inequality

Recent research on inequality focuses on the macroeconomic picture of the distribution of income and wealth. Thomas Piketty's *Capital in the Twenty-First Century* (2015) compares rising inequality in the period from the 1970s with the growth in inequality in the later eighteenth and early nineteenth centuries. Piketty compares the wealthy elites inheriting patrimonial wealth with the growth of elites from the eighteenth century whose wealth was increasingly based on interest earned on private holdings of government debt. Rentiers living off increasingly lucrative investment earnings contrasted with the labouring poor whose relative wages did not rise in any degree until after the mid-nineteenth century. Furthermore, property incomes rose from the mid-eighteenth century in Europe, and increased inequality.

Technical change during the late eighteenth and in most of the nineteenth centuries in Western Europe and in the United States reinforced this inequality, as capital was substituted for labour in many manufacturing processes. Factories employed less skilled labour; processes were simplified and products standardized for mass production in factories.

What impact did these trends to rising inequality as well as changes in technology mean for consumption? Once again the research we have is about wages with precise assumptions over what goods comprised the wage basket. Comparisons of wages and standards of living have focused on the working classes consuming ordinary commodities, and budget studies are mainly based on foodstuffs. But as we know, the rich and the poor consume different things. Philip Hoffman has argued that economic historians have been over-reliant on the price series of staple products, especially food, standardized older products, internationally traded goods, and physical goods, and they underuse luxury goods, labour-intensive goods, new products, non-traded products, retail products, and services.[35]

Luxury goods in the eighteenth century became cheaper relative to staple foods, but their impact is as hard to quantify as that for introducing new goods and services into today's cost-of-living indices. Fashion and luxury goods changed constantly, frustrating the search for consistent time series. Hoffman looked at price changes over a whole series of standardized commodities, and found the biggest advances of prices in fuel, rent, and cinnamon, and the greatest reductions of prices in textiles, sugar, silver, paper, beer, and unskilled labour. He found rising food prices and falling wages of unskilled labour. Many of those luxury products falling in price made use of factors that were getting cheaper across the seventeenth and eighteenth centuries: clothing and textiles, paper, chocolate, pewter, and sealing wax became cheaper along with the labour that went into them.[36] Adjusting the cost-of-living index with clothing, light, fuel, and beverages shows standards of living declined a little less in the period than previously estimated. But we also need to look further to class-specific cost of living indices.

Lower prices of luxury and staple goods brought real income gains for the wealthier and for richer regions. Hoffman also charted the temporal cycles in this inequality. Between 1500 and 1650, the top income groups experienced a 20 per cent reduction in their cost of living. But between 1650 and 1750, there was a reversal with the common people gaining. This swing reversed again in the second half of the eighteenth century, with wealthier groups gaining from the impact on prices of luxury goods of greater trade and new technologies. It was not until the last half of the nineteenth century that inequality moved again in favour of the lower classes.[37] In the period 1500–1650, the wealthier benefited most from cheaper new luxury goods as well as old luxuries such as domestic servants, and higher land rents added to their wealth. The poor faced scarcer food and higher costs of housing and land. In England, a second inegalitarian trend took place between 1740 and 1795–1815.

Hoffman poses that these trends favouring the wealthier classes in early modern Northwest Europe might help to explain the Great Divergence. The gains to the early phases of industrialization might well have contributed to changing behaviours associated with the 'industrious revolution'.

## The problems with budgets, probates, orphans, and thieves

Accounting for inequality addresses some of the problems we have with diametrically opposed, but equally widely accepted positions on standards of living even within Europe. But much speculation, new sources, and different data sets remain at odds. Horrell and Humphries investigated 1,350 household accounts and budgets of the labouring poor in Britain over the period 1790–1850 to draw a pessimist case on trends in family incomes over the later eighteenth and early nineteenth centuries.[38] Their results, though resting on data from the end of the eighteenth century, also led them to give little credence to ideas of an 'industrious revolution' or a 'consumer revolution' reaching below the levels of the middling classes.[39] Horrell's recent summing up reinforces earlier positions. 'Studies of the standard of living in the classic Industrial Revolution have failed to find evidence of increases in material welfare reflected in the consumption patterns of the mass of the population between 1790 and 1850.'[40] She argued that most studies based on probate inventories might support a hypothesis of rising consumption, but only for the middling classes; they anyway showed only a very gradual spread in the ownership of innovative goods across England.[41]

Wider European probate inventories, however, indicated greater ownership of new goods, both imported and British and European; these inventories were gathered from many parts of Britain and Northern Europe. They were gathered from those of the middling classes, but also included many from the labouring classes.[42] These demonstrate possession of new and imitative consumer goods, and evidence of new eating practices, with the use of ceramics, glass, and cutlery replacing pewter and wooden platters. Jan de Vries put the social history of new consumer practices in Europe together with probate accounts gathered for England and some other parts of Europe especially for the Netherlands to underpin his concept of the 'industrious revolution'.[43] This has been the one serious analysis of an economics of consumption for the early modern period that was not about prices and wages, but about changing tastes and household behaviour. De Vries drew on Gary Becker's analysis of household allocation of time to argue for a shift in household labour priorities from home-produced goods and services to market production. More within the household in early modern Europe sold their labour, and bought some of those goods they had formerly made themselves. They also worked longer and harder in order to satisfy a new taste and demand for goods imported into the locality or region, imitations of these, or entirely new goods. De Vries called this more intensive labour across the household an 'industrious revolution'. Decisions about consumption could be seen, therefore, as intra-household decisions on time use and expenditure, with wider effects on labour supply and intensity. Though wages were falling in the second half of the eighteenth century, probate inventories and other evidence of material possessions indicated that ownership of material objects was increasing. De Vries thus provided an explanation for this paradox, and one that engaged directly with an economic history of consumption. His case has been challenged by those who argue that labour intensification was driven by necessity rather than by consumer aspiration.[44]

Research on other North European data sets have, however, endorsed his position. Orphans' accounts from the Netherlands indicated wide use of tea and tea and coffee wares and ownership of a diversity of cheaper and more expensive textiles in Amsterdam and other Dutch cities.[45] Textile identifying markers from the London Foundling Hospital, thousands of swatches of mothers' clothing that were attached to records of the infants they left in the orphanage, indicated widespread ownership of printed cottons and mixed cotton and linen fabrics, fabrics that imitated more expensive imports from India, but were made in small Lancashire mills.[46] Toll records in Hamburg also indicate the rapid uptake of colonial goods, and especially coffee in Germany and Northern Europe.[47]

It was not only orphans who revealed the hidden material lives of the poor, but also thieves. Beverly Lemire and John Styles drew on the records of stolen goods in the Old Bailey to show the wide use in London of cotton textiles and of fashionable items and accessories.[48] More recent research developing these records into datasets shows a much greater impact of fashion aspiration and the desire for variety and differentiation, fashion, and taste among common people than once recognized.[49] Cotton stockings were popular items of theft from poor households as were napkins and table linen from marginally better-off households.[50]

## Where is the economic history of consumption?

We appear to have reached a stalemate on the economic history of consumption in the early modern period. Most of the research has been on Northwest Europe. It is still focused on wages and standards of living, with a great divide between those making the case for higher wages and/or more food and material possessions, and those arguing for stasis or immiseration. Wage baskets are estimated mainly on basic foodstuffs. Can an approach through large data sets take us in new directions? What analysis and questions lie behind the data sets? What was consumed, who consumed it, how and why did they consume it?

We could, instead, move down to a micro scale in order to connect an economics of consumption with the significant research on the social and cultural history of consumption. We can then engage with issues over choice and new products, encountering and integrating not only strange goods, desire, and stimulus seeking in the Scitovsky model, but also social interaction and awareness. We can investigate why and when taste mattered, the choice of qualities over quantities, and the role of fashion.

Foodstuffs are one example. Grains, as we have seen, need to be converted to flour for consumption. Food, furthermore, needs to be prepared and cooked. Even within early industrial Britain, there were great differences in cooking practices related to the availability of coal. The labouring poor in Yorkshire cooked their meals and heated their homes. Those in the South of England, though there were fewer women working in arable areas, faced much greater fuel constraints; they cooked much less and bought their bread.[51] Different food baskets also connected to different work regimes. Coffee consumption spread quickly in the proto-industrial regions of Germany. Textile workers consumed less grain and protein-rich foods than agricultural labourers. Coffee could be prepared quickly, it increased concentration in long hours of repetitive tasks, and it suppressed hunger. Merchants organizing the textile trade also dealt in coffee, and often paid their outworkers in coffee.[52]

Tastes and fashions for differentiated and exotic goods are another case. Data sets drawn from the Old Bailey records show that consumers substituted towards more expensive cotton stockings and counterpanes and away from worsted and linen. This was not about emulation, but about respectability, politeness, and differentiation. They sought greater variety and higher quality.[53] Exotic goods such as Asian imports in Jan de Vries' analysis changed tastes, and created new markets and products. Asian imports, especially textiles and the porcelain, stimulated a commercialization of societies in retailing, and drew households into the market.[54]

Lynn Hunt's *Writing History in the Global Era* (2014) links a cultural history of society and the self in late-seventeenth- and eighteenth-century Europe to how exotic goods were experienced and chosen. Internal European factors interacted with wider global connections. Europeans developed a culture in which exotic goods made sense. Larger numbers, especially in specific places with higher discretionary incomes, wanted more choice. A desiring, stimulus-seeking attitude developed in tandem with social awareness: different varieties and individual choices among these demarcated new social groups. Tastes changed as experiences of the self changed.[55]

We can thus understand the varieties of goods carried in East India Company cargoes and constantly sought in East India Company orders. This was no random collection of goods, but one constantly responding to large-scale buyers at the autumn and spring company auctions, and these were closely affected in turn by the choices of all the small retailers and peddlers they sold on to. French colourways dictated Swedish silk imports from China; East India Company orders went out with letters criticizing the colours of earlier cargoes, and demanding dynamic, responsive, and intuitive designs and patterns. Dutch and English East India companies and private European and Indian merchants competed vigorously for the finest figured jamdani muslins.[56]

## The case of textiles

A global history of the consumption of cotton textiles provides an opportunity to address some of these issues. As in the case of consumer durables in the early modern period, most of the research has focused on Europe, but there is now more on the Americas, Africa, South Asia, and East Asia. In all of these regions, fashion, sumptuary codes, tribute, and gifts provided incentives to consume a commodity that was newly traded between some large areas of the globe, and then newly manufactured in Europe and the Americas. Cotton is also the subject of two recent large-scale global histories.[57]

What are the key markers of this textile consumption across the early modern world? The entry of cotton into European ways of dress was slower than we once thought. Merchants in the sixteenth and seventeenth centuries needed to 'educate' their potential market, and cotton only became truly popular from the mid-eighteenth century. Colour fastness, novelty, and new distribution channels were all important to their uptake. The Dutch consumed the new fabrics right down the social ladder by the early eighteenth century; at least a quarter of households in the Amsterdam inventories had them. By the later eighteenth century, there were many substitutes, and cottons were widely used in the dress of wage earners in Paris and in Castille.[58]

Well before Europe's encounter with Indian cottons, Gujarati traders tapped into a lively demand in East Africa. The Portuguese traded cotton from Gujarat, Sindh, and Cambay for slaves that were then sold on at a very high profit in Brazil, Mexico, and the Caribbean. By the late seventeenth century, the Gold Coast imported 20,000 metres of European and Asian cloth a year, and between 1690 and 1800, cloth made up 68 per cent of all commodities exported from England to Africa; 40 per cent of this was from India.[59] Sumptuary codes on colour and high demand for geometric patterns and stripes in vibrant colours shaped the trade. From an early period, Indian cottons were a highly desirable luxury good in many parts of Africa.[60]

Gujarati cottons exported to East-Central and Southeast Africa responded to highly specific and changeable tastes. They were used as a currency, and were important in social, cultural, and political life in both coastal and interior areas. Cloth bestowed moral and social qualities; it marked high and low status, was a significant diplomatic gift, and marked political and cultural ceremony. Taste and fashion dictated these markets.[61]

The Latin American market was divided into higher-quality imported goods and cheaper local products. Indian cottons came to Mexico via the Pacific Manila-Acapulco route or via European imports, and were preferred in bright colours and floral patterns. Cottons entered rapidly into the wardrobes of the colonists of French and British North America and the Caribbean; consumers sought a 'more refined and expensive product'. By the last decade of the eighteenth century, one-quarter of London's cotton imports went on to Africa, and high proportions were also re-exported to the Americas. In Riello's words, 'cotton became a global commodity'.[62]

Historians are now exploring the motivations of cotton's consumption in these different regions of the world. A commodity that connected India to Europe, East Asia, Africa, and the Americas also conveyed very different meanings to its consumers. Plebeian families distinguished between 'best' and working clothes; they owned changes of clothing and duplicates, and dressed up for church and popular festivities. They focused their consumer expectations on clothes; clothes were a sign of self-respect. They chose and they benefited from new kinds of fashionable clothing made from cotton.[63]

There were also highly diverse markets for many medium-quality as well as fine-quality materials. India's cottons changed over time; they appealed to different social status and aesthetic preference. Their markets also revealed fashionability, and finishing in dyeing, printing, and embroidery appealed to consumers across India and outside.[64]

## Conclusion

An economic history of consumption has eluded many economic historians. Many have continued instead to create larger data sets and to compare like with unlike on levels of wages and standards of living. In the space left by Pomeranz in the Great Divergence debate, they have debated whether wages were different between regions of the world and whether this factor drove other economic stimulants such as technological change. But all those factors explored by social and cultural historians behind changing consumer behaviour from status and social structure to gifts, diplomacy, and display, and on to fashion, sensibility, and identity have remained beyond the purview of most economic historians. The window opened to such investigation by Jan de Vries' concept of 'industriousness' has still provided little illumination into key consumer practices. Global economic history in fact turned attention away from such investigation. The dearth of economic analysis into these many motivations behind consumer behaviour underpins an economic history which continues to avoid the history of consumption in favour of the history of wages.

A global economic history must include global connections as well as global comparisons. The impact of exotic goods and of encounters between merchants from different parts of the world helped to transform the contents of the probate inventories, toll registers, thefts, foundling hospital identifiers, and indeed food baskets. Individual, micro, and local studies are now revealing these in research such as that recounted here on cotton textiles. Different products and distinctive qualities and different preparations and presentations affected food baskets as much as domestic interiors and dress.[65] There is much for global economic historians to discover at the micro level that will move us beyond the now very dated questions and materials still informing the big data sets of wages and prices.

## Notes

1. M. J. Daunton (1995), *Progress and Poverty: An Economic and Social History of Britain 1700–1850*. Oxford: Oxford University Press; J. Mokyr (2009), *The Enlightened Economy. An Economic History of Britain 1700–1850*. New Haven: Yale University Press; R. C. Allen (2009), *The British Industrial Revolution in Global Perspective*. Cambridge: Cambridge University Press. Though the most recent edition of the *Cambridge Economic History of Britain* does have a chapter on consumption, a closer look reveals that this too is mainly about wages and the standard of living.

2. See J. Brewer (1990), *The Sinews of Power: War, Money and the English State 1688–1783*. Cambridge, MA: Harvard University Press; T. Breen (2004), *The Marketplace of Revolution: How Consumer Politics Shaped American Independence*. Oxford: Oxford University Press.

3. L. Hunt (2014), *Writing History in the Global Era*. New York: W.W. Norton.

4. D. Winch (2009), *Wealth and Life. Essays on the Intellectual History of Political Economy in Britain, 1848–1914*. Cambridge: Cambridge University Press, 149–76 and 332–66; F. Trentmann (2016), *Empire of Things: How We Became a World of Consumers, from the Fifteenth Century to the Twenty-First*. London: Allen Lane, 151–3.

5. W. Sombart (1967 [or. ed. 1913]), *Luxury and Capitalism*. Ann Arbor: University of Michigan Press; T. Veblen (1899 [ed. 1912]), *The Theory of the Leisure Class*. New York: Macmillan. Mandeville's *The Fable of the Bees*, first published early in the eighteenth century, reappeared at this time in a new American edition published by Kaye, and it was at the same time translated into German.

6. K. Lancaster (1971), *Consumer Demand: A New Approach*. New York and London: Columbia University Press; D. Ironmonger (1972), *New Commodities and Consumer Behaviour*. Cambridge: Cambridge University Press.

7. T. Scitovsky (1977), *The Joyless Economy: The Psychology of Human Satisfaction*. Oxford: Oxford University Press.

8. M. Bianchi (ed.) (1998), *The Active Consumer: Novelty and Surprise in Consumer Choice*. London: Routledge.

9. A. Offer (2012), 'Consumption and well-being', in F. Trentmann, *The Oxford Handbook of the History of Consumption*. Oxford: Oxford University Press, 653–72.

10. Offer, 'Consumption and well-being', 666.

11. K. Pomeranz (2000), *The Great Divergence: China, Europe and the Making of the Modern World Economy*. Princeton: Princeton University Press, 122.

12. Pomeranz, *The Great Divergence*, 117.

13. Pomeranz, *The Great Divergence*, 131.

14. Pomeranz, *The Great Divergence*, 144–6.

15. K. Pomeranz (2005), 'Standards of living in eighteenth-century China: Regional differences, temporal trends and incomplete evidence', in R. C. Allen, T. Bengtsson and M. Dribe (eds), *Living Standards in the Past. New Perspectives on Well-being in Asia and Europe*. Oxford: Oxford University Press, 7–10, and 21–4.

16. Pomeranz, *The Great Divergence*, 122–5.

17. J. de Vries (2015), 'Understanding Eurasian trade in the era of the trading companies', in M. Berg, et al. (eds), *Goods from the East, 1600–1800: Trading Eurasia*. Basingstoke: Palgrave, 1–39, esp. 10–11; P. Parthasarathi (2011), *Why Europe Grew Rich and Asia Did Not: Global Economic Divergence, 1600-1850*. Cambridge: Cambridge University Press.

18. de Vries, 'Understanding Eurasian trade', 11, 23–4.

19. J. de Vries (2010), 'The limits of globalisation in the early modern world', *Economic History Review*, 63 (1), 710–33.

20. de Vries, 'Understanding Eurasian trade', 15–16, 34–6.

21. de Vries, 'Understanding Eurasian trade', 17.

22. K. Pomeranz (2012), 'Commerce', in U. Rublack (ed.), *A Concise Companion to History*. Oxford: Oxford University Press, 111.

23. See Zheng Yangwen (2012), *China on the Sea: How the Maritime World Shaped Modern China*. Leiden: Brill. See R. Bin Wong (2016), 'The early modern foundations of the modern world: Recent works on patterns of economic and political change', *Journal of Global History*,

11 (2), 135–46; Also see J. de Vries (2008), *The Industrious Revolution: Consumer Behavior and the Household Economy, 1650 to the Present*. Cambridge: Cambridge University Press.

24. See for example, D. Haynes, A. McGowan, T. Roy and H. Yanagisawa (eds) (2010), *Towards a History of Consumption in South Asia*. New Delhi: Oxford University Press.

25. J. Gommans (2015), 'For the home and the body: Dutch and Indian ways of early modern consumption', in Berg et al., (eds), *Goods from the East*, 331–49.

26. C. A. Bayly (2002), '"Archaic" and "Modern" globalization in the Asian and African arena c. 1750–1850', in A. G. Hopkins (ed.), *Globalization in World History*. London: Pimlico, 52.

27. de Vries, *The Industrious Revolution*.

28. de Vries, *The Industrious Revolution*.

29. C. Shammas (2012), 'Standard of living, consumption, and political economy over the past 500 years', in Trentmann (ed.), *The Oxford Handbook of the History of Consumption*, 212.

30. Shammas, 'Standard of living', 219. Also see A. Offer (2012), 'Consumption and well-being', 653–71.

31. Shammas, 'Standard of living', 212.

32. See J. Humphries (2004), 'Household economy', in R. Floud and P. Johnson (eds), *The Cambridge Economic History of Modern Britain*, vol. 1. Cambridge: Cambridge University Press, 238–67; S. Horrell and J. Humphries (1992), 'Old questions, new data, and alternative perspectives: Families' living standards during the Industrial Revolution', *Journal of Economic History*, 52 (4), 849–80.

33. See Allen, *The British Industrial Revolution*, 106–31 and 135–55; Idem (2001), 'The Great Divergence in European wages and prices from the Middle Ages to the First World War', 38 (4), 411–47; R. C. Allen, J.-P. Bassino, D. Ma, C. Moll-Murata and J. L. van Zanden (2011), 'Wages, prices and living standards in China, 1738-1925: in comparison with Europe, Japan, and India', *Economic History Review*, 64 (Supplement 1), 8–38; See J. Humphries (2013), 'The lure of aggregates and the pitfalls of the patriarchal perspective: A critique of the high wage economy interpretation of the Industrial Revolution', *Economic History Review*, 66 (3), 693–714. Allen also refined his data to include the wages of women and children. R. C. Allen (2015), 'The high-wage economy and the Industrial Revolution: A restatement', *Economic History Review*, 68 (1), 1–22.

34. Allen, *The British Industrial Revolution*, 32.

35. T. Piketty (2015), *Capital in the Twenty-First Century*. Cambridge, MA: Belknap Press; P. Hoffman (2005), 'Sketching the rise of real inequality in early modern Europe', in Allen, et al. (eds), *Standards of Living in the Past*, 24.

36. Hoffman, 'Sketching the rise of real inequality', 25-9.

37. Hoffman, 'Sketching the rise of real inequality', 51.

38. Horrell and Humphries (1992), 'Old questions, new data', 849–80.

39. S. Horrell (1996), 'Home demand and British industrialization', *Journal of Economic History*, 56 (3), 561–604.

40. S. Horrell (2014), 'Consumption, 1700–1870', in R. Floud, J. Humphries and P. Johnson (eds), *The Cambridge Economic History of Modern Britain*, 3rd edn, vol. 1. Cambridge. Cambridge University Press, 239.

41. Horrell (2014), 'Consumption, 1700–1870', 241. Horell's findings rely on a data set compiled by C. Muldrew in his (2011), *Food, Energy, and the Creation of Industriousness: Work and Material Culture in Agrarian England, 1550–1780*. Cambridge: Cambridge University

Press. See the fundamental critique to this dataset in C. Shammas (2012), 'Review of food, energy, and the creation of industriousness: Work and material culture in agrarian England, 1550–1780', *Journal of Modern History*, 84 (4), 951–3.

42. See the table of probate inventories for early modern England in Horrell, 'Consumption', 240.

43. de Vries, *The Industrious Revolution*.

44. See Trentmann's critique of de Vries in Trentmann, *Empire of Things*, 75; P. Vries (2016), 'What we do and do not know about the Great Divergence in 2016', unpublished paper, 20.

45. Anne McCants argued there had to be a widespread consumer demand for these commodities so that they were incorporated into budgets and daily routines in sufficient amounts to alter overall standards of living. See A. McCants (2007), 'Exotic goods, popular consumption and the standard of living: Thinking about globalization in the early modern world', *Journal of World History*, 18 (4), 433–62; Idem (2008), 'Poor consumers as global consumers: The diffusion of tea and coffee drinking in the eighteenth century', *Economic History Review*, 61 (Supplement 1), 172–200; Idem (2013), 'Porcelain for the poor: The material culture of tea and coffee consumption in eighteenth-century Amsterdam', in P. Findlen (ed.), *Early Modern Things: Objects and Their Histories 1500–1800*. London: Routledge, 316–41; Idem (2015), 'Becoming consumers: Asiatic goods in migrant and native-born middling households in eighteenth-century Amsterdam', in Berg, et al. (eds), *Goods from the East*, 197–215.

46. J. Styles (2006), *The Dress of the People: Everyday Fashion in Eighteenth-Century England*. New Haven: Yale University Press; Idem (2010), *Threads of Feeling: The London Foundling Museum's Textile Tokens 1740–1770*. London: The Foundling Museum.

47. C. Fertig and U. Pfister (2016), '"Coffee, mind and body": Global material culture and the eighteenth-century Hamburg import trade', in A. Gerritsen and G. Riello (eds), *The Global Lives of Things*. Basingstoke: Routledge, 227.

48. See B. Lemire (1991), *Fashion's Favourite: The Cotton Trade and the Consumer in Britain, 1660–1800*. Oxford: Oxford University Press; Styles, *Dress of the People*.

49. J. Humphries, S. Horrell and K. Sneath (2015), 'Consumption conundrums unravelled', *Economic History Review*, 68 (3), 841 and 855.

50. Humphries, Horrell and Sneath, 'Consumption conundrums', 847 and 853.

51. D. Zyllerberg (2015), 'Fuel prices, regional diets and cooking habits in the Industrial Revolution, 1750–1830', *Past & Present*, 229, 91–122.

52. Fertig and Pfister, 'Coffee, mind and body', 229.

53. Humphries, Horrell and Sneath, 'Consumption conundrums', 853–4.

54. de Vries, 'Understanding Eurasian trade', 14 and 22.

55. Hunt, *Writing History in the Global Era*, 114–41.

56. See essays by Prakash (2015) and Berg (2015) in Berg, et al. (eds), *Goods from the East*, 119–38, and 183–96. Also see H. Hodacs (2015), *Silk and Tea in the North*. Palgrave: Basingstoke.

57. Giorgio Riello combined extensive research on museum collections of printed cotton textiles with archival research to argue for the existence of a globalized economy based in the wider world trade in printed cotton textiles from India throughout the early modern period. This trade stimulated industrialization in Europe, and especially Britain, as Europeans sought to build an industry to match the fine material attributes of these cottons at low consumer prices. G. Riello (2013), *Cotton: The Fabric that Made the Modern World*. Cambridge: Cambridge University Press. Sven Beckert's book provided another history of raw cotton and

cotton manufacture, but mainly in Europe and America in the modern period. S. Beckert (2014), *Empire of Cotton: A Global History*. New York: Alfred A. Knopf.

58. Riello, *Cotton*, 114–5.

59. Riello, *Cotton*, 137–8.

60. Trentmann, *Empire of Things*, 124.

61. P. Machado (2009), 'Gujarat, Africa and the Western Indian Ocean', in G. Riello and P. Parthasarathi (eds), *The Spinning World: A Global History of Cotton Textiles, 1200-185*. Oxford: Oxford University Press, 161–79; Idem (2009), 'Cloths of a new fashion: Indian Ocean networks of exchange and cloth zones of contact in Africa and India in the eighteenth and nineteenth centuries', in G. Riello and T. Roy (eds) (2009), *How India Clothed the World*, 53–84. Also see Trentmann, *Empire of Things*, 124–5, and 129.

62. Riello, *Cotton*, 147–8.

63. Styles, *The Dress of the People*, 241–3, 263, 307–14, 323–6; R. DuPlessis (2009), 'Cotton consumption in the North Atlantic', in Riello and Parthasarathi (eds), *The Spinning World*, 231–4. See the developing uses of cotton by gender and race in Spanish America and the Caribbean as discussed by M. Vicente (2009), 'Cottons in Colonial Spanish America', in Riello and Parthasarathi (eds), *The Spinning World*, 260. See also Rebecca Earle (2003), 'Luxury, clothing and race in Colonial Spanish America', in M. Berg and E. Eger (eds), *Luxury in the Eighteenth Century: Debates, Desires and Delectable Goods*. Basingstoke: Palgrave, 219–27.

64. P. Parthasarathi and G. Riello (2012), 'From India to the world: Cotton and fashionability', in Trentmann, *The Oxford Handbook of the History of Consumption*, 148–50.

65. On foodstuffs, see Jan de Vries' research on bread in the Dutch Republic. J. de Vries (2009), 'The political economy of bread in the Dutch Republic', in O. Gelderston (ed.), *The Political Economy of the Dutch Republic*. Aldershot: Ashgate, 85–114.

# PART II
## THE EMERGENCE OF A WORLD ECONOMY

# CHAPTER 8
# TRADE AND THE EMERGENCE OF A
# WORLD ECONOMY, 1500–2000
*Tirthankar Roy and Giorgio Riello*

The relationship between trade and the emergence of a world economy has been the subject of several differing ideas and conceptualizations over the past two generations. Economic historians have chartered the intensification of long-distance – and especially transcontinental – trade over the course of the early modern period and since the nineteenth century, but there is little consensus on the chronology and reasons for major shifts in this long period. The relative size of trade fluxes is a subject of debate especially for the pre-modern period as is a general definition of what the making of a global market might entail. Economic historians have provided rather different chronologies of the making of a global economic system of exchange. The same can be said of the relationship between trade and economic growth, a topic of disagreement especially for the period of the Industrial Revolution.

This chapter starts by charting the scale and movements of world trade over the five centuries from the start of European direct trade with Asia and the Americas to the late twentieth century. It introduces the historiography explaining these movements. It considers the complex relationship between trade, politics, and economic development. It concludes with a short overview of the points in the debates and controversies.

## The shape and scale of global trade

Historians have argued that trade can be taken as one of the indicators of the level of globalization. The exchange of goods – and more recently of an increasing amount of services – across national borders is taken to be a measure of not only economic but also social and cultural interconnection. Since 1500, world trade has mostly grown at rates far higher than those of world GDP, suggesting that national economies have become increasingly connected to each other through the trade of raw materials, foodstuffs, and manufactured commodities (Table 8.1).

With a growth rate of just under 1 per cent a year in the pre-1820 period, trade grew at three times the rate of the world GDP. In 1820, the size of world trade might have been five times larger than in 1500. Yet, this growth was modest compared to the following two centuries. It is estimated that world trade increased from $700 million (in 1970 US$) in 1700 to $38 billion in 1913.[1] On the eve of the First World War, world trade was between twenty-five and thirty-three times larger than a century earlier.[2] With a

**Table 8.1  Growth of world trade and GDP, 1500–2003  (annual average compound growth rates in percentage)**

|  | World trade | World GDP | Ratio trade to GDP |
|---|---|---|---|
| 1500–1820 | 0.96 | 0.32 | 3.0 |
| 1820–1870 | 4.18 | 0.94 | 4.4 |
| 1870–1913 | 3.40 | 2.12 | 1.6 |
| 1913–1950 | 0.90 | 1.82 | 0.5 |
| 1950–1973 | 7.88 | 4.90 | 1.6 |
| 1973–2003 | 5.38 | 3.17 | 1.7 |
| 1820–2003 | 3.97 | 2.25 | 1.8 |

*Source*: Angus Maddison, *Contours of the World Economy: Essays in Macro-Economic History* (Oxford: Oxford University Press, 2007), Table 2.6.

growth rate of over 4 per cent in the period 1820-80, there was a ninefold increase in world trade with a period of very high growth between 1840 and 1873 and slightly more contained growth over the following forty years. This was the period of liberalization of the European economies and the heyday of imperial projects on the part of European nation states.

The First World War was a moment of disruption in world trade and foreign direct investment, and it was followed by a period of slow growth. Autarchic regimes, monetary and financial instability, economic stagnation, and a weakening of empires meant in some cases an absolute reduction in world trade. It was only in the post-1945 period that trade began to grow again, indeed at a pace unmatched even during the so-called first age of globalization of the second half of the nineteenth century. Already by the early 1950s, the size of world trade had returned to 1913 levels, though it took until the mid-1970s for the level of trade as a share of world output to be back to 1913 levels.[3] At the same time, the pursuit of protectionist industrial policies in the developing world after 1950 reduced the importance of foreign trade for some of these economies (such as those of India or China), which had been highly open before 1950. The past forty years have been a period of further liberalization of commodity and financial markets and the 'multilateralization of trade'. Both world GDP and world trade grew at very high rates.

This overall picture needs however to be disaggregated in order to consider the contribution of specific countries. In 1913, the merchandise export of Britain was worth an estimated $39.35 billion (in 1990 US$), the largest in the world and just ahead of Germany, and roughly double the size of US export. Britain, the United States, and Germany – the three largest industrial economies at the time – accounted for possibly two-thirds of all trade in the world (Table 8.2). The preponderance of industrial economies has remained a feature of world trade throughout the twentieth century. In

**Table 8.2  Export of selected countries, 1820–1992  (1913 = 100)**

| | Size of the export (1913 = 100) | | | | | | | Value in 1913 (GB = 100) | Value in 1929 (US = 100) | Value in 2003 (Ge = 100) |
|---|---|---|---|---|---|---|---|---|---|---|
| | 1820 | 1870 | 1913 | 1929 | 1950 | 1973 | 2003 | | | |
| Great Britain | 3 | 31 | 100 | 81 | 100 | 240 | 816 | 100 | 105 | 41 |
| Germany | 4 | 18 | 100 | 92 | 35 | 508 | 2055 | 97 | 115 | 100 |
| France | 4 | 31 | 100 | 147 | 149 | 922 | 3578 | 29 | 55 | 51 |
| Italy | 7 | 39 | 100 | 161 | 126 | | | 12 | | |
| Russia | - | | 100 | | | | | - | | |
| United States | 1 | 13 | 100 | 158 | 225 | 909 | 4176 | 49 | 100 | 102 |
| Japan | - | 3 | 100 | 258 | 210 | 5647 | 23922 | 4 | 14 | 51 |
| China | | 33 | 100 | 149 | 151 | 278 | 10811 | 11 | 21 | 58 |
| India | | 37 | 100 | 87 | 58 | 102 | 908 | 24 | 27 | 11 |
| World | 3 | 24 | 100 | | 128 | 797 | | - | - | - |

*Source*: Angus Maddison, *Monitoring the World Economy, 1820–1992* (Paris, OECD Development Centre, 1995); Id, *Contours of the World Economy: Essays in Macro-Economic History* (Oxford: Oxford University Press, 2007), 170; Maddison, 361.

2003, the export of Great Britain was eight times larger than what it had been ninety years earlier, a modest performance compared to Germany (twenty times larger), France (thirty-five times), and the United States (forty-two times). Trade grew exponentially for China (108 times large in 2013 compared to 1914) and Japan (239 times), but enormous increases for Asian countries hide the fact of the relatively small size of their trade in 1913. At the beginning of the twenty-first century, the major Western industrial nations – the United States and Germany in particular – still controlled a large part of world trade.

## The beginning of a global economy: The early modern period

The shape of global trade in the twentieth century could not be more different from its contours just four centuries earlier. In 1500, China and India accounted for more than half of the world manufacturing output and were the engines of global trade. Silk, porcelain, iron, and copperware from China were exchanged for silver, cotton, spices, and foodstuff. Palm oil, nuts, and precious metals from Africa and the Middle East found their way to India in exchange for cotton textiles. Yet historians have disputed as to whether this was in any sense a global system of exchange. Janet Abu-Lughod put forward the idea that, already in 1250–1350, a system of global exchange existed but was neither coordinated by any specific world area nor unified into one system. She proposed instead a model based on a series of overlapping spheres of trade that included long-established routes such as the silk routes across Central Asia, the China Sea, the Indian Ocean, and the Mediterranean.[4] The work of David Christian on the silk routes showed how trade was based on a system of 'repeated transaction' with numerous disruptions caused by warfare and political instability.[5] Technology was one of the limiting factors for intercontinental trade as direct trade between the two extremes of Eurasia was all but impossible. Traders operated instead on specific segments of this Eurasian system and were organized in 'nations' or trading communities that negotiated the protection of local governments.[6]

The sixteenth and seventeenth centuries saw a restructuring of this system, though historians dispute the scale and consequences of such change. It has been suggested that the direct trade between Europe and Asia via the Cape first by the Portuguese from 1500 onwards and later by the Dutch, English, and other European companies after 1600 inaugurated a new period in world trade. This was a trade that was direct and did not have to rely on a series of intermediaries; it was in the hands of Europeans and was structured through large-scale organizations, the East India companies, that have been seen as the precursors of modern corporations.

However, the idea that Europe's direct trade with Asia and the Americas inaugurated a new era for the early modern world economy has been debated. Critics point to the fact that such a trade might have been rather modest. Extra-European markets were small and the profitability of both colonial trade and slavery remained low.[7] Over the three centuries between 1500 and 1800, just over 10,600 vessels were sent from Europe to Asia, two-thirds of which were sent in the eighteenth century.[8] At an estimated 700 tonnes per vessel, the total trade between Asia and Europe was in the region of 7.5 million tonnes, roughly fifteen present-day container ships. By contrast, coastal, short-distance, and port-to-port trade remained far more important than long-distance trade in this period. The majority of trade was carried out within the borders of specific regions. While India is often hailed as key to Britain's early modern intercontinental trade, estimates of the subcontinent's trade and GDP reveal that long-distance trade was small.[9]

Intercontinental trade was not just small but also slow as it took the best of two years for a European ship to go to China and return to Europe. It was also expensive: Although profit margins were high, recent research has underlined the cost of an 'armed trade' that relied on violence and coercion as well as a sophisticated system of diplomatic relations. This was also a trade with profound social costs as shown by de Vries' estimates of the high number of people who left Europe at the service of the East India companies. In the case of a small nation such as Portugal, this constituted in all probability a large drain of its human capital.[10]

Yet, quantities might not be the entire story. Dennis Flynn and Arturo Giráldez argue that Europeans brought together separate areas of trade into one unified system. From the 1560s onwards, vast reserves of silver mined in Latin America 'oiled' this newly integrated system of exchange and allowed it to expand in size. Because of the high value of silver in China and more generally in Asia, bullion could be used as a means of payment for a variety of Asian commodities that found their way to European and Atlantic markets.[11]

Silver was monetized and the Portuguese and Spaniards first, and later other European nations, expanded trade by integrating the American and Asian economies. The connection between the American, African, and Asian economies was furthered by the setting up of plantations in the Americas cultivating a variety of tropical commodities such as sugar, coffee, cocoa, and later raw materials such as cotton.[12] The incorporation of the Atlantic coincided with – and was fostered by – the expansion of the slave trade by the hands of European traders. It is estimated that in the period 1525–1790, up to ten million people were enslaved in Africa and transported to the Americas. Two-thirds of such slaves were transported in the eighteenth century, the period of maximum expansion of the production of tropical colonial goods.[13]

The system of intercontinental trade changed substantially over the course of the early modern period and especially in the eighteenth century. Three main changes should be underlined. First, while in the sixteenth century spices and what we might call 'traditional luxuries' had been central to global trade, by the seventeenth and eighteenth centuries their role was taken over by cheaper cotton textiles as well as tropical goods such as tea, coffee, and sugar. Tropical commodities and luxury goods were items that were, at least initially, not available or not produced within the borders of Europe and North America.

Second, over time Europe started becoming a direct competitor in the production of Asian commodities. Unlike Portugal and Spain – the key trading players of the sixteenth century – England, France, and the Netherlands possessed export-oriented industries such as the English woollens, French silks, and the Dutch lighter new draperies.[14] Over time, they started manufacturing imitations of Indian cotton textiles, Chinese porcelain, and Japanese lacquerware for domestic and export markets.[15] High tariffs and total bans were part of the mercantilist policies embraced by several, though not all, European states. The ban of import and wearing of Indian cotton and silk textiles in most European nations between 1689 and the 1770s tends to be seen, if debatably, as an example of mercantilist policies aimed at fostering local production and re-export, and extended to include colonial policies against export of manufactured commodities towards the mother country. In the case of Britain, long-distance trade had to be carried out on English ships and colonial commodities had to be sent to England before being re-exported. Duties on tobacco, tea, sugar, and spirits accounted for a quarter of government revenue in Britain in the late eighteenth century.[16] In the 1820s, British tariffs still averaged between 45 and 55 per cent.[17]

**Figure 8.1** Europe's intercontinental trade, 1501–1795.
*Source*: Jan de Vries, 'The Limits of Globalisation in the Early Modern World', *Economic History Review*, 63 (1) (2010), 720.

Over time, the Atlantic economy came to have a larger weight for Europe than the eastbound Asian trade, even though the scale of Asian and tropical trade with Europe increased substantially (Figure 8.1).[18]

## Industrialization and reconfiguration of world trade

Historians agree that the nineteenth century saw a dramatic change in both the nature and scale of global trade. The rise of the industrial West created a demand there for raw materials and produced a surplus of finished commodities that needed to find markets all over the world. If at the beginning of the seventeenth century British imports were equally divided into manufactured commodities, foodstuff, and raw materials, a century later Britain had become a net exporter of manufactured commodities with less than 10 per cent of its imports in the form of manufactured goods. By 1800, Britain relied on the import of foodstuff (45 per cent of all imports) and of a range of raw materials necessary as industrial inputs (46.5 per cent of all imports).[19] Britons in the mid-Victorian period spent one out of every four pounds sterling on foreign goods, mostly food and primary materials.[20]

As we saw earlier, the ratio of trade to GDP grew from a level as low as 1 per cent in the 1820s to ten times as much on the eve of the First World War, indicating a pronounced opening up of economies, especially those in Europe and North America (Table 8.3).[21] Besides industrialization, the transcontinental railways, transoceanic steamships with compound steam engines, and undersea telegraph cables contributed to the process. The opening of new maritime routes such as the Suez Canal in 1869 and the completion of the Union Pacific Railroad the same year allowed for cheaper and more reliable means of transport. Improvements in navigation technology and the introduction of steam decreased the cost of ocean freight by 80 per cent over the course of the nineteenth century.[22] The general peace in Europe and the balance of power in the century between 1815 and 1914 allowed for the establishment of specific imperial spheres of influence by European nations in Asia and Africa. The infrastructure of empire in turn facilitated the migration of people and the mobility of capital through foreign direct investment. Between 1870 and 1914, the stock of capital invested outside the place of origin increased from $9 billion to $44 billion.[23]

How 'free' was trade? There is a consensus that the general liberalism inaugurated with the repeal of the Corn Laws in Britain in 1846 started a new age of free trade. The Cobden-Chevalier treaty of 1860 in which Britain removed all tariffs on the import of French goods (with the exception of wine and brandy) included a 'most-favoured-nation clause' that allowed further treaties to be signed with other industrialized countries in Europe. Bairoch however insists that liberalism was more a 'myth' than a reality in nineteenth-century Europe as most economies did not readily embrace free trade. Even considering the relative relaxation of duties and other protectionist measures in the period 1860–80, Bairoch and Kozul-Wright conclude that in 1913 the developed world could be 'best described as islands of liberalism, surrounded by a sea of protectionism'.[24] The financial crisis of 1873 gave voice to those who had been arguing for protection.

Table 8.3 World merchandise export as percentage of GDP

| | |
|------|-----------|
| 1820 | 1.0 ** |
| 1850 | 5.1* |
| 1870 | 4.6 ** |
| 1880 | 9.8* |
| 1913 | 11.9 (7.9**) |
| 1929 | 9.0** |
| 1950 | 7.1 (5.5**) |
| 1973 | 11.7 (10.5**) |
| 1985 | 14.5* |
| 1993 | 17.1** |
| 1998 | 17.2* |

*Source*: *Paul Krugman, 'Growing World Trade: Causes and Consequences',
*Brookings Papers on Economic Activity*, 1 (1995), 331; ** Maddison, *The
World Economy: A Millennial Perspective* (Paris: OECD, 2001).

Three features characterized the new world trade system of the nineteenth century. The first one is the creation of markets for standardized commodities such as cotton, wool, coal, wheat, maize, and iron. Unlike the commodity exchange of the pre-modern period, this was a trade in bulk commodities. These were also no longer non-competing goods as they had been in the early modern period but competed directly with producers in different continents.[25] Chris Bayly, for instance, conceptualizes this as a shift from what he calls an 'archaic system' of exchange based on the trade of luxury items to one that can be defined as 'modern' based instead on capitalist expansion and global imperialism.[26] The interlinking of world commodity trade came to be strongly associated with international specialization of labour and, as we will see, to economic development more widely. The second element of this new system was the preponderance of Europe and Britain in particular. In 1910, 60 per cent of the tonnage passing through the Suez Canal was British. Western shipping dominated world trade.[27] The same could be said of direct foreign investment. At an estimated £4 billion, British overseas investment accounted for 43 per cent of the world total in 1913. France accounted for a further 20 per cent and Germany 13 per cent.[28] Finally, this system was based on a differentiation between industrial and primary produce economies. In 1913, primary products accounted for nearly two-thirds of all world trade, with food accounting for 27 per cent of all trade, agricultural raw materials 23 per cent, and minerals 14 per cent. While Western Europe and North America were importers of raw materials, they exported manufactured products to Africa, Latin America, Asia, and Oceania.[29]

Historians have argued that it was not just the logic of trade or its size that distinguished the nineteenth from previous centuries. O'Rourke and Williamson make a claim that a true globalization, in the sense of closer market integration driven by a sharp fall in trade and transportation cost, began only from the 1820s, whereas trade connections grew between 1500 and 1820 driven by demand and supply stimulations.[30] They take what de Vries calls a definition of 'hard globalization' and posit that the integration of markets to form an international commodity system could only happen when prices of basic commodities across the world started to converge as they did in the nineteenth century.[31] For instance, the cotton price spread between Bombay and Liverpool decreased from 57 to 20 per cent in the forty years between 1873 and 1913.[32] Other historians prefer instead a definition of so-called soft globalization based on the idea of a continuative and sustained exchange of goods across different world areas as a key identifier of a global market.[33] In defence of soft globalization, the process induced some of the key societal changes without which hard globalization would have been impossible, including financial innovation, the joint-stock company, codification of commercial law, mass demand for Asian tea or textiles, and the incentive to substitute imports and develop better ships (more on this point later). In short, the distinction between the weak eighteenth-century and the strong nineteenth-century globalization may be an artificial one.

## Trade and economic growth

The analysis of the nineteenth century brings to the fore the relationship between economic development (especially industrialization) and intercontinental trade. This topic has been at the centre of attention for economic historians for decades and has seen opposing opinions. A traditional approach going back to W. W. Rostow, and before him historians of the Commercial Revolution, argued that trade was key to capital accumulation. More recently, academic scholarship has considered a wider spectrum of socio-economic returns with C. A. Bayly arguing that merchant capitalists reaped the benefits of new global patterns of trade well before industrialization took place.[34] In the 1960s, Phyllis Deane, John Habakkuk, and Ralph Davis gave great attention to trade, but by the 1970s and 1980s, Joel Mokyr, Deirdre McCloskey, and Nick Crafts dismissed the existence of a strong connection between trade and economic growth, arguing that it was technological change rather than trade or capital accumulation that was the main driver of industrialization.[35] The Industrial Revolution became mostly an endogenous affair. In fact, they observed that Britain's terms of trade should have increased during the Industrial Revolution although in practice they fell due to cost-reducing technological innovation. They observed that trade reallocates resources to its existing optimum but does not shift that optimum itself.[36]

A more extreme position relies instead on counterfactual methodologies. Clark, O'Rourke, and Taylor show that as late as the 1850s the absence of trade with the New World would have had little impact on Britain's growth, as substitutes for the cotton, sugar, corn, and timber imported from the New World could be found in Asia and Eastern Europe. However, they also agree that after 1850 the British economy became highly dependent on foreign trade especially considering that its key sector, cotton textile manufacturing, sold 60 per cent of its production in foreign markets.[37] There is now the acknowledgement that trade in British industrial goods increased substantially during the period of the Industrial Revolution but that was due to falling prices. The overall outcome was that the value of exported goods increased at a much slower pace than the volume of traded goods.[38] O'Brien and Engerman, though sceptical of the overall importance of overseas markets for British economic growth, underline the increasing employment opportunities in export-oriented industries.[39] Furthermore, the expansion of commerce that preceded industrialization allowed the flourishing of legal, financial, and commercial institutions that underpinned the subsequent phase of industrialization and sustained growth.[40] Trade in the Atlantic strengthened the power of merchants and secured property rights.[41] Kenneth Pomeranz's ecological narrative shows through counterfactual scenarios that the imports of food and raw materials from the Americas were key to the lifting of environmental limits to growth in Europe and in Britain more specifically.[42]

A second debate on the relationship between trade and economic growth relates to the relationship between the richer industrial and the poorer economies worldwide. The nineteenth century saw a 'great specialization' of the world between the Western world (North) engaged mainly in the production and trade of industrial goods and a so-called Third World (South) specialized instead in the production of raw materials and foodstuff.[43] This is not a perfect differentiation as both Eastern Europe and the United States produced and traded extensively in raw materials and other industrial inputs. However, historians agree that in the nineteenth century trade facilitated the economic convergence between richer and poorer economies, thanks to the export growth in raw materials by non-industrialized countries.[44] Terms of trade swung in favour of non-industrial economies as the price of primary products increased over the course of the nineteenth century, while the price of manufactured commodities fell dramatically.[45]

A more cautious position is proposed by Patrick O'Brien who argues that if food and raw materials were a major import into Europe, the same could not be said of energy and minerals whose import from the other hemisphere remained negligible. Even for the case of raw materials such as cotton, oil seed, jute, hemp, dyestuffs, and wood, Europe's reliance on Asia, Africa, and Latin America decreased over the course of the nineteenth century as the supplies of these primary products from North America and Australia expanded. In 1913, Asia, Africa, and Latin America contributed less than 20 per cent of global trade, with Africa's contribution being as little as 3.7 per cent. In 1913, Europe received hardly any manufactured goods from beyond its borders, and only 20 per cent of all goods and services consumed by Europeans came from the Third World (Table 8.4).[46] Bairoch argues that we should, however, distinguish between the United Kingdom and the rest of the Western world. Britain was responsible for a large share of the trade between South and North while other 'North' economies traded more extensively between each other in both manufactured and primary products.[47]

**Table 8.4  Regional distribution of world trade in 1913  (in percentage)**

|  | World trade | World primary products exports (in %) | World manufactured exports (in %) |
|---|---|---|---|
| United Kingdom | 62 | 6.2 | 26.9 |
| Rest of Europe |  | 39.9 | 50.3 |
| North America | 13.2 | 17.2 | 11.1 |
| Asia | 11.1 | 14.7 | 6.2 |
| Africa | 3.7 | 22.0 |  |
| Rest of the world | 10 |  | 5.5 |

Source: Nicholas Crafts, 'Globalisation and Economic Growth: A Historical Perspective', World Economy, 27/1 (2004), 52; Kevin O'Rourke, 'Long-distance Trade between 1750 and 1914', in Mokyr, ed., The Oxford Encyclopedia of Economic History (Oxford: Oxford University Press, 2003), 368; Rondo Cameron, A Concise Economic History of the World (Oxford: Oxford University Press, 3rd ed. 1997), 304.

Over the twentieth century, one can observe a widening of the gap between rich and poor countries in per capita income.[48] O'Brien argues that trade did not benefit the Third World as it did not bring diversification of investment and most of the production of raw materials remained firmly in the hands of European entrepreneurs.[49] The shift in global trade in the twentieth century from primary products (64 per cent of all trade in 1913) to the trade in manufactured commodities (79 per cent of all trade in 1992) has exacerbated the isolation of Africa and parts of Asia in the post-colonial period.[50] Over the twentieth century, the North-to-North trade remained as high as 60 per cent of world trade, while South-to-South just 10 per cent. Only a third of all world trade took place between North and South.

A part of this divergence had occurred before 1950, when colonialism shaped the North–South economic exchanges, which brings us to the issue of politics.

## Trade and politics, 1500–1950

Growth of world trade between 1500 and 1930 is intimately connected with the growth of states, especially European colonial states. Why was trade and state power so closely interconnected? Did colonialism influence distribution of the gains from trade? Did politics create new patterns of international economic inequality? These three questions have been central to a number of debates on the implications of the modern world economy. Why was trade and power interdependent? The question can be approached from two ends – that of politics and that of business organization.

In the pre-industrial era, mercantilism created a reason for states to intervene in foreign trade. The European merchants needed licences and contracts to negotiate with indigenous merchants and rulers. The slave trade by its nature involved coercion as a business strategy. The slave trade in Africa was indigenous, extensive, and politically controlled before it turned into a source of supply of workers in the New World. European involvement in the African slave trade changed not only its volume but also its quality, with the introduction of a new kind of racialized chattel slavery proverbially ruthless in its instrumental brutality and unrelenting in its demand for work from these slaves, who were literally worked to death on a routine basis on British, Dutch, Portuguese, and French plantations. Such brutal and dehumanizing regimens did not exist in Africa before the arrival of Europeans. The depopulation of West Africa also had a long-term negative legacy. The trade also left a political legacy in the form of states that were readier to do opportunistic deals with the world market than to invest in the local economy and in the population living on it.[51]

European intrusion in the Indian Ocean around 1500 entailed the systematic use of gunships by the Portuguese and the subsequent attempts by them to tax trade. In the seventeenth and eighteenth centuries, naval power shifted from the Portuguese to the Dutch, the English, and the French. While these groups ordinarily relied on diplomacy and negotiation, they could in theory receive military and naval support from the sponsor states, which made them a different type of merchant group from what the region had seen before.[52] The merchant companies enjoying state monopoly can be seen as extensions of mercantilist states of Europe. Institutionally, the Dutch and the British attempts to use a more efficient and sparing use of power would suggest a successful strategy to internalize the heavy cost of protecting their monopoly from European rivals, private traders, and indigenous groups. As Findlay and O'Rourke show, in the eighteenth century, European expansion gave the English complete mastery over the slave trade, and gave the English, the Dutch, and the French territorial control in Asia and Africa.[53]

In India, the seeds of an empire were sown in the move by the British East India Company (and on a more limited scale by its rivals) to acquire sites on the coast for the creation of fortified ports. Thanks to these ports, as the Mughal Empire collapsed in the mid-eighteenth century and contests for power intensified in India, the British and the French companies found themselves well placed to join these contests and conduct proxy war between themselves. In this way, trading rivalry, combined with turmoil in India and Europe, shaped the emergence of modern imperialism. In Indonesia, the Dutch, who moved to consolidate their control on the world spice trade, saw it as a way to extend their territorial power. The consolidation of Dutch maritime power forged new links between the ports of East and Southeast Asia, even as it 'decisively decoupled historical trajectories in the archipelago from those in mainland [Southeast Asia]'.[54]

The propensity of the East India companies to engage in local politics raises the question, What kind of firms these were. Like all corporate firms, in the British East India Company too, there were 'principals' (shareholders) and 'agents' (employees stationed in trading ports). But unlike in modern firms, these two sets of actors were not located in close proximity to one another, nor were they able to communicate frequently or effectively. The limited ability of the principals to monitor the agents suggests two lessons on the nature of these firms. First, agents were given more freedom than would be allowed in a modern firm. They were more than salaried servants, and were given incentives to trade on the side, and their behaviour was monitored by an incentive-punishment mechanism. Studies on contract enforcement in the East India Company and the Hudson's Bay Company find that the incentive-punishment mechanism worked more or less effectively from the angle of the principals.[55]

Secondly, the agents' interest could differ systematically from that of the firm, partly because they were traders on the side and partly because they were exposed to certain types of political risks and opportunities that the principals did not face. Ordinarily, the divergence of interest was not a serious matter to the firm, but in the late eighteenth century, the divergence widened because the risks and opportunities involved in taking part in local politics changed. Adam Smith's famous criticism of the British East India Company in *The Wealth of Nations* (1776), in one view, needs to be seen in the context of this particular agency problem and its late-eighteenth-century manifestation.[56]

Subsequent to the formation of states, in India by the British East India Company and in Indonesia by the Dutch East India Company (VOC), economic policies in both retained a focus on trade. The influence of merchants and bankers behind British imperial policy has been explored in a well-known scholarship. The famous, if controversial, thesis of P. J. Cain and A. G. Hopkins that the support for the expansion of the British Empire formed of a coalition between landlords and capitalists is the most cited example.[57] Imperial history has also long reminded us of the deep connections that had developed between British manufacturing and services with European trading firms overseas. For example, the managing agency companies operating in India in the nineteenth century formed formal or informal partnerships with British counterparts that organized marketing and re-export businesses, and sometimes supplied finance and skilled manpower.

The British Empire functioned as if it wished to maintain open borders to trade in goods and services. Was this policy beneficial for the colonies? A recent empirical exercise shows that belonging to an empire roughly doubled trade relative to those countries that were not part of an empire. The use of a common language, the establishment of currency unions, 'the monetization of recently acquired colonies, and the establishment of preferential trade agreements and customs unions help to account for the observed increase in trade associated with empire'.[58] The finding needs to be qualified with the statement that within the British Empire, a greater share of the increased trade occurred in trade between Britain and the settler colonies of the New World.[59] But even for the non-settler colonies, the trade growth was unprecedented, not only in scale but also in a whole range of new relationships that it forged. For example, the opium trade linked China with India, while Dutch trading operations in East and Southeast Asia likewise integrated Japan and Burma in the Eurasian trade.

Was growth of trade under colonial conditions beneficial for the colonizer and the colonized peoples? For the colonizer, trade growth led to accumulation of wealth, integrated markets, and induced specialization and productivity gains. On the other hand, there is a view that the captive market of the imperial domain made the colonizer, Britain being the eminent example, less innovative than it would be otherwise. The belief feeds into an explanation of British decline in the twentieth-century world economy.[60] Of course, the strength of the belief should depend on how 'captive' or 'soft' imperial markets really were, and in turn, what we mean by these terms. One investigation concludes that it is difficult to presume that businesses could take colonial markets for granted simply because they were colonial markets.[61]

Was trade growth beneficial to the colonized people? In answer to the question, four points need to be considered. First, there was sometimes an element of pure 'extraction' using state power and institutional manipulation by the settlers or the state. But such distortions were more the exceptions than the norm.

Secondly, trade growth caused 'de-industrialization' in the colonies. The trade boom after industrialization began was driven by a large fall in the prices of manufactured goods produced in Western Europe, and a rise in the demand for primary commodities available in the tropics. So large was the rise in demand and so large the technological leap that they jointly led to a long-term increase in the terms of trade, that is, in the price of tropical exports as a ratio of the price of its imports. The tropics experienced a better utilization of idle land and mining capacity, and could buy manufactured goods in increasing quantity and increasingly better quality over time for an unchanging bundle of primary products. On the other hand, most colonies were deprived of the spillover benefits of industrialization (innovation, increasing returns to scale), experienced a decline of its own artisan manufactures, and experienced 'Dutch disease' or shift of resources away from other sectors towards exportable goods and more exposure of the export economies to commodity price fluctuations.[62] De-industrialization did occur in many primary-product-exporting economies, but not in all. In East Asia, terms of trade *fell* in the long run. In South Asia, the rise happened earlier and to a much smaller extent than in Southeast Asia, Latin America, the Middle East, and the European periphery. India did not de-industrialize as much as the other regions did, and experienced a significant growth of cotton textile mill industry.[63] The emergence of a factory textile industry shows that while trade growth might have hurt the artisans, it led to accumulation of capital by merchants, who invested money in modern factory industry.

Third, despite growth of trade, specialization in a small basket of commodities for export exposed the colonies to cyclical fluctuations. In the mid-twentieth century, these risks were a ground for trade pessimism. Individual country studies, however, show that global terms of trade boom in favour of primary commodity exporters on the whole benefited the exporting countries until the early twentieth century, even when the process increased inequality between the exporting sector and the rest of the economy.[64]

Fourth, trade growth and factor market integration were connected processes in the colonial territories. For example, British India relied heavily on net import of skilled services and capital to run public administration, to finance and then run the railways, to maintain the army, and to create and manage private businesses. To fund its deficit on the services account, the regime needed a trade surplus. Indian nationalists called the deficit a 'drain' of potential saving and investment. This interpretation remains controversial, but the interdependence of the growth of trade and services was a feature of many colonial relationships. The East India companies left a legacy on trade in services worldwide. The emergence of a secondary market in VOC shares, for example, helped establish Amsterdam as the world's leading financial centre.[65] The close interdependence between trade and investment that had developed during the first globalization is illustrated with railroad construction in India and Argentina in the late nineteenth century. With the development of a market in London for Argentine debt, foreign money then found other avenues, such as infrastructure. Analysis of the Baring crisis in the 1890s finds that trade also acted as a channel of transmission of the crisis.[66]

Migration, of course, was one of these factor market effects. Before 1800, long-distance migration flows were not always driven by market forces. New works on the early history of empires written by cultural historians shed light on movements driven by free migration, slavery, the military labour market, forced migration, exile and penal colonies, and of course settlement on new land frontiers.[67] By contrast, the sugar and cotton plantations in the Americas integrated world trade and migration closely. The largest flows of the post-1800 migration were driven by economic concerns, though not always connected with international trade.[68] After the transatlantic telegraph started working (c. 1858), it was possible for European workers in Africa and the Americas to remit money home.[69] To some extent at least, trade, by encouraging migration, stimulated factor income flows. Studies on the New World export economies suggest a link between export of goods, investment boom, migration of labour in new fields where investment took place, government expansion by borrowing abroad, migration of labour, and export of capital, though the interpretation of the causal chain between these variables remains open.[70]

What can we conclude from this discussion on the effects of trade upon the colonized world? The generalization that trade-induced poverty is hard to sustain. A cautious generalization could be that port cities gained from trade in commodities and services irrespective of where they were located. Philip Curtin's work on trade diaspora made global historians familiar with the idea that a string of cosmopolitan coastal settlements played a pivotal role in trade before modern transportation and communication technologies forged a closer link between the ports and their hinterland. Abu-Lughod's phrase 'archipelago of ports' has a similar connotation.[71] Strikingly, maritime trade and port cities retained this role in organizing world trade long after the advent of industrialization. Bayly shows in *The Birth of the Modern World* that most of the world's cities in the nineteenth century were trading cities rather than industrial ones.[72] Located in very different world regions, they collectively represented a convergence in institutions, living standards, political and cultural discourses, and bourgeois interest.

The convergence, wrought by the connections that trade created, in many cases included a late industrialization element. In this way, Bombay, Calcutta, Shanghai, Singapore, and Sao Paulo formed part of a convergent club of cities that also included New York and Liverpool. This is not to dispute that on an international scale inequality increased, but the roots of that inequality need to be searched in production conditions and resource endowments, rather than trading conditions.

## Conclusion

This chapter considers some of the main ways trade shaped a new world economy. Specialization, market integration, growth of companies, expansion in financial services, industrialization, and migration of labour and capital were some of the ways trade could have such an effect. The institutional effects, on commercial law or evolution of the company, for example, did not just follow from market integration, but also from the particular legacies of early modern trade, such as the presence of the East India companies in those parts of Asia and Africa where family firms ruled the world of trade.

Economic historians will continue to explore whether international economic inequality, the distance between rich and poor countries, also increased because of trade. While that debate remains unfinished, it is necessary to point out that whether in a richer country or in a poorer one, the cities engaged in international trade were often distinct from the rest of the country as the ones with more firms, more services, and more capitalists committed to keep the system going. Equally, there were cities and regions that were 'left out' of the capital accumulation process that trade encouraged.

Liberal regimes of the nineteenth century were strongly connected to colonial power. Liberalism as an ideal did not live easily with lack of liberty and political choices in a wide area of the globe, but since the wealthy communities in these areas developed a stake in openness and globalization, support for an independence movement was initially limited. The situation changed in the interwar period. The First World War disrupted trade completely, and empowered the wealthy indigenous businesses in the colonies. The Great Depression induced indigenous capitalists to look inward and towards the home market. Some of them were now more willing to fund the independence movement. By the mid-twentieth century, the world economy that had started taking shape from the trade between Europe and the tropical regions from the 1600s had more or less ended.

## Notes

1. P. D. Curtin (1984), *Cross Cultural Trade in World History*. Cambridge: Cambridge University Press, 251.

2. R. Cameron (1997), *A Concise Economic History of the World*, 3rd edn. Oxford: Oxford University Press, 296; V. Zamagni (2015), *Perché l'Europa ha cambiato il mondo: una storia economica*. Bologna: Il Mulino, 145.

3. M. D. Bordo (2002), 'Globalization in historical perspective', *Business Economics*, January, 22.

4. J. Abu-Lughod (1993), 'The world system of the 13th century', in M. Adas (ed.), *Islamic & European Expansion: The Forging of a Global Order*. Philadelphia: Temple University Press, 75–103; Id. (1991), *Before European Hegemony: The World System A.D. 1250–1350*. New York: Oxford University Press.

5. D. Christian (2000), 'Silk roads or steppe roads? The silk roads in world history', *Journal of World History*, 11 (1), 1–26.

6. J. de Vries (2003), 'Long-distance trade between 1500 and 1750', in J. Mokyr (ed.), *The Oxford Encyclopedia of Economic History*. Oxford: Oxford University Press, 361.

7.  R. C. Allen (2009), *The British Industrial Revolution in Global Perspective*. Cambridge: Cambridge University Press, 107.

8.  J. de Vries (2003), 'Connecting Europe and Asia: A Quantitative Analysis of the Cape Route Trade, 1497-1795', in D. O. Flynn, A. Giráldez, and R. von Glahn, (eds.), *Global Connections and Monetary History, 1470-1800*. Aldershot: Ashgate, 35–106.

9.  The debate concerns whether the axis of world trade was located in Europe or Asia, especially China. For different positions and arguments in this debate, see A. Gunder Frank (1998), *ReOrient: Global Economy in the Asian Age*. Berkeley: University of California Press, esp. ch. 2; P. Vries (2015), *State, Economy and the Great Divergence: Great Britain and China, 1680s-1850s*. London: Bloomsbury, 348–9.

10. de Vries, 'Connecting Europe and Asia'.

11. D. O. Flynn and A. Giráldez (1996), 'China and the Manila Galleons', in D. O. Flynn (ed.), *World Silver and Monetary History in the 16th and 17th Centuries*. Aldershot: Variorum; Idem (1997) (eds), *Metals and Monies in an Emerging Global Economy*; Idem (2002), 'Cycles of silver: Global economic unity through the mid-eighteenth century', *Journal of World History* 13 (1), 1–16.

12. See the chapters by Trevor Burnard and by Alejandra Irigoin in this volume.

13. For a general account of the Atlantic slave trade, see H. S. Klein (2010), *The Atlantic Slave Trade*, 2nd edn. Cambridge: Cambridge University Press. On the transition from slave trade to other types of trade in one large exporting region, see R. Law (2009), 'Introduction', in R. Law (ed.), *From Slave Trade to 'Legitimate' Commerce: The Commercial Transition in Nineteenth-Century West Africa*. Cambridge: Cambridge University Press, 1–31.

14. Allen, *Industrial Revolution*, 20.

15. M. Berg (2004), 'In pursuit of luxury: global history and British consumer goods in the eighteenth century', *Past & Present*, 182, 85–142.

16. J. Brewer (1989), *The Sinews of Power: War, Money and the English State, 1688-1783*. London: Unwin; C. Knick Harkey (2004), 'Trade: Discovery, mercantilism and technology', in R. Floud and P. Johnson (eds), *The Cambridge Economic History of Modern Britain*. Cambridge: Cambridge University Press, 188. On the role of duties, see W. Ashworth (2003), *Customs and Excise: Trade, Production and Consumption in England, 1640-1845*. Oxford: Oxford University Press; and Idem (2017), *The Industrial Revolution: The State, Knowledge and Global Trade*. London: Bloomsbury.

17. Vries, *State, Economy and the Great Divergence*, 339–41.

18. de Vries, 'Long-distance trade', 364. See also Idem (2010), 'The limits of globalisation in the early modern world.' See also M. Berg, 'Consumption in eighteenth- and early nineteenth-century Britain', in Floud and Johnson (eds), *Cambridge Economic History*, 366–7; Broadberry, et al., *British Economic Growth*, 287; C. Knick Harley (2004), 'Trade: Discovery, Mercantilism and Technology', in R. Floud and P. Johnson (eds), *The Cambridge Economic History of Modern Britain*. Cambridge: Cambridge University Press, 176; K. Pomeranz (2000), *The Great Divergence. China, Europe and the Making of the Modern World Economy*. Princeton: Princeton University Press, esp. ch. 2.

19. Berg, 'Consumption', 365.

20. Harley, 'Trade', 191.

21. P. K. O'Brien (1997), 'Intercontinental trade and the development of the Third Word since the Industrial Revolution', *Journal of Word History*, 8 (1), 77.

22. Curtin, *Cross Cultural Trade*, 252. This is a factor recently underlined by Luigi Pascali who, however, argues that the adoption of steam shipping in particular helped market integration but that the process benefited a small number of Western countries. L. Pascali (2014), 'The wind of change: Maritime technology, trade and economic development', *Warwick Economics Research Papers Series* (TWERPS), no. 1049.

23. O'Brien, 'Intercontinental trade', 80 and 84.

24. Bairoch and R. Kozul-Wright (1996), 'Globalization myths: Some historical reflections on integration, industrialization and growth in the world economy', *UNCTAD Working Paper*, 113, 5. See also Bairoch (1993), *Economics and World History: Myths and Paradoxes*. New York: Harvester, 16–29.

25. The concept of 'non-competing' good is somewhat misleading as practically all goods are substitutable. In this case, we mean the production and trade of identical goods.

26. C. A. Bayly (2004), *The Birth of the Modern World*. London: Blackwells, 44–5. See also Idem (2002), '"Archaic" and "Modern" Globalization in the Eurasian and African Arena, c. 1750–1850', in A. G. Hopkins (ed.), *Globalization in World History*. London: Pimlico, 47–73.

27. Curtin, *Cross Cultural Trade*, 252.

28. Cameron, *A Concise Economic History*, 308–9 and 311.

29. K. O'Rourke (2003), 'Long-distance trade between 1750 and 1914', in Mokyr (ed.), *The Oxford Encyclopedia of Economic History*, 367.

30. K. O'Rourke and J. G. Williamson (2002), 'After Columbus: Explaining Europe's overseas trade boom, 1500–1800', *Journal of Economic History*, 62 (2), 417–56; and Idem (2002), 'When did globalisation begin?', *Journal of Economic History*, 62 (1), 23–50. See also, Idem (2000), *Globalization and History*, esp. chs. 3–6.

31. This has been recently challenged by P. de Zwart (2016), *Globalization and the Colonial Origins of the Great Divergence*. Leiden: Brill.

32. O'Rourke and Williamson, 'After Columbus'.

33. On soft and hard globalization, see de Vries, 'The limits of globalisation'.

34. Bayly, *The Birth of the Modern World*, 52.

35. J. Mokyr (1977), 'Demand vs. supply in the Industrial Revolution', *Journal of Economic History*, 37 (4), 981–1008; D. N. McCloskey (1981), *Enterprise and Trade in Victorian Britain: Essays in Historical Economics*. London: Allen & Unwin, 139–54; D. N. McCloskey and R. Thomas (1981), 'Overseas trade and empire, 1700–1820', in R. Floud and D. N. McCloskey (eds), *The Economic History of Britain, 1700-Present*, vol. 1. Cambridge: Cambridge University Press, 87–102; N.F.R. Crafts (1985), *British Economic Growth during the Industrial Revolution*. Oxford: Clarendon.

36. P. Vries (2013), *Escaping Poverty: The Origins of Modern Economic Growth*. Vienna and Göttingen: Vienna University Press and Vandenhoeck und Ruprecht, 283.

37. G. Clark, K. O'Rourke and Alan N. Taylor (2008), 'Made in America? The New World, the Old, and the Industrial Revolution', *American Economic Review*, 98 (2), 523 and 527. See also, Idem (2014), 'The growing dependence of Britain on trade during the Industrial Revolution', *Scandinavian Economic History Review*, 62 (2), 126.

38. Harley, 'Trade', 199. One of the critiques against the approach that minimize the contribution of trade to economic growth is that it is based on static approaches that do not take into consideration both capital accumulation and technological change. K. O'Rourke, L. Prados de la Escosura and G. Daudin (2010), 'Trade and empire', in S. Broadberry and K. O'Rourke

(eds), *The Cambridge Economic History of Modern Europe*. Cambridge: Cambridge University Press, 110.

39. P. K. O'Brien and S. L. Engerman (1991), 'Exports and the growth of the British economy from the Glorious Revolution to the peace of Amiens', in B. R. Solow (ed.), *Slavery and the Rise of the Atlantic System*. Cambridge: Cambridge University Press, 177–209. See P. K. O'Brien (1982), 'European economic development; and S. L. Engerman (1972), 'The slave trade and British capital formation in the eighteenth century: A comment on the Williams thesis', *Business History Review*, 46 (4), 430–43.

40. Harley, 'Trade', 190.

41. O'Rourke, Prados de la Escosura and Daudin, 'Trade and empire', 112.

42. Pomeranz, *Great Divergence*.

43. Vries, *Escaping Poverty*, 272.

44. Bairoch and Kozul-Wright, 'Globalization myths', 5.

45. Vries, *Escaping Poverty*, 272.

46. O'Brien, 'Intercontinental trade', 88–9.

47. Bairoch and Kozul-Wright, 'Globalization myths', 9.

48. N. Crafts (2004), 'Globalisation and economic growth: A historical perspective', *World Economy*, 27 (1), 50.

49. O'Brien, 'Intercontinental trade', 95.

50. J. Foreman-Peck (2003), 'Long-distance trade since 1914', in Mokyr (ed.), *The Oxford Encyclopedia of Economic History*, 374–5.

51. Discussed in M. Vaughan (2006), 'Africa and the birth of the modern world', *Transactions of the Royal Historical Society*, Sixth Series, 16, 143–62.

52. On the Dutch case, see J. I. Israel (1989), *Dutch Primacy in World Trade, 1585-1740*. Oxford: Clarendon Press.

53. R. Findlay and K. H. O'Rourke (2007), *Power and Plenty: Trade, War, and the World Economy in the Second Millennium*. Princeton and Oxford: Princeton University Press.

54. V. Lieberman (2008), 'Protected rimlands and exposed zones: Reconfiguring premodern Eurasia', *Comparative Studies in Society and History*, 50 (3), 692–723, cit. 720.

55. S. Hejeebu (2005), 'Contract enforcement in the English East India Company', *Journal of Economic History*, 6 (2), 496–523; A. M. Carlos and S. Nicholas (1990), 'Agency problems in early chartered companies: The case of the Hudson's Bay Company', *Journal of Economic History*, 50 (4), 853–75.

56. G. M. Anderson and R. D. Tollison (1982), 'Adam Smith's analysis of joint-stock companies', *Journal of Political Economy*, 90 (6), 1237–56. P. J. Cain and A. G. Hopkins (1987), 'Gentlemanly capitalism and British expansion overseas II: New imperialism, 1850–1945', *Economic History Review*, 40 (1), 1–26.

57. For a criticism of the view, see R. Hyam (2010), *Understanding the British Empire*. New York: Cambridge University Press.

58. K. J. Mitchener and M. Weidenmier (2008), 'Trade and empire', *Economic Journal*, 118 (533), 1805–34.

59. G. B. Magee (2007), 'The importance of being British? Imperial factors and the growth of British imports, 1870-1960', *Journal of Interdisciplinary History*, 37 (3), 341–69.

60. On British declinism in general, essays compiled in J.-Dormois and M. Dintenfass (eds) (1999), *British Industrial Decline*. London: Routledge, are useful.

61. A. Thompson and G. Magee (2003), 'A soft touch? British industry, empire markets, and the self-governing dominions, c.1870–1914', *Economic History Review*, 56 (3), 689–717. See also Idem (2010), *Empire and Globalisation: Networks of People, Goods and Capital in the British World, c. 1850–1914*. Cambridge: Cambridge University Press.

62. The Dutch disease syndrome, which occurs when a specific tradeable draws resources away, can frustrate prospects of industrialization and diversification of economic activity. Angus Deaton applies the concept to post-war African development, the principle of it could apply to some tropical colonial regions as well. A. Deaton (1999), 'Commodity prices and growth in Africa', *Journal of Economic Perspectives*, 13 (3), 23–40.

63. J. G. Williamson (2011), *Trade and Poverty: When the Third World Fell Behind*. Cambridge Mass. and London: The MIT Press. See also, Tirthankar Roy (1999), *Traditional Industry in the Economy of Colonial India*. Cambridge: Cambridge University Press.

64. N. H. Leff (1973), 'Tropical trade and development in the nineteenth century: The Brazilian experience', *Journal of Political Economy*, 81 (3), 678–96.

65. O. Gelderblom and J. Jonker (2004), 'Completing a financial revolution: The finance of the Dutch East India trade and the rise of the Amsterdam capital market, 1595–1612', *Journal of Economic History*, 64 (3), 641–72.

66. K. J. Mitchener and M. D. Weidenmier (2008), 'The Baring crisis and the great Latin American meltdown of the 1890s', *Journal of Economic History*, 68 (2), 462–500.

67. For example, K. Ward (2009), *Networks of Empire: Forced Migration in the Dutch East India Company*. New York: Cambridge University Press.

68. Sunil S. Amrith (2011), *Migration and Diaspora in Modern Asia*. New York: Cambridge University Press.

69. G. B. Magee and A. S. Thompson (2006), 'The global and local: Explaining migrant remittance flows in the English-speaking world, 1880–1914', *Journal of Economic History*, 66 (1), 177–202.

70. H. W. Richardson (1972), 'British emigration and overseas investment, 1870–1914', *Economic History Review*, 25 (1), 99–113; Leff, 'Tropical trade and development'.

71. Abu-Lughod, 'The world system in the thirteenth century'.

72. Bayly, *The Birth of the Modern World*.

# CHAPTER 9
## THE GLOBAL ENVIRONMENT AND THE WORLD ECONOMY SINCE 1500
*J. R. McNeill*

The world economy and the global environment form the warp and weft of the fabric of history. Always and everywhere, the global environment has affected the world economy. Always and everywhere, the world economy has affected the global environment. Economy and environment have been tightly bound together, and have evolved together, often slowly but sometimes in leaps and bounds. This chapter will focus more on the leaps than on the pauses between them.

As a rule, the environment has shaped the economy by defining the limits of the possible. Climate, soils, vegetation, animals, diseases, waters, and winds (and a few other components of the environment) have always shaped what human communities could produce, at what costs, and in what amounts. The environment never fully determined what or how much people might produce. Culture, choice, contingency, and social circumstance (and a few other components of social systems) always played a role too. But environments did determine the limits of the possible. People might have chosen to raise camels in Iceland or build ships in the Sahara, but productivity would have been low due to environmental constraints.

As another rule, economic activity always altered the environment. Often those alterations were direct, as in the case of hunting or farming. Sometimes they were less direct, as in the case of trade. Trade, say of wine for wool, inspired one set of production decisions over all others, and thus shaped the regional environments where wine and wool were produced. In the contemporary world, some economic activities have only negligible environmental impacts – devising training plans for amateur triathletes, for example. Others have outsized impacts, magnified by powerful technologies unknown in prior times – squeezing oil out of Alberta's tar sands, for example. By and large, pre-modern economies were tied more directly to the natural environment than modern ones. Modern economies, by and large, have had larger, less local, and less consistent environmental consequences than did pre-modern ones.

This chapter takes up a small subset of the range of possible subjects involving the global environment and the world economy since 1500. They are, however, among the most consequential. First comes the intercontinental exchanges of plants, animals, and microbes following the discovery of oceanic sailing routes in the late fifteenth century. Second is the environmental implications of the creation and expansion of plantation economies, mainly in the American tropics after 1640. Third is the global environmental implications of industrialization. And fourth is a rumination upon the concept of the Anthropocene.

## Biological exchanges, 1492–1800

Nearly fifty years ago, Alfred Crosby assembled the scattered stories of the transfers of crops, weeds, animals, and microbes across the Atlantic between the Americas and (mainly) Europe into the concept of the Columbian Exchange. The concept deserves amplification, because in his day, Crosby could not do full justice to the involvement of Africa and Asia in intercontinental biotic exchanges.[1] Moreover, lesser currents of exchanges developed across the Pacific in the wake of Magellan (c. 1480–1521), important especially for the Philippines and sometimes defined as the Magellan Exchange.[2] Some scholars consider the post-Columbian epoch of biological exchange so fundamental as to merit its own term in the style of earth history's epochs: the Homogenocene.[3]

After 1450, mariners, most of them Atlantic Europeans, linked almost every nook and cranny of the humanly habitable earth into a biologically interactive web. The world's seas and deserts no longer served to isolate different biogeographical regions. The world became one without biological borders, as plants, animals, and microbes migrated wherever ecological conditions permitted their spread, although how soon and how thoroughly they did so normally depended on human factors such as transport technologies and skills, and patterns of trade, production, and politics.[4]

Columbus inaugurated regular exchanges across the Atlantic in 1492. The most conspicuous result was that Amerindians acquired a large suite of devastating diseases hitherto unfamiliar to them. Those diseases included smallpox, measles, mumps, whooping cough, and influenza, all acute viral infections which had become widespread in the sprawling interactive zone of Eurasia and northern Africa. From Japan to Senegambia, these infections were usually endemic, childhood diseases (sometimes called 'crowd diseases' because they require large, interacting populations to stay in circulation) that contributed to high rates of infant mortality. But most adults were survivors, and either resistant or fully immune to most or all of these infections. In addition to the crowd diseases, the Columbian Exchange brought some lethal vector-borne African diseases to the Americas, such as yellow fever and malaria. In the Americas, all these were new diseases, so no Amerindians carried any acquired resistance. Thus these infections ravaged the American hemisphere between 1500 and 1650. Together with widespread violence, expropriation, and famines caused by European conquests, these diseases lowered populations by 60 to 90 per cent in one of the two largest demographic disasters in world history, the other being the Black Death in the mid-fourteenth century.[5]

The sharp reduction in population in the Americas, over the period 1492–1650, carried both environmental and economic consequences on multiple scales. Within the Americas, it opened the way for the creation of new wilderness. With less farming, hunting, and fire, wild plants and animal species recolonized formerly humanized landscapes. On the global scale, resurgent vegetation in the Americas took some carbon out of the atmosphere, weakening the greenhouse effect slightly, and perhaps adding a chill to the Little Ice Age.[6] In economic terms, the population catastrophe checked global GDP growth and reduced the contributions to it made by various world regions, notably by shrinking the economy of the Americas. It also paved the way for the formation of a plantation complex, as will be discussed later in this chapter.

The Amerindians had little in the way of lethal infectious disease to export to Africa and Eurasia. When the first migrants arrived in North America some 15,000 years ago (or more), they passed through northeastern Siberia and Alaska during an Ice Age. Brutal cold is not conducive to the survival of most pathogens.[7] Beyond that filtering effect, the first Americans had left Siberia when no animals but dogs had been domesticated, so that the human infections derived from cattle, camels, and pigs (e.g. smallpox, measles, and influenza) had not yet emerged. Once arrived in the Americas, Amerindians did not domesticate any herd animals other than alpacas and llamas, which seem, by chance, not to have hosted pathogens that evolved into agents of human disease. For these reasons, as regards pathogens, the Columbian Exchange was extremely unequal: the Americas received a lot and gave only a little.[8]

The same was true of domesticated animals. The Americas had few domesticated animals, and those few (e.g. turkeys, llamas, and alpacas) did not travel well. By contrast, Eurasian species flourished when transported to the Americas. Cattle, goats, sheep, pigs, and horses were the most important animal immigrants to the Americas. The immigrant animals provided Amerindians with new sources of animal protein, hides, and wool. Horses and oxen offered an important source of traction, making ploughing feasible in the Americas for the first time, and improving transportation possibilities through wheeled vehicles and greater variety of pack animals. That extended the potential of commerce and specialization, inviting Smithian growth wherever populations recovered.

Horses in North America upset the economic and political order. The Amerindians of the North American prairies acquired horses from Spanish Mexico in the seventeenth century, and some of them quickly mastered the equestrian arts. On horseback, they became far more adept as bison hunters, solving any subsistence problems as long as the bison lasted. Moreover, those with horses easily inflicted military defeat on those without, so by the mid-nineteenth century, peoples such as the Sioux and Comanche had built considerable 'empires' on the basis of mounted warfare.[9]

Equestrian Amerindians also used their military prowess to create sizeable slave trades to Mexico. Spanish imperial legislation from 1542 had banned the enslavement of Amerindians, but did not forbid the purchase of people already enslaved. This law had the unintended effect of outsourcing the business of capture of people for the Mexican market to the horse nomads of North America, who from 1680 until 1870 or so seized women and children from communities that lacked the military power to protect them. Thus the Columbian Exchange in animals affected the Americas in political as well as economic respects.

The Columbian Exchange was more even-handed in its economic impacts when it came to crops. The Eurasian staples of wheat, rye, barley, and rice met welcoming niches in the Americas. Sometimes those niches had to be created through human (and animal) labour, as for example with rice. Some of the new crops could survive in cold and dry landscapes where indigenous crops fared poorly. Aside from grains, the Americas also acquired citrus fruits, bananas, grapes, and figs from Eurasia, and millets, sorghum, yams, okra, and watermelon from Africa. So the new food crops extended the possibilities of American agriculture and allowed a more varied diet. But they did not constitute a vast improvement, because the Americas already had maize and potatoes and plenty of fruits and vegetables.

Drug crops changed the Americas at least as profoundly as the new food crops. Sugar, both a mild drug and a food, became the mainstay of a plantation economy based on African slave labour. Coffee, from Ethiopia and Arabia, also became a plantation crop in the eighteenth century. Without these imported crops, the plantation complex of the Americas would have been much smaller (see later in this chapter and Trevor Burnard's chapter in this volume).

Maize and potatoes, together with cassava, tomatoes, cacao, peanuts, sweet potato, pumpkins, squashes, and pineapples, formed the core contribution of the Americas to global agriculture. South America also gave tobacco to the world. Some of these crops had revolutionary consequences in Africa and Eurasia. Potatoes, for example, nicely suited soil and climate conditions across Northern Europe from Ireland to Russia. In Europe, potatoes contributed to a surge of population growth in the eighteenth and nineteenth centuries, which helped supply the manpower for both overseas empires and the Industrial

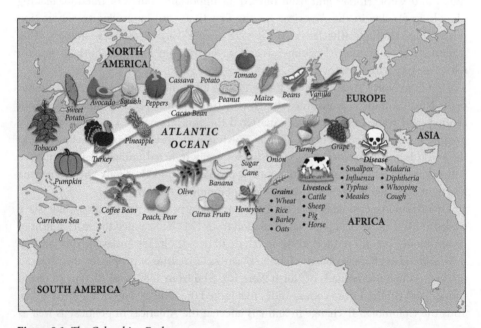

**Figure 9.1** The Columbian Exchange.

Revolution.[10] Potatoes stored well, especially in cold climates, and they provide excellent nutrition. In their native Andes, where production and storage had been raised to a high art, potatoes had helped fuel the expansion of the Inca Empire in the fifteenth century. A few centuries later they played a broadly similar role in Northern Europe.[11]

Maize, another American crop, had a more diffuse impact than the potato. It did well in conditions as varied as those of Southern Europe, China, and large swathes of Africa. Maize allowed new lands to be brought under cultivation, because it prospered where grains and tubers would not. It undergirded population growth and famine resistance in China and Southern Europe, but nowhere was it more influential than in Africa. In the two centuries after 1550, maize became a staple in Atlantic Africa, from Angola to Senegambia. Different varieties suited the several different rainfall regimes in Africa, and improved chances of surviving drought.

In addition, maize stores much better than millets, sorghums, or tubers. It thus allowed chiefs and kings to maximize their power by centralizing the storage and distribution of food. In the West African forest zone, maize encouraged the formation of larger states. The Asante kingdom embarked on a programme of expansion after the 1670s, spearheaded by armies which carried dried maize with them on distant campaigns. Maize also served well as a portable food for merchant caravans, which contributed to commercialization in Atlantic Africa, including the slave trade. The slave trade could more easily reach far inland if merchants, and their human property, had an easily portable food supply. Storehouses of maize also made it more practical to imprison large numbers of slaves in the infamous barracoons of the West African coast. Just as sugar and coffee heightened the demand in the Americas for slave imports, so too maize within Africa increased the practicality of slave exports.[12]

Cassava, also known as manioc, was the Americas' other great contribution to African agriculture. A native of Brazil, cassava is admirably suited to drought and poor soils and resistant to many crop pests. Like maize it provided a portable food that underlay state formation and expansion in West Africa and Angola. Cassava, like potatoes, need not be harvested at a particular season but may be left in the ground for weeks or more. So it is an ideal crop for people who might need to run away for their own safety, for example, people routinely subject to slave raiding. In this respect it served as a counterpoint to maize: it helped peasantries to flee and survive slave raids, while maize helped slavers to conduct and extend their business.[13] Together, maize and cassava gave Africa a much larger stock of portable and storable food, making the continent more like the rice lands of Asia and grain lands of western Eurasia, more likely to sustain long-distance trade and larger state structures. Africanists do not adopt this nomenclature, but they might well speak of pre-Columbian and post-Columbian African history.

The Columbian Exchange was the largest, fastest, and most important intercontinental biological transfer in world history, but it was not the only one. A modest trans-Pacific exchange resulted from Magellan's voyages (1519–22), at first affecting chiefly the Philippines, and intensified in the wake of Captain Cook's meanderings throughout the world's largest ocean in the late eighteenth century. The Pacific Islands, rather than the ocean's rim, felt the greatest effects. As in the Americas (or in Australia after 1788), the most striking result was sharp depopulation in the wake of repeated epidemics. Many American food crops became important in East Asia, such as sweet potatoes, maize, and peanuts in south China, but they probably arrived not across the Pacific in the wake of Magellan, but across the Atlantic and the Indian Oceans via Portuguese and Dutch traders.[14]

Taken together, the whirlwind of intercontinental biological exchange in the centuries between 1500 and 1800 brought astounding changes around the world. It led to demographic catastrophes in lands unfamiliar with the crowd diseases. It improved the quantity and reliability of food supplies almost everywhere. In cases where horses were new, it reshuffled political relations by providing a new basis for warfare.

All these early modern exchanges carried historical consequences. European imperialism, in the Americas, Australia, and New Zealand, simultaneously promoted and was promoted by the spread of European (or more usually Eurasian) animals, plants, and diseases. Europeans brought a biota that unconsciously worked as a team to favour the spread of European settlers, European power, and Eurasian species, and thereby to create what Alfred Crosby called neo-Europes – including Australia, New Zealand, most of North America, southern Brazil, Uruguay, and Argentina.[15]

Beyond the neo-Europes, something of a neo-Africa emerged in the Americas. More than ten million Africans arrived in the Americas in slave ships between 1550 and 1860. Slave ships also brought West African rice, which became not only the foundation of the coastal economy in South Carolina and Georgia in the eighteenth century, but important in Surinam as well. Other African crops came too: okra, sesame, and (although not in slave ships) coffee. All this combined to create a world where indigenous culture, including foodstuffs, was partially absorbed into a neo-African matrix. In this it resembled the neo-Europes. But at the same time neo-Africa was profoundly different from the neo-Europes: until the Haitian Revolution (1791–1804), nowhere in the Americas were Africans and people of African descent politically, economically, or socially powerful, whereas Europeans and their descendants soon dominated the neo-Europes.

As the Columbian Exchange indicates, sailing ships brought the continents together as never before. But they did not prove hospitable conveyances to every form of life. They filtered out a few species that could not survive a long journey. The age of steam, and then of air travel, broke down the remaining barriers to biological exchange, accelerating the dispersal of old and new migratory species alike. Although its greatest impacts came in the sixteenth and seventeenth centuries, in a sense the Columbian Exchange never ended. American raccoons, grey squirrels, and muskrats for example colonized parts of Europe in the nineteenth and twentieth centuries. Nor did the Magellan Exchange come to an end. If anything, it sped up in the nineteenth and twentieth centuries, not least because of deliberate introductions of species such as the kiwi fruit (from China to New Zealand to Chile and California, and Southern Europe) and eucalyptus trees (from Australia to almost everywhere). But the economically (and demographically) transformative impacts of biological globalization came mainly between 1500 and 1800.

## The plantation regime in the Americas, 1550–1850

The plantation system of the Americas, transplanted from Mediterranean and Atlantic islands in the early sixteenth century, occupied a huge zone of Atlantic America, from northeastern Brazil to Chesapeake Bay, in which the slave plantation was the primary mode of production. The ecological significance of the plantation system had several aspects.

The first point is the simplest one, one which historians and geographers have been making for twenty or thirty years now, which is that every plantation, whether of tobacco, cotton, rice, sugar, or coffee, typically required the clearing of forests to make room for planting crops. Beginning in the 1550s, a surge of deforestation swept over the coastlands of northeastern Brazil and then from the 1620s the smaller islands of the eastern Caribbean motivated by the desire to clear more space for plantation crops. The surge reached the larger Caribbean islands by the 1690s and climaxed in Cuba in the nineteenth century. The same process was under way on a very considerable scale in the American South, c. 1690–1860, where tobacco and cotton plantations likewise required the clearing of forests.[16]

One entirely inadvertent consequence of this land cover change in the Caribbean was improved breeding and survival conditions for two kinds of mosquitoes, the vectors of malaria and yellow fever. With respect to *Anopheles* mosquitoes, the vectors of malaria, deforestation in those Caribbean islands with mountains and hills changed the hydrological situation by increasing run-off, floods, siltation, and deposition in the lowlands, which in turn created more marshland, swamps, and wetlands around the coasts of the islands. Montserrat and Martinique, just to give two examples, became the perfect breeding grounds for *Anopheles* mosquitoes, which thrive in swampy terrain.

The *Aedes aegypti* mosquito, the vector for yellow fever, is particularly connected to the sugar plantation, rather than to plantations in general. *A. aegypti* is a rather peculiar mosquito; it has a strong preference for laying eggs in artificial water containers, for example, buckets, pots, and wells. It is therefore effectively a domesticated mosquito which thrives on its association with human beings – it almost never lays eggs in puddles, ponds, or ditches, as most mosquitoes do. This is the reason for its link to sugar plantations, because every sugar plantation had a great number of pots but they were in use only during the initial sugar refining phase. A large plantation might have had ten thousand or more pots, which for most of the year sat unused, some broken, many collecting rainwater, thereby providing the ideal conditions for this particular kind of mosquito to reproduce.

Plantations fed as well as bred mosquitoes. All mosquitoes like sweet liquids, which provide them with much of their energy, and female mosquitoes also require blood meals in order to make eggs. Individual mosquitoes can survive on cane juice. So a sugar plantation was a veritable smorgasbord for *A. aegypti* – all of the sweet liquid they could possibly want was easily accessible as were the blood meals needed for their reproduction, due to the proximity of the human and livestock populations. The conditions for the survival and expansion of *A. aegypti* mosquito populations were rapidly improved by the installation of plantations, specifically sugar cane plantations, in the Caribbean.[17]

The plantation system also had far-reaching consequences as far as soils were concerned. In the wake of the Columbian Exchange, the indigenous populations of the Americas – not just Atlantic America, but across continental North and South America – declined by 60 per cent to 95 per cent in most areas. This human calamity permitted forest growth and regrowth. In almost all cases, the indigenous populations of the Americas had regularly used forests and forest soils, which entailed widespread forest burning, either for agricultural clearance or else to favour the proliferation of the grazing animals which they hunted. Following the population decline, forests in the Americas grew bigger and taller than they had been for a very long time.

Big trees held mother lodes of soil nutrients. Visitors to the Atlantic American coastal regions mistook what they saw for ancient, primeval forests, but in fact the forests were usually only a century or two old, even when they included towering specimens such as the American chestnut (*Castanea dentata*) or the Venezuelan giant *Gyranthera caribensis* (one of which attained 17 metres in circumference and 63 metres in height). The tissues of these trees contained cornucopian concentrations of potential soil nutrients. In effect, the trees had been drawing up nutrients from the soil and subsoil for 100 or 200 years, largely from depths which crop roots simply could not reach. They were the functional equivalent of the water towers which are such a familiar sight in North America, pumping up ground water from the depths and storing it for later distribution.

The success of plantation agriculture in some measure depended upon the nutrients locked in these mammoth and majestic trees. Felling and burning tall forests, the chief occupation of most slaves early in the life of every plantation, unlocked stores of nitrogen, phosphorus, potassium, and a dozen other nutrients. Char and ash, mixed into topsoil, ensured the prospering of tobacco, cotton, and sugar for several years. Soon, however, the nutrient bonus was gone, carried off across the sea in tobacco leaf or raw cotton – or carried to the sea via soil erosion. Planters had to move their operations at certain intervals – after twenty, then ten or even five years – as the key nutrients that limit plant growth became ever scarcer. Evidence of this enforced mobility can be found on a small scale on individual plantations, in the way in which landowners deforested new patches of land within their holdings and planted tobacco, cotton, or sugar in them. It can also been seen on a large scale, in the migration of the centre of the plantation economy from the small islands of the eastern Caribbean to the bigger islands of the western Caribbean, including Jamaica, Hispaniola, and Cuba. The same pattern prevailed in the American South, where the cotton plantation regime migrated from the eastern seaboard of Georgia, the Carolinas, and the Chesapeake westward into Alabama, Mississippi, Louisiana, and East Texas.[18] Similarly, tobacco plantations moved from the Chesapeake area to the piedmont region of North Carolina, and even further west into Kentucky and Tennessee. Plantations were a form of shifting agriculture on a macro scale. In many environments, soils quickly became too poor to ensure profitability once the subsidy of nutrients in forest ash wore thin. Plantation agriculture as practiced in the Atlantic Americas was decidedly unsustainable due its demands on soils. By the time of the abolition of slavery (1832–88), the prospects for continued profitability of plantation agriculture in Atlantic America were very poor, as the one-off gift from the post-Columbian nutrient towers had vanished.

The plantation economy of the Americas, one of the characteristic business innovations of the early modern centuries, exemplifies the connections between ecology and economy. Its existence rested on the ecological reshuffling of the Columbian Exchange. The important plantation crops all came from the Old World. Plantation labour came mainly from Africa, serving as a replacement for the indigenous population drastically reduced by imported diseases. The plantation economy's efflorescence over two centuries (c. 1650–1850) led to sharp ecological changes in Atlantic America, notably deforestation, the entrenchment of mosquito-borne diseases, and the drawdown of soil nutrients. In short, the plantation economy of the Americas was born of unique and fragile ecological circumstances and its prosperity undermined those circumstances. It was a model unsustainable economy.

## The Industrial Revolution as global ecological change

Conventional conceptions of the Industrial Revolution consider it an English event with profound social and economic ramifications. That it was. But it was also a global event with profound ecological ramifications. From Spain to South Africa, from Argentina to Australia, lands and ecologies far from Lancashire or Tyneside took part in the Industrial Revolution.

The vast and ever-growing use of fossil fuels during the first century or so of industrialization began a permanent revolution in global environmental history. Cheap and abundant energy has probably done more to shape the human–environment relationship than anything else in the past two centuries.[19] Coal mining, oil and gas drilling, energy transport, and fossil fuel combustion help explain much of the ecological tumult since about 1850, especially in the realms of air, water, and soil pollution. But the environmental meaning of cheap and abundant energy extends well beyond the obvious to include countless 'ecological teleconnections', some of them of considerable magnitude on local and regional scales.

The phrase 'ecological teleconnections' refers to linkages that involve places far apart and carry significant environmental consequences.[20] An example, alluded to above, is the replacement of (mainly) forest land in Alabama, Mississippi, Louisiana, and East Texas by cotton plantations during 1825–60, driven (mainly) by the mounting demand for cotton in Britain. The plantation system, slavery included, colonized the warm and humid lowlands from Georgia to Texas. Tens of thousands of farmers and slaves migrated into these lands from further east. Upon settling down, their first object was to clear the existing vegetation. They slashed and burned their way through millions of hectares, and then planted maize and cotton. They arranged both crops in rows for convenience in planting and harvesting, inadvertently maximizing the susceptibility of their soils to erosion in the downpours characteristic of the humid South. One northern traveller passing through cotton country in the early 1830s noted the rapid erosion of topsoil: 'Every plough furrow becomes the bed of a rivulet after heavy rains – these uniting are increased into torrents before which the impalpable soil dissolves like ice under a summer's sun.'[21] A survey of the cotton South at the end of the nineteenth century found 'a miserable panorama of … rain-gullied fields … dirt, poverty, disease, drudgery, and monotony that stretches for a thousand miles across the cotton belt'.[22] The Industrial Revolution's demand for long-staple cotton had transformed the landscape of the American South: an ecological teleconnection.

By 1840, growing demand for cotton had begun to inspire environmental transformations elsewhere besides the American South. These transformations accelerated suddenly when the American Civil War (1861–5) and the Union blockade of the Confederacy cut North American cotton exports to a trickle. Efforts to ramp up cotton production took place in Central Asia, Tahiti, India, Anatolia, and Egypt among other lands. In Egypt, cotton's growth season did not fit the natural rhythm of the Nile flood (unlike wheat, the staple crop for forty-five centuries along the Nile). So Egyptian rulers, beginning with Muhammad Ali (r. 1805–49), undertook to impound some of the flood in order to release it when cotton in the delta needed water, and to shield the crop from potential damage from unseasonable high water. Thus mechanized cotton mills in Britain inspired the large-scale re-plumbing of Egypt that culminated in the Aswan High Dam in the 1970s.[23]

Cotton was not the only cloth whose manufacture led to conspicuous landscape change; silk did as well. In Lebanon, for example, peasant families boiled silk cocoons to disentangle the threads. The process required fuel wood, which in the early nineteenth century was still available on the slopes of Mount Lebanon. When the power looms of Lyon, Milan, and other silk-manufacturing centres geared up in the 1840s, silk cloth became cheap enough for middle-class consumers, no longer merely the raiment of the elites. Lebanese mountain families began a bonanza of silk cultivation that lasted several decades, putting mounting pressure on the fuel wood supply of Mount Lebanon. The near eradication of the famous cedars of Lebanon is often laid at the door of the Ottoman Turks and the Hejaz railway built at the end of the nineteenth century. However, the odds are that the greater part of that spurt of deforestation resulted from the efforts of rural Lebanese to take advantage of the strong market for raw silk that mechanization and cheap energy in France and Italy created: another ecological teleconnection.[24]

Cloth was only part of the story. Gutta-percha was another. The world's telegraph system took shape from the late 1840s. Outdoor wiring required insulation against the elements, a job for which tarred cotton was used at first. But engineers – notably Werner von Siemens – soon found that gutta-percha served admirably as wire insulation, suitable even for duty on the seafloor where other materials, such as rubber, suffered from salt corrosion. The first undersea cable insulated with gutta-percha made its debut at Folkestone (UK) in 1849. Between 1859 and 1900, special purpose-built ships laid about 200,000 miles of undersea telegraph cable, all of it insulated with gutta-percha.

Gutta-percha is a resinous gum found only in about eight species of trees, especially one called *Isonandra*, all of which grow exclusively in Southeast Asia. Extraction of the latex involved Dayak, Chinese, or Malay men finding and felling suitable trees, and collecting their latex in bowls. Once dried, that latex would be gathered in the ports of Southeast Asia. Raw gutta-percha was shipped from Singapore, Saigon, or Batavia to London's East End or smaller centres of gutta-percha works, where it was heated, cleaned (of mud, etc.), cooled, and applied to copper cables destined for decades of service as telegraph wire at the bottom of the sea.

A big *Isonandra* tree might yield a little more than a kilogram of gutta-percha; a typical one will yield about 300 grams. A transatlantic cable required about 250 tonnes of gutta-percha. The 200,000 miles of undersea cable in place by 1900 needed about 27,000 tonnes, or about 80 to 100 million trees' worth of gutta-percha. In 1898–9, when two trans-Pacific cables were laid, fifteen to twenty million trees were cut to supply the needed gutta-percha. Several observers noted the unsustainable character of gutta-percha exploitation. But cutting proceeded apace, to the point where the wild tree neared extinction in the accessible landscapes of Southeast Asia. Efforts at plantations of *Isonandra* and other gutta-percha trees began, unfruitfully, in the 1880s. By 1900, however, fairly successful plantations existed. Eventually, wireless telegraphy and radio (1920s) would reduce the demand for undersea cables and gutta-percha, making moot the ecological sustainability or unsustainability of gutta-percha exploitation. But in the meantime, between 1860 and 1900, an ecological teleconnection inaugurated by the desire to send information via electrons through copper wire had brought a rain forest species to the brink of extinction and made a significant dent in the forest cover of Southeast Asia.[25]

It is possible to tell other stories of ecological teleconnections created by the Industrial Revolution and cheap energy. I will quickly sketch some, beginning with two about leather. The slaughter of twenty to forty million bison on the great plains of North America between 1865 and 1881 is the largest and fastest anthropogenic reduction in wildlife biomass in history. It had several motives, but prominent among them was the demand for bison hide as leather strapping in the textile mills of New England (and to a small extent in England). Bison leather helped to make cotton. As a result, by 1882, the US bison herd amounted to about 1,000 animals, a close brush with extinction.

Tanning leather made it more flexible, suitable for fine shoes, belts, purses, and so forth. Until the invention of chemical substitutes, tanning required tannin. Suitable tannins came from a number of plants, but after 1867 among the best came from trees in South America colloquially called quebracho (*Schinopsis lorentzii*). Their heartwood, if chipped and boiled, yielded an exquisite tannin. Found in northern Argentina, southern Bolivia, and Paraguay, quebracho provided tannin to British tanneries at the end of the nineteenth century, until the tree became too rare to reward the effort. As bison helped to make cotton, quebracho trees helped to make consumer leather.[26]

Copper, tin, lead, and iron were core ingredients of the Industrial Revolution. Some of these ores lay underground not far from industrial zones, for example, Cornish tin. But most came from faraway places such as Chile, Montana, Malaya, Andalucia, or Australia.

As metallurgical industries went from strength to strength in the nineteenth and early twentieth centuries, miners hacked out more and more ore, most of which required fuel-intensive smelting or processing. Everywhere this brought a cascade of environmental consequences – more ecological teleconnections. The province of Almería, in southern Spain, provides a fine example. It was the most active lead-mining zone in the world during 1830–60, and its best customer was Britain. But lack of fuel for on-site smelting hampered the business. Bare mountains eroded quickly, filling rivers with enough silt to change the Spanish coastline.[27]

Machines of all sorts required lubricants to work properly and enduringly. Before petroleum derivatives became practical, several sorts of vegetable oils served as lubricants, not least was the palm oil. Palm oil came at first from the Niger Delta but in the early twentieth century became a plantation crop throughout West Africa and Southeast Asia. Peanut oil, mainly from Senegambia, also lubricated the Industrial Revolution. Whale oil was another important lubricant in the nineteenth century, as well as an illuminant. The quest for whale oil lay behind a determined assault on the world's right and sperm whales, led by Anglo-American whalers. Ecological teleconnections extended to the seven seas as well as to every inhabited continent.[28]

The first century of the Industrial Revolution helped to inspire changes in vegetation all around the world. Charcoal stratigraphical analysis shows that global biomass burning declined for seventeen centuries before 1750. It then spiked until 1870 or so, before again declining for several decades.[29] This spike probably represents frontier agricultural expansion in Russia, north China, North and South America, and elsewhere, places where pioneers torched vegetation in order to plant food crops. But it also represents the work of people firing woodlands in order to try to make a living providing fibres such as wool and cotton for the mills of Lancashire and New England, and the work of others cutting and burning forests for rubber or palm oil plantations. The ecological teleconnections of the Industrial Revolution helped to shape the vegetation cover of every continent.

Britain, of course, was only the first nation to experience industrialization and to scour the world for industrial ingredients. Parallel processes appeared almost simultaneously in Northwestern Europe, eastern North America, and later in Japan and Russia. All these industrial revolutions needed fibres, ores, and lubricants. Some of these ingredients came from close by. But many, perhaps most, as in the case of Britain, came from afar (even if in the case of Russia, materials came from within the Russian Empire). These later industrial revolutions also provoked ecological teleconnections, contributing to the environmental tumult of modern times.

The pell-mell industrialization of China since 1980, the fastest and largest scale such process in world history, has crafted its own environmentally consequential teleconnections, from the iron mines of Western Australia to the soybean plantations in Goias (Brazil), to the copper belt of Zambia. This latest incarnation of the general phenomenon of ecological teleconnections, like its predecessors, is predicated on fossil fuel energy, without which China would have remained the poor peasant country it was in 1950.[30]

## The Anthropocene

Since 1750, global population has grown about tenfold, energy used has increased roughly 100-fold, and the size of the world economy, if we can trust the figures assembled by Brad Delong or Angus Maddison, increased by well more than 100-fold.[31] The scale of these changes is so great, and their consequences so profound, that it may be time to reconceptualize the material relationships between economy and environment, between humankind and planet earth, and between modern history and deep history.

The term 'Anthropocene' now increasingly serves as a shorthand way to recognize the great power that humankind now exerts – clumsily – over some of the earth's basic biogeochemical systems, over life on earth, and upon the face of the earth itself. Several chemical compounds and elements, including water, nitrogen, sulphur, and carbon, are constantly moving around our planet, cycling among living things, the earth's rock and sediments, the oceans, and the atmosphere – these are some of the biogeochemical cycles. They did this planetary cycling before humans existed and they will likely do so after humans no longer exist. But for a few thousand years (just how many is a subject of debate), humans have affected those cycles. And in the last few decades, human actions have radically altered some of them (on this, there is no debate). The crux of the original Anthropocene concept is that the earth had entered upon a new interval in its history in which human actions have overshadowed the quiet persistence of microbes and the endless orbital wobbles and eccentricities, and therefore defined a new age. That new interval follows the Holocene epoch, which began 11,700 years ago.

Meanwhile, in addition to monkeying with biogeochemical cycles, humankind has also inaugurated what appears to be the sixth great mass extinction in the four-billion-year history of life on earth. This we achieve mainly by converting habitats, in which millions of species have learned to live over millions of years, into fields and pastures that help feed us.[32] And humankind has been clawing, scratching, and scraping rock and soil to such an extent that we are now, by some measures, the most active geological agent on our planet, outstripping the earth-moving work of glaciers and rivers. We have even created new 'rocks' that will survive for millions of years in the earth's crust, including half a trillion tonnes – and more each year – of concrete.[33]

To put the matter differently, in recent decades, human action has nudged the earth into a place it has never been during the Holocene. Greenhouse gas concentrations, the acidity of the oceans, and the proportion of biomass put to human use are all now outside the previous ranges of variation in the Holocene. The nitrogen and sulphur cycles are notably different from any prior incarnations at any time in the history of the earth. Global average temperatures and the share of the earth's surface covered by ice will, in all probability, soon be outside the Holocene envelope as well. It is recognition of this torrent of anthropogenic environmental change that has inspired some geoscientists to claim that the Holocene is over, to recommend formally adding the Anthropocene to the official roster of epochs and eras in earth's history, and to revise the geological timescale.

Just when the Anthropocene began (presuming it exists) is up in the air. The most common view is that the Anthropocene commenced only with the advent of sustained fossil fuel use and is only as old as coal-fired industrialization. Coal use on a global scale remained negligible until a transient process of industrialization took place in north China. Under the Song dynasty (960–1279), coal became an important fuel in a steel-and-iron complex that flourished for a century or more after 1020. Greenland's ice cap contains the wind-blown sulphurous residue of Chinese smelting during the Song dynasty. After the Chinese metallurgical boom withered, coal slipped into obscurity as regards economic and environmental history. It returned to the edge of the stage when it became a routine heating fuel in London in the sixteenth century. But the real departure came with increasingly effective steam engines, developed over the course of the eighteenth and nineteenth centuries. Steam engines could convert the chemical energy of coal first into heat energy and then – this was the revolutionary part – into kinetic energy, useful for making things and going places. As a result of the new uses for coal, British coal consumption more than doubled in 1750–1800, and then quintupled in 1800–50 and peaked in 1913.[34]

In the Anthropocene debates, coal is important mainly because when it burns it releases carbon dioxide to the atmosphere. By virtue of its abundance, carbon dioxide is the most important, although not the most powerful, of the greenhouse gases. It helps regulate the temperature of the earth's surface and lower atmosphere – where we live – and the oceans too. For the last 800,000 years – until very recently when fossil fuels entered the picture – carbon dioxide accounted for between 175 and 285 parts per million (ppm) of the atmosphere. At the very end of the eighteenth century, the carbon dioxide concentration in the atmosphere, as recorded in air bubbles trapped in polar ice, began to climb slowly. That appears as the beginning of the secular trend that continues to this day, and has brought those concentrations from about 260–280 ppm, their range for the last 11,000 years, to a little more than 400 ppm today. This is the quickest rise in the past 800,000 years. It is probably the fastest in the history of the atmosphere.

An alternative view that is gaining adherents holds that the better choice is a later Anthropocene, beginning about 1950. The subsequent decades brought tremendous surges in fossil fuel energy use, population growth, urbanization, tropical deforestation, carbon dioxide emissions, sulphur dioxide emissions, stratospheric ozone depletion, freshwater use, dam-building, irrigation, river regulation, wetlands drainage, aquifer depletion, fertilizer use, toxic chemical releases, species extinctions, fish landings, ocean acidification, and much else besides.[35]

There is, perhaps, a way to reconcile the arguments for an eighteenth-century Anthropocene and a mid-twentieth-century one. It rests upon the concept of the Great Acceleration. In effect, the Anthropocene has stages. It may have begun about 1800, but the scale, scope, and pace of anthropogenic environmental change all grew enormously from the mid-twentieth century. To offer just a few examples, primary energy use has quintupled since 1950, the number of large dams (15 metres high or taller) has sextupled, the methane concentration in the atmosphere has nearly doubled, the quantity of nitrogen flowing into coastal waters has quintupled, and marine fish harvests sextupled (and then fell off a bit). That hectic post-1945 period is the Great Acceleration, within the Anthropocene.[36] Ultimately, the distinction between an Anthropocene originating in the late eighteenth century and including within it the Great Acceleration and an

Anthropocene beginning in the mid-twentieth century is a small one, a matter of definition of terms, although fiercely fought over at the moment.[37]

Confining ourselves to planet earth may prove too narrow a view of the Anthropocene. Since 1957, earthlings have launched a few thousand rockets into nearby precincts in space. The rockets have left landing pads on Mars, Venus, and the moon. Humans have put thousands of satellites into orbit. Millions of pieces of 'space junk' now careen around the earth's general neighbourhood, ranging in size from paint flakes to rocket boosters. Two cameras, a glove, a toothbrush, and countless bits of metal, mainly aluminium, are zooming above earth in low orbit, and will do so for centuries to come. In all, about 6,000 tonnes of space junk are in earth's orbit, equivalent to a fleet of 3,000 cars parked overhead. In any case, the Space Age on our planet is also an age of anthropogenic environmental change in our solar system, and the Anthropocene concept might deservedly apply beyond the earth itself.[38]

## Conclusion

The four tales I have narrated about biological exchange, American plantations, industrialization, and the Anthropocene will suffice to sustain the case that the bond (between the world economy and global ecology) is always present, yet never constant. The two have co-evolved, inciting one another to change shape or direction, to mutate, or to grow. They always did and always will. But in the period since 1500, the bond has somehow changed. The situation is a bit like two children across from one another on a merry-go-round: if they step closer to each other, they make the merry-go-round spin faster. The scale and speed of environmental change has accelerated, and so has the pace of economic change. Both now proceed at rates unimaginable before 1500.

Whether such a pace can continue is uncertain and one of the great questions of our time. Perhaps, metaphorically speaking, the merry-go-round will spin out of control and we shall fly off. Perhaps we can carefully step further from the axis of rotation and slow to a safer speed, one we can sustain indefinitely without danger. Perhaps, somehow, we can loosen the bond between global ecology and the world economy, redesign the merry-go-round, so as to be able to enjoy the comforts of economic growth without the perils (or with reduced perils) of ecological convulsion. As usual, only time will tell.

## Notes

1. A. Crosby (1972), *The Columbian Exchange*. Westport, CT: Greenwood Press; J. Carney and R. Rosomoff (2011), *In the Shadow of Slavery: Africa's Botanical Legacy in the Atlantic World*. Berkeley: University of California Press.

2. Roughly 15–20 per cent of plant species in the Philippines today are of American origin.

3. M. Samways (1999), 'Translocating fauna to foreign lands: Here comes the Homogenocene', *Journal of Insect Conservation*, 3 (2), 65–6.

4. For details, see J. R. McNeill (2012), 'Biological exchange in global environmental history', in J. R. McNeill and E. S. Mauldin (eds), *A Companion to Global Environmental History*. Oxford: Wiley-Blackwell, 433–52.

5. A recent study is M. Livi-Bacci (2008), *Conquest: The Destruction of the American Indios*. Cambridge and Malden: Polity. Other important overviews include S. A. Alchon (2003), *A Pest in the Land: New World Epidemics in a Global Perspective*. Albuquerque: University of New Mexico Press; N. D. Cook (1998), *Born to Die: Disease and New World Conquest, 1492–1650*. New York: Cambridge University Press; Idem (2010), *La Catástrofe Demográfica Andina: Perú 1520–1620*. Lima: Pontificia Universidad Católica del Perú.

6. This idea remains controversial. See R. Dull, R. J. Nevle, W. I. Woods, D. K. Bird, S. Avnery and W. M. Denevan (2010), 'The Columbian encounter and the Little Ice Age: Abrupt land use change, fire, and greenhouse forcing', *Annals of the Association of American Geographers*, 100 (4), 755–71; S. Lewis and M. A. Maslin (2015), 'Defining the Anthropocene', *Nature*, 519, 171–80.

7. A. Drake and M. Oxenham (2013), 'Disease, climate, and the peopling of the Americas', *Historical Biology*, 25 (5), 565–97, are sceptical of the role of cold in shaping the slender disease burden of the pre-Columbian Americas.

8. The likeliest candidate for a significant disease of American origins is syphilis, but expert opinion remains divided. The debate as regards North America is presented in M. L. Powell and D. C. Cook (eds) (2005), *The Myth of Syphilis*. Gainesville: University of Florida Press. See also K. Harper, et al. (2011), 'The origin and antiquity of syphilis revisited: An appraisal of Old-World pre-Columbian evidence of treponemal infection', *American Journal of Physical Anthropology*, 146 (Supplement 53), 99–133.

9. P. Hämäläinen (2008), *The Comanche Empire*. New Haven: Yale University Press. Whether or not the word 'empire' applies to these political formations is up for debate.

10. N. Nunn and N. Qian (2011), 'The potato's contribution to population and urbanization: Evidence from a historical experiment', *Quarterly Journal of Economics*, 126 (2), 593–650.

11. The potato's impact on Northern Europe's food supply required another biological migrant: clover. Clover, although not from the Americas, was essential to the impact of the Columbian Exchange in Europe. Clover hosts microorganisms that fix nitrogen from the air in the soil, putting it where plant roots can absorb it. Potatoes are especially nitrogen-hungry, and cannot yield well consistently without nitrogen supplements to the soil. Although as yet unsung by historians, clover can claim an impact on European history as great as that of the potato. T. Kjaergaard (2003), 'A plant that changed the world: The rise and fall of clover, 1000–2000', *Landscape Research*, 28 (1), 41–9.

12. On maize in Africa, see J. McCann (2005), *Maize and Grace: Africa's Encounter with a New World Crop, 1500–2000*. Cambridge, MA: Harvard University Press.

13. J. Miller (1988), *Way of Death: Merchant Capitalism and the Angolan Slave Trade, 1730–1830*. Madison: University of Wisconsin Press, 19, 103, 193.

14. On the 'Magellan Exchange', see J. R. McNeill (1998), 'Islands in the Rim: Ecology and history in and around the Pacific, 1521–1996', in D. O. Flynn, L. Frost and A. J. H. Latham (eds), *Pacific Centuries: Pacific and Pacific Rim History since the Sixteenth Century*. London: Routledge, 70–84.

15. A. Crosby (1986), *Ecological Imperialism: The Biological Expansion of Europe, 900–1900*. New York: Cambridge University Press.

16. W. Dean (1994), *With Broadax and Firebrand: The Destruction of the Brazilian Atlantic Forest*. Berkeley: University of California Press; D. Watts (1987), *The West Indies*. Cambridge:

Cambridge University Press; R. Funes (2008), *From Rainforest to Canefield in Cuba: An Environmental History since 1492*. Chapel Hill: University of North Carolina Press.

17. J. R. McNeill (2010), *Mosquito Empires*. New York: Cambridge University Press.

18. A. Rothman (2007), *Slave Country: American Expansion and the Origins of the Deep South*. Cambridge, MA: Harvard University Press.

19. On energy and the Industrial Revolution in England, see E. A. Wrigley (2010), *Energy and the English Industrial Revolution*. Cambridge: Cambridge University Press; R-P. Sieferle (2001), *The Subterranean Forest*. Winwick: White Horse Press.

20. 'Teleconnection' is a recognized term in the atmospheric sciences and climatology, used to describe linked events thousands of miles apart.

21. J. J. Ingraham (1835), *The South-west, by a Yankee*. New York: Harper, 86, quoted in W. Johnson (2013), *River of Dark Dreams: Slavery and Empire in the Cotton Kingdom*. Cambridge, MA: Harvard University Press, 155.

22. C. Johnson, E. Embree and W. W. Alexander (1935), *The Collapse of Cotton Tenancy: Summary of Field Studies and Statistical Surveys, 1933–1935*. Chapel Hill: University of North Carolina Press, 14.

23. J. Waterbury (1979), *Hydropolitics of the Nile Valley*. Syracuse: Syracuse University Press.

24. G. Pitts (2016), *Fallow Fields: Famine and the Making of Lebanon (1914–1952)*, Ph.D. Dissertation, Georgetown University, ch. 2; Giovanni Federico (1994), *Il filo d'oro: l'industria della seta dalla Restaurazione alla Grande Crisi*. Venice: Marsilio. The energy for the silk industry often came from water power.

25. J. Tully (2009), 'A Victorian ecological disaster: Imperialism, the telegraph, and gutta-percha', *Journal of World History*, 20 (4), 559–79; L. Potter (2005), 'Community and environment in colonial Borneo: Economic value, forest conversions and concern for conservation, 1870–1940', in R. Wadley (ed.), *Histories of the Borneo Environment: Economic, Political and Social Dimensions of Change and Community*. Leiden: Verhandelingen van Het Koninklijk Instituut voor Taal, Landen Volken- kunde, 116. The 1911 *Encyclopedia Britannica* entry on gutta-percha explains some of the refining processes: https://en.wikisource.org/wiki/1911_Encyclop%C3%A6dia_Britannica/Gutta_Percha.

26. A. G. Zarrilli (2008), 'El oro rojo: la industria del tanino en Argentina (1890–1950)', *Silva Lusitana*, 16 (2), 239–59.

27. For the case of lead in southern Spain, see A. S. Picón (1983), *La Minería del Levante Almeriense, 1838–1930*. Almería: Cajal. See also J. R. McNeill and G. Vrtis (eds) (2017), *Mining North America: An Environmental History*. Berkeley: University of California Press.

28. S. M. Martin (1988), *Palm Oil and Protest: An Economic History of the Ngwa Region, South-Eastern Nigeria*. Cambridge: Cambridge University Press, ch. 1; J. N. Tønnessen and A. O. Johnsen (1982), *The History of Modern Whaling*. Berkeley: University of California Press.

29. J. R. Marlon, et al. (2008), 'Climate and human influences on global biomass burning over the past two millennia', *Nature Geoscience*, 1 (10), 697–702.

30. For a journalistic discussion of the contemporary Chinese case, see E. C. Economy and M. Levi (2014), *By All Means Necessary: How China's Resource Quest Is Changing the World*. New York: Oxford University Press.

31. J. B. Delong (2008), 'Estimates of world GDP', available at http://delong.typepad.com/print/20061012_LRWGDP.pdf; Maddison's figures: The Maddison-Project, http://www.ggdc.net/maddison/maddison-project/home.htm, 2013 version. Delong estimates the world

economy increased in size 320-fold between 1750 and 2008. Maddison's estimates do not take 1750 as a data point, but by inference it appears his estimate would be higher still.

32. By 'learned' I mean became adapted over many generations via evolution by natural selection. Only a very few species 'learn' anything in the human sense. For the ongoing extinction spasm, see E. Kolbert (2014), *The Sixth Extinction: An Unnatural History*. New York: Macmillan; G. Ceballos, et al. (2015), 'Accelerated modern human–induced species losses: Entering the sixth mass extinction', *Science Advances*, 1 (5), e1400253. DOI: 10.1126/sciadv.1400253.

33. See, for instance, the several papers in the *Philosophical Transactions of the Royal Society: A: Mathematical, Physical and Engineering Sciences*, 369 (2011); B. H. Wilkinson (2015), 'Humans as geologic agents: A deep-time perspective', *Geology*, 33 (3), 161–4.

34. Data on the quantitative history of coal in Britain are scattered throughout volumes 2 and 3 of (1983–87), *The History of the British Coal Industry*. Oxford: Oxford University Press, written by M. Flinn and R. Church, respectively.

35. A detailed argument to this effect appears in J. R. McNeill and P. Engelke (2016), *The Great Acceleration*. Cambridge, MA: Harvard University Press. A treatment that avoids all alarmism is R. DeFries (2014), *The Big Ratchet: How Humanity Thrives in the Face of Natural Crisis*. New York: Basic Books.

36. This term, intended to echo the title of Karl Polanyi's 1944 book *The Great Transformation*, which took a holistic view about the origins of modernity, made its debut (so far as I know) at a workshop in Dahlem, a Berlin suburb, in 2005. The proceedings of that workshop can be found at R. Costanza, L. Graumlich and W. Steffen (eds) (2007), *Sustainability or Collapse: An Integrated History and Future of People on Earth*. Cambridge, MA: MIT Press; for an explicit presentation of stages of the Anthropocene, see W. Steffen, P. Crutzen and J. R. McNeill (2007), 'The Anthropocene: Are humans now overwhelming the great forces of Nature?', *Ambio*, 36 (8), 614–21.

37. The debates may be followed in the pages of the *Anthropocene Review*.

38. A. Gorman (2014), 'The Anthropocene in the solar system', *Journal of Contemporary Archaeology*, 1 (1), 87–91.

# CHAPTER 10
# LABOUR REGIMES AND LABOUR MOBILITY FROM THE SEVENTEENTH TO THE NINETEENTH CENTURY

*Alessandro Stanziani*

## Why coercion?

Many economists and economic historians follow Domar's model according to which labour coercion is likely to develop when labour is scarce compared to land. This model was based largely on Russian and medieval European serfdom, but it has been since used to describe several other contexts, not only in Russia, Africa, and Asia, but also in Britain and the United States as well. Such models are interesting not so much for what they explain but for what they fail to explain.[1] Thus, Domar's model suggests that slavery and serfdom were established when labour was scarce; in contrast, Habakkuk, Postan, North, and Thomas stressed that in Western Europe, scarcity of labour accounts not for the strength but for the decline of serfdom and resulting capital intensification. In the first case, labour scarcity led to coercion, in the second, it led to increased wages and hence to capital intensification.[2] However, empirical evidence for this thesis is scanty.

Similarly diverging views and scant empirical confirmation of Domar's model emerge with regard to the colonial worlds. The cases of Australia and Canada testify to the fact that the colonization of new territories did not necessarily entail massive imports of slaves as in the United States.[3] In Russia itself, the scarcity of labour was never mentioned in sources contemporary with the emergence of serfdom,[4] while the abolition of slavery in the British Atlantic colonies had little to do with demographic trends. As Seymour Drescher puts it, there was no fundamental change in demographic patterns in the tropical world beyond Europe in the watershed period of 1760–90.[5] Wrigley and Schofield show that Britain established its overseas slave system during the very decades when the net emigration rate reached a three-century peak (1641–61); in contrast, British abolitionism took off exactly when the net emigration rate sank to a tercentennial low (1771–91).[6]

Yet, it was not just a matter of supply and demand of labour between masters and labouring people. In the period here considered, contract enforcement was a substitute for higher wages: masters used it as long as they could, in order to secure labour.[7] This was possible because of two further conditions: first, society considered labour as a service and an obligation vis-à-vis the head of the family, the village, the master, the town, and/or the state; second, labouring people had few political, civil, and legal rights compared to those of their masters.[8] In the European context, unequal political rights and the exclusion of labouring people from the benefit of the Glorious Revolution in Britain and its colonies, of the Revolution in France and its colonies as well, allowed masters to limit wage increase, despite the lack of labour. Moreover, in both areas, free labour, even where a contract existed, was considered the property of the employer and a resource for the whole community to which the individual belonged.[9] Labour was part of the broader public order. In the following pages I will discuss the relationship between labour, contract, and public order in Britain, then France, and then the colonial world. Why these areas?

In this context, the French case is of interest not because it was the land of Colbertism and opposed to liberal England, but because its labour norms in the nineteenth century were actually quite well suited both to a capitalist economy and to the heritage of the Old Regime. Highlighting the case of France and comparing it with England leads us to question the differences between liberalism and regulationism – or between free labour and guilds within the capitalist world – and from there to narrow the distance separating free labour from varieties of bondage. Contrary to widespread preconceptions, common law in England was in fact accompanied by a considerable degree of regulation and state intervention, and labour remained subject to punitive constraints until the end of the nineteenth century.

While British and French norms and perceptions translated into various forms of bondage in the Atlantic and the Indian Ocean region (thereby helping perpetuate slavery well after its official abolition), slavery nevertheless existed prior to any European intervention. The adopted solution did not result solely from British and French influences, but from the interaction between those influences and local traditions.

These comparisons on the national and imperial levels are valid only as a rough approximation. No doubt, legal rules (civil, tax, and customs laws) refer to the national and imperial dimension of these phenomena; yet those rules were only one component of economic action, along with symbolic, cultural, and political aspects. Hence we cannot ignore the importance of local components and the great differences between the dynamics of different regions. Several institutions coexisted on the local level, and even when a process of national unification took place, institutional pluralism continued. Institutional pluralism was more widespread on the level of empires, where legal pluralism was an important instrument of economic and political action.[10]

## Labour, contracts, and public order in Britain

The idea that capitalism and in particular the British Industrial Revolution was made possible thanks to institutions that facilitated free contracts and (according to some) a proletarianized peasantry is supported by a long tradition. It dates back at least to the nineteenth century and classical economists such as Smith and Marx, continuing with Tawney and Polanyi and in most works of historical sociology and economic history in the twentieth century. Even the world system approach, while stressing the existence of mixed forms of labour and exploitation on the periphery and quasi-periphery, has always assumed that free wage labour typified the 'core'.[11] However, in recent decades, several pieces of research have contested the impact of enclosures and the existence of a truly free labour market in industrializing Britain.[12]

Until at least the mid-nineteenth century, the term 'free labour' did not mean what we are now accustomed to it meaning.[13] It included indenture, debt bondage, and several other forms of unfree labour.[14] Conversely, the official abolition of slavery did not see the disappearance of forced labour, but rather the emergence of new forms.[15] Thus, from the sixteenth to the nineteenth centuries, laws on runaway slaves and indentured servants were adopted not only in the colonial Americas, but also in Great Britain, where runaway workers, journeymen, and the like were subject to quite similar laws under the Master and Servant Acts and the Statute of Artificers and Apprentices of 1562. Apprenticeship, advances in wages and raw materials, and simple master–servant relations justified such provisions. Since the mid-seventeenth century, the Poor Laws related relief directly to workhouses. Any person lacking employment or permanent residence was no longer considered simply a 'poor' person, but became a 'vagrant', and as such was subject to criminal prosecution. Anti-vagrancy laws did not decline but became stricter in the nineteenth century, particularly after the adoption of the New Poor Law in 1834. Between 1834 and the mid-1870s, there were about 10,000 prosecutions for vagrancy.[16]

In this context, the workhouse system was far from marginal: it has been estimated that in periods of crisis during the eighteenth and nineteenth centuries, about 6.5 per cent of the British population was in a workhouse at any given time.[17] Many have seen a strong influence of Bentham in the New Poor Law of 1834. The commission in charge of the New Poor Law insisted that workhouse labour would be applied for discipline rather than for profit.[18] Thus the years following the adoption of the new rules saw increasing number of paupers committed to workhouses for offences: The number of committals rose from 940 in 1837 to 2,596 in 1842, while over 10,500 committals for breach of workhouse discipline were recorded during the same period.[19]

Yet paupers and inmates increasingly resisted the Poor Laws and the workhouse principle, resorting to petitions, sabotage, and, in particular among women, self-mutilation. If one adds the massive protests against the Poor Laws in the 1830s, one would have a complex picture in which different central government orientations faced equally various local elites' attitudes and popular protests.[20]

Indeed, the history of workhouses has been one-sidedly linked to that of prisons, while the link with 'normal' labour has been ignored. This link was strong not only for the forms of discipline and rights, but also for the way wages and assistance were related. The Statute of Labourers (1350–1) was enacted two years after the Ordinance of Labourers had been put in place and was followed by a set of laws gathered under the umbrella of the Master and Servant Acts, which multiplied in the sixteenth century and accompanied the Statute of Artificers and Apprentices (1562). During the term of service, the labour of servants was legally reserved for their masters. Even at the expiration of the term of service, servants were not allowed to leave their masters unless they had given 'one quarter's warning' of their intention to leave.[21] Workers could be imprisoned until they were willing to return to their employers to complete their agreed-upon service. Any untimely breach of contract on the part of the servant was subject to prosecution. In fact, in early modern Britain, resident servants were like wives and children: all were members of the household and all were the legal dependents of its head.[22] All of them were supposed to be under his authority, the family head benefiting from a higher legal status and more legal entitlements and rights than his dependents and family. Both marriage and labour contracts were actually status contracts: they gave rise to a different legal status for wives and servants on the one hand, and for masters and husbands on the other.

In general, labour was seen as akin to domestic service, with the employer purchasing the worker's time.[23] It is important to stress the chronology of these rules: the measures of the Master and Servant Acts grew stricter starting in the 1720s, when penalties against servants who broke their contracts were reinforced. Between 1720 and 1792, ten acts of Parliament imposed or increased the term of imprisonment for leaving work or for misbehaviour. Almost all these acts were a new departure: the Master and Servant Acts not only attempted to provide for social and political stability but required tighter control of workers by their masters while guaranteeing 'fair' competition among masters (i.e. they should not try to entice away other masters' working people). Specific groups promoted these changes: tailors, shoemakers, leatherworkers, mariners, and lace makers. Monetary or raw material investments made by the employer were used to further justify such sanctions against wage earners who left their jobs.[24]

This trend had its basis in the huge expansion of the putting-out system in the eighteenth century, which added to the mounting need for agrarian labour.[25] Competition between sectors and the intense seasonality of labour strongly buttressed these new labour laws.[26] The idea that high wages were necessary to encourage technological creativity, as expressed by Habakkuk and many others, is based on the assumption that technological progress was primarily a choice between equivalent alternatives and that these choices depended on relative prices.[27] However, there is no persuasive evidence that technological progress emerged as labour-saving in the eighteenth century and the first half of the nineteenth century. Agricultural innovations in particular tended to be labour-using rather than labour-saving: the new techniques of husbandry demanded more labour, not less.[28] Recent analyses come to the same conclusion: labour and labour intensity were the main source of agricultural growth before 1850, with human and physical capital playing a secondary role.[29] Long after steam had become the dominant form of power employed in manufacturing, the major sources of energy available to farmers continued to be men, animals, wind, and water.[30] Labour-intensive techniques linked to the diffusion of knowledge and attractive markets (with increasing agriculture prices) were dominant between the seventeenth and last quarter of the nineteenth century, when this trend reversed (decreasing agricultural prices and increasing wages).[31]

This trend was not limited to agriculture. The rate of capital intensification in British industry was relatively limited until the mid-nineteenth century. [32] Unlike conventional views on the Industrial Revolution, stressing capital intensification,[33] the most frequently declared goal of innovation was either improving the quality of the product or saving on capital, not labour.[34] By 1850, there were relatively few workers employed in factories. Only a small proportion of the workforce worked in technologically advanced industries such as cotton, iron and steel, and other metalworking: the full impact of steam power in transport and production was yet to be felt.[35] The unmechanized, subcontracted work of the sweating system surely played a greater role in the intensification of work than did mechanization.[36]

De Vries' notion of an 'industrious revolution' explains this trend perfectly: even if the author mostly refers to the period between 1650 and 1750, the main features of this model were still relevant up through the mid-nineteenth century in Britain, far after that in other areas of Europe and Asia.[37]

This also contributes to explain why, contrary to E. P. Thompson's argument, working hours per day increased significantly during the eighteenth century and the first half of the nineteenth century.[38] Masters often had an incentive to increase the workday during rush periods to get the goods out and then to lay off or reduce hours in the dead season. As the pace of mechanization was slower than painted in the textbooks, the working hours increased, in particular in the textile mills.[39]

Seasonal needs in agriculture were a crucial variable. Seasonal local shortages of manpower were overcome by interregional migration and – only later in the nineteenth century – by a transformation of hand-harvesting techniques and tools.[40] In fact, the labour requirements of harvesting were particularly important since labour output peaked sharply at the harvest.[41] All this helps explain the main features of labour contracts. The labour market did not operate as an 'auction market'.[42] By the eighteenth century, an oral or written contract for workers other than day labourers was presumed to last a year, particularly in husbandry, unless specific terms had been explicitly negotiated. However, the frequency of departures, mostly in connection with the harvest, proved the relatively limited impact of the law on workers' behaviour. Masters therefore looked for other solutions, such as the possibility of workers subleasing looms and tools and finding a substitute. This solution was particularly widespread in textile mills, where family members who received a family wage usually worked small spinning mules.[43]

In general, short-term contracts allowed employers to lay off workers when there was a sudden downturn of trade or if workers became troublesome. A positive trend in business, with little unemployment, made short-term contracts favourable to workers; the reverse was true when unemployment rose. The county and police-district records for the years 1857 to 1875 show that some 10,000 people were prosecuted each year for Master and Servant offences. Overall, 5–8 per cent of servants were prosecuted, but the percentage peaked at 17 in some areas and even 20 in London in specific years. There were no significant differences between the prosecution rate under the Master and Servant Acts in rural areas as opposed to urban counties, or between agricultural, putting-out, and manufacturing areas.[44] Instead, the response to changing economic trends and the rate of prosecution was stronger in the countryside than in town, most likely because of the major impact of seasonal labour shortages on agriculture.[45] Given the strong family ties between the town and the countryside, only persistently increasing earnings would have encouraged permanent residence in town. But most masters preferred to use coercion rather than attractive wages to keep the labour force, and they thus ultimately encouraged 'fugitive' workers. The situation could change only with a new political equilibrium (increasing strength of unions land labour movement) and accelerating technical progress in both agriculture and industry, creating a capital-intensive path of growth. This occurred only after 1850, with the second Industrial Revolution and the increasing expulsion of the working force from agriculture.

## French servants

In the past, historians have been fond of opposing the persistence of guilds and the corporatist spirit in French labour law to the free market of Anglo-Saxon labour.[46] This contrast is no longer tenable as the regulation of labour in France is no longer viewed as being in opposition to market growth.[47] France, for instance, was the first country to abolish lifelong domestic service as well as criminal penalties in labour disputes.[48] The chronology of these developments requires further explanation.

As late as the eighteenth century, French official texts, estates, guilds, and local administrations considered labour to be a service provision.[49] Moreover, French case law made no clear distinction between hiring a person for services and 'hiring' a thing.[50] Although the French Revolution eliminated lifelong domestic service, it retained two forms of contracts from earlier times: hiring for labour (*louage d'ouvrage*) and hiring for services (*louage de service*). While the former brought the status of the wage earner more in line with the independent artisan, the latter represented an important legacy from earlier forms of domestic service. Cottereau has emphasized the importance of hiring for services in nineteenth-century France and its ability to protect wage earners. Such contracts and the overall attitude of *prud'homme* (law courts for labour conflicts) law courts strongly protected workers.[51] This argument, while not incorrect, is restricted to specific sectors such as the textile industry and certain urban milieus. But what about the other sectors, especially agriculture?

A variety of contractual arrangements to limit mobility existed at the time along with general provisions.[52] Thus from the sixteenth to the eighteenth century, agricultural labourers and servants were free to move about and change employers only at certain times of year – that is, according to the critical periods in the agricultural calendar. The seasonal nature of agricultural labour gave rise to a significant amount of regional mobility, which was already considerable in the seventeenth century and remained high until around the end of the nineteenth century.[53]

This mobility, together with the notion of labour as service, is precisely what helps to explain the harsh penalties imposed on labourers and servants. They were not allowed to leave their masters until the end of their contract; otherwise they lost their earnings. The master, on the other hand, could discharge them at any time.[54] The situation changed during the second half of the century, when the rate of disputes went up and the demand for agricultural wage earners and domestic servants increased due to emigration to the cities.[55]

This had an influence on industrial labour as well; about 25 per cent of labour moved from one sector to another during the summer in the mid-nineteenth century. Industrial employers could either shut down in the summer or increase wages. The adopted choice depended on the branch of the industry and the region.[56] Indeed a national market was still missing in nineteenth-century France (at least until after the 1880s) and peasant workers considered comparatively local wages in agriculture and industry. This explains why in *départments* where industrial wages were high, agricultural wages followed, and vice versa: workers compared and finally compensated the two wages. For this reason, summer shutdowns were more widespread among firms that paid their workers less than the summer wage for farm labour. This system made of local arrangements and seasonal markets left room to different kinds of farms. Smallholders and even communal fields provided seasonal work for industry and large agricultural units as well. Only between 1860 and 1890 did the earlier practice of combining agricultural and industrial employment largely come to an end. During the summer of 1860, at least 500,000 – and most probably 800,000 – workers quit their jobs. By 1890, this number had fallen to 100,000.[57] Despite important regional and sectoral differences, as a whole, the agrarian crisis and the second Industrial Revolution attracted more stable workers, who were mostly unskilled, into the towns and the manufactures.

In short, in Western Europe, between the sixteenth and the end of the nineteenth century, labour was submitted to serious legal constraints. This was so for several interrelated reasons including the fact that labour was considered a service to the community and that labour and labour intensification were the main sources of growth. National markets still lagged far behind local and international markets. These rules were hard to enforce and they were effective at keeping working people in place than to limit their voice and wages.

The major exception to this labour-intensive path and labour rules in the eighteenth and nineteenth centuries was not so much Britain but its northern American colonies, and later the United States. Since Habakkuk's work, the argument has been that scarcity of labour led to free markets, high wages, and precocious mechanization.[58] More recently, several authors have developed this argument: factor endowment and in particular the lower land-to-labour ratio in Britain compared to the United States had encouraged its agriculture sector to invest in grain; thus, a more seasonal culture was created, which in turn sustained proto-industry and multiple activity. By contrast, in the United States, scarcity of labour and agricultural diversification reduced pluri-activity and led to a quick concentration of industry.[59] Unlike Britain, increasing labour demand did not lead to coercion but to its opposite. Social and political equilibria more favourable to labour contributed to this outcome. Yet, this does not clarify the relationships between these dynamics in the north of the American colonies on the one hand, and, on the other hand, slavery in the south of the United States, and the persistent importance of the indentured labour in the North itself before, during and after the age of slavery.

## Indentured immigrants versus slaves

As the definition and practice of bonded labour in the colonies were linked to the definition and practice of wage labour in Europe, the development of labour in the two areas was interconnected. The blurred boundaries between freedom and unfreedom, property in persons and their labour, found new definitions and became closer to our understanding only in the transmutation of the English state into Imperial Britain. The same can be said of France. The British and the French exported specific notions and practices of wage earner: the servant and the indentured labour. This peculiar contract derived from two types of extant contracts: that of the sailor and that of the agrarian labourer.[60]

In the French colonies, the contract of *engagement* or indentured service was developed in the seventeenth century. It was initially intended for white settlers whose transport expenses were advanced by employers or their middlemen in exchange for a commitment to work for several years. The *engagés* were subject to criminal penalties and could be transferred along with their contract to other masters. The contract of *engagement* should not be understood in opposition to these other labour relationships, but as an extension of them in the colonial situation. Indeed, the notaries of Normandy in charge of drafting the first contracts of *engagement* in the seventeenth century explicitly relied on two types of contracts that already existed: the agricultural daily labourer's contract and the sailor's contract. It is no accident that contracts of *engagement* explicitly mention hiring for service: the *engagé* rented his services, that is, the totality of his time, to his master. Terminating a contract was therefore difficult, especially for the *engagé*. Similarly, contracts of *engagement* explicitly invoked apprenticeship contracts: the master had the same requirement to provide for the care of the *engagé* as he did for the apprentice, the same expenses in case of illness, and the same word in the margins: bondage.[61]

Two clauses differentiated the apprenticeship contract from the contract of *engagement*: the act of apprenticeship emphasized training in a trade, whereas in the contract of *engagement*, the *engagé* first owed his labour to his master who, in exchange, was to teach him about colonial farming. It was also the master who gave a lump sum to his *engagé* and not the other way around, as in the case of an apprentice.[62]

In general, the *engagés* were not allowed to marry without authorization from their masters, but an *engagé* had the right to redeem his indenture and could force his master to agree to do so. Differences nevertheless appear between the *engagés* 'with no trade' and those who left as doctors, carpenters, and so on. The latter committed themselves for three years instead of five; they received wages but were not subject to the servitude clauses imposed on the others.

In the seventeenth and eighteenth centuries, the contract of *engagement* concerned mainly whites who went not only to the French West Indies and Canada, but also to the Indian Ocean region. Between 1660 and 1715 alone, 5,200 *engagés* left for the French West Indies from La Rochelle. This figure is much smaller than the 210,000 indentured Britons who left for North America between 1630 and 1700.[63] Excluding the Caribbean, in the period 1630–1780, the colonies received between 472,000 and 510,000 migrants, 50,000 of whom were convicts and the rest were half indentured and half 'voluntary' migrants.[64]A similar relationship between mother country and colonial labour contracts existed within the British Empire. Just as a master in Great Britain had the right to pursue fugitives, so too in the colonies: indentured servants who fled were subject to criminal penalties.

Two periods can be distinguished: the first, from the seventeenth century to the 1830s, concerned some 300,000 European indentured servants. It coincided with a period when slavery was still legal and European traders engaged in the slave trade. The indentured servants were intended to be engaged in tobacco plantations and, to some degree, in manufacturing. The second phase, in the nineteenth and twentieth centuries, concerned two million indentured servants, mostly Chinese and Indians, but also Africans, Japanese, and immigrants from the Pacific Islands. They were employed in sugar plantations and in manufacturing. Unlike the indentured servants of the first phase, these new bonded labourers seldom returned to the world of free labour once their period of commitment ended. Their indenture contracts were therefore renewed.[65]

What is the relationship between indenture and slave labour? Menard argues that, in North America, indentured servants and slaves were close substitutes and that planters shifted from servants to slaves not because they preferred slaves but due to changes in the supply and cost of the two forms of labour. Around 1660, the supply of servants began to decline as in England population fell and real wages rose, thus leading to improved opportunities at home.[66] Consequently, after the mid-century, migration to America fell. However, other scholars argue that this shift reflected the planters' preferences for black slaves, whom they considered to be more docile and productive than white servants.[67]

The case of Barbados, where the development of sugar plantations transformed the island in the mid-seventeenth century, shows the relationship between the two forms of labour. With the rise of sugar, monoculture replaced diversified farming, and blacks arrived by the thousands while whites left. The island began to import food and fuel and the great planters rose in wealth and power. Because of its substantial economies of scale and large profits, sugar was most efficiently grown on big plantations that greatly increased demand for labour.[68] At the end of the seventeenth century, therefore, the influx of slaves was not a response to a general lack of labour on the island, but to a specific lack of coerced labour and indentured immigrants in particular. Increasing demand for labour was hard to meet with native Indians and white indentured and convicts. Native Indians were difficult to control and less productive than either indentured whites or African slaves.

Some significant changes appeared at the end of the seventeenth century when colonial indentured servitude began to be distinguished from other forms of resident service and, above all, from slavery. It was slavery that enabled Virginians to achieve a stable relationship between work and rights: different contracts expressed different statuses (slaves, indentured immigrants) and, starting from this, they enabled different rights to the slave on the one hand, and to the immigrant on the other hand. In the Chesapeake and the Delaware valley, the relationship between British rules and indentured immigration was reaffirmed, though in the eighteenth century it acted as a way to differentiate indentured from slave labour. Decreasing costs of transportation encouraged shipowners to enter the migration market, where labour became a tradeable commodity. William Blackstone concluded that service was temporary property of labour, while *villeinage* and slavery were perpetual conditions.[69] Progressively, indentured labour was confined to minors alone, while adult working men and women refused to accept strong hierarchical power in labour relationship that they qualified as a vestige of the British yoke. White indenture declined during the 1820s and came to an end in the following decade. By the late 1830s, penal sanctions for breach of contracts for white adult workers disappeared. It was however in this period that indentured contracts became commonplace for 'coloured' immigrants in the Americas as well as in the British and French colonies following the abolition of slavery.

While the legal and contract status of white indentured immigrants improved over time, those of servants (black until the mid-seventeenth century) progressively deteriorated into chattel slavery. This shift was the result of political and economic forces: the excess of labour demand was strong with the expansion of coffee, and then sugar and cotton cultivation in the colonies. The Restoration and then the Glorious Revolution at the end of the seventeenth century were decisive for the change of the legal status of black people in the American colonies.[70] London asserted the rights of the metropolis over its colonies. In this context, Locke, a member of this board, published his *Two Treatises of Government* (1690) in which he defended English liberty and freedom and justified slavery, to his eyes perfectly compatible with liberty.[71]

The shift from indentured labour to slavery was the outcome of a lack of labour in the colonies, aggravated by the labour-intensive path in Europe itself. The rise of the plantation system – labour-intensive and carried out on large-scale estates – bucked this trend. The sugar boom was constrained by a narrow range of technological possibilities. Crude cane-crushing mills, powered by animals, wind, or water, remained the basic forms of heavy equipment.[72] On mainland America, tobacco and then cotton plantations also relied on labour-intensive production.[73]

## Indentured after abolition

In England, many had believed that the abolition of slave trade would lead to the eventual abolition of slavery. This was not the case, as France, Spain, and Portugal continued to import slaves. A new antislavery society was founded; it shifted its agenda from gradual to immediate abolition of slavery. A period (usually six to seven years, in line with the time frame of individual emancipation and apprenticeship contracts) was imposed during which the quasi-former slaves were given apprenticeship status.[74] Slaves did not enjoy full legal status inasmuch as they were not yet 'civilized'.[75] Apprentices worked forty-five hours a week for their former owners in exchange for food, clothing, lodging, and medical care. Absenteeism or low performance (according to standards set by the planters themselves) led to severe penalties and increased the period and the amount of apprentices' obligations. Physical punishment, which had been suppressed under slavery during the 1820s, was now re-introduced for apprentices. Abuse was thus extremely frequent.[76]

Thus, even though former slave owners had received compensation of £20 million, many planters used the apprenticeship programme as additional compensation, and, to this end, they sought to extract as much unpaid labour as possible. The final social and economic outcome differed from one colony to another according to the availability of land, previous forms of bondage and types of culture, and new forms of labour and their rules (different Masters and Servants acts enacted in each colony), and to systems of credit.[77] In Barbados, the planters monopolized all the land and rented it in part to former slaves, few of whom therefore left their original plantations. In Jamaica, Trinidad, and English Guyana, many former slaves had formal access to land, but many of them ended up indebted to their former masters and found themselves back on the plantations.[78] This did not prevent former slaves (when they did not run away) from providing extremely irregular (in their masters' eyes) labour. A fall in sugar output in Jamaica was one of the major expressions of resistance.

The abolition of slavery gave new life to indentured immigration worldwide. In the nineteenth and twentieth centuries, more than 2.5 million people became indentured servants, mostly Chinese and Indian but also African, Japanese, and migrants from the Pacific Islands. They were employed in sugar plantations and in manufacturing. Unlike white settlers during the first phase of indentured immigration, during the 1850s and 1860s, many indentured migrants – especially Indians – returned home. A third of all indentured servants in Mauritius, the Caribbean, Surinam, and Jamaica and up to 70 per cent of those in Thailand, Malaya, and Melanesia returned home. Distance and the cost of transport were the two main variables affecting repatriation, though politics, concrete forms of integration, and death from disease were also important factors. Between the official abolition of slavery in 1834 and 1910, 450,000 indentured servants, mostly from India but also from Madagascar, arrived in Mauritius. Two-thirds of them remained, and as a result, the Indian population grew steadily – from 35 per cent of the island's population in 1846 to 66 per cent in 1871.[79] Numerous observers drew attention to the inhuman living conditions of these immigrants.[80] These figures must also be expanded to include other indentured servants from Southeast Asia and Africa: 30,000 in 1851 and twice that number ten years later.

The real conditions of workers depended on when they arrived, their ethnic origin, and which specific estates they worked on. Small plantation owners were more concerned about fugitive, insubordinate, and vagrant indentured servants,[81] whereas large plantation owners, who complained of the excessive cost of slave surveillance, often advocated a liberal ideology for the colonial systems. Immigrants often complained of ill treatment, withheld wages, and poor food.[82] The number of cases in which indentured servants brought proceedings against their masters – something that rarely happened in the 1850s – rose sharply thereafter. In the 1860s and 1870s, about 10 per cent of all indentured servants sued their masters, in virtually every case for non-payment or insufficient payment of wages, and they won in more than 70 per cent of cases.[83] Such a result was partly due to pressure from England and can hardly indicate that a 'march to equality' was under way. In subsequent decades, the percentage of contracts disputed by coolies declined first to 5 per cent at end of the 1870s and later dropped to a mere 0.3 per cent between 1895 and 1899, with their success rate falling to less than 40 per cent.[84] This can be explained by the fact that, after the results of the 1860s and thanks to a new law on labour contracts adopted in 1867, an increasing number of contracts were oral, making it more difficult for the coolies to produce any proof that would hold up in court. Above all, the coolies' contracts were no longer signed with plantation owners but were drawn up instead with Indian middlemen, which no doubt helped to quash many conflicts. Retention of coolies increased with the percentage of contract renewals, rising from 40 per cent in 1861 to more than 70 per cent twenty years later.[85]

In Mauritius, 14,000 indentured and domestic servants were prosecuted each year in the 1860s; during the same period in Great Britain, proceedings were brought against 9,700 servants per year for breach of contract and almost always resulted in convictions. By contrast, masters were seldom indicted and even more rarely convicted for breach of contract, ill treatment, or non-payment of wages. At the same time, even though the real conditions of indentured servants were not necessarily better than those of the slaves who preceded them, the rights they enjoyed and the fact that their status was not hereditary were essential differences that were to play an increasingly important role in the twentieth century.

## The great transformation of labour in the twentieth century

Labour contracts (*contrats de travail* in French, *contracts of employment* in English) emerged between the 1890s and the 1920s. These new legal institutions marked a departure from the forms of labour that had sustained the economic growth and societal transformation in Europe between the seventeenth century and mid-nineteenth century.

In England, at the start of the 1870s, most industrial enterprises were still independent family-run firms that employed fewer than a hundred workers. Mass production was slow in evolving and was still limited.[86] By the mid-nineteenth century, a decisive shift occurred towards an industrialized economy in which sustained increases in output per capita served to support a growing population, which, in turn, provided a source of rising demand.[87] From the mid-1880s onwards, large combinations of firms began to emerge, notably in textile manufacturing, coal mining, and engineering. Vertical integration, the welfare state, and changing labour institutions went hand in hand. Vertical integration required a stable labour force and large units; the peasant worker, the traditional poor, and Poor Laws hardly fit this process. The removal of criminal sanctions from the individual employment relationship in the 1870s was soon followed by the first legislative interventions of the welfare state.[88] These changes meant that the Poor Law remained in place but dealt only with residual cases that fell outside the range of the statutory social-insurance scheme.[89] Despite advances, seasonal and casual workers were excluded from these provisions as they were designated as independent contractors.

Litigation thus occurred over the definition of 'independent', with employers trying to avoid responsibility for the social risks of illness, injury, and unemployment.

Along an analogous path, in France, the law of 21 March 1884 legalized trade unions. The notion of the labour contract (*contrat de travail*) first appeared. The term *contrat de travail* was not in widespread use in France before the mid-1880s. However, once the term became established, it was used in turn-of-the-century legislation with respect to industrial accidents (law of 1898), which introduced the employer's objective responsibility in case of accident. This in turn opened the way to social insurances, which were being developed precisely during this period. However, the new labour law widened rather than reduced legal, social, and economic inequalities among working people. It excluded large categories, such as small enterprises, craftsmen, and peasants.[90] All these groups were marginalized as 'independent' workers.[91]

## Migration

Since the 1870s, the declining prices of these items and the joint process of mechanization led to decreasing immigration of indentured Indians, Chinese, and Africans in many production areas in the islands in the Antilles and the Indian Ocean regions. Yet migratory fluxes increased in the last quarter of the nineteenth century. In Europe, mechanization and concentration compelled people to migrate, while massive population flows helped create a single global economy for both labour and capital. Thus, between 1840 and 1940, 55–58 million Europeans and 2.5 million Africans and Asians reached the Americas; during this same period, 29 million Indians, 19 million Chinese, and 4 million Africans and Europeans moved to Southeast Asia, the Pacific Islands, and the Indian Ocean rim. Finally, forty-six to fifty-one million people from Northeastern Asia and Russia moved (or were compelled to move) to Siberia, Manchuria, and Central Asia.[92]

Economic factors were important, but they were not alone in causing this mass migration. Thanks to the transport revolution of steamboats and railroads, global migrations caused a significant shift in the distribution of the world's population. All three aforementioned destinations (Americas, Central Asia, and the Indian Ocean) experienced enormous population growth, increasing by factors of 4 to 5.5 from 1850 to 1950. Growth rates in these areas were more than twice that of world population as a whole. By comparison, growth rates in the regions of emigration were lower than world population growth and less than half of those in the regions of immigration. Taken together, the three main destination regions accounted for 10 per cent of the world's population in 1850 and 24 per cent in 1950.[93]

Even if relocation within the same empire was important (in particular, in the Russian and British empires), trans-imperial, intra-continental, regional, and local forms of migration were also important – and they clearly show the inadequacy of the Eurocentric paradigm, which consists of explaining migration as an 'expansion of the West'.[94] Indeed, migration was multi-scale and involved almost all areas of the world. Nearly four million Indians travelled to Malaysia, over eight million to Ceylon, over fifteen million to Burma, and about one million to Africa, other parts of Southeast Asia, and islands throughout the Indian and Pacific Oceans. Up to eleven million Chinese (most from the southern provinces) travelled from China to the Straits Settlements, although more than a third of these transhipped to the Dutch Indies, Borneo, Burma, and places farther west. Nearly four million travelled directly from China to Thailand, between two and three million to French Indochina, more than one million to the Dutch Indies (for a total of more than four million if transhipments from Singapore are included), and just under one million to the Philippines.[95]

At the same time, railroad construction and a relative relaxation of frontiers between Russia and China also led twenty-eight to thirty-three million northern Chinese to migrate to Siberia and Manchuria.[96] Migration within each area increased and interacted with long-distance emigration. Migrants from Ireland travelled to England for work; others moved from Eastern and Southern Europe to industrial areas in Northern Europe, especially France and Germany. In Russia, migrants moved into the growing cities and southern agricultural areas. Within India, they moved to tea plantations in the south and northeast, to the mines and textile-producing regions of Bengal, and to newly irrigated lands and urban areas throughout the subcontinent.[97]

Thus it would be reductive to explain twentieth-century migrations as simply an 'expansion of the West' and the triumph of free labour and free emigration over bondage. To be sure, whole sets of laws in defence of 'freedom' were adopted on all continents. 'Free' migration expanded with the increasing restriction of indenture contracts and their final abolition in 1920. In the United States, the Anti-Peonage Act of 1867 extended the prohibition of servitude (voluntary or involuntary) to all states in the Union. The government of India first restricted and then forbade Indian indentured contracts in 1916, while in 1874 an agreement between the Chinese and Portuguese governments stopped the transport of Chinese contract labour from Macao. Chinese authorities investigated the conditions of Chinese migrants in Cuba, Peru, and the United States, which led to the suspension of most of these contracts.

At the same time, formal rules for migration were not always supported by real legal rights granted to immigrants once they reached their destination. For example, the conditions of former indentured labourers were extremely different, precisely as they had been for former slaves. The access to landowning that one had on Mauritius and Reunion Island was hardly the rule. Elsewhere, between 1899 and 1938, most of the indentured immigrants served as day labourers in agriculture or in commerce; this was the case with Chinese, Indian, and Japanese immigrants in Cuba, British Guyana, Trinidad, and Hawaii. Servant contracts or 'independent' commercial activity was much more widespread in Cuba (40 per cent of the immigrants) and Hawaii (48 per cent) than in British Guyana (8 per cent) or Trinidad (24 per cent).[98]

Most importantly, different forms of bondage and debt obligations survived far into the twentieth century. Chinese, Africans, Indians, and, to a certain extent, even European emigrants were still subject to disguised forms of indenture contracts and bondage.[99] The same can be said for Africans, who even if officially freed from slavery were still under multiple forms of bondage in both intra-African and African-European relations. Local bondage coexisted with the intercontinental flow of free and less-free people. This was the case for various reasons: labour markets remained highly segmented, unequal skills adding to important institutional constraints. Migration was never really free; laws and reciprocal and multilateral agreements between powers obtruded and thus regulated the flow. The rise of the welfare state and protection of the 'national' working force went hand in hand with the increasing control, if not limitation of immigration and the exclusion of the colonies from the new welfare state.

## Conclusion

Unfree labour cannot exist unless political institutions intervene and limit the free market; the institutions regulating labour did not only respond exclusively to efficiency, scarcity (of labour), and profit calculations, but also to power and values. Violence, constraints, and contract enforcement were not only substitutes for higher wages, but also the expression of the belief that labour was a service to the master, the head of the family, the village, the community, and, ultimately, the state, and was accompanied by strongly unequal distribution of civil and human rights between labouring people and their masters. This global trend was at the very ground of economic growth through the seventeenth to the mid-nineteenth century, certainly in Eastern Europe and in the Western European colonial world (long after that date) and partially in the West as well. Since the mid-nineteenth century, increasing labour and civic and human rights in the West went along with capital-intensive growth, unions and political shifts more favourable to welfare capitalism. Yet, this turn consciously excluded the colonial world through the decolonization process, but even then, only for a short period, under the post-war reconstruction in Europe. Since the end of the 1970s, restrictions to the welfare state in the West went along once again with increasing restrictions to immigration and immigrants' social rights. Paradoxically, these two trends are increasingly perceived as being in opposition, the defence of national welfare being opposed to immigration.

## Notes

1. E. D. Domar (1970), 'The causes of slavery or serfdom: A hypothesis', *Journal of Economic History*, 30 (1), 18–32; E. D. Domar and M. J. Machina (1984), 'On the profitability of Russian serfdom', *Journal of Economic History*, 44 (4), 919–55. Domar's model was strongly inspired by Nieboer, a Dutch ethnographer in the late nineteenth to early twentieth century. H. Nieboer (1900), *Slavery as an Industrial System: Ethnological Researches*. The Hague: Martinus Nijhof.
2. H. J. Habakkuk (1958), 'The economic history of modern Britain', *Journal of Economic History*, 18 (4), 486–501; Idem (1962), *American and British Technology*; D. North and R. Thomas (1971), 'The rise and fall of the manorial system: A theoretical model', *Journal of Economic History*, 31 (4), 777–803; M. M. Postan (1973), *Cambridge Economic History of Europe: Expanding Europe in the Sixteenth and Seventeenth Centuries*. Cambridge: Cambridge University Press. For a more recent work, see R. C. Allen (2009), *British Industrial Revolution in Global Perspective*. Cambridge: Cambridge University Press.

3. S. Engerman (ed.) (1999), *Terms of Labor: Slavery, Freedom and Free Labor*. Stanford: Stanford University Press; M. Klein (1993), *Breaking the Chains: Slavery, Bondage and Emancipation in Modern Africa and Asia*. Madison: University of Wisconsin Press.

4. A. Stanziani (2014), *Bondage: Labor and Rights in Eurasia from the Sixteenth to the Early Twentieth Centuries*. New York: Berghahn.

5. S. Drescher (1987), *Capitalism and Antislavery: British Mobilization in Comparative Perspective*. New York: Oxford University Press; London: Palgrave, 11.

6. E. A. Wrigley and R. S. Schofield (1981), *The Population History of England: A Reconstruction*. Cambridge: Cambridge University Press, 218–21.

7. M. Huberman (1986), 'Invisible handshakes in Lancashire: Cotton spinning in the first half of the nineteenth century', *Journal of Economic History*, 46 (4), 987–98.

8. Stanziani, *Bondage*.

9. R. Steinfeld (1991), *The Invention of Free Labor: The Employment Relation in English and American Law and Culture, 1350–1870*. Chapel Hill: North Carolina University Press; Idem (2001), *Coercion, Contract, and Free Labor in the Nineteenth Century*. Cambridge: Cambridge University Press; M. Postan (1937), 'The chronology of labour services', *Transactions of the Royal Historical Society*, 20, 169–93; T. Brass and M. van der Linden (eds) (1997), *Free and Unfree Labour: The Debate Continues*. Berne: Peter Lang.

10. L. Benton (2002), *Law and Colonial Culture: Legal Regimes in World History, 1400–1900*. Cambridge: Cambridge University Press.

11. I. Wallerstein (1974), *The Modern World-System: Capitalist Agriculture and the Origins of the European World-Economy in the Sixteenth Century*. New York and London: Atheneum.

12. R. Steinfeld, *Coercion, Contract*; S. Deakin and F. Wilkinson (2005), *The Law of the Labour Market: Industrialization, Employment, and Legal Evolution*. Oxford: Oxford University Press; D. Hay and P. Craven (eds) (2004), *Masters, Servants, and Magistrates in Britain and the Empire, 1562–1955*. Chapel Hill: University of North Carolina Press.

13. Brass and van der Linden, *Free and Unfree Labour*.

14. D. W. Galenson (1981), *White Servitude in Colonial America: An Economic Analysis*. Cambridge: Cambridge University Press; D. Northrup (1995), *Indentured Labor in the Age of Imperialism, 1834–1922*. Cambridge: Cambridge University Press.

15. P. C. Emmer (ed.) (1986), *Colonialism and Migration: Indentured Labour before and after Slavery*. Dordrecht and Boston: Martinus Nijhoff Publishers; Engerman, *Terms of Labor*.

16. S. Naidu and N. Yuchtman (2009), 'How green was my valley? Coercive contract enforcement in nineteenth-century Britain', *NBUR Working Papers*: http://www.econ.ucla.edu/workshops/papers/History/Naidu.pdf?origin=publication_detail

17. D. Fraser (2009), *The Evolution of the British Welfare State*, 4th edn. London: Palgrave Macmillan, 67.

18. British Parliamentary Papers (from now on BPP) (1834), *Report from the Commissioners for Inquiring into the Administration and Practical Reform of the Poor Laws, 1834*, XXVIII, appendix A.

19. D. Green (2006), 'Pauper protests: Protests and resistance in early nineteenth-century London workhouses', *Social History*, 31 (2), 141.

20. F. Driver (1993), *Power and Pauperism: The Workhouse System, 1834–1884*. Cambridge: Cambridge University Press.

21. Steinfeld, *Invention of Free Labor*, 32.

22. A. Kussmaul (1981), *Servants in Husbandry in Early Modern England*. Cambridge: Cambridge University Press.

23. Postan, 'The chronology of labour services'.

24. D. C. Woods (1982), 'The operation of the Masters and Servants Act in the Black Country, 1858–1875', *Midland History*, 7, 93–115.

25. R. Rudolph (ed.) (1995), *The European Peasant, Family, and Society: Historical Studies*. Liverpool: Liverpool University Press.

26. Hay and Rogers, *English Society*.

27. H. J. Habakkuk (1962), *American and British Technology in the Nineteenth Century*. Cambridge: Cambridge University Press. For a critique, see J. Mokyr (1990), *The Lever of Riches. Technological Creativity and Economic Progress*. Oxford: Oxford University Press, 165.

28. C. Timmer (1969), 'The turnip, the New Husbandry, and the English agricultural evolution', *Quarterly Journal of Economics*, 83 (3), 375–95.

29. G. Grantham (1989), 'Agricultural supply during the Industrial Revolution: French evidence and European implications', *Journal of Economic History*, 49 (1), 43–72; G. Federico (2005), *Feeding the World: An Economic History of Agriculture, 1800–2000*. Princeton: Princeton University Press.

30. P. K. O'Brien (1977), 'Agriculture and the Industrial Revolution', *Economic History Review*, 30 (1), 166–81; Clark, 'Productivity growth without technical change in European agriculture before 1850'.

31. F. M. L. Thompson (1968), 'The second Agricultural Revolution, 1815–1880', *Economic History Review*, 21 (1), 62–77.

32. N. F. R. Crafts (1985), *British Economy during the Industrial Revolution*. Oxford: Clarendon Press; J. H. Williamson (1984), 'Why was British growth so slow during the Industrial Revolution?', *Journal of Economic History*, 44 (3), 687–712; C. K. Harley (1982), 'British industrialization before 1841: Evidence of slower growth during the Industrial Revolution', *Journal of Economic History*, 42 (2), 267–89; P. Deane and W. A. Cole, *British Economic Growth, 1688–1959*. Cambridge: Cambridge University Press; C. Feinstein and S. Pollard (eds) (1988), *Studies in Capital Formation in the United Kingdom, 1750–1920*. Oxford: Clarendon Press.

33. A recent summary of this approach in Allen, *The British Industrial Revolution*.

34. C. MacLeod (1988), *Inventing the Industrial Revolution*. Cambridge: Cambridge University Press.

35. Deakin and Wilkinson, *Law of the Labour Market*, 20.

36. D. Bythell (1978), *The Sweated Trades: Outwork in Nineteenth-Century Britain*. London: Batsford; J. Schmiechen (1982), *Sweated Industries and Sweated Labor: The London Clothing Trades, 1860–1914*. Urbana, IL: University of Illinois Press.

37. J. de Vries (2008), *The Industrious Revolution: Consumer Behavior and the Household Economy, 1650 to the Present*. Cambridge: Cambridge University Press.

38. H.-J. Voth (1998), 'Time and work in eighteenth century London', *Journal of Economic History*, 58 (1), 29–58.

39. E. Hopkins (1982), 'Working hours and conditions during the Industrial Revolution: A re-appraisal', *Economic History Review*, 25 (1), 52–67.

40. E. J. T. Collins (1976), 'Migrant labor in British agriculture in the nineteenth century', *Economic History Review*, 29 (1), 38–59; G. Postel-Vinay (1994), 'The dis-integration of traditional labour markets in France: From agriculture *and* industry to agriculture *or*

industry', in G. Grantham and M. MacKinnon (eds), *Labour Market Evolution*. London and New York: Routledge, 64–83.

41. K. D. M. Snell (1981), 'Agricultural seasonal unemployment, the standard of living, and women's work in the South and East, 1690–1860', *Economic History Review*, 34 (3), 407–37.

42. Huberman, 'Invisible handshakes in Lancashire'.

43. M. Huberman (1996), *Escape from the Market: Negotiating Work in Lancashire*. Cambridge: Cambridge University Press.

44. D. Hay (2004), 'England, 1562–1875: The law and its uses', in Hay and Craven, *Masters, Servants, and Magistrates*, 67.

45. Naidu and Yuchtman, 'How green was my valley?'.

46. E. Coornaert (1941), *Les corporations en France*. Paris: Gallimard; E. P. Thompson (1963), *The Making of the English Working Class*. London: Vintage Books; W. Sewell (1983), *Gens de métier et révolution. Le langage du travail de l'Ancien régime à 1848*. Paris: Aubier.

47. M. Sonenscher (1989), *Work and Wages: Natural Law, Politics and the Eighteenth-Century French Trades*. Cambridge: Cambridge University Press; P. Minard (1998), *La fortune du Colbertisme: Etat et industrie dans la France des lumières*. Paris: Fayard.

48. A. Cottereau (2002), 'Droit et bon droit. Un droit des ouvriers instauré, puis évincé par le droit du travail, France, XIXe siècle', *Annales*, 57 (6), 1521–57.

49. J. Domat (1697), *Les Lois Civiles dans leur Ordre Naturel*, reproduced in *Œuvres*. Paris: 1835, vol. 1; and R. Pothier (1861), *Traité du Contrat de Louage*. Paris: Bugnet.

50. Sonenscher, *Work and Wages*, 75.

51. Cottereau, 'Droit et bon droit'.

52. P. Hoffman (1996), *Growth in a Traditional Society: The French Countryside, 1450–1815*. Princeton: Princeton University Press, 45–6.

53. Postel-Vinay, 'The dis-integration'.

54. (1865), *Recueil des Usages Locaux en Vigueur dans le Département de la Vienne*. Poitiers: Bertrand; A. Pages (1855), *Usages et Règlements locaux, Servant de Complément à la Loi Civile et Topographie Légale du Département de l'Isère*. Grenoble: Baratier frères. See also the 1870 parliamentary enquiry in Archives Nationales de France (henceforth AN) C 1157–61.

55. Cottereau, 'Droit et bon droit'.

56. T. Magnac and G. Postel-Vinay (1977), 'Wage competition between agriculture and industry in mid-nineteenth century France', *Explorations in Economic History*, 34 (1), 1–26.

57. Postel-Vinay, 'The dis-integration'.

58. Habakkuk, American and British Technology.

59. K. Sokoloff and D. Dollar (1997), 'Agricultural seasonality and the organization of manufacturing in early industrial economies: The contrast between England and the United States', *Journal of Economic History*, 57 (2), 288–321.

60. U. Chakravarti (1985), 'Of Dasas and Karmakaras: Servile labour in ancient India', in U. Patnaik and M. Dingawaney (eds), *Chains of Servitude: Bondage and Slavery in India*. New York: Oxford University Press, 40–54; Benton, *Law and Colonial Culture*; M. Galanter (1989), *Law and Society in Modern India*. Delhi: Oxford University Press.

61. Bibliothèque Nationale de France, section des manuscrits, 'Nouvelles acquisitions de France', 9328.

62. For treatments of apprenticeship contracts, see Sonencher, *Works and Wages*.

63. Galenson, *White Servitude in Colonial America.*

64. Indentured were 60–5 per cent of all migrants in the seventeenth century and 40–2 per cent in the following century; see C. Tomlins (2010), *Freedom Bound: Law, Labor, and Civic Identity in Colonizing English America, 1580–1865.* Cambridge: Cambridge University Press, 34–5.

65. Northrup, *Indentured Labour,* 156–7, table A.1.

66. R. Menard (1977), 'From servants to slaves: The transformation of the Chesapeake labor system', *Southern Studies,* 16 (4), 366–7.

67. T. W. Allen (1994), *The Invention of the White Race,* 3 vols. New York: Verso; A. S. Parent Jr. (2003), *Foul Means: The Formation of a Slave Society in Virginia.* Chapel Hill: North Carolina University Press.

68. S. Engerman (1993), 'Europeans and the rise and fall of slavery in the Americas: An interpretation', *American Historical Review,* 98 (5), 1399–1423.

69. Sir W. Blackstone (1765–9), *Commentaries on the Laws of England,* Oxford, 4 vols., vol. 2, 16.

70. R. Blackburn (1988), *The Overthrow of Colonial Slavery, 1776–1848.* London: Verso; Tomlins, *Freedom Bound.*

71. D. Armitage (2004), 'John Locke, Carolina, and the two treatises of government', *Political Theory,* 32 (5), 602–27; B. Hinshelwood (2013), 'The Carolinian context of John Locke's theory of slavery', *Political Theory,* 41 (4), 562–90.

72. R. Sheridan (1974), *Sugar and Slavery. An Economic History of the British West Indies, 1623–1775.* Barbados: Canoe Press.

73. Fogel and Engerman (1974), *Time on the Cross;* R. Fogel (1989), *Without Consent or Contract.* New York: Norton.

74. Drescher, *Capitalism and Antislavery.*

75. BPP (1830–1), *Papers in Explanation of the Condition of the Slave Population, 5 Nov. 1831,* CCXXX, 59–88.

76. J. R. Ward (1988), *British West India Slavery, 1750–1834: The Process of Amelioration.* Oxford: Oxford University Press.

77. M. Turner (2004), 'The British Caribbean, 1823–1838: The transition from slave to free legal status', in Hay and Craven, *Masters, Servants and Magistrates,* 322.

78. T. Holt (1992), *The Problem of Freedom: Race, Labour and Politics in Jamaica and Britain, 1832–1938.* Baltimore and London: John Hopkins University Press.

79. R. Allen (1999), *Slaves, Freedmen and Indentured Labourers in Colonial Mauritius.* Cambridge: Cambridge University Press, 16–17. See also A. Toussaint (1974), *Histoire de l'Ile Maurice.* Paris: PUF.

80. Colony of Mauritius, Annual Report, 1854; *BPP,* XLII, 2050. See also, Jan Breman, *Taming the Coolie Beast.*

81. Mauritius National Archives (MNA), HA 66 (planters' petitions); BPP (1842), XXX (26), 25.

82. BPP (1842), XXX (26).

83. BPP (1875), '*Report of the Royal Commissioners Appointed to Enquire into the Treatment of Immigrants in Mauritius*', XXXIV, paragraph 704 and appendix A and B. Colony of Mauritius, printed documents, *Annual Report of the Protector of Immigrants,* 1860–1885.

84. Ibid.

85. Allen, *Slaves,* 72.

86. Mokyr, *The Level of Riches*, 114.

87. Wrigley, *Continuity, Chance and Change*.

88. Deakin and Wilkinson, *The Law of the Labour Market*, 86–7.

89. G. Bentley (1966), *The Evolution of National Insurance in Great Britain: The Origins of the Welfare State*. London: Joseph; J. Harris (1972), *Unemployment and Politics: A Study in English Social Policy, 1886–1914*. Oxford: Clarendon Press.

90. R. Salais, N. Bavarez and B. Reynaud (1986), *L'invention du chômage*. Paris: PUF.

91. A. Stanziani (2012), *Rules of Exchange: French Capitalism in Comparative Perspective, Eighteenth to Early Twentieth Century*. Cambridge: Cambridge University Press.

92. A. McKeown (2004), 'Global migration, 1846–1940', *Journal of World History*, 15 (2), 155–89; D. Treadgold (1957), *The Great Siberian Migration: Government and Peasant in Resettlement from Emancipation to the First World War*. Princeton: Princeton University Press, 33–5; T. Gottschang and D. Lary (2000), *Swallows and Settlers: The Great Migration from North China to Manchuria*. Ann Arbor: University of Michigan, Center for Chinese Studies, 171.

93. McKeown, 'Global migration'.

94. O'Rourke and Williamson, *Globalization and History*.

95. K. Singh Sandhu (1969), *Indians in Malaya: Some Aspects of Their Immigration and Settlement (1786–1957)*. Cambridge: Cambridge University Press.

96. R. H. G. Lee (1970), *The Manchurian Frontier in Ch'ing History*. Cambridge, MA: Harvard University Press.

97. A. de Haan (1999), 'Migration on the border of free and unfree labour: Workers in Calcutta's jute industry, 1900–1990', in J. Lucassen and L. Lucassen (eds), *Migration, Migration History, History: Old Paradigms and New Perspectives*. Bern: Peter Lang, 197–222.

98. Northrup, *Indentured Labor*, 150.

99. McKeown, 'Global migration'.

# CHAPTER 11
## VARIETIES OF INDUSTRIALIZATION:
## AN ASIAN REGIONAL PERSPECTIVE
*Kaoru Sugihara*

Discussion on the comparative history of industrialization usually focuses on the changes of technology and institutions, and makes a sharp distinction between the first industrializer, England, and its followers. The latter, including continental Europe, Japan, and Asia's emerging states, are often seen as having gone through a 'catch up industrialization' or 'big push industrialization'.[1] Technological and institutional innovations and mobilization of capital, among others, are highlighted as factors accounting for the first industrialization, while explanations for the diffusion of industrialization often focus on the transfer of technology, institutions, and values and norms, and the role of the state in it.

Such an approach leaves out the importance of the mobilization of natural resources and the innovative role played by local and regional forces. The recent literature on Asia's long-term path of economic development has discussed how diverse the region's resource endowments were before industrialization and how it responded to the need for procuring a much wider range and larger quantities of resources in the period of industrialization.[2] The best-known 'initial condition' in monsoon Asia was the presence of a large peasant family economy centred on rice cultivation, which could provide almost 'unlimited' supplies of labour.[3] The most-discussed constraint the region suddenly faced when industrializing was the availability of energy, especially coal, needed to serve modern industry and transport.[4] Another, equally serious constraint, emphasized in the literature, was the shortage of arable land because of population growth. Economic and social historians have discussed the widespread poverty, social inequality, and instability of the last two centuries, often by linking them to the resource shortages, especially that of land. Low agricultural productivity and a low land–labour ratio have been taken to be among the most important indicators of a resource-poor country.[5]

Asia's answer to such constraints was engaging in trade and migration within the region. The growth of intra-Asian trade and migration significantly mitigated local resource constraints, by trading coal and land-derived commodities such as rice and raw cotton and by moving labour. Monsoon Asia is richly endowed with water and biomass, but local endowment conditions vary greatly. It also suffers from the variability of water supply, acute infectious diseases, and regular natural disasters. It is this vast range of diverse environmental circumstances that offered the region opportunities for trade and migration. Yet, the impact of these local and regional resource transfers on industrialization has not been sufficiently recognized.

Asia also had to earn foreign exchange vis-à-vis advanced Western countries if it wanted to import modern machinery and associated sets of knowledge needed for industrial, urban, and infrastructural development. Exports of primary products were dependent on international demand as well as on climate variations. The longer the region took to build a competitive export sector, the more important it became to make efficient use of available local resources.

As labour was abundant and land was scarce and in order to minimize the amount of imports from the West and to exploit local resources, technology and institutions were geared towards labour-intensive and local-resource-dependent industrialization. Japan and other East Asian countries secured comparative advantage in labour-intensive industries when they were relatively free from local resource constraints, especially at the initial stage of industrialization. Where the availability of water was variable and its shortage or precariousness affected the quality of land and the environment, efforts were directed towards the more efficient governance and use of water to secure food and sustain livelihood. On the whole, the economies of India and Southeast Asia under Western domination were integrated into the international economy as exporters of primary products through the development of steamship lines and the construction of railways. While there was a significant development of labour-intensive industries in colonial India, there was also an impressive growth in the network of Asian merchants, and the migration and remittances across colonial boundaries in Southeast Asia.

In none of these countries or regions was technological and institutional innovation directed specifically towards higher labour productivity. Of course raising labour productivity is of crucial importance for any type of industrialization. But labour productivity was usually part of wider concerns about sustaining a large agrarian population and ensuring their welfare, regardless of whether the state was colonial or independent. It was important that not just a small modern sector but the local or regional economy as a whole would find its own path of economic development. Any rush for capital-intensive and resource-intensive technology would have to be financed with borrowing, often involving political costs or international risks. The adaptation of traditional or intermediate technology to serve modern needs was a great advantage, better still if it was accompanied by a fuller use of local resources. For example, where wood was plenty, timber, rather than coal, was used for heating. Charcoal could be made from timber relatively cheaply. Timber was also used instead of iron in the construction of the frame of power looms, thus lowering their cost.

This chapter considers the importance of these path dependencies for Asia's industrialization in regional perspective. The sub-regions discussed are East Asia (though Japan and China are often treated separately), Southeast Asia, and India (or South Asia). The task is twofold. First, this chapter identifies Asia's factor endowment conditions and their diversity, to describe how the sub-regions interacted to enhance the possibility of industrialization. I argue that the concurrent growth of local, regional, and global trade has been key to shaping the pattern of economic development of each sub-region in the nineteenth and the first half of the twentieth centuries. Second, the chapter traces the process of resource-intensive industrialization on a regional scale for the second half of the twentieth century, and reviews the process of diffusion and its consequences. In the last section, it compares the Asian and European regional paths of industrialization, and suggests that, while Europe initiated the diffusion of industrialization, Asia made it environmentally, technologically, and institutionally much more inclusive than the original version. This was achieved by creating the resource nexus and by exploiting, often overexploiting, the extraordinary environmental and cultural diversities of monsoon Asia and beyond.

## Initial conditions in 1820 and after

In 1820, China had 381 million people, or 37 per cent of world population; India had 209 million (20 per cent), while Japan had 31 million (3 per cent), and nine Southeast Asian states had about 38 million (4 per cent). This is obviously a crude estimate, but the difference in the size of the four sub-regions is important for the argument of this chapter. China and India had the capacity to hold a very large population, while their neighbouring sub-regions of Japan and Southeast Asia scarcely matched them but sustained distinct units as the periphery.[6] This is arguably the most important 'initial condition' for Asia's industrialization, in that the region was potentially able to both absorb the largest pool of labour on earth and connect it to the outside world.

In explaining post-war economic development up to c. 1980, Harry Oshima stressed the common socio-environmental characteristics of monsoon Asia, stretching from East and Southeast Asia to South Asia, in terms of seasonal rainfall patterns induced by monsoon winds and the centrality of the large river delta for the growth of rice farming and dense population. His formulation focuses on the sequence of intensive rice farming, population growth, availability of cheap labour, and labour-intensive industrialization leading to economic growth.[7] This sequence implicitly assumed several topics, which have been more explicitly taken up by other scholars, mainly with reference to East Asia. The development of intensive farming under land scarcity implied successful labour absorption.[8] It also implied the intensive use of water and manure required for commercial crop production.[9] Population growth also required the maintenance of social order.[10] Proto-industrialization and commercialization of agriculture meant the growth of intra-regional trade through merchant networks.[11] Finally, labour-intensive industrialization implied the capacity to engage in intercontinental trade, to exchange primary products at an initial stage and increasingly to export labour-intensive manufactured goods in return for fossil fuels, other resources, and capital-intensive goods.[12] In other words, monsoon Asia's feeding capacity came as much from the development of the ability to acquire resources as from the basic water and air circulation regime. Each country or sub-region responded to this challenge with varying difficulties and policy support, and eventually incorporated resource-intensive industrialization into its development path.

Second, maritime Asia, represented by present Southeast Asia but stretching from the coasts of the Indian Ocean to the western side of the Asia-Pacific region, was able to organize two very large sets of regional trading networks, involving local, regional, and global trade.

In the early modern period, there were a China-centred trading network east of the Malacca Straits and an Indian Ocean trade from the west of the straits to the western Indian Ocean. Together with the Atlantic trade, which was oriented more towards intercontinental trade, they comprised the three major regional networks in the world in the seventeenth and eighteenth centuries. Arab traders were extremely important in connecting Asia with Europe. Moreover, the English and Dutch East India companies conducted world trade on the basis of the two Asian trading networks locally conducted by Asian traders. Nevertheless, many would agree that the two Asian trading networks had a degree of cultural cohesiveness and diversity within it at the same time. The East Asian networks were governed by the tendency to regulate intercontinental trade, and when by the end of the seventeenth century pirate activities were curtailed, the East Asian seas became peaceful. In addition to, and partly in replacement of, tributary trade relations, China developed a more equal regime of managed trade (the Hushi system), and both Japanese and Chinese governments recognized the utility of bilateral trade relationships. In other words, Asian traders had the capacity and the environment to conduct local and regional trade comparable to European traders, though not to engage in intercontinental trade. This is the second 'initial condition' which other non-European regions did not have on a comparable scale around 1820.

It should be noted that maritime states based on port cities and surrounding rural areas grew along the coasts of the Indian Ocean, including maritime Southeast Asia. Here the key organizing agents were port cities (or port city states) and networks of merchants.[13] Even in mainland Southeast Asia, the agrarian population was not necessarily the mainstay.[14] Products derived from sea, land, and forest were all involved in the exchange economy. If the state was relatively urban or commercially oriented, it could shift its fiscal base from one commodity to another, or from one economic activity to another, relatively easily. This flexibility was one important strength for securing resources and livelihoods. The first serious economic contacts with Europe often began via these states.

## Setting up industrialization in monsoon Asia

Let me recapture the relative importance of the four sub-regions in terms of regional GDP. In 1820, China's share in Asia's GDP (sum of the four sub-regions) was 59 per cent and South Asia 29 per cent, while Japan, South Korea, Taiwan, and Hong Kong (using later territorial categories for the sake of comparison) comprised 7 per cent and Southeast Asia 5 per cent.[15] By 1950, China's share had declined to 28 per cent, while that of Japan and others rose to 21 per cent, Southeast Asia to 17 per cent, and South Asia to 33 per cent (Figure 11.1). Thus the four sub-regions became much more equal in terms of economic weight, though not concerning the size of the population. Within China and India, economic progress mainly came from the coastal regions. The weight of Asia's contribution to the world GDP shifted from the two agrarian empires in China and India to maritime monsoon Asia.

Key to this transformation was location. The economies of maritime monsoon Asia absorbed Western technology and institutions on the one hand, and mobilized local and regional resources on the other, through the development of transport networks, trade,

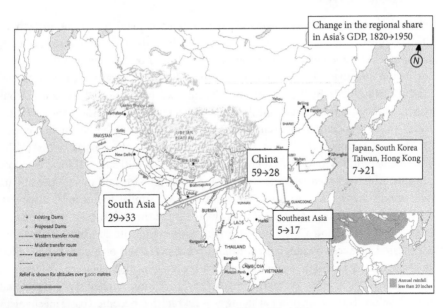

Figure 11.1  Change in the regional share in Asia's GDP, 1820–1950.

*Notes and sources*: Figures are from A. Maddison (2011), 'Statistics on World Population, GDP and Per Capita GDP, 1-2008 AD' http://www.ggdc.net/Maddison/. Map is Adapted from K. Pomeranz (2009), 'The Great Himalayan watershed: Agrarian crisis, mega-dams and the environment', *New Left Review*, 58, 5–39. K. Pomeranz (2009), 'The Great Himalayan watershed: Agrarian crisis, mega-dams and the environment', *New Left Review*, 58, 5–39.

and migration. Two paths emerged as a result. In Meiji Japan, and a little later in coastal China, commercial ports in or near major cities such as Yokohama, Kobe, and Shanghai connected imported and local resources to help modern cities and industries grow. It was important that the emerging area had both the will to industrialize (thus committed to import technology and build an infrastructure to absorb it) and the social capacity to mobilize local resources, natural and human (including the ability to import or recruit them from other places). At the same time, in India and Southeast Asia, commercial ports, built by Western colonial powers, also connected imported and local resources to develop economies centred on port cities, but driven by the exports of primary products. They included Bombay, Madras, Calcutta, Singapore, and Jakarta. Hong Kong acted as a colonial port serving both China and Southeast Asia.

The two paths were interrelated and were not necessarily geographically separate. For example, the first modern industry emerged in Bombay in the middle of the nineteenth century, and soon met competition from Japan. Both China and Japan exported tea and raw silk in large quantities to earn foreign exchange. Commercial ports in Korea and Taiwan were developed by Japanese colonial authorities, to connect their primary exports to Japan. But there was also a divergence within maritime parts of modern Asia. South and Southeast Asia tended towards the path of primary produce economies, while East Asia tended towards industrialization.

Japan's labour-intensive industrialization was both dependent on the growth of maritime economies and one of its major drivers. In the early stages of industrialization, Japan exported rice and coal, but soon became an importer of these commodities as well as raw cotton and sugar. It competed with India in the cotton yarn market of central China during the 1890s. By the early twentieth century, Japan imported raw cotton from India, rice and sugar from Southeast Asia, Korea, and Taiwan, and soybeans and their derivates from Manchuria; in exchange, it exported labour-intensive manufactured goods such as cotton yarn, cotton cloth and sundries to other parts of Asia. The environmental implication of this division of labour was a mitigation of local resource constraints, which enabled Japan to expand its industrial base, and most especially its cotton textile industry. In this respect the basic logic was similar to England's discovery of 'ghost acreages' in North America during the period of the Industrial Revolution.[16]

In the interwar period China went through import-substitution industrialization, which pressed Japanese manufacturers to find more processed or higher-value-added products for export. Under the regime of selective protectionism, Japanese manufacturers also increased the exports of textile machinery to China, which started regional industrialization. This was an original 'flying geese', which has become a basic mechanism of progressively including higher value-added commodities and commodities made with the more advanced technology in intra-regional trade. Figure 11.2 shows that Japan adopted a policy of selective protectionism, setting up tariff barriers only against imports directly competing with the domestic industry. It encouraged import substitution but pursued the benefit of free trade, and as a result its overall tariff rate remained relatively low, while China and India raised tariff rates, partly for revenue purposes but also to more comprehensively protect domestic industries. Japan's dependence upon import of raw materials was much greater than that of the other two countries.

Countries involved in intra-Asian trade included a number of European colonies in South and Southeast Asia, as well as countries of East and Southeast Asia under unequal treaties and the treaty port system. Under this system of 'forced free trade', Japanese merchants brought a wide range of cotton manufacture (cloth and apparel) and sundries (matches, soap, toothpaste and tooth brushes, traditional medicine, umbrellas, bicycles, and noodle-making machines) to Asian peoples, and they interacted with Indian, Chinese, and other Asian merchant networks. It was these networks, together with the Japanese trade associations (and government efforts to help them to compete with Asian networks), that facilitated the export of labour-intensive manufactured goods. With a time lag and political disturbances, labour-intensive industrialization spread to China and eventually to other parts of Asia.

This was also a crucial moment for modern (initially mostly colonial) states in Southeast Asia. In the late nineteenth to the first half of the twentieth centuries, most of the region was put under Western colonial rule, but it continued to interact with other Asian countries, as the region traditionally had done. In fact it developed new trade links with Japan, China, and India, roughly at the same speed as it did with the West. With the improvement of transport and information networks under Western impact, the fusion between the two former agrarian empires (of China and India) and Southeast

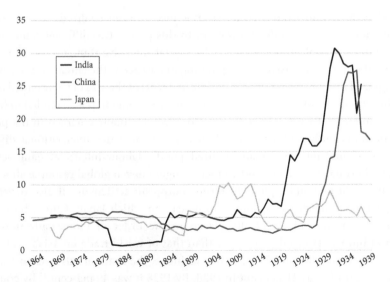

Figure 11.2  Import tariff rates in India, China, and Japan, 1868–1938.

*Notes and Sources*: India: K. Sugihara, (2002), 'Indo Kindaishi ni okeru Enkakuchi Boeki to Chiiki Koueki, 1868-1938-nen (The Long-distance Trade and Regional Trade in Modern Indian History, 1868-1938)', *Toyo Bunka*, 82, 30–1; China: Liang-lin Hsiao, (1974) *China's Foreign trade Statistics, 1864-1949*, Cambridge MA: Harvard University Press, 22–4, 132–3; Japan: Okurasho Shuzeikyoku [Japanese Ministry of Finance Government Bureau of Taxation] (1948), *Dai-15-kai Kokkai Kanzei Sankosho* (Reference Material on Customs Tariff for the 15th Parliament), Tokyo: Okurasho. Rates refer to total import revenue divided by total value of imports. The Japanese data exclude colonial imports after 1919.

Asia resulted in a massive (mostly temporary) migration of Indians and Chinese to Southeast Asia.

Furthermore, across Asia, there emerged a shared demand for modern consumption goods among ordinary peoples (from rice, dried fish, spices, and a range of non-timber forest products to Japanese manufactured goods mentioned above). The traditional commodity complex shared in the region (rice, sugar, tea, silk, and cotton) remained important, and a modern Asian consumer culture emerged. A complex set of commodity chains were created: while the growth of the market for intermediate goods (e.g. cotton yarn of low counts) meant a degree of 'culture-neutralization' of the Asian international market, these goods in turn served for a diverse range of final demand (e.g. traditional – kimono – clothing and apparel to its modernized versions). Meanwhile, unbleached cotton cloth was brought to the hinterland (and also other parts of the developing world including East Africa) by Asian merchants and enhanced the scope of regional integration. This in turn made it easier to transfer labour-intensive technology and managerial know-how to culturally diverse areas, and underpinned regionally driven industrialization in the post-Second-World-War period.

Thus, although many parts of Asia, especially India, were affected by the influx of English cotton cloth in the nineteenth century, and traditional textile industries declined to a certain extent, Asia was not just de-industrialized. It reorganized itself into a new form of industrialization. In this period two different routes of the diffusion of industrialization emerged: the capital-intensive route originating in the West and the labour-intensive one originating in East Asia. The latter was too small to be recognized by global economic historians in terms of the size of value added at this stage, but it was already an important source of employment. It also tended to be less resource-intensive than the former. Therefore, what actually emerged in the period from the nineteenth century to the 1930s was a three-tier international division of labour: capital-intensive manufactured goods, labour-intensive manufactured goods, and primary products, and an increasingly uneven global resource allocation in favour of Europe and regions of recent European settlement. It also developed an international division of labour within Asia, in which Japan, China, India, and Southeast Asia were hierarchically placed in the order of industrialization. The growth of intra-Asian trade was faster than that of world trade or Asia's trade with the West between 1880 and 1938. In one estimate, the share of intra-Asian trade in Asia's export trade was 41 per cent in 1928. By 1938 it was 49 per cent.[17] By contrast, it has been observed that 'regional integration through local and regional merchant networks appears to have been less marked in most parts of Africa, the Middle East and Latin America where the local economies were integrated into the metropolis-led international economy as satellites'.[18] However, even in Asia, the productivity of proto-industries with traditional technology, modern labour-intensive factories, and commercial agriculture built on the low land – labour ratio remained low. The standard of living rose very slowly.[19]

Finally, both intra-Asian trade and labour-intensive industrialization were severely disrupted by Japanese imperialism and territorial expansion. From 1931 to 1936, Japan grew faster than most Western countries and proceeded with heavy industrialization. This partly came from the 'import-substitution industrialization', in the sense that competitive pressure from the West was eased, largely as a result of the Great Depression. Under the collapse of world trade, the rise of protectionism and the demise of the international gold standard, an East Asian monetary order with a tendency to devalue against key currencies worked in favour of regional industrialization.[20] The intra-yen bloc trade now included a significant proportion of machinery trade. But it was also a move towards autarky, anticipating post-war India and China, in that most new industries were linked to the research and development efforts of Japan's military industries. If the direction of industrial development was driven by political and military interests (and in Japan's case without a full understanding of global military and resource balances), there was no guarantee, or even a prospect, that the country was adopting a sensible import-substitution strategy based on factor endowment considerations. To some extent, therefore, the ecologically uneven exchange between Europe and colonial Asia was extended to a similar resource transfer between Japan and other parts of Asia, not least Japan's own colonies.

Looking at the period from 1820 to 1950 as a whole, the intra-regional trading sphere of Asia showed a common tendency to expand by commercializing its agriculture and reorganizing its traditional industries, and by linking modern manufacturing to this expansion, which resulted in the evolution of the system comprising a division of labour between agriculture and industry within the region. The difference between the structure of consumption in Asia and the West was another important factor that made it possible for Asia to industrialize. Sustained by demand within the region, the traditional textile industries managed, to some extent, to develop their hand-weaving industry with the use of machine-reeled yarns and to form modern mass consumption markets somewhat different from those in the West, and thereby coped with the 'Western impact' while maintaining employment at certain levels. Such a labour-intensive path of economic development was well suited to Asia's factor endowments, and comparative advantages were established in India, China, and Japan. Although formed under many difficulties that were caused by the imposition of the free trade regime and domestic political disorders, this constituted the core part of Asia's development path, and served as the pillar for the expansion of its trade. Perhaps one of the most significant contributions from the growth of world trade, as viewed from a broader perspective that takes intra-regional transactions into due consideration, may be the fact that it triggered this type of response to the 'Western impact' and thereby helped to revitalize the region's employment absorption mechanism, which had at one time been seriously damaged.

## Post-war diffusion of industrialization

After the emergence, development, and abrupt collapse of the Yen bloc in the 1930s and the first half of the 1940s, intra-Asian trade recovered fast among a smaller number of countries. The post-war reforms under the US-led allied occupation changed the character of Japanese political, economic, and social organizations into a more democratic one. By 1950, India, China, many Southeast Asian countries, and North Korea withdrew from the regime of free trade, while the countries along the western Pacific Rim (Japan, South Korea, Taiwan, Hong Kong, and Malaya-Singapore among others) were integrated into the US-led world economy.

The post-war diffusion of industrialization, beginning in Japan and spreading to other Asian countries, followed the same interactive path between intra-regional trade and industrialization as in the pre-war years, first among a small number of countries under the regime of free trade and the technological transfer from the West, and gradually embracing others. This is the case of the 'Asian textile complex' in the 1970s, in which Japan produced rayon yarn, Taiwan wove rayon cloth, and Hong Kong made the cloth into an apparel and exported the apparel to the United States.[21] New intermediate goods included cheap plastics, man-made fibres, machine parts, and eventually IC chips. Again, we do not see such a dynamic relationship between regions in Africa, Middle East, or Latin America in this period. South Africa and Brazil proceeded with industrialization without accompanying regional integration. It is only in East Asia that economic nationalism has embraced regional integration.

Import-substitution industrialization, strictly interpreted, was based on the building of a full industrial structure equivalent to that in developed countries, by imposing very high tariffs against imports of industrial goods from the West. This strategy seemed politically viable in many countries, including India and China, though it turned out to be relatively short-lived. In India, by the Third Five-Year Plan period, it became clear that the benefits of heavy industrialization, modelled largely on the Soviet experience, did not 'trickle down', resulting in the growth of 'disguised unemployment' in rural areas and the urban 'informal sector'. In communist China during the Mao period, human development indicators improved faster than in India, but the country struggled to develop competitive heavy industries (also influenced by the Soviet experience) in the absence of technological transfer from more developed countries, especially from the West.

By contrast, some East and Southeast Asian countries – such as Japan; the newly industrializing economies (NIEs) of South Korea, Taiwan, Hong Kong, and Singapore; and the ASEAN-4 consisting of Thailand, Malaysia, Indonesia, and the Philippines – pursued an export-oriented path to industrialization. They experienced relatively high rates of growth, by taking advantage of the gains from trade more than India and China.[22] Figure 11.3 shows a further shift in the economic weight from China to Japan and NIEs between 1950 and 1980.

We record some evidence of the regional dimension of industrial upgrading. In post-war Japan, rapid technological transfer from the West led to the development of machinery industries (transport, electrical, heavy, and machine tool) along the lines of the extension of labour-intensive industries. Between 1972 and 1985, 'new' industries, driven by microelectronics technology such as computer and communication industries, grew faster in Asia than in the United States and Western Europe, although the technology originated mainly from the United States. These industries did not necessarily require industrial concentration and the kind of infrastructure which heavy industries needed such as ports and transport to carry heavy material. Nor did they need the supply of a very large amount of capital. As long as competitive labour, access to information, and commercial and financial networks were available, they would move to any location where the best combination of factor endowments and policy packages was on offer.[23] Thus semiconductor and consumer electronics factories that were established across the emerging economies became part of the 'global supply chains', and contributed to the emergence of a large, semi-skilled to skilled labour force.

ILO studies in labour-intensive industries and human resource development extensively discussed the 'matching' between the nature of new demand for skills on the one hand, and education and formal training on the other.[24] They were conscious of the transferability of the experiences of Japan and NIEs to Southeast Asia. Not many attempts were successful, nor were they comprehensively pursued by the government; however by the 1980s, the direction of thinking was clearly towards the development of human capital, or in manufacturing, that of a workforce of good quality. This was linked to a shift towards a more balanced allocation of educational expenditure between

Figure 11.3 Change in the regional share in Asia's GDP, 1950–80.

*Sources*: As per Figure 11.1.

primary, secondary, and tertiary sectors.[25] The overall result was a simultaneous rise of per capita GDP and the Human Development Index.

ASEAN-4 countries started a developmental policy under authoritarian regimes around 1965. They gradually turned to the export-oriented strategy, and proceeded to industrialization in the 1980s. This can be seen in the radical change in their commodity composition of trade. In spite of a criticism of 'shallowness' of industrialization, and limited scale of institutional reforms, such as land reform, industrialization occurred with varying degrees of success.[26] Indeed, it became a mainstay of Asia's economic policy. From a regional perspective, Southeast Asia mainly acted as an importer of East Asia's manufactured goods and capital, but was also a committed industrializer.

Under 'open regionalism', which helped the formation of ASEAN and underpinned the emergence of APEC (Asia-Pacific Economic Cooperation), the region would not discriminate against countries outside its boundaries. The underlying ideology is different from both the hegemonic regime of free trade (as in Britain and the United States) and the continental European regime of free trade through treaty networks.[27] Historically, the region was used to low tariff levels and exposure to the international economy, especially in the late nineteenth and early twentieth centuries under the regime of 'forced free trade'. It was natural for these Asian countries to engage in trade between neighbouring countries with similar economic structures, to compete for similar markets, seek complementarity in trade, and exploit regional sources of growth. China and India joined the network of trade and economic growth after policy changes in 1979 and in 1991, respectively.

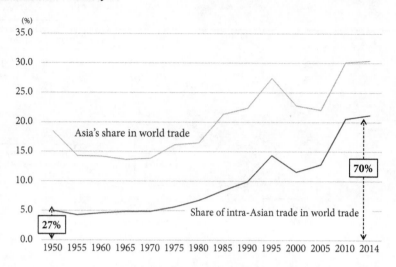

Figure 11.4 Share of Asian and intra-Asian trade in world trade, 1950–2014.

*Notes and Sources*: Percentage in box shows the share of intra-Asian trade in Asian trade. Calculated from K. Takanaka (2000), *Higashi-ajia Choki Keizai Tokei 9: Gaikoku Boeki to Keizai Hatten* (Long-term Economic Statistics of East Asia, Vol. 9, Foreign Trade and Economic Development), Tokyo: Keiso Shobo, 500–517 for 1950–99; and IMF, *Direction of Trade Statistics Yearbook* for 2000–14. Intra-Asian trade total refers to the value of exports from ten Asian countries (Japan, four NIEs, four ASEAN countries and China) and their imports from the smaller Asian countries (adjusted by FOB-CIF conversion).

In the early post-war period, the share of the United States (and other Western countries) in Asia's trade was large, and its influence in industrial development was dominant. However, the US share rapidly declined, and was replaced by the growth of regionally driven trade. In 1965, Asia's share in world exports was 14 per cent, but this share increased to 23 per cent in 2000, and to 31 per cent in 2015. More important, the share of intra-Asian trade Asia's exports increased from 35 per cent in 1965 to 51 per cent in 2000, and to 70 per cent in 2015, a figure comparable to intra-EU trade (Figure 11.4).

## Development of resource-intensive industrialization

To some extent rapid industrial upgrading in Japan along the lines of labour-intensive industrialization was complementary to the more capital- and resource-intensive industries, especially in the United States. But it also resulted in the upgrading and expansion of capital- and resource-intensive industries within Asia. Imports of fossil fuels, including oil and liquefied natural gas, and other raw materials became essential for this purpose.

In the 1950s there was a debate over how Japan's resources should be secured, especially as to whether its energy demand should depend on domestic coal or on imported oil. High economic growth and rapidly rising demand favoured the latter option. There was also a coordinated attempt by the Ministry of International Trade and Industry to spread the energy-saving methods of production in steel and electrical machinery industries. In the second half of the 1950s, serious attempts were made to develop a 'seafront industrial complex' (*rinkai kogyo chitai*) consisting of an oil refinery, and a petrochemical and electricity generation plant, among other industries. There was an accumulation of know-how prior to this period, including the idea of establishing the 'industrial port' as distinct from the 'commercial port'. International circumstances also strongly favoured this strategy. A sudden expansion of oil production in the Middle East was not being met by a matching increase of demand in Europe, and majors were looking for their customers. This gave Japanese companies the opportunity to negotiate with Western firms on technology transfer on good terms.[28]

Pursuit of the seafront complex involved a number of industrial and infrastructural developments. Against the background of low prices of resources and energy, Japanese shipbuilding companies and shipping lines attempted to utilize the latest technology of large oil tankers and other specialist bulk vessels (e.g. for iron ore) to the full. Equally important was a rapid introduction of container cargoes for other commodities, which standardized shipments across international ports and helped coordinate the transfer of goods between different means of transport in industrial ports. The seafront complex was constructed with dredging and reclamation, centred on deep harbours which could take large vessels. Railway lines and roads were built to ensure access. The establishment of the industrial site required pursuit of economies of scale on the one hand, and political and public approval on the other. In the 1960s the Japanese political will was strong enough to push the 'Pacific industrial belt' development at a speed inconceivable in the established industrial districts in the West.

Resource-intensive industries were typically located not in the central parts of major cities such as Tokyo and Osaka, but in neighbouring areas. For example, Tokyo retained employment-absorbing labour-intensive (by then mostly skill-intensive) industries within the central wards, while the bay areas of Yokohama became home to a resource-intensive cluster. After the second half of the 1960s, environmental protection movements began to spread, and the municipal government gave voice to the citizens before the central government did. Such politico-social dynamics were partly responsible for the diffusion of the industrial complex to the more distant and less politically sensitive or powerful areas, without necessarily mitigating the potential environmental damage.[29]

Unlike the 'global supply chain' – which in this context essentially consists of a network of factories (plus perhaps headquarters) scattered in various parts of Asia – the key feature here is what might be called the 'resource nexus': the creation of a spatial cluster designed for combining specific sets of resources. In particular, local and domestic resources were to be efficiently combined with imported resources. As industrialization proceeded, the resource nexus began to reorganize the entire spatial allocation of human and natural resources in the country. It encouraged the growth of cities, which provided resource-intensive industries with labour and the market (e.g. for electricity). A large proportion of the population moved to the cities, while a large part of rural areas became 'urban' at the same time. A new relationship between the city and the countryside was formed with the premise that industries would have access to global resources to lead economic growth.

Other East Asian countries also adopted the seafront industrial complex strategy. In South Korea initial conditions for heavy and chemical industries were low, because most of the colonial legacy was located in the North. In 1973, the developmental state declared the programme for 'heavy and chemical industrialization'. A series of seafront complexes were subsequently established in the far south. They were distinctly separate from the traditional light-industry zones. The new nexuses included shipbuilding, automobile, steel, and military-related machinery industries. In addition to the steel industry, which grew out of domestic demand and joined this development, petrochemical and shipbuilding industries were especially successful in exports. Meanwhile, in Seoul and its neighbouring regions and some other clusters, labour-intensive industries were transformed into 'new' industries driven by the microelectronics revolution.[30]

In Taiwan, where traditionally fragmented small and medium-sized businesses were scattered across the island, the government-led strategy for heavy and chemical industrialization lasted for a relatively short period, from the late 1960s to the early 1970s. Even so, steel, petrochemical, and shipbuilding industries were established, and they played a supporting role in the growth of labour-intensive and high-technology industries.[31]

In China, the initial phase after the policy reform of 1979 was characterized by a slow and difficult process of transition. Many heavy industries were located inland for political and strategic reasons and because of the idea that they should be developed close to where coal and other resources were found. Experts had to be persuaded that imports of resources were essential for further industrialization. The Pearl River Delta, on the strength of the rich historical tradition of Hong Kong as a major trading hub and the export-zone initiatives in Canton in the 1970s, led the development of electronics industries, while the city of Shanghai (and the Yangtze River Delta) initially suffered from the need to reorganize state-owned enterprises, heavy industries, and coal mines. The establishment of the Shanghai Baoshan Ironworks with the introduction of foreign (Japanese) technology and management was a turning point in China's commitment to the seafront development model. By the 1990s, the Yangtze River Delta had re-established itself as the main industrial complex with large imports of resources from abroad.[32]

In China the linkage between 'new' electronics-related industries and resource-intensive industries took a different form. Three 'megapolises', a chain of connected metropolitan areas, located in Pearl River and Yangtze River deltas and the national capital region (Beijing-Tianjin-Hebei), respectively, grew into a centre of progressively larger urban networks. While heavy and chemical industries, especially steel and petrochemical sectors, were concentrated on the seafront to maximize the benefits from economies of scale and access to imports, electronics and machinery industries were located across a variety of cities and the countryside, so that the region could create intra-industry linkages and links to a large consumer market.[33] This was a more embracing model for combining the strength of natural and human resources than the earlier experiments in Japan and elsewhere, with accompanying, often more serious, problems such as air pollution. It also had equally powerful political and social consequences for the inequality and uneven resource allocation with other parts of China.

## Local resources under pressure

Figure 11.5 shows a marked shift in the economic gravity from Japan and NIEs back to China, although much of this comes from the growth of coastal areas within China (and to a lesser extent India) in the period 1980–2014. It is clear by now that Asian growth began to include the 'hinterland', as well as smaller countries in the Eurasian continent. By making a vast rural population closer to trade-led industrialization, the policy changes in China and India had a major impact on the rise of emerging economies in particular and global economic development in general.

In these countries the rising export capacity made it possible to import raw materials and fossil fuels. But, while food and fossil fuels could be imported relatively easily, the resulting growth could put less tradeable factors of production under unprecedented pressure. Such resources include water for agricultural use and local biomass energy. Seasonal and annual variability of water supply could be crucial for the stability of agriculture. Nearby forests or the 'waste land' from which timber, twigs, or crop residues had been obtained could disappear as a result of population increase and expansion of arable land, and this could make it difficult for the peasant household to secure biomass energy for cooking, lighting, and heating, and for the local economy to secure

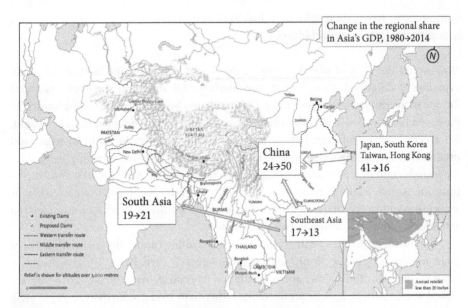

Figure 11.5 Change in the regional share in Asia's GDP, 1980–2014.

*Notes and Sources*: As per Figure 11.1. Figures for 2014 have been estimated, using *IMF, International Financial Statistics Yearbook*.

biomass resources for fuels and building materials.[34] In other words, there was a great deal of environmental diversity, which worked for sustaining a large population. As industrialization occurred and tradeable resources were brought in, however, some areas such as the Pacific coast or port cities prospered, while hinterlands, semi-arid regions, and mountainous areas took longer to meet the increased demand for local resources.

In many parts of contemporary China, water became scarce and emerged as a focal point of local, national, and regional politics. The most immediate problem was the supply of water for agriculture as well as for industrial and domestic purposes. The problem was also aggravated by the need for dam construction for electricity generation. Figures 11.1 to 11.3 outline the significance of a huge regional water and air circulation and the multi-scale character of issues involved in its governance. In contemporary India, a rapid progress in the use of tube wells solved the issue of self-sufficiency in food and raised agricultural productivity, but resulted in the lowering of water tables. Free electricity for tube-well users also distorted resource allocation, for example, by making investments in the improvement of electricity supply more difficult than otherwise.[35] Where electricity is not always available, securing local biomass energy for cooking and heating purposes could still be a matter of life and death. Vast numbers of hours had been spent on water and fuel wood collection, mainly by women.[36]

Thus the growth of the resource nexus in the core parts of Asia has been accompanied by the intensification of local resource constraints in the less developed areas, increasingly derived from multi-scale causes. In many ways they have been the two sides of the same coin.

## Conclusion: Towards a reinterpretation of Asian industrialization in global history

How would the path of global economic development look in the light of the Asian experiences described above? First, the fundamental difference between Asia and Europe in the early modern period was the population holding capacity of the former. In monsoon Asia, intensive farming, centred on rice cultivation under the scarcity of land, fed a very large population. Labour-intensive technology developed to increase land productivity and greater absorption of labour, including double-cropping, irrigation, the introduction of new seed varieties, and the use of human and animal waste. Micro-institutions such as the household and the village community helped reinforce labour absorption within the village by combining the main (farm) work with proto-industrial activities at home and during the off-peak seasons.

By contrast, in the European system of mixed farming (under the rotation system of grain and livestock production), land was less intensively used. Pasture implied a greater input of capital for the maintenance of cattle and its control, hence greater possibility for capital accumulation. Labour productivity, rather than land productivity, was pursued, both in large-scale capitalist agriculture and in peasant-based mixed farming. The result was that by 1820 the standard of living in the core regions of Western Europe was higher, while the size of the population in monsoon Asia was much larger. They could be interpreted as two different responses to the Malthusian problem of population exceeding beyond the capacity of food production.

Second, Europe offered another response to local resource constraints by developing overseas trade and capital markets and by exploiting fossil fuels, especially coal. This implied a progressive extension of its resource base to the biosphere of the New World and the tropics on the one hand and to the Asian geosphere on the other (especially on energy). War, territorial acquisition overseas, and mercantilist projects created the need for advancing scientific knowledge for navigation and military technologies. At the same time, new commodities were brought in from different parts of the world, which helped the development of consumer culture. The major urban centres acted as a 'nexus' for combining diverse resources and created the possibilities of innovation and capital accumulation. Artisans were gathered, food and raw materials for industrial products were brought from the countryside, luxuries were imported, and capital was pooled and invested for the development of infrastructure and industry. Eventually the invention of steam engines and the use of coal made a decisive impact on the increase of labour productivity in production and transport. By the time of the Industrial Revolution, the region's resource base was transformed not only into an extra-territorial one (especially through the incorporation of land and forest-derived resources of North America but more generally by engaging in intercontinental trade), but also into an extra-organic type.[37] In these two respects, Europe laid the foundations of the modern interregional system of resource exchange.

Third, the two ways of responding to local resource constraints mentioned above were combined in post-war Asia. The foundations of Asia's industrialization had been laid earlier, but the scale of post-war industrialization was different. Resource-intensive industrialization first occurred in the Pacific industrial belt of Japan in the 1960s and 1970s, and then diffused across maritime monsoon Asia and beyond. For the first time in global history, a massive population of monsoon Asia was systematically connected to the international economy and global resources. The standard of living of its large population rose, and the worsening of global income inequality was arrested.[38] The region's factor endowment regime characterized by high land productivity, a high level of labour absorption, and the original environmental characteristics of monsoon Asia such as the availability and variability of water and biomass energy were now reorganized to create a resource nexus of global reach. The region sustained the ability to imported resources, including minerals and fossil fuels, and combined them with local human and natural resources.

The key organizers of the nexus included the 'developmental state', as a substantial amount of capital and a strong leadership were needed for building large-scale infrastructure. The states were not always conscious of the environmental implications of these developments. Urban congestion and pollution and environmental degradation in the countryside also became a regional phenomenon. As the regional growth core shifted to the Chinese metropolis, the influence of the resource nexus increasingly included the Eurasian continent as well as maritime monsoon Asia.

Global environmental sustainability, including issues relating to global warming, biodiversity, deforestation and health and ecosystem protection, now largely depends on

Asia's response. The West has certainly been responsible for creating a technological and institutional path of resource exchange, but is not in a position to offer relevant historical experiences on a scale we see today.

## Notes

1. A. Gerschenkron (1962), *Economic Backwardness in Historical Perspective: A Book of Essays*. Cambridge, MA: Belknap Press; A. Suehiro (2008), *Catch-up industrialization: The Trajectory and Prospects of East Asian Economies*, trans. T. Gill. Singapore: NUS Press in association with Kyoto University Press; R. C. Allen (2011), *Global Economic History: A Very Short Introduction*. Oxford: Oxford University Press.

2. G. Austin (ed.) (2017), *Economic Development and Environmental History in the Anthropocene: Perspectives on Asia and Africa*. London: Bloomsbury Academic.

3. W. A. Lewis (1954), 'Economic development with unlimited supplies of labour', *Manchester School*, 22 (2), 139–91.

4. See K. Pomeranz (2000), *The Great Divergence: China, Europe, and the Making of the Modern World Economy*. Princeton: Princeton University Press.

5. For a brief description of the thinking of classical economy and its limits, see Y. Hayami and Y. Godo (2005), *Development Economics: From the Poverty to the Wealth of Nations*, 3rd edn. Oxford: Oxford University Press, 80–9.

6. In 1820, twelve countries in Western Europe had 115 million or 11 per cent of the world population. Data are from A. Maddison (2011), 'Statistics on world population, GDP and per capita GDP, 1–2008 AD', http://www.ggdc.net/maddison/ (Last Accessed 6 January 2018).

7. H. Oshima (1987), *Economic Development in Monsoon Asia: A Comparative Study*. Tokyo: University of Tokyo Press.

8. S. Ishikawa (1978), *Labour Absorption in Asian Agriculture: An 'Issues' Paper*. Geneva: Asian Employment Programme, ILO-ARTEP.

9. M. Elvin and Ts'ui-jung Liu (eds) (1998), *Sediments of Time: Environment and Society in Chinese History*. Cambridge: Cambridge University Press.

10. R. B. Wong (1997), *China Transformed: Historical Change and the Limits of European Experience*. Ithaca: Cornell University Press.

11. K. Sugihara (2005), 'An introduction', in K. Sugihara (ed.), *Japan, China and the Growth of the Asian International Economy, 1850–1949*. Oxford: Oxford University Press, 4–8.

12. K. Sugihara (2013), 'Labour-intensive industrialization in global history: An interpretation of East Asian experiences', in G. Austin and K. Sugihara (eds), *Labour-intensive Industrialization in Global History*. London: Routledge, 30–8, and 43–55.

13. A. Reid (1993), *Expansion and Crisis: Southeast Asia in the Age of Commerce 1450–1680*. New Haven: Yale University Press, 62–131.

14. For the Ayutthaya, see C. Baker and P. Phongpaichit (2017), *A History of Ayutthaya: Siam in the Early Modern World*. Cambridge: Cambridge University Press.

15. The territorial categories do not exactly match the ones I used for the population figures cited earlier, but the point basically stands.

16. See Pomeranz, *The Great Divergence*, 274–8.

17. Sugihara, 'An introduction', 6–7.

18. The historical presence of intra-regional networks in these regions is well known, and it is possible to reconstruct trade statistics for at least some of them for the nineteenth and early twentieth centuries from British and other Western sources; however, they do not appear to have been as large as intra-Asian trade. See K. Sugihara (2015), 'Asia in the growth of world trade: A re-interpretation of the "long nineteenth century"', in U. Bosma and A. Webster (eds), *Commodities, Ports and Asian Maritime Trade c. 1750–1950*. Basingstoke: Palgrave Macmillan, 41–51. Trade statistics assembled by the League of Nations and the United Nations for the more recent period do not show high figures either. For example, the share of intra-regional export trade in sub-Saharan Africa was 12 per cent in 2004, after which it steadily rose to 19 per cent in 2015, reflecting the progress of regional integration. Data are from IMF, *Direction of Trade Statistics Yearbook*. Asia's post-war figures, shown in Figure 11.4, essentially come from the same source.

19. An estimate suggests that a PPP (purchasing power parity)-adjusted per capita income of Japan in the mid-1930s (at current prices) was 32 per cent of the US level, which means that the gap between the two countries was greater than the Maddison estimate suggested. Since Japan's level was far higher than other Asian countries', there was no sense of 'catching up' with the West in this respect. See K. Fukao, Debin Ma and Tangjun Yuan (2007), 'Real gap in pre-war East Asia: A 1934–36 benchmark purchasing power parity comparison with the US', *Review of Income and Wealth*, 53 (3), 503–37.

20. K. Sugihara (2010), 'Formation of an industrialization-oriented monetary order in East Asia', in Shigeru Akita and Nicholas J. White (eds), *The International Order of Asia in the 1930s and 1950s*. Farnham, Surrey: Ashgate, 61–102.

21. J. S. Arpan, M. Barry and T. Van Tho (1984), 'The textile complex in the Asia-Pacific region: The patterns and textures of competition and the shape of things to come', *Research in International Business and Finance*, 4 (B), 112–7, 136–49, and 159.

22. Post-war Japan is not normally classified as 'export-oriented', as the high-speed growth was driven mainly by the domestic market. On the other hand, as we shall see below, the need to earn foreign exchange through exports to import crucial resources was so great that the strategy she developed for industrialization arguably provided a proto-type of 'export-oriented industrialization'.

23. Sugihara, 'Labour-intensive industrialization in global history', 50–1.

24. R. Amjad (1981) 'The development of labour intensive industries in ASEAN countries: An overview', in R. Amjad (ed.), *The Development of Labour Intensive Industries in ASEAN Countries*. Geneva: ILO, 1–28; Idem (1987), 'Human resource development: The Asian experience in employment and manpower planning: An overview', in R. Amjad (ed.), *Human Resource Planning: The Asian Experience*. Geneva: ILO, 1–37.

25. Many developing countries in Asia overspent on tertiary education, while spending too little on primary education at the early stage of industrialization. See P. H. Lindert (2003), 'Voice and growth: Was Churchill right?', *Journal of Economic History*, 63 (2): 315–50; Idem (2004), *Growing Public: Social Spending and Economic Growth*, Vol. 1, *The Story*. Cambridge: Cambridge University Press.

26. A. Singh (1979), 'The 'Basic Needs' approach to development vs the new international economic order: The significance of third world industrialization', *World Development*, 7 (6), 585–606; E. Lee (1979), 'Egalitarian peasant farming and rural development: The case of South Korea', *World Development*, 7 (4–5), 493–517.

27. Sugihara (2015), 'Asia in the growth of world trade', 34–8.

28. S. Kobori (2010), *Nihon no Enerugi Kakumei: Shigen Shokoku no Kingendai* [The energy revolution in Japan: The modern and contemporary history of a resource-poor country]. Nagoya: Nagoya Daigaku Shuppankai.

29. S. Kobori (2017), 'Rinkai Kaihatsu, Kogai Taisaku, Shizen Hogo: Kodo Seicho-ki Yokohama no Kankyoshi' [Seafront development, anti-pollution policy and nature conservation: An environmental history of Yokohama in the period of high-speed growth], in S. Shoji (ed.), *Sengo Nihon no Kaihatsu to Minshushugi: Chiiki ni Miru Sokoku* (Development and Democracy in Post-war Japan: Conflicts at Local Settings). Kyoto: Showado.

30. H. Hashiya (1995), 'Kankoku, Taiwan no Nizu-ka to Toshika' [Development of newly industrializing economies and urbanization in South Korea and Taiwan], in R. Kojima and N. Hataya (eds), *Hatten Tojokoku no Toshika to Hinkonso* (Urbanization and the poor in developing countries). Tokyo: Ajia Keizai Kenkyusho, 43–6; N. Ishizaki (1996), 'Kankoku no Jukagaku Kogyo Seisaku: Kaishi no Naigai Joken to Jisshi Shutai' [South Korea's policy for heavy and chemical industries: Internal and external conditions for its establishment and actors for implementation], in T. Hattori and Y. Sato (eds), *Kankoku, Taiwan no Hatten Mekanizumu* [Patterns of development of South Korea and Taiwan]. Tokyo: Ajia Keizai Kenkyusho, 65–86.

31. R. Wade (1990), *Governing the Market: Economic Theory and the Role of Government in East Asian Industrialization*. Princeton: Princeton University Press, 86–112; Hashiya, 'Kankoku, Taiwan no Nizu-ka to Toshika', 46–9; H. Sato (1996), 'Taiwan no Keizai Hatten ni okeru Seifu to Minkan Kigyo: Sangyo no Sentaku to Seika' [Government and private enterprises in the economic development of Taiwan: Choice of industries and their performance], in Hattori and Sato (eds), *Kankoku, Taiwan no Hatten Mekanizumu*, 96–101.

32. M. Zhou (2007), *Chugoku Keizairon: Kodo Seicho no Mekanizumu to Kadai* [Essays on the Chinese economy: The mechanism of high-speed growth and its problems]. Tokyo: Nihon Keizai Hyoronsha, 81–4, and 119–21.

33. Zhou, *Chugoku Keizairon*, 72–128.

34. K. Sugihara (2012), '"Kaseki Shigen Sekai Keizai" no Koryu to Baiomasu Shakai no Saihen' (The rise of the fossil-fuel-driven world economy and reorganization of the biomass society), in K. Sugihara, K. Wakimura, K. Fujita and A. Tanabe (eds), *Rekishi no nakano Nettai Seizonken: Ontai Paradaimu wo Koete* (The Tropical Humanosphere in Global History: Beyond the Temperate Zone Paradigm). Kyoto: Kyoto Daigaku Shuppankai, 164–79.

35. N. K. Dubash (2002), *Tubewell Capitalism: Groundwater Development and Agrarian Change in Gujarat*. New Delhi: Oxford University Press; T. Shah (2009), *Taming the Anarchy: Groundwater Governance in South Asia*. Washington, DC: Resource for the Future Press.

36. B. Agarwal (1986), *Cold Hearths and Barren Slopes: The Woodfuel Crisis in the Third World*. London: Zed Books.

37. See E. A. Wrigley (2016), *The Path to Sustained Growth: England's Transition from an Organic Economy to an Industrial Revolution*. Cambridge: Cambridge University Press; and S. Pollard (1981), *Peaceful Conquest: The Industrialization of Europe, 1760–1970*. Oxford: Oxford University Press.

38. The GINI coefficient appears to have worsened since the diffusion of industrialization began in the nineteenth century, but stopped worsening around the middle of the twentieth century, largely as a result of the high economic growth of Asian countries. However, a further 'equalization' does not appear to have occurred over the last twenty years or so. Calculated from Maddison (2011), 'Statistics on world population'.

# CHAPTER 12
# GLOBAL COMMODITIES AND COMMODITY CHAINS
*Bernd-Stefan Grewe*

Since the 1940s, it has been customary for most married people in Europe and America to wear a golden ring, a symbol of eternal love. In India, a Hindu bride is also offered golden jewellery, not as a symbol of eternal love, but as a dowry. Usually such a dowry plunges a family into debt. On the other side of the Indian Ocean, in the Transkei in South Africa, a Mpondo groom has to pay a *lobola* to the bride's family. This bride-price is not paid with gold, but with cattle. Nonetheless this marriage is as much linked to gold as the others, because the cattle for the *lobola* is mostly earned by young Mpondos employed as mineworkers in the Witwatersrand gold industry near Johannesburg.

In the Americas as in Europe, South Asia, and Southern Africa, gold clearly plays a major role in weddings, but a different one in each case. The practices and meanings people attribute to this metal may also change over time, and such changes can have major repercussions on the demand for gold on international markets. For example in the first decade of the twenty-first century, each year about ten million weddings took place in India alone at which jewellery – mostly gold and to a lesser extent diamonds of an estimated value of more than US$8 billion – was purchased. Yet in most economic history textbooks there is no indication of such large-scale demand and use, as gold is only mentioned in chapters on monetary history and especially in relation to the history of the gold standard.

Gold is a fascinating commodity and is here used to illustrate the potential and limits of approaches in global economic history based on the study of commodities. I focus on three approaches in particular: first on so-called *history of commodities*; second on *commodity-chain approaches*; and finally on *value-chain approaches*. I argue that commodity-based narratives provide unique insights into global economic processes but struggle to generalize or provide historians with suitable tools of analysis. In the past thirty years, economic historians have borrowed the concept of the commodity chain from sociology and political science. Here too one can see limitations both at a methodological and at an historical level. I therefore consider the concept of the global value chain and evaluate whether this might be a useful tool for economic historians.

## Histories of global commodities

Histories of global commodities are not new. Several such histories were written many decades before the term 'globalization' was coined. Gold, for instance, is mined in specific areas of the world and over the centuries has been treasured and used by different world societies. It has been used not only for jewellery and precious objects but also, and in tandem, as a currency and as a form of treasure (either by rulers and merchants or as gold reserves held by central banks). Gold like silver has been essential for the development of global trade between America, Europe, and Asia, since the fifteenth century. The two precious metals were the material base for payment in far distant trade. Gold from Brazil and silver from Peru circulated around the globe and linked colonial Latin America with Europe and Asia in the early modern period. The form of labour exploitation changed over time – from slavery and forced labour to wage labour or free labour – but far too often people who worked in the mines had little choice but to work under harsh, unhealthy, and dangerous conditions for little or no salary.

The case of gold alerts us to the fact that there are different ways to write about commodities: in particular we can distinguish three groups of commodity histories. First, commodity histories often describe the origins of a certain good, how it was discovered in ancient times, how different cultures and societies made use of it, how it was eventually reframed and remodelled during and after the Industrial Revolution, and how it was finally consumed. Early commodity histories and more recent coffee-table books contain information that can be of great value for historians today. A second group of commodity histories are of popular appeal and include titles such as Mark Kurlansky's *Cod* (1997), *Salt* (2002), or *Big Oyster* (2006), and Mark Pendergrast's *Uncommon Grounds* (1999) on coffee and *For God, Country and Coca-Cola* (1993). Finally, a third group of commodity histories is based on academic research and contributes to scholarly discussions.

One of the pioneering publications within this last group of academic commodity histories was *Sweetness and Power* (1985) by the anthropologist Sydney Mintz. His history of sugar starts with the cultural and social history of food in eighteenth- and nineteenth-century Britain interlinking it with its production in the Caribbean. Mintz studied the anthropology of food in Europe and how sweetness slowly gained importance from the Middle Ages, its use rapidly developing from the nineteenth century onwards. Sugar changed its character from a former luxury good for the elite that was presented in silver or golden sugar bowls to a staple product and important food that even the working classes could afford to sweeten their tea or coffee. Sugar provided an increasing share of the calorie intake of common people in the nineteenth century. This change in relevance was closely linked to the plantation economy, of how sugarcane was cultivated, harvested, and quickly processed into raw sugar. The increase in consumption provided an impetus for a capitalistic and intensified production process based on slave labour. The labour-intensive organization of the sugar plantations in the Caribbean attracted capital from Europe and further encouraged the development of capitalist economies.

More recent research on commodity history has evolved around the London-based network 'Commodities of Empire'.[1] Inspired by Mintz and already working on the economic history of colonialism in Latin America, Africa, and South Asia, several researchers have started to investigate the commodity history of typical colonial products like sugar, tobacco, palm oil, cotton, rubber, cocoa, coffee, and tea. These studies have offered new insights into the functioning of the global economy and its various and often surprising effects on distant corners of the earth, like the example of coffee production in Kenya. Here, the overproduction of coffee in Brazil and Colombia endangered the colonial tax revenues derived from coffee sales. To preserve the coffee sector and the tax income from it, the colonial administration broke the former monopoly on coffee production of the white settlers and allowed African farmers to grow Arabica coffee. This case shows an active strategy of a colonial government to reorganize the commodity chain in order to raise production while maintaining quality but at lower costs.[2]

Other studies on commodity chains reveal new global connections with other chains that have often been ignored by traditional economic history. Since the publication of Mintz's *Sweetness and Power*, historians have acknowledged the role of sugar cultivated in the Caribbean plantations to the nutrition of British workers in the classic period of the Industrial Revolution. It is much more surprising to discover the extent to which North Atlantic salted cod was important for the feeding of slaves in the Caribbean and in Brazil. Taste and low price made it possible for salted cod to become a major staple in the West Indies and Brazil although ample supplies of fresh fish existed locally.[3] So cod fished by British fishermen off Newfoundland and Nova Scotia was salted and brought to the sugar plantations, which in turn produced sugar for British workers. Another overseen commodity chain linked Argentina with Europe through the export of skins and leather. Herds of cattle in the Argentine Pampa also delivered meat that was dried and salted in meat-salting plants, differentiated into standardized classes of quality, and then exported – like cod – to Cuba and Brazil to feed slaves on sugar plantations. The introduction of new technologies to produce corned beef and refrigerated ships to export frozen beef reshaped the commodity chain in the nineteenth century.[4]

Another recent variety of commodity history is Sven Beckert's *Empire of Cotton* (2014).[5] His book uses cotton as a lens through which to read the development of the modern economy. He reconstructs the rise of cotton from a locally cultivated crop that was hand-spun and woven into textiles for the same region where it was produced, to one of the most important commodities of the nineteenth century. The book shows the connection between cotton and the invention of new machinery and the development of industrialized production. Beckert distinguishes a phase of what he calls 'war capitalism', during which slavery and colonialism prepared the ground for a globalized cotton industry. This led to a phase of 'industrial capitalism' which involved the processing of fibres and the manufacturing of textiles. The author shows how both stages of industrialization rested on violence: on the militarization of the trade (with the East India companies), massive land expropriation in the Americas, genocide (of Native Americans), and the enslavement of millions of Africans. He also shows how 'industrial capitalism' depended on a strong, interventionist state 'capable of forging and protecting global markets, policing its borders, regulating industry, creating and then enforcing private property rights in land, enforcing contracts over large geographical distances, forging fiscal tools to tax populations, and building a social, economic, and legal environment that made the mobilization of labor through wage payments possible'.[6]

These types of commodity histories are based on many years of research. Mintz, for instance, started his archival research in Puerto Rico in the late 1940s, working on the lives of workers on sugar plantations.[7] Perhaps one criticism that can be made of commodity-based studies is that they rarely reflect on the methodological approach they adopt. Often, they rely on a synthesis of current historic knowledge, integrating different viewpoints and showing parallel developments in different parts of the world.

## Commodity chains

A commodity chain can be defined as the production of a tradeable good from the extraction of its raw materials through to its design and elaboration, followed by its transport and sale into the hands of the consumer. What would the commodity chain of gold look like? In the 1960s, this chain might have begun more than 2,000 metres underground in a South African gold mine in the Orange Free State from where the ore was hewn and brought to the surface. The ore was milled in large plants and then treated with cyanides to extract the gold, which was smelted into raw bars. These bars which still contained other metals were transported to the Rand Refinery at Germiston close to Johannesburg where the gold was refined out and melted into so-called London Good delivery bars of 995.0 per thousand purity. This bullion was shipped via plane to London, the leading international market for gold. Here the gold was bought either by one of the national reserve banks for its gold reserves or by a Swiss bullion dealer who resold and transported it to Dubai. The bars were then smuggled with dhows across the Indian Ocean to secret places on the Indian coast close to Mumbai. Only a few hours after its arrival, the gold was melted again, resold, and distributed in small lots to local goldsmiths who worked and sold it to local consumers.

Gold is an example of the long-standing interest in commodity chains that goes back to times before the very label 'commodity chain' was invented. The work of Frank Taussig in the early years of the twentieth century reflected on the relationship between labour and production and investigated geographical divisions of labour.[8] John Davis and Ray Goldberg integrated different steps of production, distribution, transportation, and marketing in a single analytical framework.[9] The interest in investigating commodity histories beyond national borders was further developed in the 1970s in the context of world-systems theory. Terence Hopkins and Immanuel Wallerstein were probably the first to use the expression 'commodity chains' and to think of them in a decidedly historical perspective.[10] Hopkins and Wallerstein proposed the analysis of commodity chains in order to overcome the distinction between different market levels ranging from national to international. Their concept was designed to dismiss the assumption that 'commodity chains developed first of all within the boundaries of the state and later began to cross state frontiers'.[11] Commodity chains cut across state boundaries and were thus of fundamental importance in the analysis of world systems and their core–periphery relations.[12] Wallerstein's concept of the world economy as being structured into core, semi-periphery, and periphery could be substantiated through the study of commodity chains. Wallerstein showed that core activities commanded a large share of the surplus produced within a commodity chain while peripheral activities commanded only little or no surplus.[13]

The interest in commodity chains resurfaced in full in the 1990s when Gary Gereffi and Miquel Korzeniewicz published an edited volume entitled *Commodity Chains and Global Capitalism* (1994). Similar to Wallerstein's initial definition, their concept of a 'global commodity chain' (GCC) referred to the whole range of activities involved in the design, production, and marketing of a product across national boundaries. Yet, their definition of commodity chain differed from that of world-system scholarship in several respects.[14] First, GCC is much more contemporarily oriented than Wallerstein's historical study which started in the long sixteenth century. GCC concentrates on the study of the contemporary apparel and automobile industries, as well as chains of production of foodstuffs such as bananas and tea or natural resources such as timber. Second, the GCC approaches are specifically interested in inter-firm networks and examine how global industries are organized. In opposition to the macro-focus of the world-system analyses that study the world capitalist order and how commodity chains structured and reproduced a stratified and hierarchical world system, GCC considers the macro–micro links between global, national, and local units of analysis. Third, the GCC framework is a network-based and organizational approach. The GCC method helps to analyse processes of globalization in specific locations where production and related services occur and to understand how these locations and activities are connected to each other. GCC pays more attention to the specificity of locality and place than world-system approaches, and is therefore conducive to the study of local cultural or social aspects.[15]

Gereffi and his co-authors developed this approach primarily to analyse the power relations that are embedded in commodity chains and their governance. Overall, they defined four dimensions of the GCC framework: first, an input–output structure (a set of products and services linked together in sequence of value-adding economic activities); second, a territoriality (spatial dispersion or concentration of enterprises in production and distribution networks); third, the governance structure (authority and power relationships); and finally, the institutional context.[16]

GCC research starts from the assumption that a lead firm dominates the character of the chain. For the 1980s and 1990s, they identify in particular two types of governance structures for networked GCCs, which they call 'producer-driven' and 'buyer-driven' global commodity chains. The difference resides in the location of key barriers to entry. Producer-driven commodity chains are those in which large, transnational corporations play a key role in coordinating production networks. This type of GCC can typically be found in capital- and technology-intensive industries such the automobile, aircraft, computers, and heavy machinery sectors where profit is generated by productive scale, volume, and technological innovation. In buyer-driven GCCs, large retailers, marketers, and branded manufacturers take the role of key agents and set up decentralized production networks in a variety of countries, typically located in the Global South. This is a typical pattern in relatively labour-intensive consumer goods such as garments, footwear, toys, and housewares. The companies that develop and sell brand-named products exert control over how, when, and where manufacturing takes place, and how much profit accrues at each stage of the chain. The dominant enterprises transfer economic competitive pressures to peripheral areas of the world economy.[17]

One of the most debatable aspects of the GCC research is that the control of commodity chains, and therefore the profit generated by the process, is considered to be in the hands of so-called key agents. Take for instance the case of gold in the late nineteenth and early twentieth centuries. Following the flows of gold, much of the gold from the late nineteenth-century rushes in California, Australia, and South Africa was channelled to London from where it was sold and distributed to the rest of the world. Before the First World War, the City of London and the Bank of England had a hegemonic position in world finance and much gold was shipped to London in order to pay for credit and for hoarding. London attracted more than a third of all the gold mined in this period, thus acting as the 'key agent' in this commodity chain. But did the bankers and bullion dealers exert any control of the global flows of gold? The key agents in the City of London comprised not only the Bank of England and large merchant banks such as Rothschild's but also a group of five bullion brokers who later became members of the London Gold Market Fixing (Mocatta, Rothschild, Sharps Pixley & Co, Johnson Matthey, and Samuel Montagu). Although the Californian and the other gold rushes in America did not take place within the British Empire, the American need for credit brought much of its gold to London. For the Australian and South African gold, the most important factor was not that both territories were part of the British Empire but the fact that the big mining companies that ran the mines were financed by the City of London. Not only the gold but also most of the profits from gold mining flew to London, which was distributed as a dividend to stockholders.

One disadvantage of the GCC approach as exemplified through gold is that much research has a strong European or American orientation.[18] Few studies examine in detail the agency and interests of stakeholders in other world locations. Hence in the case of gold, the role of Indian, South African, and Australian actors is rarely given as much prominence as that of Western reserve banks.[19] A closer inspection of the GCC of gold in the 1920s, for instance, reveals that the control of the different segments of the chain was far from the prerogative of a single 'key agent' (such as the Bank of England or Rothschild's), and chains could be organized without any major driver. This does not mean that these chains are necessarily organized in a more equal way without major players or imbalances of power, but it is not necessary to assume the presence of either a visible hand to manage and control the whole of a chain or the invisible hand of markets. Power and control are surely not absent from markets and in commodity chains, but they are not necessarily concentrated in one key agent.

A second problem with a GCC approach is that it often implies that initiatives for change in the chain originate mainly from the industrialized countries in the North (or as Wallerstein calls it, the core). In this perspective, the role of actors from the Global South (Wallerstein's periphery) is seen as passive. This may be due to the fact that most commodity-chain studies concentrate on commodities that are consumed in the developed countries of the northern hemisphere, ignoring the fact that many chains find final consumers in the so-called 'developing countries' (or colonized areas). Populations in former colonies and in the Global South are often considered as producers, leaving researchers with little knowledge of their consumption patterns. For gold, two observations from the 1920s illustrate this issue. Once the gold mining houses in Johannesburg had erected their own refinery – the Rand Refinery in Germiston – they became technically independent from the London refiners and market. As they could guarantee the purity of the gold themselves, they sold it directly to the United States and to the Indian subcontinent, thus circumventing the London market. The London network of bankers, bullion dealers, and insurance brokers continued to manipulate prices, shipment tariffs, and insurance rates; yet in the second half of the 1920s, South Africa started to export its gold directly from Durban to Bombay. But shortly afterwards, in 1931, it was forced again to sell its gold in London when Indian demand collapsed due to bad harvests and falling agricultural prices. The flow of gold was therefore determined not by key agents in London, but by other economic factors in South Asia.[20]

A third critical aspect of the GCC approach is the assumed imbalance of power within the chain. Indeed, many studies have shown the power of leading firms and how these so-called drivers reaped the largest share of profits in the chain. However, a group of Latin American historians – including Steven Topik, Carlos Marichal, and Zephyr Frank – has rejected the claim that profits invariably accrued in the more developed countries. Instead they have shown that the arrangement of production and the distribution of profit were dependent on the endowment of the different actors in the commodity chain. They have showed, for instance, how Brazilian coffee producers have been able to get a high share of profit.[21]

Notwithstanding these caveats, GCC provides an alternative method for the economic analysis of global economic processes that link industrialized and developing countries both at a macro and at a micro level. GCC methods of analysis have continued to develop theoretically and empirically over the past quarter of a century. By the early 2000s however researchers became interested in a subfield that has come to be known as the 'global value chain'.

## Global value chains

A new interdisciplinary and international initiative to examine different approaches of global production networks started in 2000. Its main objective was to create a new theory of governance to help policymakers explain and predict governance patterns in cross-border production networks. Global value chain research was designed to study the different ways in which global production and distribution systems are integrated in the global economy. The intention was to explore the possibilities for firms in developing countries to enhance their position in global markets. Thus the authors hoped that the theory of global value chain governance would be useful for the crafting of effective policy tools related to industrial upgrading, economic development, employment creation, and poverty alleviation.[22] Therefore it was claimed that this new model of analysis should be robust, relevant, and easily applicable to real-world situations.[23]

The shift from 'commodity chains' to 'value chains' is not simply a terminological one as some critics first suggested.[24] Many empirical studies observed that an increasing number of producer-driven chains were changing as lead firms started to outsource large parts of their global production to external manufacturing firms. Some chains became more buyer-like. The distinction between the two types of producer- and buyer-driven chains was no longer sufficient and other network types were needed. The GCC typology was based on a rather static view of technology and barriers to entry, but technological change and firm- and industry-level learning stimulate change and make chains rather dynamic. Many industries showed a clear shift away from vertically integrated producer-driven chains, while buyer-driven chains could not encompass all the different networks observed in the field. The decision to replace the term 'commodity' with 'value' was taken because commodities are too often identified with undifferentiated products, mainly primary products (i.e. crude oil) or agricultural products (such as coffee, cocoa, wheat, or jute).[25] Another reason to choose 'value' is that the term captures the notion of 'value added' and thus the application of human effort to generate profit on invested capital.

The building of a new global value chain (GVC) theory rests on the centrality of 'nodes' considered to be 'the pivot points in transformation sequences: extraction and supply of raw materials, the stages of industrial processing, exports, and final marketing'.[26] GVC addresses in particular three questions related to nodes: first, what kind of activities are bundled up in one node of the chain or split among various nodes? Second, how are knowledge, information, and materials passed from one node to the next? And finally, where are these nodes located? Based on a comparison between case studies, a GVC working group was able to identify five ways in which firms governed or coordinated the linkages between value chain activities:

1. *Market linkages* that are governed by price, and in which the costs of switching to new partners are low for both parties.

2. *Modular linkages* in which suppliers make products to a customer's specifications. Complex information regarding the transaction is codified and digitized before it is passed to highly competent suppliers.

3. *Relational linkages* in which complex interactions between buyers and sellers take place, creating mutual dependence and high levels of asset specificity. Trust and relationship are often built over time and might work in spatial proximity as well as in spatially dispersed networks. Tacit information is exchanged between buyers and highly competent suppliers.

4. *Captive linkages* in which less competent suppliers are provided with detailed instructions and are dependent on much larger buyers. Suppliers have to face significant switching costs and are therefore 'captive'. These linkages are often characterized by a high degree of monitoring and control by lead firms.

5. *Hierarchical linkages* which are a governance form characterized by vertical integration and managerial control, flowing down from headquarters to subsidiaries and affiliates.[27]

This typology is the first step towards an operational theory of global value chain governance and helps us to study under which conditions market, modular, relational, captive, or vertically integrated chain governance arise. GVC identifies three key determinants of governance patterns: complexity of information and knowledge transfer that are required to sustain a particular transaction, particularly with respect to product and process specifications; the extent to which information and knowledge can be codified and efficiently transmitted; and the capabilities of suppliers in relation to the requirements of the buyers.[28]

What makes GVCs attractive for economic historians is that the evolution of governance structures over time is integral to their study. By considering several sectors, GVC observes a trajectory from one type of governance to another and identifies causal factors in the hope of being able to anticipate future change in GVC. The evolution of the bicycle industry serves as example of how hierarchies and vertical integration in the early years of the industry (in the 1890s) evolved towards inter-firm governance and reliance on market mechanisms. In this GVC, specialist firms such as Sachs, Shimano, or later SRAM producing just one component of a bicycle became more competitive than vertically integrated producers of complete bicycles. Another example is provided by the apparel industry whose governance changed from captive to relational value chains. The suppliers in many East Asian countries moved in a few decades from simply assembling imported inputs to full-scale supply as they learned how to make internationally competitive consumer goods. This however requires the capacity to interpret designs, to produce samples, to source all needed inputs, to control product quality, not to exceed the buyer's price, and to guarantee on-time delivery.

Other value chains changed in a different direction, as in the case of fresh vegetables. As a primary product, the GVC of fresh vegetables in Kenya had for a long time been the typical example of a market-based form of governance. But this changed in the 1980s when large UK supermarket chains (Tesco, Asda, and Sainsbury's) wished to attract new customers by offering year-round supply and guarantee them high quality. At the same time, they had to meet stronger standards of food safety, especially concerning pesticide residues. The supermarkets' strategy was to increase their control over the chain and to explicitly coordinate their supply. They therefore signed renewable annual contracts with their suppliers and monitored the entire chain.

The differentiation of the GVC model between five different governance types (market, modular, relational, captive, and hierarchical) is useful in the analysis of global economic connections. The example of the commodity chain of gold in the 1960s illustrate this: at the production end of the chain in South Africa, most of the mines were directed by a handful of large 'mining houses' (who also controlled about three-quarters of all the joint-stock companies listed in the Johannesburg stock exchange – an enormous concentration of economic power). Most of the mines were organized as stock companies and run by these so-called mining houses. These holdings took care of the transactions of their shares at stock exchanges in Europe and the United States and to a smaller extent in Johannesburg. They had the know-how to run a mine and therefore appointed the directors and mining engineers. This was obviously a hierarchical linkage. However, most of the profits from these mines left South Africa as dividends were paid to the shareholders located overseas. The mining houses were able to govern their business with as little as 30 per cent of the shares as most international investors did not attend shareholders' meetings in Johannesburg.

Often GVC studies focus on the vertical direction of a network paying little attention to the horizontal dimension of such linkages. Although the control of the individual mines by the holdings was hierarchical, at the same time the different mines and mining houses did not compete on a market for gold. In an atmosphere of mutual trust, they shared technical information and mining innovation. This was greatly facilitated by the fact that the mines did not have to compete for a lower price of gold when their product did not differ in quality and when the market absorbed any amount of gold for a guaranteed price (under the gold standard, the central banks of the gold pool countries guaranteed the price of the gold). Cooperation allowed firms to save on costs and even to coordinate their sales. The gold derived from the ores that lay many thousands of feet underground, that the miners brought to the surface, was milled, treated with chemicals, and refined at the Rand Refinery. This refinery was run by the Chamber of Mines of South Africa and was deemed to embody the cooperation of the mining houses in Johannesburg. The bars were then shipped via Durban to Southampton and London. The gold was then either sold for a fixed price to the Bank of England or on the gold market. It is highly questionable whether the London gold market was governed by market linkages as the volatility of the gold price was limited within a small range of fixed prices. Under the Bretton Woods system, the reserve banks of the gold pool countries stabilized the gold price and thus the value of their currencies by selling gold to the market or buying it whenever it was necessary to stabilize its price.

As stated above, the biggest demand for gold for private purposes came from India. But after the military conflict with China in 1962, the Indian government completely banned the import of gold in an attempt to shift the capital spent on jewellery towards investment for the development of Indian industry. However, what came to be known as the 1963 Gold Control Act did not affect the demand for gold in India at all. The uncurbed demand stimulated a black market and the smuggling of gold via the Indian Ocean, with Dubai as a major connecting port. As the price of gold was 75 per cent higher in India than on international markets, smuggling was extremely lucrative.[29] It is estimated that between 107 and 217 tonnes of gold were smuggled into India annually between 1968 and 1972.[30] The sophisticated smuggling business was not run by individuals, but by professional cartels operated from Dubai. Thus, the little sheikdom of Dubai that in the 1960s had less than 60,000 inhabitants became the single largest gold buyer at the London gold market. As this cursory analysis of gold reveals, the GVC model proofed to be a useful analytical tool to better understand global interconnections.

## Critiques

However, for historians wishing to adopt a commodity-chain or value-chain approach, there are several methodological problems and challenges to overcome: First, most studies present the commodity and value chains in a linear form. Several authors have stressed the problem of the linearity of commodity chain studies.[31] They question how chains are presented and argue that the competitive position of various actors at specific nodes of the chain is excluded.[32]

Second, a possible solution to the problem of linearity could be to scrutinize the construction of chains and question the decision-making processes in the identification of chains. Most chains are presented as linking different nodal points at which new actors enter the chain and participate in different ways. Historians, who often tend to make their decision depending on the availability of sources, should openly discuss the ways in which the haphazardness of recordings has effects on the results they produce.

Third, historians have favoured certain commodity chains, especially luxury goods, exotic commodities, or strategic resources like rubber and oil. When they have considered agrarian products, most historians preferred the products of the plantation complex (sugar, coffee, tea, cocoa, cotton, and rubber) but for a long time ignored the contribution of the small farmers to the same commodity chain. This raises fundamental questions not only in which direction to orientate the research at the nodal points, but also which commodities we should study: The study of rice, maize and potatoes, silicon, cobalt, copper, aluminium, and uranium might be of greater relevance for global history than the study of luxury goods or even gold.[33]

Fourth, entire segments of commodity chains are organized in ways that defy formal control on the part of states or of any other formal institutions. This informal part of the economy does not just exist in countries of the economic periphery where the power of the state is supposed to be weaker than in the industrialized countries. Informal relations are the domain of cities not only in developing countries such as Bangladesh, Pakistan, Vietnam, or Indonesia, but can be found also in Western metropolises as for example within sweatshops that produce haute-couture textiles in Paris and New York.

Finally, GCC and GVC approaches and sometimes historic studies making use of these methods ignore the cultural dimension of economic interaction.[34] The action is often conceived in a way as if the origin of the actors involved, their language, their conceptions of work and leisure, their ideas of dignity and honour, their estimations of goods and services, and many other cultural aspects are of no importance to the functioning of commodity chains. GCC and GVC overlook the relevance of cultural patterns because they seem to have little bearing on the distribution of power and wealth.

## Conclusion

The study of global commodities and of value chains has slowly gained acceptance among historians and is now shaping a new research field at the intersection between economic and global history.[35] Commodity-chain and value-chain approaches offer many new insights on global economic processes that link industrialized and developing countries. Furthermore, they help us to overcome the traditional opposition between micro versus macro approaches to economic history as they consider processes and decision-making practices at different levels. The somewhat naïve assumption of early commodity-chain approach (GCC) that such chains were managed by key agents has been refuted both theoretically and empirically. Yet, the legacy of GCC is still important as it investigates systematically the different ways in which global commodity and value chains were governed at different levels and under a variety of conditions. Historical studies of commodities and their chains have shown their potential for gaining a better understanding of the basic characteristics of global economic interconnections. The metaphor of chain helps us to develop a comprehensive narrative that is never simplistic.

## Notes

1. Commodities of Empire. A British Academy Research Project. https://commoditiesofempire.org.uk/. See also the special issue of the *Journal of Global History* (4) published in 2009.
2. David Hyde (2008), 'Global coffee and decolonisation in Kenya: Overproduction, quotas and rural restructuring', *Commodities of Empire Working Paper* No. 8, https://commoditiesofempire.org.uk/publications/working-papers/working-paper-8/
3. M. W. Herold (2015), 'Nineteenth-century Bahia's passion for British salted cod: From the seas of Newfoundland to the Portuguese shops of Salvador's Cidade Baixa, 1822–1914', *Commodities of Empire Working Paper* No. 23, https://commoditiesofempire.org.uk/publications/working-papers/working-paper-23/
4. A. Sluyter (2010), 'The Hispanic Atlantic's Tasajo trail', *Latin American Research Review*, 45 (1), 98–120; A. Sluyter (2012), *Black Ranching Frontiers: African Cattle Herders of the Atlantic World, 1500–1900*. New Haven and London: Yale University Press, 169–210.
5. Sven Beckert (2014), *Empire of Cotton: A Global History*. New York: Alfred A. Knopf.
6. Beckert (2014), *Empire of Cotton*, 76.
7. S. Mintz (1960), *Worker in the Cane: A Puerto Rican Life History*. New Haven: Yale University Press.
8. F. W. Taussig (1911), *Principles of Economics*, Vol. 1. New York: Macmillan, 15 and 30–48. See also, M. van der Linden (2007), 'Labour history: The old, the new and the global', *African Studies*, 66 (2–3), 169–80.
9. John H. Davis and Ray A. Goldberg (1957), *A Concept of Agribusiness*. Boston: Harvard University Press, vii, 1–2, thank explicitly the Russian economist Wassily Leontief who had designed a related approach in the 1920s. There is an (shortened) English reprint of his article (German original in *Archiv für Sozialwissenschaft und Sozialpolitik*, 60 (1928), 577–623): W. Leontief (1991), 'The economy as a circular flow', *Structural Change and Economic Dynamics*, 2 (1), 181–212, 182: 'At this point the concept of a circular flow comes into play as a tool which enables us to identify those causal relationships that are specific to the economic sphere. Circular flow analysis only takes into account those relationships which allow us to return to the initial starting point.'
10. T. K. Hopkins and I. Wallerstein (1977), 'Patterns of development of the modern world-system', *Review: Fernand Braudel Center*, 1 (2), 128.

11. Hopkins and Wallerstein, 'Patterns of development', 128–9.

12. I. Wallerstein (1974–2011), *The Modern World-System*, 4 vols. New York: Academic Press, (vols. 1–3) 1974–89. Berkeley: University of California Press (vol. 4), 2011.

13. G. Arrighi and J. Drangel (1986), 'The stratification of the world-economy: An exploration of the semiperipheral zone', *Review: Fernand Braudel Center*, 10 (1), 11–12.

14. An excellent comparison between these concepts can be found in J. Bair (2005), 'Global capitalism and commodity chains: Looking back, going forwards', *Competition & Change*, 9 (2), 153–80.

15. Bair, 'Global capitalism', 159.

16. The last dimension was added later and is still the less developed, as the governance structure is by far dominant in GCC research. G. Gereffi, M. Korzeniewicz and R. P. Korzeniewicz (1994), 'Introduction: Global commodity chains', in G. Gereffi and M. Korzeniewicz (eds), *Commodity Chains and Global Capitalism*. Westport CT: Praeger, 7; G. Gereffi (1995), 'Global production system and Third World development', in B. Stallings (ed.), *Global Change, Regional Response*. Cambridge: Cambridge University Press, 100–42.

17. Gereffi underlines the similarities with Michael Porter's value-chain approach. See M. Porter (1985), *Competitive Advantage: Creating and Sustaining Superior Performance*. New York: Free Press. This value-chain approach is also recommended in Michael Porter's 'Competitive Advantage and Business History', *Business and Economic History*, 21 (2), 228–36. P. Scranton and P. Fridenson (2013), *Reimagining Business History*. Baltimore: John Hopkins University Press; R. Kaplinsky (2004), *Competitions Policy and the Global Coffee and Cocoa Value Chains*. Brighton: Institute of Development Studies.

18. For gold, see the excellent study by B. Eichengreen (1992), *Golden Fetters: The Gold Standard and the Great Depression, 1919-1939*. New York: Oxford University Press.

19. J. McGuire, P. Bertola and P. Reeves (eds) (2001), *Evolution of the World Economy, Precious Metals and India*. New Delhi: Oxford University Press.

20. B.-S. Grewe (2013), 'The London Gold Market, 1910–1935', in C. Dejung and N. P. Peterson (eds), *Power, Institutions and Global Markets: Actors, Mechanisms and Foundations of World-Wide Economic Integration, 1850-1930*. Cambridge: Cambridge University Press, 112–32.

21. S. Topik, C. Marichal and Z. Frank (eds) (2006), *From Silver to Cocaine: Latin American Commodity Chains and the Building of the World Economy, 1500--2000*. Durham, NC and London: Duke University Press.

22. G. Gereffi, J. Humphrey and T. Sturgeon (2005), 'The governance of global value chains', *Review of International Political Economy*, 21 (1), 79.

23. A very concise presentation of the GVC theory and the scientific context from which it was derived can be found in T. J. Sturgeon (2009), 'From commodity chains to value chains: Interdisciplinary theory building in an age of globalization', in J. Bair (ed.) (2008), *Frontiers of Commodity Chain Research*. Stanford: Stanford University Press, 110–34.

24. B. Daviron and S. Ponte (2005), *The Coffee Paradox: Global Markets, Commodity Trade and the Elusive Promise of Development*. London: Zed Books, 27.

25. For this type of commodity chain, John Talbot proposed the term 'tropical commodity chain'. J. M. Talbot (2002), 'Tropical commodity chains, forward integration strategies and international inequality: Coffee, cocoa and tea', *Review of International Political Economy*, 9 (4), 701–34.

26. Bair, 'Global commodity chains', 66.

27. Sturgeon, 'From commodity chain to value chain', 119.

28. Out of the eight possible combinations of the three variables, there are only five value chain types that the group can actually find. It is unlikely to find a combination of low complexity of transactions and low ability to codify which excludes two combinations. If the complexity of the transaction is low and the ability to codify is high, then low capacity suppliers would be excluded from the chain.

29. See T. Green (1981), *The New World of Gold*. Johannesburg: Jonathan Ball, 172–5.

30. A. Sarma, et al. (1982), 'Gold mobilisation as an instrument of external adjustment: A discussion paper', Bombay: Reserve Bank of India, 29. According to estimates of Consolidated Gold Fields Ltd, the total illegal gold imports amounted to an estimated 4,770 tonnes of gold between 1958 and 1990. For comparison: at the end of 1991 the largest gold reserves in a central bank amounted to 8,146 tonnes (the United States), and the second largest 2.960 tons (Germany). See G. O'Callaghan (1983), 'The structure and operation of the world gold market', *IMF Occasional Paper*, no. 105, 11.

31. J. Henderson, P. Dicken, M. Hess, N. Coe and H. Wai-Chung Yeung (2002), 'Global production networks and the analysis of economic development', *Review of International Political Economy*, 9 (3), 442; Bair, 'Global commodity chains', 16; Sturgeon, 'From commodity chains to value chains', 126.

32. Bair, 'Global commodity chains', 15.

33. B.-S. Grewe (2016), 'Raum und Macht – Eine Stoffgeschichte des Goldes im frühen 20. Jahrhundert', *Jahrbuch für Wirtschaftsgeschichte*, 57 (1), 59–89.

34. M. Granovetter (2005), 'The impact of social structure on economic outcomes', *Journal of Economic Perspectives*, 19 (1), 33–50.

35. See the calls for papers of the IISH Amsterdam 'Commodity Frontiers' (Amsterdam, July 2015), ITH conference 'Commodity Chains and Labour Relations' (Linz, September 2016), and 'Global Commodity Frontiers in Comparative Historical Context' (London, December 2016).

# CHAPTER 13
# THE RISE OF GLOBAL FINANCE, 1850–2000
*Youssef Cassis*

What is global finance? At its roots lie international capital flows – the export of capital from some countries and the import of capital from others. However, global finance is more than that. It should be considered as the plant rather than simply the roots. It could be described as the complex web of financial institutions, markets, and agents involved in moving capital across nations and regions, each fulfilling a set of functions in the nations and regions connected by these multiple transactions. Within these nations and regions, global financial transactions have concentrated in specific places, usually cities, where the various financial services required by these transactions have gathered, primarily in order to achieve external economies of scale. International financial centres thus form the fabric of global finance.

This chapter takes the third quarter of the nineteenth century as its point of departure, because of the extent – both quantitative and qualitative – of finance in the age of industrial capitalism. International capital flows started their long upswing wave, which would continue until 1914 (perhaps even 1931) when new financial institutions and markets emerged in all advanced economies, in particular with the rise of the big banks and the development of the securities markets. However, the rise of global finance has not continued unabated from the mid-nineteenth century to the early twenty-first century. World wars, financial crises, and economic nationalism have led to periods of domestic (or imperial) withdrawals or the exclusion of nations or regions from international financial exchanges – especially during the decades from the early 1930s to the late 1970s. And the resumption of global finance from the 1980s has taken new forms as a result of technological and financial innovations as well as the transformation of the world economy.

The chapter follows a chronological order and is divided in three parts: the first deals with the first era of modern globalization, from the 1850s to 1914; the second with the era of wars, depression and regulation, from 1914 to 1973; and the third with the wave of deregulations and innovations that marked the second globalization, from 1973 to 2000 and includes a brief epilogue discussing the effects of the financial debacle of 2008 and the rise of new economic powers, above all China, in global finance. It is structured around the development of financial centres in both the core industrial countries and the periphery, paying particular attention to their differences and similarities as well as the interactions between them.

## The first modern globalization, 1850–1914

Foreign investment began to grow substantially from the mid-1850s, the capital stock invested outside its country of origin going from just under $1 billion in 1855 (it was at the same level thirty years earlier) to $7.7 billion in 1870. It then rose to $23.8 billion in 1900 and to $38.7 billion in 1914.[1] Throughout these years, Britain was the largest exporter of capital, followed by France, and, later in the nineteenth century, Germany. Small European countries (the Netherlands, Belgium, and Switzerland) exported substantial amounts of capital, especially when measured as a proportion of their GDP. The United States became a capital exporting country by the turn of the twentieth century, even though it remained a net debtor until the end of the First World War.

While Britain maintained its lead during the long nineteenth century, it was seriously challenged by France during the 1850s and 1860s. The two countries exported similar amounts of capital ($75–$100 million per year in the 1850s and $150–$175 million in the 1860s), with a slight advantage for France, though Britain still held a larger stock of foreign investments.[2] Following its defeat by Prussia in 1871, France was no longer able to challenge Britain but retained its second place. The volume of capital exports increased markedly from the beginning of the twentieth century, having fallen in the 1890s in the wake of the Baring Crisis. Between 1880 and 1913, capital exports amounted to 40 per cent of available savings for Britain and between 20 and 25 per cent for France.

Figures are less reliable for the destination of capital exports, especially before 1900. The United States was definitely the largest recipient, with 16 per cent of the world's total in 1913 (40 per cent of which came from Britain), followed by Canada and Russia (each with 8 per cent), Argentina (7 per cent), and Brazil, Mexico, India, Australia, China, South Africa, Spain, and the Austro-Hungarian Empire (with 4–6 per cent).

International capital flows were part of a broader globalization of the world economy, in particular free movements of people, transport facilities, speed of communication, and expanding trade, which required huge transfers of capital and/or facilitated international financial transactions. From 1850 international migration increased on an unprecedented scale: Thirty-six million Europeans left the Old Continent between 1870 and 1915, most of them, some 70 per cent, heading for the United States and almost all the others for Argentina, Australia, Canada, and Brazil – in other words mainly to temperate regions where European immigration was still recent. Advances in transport and communication made the world smaller and brought countries and continents closer together. The building of railway lines, starting in the 1830s, continued on a much larger scale, world mileage increasing from 205,000 kilometres in 1870 to 925,000 kilometres in 1906. Maritime transport also made considerable progress with the development of oceanic steamships, which really got under way in the 1890s, when steam tonnage finally overtook that of sailing ships. Telecommunications sped up to the point of becoming instantaneous, first with the telegraph (a cable linked Britain to the European continent as early as 1851, and the first transatlantic cable between London and New York was laid in 1866), then with the telephone (Paris and London were connected in 1891, transatlantic links having to wait until the 1920s), and finally with wireless telegraphy (messages were transmitted across the Atlantic from 1901).[3] Foreign trade grew dramatically in the nineteenth century. In the case of Europe, the proportion of exports, measured as a percentage of GDP, went from 9 per cent in 1860 to 14 per cent in 1913.[4]

The global financial order was organized around a dominant economy: Great Britain – even though it was challenged and then overtaken by the United States (in industrial output in the 1880s and GDP by 1900) and Germany (in industrial output in around 1905). Britain's position rested on the leadership it retained in foreign trade (still 14 per cent of world trade in 1913, down from 20 per cent in the mid-nineteenth century) and services and finance (as the largest capital exporter and the largest provider of trade finance), as well as its key position in the system of multilateral trade, on account of its deficit with the major industrial countries and its surplus with its colonial empire.[5] Britain's weight in the world economy was thus primarily due to the role of the pound sterling – the main international trading and reserve currency and the cornerstone of the international monetary system in force at that time, the gold standard.

Britain's financial pre-eminence was embodied in the global role played by the City of London, the world's leading financial centre.[6] The City offered an unrivalled range of financial services, which made it the principal engine of financial globalization. First, the bulk of world trade was financed through the medium of bills of exchange drawn on London. And second, with nearly 50 per cent of foreign capital stocks held by British investors, London was the main centre for the issue of foreign loans. These two essential functions were carried out by a group of private banks, known as merchant banks.[7] The issuing business, the most prestigious activity in international finance, was the preserve of the most select houses (Rothschilds, Barings, Morgan Grenfell, Hambros, Schroders, and a few others, including Kleinworts, the leading accepting house). The accepting business (in other words guaranteeing the payment of a bill exchange when it came to maturity) was the bread and butter of a growing number of firms, possibly as many as 105 in 1914, several of them from abroad. In the heart of the world's financial capital, the wheels of global finance were thus activated by old-established family-owned private banks rather than by the new joint-stock banks that had emerged in the mid-nineteenth century. The latter (Lloyds Bank, Midland Bank, London County and Westminster, and National Provincial Bank, to name but the four largest in 1913), known as the clearing banks, confined themselves to deposit banking activities within the domestic economy, but they provided the cash credit required by the merchant banks' operations.

Another group of newly formed joint-stock banks, known as overseas banks (London and River Plate Bank; Hong Kong and Shanghai Banking Corporation; Chartered Bank of India, Australia and China; Standard Bank of South Africa; and others) were directly involved in international finance. They usually had their head office in London (one exception was the Hong Kong and Shanghai Banking Corporation), but operated a network of branches in the formal and informal empire. Their goal was to provide facilities, especially foreign exchange, to merchants in the regions in which they were established. They also offered financial services in regions often lacking in banking infrastructure, thus winning a clientele from among well-off members of the local community. While the number of overseas banks doubled between 1860 and 1913 (from fifteen to about thirty), the number of branches increased more than tenfold (from 132 to 1,387).[8] But there was also a movement in the opposite direction. As a result of its financial predominance, the City attracted large foreign banks that came there to seek profitable business opportunities. Thirty of them – more than in any other centre – had opened an office by 1913, belonging to twelve different countries, and included the major French and German banks.

The City of London's other major activity as an international financial centre was the London Stock Exchange – a secondary market where the securities issued on the primary market could be negotiated. The nominal value of the securities listed there went from £2.3 billion in 1873 to £11.3 billion in 1913, more than the New York Stock Exchange and the Paris *Bourse* combined.[9] As evidence of its highly cosmopolitan character, foreign stocks, which represented between 35 and 40 per cent of the total in 1873, exceeded 50 per cent from 1893 onwards. By 1914 one-third of all securities in the world were quoted on the London Stock Exchange. The City hosted major commodity markets, such as the London Metal Exchange and the Baltic Exchange; and it provided specialized professional services, especially legal and accounting, whose leading firms soon expanded abroad to follow their clientele or to build up a new one. Price Waterhouse, for example, opened a branch in New York in 1890 and another in Chicago in 1892, where its business took off very quickly. Finally, in the centre of global finance, the Bank of England was, to use Keynes' words, the 'conductor' of the international monetary system, whose leadership the other central banks were prepared to follow in order to maintain monetary stability.[10]

No other centre had the same global range of services as London. Paris has been accurately described by Alain Plessis as a 'brilliant second'.[11] Its strength lay above all with its long-term capital market, especially for foreign securities, which was second only to London. Until the negotiation of the war indemnity loans in 1871–2, the issuing business had remained in the hand of the *Haute Banque* (Rothschilds, Fould, Mallet, Hottinguer, Seillière, and a few others), a group of private banks akin to the London merchant banks. From then on, it was taken over by the new joint-stock banks – the investment banks (Paribas) as well as the big commercial banks (Crédit Lyonnais, Société Générale, and Comptoir National D'escompte de Paris) which, unlike their English counterparts, were involved in international finance, especially the placing of foreign loans. They also established a network of foreign branches: in 1913, the Crédit Lyonnais owned twenty, compared with eight in 1878, and the Comptoir d'Escompte owned twenty-eight. Overseas banks were far less prominent than in the City of London, owing partly to competition from the commercial banks but mainly to France's weaker presence in the world. However, the most important among them (Banque Impériale Ottomane and Banque de l'Indochine) were forces to be reckoned with in international finance. Paris also attracted foreign banks, though less than London (around fifteen in 1913). And the Banque de France, with its large gold reserves, played a key role in the international monetary system alongside the Bank of England, maintaining regulation and stability by allowing its gold to flow to London when the need arose.

The rise of global finance coincided with the rise of new financial powers. Frankfurt, Hamburg, and Cologne had been European financial centres of some significance since the seventeenth century, but it was only after German unification in 1871 and rapid industrialization in the following decades that Germany and its new political and financial capital, Berlin, rose to financial prominence. More than anywhere else, business was dominated by the big banks (Deutsche Bank, Dresdner Bank, Disconto-Gesellschaft, and Darmstädter Bank). They were universal banks, engaged in both commercial and investment banking, and controlled most international financial transactions. In addition to a number of foreign branches, they also established subsidiaries to conduct business in less developed countries. The Deutsche Bank, for example, created the Deutsche Überseeische Bank (active in Latin America) and the Deutsch-Asiatische Bank, the latter in conjunction with the Disconto-Gesellschaft and Bleichröder, a private bank.[12] However, Berlin was not in a position to rival seriously London or even Paris, if only because Germany invested far less capital abroad than Britain and France did. Moreover, the Berlin Börse was strictly regulated in order to curb speculation and combat fraud – the law of 1896 considerably limited forward transactions, and actually prohibited them on the securities of mining and manufacturing companies. As a result, speculative transactions, which represented the bulk of stock market business, moved out of Germany, towards Amsterdam and London in particular.

Specialized services were offered by lesser European financial centres – a broad and diverse secondary market in Amsterdam; finance companies in Brussels and Switzerland (Zurich, Geneva, and Basel) that contributed to the development of the power industry worldwide by transferring funds provided by the big German banks and electrical engineering companies.[13] All in all, the bulk of international financial business was conducted in the financial centres of the leading capital exporting countries.

New York's position was somewhat peculiar. Its arrival among the leading financial centres was more as an entry point for foreign funds than as a point of departure for capital exports – though the situation had changed by 1900. New York's importance became increasingly decisive because of the massive amount of foreign investment in the United States, the dynamism of the American economy (foreign investment only made a small contribution to the huge domestic accumulation of capital), and the city's position as the country's financial centre. Like the City merchant banks, the Wall Street investment banks (J. P. Morgan, Kidder Peabody, Lee Higginson, Kuhn Loeb, and Seligman and Speyer), also family-owned private banks, formed the cornerstone of New York's financial centre.[14] Revealingly, they had close links to foreign financial centres, above all the City of London. Unlike in London, the largest national banks were themselves involved in investment banking, with the National City Bank in the lead.[15] Nevertheless, New York's international influence was still limited and it was dependent on London for the financing of American foreign trade, but the institutional foundations of its future predominance were laid during the pre-war years.

International financial centres developed in other borrowing countries, but with different characteristics from the providers of global finance. Centres such as Hong Kong, Shanghai and Peking, Bombay and Calcutta, Cairo and Alexandria, Sydney and Melbourne, Yokohama, Buenos Aires, Rio de Janeiro, Constantinople, and St Petersburg all hosted between six (St Petersburg) and twelve (Shanghai) 'transnational' banks.[16]

By comparison London had sixty-two, Paris thirty-one, and New York twenty. Other centres in advanced economies were well behind: Brussels and Hamburg had ten, Berlin nine, and Amsterdam eight. Other European centres, such as Vienna, Milan, Madrid, Stockholm, and Zurich, hardly featured at all. Emerging centres, including New York, tended to attract foreign banks rather than host the head office of multinational banks. In China, India, the Middle East, Latin America, and Australasia, virtually all 'transnational' banks were branches of foreign banks that primarily financed foreign trade. With the exception of London, which combined the two, capital exports were the dominant feature of established financial centres, and trade finance that of emerging ones, especially in Asia.

The position of financial centres in less developed countries points to an important feature of global finance before 1914 – the fact that opening up the world went hand in hand with the establishment of colonial empires and the imperialist powers' direct or indirect domination over most of the world on an unprecedented scale. In 1914, the British Empire stretched over 30 million square kilometres and included 450 million inhabitants, while the French colonial empire stretched over 10 million square kilometres with 50 million inhabitants. On top of this, they informally held sway over regions as vast as China, the Ottoman Empire, and Latin America.

The costs and benefits of global finance must be considered in this context. There is no doubt that capital transfers played a positive role in the economic development of capital importing countries – though with major differences between countries and regions. Government loans were certainly not always put to productive use, whether in connection with military expenditure or, more often, with servicing an already contracted debt. Yet significant achievements were made, especially in infrastructure: railways, roads, docks, ports, power stations, and urban development. These achievements enabled natural resources to be developed and exported, thus stimulating economic growth; and only foreign capital could ensure their success. Recent research has emphasized, from a strictly financial perspective, the links between the cost of a loan and the risks associated to it.[17] Favourable conditions included the borrowing country's adherence to the gold standard, which was seen as a guarantee of good financial order, or membership of the British Empire, which provided additional assurance.[18] Borrowing on the international capital market was more expensive for Turkey than for Argentina or Russia, and even more expensive than for Australia or Japan. Indebtedness could, however, have another cost, and, even allowing for the complexities of the relationships between political and financial interests, it did contribute to the partial or total loss of political independence – from the occupation of Egypt and the foreign interference in the Ottoman Empire's finances to the division of China into 'spheres of influences'.

## Wars, depression, and regulation, 1914–73

The First World War did not put an end to capital exports. Between 1914 and 1918, debts totalling nearly $20 billion – in other words an amount equivalent to the stock of

British foreign assets on the eve of the war – were incurred among the Allies. The two main creditor countries were the United States ($9.2 billion) and the United Kingdom ($8.5 billion), with France ($1.7 billion) trailing far behind – although Britain also had to borrow from the United States ($4.2 billion) and the French from both the United States ($2.7 billion) and the United Kingdom ($2.5 billion), while the other Allies (Italy and Russia) were only borrowers.[19] However, despite these vast amounts of capital transfers, one cannot talk of a global market. These loans were essentially contracted between governments and did not activate the mechanisms usually associated with credit transfers between international financial centres. France, for example, borrowed $2.9 billion from the American government compared with only $336 million from banks, and $2.1 billion from the British government, compared with $625 million from banks, including the Bank of England. Only a few intermediaries and privileged partners were involved in these operations, most of which were managed from New York and London, from where they continued to offer their expertise and their network of relationships. In this respect, the First World War marked the end of the Rothschilds' supremacy in government loans and the advent of the House of Morgan, which was responsible for issuing the first Anglo-French loan for $500 million in October 1915, followed by four more loans amounting to a total of $950 million on behalf of Britain in 1916 and 1917, and was to dominate global finance in the 1920s.

Global financial transactions, both capital exports and trade finance, resumed after the war. Some $10 billion flowed from creditor to borrowing nations during the second half of the 1920s. One major difference with the pre-war years was the proportion of short-term capital – about half the total in the case of European borrowers, not least Germany.[20] Another difference was the respective position of the financial powers. The great victor was the United States, which in a few years changed from a debtor country to a creditor country (having net private liabilities in excess of $3 billion in 1913 to net assets of $4.5 billion in 1919). Europe was no longer the world's banker. Germany lost nearly all its foreign assets; France most of it, probably three-quarters of its assets in Europe, mainly in Russia; and Britain some 20 per cent, essentially the $3 billion worth of American stock that it was obliged to sell. The situation was complicated by the questions of war debts ($19.4 billion in total, mainly due to the United States and Great Britain) and reparations (132 billion gold German marks – three times Germany's GDP). There was thus no return to pre-war stability. The gold standard was finally restored between 1924 and 1926, but its functioning was beset with difficulties and unable to achieve its objective, namely to permit balance-of-payments adjustments. This was caused by the overvaluation of the pound and the undervaluation of the French franc, the uneasy cooperation between central banks, and insufficient expansionary policy in the surplus countries (France and the United States).

Nevertheless, London remained the world's leading financial centre in the 1920s, having soon regained its predominance in most activities, despite the success of acceptances drawn on New York, thanks to the establishment of the Federal Reserve in 1913, which allowed national banks to accept bills of exchange. However, it had to cede first place to New York in foreign issues. Britain remained the largest holder of foreign investment in terms of stocks, but no longer the largest capital exporter in terms of annual flows, because of the constraints weighing down its balance of payments. This role was now devolved to the United States. During the second half of the 1920s, foreign issues placed in New York generally exceeded those offered in London by 50 per cent (respectively, $969 and $592 million in 1924, $1,337 and $676 million in 1927, and $671 and $457 million in 1929). Overall, New York ranked number two, but it should not be forgotten that in spite of its new world role, it remained as much an American as an international financial centre. Foreign issues played a secondary role to domestic issues and accounted for only 15 per cent of the total amount of new issues in the 1920s. In addition, foreign capital continued to be invested in the United States, both long term and short term, especially with the bullish trend that marked the decade. This interaction between national and international business was one of the main characteristics of New York when compared to London.[21]

Paris was weakened by the war and dropped from second to third place. France was crippled by the weakness of the franc, capital flight, and reconstruction requirements. However, the stabilization of the franc by Raymond Poincaré in December 1926 marked a turning point: Paris recovered part of its pre-war vitality, rekindling ambitions to compete with London and New York. Berlin paid the price of defeat and hyperinflation in 1923. Germany became the world's largest capital importing country in the 1920s, and it is mainly in this capacity that the German capital remained a significant international financial centre. Amsterdam, on the other hand, was commonly described as Germany's effective financial centre during the years of inflation and hyperinflation. All the major banks set up there after the end of the war and were active on the foreign exchange market and later in the acceptance market, and Amsterdam enjoyed spectacular growth during the 1920s and established itself as the foremost centre in continental Europe. Zurich and the other Swiss centres (Geneva and Basel) played a lesser though not insignificant role in attracting foreign capital and redirecting it abroad – mainly to Germany.

Financial institutions played fundamentally the same role as before the war. Foreign issues continued to be handled by the merchant banks in the City, with limited competition from the clearing banks; and by the investment banks in Wall Street, with increasing competition from the securities affiliates of the big banks, with National City Bank in the lead. As before the war, both merchant and investment banks were in family hands, some organized as partnerships, others as limited companies but still controlled by their owners. With the exception of J. P. Morgan which towered above the rest, they were small or medium-sized companies. Their global transactions were conducted from New York or London, without a significant presence abroad – some had a branch or a subsidiary in another centre (J. P. Morgan, for example, held a majority stake in Morgan Grenfell in London and Morgan Harjes in Paris), but most worked through correspondents.

The big banks somewhat retreated on the global financial front. The emergence of the 'Big Five' in England in 1918, which became the world's largest banks, did not fundamentally alter their functions. The French banks were weakened by the depreciation of the franc, the loss or closure of several foreign branches (in Russia, the Middle East, and Latin America), and the slow resumption of foreign investment. The German banks were stripped of their foreign assets (foreign branches and subsidiary companies). The American banks made only a short-lived attempt at expanding abroad in the early 1920s: Their total number of foreign branches soared to 181 in 1920 though it decreased to 107 by 1925. In the end, British overseas banks were the only ones to expand: their network of branches increased by nearly a thousand to reach 2,353 in 1928, almost exclusively in their areas of specialization.

The Great Depression was a watershed in the history of global finance. It consisted of four interrelated shock waves: the Wall Street Crash of October 1929, by a series of banking crises occurring over a period of five years, the collapse of the world monetary order, and an economic slump of dramatic proportions. Long-term capital investments almost completely stopped in the 1930s. New York saw its role as an international financial centre shrivel: foreign loans, which had been its speciality, fell to less than $300 million in 1931 – less than the issues offered in London – and to less than $100 million in 1932 and 1933. But the domestic capital market was also shaken, issues on behalf of companies going from $8 billion in 1929 to $160 million in 1933. In London, foreign loans outside the British Empire ceased almost completely after September 1931, adding up to a mere £28.5 million between 1932 and 1938 – that is to say less than 3 per cent of the total amount of issues in London, as against 17 per cent for imperial issues (£186.7 million), which continued throughout the decade.[22] The number of foreign issues as a whole, including in the empire, thus dropped considerably in the 1930s. However, Britain's imperial retreat, strengthened by the formation of the sterling area, made it possible to conduct international financial transactions from London. Overseas banks, for example, added another thousand branches to their worldwide, mainly imperial, network.

From the perspective of global finance, the Second World War was different from the First if only because global financial activities had started to decline several years earlier. Moreover the state's hold over the economy was stronger than it had been during the Great War, leaving hardly any opportunity at all for bankers and financiers to take charge of the large financial transactions required by the war effort. Capital transfers mainly took place within each of the two camps and consisted of state-to-state transactions, or exactions – the American lend–lease programme on the Allied side and the extensive use of resources from the occupied territories made by the Reich on the Axis side.[23]

Global finance did not rise from the ashes after the Second World War. The regulations inherited from the 1930s and those established in the immediate post-war years, including exchange controls, contributed to financial stability but hampered the re-emergence of a globalized financial world. Until the 1960s, or in some cases the 1970s, the international financial centres' business remained mostly confined within national borders: the golden age of economic growth, between 1950 and 1973 when annual GDP growth averaged 5 per cent in Europe and 8 per cent in Japan, was not accompanied by intense international movements of private capital. The largest capital transfers were not left to the private sector, but were undertaken by governments, state bodies, and, to a lesser extent, multilateral agencies like the International Monetary Fund or the World Bank. Between 1955 and 1962, foreign issues floated in New York barely reached $4.2 billion – a feeble sum compared with the $126.5 billion for domestic issues, or the $98 billion in economic and military aid granted by the United States to foreign countries between 1945 and 1952.[24]

New York emerged as the world's financial capital and its position remained unchallenged until the 1960s. However, New York's pre-eminence corresponded to a period in which international capital flows were far smaller than before 1931 or after 1980. London's position was considerably weakened after the war, but it refocused on the Commonwealth and, particularly, on the sterling area, which enabled it to resume, in a more limited way, the role it had played on the world stage prior to 1914.[25] Paris' international position after 1945 was a mere shadow of what it had been only some thirty years earlier. Even more than in Britain, the state's grip ended up stifling the Parisian capital market, with foreign issues practically nil during this period.[26] In Germany, Frankfurt took over from Berlin as the country's financial centre but remained a centre of national rather than international significance until the late 1970s.[27] Zurich was one of the rare financial markets, along with New York, to strengthen its international position, probably ranking third (together with Geneva, Basel, and to a lesser extent Lugano) behind New York and London in the 1960s as the Swiss markets quickly developed their role for accommodating and investing foreign capital, through international issues and wealth management.[28]

In a climate of state intervention and regulation, global business and finance resurfaced in the late 1950s with the advent of the Euromarkets. The Euromarkets are markets for transactions in dollars taking place outside the United States, free of American regulations. For various reasons, dollars started to accumulate in Europe, especially in London, in the 1950s – the Cold War and the Soviet Union's fears of having its dollar deposits frozen in the United States; the overseas investment and growing payment deficit of the United States; banking regulations, especially Regulation Q, which put a ceiling on the rate of interests which US banks paid on domestic bank deposits. The Eurodollar market, a short-term money market, was the first to develop, when London banks began to use dollars rather pounds to finance third-party trade, after the British government had banned the use of sterling instruments for such purposes following the sterling crisis of 1957.[29] With the European currencies' return to external convertibility in December 1958 and, from the early 1960s, the gradual relaxing of controls on capital flows, the Eurodollar market expanded rapidly. It was supplied mainly by American multinationals and by European central banks and provided credit on a worldwide scale and in hitherto unprecedented proportions, mainly to finance international trade and other short-term loans. From approximately $1.5 billion when it started in 1958, this market reached $25 billion ten years later and $130 billion in 1973.[30]

The Eurodollar market quickly gave birth to the Eurobond market, a long-term capital market using Eurodollars not only for bank loans but also for issuing dollar-denominated bonds, in London rather than in New York. The first Eurobond was issued in London in July 1963 to Siegmund Warburg, on behalf of Autostrada Italiana, a subsidiary of the state holding company IRI.[31] Eurobonds quickly proved very popular, especially as they were issued to bearer, which means that they were anonymous and exempt from withholding tax. The Eurobond market grew from about $250 million in 1963 to a yearly average of over $4 billion ten years later.

A third form of Euro credit – medium term this time, lasting from three to ten years – developed in the mid-1960s, between short-term, mainly interbank, Eurodollar deposits, and long-term Eurobonds. These were international bank loans wholly financed by resources in Eurodollars and generally granted on the basis of floating interest rates. In view of the growing demand for these loans and the size of the amounts required, they took the form of syndicated loans bringing several banks together. Despite the risks associated with interest rate fluctuations, the borrower found this a more flexible source of funding than a bond issue. From barely $2 billion in 1968, Euro credits quickly swelled to exceed $20 billion in 1973 – or more than four times the amount of Eurobonds.

The Euromarkets reshaped the world of international finance. They marked the start of the huge multinational expansion of American banks. They went from having 131 branches abroad in 1950 to having 899 in 1986, in addition to their 860 foreign subsidiaries. Europe was the preferred destination: By 1975 the eight largest American banks had set up 113 branches and 29 representative offices there, London alone having 58 of them.[32] Competition from American banks was particularly strong. While London bankers were the founders of the Euromarkets, American banks soon dominated it. The rise of the Euromarkets also signalled the rebirth of the City of London, which quickly became their natural home. London was certainly well equipped for hosting these new financial activities – because of the age-old experience of its bankers, their expertise in international finance, and the diversity and complementarity of its institutions and markets. The positive attitude of the British monetary authorities, in contrast to that of their European counterparts, also made a difference. The first sign of the rebirth of the City was the attraction that it held for banks throughout the world: The number of foreign banks represented in London went from 59 in 1955 to 159 in 1970 and 243 in 1975 – that is to say, nearly twice the corresponding number in New York.[33]

The City merchant banks and the Wall Street investment managed to retain a share of the Eurobond market – the issuing business was one of their historical specialities – but they faced strong competition from both American and European, and later Japanese, big banks in an increasingly global market. While twelve of them (including Kuhn Loeb, SG Warburg, Hambros, Morgan, and NM Rothschild) featured among the top twenty co-lead managers of Eurobond issues in the market's first five years, between 1963 and 1967, their number had fallen ten years later to six, between 1973 and 1977. In both periods, the ranking was headed by Deutsche Bank.[34] Investment banks and merchant banks were still dominant in corporate finance, especially mergers and acquisitions, an activity that took off in the 1960s but was not to become global for another twenty years.

However, they were starting to lose their private bank character as most of them not only converted into public companies (some had done so earlier) but opened ownership and control to outside interests.

## Innovations and deregulations, 1973–2000

The end of the Bretton Woods system in 1971–73 opened a new era of international capital flows. According to recent estimates, in 2000 foreign assets (\$28,984 billion) represented 92 per cent of world GDP, up from 25 per cent (with \$2,800 billion) in 1980 and barely 6 per cent (\$147.7 billion) in 1960.[35] At the turn of the twenty-first century, the United States was – as indeed it had been since the end of the Second World War – the largest holder of capital outside its territory, ahead of Britain, Japan, Germany, and France – the same countries, in a different order, as before 1914, with the addition of a newcomer, Japan. The destination of foreign investment, on the other hand, had changed. At the beginning of the twentieth century, it was the colonies and new countries that received the bulk of these transfers. A century later, it was the rich countries of Europe and North America that, with Japan, absorbed more than 80 per cent of foreign investment.

The upsurge in capital exports started with the demise of the Bretton Woods system in 1971–73. With the end of fixed exchange rates, free movements of capital became compatible with an independent monetary policy – in line with the Mundell-Fleming's trilemma, according to which only two of these three policy options can be pursued together. Their continued expansion took place within a new climate marked, in particular, by financial deregulations and innovations.

The deregulation movement started in the United States, with the liberalization of the New York Stock Exchange (abolition of fixed commissions) in May 1975, making competition keener and leading to a consolidation in investment banking. The City of London followed in October 1986 with 'Big Bang', also a reform of the stock exchange (abolition of fixed commission and of the separation, unique to the London Stock Exchange, between the functions of brokers, who acted on behalf of clients, and jobbers, who were market-makers); it was also decided to open the London Stock Exchange, and by extension the City, to the outside world by permitting banks, both domestic and foreign, to buy member firms, hitherto banned. In Paris, the stockbrokers' monopoly was abolished in 1992. In Germany, the Bundesbank authorized floating-rate issues in 1984–5, despite its distrust of financial innovation, and allowed foreign banks to act as lead banks for foreign issues in Deutsche marks.[36] The wave of deregulation culminated in 1999 when the Glass-Steagall Act of 1933 was repealed by the Financial Modernization Act. Commercial banking and investment banking could again be brought together on the grounds that new financial instruments justified greater concentration among the various intermediaries in the world of finance.

Financial innovation became, as never before, an integral part of global finance. Three main factors account for this development. One was the incredible progress made in computing, which enabled the new financial products to reach an otherwise impossible degree of sophistication. Another was the application to the market of theoretical advances made in the field of financial economics (Markowitz and Sharpe's modern portfolio theory, Fama's efficient market hypothesis, Black and Scholes options pricing model, and others), opening the way for the design of ever more complex financial products. And a third was the liberalization of the financial markets, whose aim was to improve their efficiency by encouraging financial innovations – which remained very lightly, if at all, regulated.

The end of Bretton Woods offered an incentive. Modern derivatives, which have been at the heart of the financial revolution of the late twentieth century, came into being in Chicago in 1972 with the creation of the International Monetary Market, where currency contracts were traded – the initiative was taken to provide facilities for hedging against foreign exchange fluctuations. The Chicago Board Options Exchange, where options were traded on shares, was founded a year later. Europe followed with LIFFE (London International Financial Future Exchange) in 1982, MATIF (Marché à Terme des Instruments Financiers) in Paris in 1986, and DTB (Deutsche Termin Börse) in Frankfurt in the early 1990s.

Derivatives were also combined with a new investment medium: alternative management funds, better known as hedge funds, which appeared in the 1980s.[37] They were usually domiciled in an offshore centre, were highly leveraged, and took short positions, through derivatives or forward operations. Their managers, who often made the headlines in the financial press, earned high bonuses – generally reaching 20 per cent of profits above a certain threshold plus 1.5 to 2 per cent management fees – and, as a rule, invested their own funds alongside those of their clients. Their growth was phenomenal during the 1990s, from a few hundreds to nearly 3,000 by 2006, with nearly $1,000 billion of funds managed. And if they enjoyed spectacular successes (with George Soros allegedly making £1 billion in 1993), they also suffered severe setbacks, most spectacularly with the failure of LTCM (Long-Term Capital Management) in 1998, which had a debt-to-equity ratio of 25 to 1 and two economics Nobel Prize winners (Robert Merton and Myron Scholes) on its board of directors.

Banking and financial practices have been deeply transformed by what has become known as securitization – the conversion of various types of debt, especially loans, into marketable securities. Its novelty resided in the type of assets converted into securities and the type of 'financial products' emerging from this conversion. Typically, they were derivatives. Mortgages were the first debts to be securitized, in the form of mortgage-backed securities; other assets, in particular consumer debt (insurance policies, car loans, credit card loans, student loans, and so on), were in turn securitized, bearing the generic name of assets-backed securities; credit derivatives were also developed, in the first place Credit Default Swaps, which offered protection against the risk of default on a debt through a contract between two parties, the seller as it were insuring the buyer in return of the payment of a regular fee.

The securitization process was mainly undertaken by investment banks in New York and London, thus enhancing the position of these two centres in the age of global finance. By the turn of the twenty-first century, New York was still in the first place, by far the largest capital market, even if London had the edge in direct international financial activities, ranking first for international banking, asset management, and foreign exchange, and attracting the highest number of foreign banks (481 as against 287 in New York). These two centres were well ahead of the pack. New York clearly set the tone in international banking and financial business, if only because of the might of the American banks, mostly based in New York, and on which a great deal of London's international influence depended. London's policy of opening up to the world had been kept up relentlessly and had borne fruit, at the cost, however, of a certain eclipse of British financial institutions and the City's dependence on foreign banks – what has sometimes been called the 'Wimbledon effect'.[38]

The major newcomer of the post-war era was Tokyo. As a result of Japan's rise to the rank of economic superpower, Tokyo established itself as a major international centre during the 1970s, going in twenty years from being a regional financial centre to a centre of world dimensions. And the possibility that Tokyo might overtake New York and become the world's leading financial centre did not seem entirely fanciful at the end of the 1980s, though such judgements proved too hasty. The American economy, far from declining, enjoyed spectacular growth in the 1990s whereas the Japanese economy went into a long slump after the burst of the stock exchange and property bubbles in 1990, which had severe repercussions for Tokyo's international position.

Frankfurt only overtook Zurich and Paris to become continental Europe's leading financial centre in the late 1980s. The decision in 1992 to establish the headquarters of the new European central bank in Frankfurt gave it a further boost, raising hopes that it might eventually overtake London, but this appeared highly unlikely a decade later. Paris regained some ground from the 1980s, without, however, really finding its role. Paris did not dominate any of the main fields of international financial activity, but held some aces, especially in asset management as well as in the bond market and derivatives. Zurich and Geneva continued to figure among the leading centres, increasingly specializing in wealth management, with 35 per cent of the world's private offshore wealth in the early 2000s, as against 21 per cent for Britain and 12 per cent for the United States.

The number of emerging, or rather aspiring, international financial centres increased significantly in the last two decades of the twentieth century. Several cities, especially in emerging economies, were actively promoted with the aim of their gaining the status of regional or even global international financial centre. Two centres were particularly successful in managing this transition: Singapore and Hong Kong, both with solid banking institutions, inherited from the British overseas banks, advantageous geographical location, and stable political regimes, despite the uncertainties related to Hong Kong's return to its big neighbour in 1997 – all essential requirements for the rise of an international financial centres, which were rarely met in most emerging economies.

Singapore's development was nonetheless the result of a systematic effort made on the part of the authorities, immediately upon the country's independence in 1965, to turn it into an international financial centre by hosting the nascent Asian dollar market (the counterpart of the Eurodollar market in London) and encouraging the emergence of a bond market. Singapore's financial markets really took off in the 1980s, and the foreign exchange market grew in its wake to reach fourth position in 1998, behind London, New York, and Tokyo; derivatives started being traded in 1984 with the foundation of SIMEX; and as a result, an increasing number of foreign banks set up there, reaching 260 in 1995.[39] In Hong Kong, by contrast, the authorities adopted a non-interventionist stance, at the same time creating conditions conducive to developing financial activities, notably a favourable tax system and modern infrastructure, in addition to the absence of exchange control, a robust legal system, the existence of the rule of law, and its position as the door for a China that began to open up to the world at the end of the 1970s.[40] Syndicated Euro credits found a home here, with operations on behalf of enterprises and governments in the region's main economies – Japan, Taiwan, South Korea, Australia and New Zealand, later joined by Thailand, the Philippines and, above all, China. In the space of about ten years, Hong Kong established itself as the world's third centre for Euro credits, behind London and New York. Its international status was mirrored in the presence of foreign banks, numbering 357 in 1995, that is to say more than any financial centre except for London.[41]

New York, London, Hong Kong, and Singapore stood at the apex of a hierarchy of financial centres. The Global Financial Centres Index listed forty-six centres when it was first published in 2007, with London ranked first (in terms of competitiveness) and Athens forty-sixth. The number had nearly doubled nine years later. Multinational banks considerably expanded in the second age of global finance, with a much stronger presence in the financial centres of both advanced and emerging economies – from about 20 per cent, in terms of number, in 1995, to 34 per cent in 2009, with some countries, especially in Eastern Europe, having more than 50 per cent of assets controlled by foreign banks.

These developments were at once the cause and the consequence of the emergence of a new type of multinational banks, that some have called 'transnational banks', in a different meaning from the one used earlier in this chapter, to underline both the quantitative and qualitative differences with their predecessors – in terms of size, internal organization, geographical spread, and range of activities.[42] The specialized British overseas banks, which had dominated multinational banking since the mid-nineteenth century, had lost their competitive advantage by the 1960s. By the turn of the twenty-first century, global finance was dominated by the world's leading universal banks (Citigroup, J. P. Morgan Chase, Bank of America, HSBC, RBS, Barclays, Deutsche Bank, BNP Paribas, UBS, Credit Suisse, and a few others). The largest, Citigroup, had offices in over 100 countries and employed nearly 370,000 people in 2007, before the crisis. It was engaged in all types of banking and financial activities, including retail banking, investment banking, trading, wealth management, and alternative investments such as hedge funds and private equity. Even more significantly, the bank had internalized its international activities, and was able to draw resources from one place and exploit them in another. All universal banks had more or less adopted this model.

## Conclusion

This chapter, like the rest of the book, ends around 2000, in other words before the financial crisis of 2008. However, it is impossible to end this overview of the rise of global finance since the mid-nineteenth without briefly considering the effects of the most severe *financial* crisis in modern history – the result of global imbalances and low interest rates, highly complex and not always well-understood financial instruments, and irresponsible risk-taking reflected in exceptionally high leverage ratios hidden in off-balance-sheet operations. At the time of writing, in summer 2016, two points are worth highlighting.

The first is that the financial crisis has slowed down the tremendous rise of finance – as an economic, social, political, and cultural phenomenon, sometimes called 'financialization'. However, despite the regulatory measures taken at both national and international levels, the financial sector, in other words global finance, as the two have been inextricably linked since the end of the twentieth century, has continued to grow – in contrast with what happened during the half-century that followed the Great Depression. There are several reasons for this: the costs of cutting the financial sector down to size, if only because of its share of national income and employment; the political climate in the advanced economies most affected by the crisis, which has been able to accommodate protest against financial abuses; and the international context, where old and new tensions have not threatened the globalization of the world economy.

The second point is that the financial crisis has not fundamentally altered the balance of power in global finance. New York and London have remained the two leading international financial centres and have not been toppled by Hong Kong, Singapore, Shanghai, or Dubai. Changes of this magnitude have occurred very rarely in history – only three cities (Amsterdam, London, and New York) have in turn been the world's leading financial centre in the last 300 years – and were very slow processes – as witnessed for example by the replacement of London by New York as the nerve centre of world finance. Emerging markets will have to meet several conditions, not least in terms of wealth, depth of skill, and openness, before claiming the mantle.

The financial debacle of 2008 may have undermined global finance, but it did not kill it. It is to be hoped that the crisis was severe enough to serve as a warning and ensure that the global financial system rests on more solid grounds. A retreat from global finance has never been a natural swing of the pendulum. It has always been the result of a devastating financial crisis. And the upheavals of the world's financial order have tended to take place in the midst of military cataclysms.

# Notes

1. M. Obstfeld and A. Taylor (2004), *Global Capital Markets: Integration, Crisis and Growth*. Cambridge: Cambridge University Press, 52.

2. Estimations based on A. Imlah (1952), 'British balance of payments and the export of capital, 1816-1913', *Economic History Review*, 2 (2), 235–6; and M. Lévy-Leboyer (1977), 'La balance des paiements et l'exportation des capitaux français', in M. Lévy-Leboyer (ed.), *La position internationale de la France: Aspects économiques et sociaux XIXe-XXe siècles*. Paris: Editions de l'École des Hautes Études en Sciences Sociales, 119–20.

3. P. Bairoch (1997), *Victoires et Déboires: Histoire Economique et Sociale du Monde du XVIe Siècle à Nos Jours*, 3 vols. Paris: Gallimard, vol. 2, 123, 127, 175–9.

4. P. Bairoch (1976), *Commerce Extérieur et Développement Economique de l'Europe au XIXe Siècle*. Paris: La Haye Mouton.

5. See S. B. Saul (1960), *Studies in British Overseas Trade, 1870-1914*. Liverpool: Liverpool University Press; and F. Crouzet (1964), 'Commerce extérieur et empire: l'expérience britannique du libre-échange à la Première Guerre mondiale', *Annales E.S.C.*, 19 (2), 281–310.

6. See D. Kynaston (1994), *The City of London. Volume I: A World of Its Own 1815-1890*. London: Chatto & Windus; Idem (1995), *The City of London. Volume II: Golden Years, 1890-1914*. London: Chatto & Windus; R. Michie (1992), *The City of London: Continuity and Change, 1850-1990*. Basingstoke and London: Macmillan; Y. Cassis (2006), *Capitals of Capital: A History of International Financial Centres 1780-2005*. Cambridge: Cambridge University Press.

7. See S. D. Chapman (1984), *The Rise of Merchant Banking*. London: Allen & Unwin.

8. G. Jones (1993), *British Multinational Banking 1830-1990*. Oxford: Clarendon Press.

9. R. Michie (1999), *The London Stock Exchange: A History*. Oxford: Oxford University Press, 88.

10. B. Eichengreen (1996), *Globalizing Capital: A History of the International Monetary System*. Princeton: Princeton University Press.

11. A. Plessis (2005), 'When Paris dreamt of competing with the City', in Y. Cassis and E. Bussière (eds), *London and Paris as International Financial Centres in the Twentieth Century*. Oxford: Oxford University Press, 42–54.

12. P. Hertner (1990), 'German banks abroad before 1914', in G. Jones (ed.), *Banks as Multinationals*. London: Routledge, 99–119.

13. W. J. Hausman, et al. (2008), *Global Electrification: Multinational Enterprise and International Finance in the History of Light and Power, 1878-2007*. New York: Cambridge University Press.

14. V. Carosso (1970), *Investment Banking in America: A History*. Cambridge, MA: Harvard University Press.

15. H. van B. Cleveland and T. H. Huertas (1985), *Citibank 1812-1970*. Cambridge, MA: Harvard University Press.

16. For the purpose of this study, 'transnational banks' has been defined as comprising both the multinational banks headquartered in a financial centre and the branches/subsidiaries of foreign banks established in that centre. See Y. Cassis (2016), 'International financial centres', in Y. Cassis, R. Grossman and C. Schenk (eds), *The Oxford Handbook of Banking and Financial History*. Oxford: Oxford University Press, 302–3.

17. M. Flandreau and D. Zumer (2004), *The Making of Global Finance 1880-1913*. Paris: OECD.

18. M. Bordo and H. Rockoff (1996), 'The Gold Standard as a "Good Housekeeping Seal of Approval"', *Journal of Economic History,* 56 (2), 389–428; N. Ferguson (2005), 'The City of London and British imperialism: New light on an old question', in Cassis and Bussière (eds), *London and Paris,* 57–77.

19. D. Artaud (1978), *La Question des Dettes Interalliées et la Reconstruction de l'Europe (1917–1929).* Paris: Champion.

20. C. H. Feinstein and K. Watson (1995), 'Private international capital flows in Europe in the inter-war period', in C. H. Feinstein (ed.), *Banking, Currency and Finance in Europe between the Wars.* Oxford: Oxford University Press, 94–130.

21. M. Wilkins (1999), 'Cosmopolitan finance in the 1920s: New York's emergence as an international financial centre', in R. Sylla, R. Tilly and G. Tortella (eds), *The State, the Financial System and Economic Modernization.* Cambridge: Cambridge University Press, 271–91.

22. T. Balogh (1947), *Studies in Financial Organization.* Cambridge: Cambridge University Press, 250.

23. A. S. Milward (1977), *War, Economy and Society, 1939–1945.* London: Allen & Unwin.

24. M. Nadler, S. Heller and S. Shipman (1955), *The Money Market and Its Institutions.* New York: Ronald Press, 290–1; R. Orsingher (1964), *Les Banques dans le Monde.* Paris: Payot, 140–1.

25. Michie, *The City of London;* D. Kynaston (2001), *The City of London: Volume IV: A Club No More 1945–2000.* London: Chatto & Windus.

26. L. Quennouëlle-Corre (2015), *La Place Financière de Paris au XXe Siècle: Des Ambitions Contrariées.* Paris: Comité pour l'Histoire Economique et Financière de la France.

27. C.-L. Holtfrerich (1999), *Frankfurt as a Financial Centre: From Medieval Trade Fair to European Banking Centre.* Munich: C. H. Beck.

28. M. Iklé (1970), *Die Schweiz als Internationaler Bank- und Finanzplatz.* Zurich: Orell Füssli.

29. C. Schenk (1998), 'The origins of the Eurodollar market in London, 1955–1963', *Explorations in Economic History,* 35 (2), 221–38; S. Battilossi (2002), 'Introduction: International banking and the American challenge in historical perspective', in S. Battilossi and Y. Cassis (eds), *European Banks and the American Challenge Competition and Cooperation in International Banking Under Bretton Woods.* Oxford: Oxford University Press, 1–35.

30. (1996), *International Capital Markets Statistics, 1950–1995.* Paris: OECD.

31. I. M. Kerr (1984), *A History of the Eurobond Market: The First 21 Years,* London: Euromoney Publications; N. Ferguson (2010), *High Financier. The Lives and Time of Siegmund Warburg,* London: Allen Lane.

32. T. F. Huertas (1990), 'U.S. multinational banking: history and prospects', in Jones, *Banks as Multinationals,* 253.

33. M. Baker and M. Collins (2005), 'London as an international banking centre, 1950–1980', in Cassis and Bussière (eds), *London and Paris,* 248–53.

34. Kerr, *A History of the Eurobond Market,* 29 and 53.

35. Obstfeld and Taylor, *Global Capital Markets,* 53.

36. G. Franke (1999), 'The Bundesbank and financial markets', in Deutsche Bundesbank (ed.), *Fifty Years of the Deutsche Mark.* Oxford: Oxford University Press, 246–53.

37. S. Mallaby (2010), *More Money than God: Hedge Funds and the Making of the New Elite.* London: Bloomsbury.

38. R. Roberts and D. Kynaston (2001), *City State. How the Markets Came to Rule Our World*. London: Profile Books.

39. R. C. Bryant (1989), 'The evolution of Singapore as a financial centre', in K. S. Sandhu and P. Wheatley (eds), *Management of Success: The Moulding of Modern Singapore*. Singapore: Institute of Southeast Asian Studies, 337–72; D. R. Lessard (1994), 'Singapore as an international financial centre', in R. Roberts (ed.), *Offshore Financial Centres*. Aldershot: Edward Elgar, 200–35.

40. Y. C. Jao (1983), 'Hong Kong as an international financial centre: Evolution and prospects', in R. Roberts (ed.), *International Financial Centres of Europe, North America and Asia*. Aldershot: Elgar, 491–534; C. Schenk (2001), *Hong Kong as an International Financial Centre: Emergence and Development, 1945–1965*. London: Routledge.

41. R. Roberts (1998), *Inside International Finance*. London: Orion.

42. C. Kobrak (2016), 'From multinational to transnational banking', in Cassis, Grossman and Schenk, *The Oxford Handbook of Banking*, 163–90.

# PART III
## REGIONAL PERSPECTIVES TO GLOBAL ECONOMIC CHANGE

# CHAPTER 14
## AFRICA: ECONOMIC CHANGE SOUTH OF THE SAHARA SINCE C. 1500
*Gareth Austin*

This chapter tries to identify the major sources of economic change in sub-Saharan Africa from the external slave trades onwards, to highlight the implications for the global debates about the evolution of inequality between different world regions, and assess the respective importance of resources and institutions as engines of economic change.[1] It will be argued that, while external influences have often facilitated and triggered economic change in Africa, internal influences have been crucial to the extent and shape of those changes. It will also be suggested that it is neither resource endowments nor institutions as such that have usually been decisive, but rather the interaction between them: with institutions generally not only responding to the resources available, but also gradually changing them.[2]

The main discussion is organized in four sections. As a preface, the first problematizes the traditional Eurocentric periodization of Africa's economic past. The second section focuses on the internal variables by summarizing the main features of Africa's changing resource ('factor') endowment from the sixteenth to the early twentieth century, and tracing a cluster of institutions with which that resource complex was associated. The third section considers the impact on African economies of the combination of external changes in technology and patterns of demand. The fourth section discusses what otherwise contrasting literatures consider to be the most important set of institutional changes: those in property and labour regimes associated with capitalism (arrangements which in Africa are traditionally seen as imported innovations and whose implementation and evolution have, however, been strongly shaped by the land–labour ratio within the region) and its transformation over the last century. The conclusion draws the threads together, emphasizing their entanglement, and reflects on their implications for the global issues.

## Period and agency in African history

Over the last sixty years, specialists in African history have challenged the traditional perception that economic change in the sub-Saharan subcontinent was largely absent or essentially exogenous. In this view, a long-term stagnation was initially modified by North African, Asian, and especially European commercial contact, most notoriously the external slave trades; with major economic and demographic change starting under colonial rule and continuing since independence – still in the context of continued dependence on external relationships, with disappointing welfare results often accompanied by political instability and violence. In contrast, the historical research conducted in recent decades generally emphasizes the importance of African agency (Africans making, or actively participating in making, their own histories) and change and variation within African economies. Yet to a certain extent, the old view, in various forms, continues to frame the ways in which most scholars in various disciplines view African history. This is partly because the revisionist research has tended to be relatively local in focus, whereas the older views have been restated at a general level, in the categories of successive theories (dependency and world systems[3] and some forms of rational-choice institutionalism[4]) that have themselves functioned to re-dress (rather than redress) the narrative of European (or North Atlantic) exceptionalism against which sub-Saharan Africa continues to be used as a convenient 'other'.

The continued priority of external sources of change in contemporary understandings of African economic history is expressed most strongly in the persistence of the traditional tripartite political periodization: pre-colonial, colonial, and post-colonial. For economic history, this has been questioned, but the most influential challenges tend to be at sub-regional level. For South Africa, it is widely accepted that a critical watershed was the mineral revolution of the 1860s–1880s, without which the subsequent growth of manufacturing would have been greatly attenuated.[5] Again, A. G. Hopkins made an influential proposal that 'the modern economic history of West Africa' should be dated not from colonization in the late nineteenth century but from the early-nineteenth-century transition in the Atlantic trade, from the export of slaves to that of agricultural produce. This was a defining watershed in that it involved the entry of small-scale producers into intercontinental trade for the first time on a wide scale.[6] But the only commonly accepted challenge to the traditional periodization for the region as a whole is the view that the independence of most of tropical Africa, around 1960, was a lesser turning point than the growth of state intervention in African economies, dating from the Second World War and its immediate aftermath, or indeed from the 1930s.[7]

Let us consider the respective roles of external and domestic influences on the turning points of African economic history in more detail, taking as an example the post-independence era. Within this, it makes sense to identify the 1980s as a policy watershed: when state-led development policies gave way, via 'Structural Adjustment', to the liberal economic regimes that have characterized the region ever since. Regarding economic growth, three periods can be distinguished at the level of the region as a whole: relatively slow growth of output (in real GDP per capita), averaging little more than 1 per cent per year c. 1960 to 1975; stagnation over the following two decades, with some years of actual decline; and a general expansion over the twenty-plus years from c. 1995, at about 2 per cent per capita. The external influence on this regional growth record is palpable: the first OPEC oil price shock, in 1973, was a brake on economic growth in most sub-Saharan countries, few of whom were yet oil exporters. Conversely, the recent general economic expansion – spread more widely across the region than earlier booms – was at least initially stimulated by the rise in world commodity prices led by China's industrialization. Yet, at least until that boom, shifts in interregional terms of trade correlate rather weakly with the records of individual national economies. Most African economies did relatively well in part of their post-independence history, but almost all of them also had at least one period of stagnation or even decline.[8] Côte d'Ivoire and Ghana, cocoa-growing neighbours with similar factor endowments, followed almost opposite trajectories for half a century: a contrast which cannot be explained primarily by external influences, but rather owes much to very different policy choices in the early decades of independence.[9]

The general policy shift that was Structural Adjustment is often casually attributed entirely to external pressure, from the International Monetary Fund (IMF) and the World Bank. They provided loans in return for which national governments accepted packages of economic liberalization, shifting the mechanism of allocation of resources and goods from administration to markets. Certainly, the Washington-based institutions were crucial to the process, but it is important not to overlook the domestic pressures, which in many countries led governments to embark on Adjustment. In contrast to Latin America, at the beginning of the 1980s, few African governments had big debts to foreign banks, because the banks would not lend to them. Indeed in Africa huge sovereign debt to export ratios were usually a consequence of Adjustment rather than a cause. Between 1980 and 1995, for sub-Saharan Africa, the ratio of external debt to exports jumped from 90 per cent to 241 per cent, whereas for Latin America and the Caribbean the rise was from 206 per cent to 212 per cent.[10] A bigger problem for many African countries at the start of the 1980s was profound shortages of government revenue and import-purchasing power as a result of having increasingly overvalued, more or less non-convertible, currencies that acted effectively as instruments of penal taxation on their exporters (this did not apply to nearly the same extent, nor in the same way, to the franc zone countries, for whom Adjustment was less radical because their currency was already fully convertible). Faced with official prices that made it unprofitable to produce or sell, including for domestic markets, farmers and traders in countries from Guinea to Tanzania to the then (Congo) Zaire bypassed official markets.[11] This unorganized economic resistance from below did much to end the era of state-led development policy. It does much to explain why the governments concerned reluctantly decided to accept the IMF and World Bank's offer of credit to assist them to shift from state to market-based development policies. Thus, for both policy and performance, the major trends and turning points of post-independence economic history have been very much the outcome of interactions between external and internal variables.

## Resources, techniques, and institutions within Africa, 1500–c. 1918

Most of sub-Saharan Africa, most of the time, was characterized by a relative abundance of cultivable land in relation to labour, often until far into the twentieth century, and in some areas, even until today. That is to say, over any period longer than it took to clear the bush, the expansion of agricultural output was unconstrained by the physical availability of land. Because most of the capital goods used in arable agriculture, handicraft production, and small-scale mining were created by simple tool-aided labour, output was mainly a function of labour inputs. In much of tropical Africa, labour scarcity was relieved by an extremely uneven seasonal distribution of rainfall: for much of the dry season, there was (as of 1500 and, in most areas, even 1850) little that could be done in agriculture, freeing labour variously for hunting, mining, and handicraft production. Meanwhile, sleeping sickness made the use of large animals unsustainable, whether for transport or ploughing, wherever the parasite's host, the tsetse fly, was endemic: the forest zones and shifting zones within the savannas.[12] In this forbidding context, it is almost superfluous to add that, of two geographical features particularly favourable to early industrialization, Africa was short on one, navigable rivers, and completely lacking in the other, large supplies of coal and iron ore in close proximity to each other. The physical abundance of land at least reduced certain sources of risk to food security. The downside was that the fertility of the soils, derived from one of the oldest bedrocks on the planet, was often low; and where it was high, it tended to be easily exposed to degradation from severe rain or sun.[13]

While agricultural techniques varied across Africa, it is difficult not to see their prevailing features as specific responses to these physical conditions: a preference for land-extensive methods in the prevalence of itinerant pastoralism in herding areas, and various forms of hoe-based land rotation in arable ones, with the largest trees often being left to stand in cultivated fields. Conversely, the low opportunity cost of dry season labour facilitated labour-intensive production off the farm, notably a preference (especially in West Africa) for cloth woven on the narrow loom.[14]

Despite the prevalence of land-extensive techniques in agriculture, intensification (defined as raising the ratio of capital and/or labour inputs per unit of land) in such forms as terracing and irrigation was ancient in parts of eastern, southern, and even western Africa. It was used to be thought that, nevertheless, there was no cumulative trend towards intensification, because irrigation or terracing came and went in particular sites, albeit in some cases lasting centuries before their demise. Recent research suggests, however, that there was a net expansion of intensive agriculture during the sixteenth to nineteenth centuries,[15] though the extensive methods mentioned above remained predominant until land became scarce, which it did it in many countries in the twentieth century.

Alongside the general (though not universal) preference for land extensiveness in agriculture was a cluster of very widespread institutional features, notably strong social approval for mothers (and fathers) who had many children;[16] broadly defined kinship groups and diverging inheritance;[17] relatively open access to land, in the sense of readiness to grant use rights in land even to strangers providing they acknowledged the ultimate ownership of the existing owners, who were often a lineage or chieftaincy;[18] widespread property in people, including children, wives, subjects, and also slaves and pawns;[19] and the persistence of 'stateless' (segmentary lineage) societies and small states alongside large kingdoms and empires, through to the European partition of Africa from 1879.[20] These institutional patterns, like the characteristic choices of technique, can be understood as reflecting the combination of land abundance and constraints upon intensification: settings in which the production of large grain surpluses was unnecessary (given low population density and widespread self-sufficiency in basic staples) and/or difficult (where soils did not readily support short fallowing cycles). In such contexts, there was usually no market in land rights (any payments were token or customary) but people – not only children and adults, kin, but also immigrants – especially people who were in some sense dependents, were valued as current or future producers and reproducers, and possessing them raised the owners' prestige. Inheritance systems were organized not to transmit capital to narrowly specified heirs, but rather to spread what property there was widely, the better to reinforce alliances and thereby share and reduce risks, whether to nutritional or physical security. State formation was inhibited (though not prevented) by the difficulty in concentrating the means to support political and military specialists. Meanwhile, long-distance trade, spanning polities (large or small) and cultures, could be facilitated by the construction of ethnic and religious trading diasporas, which created internal moral communities, offering gains from (otherwise much more limited) trade to producers and consumers at the cost of some monopoly profit for the intermediaries.[21]

The argument for seeing these institutional patterns as responses to the characteristic complex of resource conditions described above is borne out by what happened where resources were different, or when they changed. The most enduring exception to the difficulty of political centralization was the kingdom of Abyssinia in what is now northern Ethiopia. This was indeed an 'exception that proves the rule' as its fiscal and logistical base was grain surpluses paid as tribute by a peasantry in an environment supportive of at least semi-intensive agriculture, with a long history of plough use.[22] Where land rights became locally scarce, land markets could emerge, as in Akwapim district in southern Ghana in the pre-colonial and early-colonial nineteenth century,[23] and access to land could be newly restricted to close kin, as on the 'Kikuyu reserve' in central Kenya in the 1940s, when young, unmarried adults who had been 'squatting' on land reserved for European settlers returned home to find that cash crops and population growth had made previously cheap and abundant land economically valuable.[24]

Conflicts of interests, in some cases violent, were not limited to when the older institutions broke down or were transformed. High social valuation of children was one of the motives for polygamy, which tended to promote the concentration of wives among older, wealthier men.[25] In certain circumstances the value of labour was converted into slavery and debt bondage, especially when the demand for labour for commodity production rose, as in both West and East Africa during much of the nineteenth century.[26] The widespread survival of stateless societies and small states owed much to the determination of some small-scale societies to resist incorporation,[27] combined with the failure of state-builders to establish or extend their boundaries as far as they wished: reflecting the widespread difficulty of extracting regular grain surpluses sufficient to support a substantial class of military specialists.

The propensity to use land-extensive methods of production, noted above, is best seen not as a static residual but as a path of development. Specifically, for most of sub-Saharan Africa, the pattern of endogenous change from the fifteenth century to the late nineteenth or twentieth century can be described as following an overarching land-extensive path of economic development within which, however, there were intensive elements.[28] The land-extensive path may be defined as 'a general, long-term revealed preference for methods which used additional land where that would raise returns on labour or capital, or conserve the latter'.[29] To enlarge on a point introduced above, this preference could be seen most widely and importantly in arable farming, notably with the predominance of the hoe over the plough, the avoidance of clear felling, and the preference for polyculture (planting more than one crop in the same field) over monoculture. In pastoralism it was found, albeit to a large extent of necessity, in the widespread practice of transhumance, motivated especially by the need to keep the cattle away from the tsetse flies when the latter advanced during the rainy season. Even slave raiding can be viewed as a form of land extensiveness, albeit with extremely high costs to the region as a whole.

A land-extensive *path* of development, as distinct from a land-extensive strategy at a given moment, actually entails phases of intensification: when it was necessary to increase the ratio of labour and/or capital per hectare in order to take a step forward in total factor productivity. This is not to be confused with labour intensity by default, as in the reliance on headloading in the tsetse-fly zones, where pack animals were unavailable. It is also not to be confused with the labour intensity in dry-season occupations, such as mining and handicrafts, made possible by the low opportunity cost of labour during the agricultural off season. Rather, the most general example of a phase of intensification within an overarching path of land extensiveness was the transition from hunting and gathering, or even from itinerant pastoralism, to settled agriculture, though the former transition had mostly occurred before our period. The most important example in the early colonial period was the adoption of tree crops in certain colonies, notably cocoa beans in Ghana and Nigeria. This entailed a new production function and much fixed capital formation.[30] Even so, West African farmers chose to farm cocoa in as land extensive a fashion as possible, planting trees close together to minimize weeding at the cost of lower output per hectare, and temporarily abandoning capsid-infested farms so that the cocoa trees became overshadowed by the returning bush, leading to the disappearance of the pests. The farm could then be literally cut out of the bush and restored to production; this practice is distinct from the intense application of sprays and labour time to direct but unsuccessful action against the infestation. The efficiency of this approach, under tropical African conditions, was demonstrated by the comprehensive victory of Ghanaian cocoa farmers, large and small scale, in competition with European planters during the early colonial period.[31]

Given the relative scarcity of labour, there were three major ways of raising the rate of return for principals, whether they were individual farmers, household heads, or rulers.[32] The first was raising labour productivity in agriculture. African farmers did this, above all, through trial and error with crops and crop varieties, resulting in the selective adoption and adaptation of a range of exotic cultigens, on which more in the next section. Agricultural productivity was also raised in some contexts by the adoption of the plough: where soils were thick enough and demand high enough, as in the Cape and Natal in the mid-nineteenth century. The second approach to increasing the rate of return was to raise the productivity of labour outside the traditional agricultural year. There are a range of examples of how this was done before colonization, including double-cropping where new crops made that possible. In the twentieth century, the most important contribution was the mechanization of transport. The third strategy was to reduce the supply price of labour by coercion. The Nieboer-Domar hypothesis, that coercion of labour paid under conditions of land abundance in the absence of sizeable capital formation or economic advantages of scale, applied strongly to tropical Africa before colonization and again into the early twentieth century.[33] From the fifteenth to the end of the nineteenth century, in arable and mixed farming areas, increases in demand for commodities tended to be met by the acquisition of slaves, usually by purchase from the original captors, often via more than one set of intermediaries. The nineteenth century saw a major increase in the scale of slavery in West Africa and parts of East Africa, such as the kingdom of Buganda.[34] The same logic was operative under colonial rule, where, if slavery was forbidden, other forms of coercion could be applied to the same end, as will be highlighted below.

The overall effect of the non-coercive human responses to relative scarcity of labour in relation to land, limited soil fertility, and the other features of the physical environment of fifteenth- to early-twentieth-century Africa was to loosen – and ultimately to transform – the resource constraints: extending the effective agricultural year, raising productivity in and outside agriculture, and, after 1918, beginning to move the overall factor ratio from land abundance to land scarcity. High social approval of large families contributed to the demographic expansion that improving public health made possible over subsequent decades.[35] In the twentieth century as a whole, the population of sub-Saharan Africa rose by perhaps six times. In much of this, however, interaction with external influences was critical.

## External influences: Technology and demand from 1500 to the present

Let us turn to the interaction of African economies with external markets and, relatedly, external technological changes. While sub-Saharan Africa had an endogenous trajectory of land-extensive economic growth, however intermittent and long-term, the growth that was achieved, and the costs involved, owed greatly to its involvement in trade between different regions of what became the world economy. Three features stand out.

First, and most positively, as Paul Richards has phrased it, the present crop repertoire of African agriculture reflects selective adoptions and adaptations, via local trial and error – natural and cultural selection – over many centuries.[36] Sub-Saharan Africa was an integral part of the Old World, and the initial borrowings were from Asia: notably the banana-plantain family, which was eventually adopted throughout the tropical latitudes of the continent, and beyond. In the Bugandan environment, for example, it made possible an exceptionally high productivity food culture, covering nutritional requirements with labour inputs that were unusually small by African standards.[37] After the Portuguese connected Africa and the New World, effectively from the sixteenth century, a series of crop imports from the Americas began, including maize and cassava (manioc), groundnuts (peanuts), different varieties of cotton, and in the nineteenth century, cocoa beans, while some rice varieties moved in the opposite direction. For the productivity of both labour and (less important at the time) land in African agriculture, maize in particular was 'revolutionary', according to major sub-regional histories.[38] Cassava was adopted more selectively and gradually, and incorporated into local diets in differing ways. Crucially, its drought resistance improved food security, and its tolerance of relatively poor or depleted soils prompted a further round of adoption in the mid-twentieth century, in export-crop-growing areas in which fertile land was becoming scarce.[39] This long-standing readiness to experiment with, and selectively adopt, exotic cultigens is a reason for optimism about the prospects for raising agricultural productivity in contemporary Africa.

The second feature of sub-Saharan Africa's external trade is notorious: the longevity and geographical breadth of slave exports. The Atlantic trade alone accounted for about thirteen million captives forcibly embarked, from its beginning in 1441 to the last voyage in 1866. The trades across the Sahara, through the Nile Valley, and from the Indian Ocean and Red Sea coasts were both older and longer lasting, though less intense. A combination of estimates for the Atlantic trade, and guesstimates for the other trades, puts the grand total of slaves shipped or walked out of sub-Saharan Africa between 1500 and 1900 at nearly eighteen million.[40] The available figures for pre-colonial populations are almost entirely dependent on backward projection from colonial censuses.[41] Thus we have only a rough sense of the size of the populations from which these people were taken – and of the collateral losses, in deaths in raids and slave-trade-inspired wars, plus deaths en route to the coast or to the starting points for the Saharan crossing, and while awaiting the final journey. The margin of error is such that it is impossible to be sure of the scale of actual depopulation.[42] The latter may have been specific to particular areas, given that the biggest slave-exporting parts of West Africa were among the more densely populated in the early twentieth century. Even so, the removal of many millions of people from a labour-scarce region, which probably had only about 100 million people by 1900,[43] can only have been damaging for its long-term economic development; much more so, given the violence and insecurity that resulted from the slave trades, causing casualties, and requiring communities and traders to give priority to defence. A particular politically decentralized society based near Rufisque in Senegal cultivated a reputation for killing strangers on sight.[44] While rational as a defence mechanism this was hardly conducive to 'Smithian' growth, that is, the trade-based pattern of economic growth and specialization often seen as crucial in the early modern world. It seems, as Joseph Inikori argues, that the intensification of the Atlantic slave trade from the 1680s put a stop to what was otherwise a general tendency for production and exchange to expand in West Africa, a stop that was itself ended only by the abolition of the trade, a gradual and uneven process which effectively began in 1807.[45] The external slave trades had major repercussions for social structure and institutions. The nature of the activity meant that it was virtually monopolized by large traders and rulers, and thereby was a force for inequality, over hundreds of years.[46] It also rewarded militarism; conversely, when the Atlantic slave market was closed to the kingdoms of Asante and Dahomey, 'peace parties' emerged in both, advocating a reorientation away from wars and slave exports to peaceful trade.[47]

In a sense, it was paradoxical that the external slave trades were profitable even to the sellers and buyers themselves, given labour scarcity within the region and the existence of an intra-regional market for slaves, which competed with the overseas and cross-desert demand. Part of the demand from the Ottoman Empire was for girls and eunuchs for harems, but otherwise African slaves were wanted mainly for agriculture, on New World plantations and North Africa, and for specialized roles such as (in the case of Somali boys) pearl diving in the Gulf of Arabia. One motive for selling captives to ship or camel-borne merchants was to obtain state-of-the-art military tools, especially firearms from Europe and horses from North Africa. But the majority of imports comprised the kinds of commodities that were also produced widely in sub-Saharan Africa, such as textiles. This makes it hard to avoid the conclusion that, over several centuries and much of the continent, the productivity of (even enslaved) African labour was lower within sub-Saharan Africa than in the areas to which African slaves were taken.[48] Part of this may have been a function of effective proximity to markets, raising the unit price of the commodities produced by Africans in the unfree diaspora compared to the prices obtainable at home. But the productivity gap was also partly a function of relatively low physical productivity of labour in Africa, because of environmental constraints in agriculture and transport, as well as the low labour productivity of labour-intensive, dry-season handicraft production.[49] Thus the geographical breadth and chronological length of the slave trades across ocean and desert was made possible – made privately profitable – by supply-side elements. These trades were external but by no means entirely exogenous.

The last comment applies also to the political conditions that permitted and sustained the sale of captives outside the region. In sub-Saharan Africa, as usual in the world history of slavery, the vast majority of enslaved people were outsiders, foreigners, to the society that originally enslaved them, and in the society (which was very often a different one, in the intra-regional as well as interregional trades) where they were eventually set to work. A crucial difference was that by 1500 in Europe, the Middle East, and North Africa, intra-regional slave procurement had been greatly reduced or eliminated where the emergence of huge empires and 'world' religions obliged would-be slave owners to obtain slaves from much greater distances: the foreigners and unbelievers were much further away than before.[50] This externalized the collateral casualties of slaving, in that the initial violence took place far away. In contrast, the multitude of polities in sub-Saharan Africa meant that enslavable people – 'aliens' – were often relatively near in physical terms, bringing the mayhem and insecurity of slaving close to home.[51] The problem was compounded by military competition between African polities, small and large alike. To refuse to sell people to the Europeans would reduce a ruler's access to firearms and gunpowder.

Besides the selective importation of exotic cultigens, and the external markets for slaves, there has been a third major feature of Africa's long-term incorporation in the world economy: a succession of technological innovations overseas altered the content and scale of external markets for African products, in ways that contributed to the progress of African economies along the land-extensive path of economic development. It was the first industrial revolution that created or greatly enlarged the markets for groundnuts and palm oil in Europe, commodities that could be grown profitably by land-extensive methods in West African soils. Likewise, the inventions of the second Industrial Revolution, notably milk chocolate, the bicycle, and the internal combustion engine, created a new and vast market for rubber, and greatly enlarged the demand for cocoa beans. Tyres made wild rubber valuable: eliciting responses not only by Leopold's armed adventurers in the Congo but also by small-scale African migrant tappers in West Africa.[52] The emergence of a mass market for chocolate made it profitable for African entrepreneurs to initiate a major innovation in Ghana and Nigeria, adopting an exotic crop, and a tree crop at that, changing the factor ratios in forest zone agriculture, while finding methods of production which adapted the product to the kinds of soils available.[53] This pattern has continued to the present, from the advances in the technology of extracting and transporting petroleum that made Africa's oil deposits commercially valuable, to the invention of the mobile phone, which made coltan a mineral to kill for in Congo-Kinshasa in the later 1990s and 2000s. Economically, the most important category of imports paid for by these primary product exports was surely the tools of mechanized transport: loosening, and ultimately releasing, the vice in which the constraints on the use of animals had held the majority of Africa. A range of other imports have helped make African economies more efficient, among which the most recent major example is again the mobile phone, the widespread adoption of which has greatly improved information flows in local markets.

## The emergence of capitalist institutions during and since colonial rule

The otherwise often contrasting Marxist, dependency, and rational-choice institutionalist schools of thought on economic development south of the Sahara implicitly agree on one thing: that such development has depended and continues to depend on the extent of the establishment within the region of a particular complex of institutions often associated with capitalism: individual ownership of land, labour that is free of coercion but 'unencumbered' by the possession of land rights, and a system of government and law that upholds private property.[54] These institutions have traditionally been seen as essentially exotic to Africa. Historians have increasingly qualified this: labour markets and, though only rarely, wage labour preceded colonial rule; land tenure was often individual at the point of agricultural use and, as we have seen, land markets might emerge where land became scarce; and pre-colonial states defended certain forms of private property, including in people.[55] But it remains true that widespread individual title in land and the near-ubiquity of free labour, where they have emerged in sub-Saharan Africa, did so during or after colonial rule. To be sure, capitalism was compatible with slavery and other forms of labour coercion, as was indeed shown again in the early colonial period; but by then free labour was at least considered as part of the ideology of capitalism, or of self-consciously 'modern' societies, as colonial administrations were frequently reminded by the international abolitionist movement and the International Labour Organization.

Before going further, it is necessary to highlight the lateness and brevity of colonial rule in most of sub-Saharan Africa: sixty or seventy years in many countries, roughly half a millennium after the beginning of European overseas colonialism. When it finally arrived, European rule in Africa proved to be colonialism on the cheap. Governors were expected to balance their budgets, rather than ask for money from the metropole. In a chicken-and-egg fashion, under-resourced administrations then imposed relatively limited tax demands on their populations. For the largest empire, Ewout Frankema has calculated that the tax demand on an unskilled wage earner in the interwar period amounted to only a few days a year in some of the British colonies in Africa. While that burden could be painful at the margin, the fiscal ambitions of the colonial administrations were strikingly low compared to the white dominions, such as Australia.[56] In part, this was a response to the weakness of colonial coercive power on the spot: troops could be shipped in to suppress a rebellion, but the ratio of European officials, police, and soldiers to the population over which they presided was tiny: in the 1930s, 1:19,900 in British tropical Africa and 1:27,000 in French West Africa.[57] In this context, it is not surprising that, in the non-settler colonies, early imperial ambitions to transform African societies quickly gave way to a pragmatic gradualism.

Individual land ownership was a key part of what A. G. Hopkins has called 'Britain's first development plan for Africa', a mid-Victorian enthusiasm for private property rights as the key to economic advance anywhere in the world.[58] The British imposition of a protectorate on Lagos in 1851, and the annexation of that city state a decade later, was indeed motivated in part by calls from British and some African traders for the British to impose private ownership in land and real estate, in order to animate the credit market by providing good security for loans. By the time Britain came to annex the rest of Nigeria, during the general European partition of the continent, officials had abandoned such ambitions. Only in settler colonies did the British introduce compulsory registration of title before 1945, and then only on land reserved for Europeans.[59] Elsewhere, the British invoked 'customary' law, which they generally interpreted as forbidding land sales or mortgages. The result in some cash-cropping areas was to freeze the existing land tenure systems at a moment when some of them had been evolving to permit land alienation, as in the Akwapim case noted above. Part of the British reticence was economic: in southern Ghana and southwest Nigeria, the rapid expansion of African investment in tree crop agriculture proved that the existing systems were capable of providing reassurance to investors that their property rights were secure (in Akan land tenure in southern Ghana, for instance, the farmer who planted a crop was secure in possession of the crop, even if the land on which it grew was litigated over by rival chiefs). Thus it was a case of 'if it ain't bust, don't fix it'.[60] But there was also a powerful social and political reason to discourage land sales among Africans, a consideration which applied both to the so-called peasant colonies, where Africans retained virtually all the land under their ownership and control, and to the 'reserves' into which Africans were crowded in settler colonies. This was the fear that a land market would result in the poorer farmers selling up and moving to the towns, creating dangerous problems of social control. In practice, though less so in law, the story was similar in the French colonies. There were partial exceptions in the late-colonial period, notably in central Kenya, where the British reacted to the Mau Mau revolt by adopting a rather Stolypin-like land reform, designed to reward and strengthen the wealthier cash-cropping peasants, as opposed to the landless former squatters who provided a disproportionately large number of recruits for the guerrillas.[61] The case for colonial promotion of individual land ownership was made strongly and repeatedly within colonial administrations, but the reality of African enterprise on the ground, and the fear that the population might get out of control, ensured that it was not much acted upon.

Indeed, colonial officials, of all nationalities, were not keen to see the mass of the population lose their land rights completely and move to the towns. But the imperial governments had justified their annexations in Africa partly by the promise to implement in their new colonies the abolition of slave trading and slave holding that they had already applied in their existing colonies. They had to contend with the fact that colonization had not abolished the Nieboer-Domar problem: at the beginning of the twentieth century labour coercion remained profitable to employers. In much of tropical Africa, colonial administrations responded with a policy that can be described as gradualist: banning the slave trade, in some cases (e.g. Northern Nigeria), announcing that no one could be born a slave, but taking a decade or two (sometimes more) before making slaveholding illegal. In French West Africa, emancipation was proclaimed only in 1905, perhaps precipitated by mass walkouts of slaves, leaving their masters, in parts of what is now Mali.[62] The problem for masters (and in French West Africa about 30 per cent of the population were estimated to be slaves at the beginning of the colonial period) was real: How could they afford to become employers instead? The answer depended on whether they were able to enter export agriculture and, if so, on the profitability of the crop concerned. In the cocoa belt of southern Ghana and southwestern Nigeria, the transition to hired labour was relatively smooth, with the workers migrating seasonally from areas where the soils and/or transport costs made export agriculture unaffordable. In some other cases, including southeast Nigeria, former slave owners were reduced to reliance on family labour.[63] On the desert edge in what is now the Republic of Niger, lack of fertile soil and lack of cheap transport combined to encourage states and, later, also a foreign development agency to demand unpaid labour from the population.[64] Overall, the transition to free labour in West Africa, and parts of East Africa, was thus the result of the interaction of government policy and the geographically uneven spread of export agriculture, spearheaded by African enterprise. In British West Africa, especially, freedom proved no euphemism: workers in these non-settler colonies were able to obtain wages that were relatively high by comparison with labour-abundant parts of Asia.[65] In the cocoa-growing areas, they went on in subsequent decades to negotiate successively more favourable contracts, crucially including – at their insistence – a switch from annual wage contracts to a form of sharecrop labouring. Thus, at the initiative of the workers, West Africa reversed the conventional model of labour market development, from sharecropping to wage labour.[66]

Besides going slow on abolishing slavery, colonial governments all over sub-Saharan Africa resorted to various forms of forced labour. This was least so – though it still happened[67] – in the more prosperous export-crop zones, where it was both least necessary and hardest to enforce, because the opportunity cost was higher. The International Labour Organization adopted a Forced Labour Convention in 1930, which turned up the international and metropolitan pressure on the supposedly more liberal colonial regimes to match their own rhetoric of liberty. But it was only in 1945 that the post-liberation assembly in Paris passed a law, moved by the young Felix Houphoet-Boigny, future president of Ivory Coast, abolishing forced labour throughout the French Empire.[68]

In the settler colonies (among which South Africa became politically independent in 1910, and Southern Rhodesia partly autonomous in 1923, both under white minority rule), the solution had been found as far back as the seventeenth century, in the Cape: a policy of denying Africans access to land in order to force them to sell their labour. The classic embodiment of the policy, implemented also in Rhodesia and Kenya in particular, was the 1913 Natives Lands Act, which extended to the whole of South Africa the two prongs of the policy: 93 per cent of land was reserved for whites, and Africans were not allowed to work on white-owned land except as wage labourers. Though by no means fully implemented (the abolition of black sharecropping tenancy threatened the economic survival of many poor white farmers, who depended on their tenants for capital as well as labour),[69] it was sufficiently enforced to be the cutting edge of an ambition to drive Africans out of the market for agricultural produce and into the labour market. They were not supposed, however, to form a proletariat. Hence, under the policies of segregation and later of apartheid, in principle blacks were prohibited from living permanently in towns. Even in the 'peasant' colonies, where there was no such law, it was not until the 1940s that colonial officials began to abandon the conviction that Africans were essentially rural folk.[70]

Thus, as far as land and labour relations were concerned, colonial governments in Africa hardly fulfilled the orthodox Marxist expectation that the imperialism of capitalist powers would comprehensively destroy pre-capitalist social relations and establish the most modern of capitalist ones. Their legacy as state-builders was no more convincing from a market perspective. On paper, they brought to an end the long history of stateless societies and micro-states. But the purpose of the Berlin conference of 1884–5 which formally partitioned Africa was to prevent European powers fighting each other in Africa and – with exceptions during the world wars, especially Tanganyika – that aim was largely fulfilled. As Jeffrey Herbst pointed out, the guarantee that they would respect each other's borders, even when the details were yet to be fixed on the ground, reduced the incentive to colonial powers to establish firm state control right up to their frontiers. At a lower level of centralization, the reliance of colonial powers on governing through African intermediaries such as chiefs and emirs ('indirect rule' applied to a greater degree in the British case but to some extent in all the empires), combined with the preservation or ossification of customary land law, prevented the emergence of national land markets and ensured that collective identities would be, in future, more rather than less strongly 'ethnic', and only weakly national.[71]

During the first twenty years after colonial rule, any spread of land titling was rather sporadic, and actively rejected by left-leaning governments. With Structural Adjustment in the 1980s, the World Bank managed to engineer a liberal land reform in the republic of Guinea,[72] but a general, Africa-wide shift towards intensified buying and selling of land, with or without formal title, seems to have waited for the post-1995 boom. The subsequent 'land rush' has been propelled partly by a renewed external demand for African lands, for growing food and fuel crops for overseas markets, which 'structurally adjusted' governments have tended to try to satisfy. But it has also been driven by the growth of commercial agriculture supplying the rapidly urbanizing populations of African countries.[73] The poor in Africa used to be people mainly with insufficient labour power at their free disposal to use the land which they were entitled to use. Now they are, in effect, increasingly landless, and looking to the cities for their subsistence.[74] The resource ratio hindered the growth of wage labour in the early colonial period, when land was still overwhelmingly abundant except where settler regimes made it artificially scarce. But by the twenty-first century, the growth of population, as well as export agriculture and especially the cities, favoured the free labour market: on the supply side at least.

## Conclusion

This chapter has emphasized the interaction of African and external agency in African economic history, arguing that the endogenous propensities towards a land-extensive path of development were energized at various points by exchange with other world regions, with results more negative than positive (during the slave trades) or the other way around (during the export-crop revolution of the early colonial period in non-settler colonies, and in the recent general African boom). Africa was 'developing' before the Great Divergence, increasing food security and agricultural productivity, and with a resilient handicraft manufacturing sector, especially in West Africa. The Atlantic slave trade, and the intensification of the other slave trades during the nineteenth century, surely hindered the economic progress of the region as a whole. But the very fact that the export of slaves was so widespread, and lasted so long, suggests that labour productivity in the region tended to be lower than in the solely slave-importing parts of the world, even if the gap was aggravated by the slave trades themselves. Thus, it is argued here that Africa was on a development path, of a specific kind – land-extensive – but it is not suggested that even West Africa, the strongest candidate to be an economic 'core' in the Pomeranz sense, was on course for an indigenous industrial revolution before the intensification of the Atlantic slave trade in the late seventeenth century.

Following the beginning of industrialization in Europe, interactions with technologies of overseas origin, and relatedly with overseas markets, encouraged Africans to specialize in agricultural exports, especially in West Africa, even before colonial governments arrived to invest further in the transport infrastructure of the import–export economy. There were some successes in the nineteenth century and since. Africa has experienced intermittent episodes of economic growth per capita,[75] though they were mostly specific to particular sub-regions (such as West Africa in the decades between the beginning of the end of the Atlantic slave trade and the outbreak of the First World War, and South Africa following the mineral revolution) until the post-1995 boom. It should also be noted that the mere fact of having increased per capita income at all during the twentieth century, when child-friendly social values combined with public health advances to produce perhaps a sextupling of population, is an impressive case of what Kuznets called 'extensive growth'.

It is possible to view African economic history as to a large extent a story of resource rents, and African political economy as the struggle over them.[76] But raising productivity has also been part of the story, though mostly in very particular contexts. As land has become scarcer, and as urbanization has proceeded, over the last century, poverty has increasingly ceased to be associated with lack of access to labour. Historical comparisons, especially with Southeast Asia, suggest that the prospects for a general breakthrough to much higher living standards in a region that is well advanced in transition from labour scarcity to (an increasingly educated) labour surplus depends greatly on whether at least some African economies can industrialize.[77]

## Notes

1. In thematic emphasis, and also in being more discursive and less formally quantitative and chronologically organized, this chapter complements G. Austin (2016), 'Sub-Saharan Africa', in J. Baten (ed.), *A History of the Global Economy from 1500 to the Present*. Cambridge: Cambridge University Press, 316–50.

2. 'Institutions' is used here in the sense of the formal and informal rules surrounding economic activity. D. North (1990), *Institutions, Institutional Change and Economic Performance*. Cambridge: Cambridge University Press, 3–4.

3. W. Rodney (1972), *How Europe Underdeveloped Africa*; I. Wallerstein (1976), 'The three stages of African involvement in the world economy', in P. Gutkind and I. Wallerstein (eds), *The Political Economy of Contemporary Africa*. Beverly Hills: Sage, 30–57.

4. D. Acemoglu, S. Johnson and J. A. Robinson (2001), 'The colonial origins of comparative development: An empirical investigation', *American Economic Review*, 91 (5), 1369–401. For a critique of this and related work, see G. Austin (2008), 'The "reversal of fortune" thesis and the compression of history: Perspectives from African and comparative economic history', *Journal of International Development,* 20 (8), 996–1027. For a distinctly different rational-choice institutionalist perspective on African political economy in the twentieth century and before, see R. H. Bates (1983), *Essays on the Political Economy of Rural Africa*, Cambridge: Cambridge University Press; and Idem (2008), *When Things Fell Apart: State Failure in Late-Century Africa*. New York: Cambridge University Press. Bates focuses on internal sources of political-economic change.

5. C. H. Feinstein (2005), *An Economic History of South Africa: Conquest, Discrimination and Development*. Cambridge: Cambridge University Press.

6. A. G. Hopkins (1973), *An Economic History of West Africa*. London: Longman, 124–35. See also R. Law (ed.) (1995), *From Slave Trade to 'Legitimate' Commerce: The Commercial Transition in Nineteenth-Century West Africa*. Cambridge: Cambridge University Press.

7. This sense of period is represented in a history of contemporary Africa which sets economic change in a broader context. F. Cooper (2002), *Africa since 1940: The Past of the Present*. Cambridge: Cambridge University Press.

8. J. C. Bertélemy and L. Söderling (2001), 'The role of capital accumulation, adjustment and structural change for economic take-off: Empirical evidence from African growth episodes', *World Development*, 29 (2), 323–43. See, further, M. Jerven (2014), *Economic Growth and Measurement Reconsidered in Botswana, Kenya, Tanzania, and Zambia, 1965–1995*. Oxford: Oxford University Press.

9. J. C. W. Ahiakpor (1985), 'The success and failure of dependency theory: The experience of Ghana', *International Organization*, 39 (3), 535–52; M. Eberhardt and F. Teal (2010), 'Ghana and Côte d'Ivoire: Changing places', *International Development Policy*, 1 (1), 33–49.

10. N. van de Walle (2001), *African Economies and the Politics of Permanent Crisis, 1979–1999*. Cambridge: Cambridge University Press, 221.

11. V. Azarya and N. Chazan (1987), 'Disengagement from the state in Africa: Reflections on the experience of Ghana and Guinea', *Comparative Studies in Society and History*, 29 (1), 106–31; J. MacGaffey (1987), *Entrepreneurs and Parasites: The Struggle for Indigenous Capitalism in Zaire*. Cambridge: Cambridge University Press.

12. G. Austin (2008), 'Resources, techniques, and strategies south of the Sahara: Revising the factor endowments perspective on African economic development, 1500–2000', *Economic History Review*, 61 (3), 587–624.

13. Austin, 'Resources, techniques, and strategies'. The soil quality issue is discussed further in Austin (2017), 'Africa and the Anthropocene', in G. Austin (ed.), *Economic Development and Environmental History in the Anthropocene: Perspectives on Asia and Africa*. London: Bloomsbury, 95–118. My friend Joseph Inikori claims that soil scientists take a much more optimistic view: J. E. Inikori (2014), 'Reversal of fortune and socioeconomic development in the Atlantic world: A comparative examination of West Africa and the Americas, 1400–1850', in E. Akyeampong, R. H. Bates, N. Nunn and J. A. Robinson (eds), *Africa's Development in Historical Perspective*. New York: Cambridge University Press, 79–80. But this is contrary to the soil science studies cited in my own earlier work, and indeed to the volume on which he relies: B. Vanlauwe, J. Djiels, N. Sanginga and R. Merckx (eds) (2002), *Integrated Plant Nutrient Management in Sub-Saharan Africa: From Concept to Practice*. Wallingford, Oxfordshire, UK: CABI Publishing and the International Institute of Tropical Agriculture. For example, the chapter by U. Mokwunye and A. Bationo (2002), 'Meeting the phosphorus needs of the soils and crops of West Africa: The role of indigenous phosphate rocks', provides a quantitative survey of the characteristics of West African soils, concluding 'Across all agroecological zones, the soils are poor in organic matter content, base exchange capacity and available phosphorus' (p. 209).

14. Austin, 'Resources, techniques, and strategies'.

15. M. Widren (2017), 'Agricultural intensification in Sub-Saharan Africa, 1500 to 1800', in G. Austin (ed.), *Economic Development and Environmental History in the Anthropocene: Perspectives on Asia and Africa*. London: Bloomsbury, 51–67.

16. J. Iliffe (1989), 'The origins of African population growth', *Journal of African History*, 30 (1), 165–9.

17. J. Goody (1976), *Production and Reproduction: A Comparative Study of the Domestic Domain*. Cambridge: Cambridge University Press.

18. C. H. Perrot (ed.) (2012), *Lignages et territoires en Afrique aux XVIIIe et XIXe siècles: Stratégies, compétition, intégration*. Paris: Karthala; G. Austin (2004), 'Sub-Saharan Africa:

Land rights and ethno-national consciousness in historically land-abundant economies', in S. L. Engerman and J. Metzer (eds), *Land Rights, Ethno-Nationality, and Sovereignty in History*. London: Routledge, 276–93.

19. G. Austin (2017), 'Slavery in Africa', in D. Eltis, S. L. Engerman and D. Richardson (eds), *The Cambridge World History of Slavery*, vol. 4, *Slavery since 1804*. Cambridge: Cambridge University Press, 174–96.

20. J. Herbst (2014), *States and Power in Africa*. Princeton: Princeton University Press, 2nd edn.

21. P. D. Curtin (1984), *Cross-Cultural Trade in World History*. Cambridge: Cambridge University Press, 38–57; G. Austin (2002), 'African business in nineteenth-century West Africa', in A. Jalloh and T. Falola (eds), *Black Business and Economic Power*. Rochester NY, 114–44.

22. D. Crummey (1980), 'Abysinnian feudalism', *Past & Present*, 89, 115–38.

23. G. Austin (2007), 'Labour and land in Ghana, 1879–1939: A shifting ratio and an institutional revolution', *Australian Economic History Review*, 47 (1), 95–120.

24. R. H. Bates (1990), 'Capital, kinship, and conflict: The structuring influence of capital in kinship societies', *Canadian Journal of African Studies*, 24 (1), 145–64.

25. A neat abstract analysis is C. Meillassoux (1972), 'From reproduction to production: A Marxist approach to economic anthropology', *Economy and Society*, 1 (1), 93–105.

26. Austin, 'Slavery in Africa'.

27. See, for instance, J. F. Searing (2002), '"No kings, no lords, no slaves": Ethnicity and religion among the Sereer-Safèn of Western Bawol, 1700–1914', *Journal of African History*, 43 (3), 407–30.

28. This argument is developed, successively, in Austin, 'Resources, techniques and strategies'; G. Austin (2013), 'Labour-intensity and manufacturing in West Africa, c.1450-c.2000', in G. Austin and K. Sugihara (eds), *Labour-Intensive Industrialization in Global History*. London: Routledge, 201–30; and Austin, 'Africa and the Anthropocene'.

29. Austin, 'Africa and the Anthropocene', 102.

30. G. Austin (2014), 'Vent for surplus or productivity breakthrough? The Ghanaian cocoa take-off, c. 1890-1936', *Economic History Review*, 67 (4), 1035–64.

31. G. Austin (1996), 'Mode of production or mode of cultivation: Explaining the failure of European cocoa planters in competition with African cocoa farmers in colonial Ghana', in W. G. Clarence-Smith (ed.), *Cocoa Pioneer Fronts: The Role of Smallholders, Planters and Merchants*. Basingstoke: Macmillan, 154–75.

32. The first part of this paragraph is based on Austin, 'Resources, techniques, and strategies'.

33. For an exposition of the concept and a case study, see G. Austin (2005), *Labour, Land and Capital in Ghana: From Slavery to Free Labour in Asante, 1807–1956*. Rochester, NY: University of Rochester Press, 155–70, 236–49, 495–8, 512–15.

34. Austin, 'Slavery in Africa'; P. E. Lovejoy (2012), *Transformations in Slavery: A History of Slavery in Africa*, 3rd edn. Cambridge: Cambridge University Press, 160–243, 327–44. For Buganda, see R. Reid (2002), *Political Power in Pre-Colonial Buganda: Economy, Society and Warfare in the Nineteenth Century*. Oxford: James Currey.

35. Iliffe 'The origins of African population growth'.

36. That was an oral observation in a presentation at the West Africa Seminar in the Anthropology Department of University College London in 2010. See further, Richards, 'A Green Revolution from Below? Science and Technology for Global Food Security and

Poverty Alleviation', retirement address, Wageningen University, 18 November 2010, published online at http://edepot.wur.nl/165231.

37. D. L. Schoenbrun (1998), *A Green Place, a Good Place: Agrarian Change, Gender, and Social Identity in the Great Lakes Region in the 15th Century*. Portsmouth, NH: Heinemann, 79–83.

38. For an overview, see J. C. McCann (2005), *Maize and Grace: Africa's Encounter with a New World Crop, 1500-2000*. Cambridge MA: Harvard University Press.

39. For example, in the Ghanaian cocoa belt: Austin, *Labour, Land and Capital*, 66, and 474.

40. See Lovejoy, *Transformations in Slavery*, 19, 46, 138. For the Atlantic slave trade, see further *Voyages: The Trans-Atlantic Slave Trade Database*, http://www.slavevoyages.org, launched in 2008 by a team led by David Eltis.

41. For the state of the debate about how to interpret colonial censuses, see P. Manning (2014), 'African population, 1650-2000: Comparisons and implications of new estimates', in E. Akyeampong, R. H. Bates, N. Nunn and J. A. Robinson (eds), *Africa's Development in Historical Perspective*. New York: Cambridge University Press, 131–50; E. Frankema and M. Jerven (2014), 'Writing history backwards and sideways: Towards a consensus on African population, 1850-2010', *Economic History Review*, 67 (4), 907–31.

42. D. Henige (1986), 'Measuring the immeasurable: The Atlantic slave trade, West African population and the Pyrrhonian critic', *Journal of African History*, 27 (2), 295–313.

43. Austin, 'Resources, techniques, and strategies', 590–1; and references in n. 41 above.

44. Searing, "'No kings, no lords, no slaves'".

45. J. E. Inikori (2007), 'Africa and the globalization process: Western Africa, 1450-1850', *Journal of Global History*, 2 (1), 63–86; Inikori (2009), 'The economic impact of the 1807 British abolition of the transatlantic slave trade', in T. Falola and M. D. Childs (eds), *The Changing Worlds of Atlantic Africa: Essays in Honor of Robin Law*. Durham, NC: Carolina Academic Press, 163–82.

46. Hopkins, *Economic History of West Africa*, 125; E. Evans and D. Richardson (1995), 'Hunting for rents: The economics of slaving in pre-colonial Africa', *Economic History Review*, 48 (4), 665–86.

47. I. Wilks (1975), *Asante in the Nineteenth Century*. Cambridge: Cambridge University Press; R. Law (1997), 'The politics of commercial transition: Factional conflict in Dahomey in the context of the ending of the Atlantic slave trade', *Journal of African History*, 28 (2), 213–33.

48. S. Fenoaltea (1999), 'Europe in the African mirror: The slave trade and the rise of feudalism', *Rivista di Storia Economica*, 15 (2), 123–65.

49. Austin, 'Resources, techniques, and strategies'.

50. J-F. Paul (2009), 'Empire, monotheism and slavery in the Greater Mediterranean region from antiquity to the early modern era', *Past and Present*, 205, 3–40.

51. J. I. Inikori (2003), 'The struggle against the transatlantic slave trade: The role of the state', in S. A. Diouf (ed.), *Fighting the Slave Trade: West African Strategies*. Athens, OH: Ohio University Press, 170–98.

52. Leopold's regime needs no introduction; on African enterprise in the wild rubber boom in West Africa, see K. Arhin (1980), 'The economic and social significance of rubber production and exchange on the Gold and Ivory Coasts, 1880-1900', *Cahiers d'études africaines*, 20 (77–78), 49–62; E. Osborn (2004), "'Rubber fever", commerce and French colonial rule in Upper Guinèe, 1890-1913', *Journal of African History*, 45 (3), 445–65.

53. A. G. Hopkins (1978), 'Innovation in a colonial context: African origins of the Nigerian cocoa-farming industry, 1880-1920', in A. G. Hopkins and C. Dewey (eds), *The Imperial*

*Impact*. London: Athlone, 83–96, 341–2; P. Hill (1997), *The Migrant Cocoa-Farmers of Southern Ghana: A Study in Rural Capitalism*. Hamburg: LIT; first published Cambridge 1963.

54. J. Sender and S. Smith (1986), *The Development of Capitalism in Africa*. London: Methuen; S. Amin (1976), *Unequal Development: An Essay on the Social Formations of Peripheral Capitalism*. Hassocks, UK: Harvester; Acemoglu, Johnson and Robinson, 'Colonial origins'.

55. S. J. Rockel (2006), *Carriers of Culture: Labor on the Road in Nineteenth-Century East Africa*. Portsmouth, NH: Heinemann; G. Austin (2009), 'Factor markets in Nieboer conditions: Pre-colonial West Africa, c.1500-c.1900', *Continuity and Change*, 24 (1), 23–53.

56. E. Frankema (2010), 'Raising revenue in the British empire: How "extractive" were colonial taxes?', *Journal of Global History*, 5 (3), 447–77. See also L. A. Gardner (2012), *Taxing Colonial Africa: The Political Economy of British Imperialism*. Oxford: Oxford University Press.

57. A. H. M. Kirk-Greene (1980), 'The thin white line: The size of the British colonial service in Africa', *African Affairs*, 79 (314), 25–41.

58. A. G. Hopkins (1995), 'Britain's first development plan for Africa', in Robin Law (ed.), *The Commercial Transition in West Africa*. Cambridge: Cambridge University Press. See also A. G. Hopkins (1980), 'Property rights and empire building: Britain's annexation of Lagos, 1861', *Journal of Economic History*, 40 (4), 777–98.

59. Though African land purchases were permitted in certain contexts. See, for instance, A. K. Shutt (2002), 'Squatters, land sales and intensification in Marirangwe Purchase Area, colonial Zimbabwe, 1931–65', *Journal of African History*, 43 (3), 473–98.

60. Austin, *Labour, Land and Capital*, 339–48, 531–3.

61. D. Branch (2009), *Defeating Mau Mau, Creating Kenya: Counterinsurgency, Civil War, and Decolonization*. Cambridge: Cambridge University Press, 120–5.

62. M. A. Klein (1998), *Slavery and Colonial Rule in French West Africa*. Cambridge: Cambridge University Press.

63. D. C. Ohadike (1999), '"When the slaves left, the owners wept": Entrepreneurs and emancipation among the Igbo people', in S. Miers and M. A. Klein (eds), *Slavery and Colonial Rule in Africa*. London: Frank Cass, 189–207; generally, G. Austin (2009), 'Cash crops and freedom: Export agriculture and the decline of slavery in colonial West Africa', *International Review of Social History*, 54 (1), 1–37.

64. B. Rossi (2015), *From Slavery to Aid: Politics, Labour, and Ecology in the Nigerien Sahel, 1800–2000*. Cambridge: Cambridge University Press.

65. E. Frankema and M. van Waijenburg (2012), 'Structural impediments to African growth? New evidence from real wages in British Africa, 1880–1965', *Journal of Economic History*, 72 (4), 895–926.

66. Austin, *Labour, Land and Capital*, 315–24, 401–30, 442–3, 452–4, 527–9, 540–6.

67. For example K. O. Akurang-Parry (2000), 'Colonial forced labor policies for road-building in southern Ghana and international anti-forced labor pressures, 1900–1940', *African Economic History*, 28 (1), 1–25.

68. F. Cooper (1996), *Decolonization and African Society: The Labor Question in French and British Africa*. New York: Cambridge University Press.

69. A marvellously thought-provoking case study is C. van Onselen (1990), 'Race and class in the South African countryside: Cultural osmosis and social relations in the sharecropping economy of Transvaal', *American Historical Review*, 95 (1), 99–123.

70. M. Lipton (1985), *Capitalism and Apartheid*. Aldershot: Gower; Cooper, *Decolonization*.

71. M. Mamdani (1996), *Citizen and Subject: Contemporary Africa and the Legacy of Late Colonialism*. Princeton: Princeton University Press. For a highly perceptive recent analysis see C. Boone (2014), *Property and Political Order in Africa: Land Rights and the Structure of Politics*. New York: Cambridge University Press.

72. J. Clapp (1997), *Adjustment and Agriculture in Africa: Farmers, the State and the World Bank in Guinea*. London: Macmillan.

73. C. Oya (2013), 'The land rush and classic agrarian questions of capital and labour: A systematic scoping review of the socioeconomic impact of land grabs in Africa', *Third World Quarterly*, 34 (9), 1532–57.

74. Compare J. Iliffe (1987), *The African Poor: A History*. Cambridge: Cambridge University Press.

75. Austin, 'Resources, techniques, and strategies', 610–14; further, M. Jerven (2010), 'African growth recurring: An economic history perspective on African growth episodes, 1690–2010', *Economic History of Developing Regions*, 25 (2), 127–54.

76. I owe this thought to William Gervase Clarence-Smith, in a conversation many years ago.

77. Austin, 'Labour-intensity and manufacturing'; G. Austin (2016), 'Is Africa too late for "late development"? Gerschenkron south of the Sahara', in M. Andersson and T. Axelsson (eds), *Diverse Development Paths and Structural Transformation in the Escape from Poverty*. Oxford University Press, 206–35; G. Austin, E. Frankema and M. Jerven (2017), 'Patterns of manufacturing growth in Sub-Saharan Africa: From colonization to the present', in K. O'Rourke and J. G. Williamson (eds), *The Spread of Modern Industry to the Poor Periphery since 1870*. Oxford University Press, 345–73.

# CHAPTER 15
## THE NEW WORLD AND THE GLOBAL SILVER ECONOMY, 1500–1800
*Alejandra Irigoin*

According to Adam Smith, the discovery of the Americas and the discovery of a passage to the East Indies by the Cape of Good Hope were the 'two greatest and most important events recorded in the history of mankind'.[1] Economic historians of the pre-modern period have emphasized one or the other of these two events leading alternatively to what we might call a Euro-Atlantic centrism (as for instance in the triangular trade concept proposed by Eric Williams) or to a Sino-Asian centrism (for instance in the Great Divergence debate). Yet, many of these narratives have provided little help in understanding why Adam Smith's East and, most especially, West Indies were so crucial to the development of the European economy.

The incorporation of the New World into the pre-modern international economy has been the subject of several recent studies in global economic history. Kenneth Pomeranz and Hersh and Voth underline the contribution of the Americas in terms of ghost acreage for the production of food and fibres for differential European consumption and living standards.[2] A vast literature discusses the Columbian Exchange as detailed in John McNeill's chapter in this volume. Factor endowment and a particular European political economy have created a narrative that associates colonialism with the exploitation of New World riches and peoples as described by Trevor Burnard. Finally, the trade of people (slaves) and commodities is also central to economic narratives of the New World and the Atlantic, although recent growth theories have focused on endogenous sources of development, and few economic historians today think of trade as the engine of economic growth.

Yet trade matters and arguably the Americas are intimately associated with the production and trade of silver, a commodity which became fundamental for the subsequent development of the global economy after 1500. This chapter charts the role of the Americas in global economic history by concentrating on the role of silver. Silver had no substitute and was available in large quantities in Spanish America. This is a well-known topic in European economic history; however recent developments in Asian economic historiography have stimulated a revision of the extraction, processing, and exchange of American silver in the early modern world economy. American silver was used in the form of coins as the preeminent global currency. It remained a currency standard for more than two centuries before a gold standard came to define the classic economic globalization of the late nineteenth and twentieth centuries. This chapter considers the Americas' contribution to the world economy through the lens of silver in order to reassess some of the factors that drove the expansion of trade and integration of markets to an unprecedented level in the three centuries after 1500. It revises conventional interpretations of the development of the early global economy away from views centred either in Asia or in Europe.

## Silver, trade, and the early modern world economy

Monetary historians explain the stream of silver flowing towards Asia as the result of a difference in gold-to-silver ratios within Eurasia.[3] For reasons not yet explored, unlike Europeans, Asians preferred silver as money over gold.[4] The New World produced large quantities of silver – and to a lesser extent gold in the early eighteenth century – that added to the availability of world silver from the rich mines of Central Europe estimated at 50 tonnes per year at its peak in the 1540s.[5] By the early sixteenth century, the Japanese had adopted the technology of cupellation (the process of separating precious metals from ore) from Korea; production boomed and Japan supplied silver to China, the world's largest economy. The Japanese silver output peaked in the 1620s at 130–60 tonnes per annum.[6] Although production continued into the eighteenth century, the level of exports declined so dramatically that Japanese silver was all but absent from China by the 1680s. The 'Japanese silver century' (1580–1680) paled however in comparison with the large quantities and higher quality of Spanish American silver that arrived in Asia.[7] The New World aggregate output was 280–300 tonnes a year by the early seventeenth century and it doubled in the following century. All of Spanish American mining combined might have produced 75–80 per cent of world output in the pre-modern period.[8]

Between 1500 and 1820 global trade grew at an aggregate 1 per cent per annum and European intercontinental trade in the eighteenth century grew at 1.26 per cent.[9] The aggregate production of Spanish American silver grew at 1.09 per cent a year in the same period. European tonnage to Asia grew at 1.16 per cent and Mexican silver production at 1.35 per cent over the course of the eighteenth century.[10] Whereas there are a number of theories which might explain the relation between the growth trends of world trade and the expansion of European commerce, there is little exploration of the co-evolution of the development in the extraction and trade of silver and world trade.[11]

Global monetary historians point to the arbitrage – that is, buying cheap in one market for sale in another where the goods are expensive – that the Europeans carried out in their commerce with Asia and especially with China.[12] The relative abundance or scarcity of a specific metal can explain the different bimetallic rates in America, Europe, and Asia. However the gold–silver ratio in China had equalized to that of Europe by 1750 though the silver trade not only continued but also expanded further with significant increases in the latter part of the century.[13] As argued elsewhere, by 1800 it was apparent that what China, and perhaps Asia at large, demanded was not silver bullion per se, but specie, a universally reliable means of payment made of silver.[14] Without its own coinage of silver, China became reliant on the currency standard that the Spanish American coin provided.

It remains true, however, that the arbitrage between rich and poor silver markets produced a windfall for Europe. Palma estimates that a 10 per cent increase in the production of precious metals in the New World increased in any given year the real GDP in Europe by 1.3 per cent within four years – because prices responded to monetary injections with considerable lags.[15] To Europe, American silver was the means to trade in Asia. Silver accounted for 93 per cent of the European cargo values to China and 79 per cent of the India-bound cargo.[16] With American silver, the European companies in Asia bought cotton and silk textiles not just for European consumers but also to trade for slaves and gold in Africa.[17] In the Americas, African slaves cultivated commercial crops such as sugar and coffee that were shipped to Europe, thus establishing a truly global multilateral trade in people, goods, and money.[18] Later, American foodstuff, dyes, and cotton found a market in Europe, but silver and gold were the main returns of the New World until well in the late eighteenth century.

Acting as intermediaries in this extensive global commerce, European traders linked different parts of the early modern world economy. In a well-known article, Patrick O'Brien argued however for a peripheral role for the New World in the economic development of Europe when he observed that three-quarters of the commodity exports in Europe had another European port as destination.[19] However he did not consider the actual composition of such intra-European trade: American and Asian commodities such as textiles, tea, sugar, slaves, and silver were key to European trade as they were re-exported within and indeed beyond Europe. Along the way, European states taxed their import and consumption, thus creating much-needed revenue for the developing European nation states.[20] The old mercantilist idea that precious metals were to be stocked did not account for the profits derived in the intermediation of all these goods. A more modern understanding of mercantilism can explain how specialization and trade contributed to the growth in Europe. Without silver, the scale of European commerce would have been much smaller and any resulting Smithian growth improbable.[21]

## The production of silver in Latin America

But how was silver obtained from the New World? Mining in Spanish America was a wholly private enterprise which enjoyed state support for taxes paid to the King on the volume produced. Spanish colonialism imposed a royal domain over land and the subsoil. Thus the King allocated the right to mine the precious metals to individuals – and even to indigenous communities for a direct taxshare – on the production. So mining, smelting, refining and even minting, were all private affairs. Because of the demographic collapse, coerced labour was the exception rather than the norm despite the emphasis by both neo-institutionalist and Marxist economic historians on the exploitative nature of Spanish colonialism.[22] They made up only half or less of the Potosi workforce – that is, less than unskilled 3,000 workers in the eighteenth century – and worked in Huancavelica quicksilver mines.[23] The pre-Hispanic tributary system persisted under the Spanish rule, known as the Mita (quechua for 'shift', 'turn'). It performed more as a subsidy to miners than a core input to mining (Tandeter, 1993). The great silver mines of Mexico employed overwhelmingly free wage labour – a total workforce of around 50,000 men in the eighteenth century.[24]

The largest mining site of all, Zacatecas in the northern periphery of the Spanish settlement, developed from the mid-sixteenth century in an area without a sizeable native population. Indigenous and increasingly mixed-race people made a very (spatially) mobile labour force in mining. African labour, by contrast, was not the best suited for mining at more than 2,500 metres altitude as in Zacatecas (or for that matter at the 4,000 metres altitude of Potosí) but slaves and wandering labourers worked the gold mines of Colombia and Brazil. Indigenous people and increasingly mestizos provided the bulk of the labour force in silver mining. Spaniards were relatively more numerous among refiners, smelters, and renters of mines, and definitively controlled the exchange of ore and bars for coin as they ran the financing of mining.

The persistence of communal property rights to land by the indigenous communities increased the opportunity cost of wage labour even in the most populated regions of the New World. Nominal wages were very high and stable over time. Indeed, earnings were adjusted by sizeable non-monetary compensation that followed declining demographic trends. Their reduction starting in the 1780s followed population recovery. This explains the extraordinarily high (and steady) nominal wage of compulsory labourers in Potosí; they received about 12.5 grams of fine silver a day, a rate comparable to skilled labourers in late-eighteenth-century London.[25] The combination of indigenous property rights, guaranteed urban food supplies, and the peculiarity of a silver-abundant economy shaped a very different labour market and higher standards of living in Spanish America than most recent studies posit.[26]

Mining was widespread both geographically and socially. The location and size of mines were more varied in Mexico than in Spanish Peru, where Potosí produced by far the largest volume of silver in the seventeenth century. With a faster population recovery and more numerous and dispersed silver deposits, Mexico became the dominant world supplier of silver in the eighteenth century, producing according to Soetbeer 45–55 per cent of the world silver.[27] Potosí continued producing silver, though with marginal decreasing profits. Europeans had originally relied on indigenous technology for the extraction, smelting, and casting of silver in wind-blown furnaces.[28] The incorporation of amalgamation – the blending of pulverized ore with mercury – and the availability of mercury in Huancavelica in the Andes or from Almaden in Spain secured indispensable inputs and fostered a steady growth in production from the late sixteenth century. To some Andean historians, the new technology also was prejudicial to indigenous miners, subjecting them to a wage labour relation in lieu of a former sharing system. This, together with the commutation of tribute in kind for cash payments, established market relations for production factors and goods very early in the Spanish New World (Figure 15.1).

Yet, the volumes produced are extraordinary. Throughout the period, the combined output of Mexican and Peruvian mines added 300 tonnes a year to a stock that largely exceeded the contemporary Asian demand. At its peak in the 1780s–1800s, silver output in Spanish America totalled 600 tonnes a year. Precious metals accounted for around 60 per cent of the value of the New World exports throughout the 1740s. Even at the peak of gold production in Brazil in the 1730s and 1740s, silver never represented less than 60 per cent of precious metals' total output. This proportion diminished with the growth

**Mining Quantities (kg) - 1493 to 1801**

GOLD
- 168 001 - 708 752
- 98 501 - 168 000
- 27 001 - 98 500
- 26 - 27 000

SILVER
- 11 053 001 - 22 686 817
- 2 195 001 - 11 053 000
- 107 001 - 2 195 000
- 18 023 - 107 000

**Figure 15.1** Composition and geographical distribution of the precious metal Production in the New World.
*Source*: N. Palma (2015), 'Harbingers of Modernity: Monetary Injections and European Economic Growth, 1492–1790', Unpublished PhD. thesis, London School of Economics, fig. 2. p. 63. I thank Nuno Palma for allowing the reproduction of this updated version of the map.

of exports from the British colonies in the mainland and record sugar production in the West Indies by the 1760s. Yet silver made at least a third or more of the total New World exports. The rise in the international price of silver between the 1790s and 1810s lowered the price of imports, giving an additional boost to the production of non-precious metals commodities in Spanish America. The production of silver collapsed only with the implosion of Spanish governance in the 1820s.[29]

More importantly, silver was obtained by means of trade and not from extraction. Historians like Hamilton for the seventeenth century, and Morineau and Garcia Baquero for the eighteenth century, agreed that until the late 1770s at least 70 per cent of the 'treasure imports' to Spain was made of privately owned silver. Moreover, at around twenty million pesos, private remittances reached up to 90 per cent of total silver sent to Europe in the 1790s when exports boomed.[30] So the extraordinary volume of silver shipped out of the New World, which by and large was private property, reflects the levels of private consumption attained in the Americas.[31]

## The Spanish silver trade

Between the 1580s and 1730s, export values increased tenfold, from around a million pesos a year in the 1580s to ten million (250 tonnes of pure silver) in the 1730s. These volumes doubled after the 1750s and neared thirty million (750 tonnes) in the 1770s. Thus the European re-export of silver to China – estimated at an average of 114 tonnes of silver a year between 1719 and 1833 – becomes less important in this light. By and large the main destination of silver was Spain, a trade carried out via the few authorized ports – Seville first and Cadiz from 1700 from where silver was re-exported into Europe and beyond. Figure 15.2 shows the relation between output and coinage of silver and shipments to Europe throughout the eighteenth century.

For most of the eighteenth century, for when data is available, the relation between the pace of mining and minting and the shipment of silver to Europe was weak.[32] The export of precious metals to Europe was not immediate or automatic as often assumed. Instead, most of the silver remained in circulation in the domestic economy before it was traded for goods and services overseas. Although agriculture accounted for the largest share of the colonial economy, mining was its engine. Provisioning, labour, and services such as transport circulated silver domestically throughout the empire. Internal and external commerce was the main source of revenue for the Spanish administration as trade and consumption taxes became the fiscal backbone of the empire in the eighteenth century.[33] Concerned with the supply-side aspects of the silver trade, economic historians have underestimated the importance of silver in the New World.

Surely the markup price of goods exported to Spanish America was huge considering the various costs incurred: transportation costs within and outside Europe, trading costs, and taxes as most of these goods were re-exports from Asia and other European countries, plus the intermediation costs charged by the Spanish privileged participants in the American trade. Economic historians have assumed that this trade was driven by the need for imported commodities. However, the Spanish settlements in the mainland and in the Caribbean islands were self-sufficient in food and plenty of high-quality foodstuffs like sugar and meat. There is also an idea that this was a commercial system organized for the profit of the Spanish king and metropolitan merchants, which prejudiced economic devel-

Figure 15.2  Silver output and trade in the eighteenth century.
*Sources*: For silver output, J. TePaske, and K. Brown (2010), *A New World of Gold and Silver*, Leiden, Brill. For silver trade at Cadiz: A. Garcia Baquero (1996), 'Las remesas de metales preciosos americanos en el siglo XVIII: Una aritmética controvertida', *Hispania*, Appendix. For silver arrivals in Europe, M. Morineau (1986), *Incroyables gazettes et fabuleux métaux: Les retours des trésors américains d'après les gazettes hollandaises, 16e-18e siècles*. Paris: Editions de la MSH. For coinage, author's elaboration from G. Cespedes (1996), *Las Cecas Indianas en 1536-1825*. Madrid: Fabrica de Moneda y Timbre.

opment in the region. But the structure of this trade is poorly known. Indeed, as in Africa, European merchants were price takers in the commerce for silver in Spanish America.[34]

For all the bad reputation of their monopolistic practices, the Spaniards had limited control on the commerce with their possessions. A maritime empire without a fleet might appear an oxymoron. Yet, Spain's shipping capacity did not match the geographical and maritime extension of its empire. Remarkably, trade to the Spanish East Indies – the so-called Manila Galleon – was 'rationed' to only one or two ships of c. 1,200 tonnes a year.[35] The size of the two fleets convoyed over the Atlantic in the 1720s and 1730s averaged barely 10,000–12,000 tonnes on a dozen vessels respectively on each journey. At arrival, the fleet and galleons traded their goods for silver at fairs in Jalapa/Veracruz and Portobello/Cartagena and in Acapulco, where similarly privileged cartels of local merchants controlled the supply of silver and the sale of imports further inland. From the 1760s, fleets were discontinued; hence individual vessels doubled in number and more ports were licensed in the metropolis and colonies to trade, legalizing de facto an existing large irregular trade.[36] This 'liberalization' eroded the rents of cartels that controlled each step of the trade. This increased further the number and frequency of vessels bringing in some competition. When ships from the United States were allowed as neutrals to carry on the Spanish commerce after 1797, they were already regulars: more than 200 foreign ships a year called at Havana in the 1800s.[37] The Napoleonic Wars threw the Spanish American trade open to the US vessels in the 1790s and to the British after Trafalgar. This explains why US merchants became dominant in the silver trade to Asia after the 1780s. They supplied 80 per cent of the 3,800 tonnes of silver that China imported after 1790 and were large exporters to India too into the nineteenth century.

Formally, until 1778, Andalusian ports enjoyed the privilege of organizing the trade with America. Subsequent 'liberalization' did not change Cadiz's primacy among Spanish ports as the city continued sending 75–80 per cent of all American imports in the last two decades of the eighteenth century. In reality, Spanish colonial commerce had always been dominated by foreigners. The *Catastro de Ensenada*, a census of the 640 traders in Cadiz compiled in 1762, reveals that around 80 per cent of the commerce was in foreign hands, 42 per cent controlled by French mercantile houses, 15 per cent by English/Irish and Dutch/Flemish merchants, respectively, and 10 per cent by Italians.[38] Spaniards were numerous among the smallest freighters or acted as figureheads for foreign houses.[39] Indeed the Cadiz merchant guilds (Consulado) were constantly at odds with similar corporations in the New World as they competed for the control of silver returns for foreign goods.[40]

Yet, direct trade resulted in more and relatively cheaper silver traded to Europe. Neither the composition nor the origin of goods changed, but terms of trade improved for New World producers, and gave a boost to non-precious metal commodities. Access to direct shipping opened a cleavage between new commercial interests and the established merchant networks which controlled inland commerce. Thus the clout of the powerful Consulados of Mexico and Lima started to wane and in the 1790s Caracas, Guatemala, Guadalajara in Mexico, and Buenos Aires, Cartagena, Veracruz, Havana, Santiago de Chile, and Manila obtained the royal charter for their own mercantile jurisdiction. The carry trade by the United States and Britain catalysed the competition into the civil conflict that followed the collapse of the Spanish government in the 1810s.

Silver allowed Europeans to participate in the Baltic and Hanseatic trades, and trade with the Ottoman Empire, Central Asia, and certainly with maritime Asia.[41] But its persistence beyond the equalization of the bimetallic ratios within Eurasia requires a further inquiry. The geographical distribution – and size – of the silver flows cannot conceal the significance of consumption in Spanish America. With a total population of twelve million people by 1800 and fabulous silver endowments, the 'silverization' of the world economy had an equivalent in the extraordinary levels of private consumption in the New World, high inequality notwithstanding. The production of local manufactures there was characterized by the 'protection' of high transport costs (both overseas and overland) and the costs of intermediation of several rent-seekers, as well as a growing 'Dutch Disease' effects from the world demand of silver.

The quantity of silver was probably less important than – and of secondary importance to – the profits Europeans made in its global re-export. These were not 'super-profits' derived from their exploitation of extra-European people and riches. They were the rents that all mercantilist states in Europe competed for in order to obtain a less costly and more direct access to silver. So silver as the driver of global trade was also the driver of institutional and production changes in European economies introduced to secure cheaper goods and more profitable trade. That meant the increasing substitution of imports and lower domestic financial costs of war making. Ultimately it was the marginal acquisition of silver which allowed the continuation of trade; and trade was the means to increase the elasticity of supply and demand in the European economy. Mercantilism might have been a zero-sum game within Europe, but the process of Smithian growth worldwide since 1500 owed a great deal to the intermediation of silver and the trade it fostered.

## Silver in Europe and Asia

Silver was exported as a commodity out of Spanish America.[42] It is unclear whether silver was imported into Europe and Asia as a commodity or money, as the overwhelming proportion of it was coined with very consistent pure silver content, size, and weight.[43] Historians use the term 'silver' to indicate bullion or specie. However private agents, bankers, and states beyond the Spanish American world had a more informed view: the Genoese, for instance, financed the Spanish king and traded a great deal of silver into Europe in the mid-seventeenth century, and valued the piece of eight (the Spanish coin)[44] over its intrinsic content of pure silver. In the 1640s the price for the Spanish coin oscillated between 103.35 and 108.11 soldi, which was their money of account. Their own silver coin, the scudo, had 36.7929 grams of pure silver and was quoted to be worth between 117.75 and 122.33 soldi, while the exchange rate with the peso hovered between 1.12 and 1.14 per scudo.[45] Given that the piece of eight had 25.560 grams of pure silver, the exchange rate at silver parity was 1.4394 soldi, indicating that the piece of eight as specie enjoyed 20 per cent premium in Genoa.

Seafarers on English ships in the mid-seventeenth century demanded pieces of eight for their wages; lawsuit records at the High Admiralty Court show the variation in the exchange rate to sterling depending on the distance from Cadiz where it was exchanged at 48 pence, to Smyrna at 57–67 pence, and Mozambique at 78 pence, for instance.[46] However it is doubtful that these rates reflected the gold price of silver in each place. The exchange rate in sterling at Malaga in the same years was 54 pence and in Genoa it fluctuated mirroring the particular local market conditions.[47] It should not be surprising that sailors demanded pieces of eight for wages in international shipping; they also hoarded pieces of eight – or pesos after 1732 – for savings as the Old Bailey records in London attest.[48] Chinese seamen engaged in the junk trade to Batavia in the eighteenth century preferred this coin as a means to send remittances home and according to the historian of the Xianfeng inflation Jerome Ch'en 'fearing the eventual collapse of the Qing regime' at the time, people hedged against inflation and turmoil transfer(ing) 'their savings into silver, mostly in the form of the Spanish Dollar (peso)'.[49]

Individuals were not the only ones who invested in pieces of eight or Spanish pesos. European rulers had different ways to taking part in the intermediation of specie. The Spanish monarchy had no means to control the rates at which her American specie was to be transacted in Cadiz or in the colonies. Exchange was a private open business and subject to royal licenses granted to export silver out of Spanish America. Eventually the market came to be controlled by different sets of foreigners who obtained one privilege or another to import goods and slaves, or victualled the Spanish 'contractor state'. Amsterdam, by contrast, was a free market for specie slightly above the mint price and France struggled during the *ancien regime* to stabilize the silver price of her currency. Napoleon took pains to move the French monetary system to a silver-based currency in the first decade of the nineteenth century, leading to the establishment of the modern Banque of France. Even then, *piastres* imported from Spain continued to reach Amsterdam and beyond.[50] Some European countries smelted the imported silver and cut their own specie, but debasements and recoinages were frequent.

In the seventeenth century, South Asia operated with multiple metallic currencies, but used the piece of eight to fix different exchange rates as reported by the East India Company's factors. One of them, Charles Lockyer, in 1711 indicated that the 'pillar dollars are the most esteemed and therefore bear the highest price (at St George's fort)'. In Madras 'silver in any form passes currant [*sic*] by weight instead of money, reckoning from a take decimally to the smaller matter imaginable, in payments made with tankards, dishes, bowls, plates, spoons and silver porringers'. According to Lockyer, the Chinese however were well acquainted with the English marks guaranteeing the quality of the metal; therefore 'old plate is the most profitable silver you can carry with you, *when dollars are dear*.'[51] Most rulers in Southeast Asia considered the Spanish American peso legal tender of sorts, even if they were seldom seen in their markets, as late as in 1820s' Penang or Singapore.[52]

Some economies involved in silver exchange were exceptional in their own way. In China, from the 1780s at least, silver specie circulated as money in the southern region, adding another layer of complexity to the peculiar monetary system of an empire that did not coin silver but relied on imported specie.[53] In England, silver coinage was drastically reduced in quantity after 1696. Thereafter, gold and small change in copper formed the nation's currency. Goldsmiths continued producing silver plate in sizeable quantities through the eighteenth century and the East India Company exported silver to record levels.[54] Until the 1740s, in England the exchange business with bullion and specie was in the hands of goldsmiths. Thereafter, the Bank of England took over the market aligning the private rates by setting an official rate for the silver peso along with the exchange rate for gold and silver bullion.[55] Notably the banking services that goldsmith bankers had offered declined in favour of discount banks.

Figure 15.3 shows the relation between the market rates of the silver peso in sterling and the silver/gold ratio in England. It is apparent that the market price of specie in London in the eighteenth century did not bear any relation to the silver/gold ratio in England. Obviously Figure 15.3 encompasses the period when sterling was inconvertible, yet at the time the depreciation of sterling to the silver peso was higher than to gold.[56] It is worth exploring the role of the bank in steering the market for specie and the business with the company. A particular cooperation between three major institutions at the time made the English the providers of an incomparable arrangement for the market of specie.[57] Remarkably the English East India Company replicated the mechanism in India; it fixed a standard rate for the silver peso/Spanish

Figure 15.3 The market price of silver peso in sterling, in London, 1717–1818.
*Sources*: Silver/Gold Ratio from L. H. Officer (2016), *Between the Dollar-Sterling Gold Points: Exchange Rates, Parity, and Market Behavior*. Cambridge: Cambridge University Press; Exchange rate from E. M. Kelly (1976), *Spanish Dollar and Silver Tokens, An Account of the Issues of the Bank of England, 1797–1816*. London: Spink & Son.

dollar for its accounts in transactions which involved silver and a variety of currencies. This was the rate which set discounted bills in London, and priced goods in India, suggesting that the company dealt with treasure exports in a similar fashion to the bank-run market for exchange in London.[58]

The Mint, the Bank of England, and the East India Company concurred to stabilize and develop a market for bullion while the silver commerce with Asia expanded; at the same time a particular monetary regime and banking practices were established, foreshadowing a new international currency standard. The gold standard of the British pound eventually replaced the currency standard that the silver peso had created in the mid-seventeenth century. The Napoleonic Wars in Europe, which led both to the Restriction Period and the implosion of the Spanish rule in America, resulted in a definitive cleavage in monetary matters too.

As pointed by Michel Morineau twenty years ago, 'the incorporation of precious metals in the general circulating medium of European economies, their effective role in the development of the economy and of the armed forces, the concurrence with other means of payment, and the transition to the different modern monetary regimes of the 19th century' remains to be explained.[59] His research on silver import to Europe was crucial to debunk Hamilton's ideas about the price revolution and the crisis of the seventeenth century, which persisted in the economic historiography for a long while.

## Conclusion

For Adam Smith, New World commodities were 'new values, new equivalents' in the global economy to be exchanged for the surplus of each intervening country – even in those which 'never sent any commodities to America, (and) never received any from it'.[60]

Among those, silver, in his words, was 'one of the principal commodities by which the commerce between the two extremities of the Old (world) is carried on, and by means of it, in a great measure, that those distant parts of the world are connected with one another'.[61] Moreover, he pointed at 'what has been said of the East India trade might possibly be true of the French; that though the greater part of the East India goods were bought with gold and silver, the re-exportation of a part of them to other countries brought back more gold and silver to that which carried on the trade than the prime cost of the whole amounted to', revealing the crucial importance of the carry trade among European nations and of silver as underlying factor in the contemporary process of Smithian growth in Europe.[62]

Therefore the 'general advantage which Europe, considered as one great country' derived from the discovery of America and of the passage to the East Indies 'consisted first, in the increase of its enjoyments, and secondly, in the augmentation of its industry'. Despite the largesse of its production and exports to the world, Spanish American silver did not have persistent inflationary effects on prices worldwide. On the contrary, it was for Smith 'the gradual enlargement of the market for the produce of silver mines in America, probably the cause which has not only kept up the value of silver in the European market, but has perhaps even raised somewhat higher than it was about the middle of last century'. The market had become ever 'more extensive' in America – as in Asia – and the 'greater part of Europe has been much improved, England, Holland, France and Germany, even Sweden and Denmark and Russia have all advanced considerably both in agriculture and in manufactures..[63]

For Smith, these improvements 'must necessarily have required a gradual increase in the quantity of silver coin to circulate it; and the increasing number of wealthy individuals must have required the like increase in the quantity of their plate and ornaments of silver'.[64] He flagged that 'America is itself a new market for the produce of its silver mines; and its advances in agriculture, industry and population are much more rapid that those of the most thriving countries in Europe; its demand must increase much more rapidly'.[65] However, scholars within and outside the region have overlooked this relation – or result – between silver and the development of the global economy because of an inaccurate understanding of the colonial economy in Spanish America.

Thus the role of the global silver trade is still little understood. The incorporation and circulation of silver and specie in the European economy and the importance of the New World demand – and of Spanish America in particular – are aspects yet to be mined by global economic historians.

## Notes

1. A. Smith (1776/1979), *An Inquiry into the Nature and Causes of the Wealth of Nations.* London: The Electric Book Company, http://www.myilibrary.com?ID=124076 Book IV, part III, ch 7: 829.

2. K. Pomeranz (2001), *The Great Divergence: China, Europe, and the Making of the Modern World Economy.* Princeton: Princeton University Press; J. Hersh and H. Voth (2009). 'Sweet

diversity: Colonial goods and the rise of European living standards after 1492', *Discussion Paper CEPR* 7386.

3. D. O. Flynn and A. Giráldez (1996), *World Silver and Monetary History in the 16th and 17th Centuries*. Aldershot: Variorum; Ibid. (1997), *Metals and Monies in an Emerging Global Economy: Expanding World*. Brookfield: Variorum.

4. I. Habib (1982), 'Monetary system and prices', in T. Raychaudhuri and I. Habib (eds), *The Cambridge Economic History of India*. Cambridge: Cambridge University Press, 360–81; R. von Glahn (1996), *Fountain of Fortune: Money and Monetary Policy in China, 1000–1700*. Berkeley: University of California Press. Copper, tin or brass also circulated as small change in different Asian states. R. von Glahn (2014), 'Chinese coin and changes in monetary preferences in maritime East Asia in the fifteenth-seventeenth centuries', *Journal of the Economic and Social History of the Orient*, 57 (5), 629–68.

5. Soetbeer (1886), cited by J. Nef (1941), 'Silver production in Central Europe, 1450–1618', *Journal of Political Economy*, 49 (4), 589.

6. I. Seiichi (1976), 'Japanese trade in the 16th and 17th centuries', *Acta Asiatica,* 30, 1–18 who estimated this volume equivalent to the 30–40 per cent of the world production at the time.

7. R. Innes (1980), 'The door ajar: Japan's foreign trade in the seventeenth century', Unpublished PhD Thesis, Ann Arbor: University of Michigan, 379, and 582.

8. J. TePaske and K. Brown (2010), *A New World of Gold and Silver*. Leiden: Brill, table 3.20.

9. A. Maddison (2007), *Contours of the World Economy, 1-2030 AD: Essays in Macro-Economic History*. Oxford: Oxford University Press; K. O'Rourke and J. G. Williamson (2002), 'After Columbus: Explaining Europe's overseas trade boom, 1500–1800', *Journal of Economic History*, 62 (2), table 1, 421.

10. J. De Vries (2003), 'Connecting Europe and Asia: A Quantitative Analysis of the Cape Route Trade, 1497-1975', in D. Flynn, A. Giráldez, and R. von Glahn (eds), *Global Connections and Monetary History 1470-1800*. Aldershot: Ashgate.

11. Williamson and O'Rourke did not consider precious metals because of their monetary role or think their 'impact of intercontinental silver flows on aggregate price levels' was relevant. O'Rourke and Williamson (2002), 'After Columbus', fn. 4. See D. O. Flynn and A. Giráldez (2004), 'Path dependence, time lags and the birth of globalization: A critique of O'Rourke and Williamson', *European Review of Economic History*, 8 (1), 81–108.

12. A. Gunder Frank (1998), *ReOrient: Global Economy in the Asian Age*. Berkeley: University of California Press; and Flynn and Giráldez (various years).

13. In India, the ratio had equalized by 1670 at 15/16:1, but reverted to 13:1 and even 11.5:1 in the early eighteenth century; it remained below the European ratio for remainder of the century. Habib, 'Monetary system', table 9.

14. A. Irigoin (2013), 'A Trojan horse in Daoguang China? Explaining the flows of silver in and out of China', *LSE Economic History Working Papers* 173/13.

15. N. Palma (2015), 'Harbingers of modernity: Monetary injections and European economic growth, 1492–1790', unpublished Ph.D. thesis, London School of Economics. Another argument about the importance of liquidity in Europe and Asia can be found in R. Findlay and K. O'Rourke (2009), *Power and Plenty: Trade, War and the World Economic in the Second Millennium*. Princeton: Princeton University Press, 212.

16. L. Dermigny (1964), *La Chine et l'Occident; le commerce à Canton au XVIIIe siècle*, 1719-1833. Paris: SEVPEN II, 686.

17. H. Klein (1990), 'Economic aspects of the eighteenth-century Atlantic slave trade', in J. Tracy (ed.), *The Rise of Merchant Empires: Long Distance Trade in the Early Modern World*

*1350–1750.* Cambridge: Cambridge University Press, 287–310; K. Weber (2002), 'German rural industry and trade in the Atlantic, 1680–1840', *Itinerario*, 26 (2), 99–119.

18. Cotton from the United States became a prime export commodity after 1815, but, strictly speaking, it was cultivated with home-grown slave labour of African descent, which makes this crop distinct from the traditional West Indies exports.

19. P. K. O'Brien (1982), 'European Economic Development: The Contribution of the Periphery', *Economic History Review* 35 (1), 4.

20. P. K. O'Brien (1998), 'Inseparable connections: Trade, economy, fiscal state and the expansion of empire', in P. J. Marshall and A. Low (eds), *The Oxford History of the British Empire. Vol. 2. The Eighteenth Century*, 53–78; P. K. O'Brien (2014), 'The formation of states and transitions to modern economies', 357–64.

21. Findlay and O'Rourke, *Power and Plenty*, 210.

22. M. Dell (2010), 'The persistent effects of Peru's mining mita', *Econometrica*, 78 (6), 863–903; M. Van der Linden (2011), *Workers of the World: Essays toward a Global Labor History.* Leiden: Brill.

23. E. Tandeter (1981), 'Free and forced labour in late Colonial Potosí', *Past & Present*, 93, table 2; P. Bakewell (1984), *Miners of the Red Mountain, Indian labour in Potosí.* Albuquerque: University of New Mexico Press; R. Barragan (2017), 'Working Silver for the World: Mining Labor and Popular Economy in Colonial Potosí', *Hispanic American Historical Review*, 97 (2), 193–222.

24. C. Marichal (2006), 'The Spanish American silver peso: Export commodity and global money of the ancien regime (16–18th centuries)', in S. Topik, C. Marichal and Z. Frank (eds), *Latin American Commodity Chains and the Building of Global Economy.* Durham: Duke University Press, 30.

25. E. Tandeter (1993), *Coercion and Market: Silver Mining in Colonial Potosí, 1692–1826.* Albuquerque: University of New Mexico Press; Allen, 'The Great Divergence in European wages and prices from the middle ages to the First World War'.

26. Allen, et al. (2012), 'The colonial origins of the divergence in the Americas: A labor market approach', *Journal of Economic History*, 72 (4), 863–94; A. Arroyo and J. L. Van Zanden (2011), 'Between conquest and independence: Real wages and demographic change in Spanish America, 1530–1820', *Explorations in Economic History*, 49 (2), 149–66; R. Dobado and G. Montero (2014), 'Neither so low nor so short: Wages and heights in Bourbon Spanish America from an international comparative perspective', *Journal of Latin American Studies*, 46 (2), 291–321; and A. Challú and A. Gómez-Galvarriato (2015), 'Mexico's real wages in the age of the Great Divergence, 1730–1930', *Revista de Historia Economica/Journal of Iberian Latin American Economic History*, 33 (1), 83–122 for a different view.

27. TePaske and Brown, *A New World*, 140.

28. C. S. Assadourian (1982), *El Sistema de la Economía Colonial. El Mercado interior. Regiones y Espacio Económico.* Mexico: Nueva Imagen, 22.

29. A. Irigoin (2009), 'Gresham on horseback. The monetary roots of Spanish America political fragmentation in the nineteenth century', *Economic History Review*, 62 (3), 551–75.

30. J. Cuenca (2008), 'Statistics of Spain's colonial trade, 1747–1820: New estimates and comparisons with Great Britain', *Revista de Historia Economica/Journal of Iberian and Latin American Economic History*, 26 (3), 323–54.

31. Significantly this data do not include Brazilian gold exports or the silver smuggled by European interlopers or traded in Pacific commerce. Gold was also produced in Peru, Colombia, Chile, and Mexico.

32. The r² is 0.30, whereas the correlation between output and coinage is 0.94.

33. R. Grafe and A. Irigoin (2006), 'The Spanish Empire and its legacy: Fiscal redistribution and political conflict in colonial and post-colonial Spanish America', *Journal of Global History*, 1 (2), 241–67. In the eighteenth century, the growth of population and of mining, together with the expansion of the Europeanized economy over the territory, fostered some Smithian growth empire-wide. By taxing commerce, a 'developmentalist' state enlarged its fiscal base along the way. Grafe and Irigoin, 'A stakeholder empire'.

34. J. Baskes (2005), 'Risky ventures: Reconsidering Mexico's colonial trade system', *Colonial Latin American Review*, 14 (1), 27–54; D. Brading (1971), *Miners and merchants in Bourbon Mexico, 1763-1810*. Cambridge: Cambridge University Press, 97.

35. Findlay and O'Rourke attribute this restraint to a compromise between 'a permit to trade, but to restrict it to a prescribed level permitting the survival of the import competing silk industry' (in Mexico and Spain). Findlay and O'Rourke, *Power and Plenty*, 168.

36. Numbers compare with the English East India Company's commerce in the East Indies and China.

37. L. Salvucci (2005), 'Atlantic intersections: Early American commerce and the rise of the Spanish West Indies (Cuba)', *Business History Review*, 74 (9), 781–809.

38. D. Ozanam (1968), *La Colonie Francaise de Cadiz au XVIII siècle*. Madrid: Melanges de la Casa de Velazquez.

39. M. Bernal (1992), *La Financiación de la Carrera de Indias (1492-1824): Dinero y Crédito en el Comercio Colonial Español con América*. Cadiz: Fundacion El Monte.

40. Litigations before the court between the different Consulados in Seville, Mexico, Lima, and Manila were constant. Probably the dispute around the introduction of Asian silks and textiles to the New World over a period of 150 years recapitulated by A. Alvarez de Abreu (1736/1977), *Extracto Historial del Comercio entre China, Filipinas y Nueva España*, Mexico: Instituto Mexicano de Comercio Exterior, is the best example.

41. M. Malowist (1958), 'Poland, Russia and Western trade in the 15th and 16th century', *Past & Present*, 13, 26–41; S. Pamuk (1994), 'Money in the Ottoman Empire, 1326–1914', in H. Inalcik and D. Quataert (eds), *History of the Ottoman Empire, 1300-1914*. Cambridge: Cambridge University Press, 947–85.

42. The section builds largely on my paper 'Standard error: The problems for economic historians from (mis)taking Spanish American silver as commodity money, 1700s-1830s' presented at the Economic History Society Congress on Iberometrics, Pamplona 2017.

43. Mintage was done locally and overwhelmingly made of one-peso coin. R. Romano (1998), *Moneda, Seudomoneda y Circulación Monetaria en la Economía de México*. Mexico: Fondo de Cultura Económica.

44. The coin had a fractional equivalent to 8 reals. It was called the *peso de a ocho* until 1732 when it started to be milled. Henceforth it was known as the Spanish dollar in English and the *piastre* in French.

45. Thanks to Claudio Marsilio for sharing the exchange rates information.

46. R. Blakemore (2017), '"Pieces of eight, pieces of eight": Seamen's earning and the venture economy in early modern seafaring', *Economic History Review*, 70 (4), 1153–84. See his 'Descriptive Report' in http://humanities.exeter.ac.uk/history/research/centres/maritime/resources/sailingintomodernity/datasets/ accessed 16/08/2017.

47. C. Marsilio (2012), 'The Genoese and Portuguese financial operators' control of the Spanish silver market (1627-1657)', *Journal of European Economic History*, 41 (3), 67–89.

48. A. Dolan (2015), 'The fabric of life: Linen and life cycle in England, 1678–1810', Unpublished Ph.D. Thesis, University of Hertfordshire.

49. L. Blussé (2011) 'Junks to Java: Chinese shipping to the Nanyang in the second half of the eighteenth century', in E. Tagliacozzo and W. Chang, *Chinese Circulation. Capital Commodities and Networks in South East Asia*. Durham: Duke University Press, 285; J. CH'en (1958), 'The Hsien-Feng inflation', *Bulletin of the School of Oriental and African Studies*. University of London, 21 (3), 580.

50. M. Zylberberg (1993), *Une si douce domination. Lex milieux d'affaires françaises et l'Espagne vers 1780–1808*. Paris: Comité pour l'histoire économique et financière de la France.

51. C. Lockyer (1711), *An Account of the Trade in India*. London: Samuel Crouch, 136 and 140.

52. L. Wong (1960), 'The trade of Singapore, 1819–69', *Journal of the Malayan Branch of the Royal Asiatic Society*, 33 (4), 4–135; A. Reid and F. Radin (1996), 'Shipping on Melaka and Singapore as an index of growth, 1760–1840', *Journal of South Asian Studies*, 19 (1), 59–84.

53. Irigoin (2013), 'A Trojan horse in Daoguang China?'; R. von Glahn (2013), 'Cycles of silver in Chinese monetary history', in Billy K. L. So (ed.), *The Economy of Lower Yangzi Delta in Late Imperial China*. London, Routledge, 17–71.

54. N. Mayhew (2012), 'Silver in England, 1600–1800: Coinage outputs and bullion exports from the records of the London Tower Mint and the London Company of Goldsmiths', in J. H. Munro (ed.), *Money in Pre-Industrial World: Bullion, Debasements and Coin Substitutes*. London: Pickering & Chatto, 97–108.

55. J. H. Clapham (1941), 'The private business of the Bank of England, 1744–1800', *Economic History Review*, 11 (1), 77–89; A. Hotson and T.C. Mills (2015), 'London's market for bullion and specie in the 18th century: the roles of the London Mint and the Bank of England in the stabilization of prices', in M. Allen and D. Coffman (eds), *Money, Prices and Wages; Essays in Honour of Prof. Nicholas Mayhew*. Basingtoke: Palgrave, 217–27.

56. J. N. Silberling (1919), 'British prices and business cycles, 1779–1850', *Review of Economics and Statistics*, 1 (10), 282–97.

57. A. Irigoin (forthcoming), 'The Rise and Decline of the Global Silver Standard' in S. Battilossi, Y. Cassis and K. Yago (eds) *Handbook of the History of Money and Currency* (Springer).

58. K. N. Chaudhuri (1968), 'Treasure and trade balance: The East India Company's export trade, 1660–1720', *Economic History Review*, 21 (3), 480–502.

59. Morineau cited in A. García-Baquero González (1996), 'Las remesas de metales preciosos americanos en el siglo XVIII: Una aritmética controvertida', *Hispania: Revista Española de Historia*, 56 (192), 266.

60. Smith, *Wealth of Nations*, Book IV, chapter 7, 782.

61. Smith, *Wealth of Nations*, Book I, chapter 11, 287.

62. Smith, *Wealth of Nations*, Book IV, chapter 3, 629, 621–25.

63. Smith, *Wealth of Nations*, Book IV, chapter 7, 780.

64. Smith, *Wealth of Nations*, Vol III, chapter 11, 282–3.

65. Smith, *Wealth of Nations*.

# CHAPTER 16
## ECONOMIC CHANGE IN EAST ASIA FROM THE SEVENTEENTH TO THE TWENTIETH CENTURY
*Debin Ma*

### What is East Asia?

Although defying precise demarcation, East Asia can be defined in geographic, political, and cultural terms. Situated largely at the eastern end of the Asian continent, East Asia is more closely associated with today's nation states or regions of China, Japan, North and South Korea, and Northern Vietnam but could, for cultural reasons, include the far-flung city state of Singapore. Three interrelated historical identities are shared in varying degrees across East Asia. First is the use of classical Chinese characters among the educated elites and the corresponding adoption of the teachings of Confucius as the ruling ideology. This is coupled with a hierarchical civil bureaucracy inculcated in the teachings of Confucian classics and superimposed upon a predominantly agrarian economic structure. And finally, East Asia is an international order based on what is called a 'tributary system'.

As a reflection of a Neo-Confucian cosmology, the political order of the tributary system consisted of radiating concentric rings, with political power emanating from the imperial seat of the Chinese emperor out towards administrative provinces, tributary or vassal states, and mutual trade zones. The tributary states system created a political framework in which neighbouring small states maintained a status of near protectorate and within which cross-national trade, although restricted, was conducted. This China-centred hierarchical worldview was internalized by periphery states such as Korea, Northern Vietnam, and to a certain extent, Japan, who, in turn, imposed a 'satellite tributary system' upon other smaller states.[1] East Asian states prevailed within the tributary system until aggressive Western imperialism reached China's shore by the mid-nineteenth century.

### East Asia in the seventeenth to the nineteenth centuries

The seventeenth century saw the onset of new political regimes in Qing China (1644–1911), Tokugawa Japan (1603–1868), and the consolidation of the Choson dynasty in Korea (1392–1897). Despite being a minority tribe hailed from China's northeastern border, the Manchu rulers turned Qing China into a mature, highly centralized, unitary political regime governed by an absolutist emperor at the top of the power pyramid, aided by a formal bureaucracy recruited through a highly structured national civil service examination based on Confucian classics. The formal imperial regime coexisted alongside the emperor's personal rule, his personal entourage of eunuchs, consort, and other inner court staffs.[2] While Korea more faithfully reproduced the Chinese system of governance with variation and adaptations, the Japanese system of governance remained far more fractured and decentralized under the Tokugawa regime when the emperor was sidelined in Kyoto as a symbolic figure. The real power resided instead in the hands of a military general-bureaucrat (the Shogun) in Tokyo. But even the Shogunate's rule only directly controlled part of the Japanese territory and coexisted with 300 autonomous daimyos.[3]

Both cohesion and diversity characterized East Asia as an integrated cultural zone or sphere. Firstly, despite the dominance of Chinese classics across the entire area, the diversity of ethnic and national identities remained important. Indeed, the Qing Empire was ruled by a non-Han minority group from Manchuria (in northeastern China) who had had a long-standing engagement with the Han Chinese over the centuries. The interaction between Han Chinese or Confucian cultures and other cultures in the region should be viewed as a bi-directional flow rather than that of Han Chinese dominance.[4] Secondly, connected with political and ideological exchange was the trade in goods and perhaps more importantly in technology – both formally and informally – under the tributary system. Despite the relative isolation, exchange led to the diffusion of technology that allowed regions and states of East Asia to catch up economically and technologically through import substitution during the early modern period. Among the outcomes was the creation of a well-articulated intra-Asian trading network somewhat independent of the Western trade systems that made serious inroads into East Asia only after the mid-nineteenth century.[5] Trade between East Asia and the world beyond remained limited though of critical importance. The export of Chinese silks and tea fuelled a passion for Chinoiserie in the West that eventually led to imitation and import substitution of Chinese products in Europe and India. In the opposite direction, the inflow of Latin American silver ingots and coins lubricated the engine of Chinese commerce and supported the monetization of public finance from the sixteenth century onwards. The introduction of New World crops such as maize, peanuts, and potatoes sustained the population, which tripled during the Qing Empire.

The beginning of the nineteenth century may have seen the turn of the tide that had once favoured the fortune of Qing China. Population growth sustained by rising agricultural land productivity and the introduction of new crops may have finally stretched the limits of the constraints on resources. Beginning with the White Lotus (1796–1804), a series of domestic rebellions culminating in the vast Taiping uprising (1851–64), one can observe an erosion of the Qing regime. Externally, following the collapse of East India Company's monopoly in 1833, British imperialism driven by private commercial interest intensified to the detriment of Chinese trade. The rise of the trade in Indian opium to China reversed China's long-standing trade surplus, draining silver specie out of the empire. The increasing scarcity of silver specie caused havoc across the economy, diminished the government's capacity to collect taxes, and decreased the morale of the military.[6] This occurred because during the sixteenth and seventeenth centuries, mid-Ming reforms had led to the silverization of tax revenue and the use of silver as one of the mediums of exchange in the economy. Prompted by an urge to act, but armed with little understanding of the might of the rising Western imperialism, the Qing's military confrontation with England in the now famous Opium War of 1842 turned out to be a humiliating defeat. It also marked the fall of the world's largest and most remote empire into the orbit of Western imperialism. British arms forced the Qing to accept the Treaty of Nanking (1842), which ceded Hong Kong to the British, imposed a regime of virtual free trade, and initiated the 'treaty port' system by opening five Chinese ports to British and other Western merchants. This agreement, which set the tone of China's international economic relations during the century prior to the Pacific War (1941–5), subsequently expanded to include dozens of treaty ports where foreign residents were protected by extraterritoriality at the expense of Chinese sovereignty.

In the eighteenth and nineteenth centuries, Tokugawa Japan shared commonalities as well as differences with Qing China. In contrast to the eighteenth-century population growth of Qing China, Japan's population remained stable. This led an early generation of historians to interpret this as a form of early modern Japanese exceptionalism vis-à-vis other Asian countries, creating a unique 'social structure' that allowed a precocious demographic transition for Japan. However, population stagnation can similarly be interpreted as the result of Japanese population being trapped by its land territory, which – unlike Qing China which saw a doubling of its territory – was circumscribed by its coastal borderlines.[7] However, there is little dispute that Japan diverged from China at the beginning of the nineteenth century as the country remained relatively peaceful, and sheltered from the dual crisis of opium and silver outflows that had gripped China. But this divergence should not be overstated as the onslaught of Western imperialism exerted equal if not more pressure on isolationist Tokugawa Japan. Indeed, after the opening up of East Asia to free trade under Western imperialism in the mid-nineteenth century, during their early attempts to expand business overseas, the Japanese suddenly found themselves under the pressure of a remarkable resurgence of China-based mercantile dominance across regions of East and Southeast Asia. In particular, Shanghai, as a newly opened treaty port, rapidly emerged as an important node in a vast trading network that enveloped, among others, the Japanese treaty ports of Yokohama and Kobe. The dominance and cohesion of Chinese merchant networks throughout Asia posed a challenge to the young Meiji government as formidable as the agenda of catching up with the West.[8]

Recent attempts at constructing new long-term Chinese GDP series seem to confirm earlier estimates by Maddison.[9] The claim that China was the world's leading economy in the seventeenth and eighteenth centuries was somewhat misleading based on a conflation of aggregate and per capita figures. Based largely on guesstimates, Maddison put China's annual per capita income at about $500–600 (international $ in 1990 prices), a level that was about 80 per cent (in 1500) and 35 per cent (in 1700) of the world's leading but much smaller economies of Britain and the Netherlands, respectively. But Maddison was right in trumpeting the aggregate size of the Chinese economy.[10] With a doubling of its territory and a tripling of its population between the fifteenth and the eighteenth centuries, no other early modern political entity achieved such size in both territory and population under a single political regime. But it will be a far cry to claim that any of this gave the Chinese economy the leading position that it may have held in the early centuries of the second millennium as under the Song dynasty (960–1279 CE). The commercial, financial, political, technological, and scientific revolutions that characterized a fragmented and quarrelsome Europe largely sidestepped the centralized but rigid Qing state, only to haunt it by the mid-nineteenth century. We can get a more comprehensive profile of the evolution of Chinese living standards and human capital in the nineteenth and twentieth centuries based on integrated estimates of real wage and anthropometric evidence. They confirm a general decline in living standards and human capital after the mid-nineteenth century followed by a recovery only at the turn of the twentieth century (Figure 16.1). The real wage data also reveal that in the eighteenth and nineteenth centuries Chinese living standards were probably closer to the relatively underdeveloped parts of Europe but lower than Northwestern Europe. They confirm that a divergence in living standards and per capita income between Europe and China already existed before the Industrial Revolution and only widened from the nineteenth century onwards.[11] However, in contrast to the findings based on real wages and heights, the basic numeracy index reveals a relatively high level of Chinese human capital, which in the eighteenth and nineteenth centuries was closer to that of Northwestern Europe than countries with a comparable low level of living standards such as India or Turkey.[12]

**Figure 16.1** Real wages in Asia and England, 1738–1914.
*Source:* R. Allen, J.-P. Bassino, D. Ma, C. Moll-Murata and J. L. van Zanden (2011), 'Wages, Prices, and Living Standards in China, Japan, and Europe, 1738–1925', *Economic History Review*, 64 (S1), pp. 8–38.

## Economic change in modern East Asia

Western imperialism represented an external threat drastically different from China's traditional nemesis on its Northern frontier and was therefore a watershed in Chinese history. The challenge was economic, political, institutional, and ideological. The new era saw China start off disastrously with the outbreak of the devastating Taiping Rebellion (1850–62). It must be said that the Qing under the so-called Tongzhi Restoration (1861–75) engineered a remarkable economic recovery through the revitalization of traditional institutions: the reinstatement of Confucian orthodoxy, the restoration of the national civil service examination (largely interrupted during the Taiping Rebellion), and the initial exemption from land taxes to lure cultivators back to war-torn agricultural regions.

The Qing did not remain entirely passive to Western incursions. As a natural extension to the Tongzhi Restoration, powerful regional bureaucrats such as Li Hongzhang and Zhang Zhidong sponsored the Self-Strengthening Movement (1860–94), a programme that aimed to expand Chinese military strength by developing a small number of Western-style, capital-intensive enterprises financed by the state and directed by eminent officials who possessed the highest credentials awarded under the Confucian academic system. Although these enterprises – which included arsenals, factories, and shipyards – were fraught with inefficiency and corruption, they did manage to record modest achievements. Nonetheless, the overall ideological orientation during this period remained conservative. In contrast to the concurrent Meiji reforms in Japan, no Chinese reform touched the fundamentals of the traditional regime: there was no introduction of modern constitution or commercial law; no reform in the currency system; modern banks or modern infrastructures such as railroads were expressly prohibited; and steamships were limited to major riverways such as the Yangzi River.

The direct impact of the treaty port system according to which Chinese trade tariffs were restricted to a modest 3–5 per cent was the expansion of China's international trade. China's maritime customs data show how real imports more than doubled in the quarter of a century prior to 1895, with exports increasing by half of that. Trade statistics suggest that after 1895 trade grew at a slower pace, around 2–3 per cent per annum. Despite its modest scale, trade gradually integrated major domestic commodity markets into the international exchange system of the Pacific Basin.

The treaty system accelerated the arrival of new technologies, initially to the treaty ports themselves, which became staging points for the diffusion of technologies into the domestic economy. However, industrialization continued to lag behind the opportunities opened up by trade and the inflow of new technology partly due to powerful obstacles to innovation that existed within China's domestic economy. These barriers, which negatively affected the expansion of infrastructure such as modern railroads and inland steam shipping, are most clearly visible in the history of private efforts to introduce new technologies and new business arrangements in the processing of agricultural commodities like soybeans and silk larvae.[13]

In sharp contrast to Qing China, the Samurai clans that overthrew the old Tokugawa regime and came to power with the 1868 Meiji Restoration made no pretence to 'restore' Japan to her old days, but instead proclaimed to seek knowledge throughout the world. They embarked on a reform programme to forge a modern nation state modelled after the West. Japan's decisiveness in turning outwards in facing the Western imperial challenge stood in stark contrast to the contemporaneous Qing's determination to reinstate an orthodox Neo-Confucian ruling ideology to an empire that had been brought to the brink of collapse. In contrast to the Self-Strengthening Movement (1860–94) that pursued the modernization of the Chinese military through a series of either government-financed or government-controlled Western-style industrial enterprises, Meiji Japan threw its full support behind the private sector, which – with the sell-off of the limited number of government enterprises in the 1880s – was designated as the mainstay for Japan's industrialization. The self-strengtheners in China displayed either indifference or hostility towards private enterprise in modern sectors, supplied few critical modern public goods, and in most cases even opposed private efforts to build public infrastructure such as railroads and inland steam shipping. By contrast, the Meiji leaders engaged in the build-up of crucial social and physical infrastructures such as a modern legal system, public education, research and technological diffusion, a modern monetary and banking system, and modern transportation and communications. While there was little overhauling of its traditional political, legal, monetary, and education system in nineteenth-century Qing China, the 1890s saw the birth of a newly transformed modern constitutional monarchy in Japan.[14]

Available macroeconomic statistics give an annual growth rate of Japanese per capita GDP at 2.25 per cent between 1887 and 1897. By 1910 the Japanese economy was 50 per cent larger than it had been in 1887. Japan's share of manufacturing and mining in total GDP rose from 8.7 per cent in 1887 to 11 per cent in 1897, and to 16 per cent in 1910.[15] Although rigorous quantitative comparison with Qing China are impossible due to the lack of reliable macroeconomic statistics for the late nineteenth century, it is clear that in China there was little industrial expansion except for government-sponsored enterprises which, however, created little spillover effect across the economy. As for agriculture, technological progress and productivity gains were largely absent while the effects and degrees of commercialization during this period were mixed.[16]

The absence of macroeconomic statistics hinders any attempts to pinpoint the critical historical moment when Japan overtook China in economic terms. However, China's humiliating naval defeat by Japan in 1894–5 serves as the litmus test of the merits of almost three decades of contrasting political and economic policies. This ignominious military defeat by a nation long regarded as China's minor tributary neighbour inflicted a profound mental shock on Chinese elites and the public at large. An immediate economic impact followed the 1895 signing of the Treaty of Shimonoseki, which granted foreigners the right to establish factories in the treaty ports. Eliminating the prohibition against foreign factories in treaty ports sparked a rapid expansion of foreign direct investment in China. This new arrangement indirectly legitimized Chinese modern enterprises. Despite some setbacks from the repression of the Hundred Days' reform centred in the southern province of Hunan in 1898, followed by the subsequent debacle surrounding the Boxer Rebellion in 1900, the Qing constitutional movement of 1903–11 was a far more comprehensive and ambitious initiative. It aimed at steering China towards a constitutional monarchy by drafting a formal modern constitution with national, provincial, and local level parliaments. Military modernization was high on the reform agenda. Administrative reform sought to modernize public finance and adopt a national budget, as well as the setting up of new ministries of education, trade, and agriculture, and encouraged the founding of local chambers of commerce.

From the very end of the nineteenth century, Chinese activity in mining and manufacturing accelerated sharply from its small initial base. Overall industrial output showed double-digit real annual growth during the period 1912–36, a phenomenal result for that period, especially in view of China's turbulent political scene and the impact of the Great Depression. Factory production, initially focused on textiles, food processing, and other consumer products, concentrated in two regions: the Lower Yangzi area, where both foreign and Chinese entrepreneurs pursued factory expansion in and around Shanghai; and China's northeast or Manchurian region, where Japanese initiatives predominated. By 1935, Chinese factories, including some owned by British and Japanese firms, produced 8 per cent of the world's cotton yarn (more than Germany, France, or Italy) and 2.8 per cent of global cotton piece goods production. Despite the importance of foreign investment in Shanghai and especially in Manchuria, Chinese-owned companies produced 73 per cent of China's 1933 factory output. The growing production of light consumer and industrial goods, combined with the accumulation of experience in operating and repairing modern machinery, generated backward linkages that spurred new private initiatives in machinery, chemicals, cement, mining, electricity, and metallurgy. Official efforts (including semi-official Japanese activity in Manchuria) also promoted the growth of mining, metallurgy, and arms manufacture. [17]

China's economic prospects acted as a magnet for trade and investment during the pre-Second-World-War decades. China's foreign trade rose to a peak of more than 2 per cent of global trade flows in the late 1920s, a level that was not regained until the 1990s. Between 1902 and 1931, inflows of foreign direct investment grew at annual rates of 8.3 per cent for Shanghai, 5 per cent for Manchuria, and 4.3 per cent for the rest of China. By 1938, China's stock of inward foreign investment amounted to US$2.6 billion – more than any other underdeveloped region except for the Indian subcontinent and Argentina. Although estimates of pre-war capital flows often blur the distinction between direct and portfolio holdings, it is evident that China played a substantial role in global capital flows. The above-mentioned 1938 figure of US$2.6 billion for China's stock of foreign investments amounts to 8.4 per cent of worldwide stocks of outward foreign investment and 17.5 per cent of outward foreign direct investment in that year. By contrast, China's 2001 share of worldwide inward foreign direct investment was only 2.1 per cent. Domestic investment also showed substantial growth. 'Modern-oriented' fixed investment (calculated from consumption of cement, steel, and machinery) grew at an average annual rate of 8.1 per cent between 1903 and 1936, outpacing Japanese gross domestic fixed capital formation in mining, manufacturing, construction, and facilitating industry, which advanced at an annual rate of 5 per cent. Despite the effects of the Great Depression and political tumult, economy-wide gross fixed investment exceeded 10 per cent of aggregate output during 1931–6.[18]

Transport development contributed substantially to economic expansion. China's railway track length grew from 364 kilometres in 1894 to over 21,000 by 1937, and newly constructed north–south lines slashed economic distances across a landscape dominated by rivers flowing from west to east. The completion of railway and telegraph connections linking Peking (now Beijing) and the central China river port of Wuhan in 1906 reduced the time needed to ship commodities between these cities. In a remarkable triumph of a free-banking version of the silver standard, privately owned Chinese banks, often cooperating with foreign financial institutions and traditional money lenders, transformed the financial face of China by persuading households and businesses to transact with paper banknotes that were convertible into silver on demand. This monetary transformation reduced transaction costs. The expansion of branch networks allowed major domestic banks to attract deposits from all regions and recycle them to the areas of greatest demand, contributing to the emergence of an embryonic national market for funds. All in all, these developments in industry, transport, and finance precipitated an episode of modern economic growth at the national level during the early decades of the twentieth century.

These forces resulted in increased per capita output and structural changes of the sort associated with Simon Kuznets' concept of 'modern economic growth'. This was the case in two major regions: the Lower Yangzi, where private domestic and foreign investment in and around Shanghai served as a key driver, and the northeast (Manchuria), where Japanese investment and eventual takeover provided momentum for economic development. Table 16.1 details the comparative growth pattern in modern industries in Japan and China. It shows that growth rates in China (including Shanghai) were comparable for the 1895–1911 and 1912–36 periods, and were possibly matched only by those of Korea in the period 1912–36.[19] Tables 16.2 and 16.3 show the changing economic structure and per capita GDP levels of China, Japan, Taiwan, and Korea during the 1930s at the national level. Clearly, sectoral structural change came much faster in the smaller economies of Taiwan and Korea than that of China.[20] Overall,

### Table 16.1 Annual real growth rates of modern industry output in China and Japan, 1880–1936

|  | China (%) | Shanghai (%) | Japan (%) |
|---|---|---|---|
| 1880–1895 |  |  | 10.0 |
| 1895–1912 |  | 9.4 | 5.7 |
| 1912–1925 | 10.0 | 12 | 8.6 |
| 1925–1936 | 5.4 | 6.5 | 9.5 |

*Source*: D. Ma (2008), 'Economic growth in the Lower Yangzi region of China in 1911–1937: A Quantitative and Historical Perspective', *Journal of Economic History*, 68 (2), pp. 385–92, and sources cited therein.

**Table 16.2 GDP structure in East Asian countries**

|  |  | China (percentage of total) | Japan (percentage of total) | Taiwan (percentage of total) | Korea (percentage of total) |
|---|---|---|---|---|---|
| 1914–18 | Agriculture | 71 | 29 | 48 | 66 |
|  | Industry | 8 | 20 | 29 | 7 |
|  | Services | 21 | 51 | 23 | 24 |
| 1931–36 | Agriculture | 65 | 19 | 44 | 53 |
|  | Industry | 10 | 28 | 27 | 13 |
|  | Services | 25 | 53 | 29 | 34 |
| Annual per capita NDP growth rate in 1914–18 and 1931–36 |  | 0.53 | 1.4 | 1.5 | 1.1 |

*Source*: D. Ma (2008), 'Economic Growth in the Lower Yangzi Region of China in 1911–1937: A Quantitative and Historical Perspective', *Journal of Economic History*, 68 (2), pp. 385–92, and sources cited therein.

**Table 16.3 East Asian per capita GDPs in 1934–6 (in 1934–6 US dollars) and relative to the United States**

|  | United States | Japan | Taiwan | Korea | China |
|---|---|---|---|---|---|
| Per capita GDP (exchange rate conversion) | 574.7 | 77.1 | 49.2 | 29.1 | 20.1 |
| As percentage of US GDP | 100.0 | 13.4 | 8.6 | 5.1 | 3.5 |
| Per capita GDP (purchasing power parity conversion) | 574.7 | 180.8 | 129.6 | 70.9 | 63.6 |
| As percentage of US GDP | 100.0 | 31.5 | 22.6 | 12.3 | 11.1 |

*Source*: K. Fukao, D. Ma and T. Yuan (2007), 'Real GDP in Pre-war East Asia: A 1934–36 Benchmark Purchasing Power Parity Comparison with the U.S.', *Review of Income and Wealth*, 53 (3), Table 8.

Japanese economic development preceded that of China by nearly two decades and emerged as three times of that of China in the 1930s in purchasing power parity terms after controlling for domestic price differences.

## East Asia in the shadow of the Japanese Empire

The rapid modernization of Japan is one of the most significant events in world history. Accompanying this modernization was its immediate impact across East Asia, particularly across areas of shared cultural heritage. Japan's emergence on the international scene was initially seen as a challenge to the China-dominated tributary order. Being subject to a similar treaty port system, Meiji Japan manoeuvred itself from a semi-colonial status onto a relatively independent sovereign state, which, like all other 'civilizing European states', developed its own forms of imperialism in the region. Japanese imperialism in East Asia developed within the context of the unequal treaty port system (under the cloak of free trade) imposed by European imperialism. Slowly, however, Japanese imperialism became increasingly formal with the acquisition of Taiwan and Korea following the Sino-Japanese War of 1894–5 and the Russo-Japan War of 1904–05, respectively. It was in these two territories on the Chinese peripheries that Japan began a massive transfer of the Meiji modernization programme. Such a programme included the full-scale transplant of Japanese monetary and banking institutions, public infrastructural investment, and the transfer of industrial and agricultural technologies. It was later extended to include the education system. Both Korea and Taiwan were developed into major agricultural and raw material producers for the benefit of Japan.[21]

In the end, Japan's relationship with China was qualitatively different from that imposed on China by the Western powers through the treaty port system. The two countries shared a common culture and linguistic similarities and both had been the objects of Western gunboat diplomacy. Indeed, following Japan's victory over China in the 1890s, there emerged the notion that the Japanese, in repayment of their cultural debt to China, should help pull China up in the path of 'civilization'. Many Japanese felt empowered or even obliged by their successful modernization to help the Chinese climb the path to national wealth. But these yearnings for solidarity with China were often confounded by a sense of Japanese superiority, which partly laid an ideological basis for Japanese imperialism in China.

Equally important to the rise of Japanese imperialist sentiment is the country's changing economic structure. In 1902, Japanese investment in China was a mere 0.1 per cent of total foreign investment, but by 1931 it formed more than 50 per cent of total foreign investment in China. The total number of Japanese residents in China dwarfed the Western residents in China. In 1910, the total volume of Japanese commodity trade with China was about five times that of Korea and Taiwan combined. While that disparity declined over time as Japanese colonies developed important food crops, China remained an important exporter of key raw materials and a consumer market for Japanese manufactured goods.[22] The Japanese production and trade structure were maturing: while Japanese exports to Western Europe and North America remained confined to labour-intensive products, Japan became a major and highly competitive exporter of (capital and skill-intensive) manufactured goods to other parts of Asia.[23]

Japan's increasing penetration of the China market came at a time when Western powers were beginning to retreat and compromise with Chinese nationalism after the fall of Qing in 1911. More importantly, while British investment in China was only about 7 per cent of its overall foreign direct investment in 1929, Japanese investment in China reached about 90 per cent of the country's foreign direct investment in the 1930. According to Peter Duus, this may have prompted Japanese imperialism to turn from informal (maintained jointly within China by all the powers) to direct control (and a later full-scale invasion). This direct control started with the full annexation of Manchuria and the establishment of the puppet state there in 1931. The Japanese aggression however coincided with a global downturn. Beginning in 1929, China's economy faced a succession of shocks caused by the Great Depression and falling export demand, the severance of Manchuria in 1932 by the Japanese, and rapidly rising silver prices triggered by Britain's decision to exit the gold standard and the US Silver Purchase Act of 1934.

Considerable debate remains over how well the Chinese economy weathered the storm and the severity of the combined impact of these events on aggregate economic activity. But there is no dispute about what happened afterwards: the disastrous full-scale invasion of mainland China in 1937 degenerated into a protracted and brutal eight-year war, which spelled the end of nearly three decades of economic growth in East Asia. It is also ironic that the Sino-Japanese War marked the direct confrontation of Japanese imperialism against the newly risen Chinese nationalism, itself inspired by Japan's modernization success.

## Conclusion

An integrated global history is critical to our understanding of the past, present, and future of East Asia. In the absence of a single unified religion, East Asia was forged by shared culture and writing scripts which defined some important economic and social features. These in turn directed the long-term economic trajectory of this region. A shared identity served to enhance the diffusion of modernization and industrialization but also led to conflicts and warfare. In the aftermath of the Second World War, East Asia witnessed economic miracles in Japan and two of her former colonies, South Korea and Taiwan. The last three decades have also seen China's miraculous emergence as the world's second largest economy. These miracles would have been impossible without the positive cooperation and competition among East Asian countries. But changing political and economic imbalances could also lead to renewed tension or conflict. It is hoped that the shared heritage and identities will become the source of future cooperation rather than conflict in East Asia.

## Notes

1. E. Rawski (2015), *Early Modern China and Northeast Asia, Cross Border Perspectives*. Cambridge: Cambridge University Press.

2. D. Ma (2012), 'Political institution and long-run economic trajectory: Some lessons from two millennia of Chinese civilization', in M. Aoki, T. Kuran and G. Roland (eds), *Institutions and Comparative Economic Development*. Basingstoke: Palgrave Macmillan, 78–98.

3. Rawski, *Early Modern China*.

4. Rawski, *Early Modern China*.

5. T. Hamashita and H. Kawakatsu (1991), *Ajia Koekiken to Nihong Kogyoukyoka* [Asian Trading Networks and Japanese Industrialization 1500–1900]. Tokyo: Libro.

6.  Man-houng Lin (2006), *China Upside Down: Currency, Society, and Ideologies, 1808–1856*. Cambridge, MA: Harvard University Asia Center: Distributed by Harvard University Press.

7.  For a reinterpretation of the comparison between China and Japan based on a regional perspective, see D. Ma (2008), 'Economic growth in the Lower Yangzi region of China in 1911–1937: A quantitative and historical perspective', *Journal of Economic History*, 68 (2), 385–92.

8.  T. Hamashita, and H. Kawakatsu (1991), *Ajia Koekiken to Nihong Kogyoukyoka* [Asian Trading Networks and Japanese Industrialization 1500-1900]. Tokyo: Libro.

9.  J. Bolt and J. L. van Zanden (2014), 'The Maddison Project: Collaborative Research on Historical National Accounts', *Economic History Review*, 67 (3), 627–51.

10. A. Maddison (2007 [2nd ed.]), *Chinese Economic Performance in the Long Run*. Paris: Development Centre of the Organisation for Economic Co-operation and Development.

11. R. Allen, Jean-Pascal Bassino, Debin Ma, Christine Moll-Murata and Jan Luiten van Zanden (2011), 'Wages, prices, and living standards in China, Japan, and Europe, 1738–1925', *Economic History Review*, 64 (Supplement 1), 8–38.

12. It should be said that in comparison to the high level of Japanese numeracy, Chinese numeracy displayed great volatility during the nineteenth century. J. Baten, D. Ma, S. Morgan and Q. Wang (2010), 'Evolution of living standards and human capital in China in 18th–20th century', *Explorations in Economic History*, 47 (3), 347–59.

13. See L. Brandt, D. Ma and T. Rawski (2014), 'From Divergence to Convergence: Re-evaluating the History behind China's Economic Boom', *Journal of Economic Literature*, 52 (1), 45–123, for details.

14. Ma, 'Economic growth in the Lower Yanzi'.

15. Ma, 'Economic growth in the Lower Yanzi'.

16. Ma, 'Economic growth in the Lower Yanzi'.

17. Brandt, Ma and Rawski, 'From divergence to convergence'.

18. Brandt, Ma and Rawski, 'From divergence to convergence'.

19. For industrial growth in Taiwan and Korea during this period, see T. Mizouchi and M. Umemura (ed.) (1988), *Basic Economic Statistics of Former Japanese Colonies, 1895–1938*. Tokyo: Toyo Keizai Shinposha, 273 and 276, respectively. Note that as the growth spurt of modern industry in Japan started well before 1895, Japanese industrial expansion in twentieth century expanded from a larger base than Shanghai.

20. For the importance of Japanese imperial investment in social overhead capital and education in Korea and Taiwan in the facilitation of this rapid sectoral transformation and growth in GDP, see Anne Booth (2007), 'Did it really help to be a Japanese colony? East Asian economic performance in historical perspective', *Asia-Pacific Journal*, 5 (5), 1–26.

21. Mizouchi and Umemura (ed.), *Basic Economic Statistics*. Clearly in the long-run investment in education and infrastructure also provided a basis to support the rapid independent economic development of both regions after 1960. See Booth, 'Did it really help?'.

22. P. Duus (1989), 'Japan's informal empire in China, 1895–1937: An overview', in P. Duus, R. Myers and M. Peattie (eds), *The Japanese Informal Empire in China, 1895–1937*. New Jersey: Princeton University Press, xiii.

23. Duus, 'Japan's informal empire', 3.

# CHAPTER 17
# EUROPE IN THE WORLD, 1500-2000
*Peer Vries*

## A diverse continent

Europe's history of the last half millennium is one of almost uninterrupted warfare, culminating in the twentieth century in two disastrous world wars.[1] These violent conflicts were the main cause of the marked reduction in number of the continent's polities. At the end of the Middle Ages, Europe counted several hundred of them; immediately after the Second World War, only some thirty. At the very end of the period under discussion we see two trends: an increase of the number of polities because of the disintegration of the Soviet Union, Yugoslavia, and Czechoslovakia and a further reduction of the number of fully sovereign states as Europe's economic and political integration became deeper and wider. This increasing integration, however, did not create a homogenous economic entity, as will be pointed out at several occasions in this text. Differences in wealth, development, and growth between countries have continued to be substantial and in several cases even increased.

The units of analysis and comparison in this chapter will almost exclusively be states, as we currently know them. There are disadvantages to such a focus. It can easily become anachronistic and even in relatively tiny states in Europe regional differences were and often are substantial. The decision to nevertheless focus on states has been made for pragmatic reasons – the number of pages available, intelligibility and comparability, and the available data.

Until the sixteenth century the centre of gravity of Europe's civilization and economy had primarily been the Mediterranean area. In that century, the slow and protracted process started in which the region lost its primacy.[2] It became less 'integrated' because of the rise of the Ottoman Empire just when with the increasing importance of the Atlantic world the centre of the European economy shifted northwest. The Mediterranean economies, moreover, had few direct exchanges with the emerging Atlantic economy, and their overseas connections to East and Southeast Asia were less tight than those of the Dutch, the British, or the French. Southeastern Europe became part of the Ottoman Empire, which most scholars regard as retarding for its economy. That empire never directly engaged in the upcoming Atlantic economy. Its exchange with the Far East never became intense. The parts of Southeastern Europe that came under its rule were also only weakly integrated in the European economy as a whole, even in the nineteenth century, not least because of geographical reasons. Much of the rather low amount of their international trade, moreover, was in foreign

**Table 17.1 The position of the region 'Europe'* in the world (Europe as a percentage of the world)**

| Year | Land surface | Population | GDP** |
|------|-------------|-----------|-------|
| 1500 | < 4 | 16 | 20 |
| 1820 | < 4 | 16 | 27 |
| 1913 | < 4 | 19 | 38 |
| 2003 | < 4 | 8 | 21 |

* Here as in the entire chapter, without Russia, the Russian Empire, or the Soviet Union.

** The figures for GDP are, of course, for the period until 1913 estimates.

Source: A. Maddison (2007), *Contours of the World-Economy, 1–2030 AD. Essays in Macro-Economic History*. Oxford: Oxford University Press, 378 and 381, for population and GDP.

hands. The region became one of the poorest of Europe, which it still is.[3] Other parts of the Mediterranean world also saw their position change: the economy of Italy was probably already stagnating at the beginning of the early modern era. A widening gap emerged between a North that continued to be relatively speaking quite wealthy and a relatively poor South. Spain and Portugal became the centres of huge, primarily Atlantic, empires but nevertheless their economies faltered. Incomes per capita tended to stagnate or even decrease. Compared to Northwestern Europe they began to look poor and backward.[4] At the end of the twentieth century, notwithstanding sometimes quite impressive efforts at catching up, their income still was below the average of the Euro area.

Overall from the end of the sixteenth century onwards we see a retreat of the Mediterranean and a rise of the Atlantic. Northwestern Europe, which had been fairly marginal until the later Middle Ages – in particular in the case of the later Dutch Republic and the British Isles – became Europe's wealthiest and most dynamic region. Because of the British and Dutch role in European economic development they will receive quite some attention in the rest of this text, so I confine myself to this brief comment here.

Overall Central Europe – here for convenience defined as the lands of the Holy Roman and Habsburg empires – became more peripheral during the early modern era, although with important regional differences. Trade connections with Northern Italy, Castile and Aragon, and the Southern Low Countries became less intense. Its importance as producer of silver and iron declined. The German, non-Habsburg, regions of the Holy Roman Empire politically and economically lost leverage. Their economies were severely damaged during the Thirty Years' War (1618–48). In the eighteenth century, Prussia started to fill the political void, but it was only after 1870 that a unified Germany with a dynamic and strong economy emerged. From then onwards, Germany almost without interruption had the strongest single economy of Europe. The Habsburg Empire had great power status but apart from some regions – all in its Western half – like Bohemia, Silesia, and parts of present-day Austria, it continued to be relatively poor.[5] Yet, at the end of the twentieth century Austria had become one of the wealthiest countries in Europe. This is also the case for Switzerland that deserves separate mention here as a central European country that enjoyed autonomy for seven centuries and industrialized quite early.[6]

The economies of most of East, Central, and Southeastern Europe overall developed differently from those of North and Northwestern Europe. From the early sixteenth century, if not earlier, the region became more 'peripheral' and 'fell behind'. Previously existing states lost their independent statehood and became part of more 'coercion-intensive' polities like the Habsburg, Russian, or Ottoman empires, just when in Western Europe polities emerged with more potential for development that started reaping benefits of overseas expansion. There, however, also existed internal reasons. First and probably foremost is the re-institution or strengthening of 'feudal' structures. In particular, east of the Elbe, unfree labour became the rule in agriculture, where many scholars speak of a 'second serfdom' and in several other sectors of the economy. In towns, a more restrictive guild system began to prevail. Levels of urbanization were low and there was no strong modernizing bourgeoisie. The region participated in international trade, but it did so as a periphery. Intercontinental trade was all but absent.[7] After the Second World War, there was a major – but ultimately unsuccessful – effort to 'catch up' behind an Iron Curtain in a communist setting of planned development. When the curtain fell, most of the region returned to a peripheral position. Several countries even saw a sharp decrease in their GDP per capita.

The history of Northern Europe here defined as Scandinavia, including Finland and Iceland, has its ups and downs. It has never been economically or politically a powerful European 'core' region, although Sweden in the seventeenth century came close to it. Things have fundamentally changed here, in particular during the twentieth century. Over the last decades it has even become one of the richest and most developed parts of Europe.[8]

Differences in wealth in Europe in the period discussed here have always been substantial, as Tables 17.2 and 17.3 show. In the case of Table 17.2 they provide no more than very rough estimates, which, moreover, in several instances are not completely identical to those of the Table 17.3 for the years 1820 and 1870. For many countries we still lack sufficient good statistical information. Differences in patterns of development and levels of wealth are striking.[9] Eastern and Southeastern Europe, of which only the Polish case is presented in Tables 17.2 and 17.3, did not catch up with Western Europe since the beginning of the nineteenth century, while Southwestern Europe and certainly Northern Europe did manage to diminish or even close the gap.

The concept of Europe is not only problematic because of the substantial and shifting cleavages within the geographical entity that bears that name, but also because Europeans, over almost the entire period discussed here, held sovereignty over large regions outside their continent. By 1800 Western states – European states and their overseas settler

**Table 17.2 Comparative levels of GDP per capita in Europe, in real terms (United Kingdom in 1820 = 100)**

|                 | c. 1500 | c. 1700 | c. 1750 | 1820 | 1870 |
|-----------------|---------|---------|---------|------|------|
| United Kingdom  | 57      | 73      | 87      | 100  | 187  |
| The Netherlands | 67      | 109     | 109     | 107  | 162  |
| France          | n.a.    | n.a.    | n.a.    | 72   | 110  |
| Italy           | 83      | 71      | 76      | 65   | 88   |
| Spain           | 63      | 61      | 58      | 62   | 71   |
| Sweden          | 64      | 66      | 67      | 70   | 97   |
| Poland          | 50–54   | 38–42   | 34–37   | 41   | 55   |

*Source*: S. Broadberry and K. O'Rourke (2010), 'Introduction to Volume 1' in S. Broadberry and K. O'Rourke (eds), *The Cambridge Economic History of Modern Europe. Volume I: 1700–1870*. Cambridge: Cambridge University Press, p. 2.

**Table 17.3 GDP per capita in several European countries, 1820–2000, in real terms (Great Britain in 1960 = 100)**

|                 | 1820 | 1870 | 1910 | 1960 | 2000 |
|-----------------|------|------|------|------|------|
| Great Britain   | 23   | 37   | 53   | 100  | 243  |
| The Netherlands | 21   | 36   | 43   | 96   | 256  |
| France          | 13   | 22   | 34   | 86   | 235  |
| Italy           | 17   | 18   | 25   | 63   | 217  |
| Spain           |      | 14   | 22   | 36   | 182  |
| Sweden          | 10   | 16   | 29   | 100  | 241  |
| Poland          |      | 11   |      | 37   | 84   |

Calculated on the basis of J. L. van Zanden et al. (eds) (2014), *How Was Life? Global Well-Being since 1820*. Paris: OECD, p. 67.

colonies' offshoots – controlled some 35 per cent of the world's land surface. By 1914 they had increased that total to almost 85 per cent. In 1500 it had only been 7 per cent.

For many people all around the world globalization took the form of being colonized by Europeans (Table 17.4).[10] But when it comes to importance and size of their empires we again see big differences between different parts of Europe.

The economic consequences of being absorbed into a European empire differed too. The so-called Western offshoots (the settler colonies in the United States, Canada, Australia, and New Zealand) in the end all became rich. The United States became

**Table 17.4 Size and population of the overseas empires of the main colonial powers of Europe**

| | | | In 1760 | | |
|---|---|---|---|---|---|
| | Spain | Portugal | United Kingdom | The Netherlands | France |
| Area | 12.3 | 8.5 | 3.2 | 0.2 | 0.065 |
| Population | 18.8 | 1.6 | 2.8 | 3.3 | 0.6 |

| | | | In 1938 | | |
|---|---|---|---|---|---|
| | United Kingdom | France | Italy | Belgium | The Netherlands |
| Area | 33.6 | 12.2 | 3.4 | 2.4 | 2.1 |
| Population | 496.8 | 70.6 | 12.9 | 14.3 | 68.4 |

Data in million of square kilometres and million inhabitants.

*Source:* B. Etemad (2007), *Possessing the World: Taking the Measurements of Colonisation from the Eighteenth to the Twentieth Century.* New York: Berghahn Books, 135–136, 167, 171, 174 and 178.

independent already in the 1770s. The other three countries were integrated into the British Empire quite differently from 'normal' colonies. As a rule, colonies, British and otherwise, did *not* develop into wealthy countries.[11]

Discussing Europe in a global context over the period of half a millennium requires making clear choices. This text sets out to discuss developments that occurred in Europe's economic history over the last 500 years that are of worldwide relevance. I single out three: first, Europe's dominant role in creating a global economy; second, the fact that Europe became the first region in the world characterized by modern economic growth; and finally, Europe's political economy, in terms of how it actually worked and in terms of the prevailing ideas about it.

## Europe and globalization

Let us begin with economic globalization, that is, the increase in intensity, extent, speed, and impact of intercontinental economic contacts. Some caveats are in order. Firstly, the fact that focusing on Europe's intercontinental exchanges with the rest of the world can easily be misleading. Those exchanges were important but must be put into perspective. Trading bulk goods over a long distance, even over water, continued to be expensive and laborious until at least the second half of the nineteenth century. Even in Europe with its many waterways and its long coasts, regions in the interior often were hardly integrated in intercontinental networks of exchange.[12] Even at the very end of the twentieth century the bulk of trade by Europeans still was with other Europeans. For most of the period discussed, long-distance and certainly intercontinental trade was only a small fraction of total trade. Secondly, the focus in this text will be on European particularities and on European agency. That is because this is a text about Europe not because Europe would be exceptional in all respects or because the rest of the world would be without any agency.

Economic globalization was not a unilinear process. From Columbus and Vasco Da Gama onwards, it intensified. During the seventeenth century there was a setback, after which it got a new impulse in the next century. In the nineteenth century a major intensification of intercontinental exchanges set in that was only interrupted during the period between the two world wars. From the 1970s onwards, it became very intense.

The so-called Columbian Exchange of flora, fauna, and diseases between the Old and the New Worlds was probably the most consequential form of pre-industrial intercontinental exchange.[13] There was also an intercontinental transfer of people, first and foremost the transatlantic slave trade that brought enslaved people from Africa to the Americas. Europeans were heavily involved in it as slave traders and as consumers and sellers of the goods made through the use of slave labour. Between 1519 and 1867, some eleven million enslaved Africans were shipped from Africa to the Americas, almost half of them by Portuguese and Brazilians, some 28 per cent by British traders and some 13 per cent by French carriers, and the rest by people from the Dutch Republic, Spain, or the United States.[14] Europeans not only brought slaves to the Americas. They also traded slaves in Asia.[15] On top of that, over the entire early modern period, they imported in total some 600,000 enslaved people to Italy and some 375,000 enslaved Africans to the Iberian Peninsula. Less well known is the fact that Europeans could be enslaved by others: more than one million white Christian Europeans were enslaved by traders from North Africa, whereas some three million East Europeans were sold on slave markets in the Middle East.[16]

The number of people who left Europe for other continents over the entire pre-industrial period was rather small: for the Americas before 1820 only an estimated three million, and for Asia before 1800 only some two million, and for Africa certainly not more than 100,000 (Figure 17.1).

In discussing the main routes of pre-modern commodity trade, one must differentiate between the triangular trade between Europe, Africa, and the Americas, and the trade between Europe and Asia along the Cape.[17] In quantitative terms, the Atlantic world was more important as a trading zone for Europe than Asia. The goods exchanged between these zones were different too. From South and Central America, Europe imported bullion, sugar, and cotton. Together with tobacco, cotton also came from the southern states of what is now the United States. From the 1820s onwards, coffee was imported from Brazil. Europeans brought slaves and manufactured goods in return. From the northern half of the American continent came fish, furs, and wood. In return that region imported primarily manufactured goods from Europe. Africa provided mainly slaves and at times gold and ivory. It received mainly textiles, weapons, and also alcoholic drinks.

Asia provided 'Oriental' luxuries. It all began with spices coming from what now are Indonesia and India. Over time cotton textiles became India's most important export

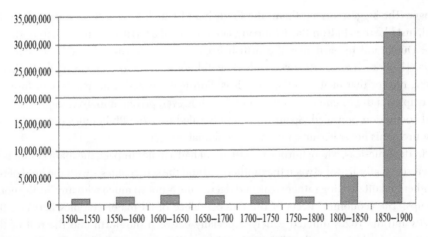

**Figure 17.1** European migration to other continents, 1500–1900.
*Source:* J. Lucassen and L. Lucassen (2009), 'The Mobility Transition Revisited, 1500–1900: What the European Case can Offer to Global History', *Journal of Global History*, 4 (3), p. 356.

product to Europe. In return Europeans mainly sent bullion. China's main exports to Europe consisted in porcelain, silk, raw as well as in the form of textiles, and from the last decades of the eighteenth century onwards almost exclusively tea. In return it received mainly American silver, directly from Mexico or indirectly via Europe. Japan for some time was an important exporter of silver. Later copper became its main export. Imports from Europe via the Dutch were confined to a variety of specific manufactured 'luxury' products. Closer to home the Ottoman Empire increasingly provided Europe with raw materials, over the eighteenth century in particular cotton. It imported mainly manufactured goods and colonial re-exports from Europe. The impact of Asian trade on Europe's economy as a whole continued to be quite confined till the end of the eighteenth century. The lubricating oil of this intercontinental trade consisted of bullion from Latin America. The drain of it to Asia certainly was substantial, but the bulk of the gold and more than half of the silver that Europe got from the Americas stayed in Europe.

Europe's trade tended to be organized differently depending on its trade partners. Spain's (or rather Castile's) and Portugal's governments as colonial rulers tried to regulate or in any case skim the trade between mother country and colonies. Full control was impossible especially in the Americas. Barriers to entry were low and smuggling, privateering, and piracy too attractive. Governments of other European countries faced the same problems. Overall, trade with 'the West' was less regulated and restricted than trade along the Cape. Chartered companies, for example, were less prominent in it. True enough, England's Hudson Bay Company continued to exist till the 1860s, but it was as much a territorial ruler – over a huge territory in what now is Canada – as an enterprise. In European trade with the East, the role of such companies – a kind of company-states that combined private enterprise and sovereign rights like the right to conclude treaties, have armies and navies, wage war, or coin money – was more substantial and lasted longer. The biggest among them, the English and Dutch East India companies, in the end, just like the Hudson Bay Company, acted more like territorial rulers than traders.[18] The Dutch and in particular the British became major territorial powers in parts of Asia. The French were less successful: They did not manage to keep strong footholds in India, nor for that matter in the Americas. Portugal was active in Asia too, in India in principle via the *Estado da India*. In practice, however, private initiative, improvisation, and corruption prevailed. Spain in Asia only ruled over the Philippines but for lack of resources this never became a successful colonial project.

In the Americas, where European settlement had a major impact, the main conflicts of interest actually arose between the motherland and the settler elites – with the hold of the motherland often being rather weak and decreasing – not so much with any 'indigenous' groups. The economic effects of the independence of all major colonies between the 1770s and the 1820s differed widely, especially between the north and the rest of the continent. In Africa, until well into the nineteenth century, European direct political leverage was marginal. European settlements were tiny. The Dutch settlement in South Africa with some 60,000 settlers of European descent was the only relative exception. In the big empires in Asia, Europeans for a long time were only on sufferance. Imperial China did trade with them but allowed them hardly any freedom of movement and manoeuvre on its territory. That would only change with the Opium Wars of the 1840s and 1850s. In Japan, between 1633 and 1639, the Tokugawa Shogunate enacted what has become known as the *sakoku* or 'locked country policy'. That stayed in effect until 1853. Except to some extent for the Dutch, the country became forbidden territory, at least for Europeans. Korea was even more closed to the outside world. The Mughal rulers initially considered the Europeans at best useful suppliers of goods and services and at worst a nuisance, but certainly not a serious threat. In particular in the case of the English, that proved to be a mistake. In the Ottoman Empire economic power relations changed too. In the beginning, with the Ottoman Empire at its heights, the so-called capitulations, grants by successive sultans to Christian nations conferring rights and privileges in favour of their subjects resident or trading in Ottoman dominions, were voluntary gifts. Over time, however, they became signs of European penetration and encroachment.

If possible Europeans tried to manipulate exchange. In particular overseas trade and politics were mixed up. Distinctions between the private and the public, including those between private and public violence, were blurred. Only a thin line separated trade, privateering, and piracy. Trade and empire building often went hand in hand. In particular European overseas imperialism had a peculiar twist. It combined exploration, control, and utilization[19] and involved sustained efforts to create a division of labour in which a European motherland functioned as 'core' and its overseas trade partners as peripheries.[20]

Until the second half of the eighteenth century, these peripheries were located first and foremost in the Americas, in small parts of Asia, in the slave-exporting regions of Africa whose 'slave-production' became an integral part of the emerging Western world system, and in those parts of Europe that had become peripheral to Northwestern Europe. Examples here are the Baltic region that provided the Dutch Republic with rye and materials needed for its fleet; Russia that exported flax, hemp, rye, and wood to Great Britain; Hungary that provided Northwestern Europe with cattle, or Ireland that until well into the nineteenth century functioned as a semi-colony of Britain.

In the European core the import of 'exotic' commodities like cocoa, coffee, spices, sugar, tea, tobacco, textiles, and porcelain led to changing patterns of consumption. Several scholars even speak of a 'consumer revolution'.[21] In the wealthier parts of Northwestern Europe the wish to consume Asian 'novelties' often acted as a driving force behind another revolution, the so-called industrious revolution: a substantial increase of the total supply of labour on the labour market as more people began to work longer and harder in order to earn more monetary income. Such industriousness often was accompanied by specialization, increasing market integration, and growth.[22] A third effect of imports from overseas consisted in the efforts undertaken to produce substitutes and sometimes export previously imported commodities as for example silk and cotton textiles and porcelain. When it was not possible to transfer production to the mother country, European merchants often transferred it to extra-European regions they controlled. Examples here would be the Dutch who began to grow coffee on Java or the British who started growing tea in India.

Between 1750 and 1850, that is, still before Western Europe could be called 'industrial', the global economic position of Europe or more generally 'the West' underwent major strengthening. In the Americas, the United States became politically independent but intensified its economic ties with its former colonizer Great Britain. Most of the Spanish colonies – but also Brazil – became part of the 'informal empire' of the United States and the United Kingdom. In Asia, too, Europeans increased their leverage. The Battle of Plassey in 1757 has become the symbol of Great Britain's rise in India, that actually had already begun earlier. With increasing political power, the British changed their trade relations with the country and also got some grip on production there.[23] The Ottoman Empire was 'opened' in 1838 by the Treaty of Balta Limani – with the United Kingdom – that stated that the empire would abolish all monopolies, allow British merchants and their collaborators full access to all Ottoman markets, and tax them equally to local merchants. Already from the first decades of the nineteenth century, silver had started leaving China as payment for opium, but the turning point here was the First Opium War (1839–42). After that war, the Qing Empire retained its formal independence, but lost much of its sovereignty. Japan was 'opened' from the 1850s onwards. It, too, signed unequal treaties but it never became a real periphery. In Southeast Asia, Great Britain, France, and the Netherlands further expanded their empires into what is today Malaysia, Cambodia, Laos, Vietnam, and Indonesia.

From the end of the eighteenth century and even more so after 1850 when industrialization deepened, the gap in wealth and power between 'the West' and 'the Rest' became so big that Western countries could start a new round of empire building. The clearest victim was Africa. The fact that parts of Europe industrialized would already have sufficed to create a worldwide 'Great Divergence'.[24] But its effect became even bigger because the industrializing countries in Europe also dominated global trade, transport, communication, and finance at a time when economic globalization switched into a higher gear. Global trade, to confine us to that aspect, not only increased but also changed character. Before, a very substantial part of what Europeans exported to other continents had not been produced by themselves. Now for about a century global trade became characterized by the 'Great Specialization', a global division of labour in which developed, 'industrialized' countries produced and exported manufactured goods while non-developed countries produced and exported primary commodities.

In order to facilitate their imports from their peripheries, European core countries invested enormous sums of money to create the relevant infrastructure there. Moreover, in the century between 1815 and 1914, more than forty million migrants left Europe for other continents, in particular the Americas and so provided extra labour for producing export commodities. The effects varied according to the region, but overall the outcome of this 'division of labour' was not positive for the non-developed countries. With the exception of Japan, countries outside the West not only 'failed' to industrialize; their manufacturing sector was also severely damaged by Western competition.[25]

The exact impact on the economies of European core countries of this global division of labour – that for 'old' peripheries had already originated before industrialization and the heydays of European imperialism – continues to be subject of acrimonious debate. The focus has long been on the extent to which 'unequal exchange' – and sheer coercion and extraction – enabled Western accumulation of capital.[26] With the increasing awareness that the motor of modern growth is innovation rather than accumulation, research now has broadened and takes on board all potential positive and negative effects of specializing in the production of certain goods.[27]

In global economic history, understandably, the focus is on the Great Divergence and the Great Specialization on a global scale. But economic development over roughly the last two centuries was not an even process in Europe itself either. There have also been shifts within the core of the 'Western' world itself. Until the First World War, Europe's industrial nations held global economic global primacy. After 1918, the United States took over and became not only the world's largest, but also increasingly its leading economy. The period of the Great Depression of the 1930s was an era of de-globalization in which intercontinental trade, investment, and migration decreased and the economies of European countries tended to become more closed.[28] The boom of the economies of Western Europe in the period 1945–73, after the backlash of the Great Depression and the Second World War, in a context of increasing trade between developed countries primarily was a matter of successfully catching up with the United States.

Several of the previous comments already took us to the last decades of the twentieth century. In the second half of that century, three major changes in Europe's global position occurred. Firstly, in a few decades, the decolonization of Europe's overseas empires unfolded. One of the effects was that between 1945 and the beginning of the 1990s, some five to seven million Europeans and non-Europeans alone left the (former) European colonies for Europe. They were joined by labour migrants from North Africa and Turkey. Secondly, the Great Specialization came to an end. Non-Western countries increasingly began to massively produce and export manufactured goods, whereas the most advanced parts of Europe 'de-industrialized'. And finally, the increasing integration of European economies into a common market allowed the continent to become a big global player. In 2000, the GDP of the countries of the European Union was about a quarter of global GDP, their exports some 40 per cent of global exports. But as indicated earlier on, integration did not mean convergence.

## Modern economic growth

Europe became the cradle of modern economic growth, that is, a sustained and substantial increase of GDP per capita in real terms. Before industrialization, the available natural resources set fairly strict limits to its economic growth and development. It experienced periods of 'efflorescence', but growth in such periods was fragile and as a rule short-lived.[29] The direct and overwhelming dependency on nature made the economy vulnerable and 'volatile' in the short run, and fairly stagnant in the long run. Even its most advanced economies, Great Britain and the Dutch Republic, increasing population easily led to economic problems or stagnation.[30]

Modern economic growth has taken different shapes but the same fundamental changes underlie all its varieties.[31] One is a major change in sources and use of energy away from the traditional energy sources such as muscle power, water, wind, and wood. Industrializing Europe increasingly began to rely on fossil fuels like coal, later oil and natural gas, and later still nuclear power as its main sources of energy, producing heat *and* power.[32] A second major change was in the materials used: Europe's modern economies began to thrive on iron, steel, concrete, and (mineral-based) synthetic materials instead of organic materials. The third major change was the fact that innovation became the most important motor of growth.

When industrialization began in Great Britain, waterpower still was important, but from the first decades of the nineteenth century, steam power became omnipresent in mechanized production and transport as for instance the railways. Steel, heavy engineering, electricity, and chemical industry were central in what is often called the 'Second Industrial Revolution' from roughly 1870 to 1914. After the First World War, oil, automobiles, and motorization held centre stage. After the Second World War, developed economies entered the age of mass production for mass consumption. With the digital revolution yet another new leading sector came to the fore.[33]

The emergence of modern growth is normally identified with industrialization. Clearly industry as such was very important, but innovation and the use of new sources of energy and new technologies can also lead to ever-increasing productivity in agriculture and services. The shift from the primary to the secondary and then tertiary sector, that is considered characteristic for modernizing economies, did indeed occur in all of Europe but with major differences in timing and intensity. Only rarely did industry employ over 50 per cent of the total labour force. The service sector eventually became by far the biggest sector in all advanced European economies. The growth of employment in the government sector, at least when it comes to civilian employment, needs separate mention. In several European countries, it employed up to 20 per cent of the labour force at the end of the twentieth century.[34]

There has never been one model of European industrialization. Ivan Berend distinguishes three varieties.[35] The first one is a fairly close and relatively early imitation of the British example characterized by the use of coal and the mechanized production of textiles and iron, using British technology. This route was taken in Great Britain, France, Switzerland, and to some extent in Austria and Bohemia after 1880. The second one, a route usually described as the 'the Second Industrial Revolution' with an emphasis on chemical industry, electricity, and automobiles, was best exemplified in Western parts of Germany but in the later phases of their industrialization France, Switzerland, and Northern Italy also followed it, just like Great Britain and Belgium, and Scandinavia after 1870. The third one is characterized by industrialization based on agricultural products and food processing. Classic examples would here be Denmark and the Netherlands, and to a lesser extent Switzerland and Austria /Bohemia, in particular in the period 1840–80.

Differences in wealth, growth, development, and economic 'modernity' did not disappear with industrialization (Table 17.5). Over the long nineteenth century (1780s–1914) attempts at economic modernization in Europe were successful in Western Europe including Switzerland, Austria, Bohemia, and Silesia, and with some retardation in Scandinavia. The industrial trajectory of Ireland, Eastern parts of Germany, and Southern Italy long was much less successful. Medium income levels as compared to Western Europe and a certain level of industrialization were reached in most of Central Europe, the Baltic region, Finland, and Ireland. Then there was a third group of countries with some islands of modernity but where, overall, modernization failed. That group would include Russia, the Iberian Peninsula, and Southern Italy. A lack of industrialization, only a semblance of economic modernization, and the lowest income levels of Europe

**Table 17.5  Levels of industrialization in Europe, 1750–1900  (United Kingdom in 1900 = 100)**

|  | 1750 | 1800 | 1830 | 1860 | 1880 | 1900 |
|---|---|---|---|---|---|---|
| Europe as a whole | 8 | 8 | 11 | 16 | 24 | 35 |
| United Kingdom | 10 | 16 | 25 | 64 | 87 | 100 |
| Habsburg Empire | 7 | 7 | 8 | 11 | 15 | 23 |
| France | 9 | 9 | 12 | 20 | 28 | 39 |
| German States/Germany | 8 | 8 | 9 | 15 | 25 | 52 |
| Italian States/Italy | 8 | 8 | 8 | 10 | 12 | 17 |

Source: P. Bairoch (1982), 'International industrialization levels from 1750 to 1980', *Journal of European Economic History*, 11 (1/2), 269–333.

could be found in the Balkans and the easternmost and southernmost borderlands of the Habsburg Empire. With some exceptions, a listing of regions in 'order of development' at the end of the twentieth century would be fairly similar. Levels of industrialization and development *inside* countries as a rule also were quite different, as the process of development often knows virtuous and vicious circles.

## Europe's political economy

Scholars claiming that Europe's economy was exceptional in its institutional set-up almost without exception refer to the fact that it was the continent where 'capitalism' first came to full maturity. As long as capitalism is not simply equated with a market economy based on private property and private enterprise with 'free' and, as mainstream economics defines it, 'fair' competition, that indeed seems correct. Market economies, especially for consumer goods, have been fairly normal throughout global history. In the variety of capitalism that was unique to certain parts of Europe, markets, private property, and private enterprise indeed were prominent. But those markets often did *not* function according to the logic of 'perfect' competition. They existed in combination, in particular in certain sectors, with state intervention going far beyond just enabling the market to work. The driving forces of modern capitalist development – large-scale capital accumulation and major technological innovations – do not easily flourish in a setting characterized by completely open and fair competition. Most scholars would now agree that competition was important in pushing innovation and creating growth in Europe. The wealthiest parts of Europe were regions with high levels of market integration.[36] Although the market mechanism was often tampered with, apart from some specific instances, it was not eliminated in Western Europe. But one should not underestimate the importance of forms of market manipulation and regulation like monopolies, oligopolies, and cartels, and of protectionism and government regulation.

One must differentiate according to time and place and realize that there were different kinds of markets. Scholars like Marx and Weber claiming that Europe was 'the cradle of capitalism' have always emphasized the fundamental importance of a labour market with free labour. Yet, even in Europe such free wage labour was far from normal. Simplifying to the extreme, one can distinguish three labour regimes in agriculture, the main sector of production, until well into the nineteenth century: a regime with chiefly unfree, manorial subordination; one in which peasants and their families constituted the main labour force; and one with chiefly wage labour.[37] The first regime was predominant in Central and Eastern Europe, but certainly not unknown elsewhere in Europe. In Prussia serfdom was only formally abolished in 1806 and in Austria-Hungary only in 1848. The second regime became predominant in England and the western and northern parts of what is now the Netherlands, but also on large *latifundia* in, for example, Southern Spain, Portugal, or Italy. A peasant, household mode of production could be found all over Europe but was predominant in most of France, present-day Germany, and Scandinavia.[38] City air did not always make you free in every respect. Until 1810 only members of a guild could practise a certain trade in Prussia. That rule was only abolished in the rest of Germany in 1869, and even then not entirely. In Austria it existed till 1859. Free wage labour, that 'even' in Europe for very long coexisted with all sorts of un-free labour, certainly was not uniquely European but it probably was more common there than elsewhere in the world and the number of wage labourers increased over the eighteenth and nineteenth centuries. In Great Britain, the first industrial nation, it was already common before industrialization.

In practice, occupations – and economic sectors – were not neatly distinguishable. Manufacturing and later industry tend to be associated with towns and factories, but for very long they continued to be found in the countryside, with towns specializing in processes that required skilled labour and advanced implements. Many people, in particular in the countryside, operated in an 'economy of makeshifts', switching between activities like taking care of their own tiny farms (if they still had land) and selling some of their produce or their labour. By far the majority of them worked in a system called 'putting out', in which they got raw materials from merchants, processed them, and returned the processed materials to those same merchants, who then paid them a piece rate. Less common was the so-called *Kaufsystem* in which the actual producers themselves acquired the raw materials, processed, and sold them. Although in particular the first form of domestic manufacturing has been described as 'proto-industry', it often was not a preparatory stage of industrialization at all.[39] Next to markets for labour, there also emerged markets for land and money. Overall, land markets continued to be subject to restrictions for very long – in several countries till far into the nineteenth century – as land owned by the Church or aristocrats often was all but inalienable. Money markets apparently worked quite well. Interest rates in any case, overall, first and foremost in Northwest Europe, were relatively low.

A second claim that is often made with regard to European capitalism is that it was characterized by exceptionally well-described and protected property rights.[40] That claim exaggerates 'European exceptionalism' and assumes that securing property rights suffices to create modern growth, which is incorrect. That some sort of protection of property is indispensable for sustained growth is not disputed.

This emphasis on protection highlights the role of the modern state as a guarantor of those property rights and creator of institutional arrangements without which economic growth cannot be sustained. The fact that Europe over the past two centuries has had so many functioning states is already fairly exceptional: the world is full of 'failed' states. In such states chances of having modern economic growth are nil. But what is striking is that in those parts of Europe that first knew modern economic growth the state actually was very present and active in the economy. In most European countries rulers have always tried to influence and change the economy. Innumerable examples exist of government initiatives and policies that failed completely. But the wealthiest European countries all had states that at one time or another wanted to be and effectively *were* 'developmental'.

The modern state as we now define it was a European invention that slowly took shape and only really 'matured' after the French Revolution.[41] Its actual policies and power differed substantially according to time and place. Most European polities *before* the first decades of the nineteenth century are described as 'fiscal-military states' and their policies as 'mercantilist'. The expression 'fiscal-military state' speaks for itself. Such states – or maybe better 'proto-states' – had levels of government revenue (and expenditure and indebtedness) that were higher than in any of the major world empires, and spent the bulk of their revenues on war.[42] Obviously high taxes and high spending on the military are not necessarily good for the economy, even though high deficit spending may have had 'Keynesian' effects. But in several European states, first and foremost those with some form of political representation for those who provided the state with substantial amounts of taxes and especially loans, the permanent bargaining over claims and counterclaims between rulers and the ruled embedded the state in society, which often led to institutional innovations, strengthening of the economy, and higher revenues.[43]

Most of the fiscal-military states pursued mercantilist policies. There has never been an elaborate system of thought called 'mercantilism', but there is a set of core notions that are referred to time and again. They have to be understood against the background of fierce competition between states in which increased production and trade counted primarily as means to strengthen the state. Domestically mercantilist rulers strove to eliminate hindrances to production and trade and to create efficient markets. That as such could already help strengthen the state. The most effective way to do that, so it was claimed, was to stimulate, protect, *and* tax the production and export of high value-added goods and confine imports to raw materials. As far as possible, domestic products should substitute for expensive imports. In their view, competitiveness of the national economy and the military strength of their states could further be enhanced if subjects worked hard and at low wages. Labour therefore had to be disciplined. Creating monopolies, such as the chartered companies, was also supposed to make the country more competitive. Besides, it made revenue collection easier for government.[44] Mercantilists were permanently 'benchmarking' and comparing their state and economy with that of others, something which European rulers and ruled have continued to do ever since.[45] Often the effects of mercantilist policies on the economy were negative, and many of the positive 'developmental' effects actually unintended and indirect. Such policies, moreover, were not, as often suggested, typical only for seventeenth- and eighteenth-century Europe. Even in Great Britain, the home country of Adam Smith, mercantilist measures, for example, very high tariffs, remained in force well into the nineteenth century. But often mercantilism 'worked'.

After the Napoleonic Wars, the nature of the state and of state spending began to change. The fiscal-military state seemed to have reached its limits. No longer were the bulk of expenditures for the military. Civil spending on material (transport and communication) and immaterial infrastructure (first and foremost education) became much more important. In the period from c. 1820 to 1870 states tended to become somewhat leaner and less interventionist, especially when it comes to international trade. From the 1870s onwards, however, many countries in Europe – though not the United Kingdom – again became more protectionist, in particular because of pressure by agricultural interests that felt threatened by imports from the New World and Russia. The growth in the volume of international trade slackened. Domestically governments could no longer ignore the 'social question' and had to care more about the welfare of their citizens. Ideologies and scholarly disciplines emerged that claimed to know how 'the economy' worked.

With the First World War, state intervention reached an unprecedented level of intensity as war more than ever depended on total mobilization of resources. In particular in Germany the war economy came close to what would later be called a 'planned economy'. During what turned out to be the interwar period, the Great Depression in particular hit Western Europe, but the ensuing problems led to a Europe-wide new wave of large-scale state intervention. In the few European countries that continued to be parliamentary democracies, governments attempted to combat unemployment and protect their economies. In some cases they cautiously experimented with 'Keynesian' policies. In countries that had authoritarian, fascist/national-socialist, and communist rule, dictatorial intervention in or even control of the economy became normal to make the country strong and catch up with potential enemy countries. The Second World War, of course, again meant massive state planning and control.

The post-war period saw the gradual emergence of the welfare state in Western Europe.[46] Thinking in terms of laissez-faire had lost most of its attraction during the Great Depression. Recovering from the massive destruction of the Second World War required massive state intervention. Citizens in now democratic states increasingly regarded the state as guarantor of basic welfare and promoter of growth. Advanced economies also required a quickly expanding infrastructure in the form of transport, communication, and education. Government expenditure and the presence of the government in the economy increased accordingly. Whatever the political colour of government and whatever its plans or claims, the state in terms of taxes, expenditures, debts, or employment continued to grow almost without interruption (Table 17.6).

In the 1980s, there was increasing talk of liberalizing the economy. In the sphere of banking and finance that certainly occurred, though for the rest of the economy it proved very hard to tame the Leviathan.

Modern economic growth in Europe never was simply the result of a rise of the market and laissez-faire. It required a state that did not confine itself to being night watchman. State intervention played a role in *all* successful and unsuccessful processes of industrialization and economic modernization. The connection between power and profit moreover was never severed. Countries that wanted to catch up realized that it would require a strong, modern and active state. This suggests that Europe's impact on the world economy was not confined to the realm of the economic and the material. The global impact of its thinking about 'the economy', the way it should be organized, and its economic policies were just as pervasive. Between the French Revolution till at least the Second World War, Europe was by far the major producer and exporter of economic doctrines and practices. Economists like to focus on materialist factors but actually the global impact of European economic ideas like mercantilism, laissez-faire liberalism, socialism and communism, and Keynesianism can hardly be overestimated.

Table 17.6  Government spending* as a percentage of GDP, 1870–2009

| | 1870 | 1913 | 1920 | 1937 | 1960 | 1980 | 1990 | 2000 | 2005 | 2009 |
|---|---|---|---|---|---|---|---|---|---|---|
| Austria | 10.5 | 17.0 | 14.7 | 20.6 | 35.7 | 48.1 | 38.6 | 52.1 | 50.2 | 52.3 |
| Belgium | n.a. | 13.8 | 22.1 | 21.8 | 30.3 | 58.6 | 54.8 | 49.1 | 52.0 | 54.0 |
| Britain | 9.4 | 12.7 | 26.2 | 30.0 | 32.2 | 43.0 | 39.9 | 36.6 | 40.6 | 47.2 |
| France | 12.6 | 17.0 | 27.6 | 29.0 | 34.6 | 46.1 | 49.8 | 51.6 | 53.4 | 56.0 |
| Germany | 10.0 | 14.8 | 25.0 | 34.1 | 32.4 | 47.9 | 45.1 | 45.1 | 46.8 | 47.6 |
| Italy | 13.7 | 17.1 | 30.1 | 31.1 | 30.1 | 42.1 | 53.4 | 46.2 | 48.2 | 51.9 |
| The Netherlands | 9.1 | 9.0 | 13.5 | 19.0 | 33.7 | 55.8 | 54.1 | 44.2 | 44.8 | 50.0 |
| Spain | n.a. | 11.0 | 8.3 | 13.2 | 18.8 | 32.2 | 42.0 | 39.1 | 38.4 | 45.8 |
| Sweden | 5.7 | 10.4 | 10.9 | 16.5 | 31.0 | 60.1 | 59.1 | 52.7 | 51.8 | 52.7 |
| Switzerland | 16.5 | 14.0 | 17.0 | 24.1 | 17.2 | 32.8 | 33.5 | 33.7 | 37.3 | 36.7 |

*1870–1937 central government; 1960–2009 general government.

Source: 'Taming Leviathan: A Special Report on the Future of the State', *The Economist*, 19 March 2011, p. 4.

## Conclusion

At the beginning of the twenty-first century the relative decline of 'Europe' on the global scene is undeniable. Its military and political power has dwindled and it certainly no longer rules the waves. It still is an economy of major global importance but even if it actually were an economic unity, it no longer can be called 'dominant'. Modern economic growth no longer is a Western monopoly. Other parts of the world show more impressive growth figures and more dynamism than Europe. Europe's states and economies and mainstream European ideas about the economy are no longer a source of inspiration.

## Notes

1. My definition of Europe is strictly geographical. It encompasses the westernmost part of Eurasia without Russia/the Russian Empire/the Soviet Union. For debates on the question *what* and *where* Europe is, see K. Wilson and J. van der Dussen (eds) (1993), *What Is Europe?* Milton Keynes: The Open University.

2. F. Tabak (2008), *The Waning of the Mediterranean, 1550–1870: A Geohistorical Approach.* Baltimore: Johns Hopkins University Press.

3. For the economic history of the Ottoman Empire, see H. Inalcik and D. Quataert (eds) (1994), *An Economic and Social History of the Ottoman Empire.* Cambridge: Cambridge University Press. Two volumes. For the situation since 1800, see M. Morys (ed), *Economic History of Central, East and Southeast Europe, 1800 to the Present Day,* forthcoming.

4. See C-A. Nogal and L. Prados de la Escosura (2012), 'The rise and fall of Spain 1270–1850', *Economic History Review,* 66 (1), 1–37; N. Palma and J. Reis, *Portuguese Demography and Economic Growth, 1500–1850,* http://studylib.net/doc/12315291/portuguese-demography-and-economic-growth--1500-1850--1; P. Malanima (2011), 'The long decline of a leading economy: GDP in Central and Northern Italy, 1300–1913', *European Review of Economic History,* 15 (3), 169–219.

5. For the economic history of 'Germany', see M. North (2005), *Deutsche Wirtschaftsgeschichte. Ein Jahrtausend im Überblick,* 2nd rev. edn. Munich: C.H. Beck. For the economic history of the Habsburg Empire, I refer to general histories of this empire.

6. For Austria, see for example, R. Sandgruber (1995), *Ökonomie und Politik. Österreichische Wirtschaftsgeschichte vom Mittelalter bis zur Gegenwart.* Vienna: Ueberreuter. For Switzerland, see for example, J.-F. Bergier (1983), *Wirtschaftsgeschichte der Schweiz: Von den Anfängen bis zur Gegenwart.* Cologne and Zurich: Benzinger.

7. I. Berend (2003), *History Derailed: Central and Eastern Europe in the Long Nineteenth Century.* Berkeley, Los Angeles and London: University of California Press; M. Cerman (2012), *Villagers and Lords in Eastern Europe, 1300–1800.* Basingstoke: Palgrave Macmillan; D. Chirot (ed.) (1989), *The Origins of Backwardness in Eastern Europe. Economics and Politics from the Middle Ages until the Early Twentieth Century.* Berkeley, Los Angeles and London: University of California Press. For the situation during communist times, see I. Berend (2006), *An Economic History of Twentieth-Century Europe: Economic Regimes from Laissez-Faire to Globalization.* Cambridge: Cambridge University Press.

8. See the references to Scandinavia in Berend, *Economic History of Twentieth-Century Europe.*

9. See Berend, *Economic History of Twentieth-Century Europe*, chs. 4–6, and G. Therborn, (1995), *European Modernity and Beyond: The Trajectory of European Societies, 1945–2000*. London, Thousand Oaks and New Delhi: Sage Publications Ltd.

10. D. Abernethy (2000), *The Dynamics of Global Dominance. European Overseas Empires 1415–1980*. New Haven and London: Yale University Press.

11. See G. Bertocchi and F. Canova (2002), 'Did colonization matter for growth? An empirical exploration into the historical causes of Africa's underdevelopment', *European Economic Review*, 46 (10), 1851–71, and G. Gozzini (2010), *Un'idea di giustizia. Globalizzazione e ineguaglianza dalla rivoluzione industriale a oggi*. Turin: Bollati Boringhieri, ch. 4.

12. See Studer, *The Great Divergence Reconsidered*, ch. 4, and V. Bateman (2012), *Markets and Growth in Early Modern Europe*. London: Pickering and Chatto.

13. N. Nunn and N. Qian (2010), 'The Columbian Exchange: A history of disease, food and ideas', *Journal of Economic Perspectives*, 24 (2), 163–88. See also, J. R. McNeill's chapter in this volume.

14. R. Findlay and K. O'Rourke (2007), *Power and Plenty. Trade, War, and the World Economy in the Second Millennium*. Princeton and Oxford: Princeton University Press, 228.

15. For European slave trade in the Indian Ocean region, see R. Allen (2015), *European Slave Trading in the Indian Ocean, 1500–1850*. Athens: Ohio University Press.

16. L. Lucassen (2016), 'Connecting the world: Migration and globalization in the second millennium', in C. Antunes and K. Fatah-Black (eds), *Explorations in History and Globalization*. Abingdon and New York: Routledge, 19–46, 29–30.

17. I focus on Europe's role in intercontinental trade. For intercontinental trade in a more global perspective, see the chapter by Giorgio Riello and Tirthankar Roy in this volume.

18. See P. J. Stern (2011), *The Company-State: Corporate Sovereignty and the Early Modern Foundations of the British Empire in India*. New York: Oxford University Press

19. Abernethy, *Dynamics of Global Dominance*.

20. I. Wallerstein (1974, 1980, 1989 and 2011), *The Modern World-System*. The volumes have been published in different places and not all by the same publisher.

21. F. Trentmann (2016), *Empire of Things: How We Became a World of Consumers, from the Fifteenth Century to the Twenty-First*. London: Allen Lane. See further the contribution by Maxine Berg to this volume.

22. J. de Vries (2008), *The Industrious Revolution: Consumer Behavior and the Household Economy, 1650 to the Present*. Cambridge and New York: Cambridge University Press.

23. See the chapter by Giorgio Riello and Tirthankar Roy in this volume.

24. See the chapter by Prasannan Parthasarathi and Kenneth Pomeranz in this volume.

25. Findlay and O'Rourke, *Power and Plenty*, ch. 7; J. G. Williamson (2011), *Trade and Poverty: When the Third World Fell Behind*. Cambridge, MA and London: MIT Press.

26. P. Emmer, O. Pétré-Grenouilleau and J. Roitman (eds) (2006), *A Deus ex Machina Revisited. Atlantic Colonial Trade and European Economic Development*. Leiden: Brill; P. O'Brien and L. Prados de la Escosura (eds) (1998), *The Costs and Benefits of European Imperialism from the Conquest of Ceuta, 1415, To the Treaty of Lusaka, 1974. Proceedings of the Twelfth Economic History Congress*. Madrid: Published as *Revista de Historia Económica*,16, first issue of 1998.

27. E. Reinert (2007), *How Rich Countries got Rich ... and Why Poor Countries Stay Poor*. New York: Caroll and Graf, chs. 4, 5 and 8; and Williamson, *Trade and Poverty*.

28. Findlay and O'Rourke, *Power and Plenty*, ch. 8.

29. See the contribution by Jack Goldstone in this volume.

30. For the logic of pre-industrial (advanced) organic economies, see E. A. Wrigley (2016), *The Path to Sustained Growth: England's Transition from an Organic Economy to an Industrial Revolution*. Cambridge: Cambridge University Press.

31. For the concept 'modern economic growth', see P. Vries (2013), *Escaping Poverty. The Origins of Modern Economic Growth*. Vienna and Göttingen: Vienna University Press and Vandenhoeck und Ruprecht.

32. A. Kander, P. Malanima and P. Warde (2013), *Power to the People: Energy in Europe over the Last Five Centuries*. Princeton and Oxford: Princeton University Press.

33. C. Freeman and F. Louçã (2001), *As Time Goes By. From the Industrial Revolutions to the Information Revolution*. Oxford and New York: Oxford University Press.

34. For changes in sectorial employment, see A. Carreras (2003), 'El siglo XX, entre rupturas y prosperidad (1914–2000)' in A. di Vittorio (ed), *Historia Económica de Europa*. Barcelona: Critica, 303–435, 324 and 327, and Therborn, *European Modernity and Beyond*, ch. 4.

35. I. Berend (2013), *An Economic History of Nineteenth-Century Europe: Diversity and Industrialization*. Cambridge: Cambridge University Press, ch. 5.

36. V. Bateman (2012), *Markets and Growth in Early Modern Europe*. London: Pickering and Chatto.

37. See the chapter by Alessandro Stanziani in this volume.

38. For the situation in Central and Eastern Europe, see note 7. For the emergence of capitalist agriculture in Great Britain and the Netherlands, see M. Overton (1996), *Agricultural Revolution in England. The Transformation of the Agrarian Economy 1500-1860*. Cambridge: Cambridge University Press; and J. de Vries (1974), The *Dutch Rural Economy in the Golden Age, 1500–1700*. New Haven: Yale University Press. Very informative and detailed is T. Scott (ed.) (1998), *The Peasantries of Europe: From the Fourteenth to the Eighteenth Centuries*. London and New York: Longman.

39. M. Cerman and S. Ogilvie (eds) (1996), *European Proto-Industrialization: An Introductory Handbook*. Cambridge: Cambridge University Press.

40. See for example D. Acemoglu and J. Robinson (2012), *Why Nations Fail. The Origins of Power, Prosperity and Poverty*. London: Profile.

41. P. Vries (2016), 'States: A subject in global history', in C. Antunes and K. Fatah-Black (eds), *Explorations in History and Globalization*. London and New York: Routledge, 155–76.

42. P. Vries (2015), *State, Economy and the Great Divergence. Great Britain and China, 1680-1850s*. London: Bloomsbury Academic, under 'fiscal-military state'.

43. M. Dincecco (2011), *Political Transformations and Public Finances. Europe, 1650-1913*. Cambridge: Cambridge University Press; D. Stasavage (2011), *States of Credit. Size, Power and the Development of European Polities*. Princeton and Oxford: Princeton University Press.

44. P. Roessner (ed.) (2016), *Economic Growth and the Origins of Modern Political Economy: Economic Reasons of State, 1500–2000*. Abingdon and New York: Routledge.

45. S. Reinert (2011), *Translating Empire: Emulation and the Origins of Political Economy*. Cambridge, MA and London: Harvard University Press.

46. For a short introduction, see D. Garland (2016) *The Welfare State: A Very Short Introduction*. Oxford: Oxford University Press. A quantitative analysis is provided by P. Lindert (2004), *Growing Public. Social Spending and Economic Growth since the Eighteenth Century*. Cambridge: Cambridge University Press.

# CHAPTER 18
## SOUTH ASIA IN THE WORLD ECONOMY, 1600–1950

*Bishnupriya Gupta and Tirthankar Roy*

### Defining South Asia

The South Asian Association for Regional Cooperation demarcates South Asia as a world region consisting of six large countries, Afghanistan, India, Pakistan, Bangladesh, Nepal, and Sri Lanka, and two smaller ones, Bhutan and Maldives. Together these countries contain about a fifth of the world's population today. Most historical debates on economic change and globalization in this territory, however, relate to the area now included in India, Pakistan, and Bangladesh. This is so because the rule of two long-lasting powerful empires, the Mughal (1526–c. 1720) and the British empires (c. 1765–1947), extended over a large part of the combined territory of the three countries, imparting a certain consistency in the political and economic history of these countries. The imperial connection extended to Afghanistan in an uneven fashion. The history of lower Burma (Myanmar), which was ruled by the British, also overlaps with the history of mainland South Asia in important ways. Yet these two countries were also distinct from the mainland on many points. Sri Lanka or Ceylon was ruled by a different entity from that of British India. Nepal, Bhutan, and Maldives were not colonized. The historical scholarship centred on these countries, therefore, does not speak directly to the scholarship that has developed on mainland South Asia. This chapter, therefore, will define South Asia as the combined territory of India, Pakistan, and Bangladesh. The term 'India' will be used interchangeably with South Asia to refer to the Indian subcontinent under the two empires of the Mughal and British.

Even this region demonstrates diversity in geographical and political terms, and it will be useful to examine this briefly before discussing the major debates and controversies about the region's economic history. Geographically, the region can be divided into four zones – the Himalayas, the Indo-Gangetic Basin (the floodplains of the Ganges and the Indus), the arid or semi-arid areas including the Deccan Plateau, and the littoral. Much of South Asia has a tropical climate, with a hot season that lasts half the year, broken by the southwest and northeast monsoon rains. The monsoon, the rivers that flow through the Indo-Gangetic Basin, and good soil conditions in the floodplains make agriculture possible, but extreme aridity also makes it seasonal and often dependent on expensive irrigation systems. Yet although agricultural conditions are uneven, South Asia's position in the middle of the Indian Ocean sustained a great maritime trade with West and East Asia along the coastal zone. The integration of markets away from the coast depended on navigable rivers in the north and land routes used by pack bullocks before the advent of the railways from the middle of the nineteenth century. The region saw large variations in prices across regions as well as frequent famines, driven by the weather and political conflicts.

Politically, the region can be divided into two types. The Indo-Gangetic Basin forms one type. The flat terrain and good agriculture supported a lot of overland trade, as well as wheeled and river traffic, urbanization, and thus strong states for centuries. The empires sustained themselves by means of agricultural taxation. Not all of the 700,000 square kilometres of the basin was integrated; the Bengal Delta in particular was intermittently part of imperial states that formed in north India. But a great deal of this zone was politically integrated. These conditions occurred in the Deccan Plateau to a more limited extent. In the arid areas, the uplands, and near the coasts, states tended to be smaller in extent and less powerful. Political and military power was more contested. Agriculture was more precarious, and overland trade dependent on the expensive and inefficient system of bullock caravans.

This brief overview of geography and politics should give us a sufficient backdrop for introducing the key historiographical debates around South Asia's encounter with the world economy from the seventeenth century. Two sets of historiographical debates will frame this chapter: one relating to the eighteenth-century passage of empires and the other on the impact of colonialism on development. The context for both the debates is set within the European expansion in the Asian commercial world.

## Europeans in South Asian trade

South Asia had been a trading zone for millennia. The Mughal Empire traded a great deal with West and Central Asia by road and by sea. The coastal areas, as we have seen, traded with maritime Asia on both sides of the Indian Ocean.

The *bazaars* symbolized a well-developed commercial system. Local communities of traders engaged in internal trade in grain and industrial goods. Some artisans worked directly for the nobility or the government; others sold to the merchants involved in long-distance trade. There was widespread use of 'hundis' or bills of exchange reflecting the well-developed network of banking and commerce. Indian merchant ships carried goods to Alexandria, Basra, and Baghdad to the west and to Sumatra in the east, but were not sturdy enough to sail the China seas. Commodities traded included not only raw silk, but also manufactured goods such as textiles. Both China and India imported bullion from outside, spices from Southeast Asia, horses from West Asia, and ivory from East Africa.

This booming trade in the Indian Ocean and South China Sea was comparable to the European trade. One key difference in the institutional setting between India and Europe was that customary community laws and the long-term relationship between members of the same social network governed the system of trade and commerce in India rather than a formal system of universal law as in Europe. The contract enforcement mechanism of the Indian trading communities was similar to the private order institution highlighted by the work of Avner Greif.[1] Caste- and community-based networks of Hindus, Muslims, Jains, Parsis, and Baghdadi Jews specialized in different trading operations at different locations.[2] Their commercial exchange depended on maintaining trust and reputation of members who belonged to the community, and exercised the primary means of contract enforcement.

From the 1600s, a new element was added to this picture: European merchants, some of whom operated as employees of highly organized companies. The arrival of the European trading companies disrupted the existing trading pattern, though only gradually. Indian cotton textiles were previously traded all over the Indian Ocean region. Increasingly in the early eighteenth century, Indian textile exports were directed to European markets.[3] This trade was in the hands of the European trading companies from the seventeenth century through monopoly trading rights granted by European governments. Like many other merchant communities in the area, the European companies negotiated with the local rulers the right to conduct trade and sign treaties. The treaties allowed trading posts to be established along the Indian littoral. The two main organizations were the Dutch and the English East India companies. They imported silver from Europe to purchase cloth, silk, and spices. The textile weavers entered into contracts with the companies to supply specified types of cloth over a period of time. In return the companies provided them with advances to buy raw material and cover their living costs. Indian calicoes and muslins became items of fashion and were sold in European, African, and American markets as well as in East Asia. Trade in textiles began to rapidly increase, and rising exports from India created a picture of prosperity in the urban centres.

European expansion and Indian Ocean trade joined in the early seventeenth century along the South Asian coast. Intense rivalry among Europeans and the British East India Company's need to protect a trade monopoly also drew the Europeans into politics from time to time. The political engagement involved mainly the Mughals or their vassals until the early eighteenth century. From about 1720, the Mughal Empire started breaking apart into a number of 'successor' states, and the field of political engagement shifted to these states. Anglo-French conflict in Europe spilled over into India, and complicated these processes. In the 1760s, the British East India Company had established areas of strong influence, even indirect rule, in Bengal and in the state near Madras known as Carnatic. By 1800, the British Empire was more or less an accomplished fact.

Two major historical debates about South Asia address the causes and consequences of these eighteenth-century shifts. One questions whether the eighteenth century was a period of decline or a period of growth, the other why Indo-European trade led to a new empire. In other words, why did British merchants take over state power?

## The eighteenth-century transition

The context of the former question lies in the nineteenth-century account of how the British came to acquire state power, emphasizing that anarchy and warfare among successor states made a third-party intervention likely. A state of anarchy points at a dark age in economic history, followed by a new era of flourishing enterprise after the takeover of power by the British. However, was the eighteenth century really a time of decline? This 'imperialist' narrative of how India came to be ruled by the British stayed more or less intact until the 1970s. Some historians of imperialism used Karl Marx's notion of a 'primitive accumulation' to suggest that officers of the company were driven by a desire, not to save India from anarchy, but to plunder its wealth. However, they did not challenge the orthodox view of the eighteenth century as a dark age.

That idea was questioned in the 1980s, through new accounts of the eighteenth century offered by historians at Cambridge, notably C. A. Bayly and David Washbrook.[4] Their work revealed the significant extent of capital accumulation by Indian merchants and bankers in the eighteenth century. Some of the successor states ruled over rich territories with lots of trade. Warfare and revenue farming improved the political clout of bankers. European enterprise needed the association with, and partnership of, Indian merchants. Almost the entire credit of the East India Company (hereafter Company), until the Indian Mutiny in 1857, came from Indian bankers. These historians, in other words, described a world in which overseas merchants and capitalists in the interior zones developed compatible interests, and both seemed to do better, not worse, in the eighteenth century.[5]

A deeper view of the emergence of an empire from trade began to form out of this reinterpretation, giving birth to the second of the two main debates on the eighteenth century, questioning why trade led to an empire, or why European merchants took over state power. Older views of the Company's successes on the battlefield during the imperialist wars focused on the imbalance of military strength or the disunity among the Indian rivals. Newer perspectives helped change the existing discourse in at least three ways.

First, to a significant extent, warfare in eighteenth-century India was a reflection of warfare in contemporary Europe. The two huge processes of state formation were more interdependent than it might seem from the Indian-bound explanations of the Company's rise. The eighteenth-century political process in South Asia was a chapter in what Bayly calls The Birth of the Modern World, in which Europe's own state-making and commercial expansion into Asia was a part.[6] Second, whereas historians previously saw conflict, in the new interpretations, they now saw consensus in the form of alliances. The Company's acquisition of state power between the 1740s and the 1770s did not happen through outright conquest. And therefore, the idea of alliance is an attractive one. It works particularly well in the context of Bengal, where a palace intrigue involved a section of the Company officers. This idea also has possibilities as a broader paradigm for understanding Indo-European relationships at this time.

Some of these revisionist writings suggest a broad continuity between Indian history before and after the collapse of the Mughal Empire. The Company could be seen as just another Indian type of state. As will be discussed more below, other contributors to these debates emphasize discontinuity and the European origin of the new state to explain its success.

Third, whereas the older views of Company's ascendance focused on military capability alone, new works interpreted the Company's comparative advantage in the battlefields differently. We should add that the theme of military capability has also received an emphasis in Phil Hoffman's recent work, which connects European history and global economic history in a new fashion.[7] On the other hand, research using South Asian data points at two ways the Company represented a distinctively European state in the South Asian setting. The oversight the British Parliament exercised over its operations in India made the Company a more credible ally among contending powers in the late-eighteenth-century South Asia.[8] Military conquest came with the right to revenue collection, and changed the nature of trade between Britain and India. The East India Company, as a trading agent, exchanged bullion for textiles. Now the textiles could be bought by tax revenues paid to the Company as the ruler.

The Company marked itself out as a distinctively European power in the way it undertook institutional reforms to the land ownership structure in Bengal. This process had begun between 1772 and 1793, when the rulers of the Indian territories acquired by the British East India Company set up a centralized land tax collection system replacing the old feudal system that relied on warlords and intermediaries to do the job for the ruler. The transition owed not only to the capacity of the Company to coerce and threaten the intermediaries, known as the zamindars, but also to an understanding reached with them. In Bengal, the understanding took the form of the Permanent Settlement, where the zamindars received ownership rights over the land they once collected taxes from, but ceased to enjoy sovereign and military power over them. The move had complex origins, including, as Ranajit Guha had shown, the influence of physiocrat doctrines that privileged private land ownership.[9] However fiscal and military motives also played roles, and evidently paid off when there was a sharp rise in tax collection in the early nineteenth century. The Company used the fiscal capacity to create a standing army, ending dependence on allies and mercenaries, who still ruled in other states. According to this second approach, a superior ability to raise resources was the reason why the British succeeded in establishing a stable rule, which lasted for so long in South Asia, and why it prevailed over its rivals and imposed its command on the princely states.[10]

## British Empire and the economy of South Asia

The British Empire in South Asia, which rose to power between the mid-eighteenth and mid-nineteenth centuries, achieved a degree of political, bureaucratic, and military centralization that the region had not seen before. Britain by this time had abolished Corn Laws and with that protective tariffs. As the first country to embrace the doctrine of free trade, it imposed it on India. As South Asia integrated into the world economy, trade, investment, and migration rose to far higher levels than before. The trade to GDP ratio increased dramatically, from 2–3 per cent in the mid-1800s to 20 per cent on the eve of the First World War. Though only a small proportion of British capital went to land scarce colonies,[11] South Asia received a large share of this investment. British capital went mainly into the railways to develop a modern transport network.

Nationalist historians have argued that the railways connected the agricultural hinterland to the ports and paved the way for the rising volume of trade in agricultural goods that met the demand for food and raw material in industrial Britain.[12] India also provided the much-needed outlet for industrial goods, in particular textiles. Millions of Indians emigrated to work in the plantation colonies of the British Empire in the far away tropical lands of Fiji and the West Indies as well as closer to home in Malaya and Ceylon. Consequently, the Indian economy de-industrialized and became more agricultural. There is a counternarrative, however, one that points out that the scale of the de-industrialization cannot be precisely measured and that there was a reversal in the fortunes of traditional industry including textiles from around 1900, thanks to product differentiation. Only some product groups competed with machine-made alternatives.[13]

## Measures of globalization: Volume and composition of trade

The first phase of globalization began in 1870 with the introduction of new technology in intercontinental telegraph, shipping, the opening up of the Suez Canal, and thousands of miles of railway networks built in different parts of the world with British capital. Sailing ships were replaced by steam, bringing down transport costs together with the shortening of the trade route from Europe to Asia. Conditions to bring about a fast increase in trade were all there. The British Empire also removed another barrier to trade: tariffs and trading rules. The creation of an international market under the hegemony of Britain brought with it an international division of labour defined by comparative advantage.

The decline of Indian textile exports, faced with cheaper textiles of the modern cotton industry, and the integration of the Indian economy into the empire created new sectors of export. South Asia's comparative advantage was in the production of agricultural commodities, while British advantage lay in manufacturing. As the British economy became more industrial, it relied on imported food and raw materials from the rest of the world. South Asia became an important supplier. This was reflected in the changes in the composition of Indian trade. Figures 18.1a and 18.1b show the rise in the merchandise trade from 1840 to 1914. Both imports and exports rose, but the share of trade with Britain did not rise comparably. India's exports were more diversified by country than Indian imports. Total imports and imports from Britain rose in line until the end of the nineteenth century. Thereafter, India began to import more from the rest of the world. For exports, Britain was less important in the Indian merchandise trade after the end of the American Civil War, during which most of the raw cotton used in the British cotton textile industry was supplied by India.

India's net exports were positive all through this period and rising as shown in Figure 18.1c. However, the net exports with the United Kingdom turned negative from 1870s. India's reliance on British imports was larger than Indian exports to Britain, suggesting that imperial connections in trade may have been more advantageous to Britain. India

**Figure 18.1** (a) Merchandise exports from India, 1840–1920 (in millions GB£); (b) Merchandise Imports to India, 1840–1920 (in millions GB£); and (c) Indian net exports, 1840–1920 (in millions GB£). *Source*: Constructed from Statistical Abstracts of British India.

imported mainly industrial goods. The import of machinery from Britain rose with the rise of modern industry in India. The Indian railway infrastructure was set up through British investment and also relied on the import of rolling stock and other equipment from Britain.

Table 18.1 shows that the composition of exports underwent significant changes. Cotton piece goods accounted for the largest share in exported merchandise in 1811, yet by 1850 this was insignificant. Raw cotton, indigo, and opium constituted 80 per cent of total exports. In half a century, the composition of India's export trade had changed dramatically. By 1935, tea had emerged as the second largest export after raw cotton. New products emerged such as raw jute and manufactured jute goods. Indigo, opium, and sugar declined as exportables. The rise in exports of cotton goods from the late nineteenth century reflected the growing importance of the domestic modern industry and its competitive advantage in markets in Asia. Agricultural exports increased at 4 per cent per year between 1876 and 1913.

## The impact of globalization on the economy of South Asia

What effect did this have on production and productivity?

The effect of trade on growth and the implications of trade in agricultural goods as opposed to trade in manufactured goods are debated topics. The literature on trade and growth suggests that specialization by comparative advantage increases welfare. What matters is factor endowment-based specialization. Countries with abundant land relative to labour gain by specializing in agricultural products, while labour abundance provides comparative advantage in industrial products. Both countries can gain by specializing and trading. The Prebisch-Singer thesis cautioned us against this by showing empirically that terms of trade of agricultural products relative to industrial products have declined from the middle of the nineteenth century to the middle of the twentieth century.[14] Therefore specialization in agricultural production can adversely affect economic development. Since then, Frankel and Romer have showed, using cross-country data from the second half of the twentieth century, that trade has a causal positive effect on economic growth. Output per capita depends on the volume of trade. Evidence from nineteenth century is much more mixed.[15] Mitchener and Weidenmier show that being a colony increased the volume of trade.[16] Pascali uses cross-country data to show that for the colonies trade had a negative effect on indicators of economic development.[17]

From within Indian economic history, a few other dimensions of the globalization process have generated a great deal of controversy. Three such debates are especially important. First, if free trade destroyed a part of the indigenous textile industry, how large and how bad was the impact? Second, if average levels of living standards in India rapidly fell behind Western European levels from the 1800s, was this 'divergence' due to globalization? Did colonization contribute to the divergence? Third, although a great deal of the exports came from agriculture, why did peasants not seem to gain from the process? Let us consider these three aspects separately.

**Table 18.1  Changing composition of Indian trade, 1811–1935**

| | Raw cotton | Cotton goods | Indigo | Raw silk | Food grains | Raw jute | Jute goods | Opium | Sugar | Tea |
|---|---|---|---|---|---|---|---|---|---|---|
| 1811 | 4.9 | 33.0 | 18.5 | 8.3 | | | | 23.8 | 1.5 | |
| 1828 | 15.0 | 11.0 | 27.0 | 10.0 | | | | 17.0 | 4.0 | |
| 1850 | 19.1 | 3.7 | 10.9 | 3.8 | 4.1 | 1.1 | 0.9 | 30.1 | 10.0 | 0.2 |
| 1870 | 33.2 | 2.5 | 5.8 | | 8.1 | 4.7 | 0.6 | | | 2.1 |
| 1890 | 16.5 | 9.5 | 3.1 | | 19.5 | 7.6 | 2.5 | | | 5.3 |
| 1910 | 17.2 | 6.0 | 0.2 | | 18.4 | 7.4 | 8.1 | | | 5.9 |
| 1935 | 21.0 | 1.3 | | | 13.5* | 8.5 | 14.5 | | | 12.3 |

*Source:* K.N. Chaudhuri (1983), 'Foreign Trade and Balance of Payments', in Dharma Kumar and Meghnad Desai (eds), *The Cambridge Economic History of India*, Vol. 2. Cambridge: Cambridge University Press, Tables 10.10 and 10.11.

## De-industrialization

In the first half of the nineteenth century, there was a fall in industrial employment, at first driven by the decline of textile exports and then by the rising market share of British industrial goods. The penetration of British textiles in the Indian market followed a slightly different chronology. Several authors show that the decline in the share of Indian textiles in the domestic market occurred mainly between 1850 and 1880.[18] In 1850 imports were roughly 10 per cent of domestic consumption, but by 1880 imports supplied 60 per cent of domestic consumption. Thereafter Indian cotton mills began to take over a share in the Indian market. The textile market expanded not only in response to population growth but also due to a rise in per capita cloth consumption as the relative price of textiles declined.

The decline of traditional industries and the loss of industrial employment is known as de-industrialization. There have been several notable attempts to measure the extent of the decline; the majority of these deal with eastern India.[19] Bagchi showed that the proportion of the working population engaged in industry was higher in 1800 at around 15–18 per cent, compared to 9–10 per cent in 1900. The most recent of these estimates by Ray shows that de-industrialization affected 4 per cent of the workforce over several decades in the nineteenth century. This was a significant figure, but not a catastrophe. Another recent paper by Clingingsmith and Williamson reaches the same conclusion, calling the early nineteenth century a period of 'weak de-industrialization' that shows a relative, rather than an absolute, decline of industry.[20]

The corresponding loss of income is harder to measure because the large hand-spinning industry mainly employed part-time domestic workers. The opportunity cost of shifting out of this activity was low. The income loss, therefore, should be smaller than the employment loss. The effect of de-industrialization on social welfare is also difficult to measure. There was a rise in unemployment. At the same time the massive fall in yarn and cloth prices arising from the higher productivity of the British industries enabled more consumption of cloth. Handloom weavers started to use imported yarn, which increased the profitability of cloth production. Per capita consumption of cloth rose from 11 yards in 1880 to 15 in 1913 and to 17 in 1930. The net effect is therefore ambiguous.

New research by Broadberry and Gupta sheds light on the chronology of changing comparative advantage of British textiles in India.[21] The textile industry in Britain saw total factor productivity growth with the introduction of new technology, while textile technology in Indian industry changed little. British products became competitive in the home market between 1770 and 1790. British products became competitive in third markets between 1790 and 1820. Consequently, India's exports began to decline. It was only after 1830 that British goods saw a high enough productivity increase to displace Indian goods in the Indian market. British total factor productivity was twice as high as that of Indian products and increased to three and a half times between 1680 and 1790. The price of British goods was twice as high in 1680, but only 35 per cent as that of Indian textiles goods in 1820 (Table 18.2).

Table 18.2  Productivity and price advantage of British textile goods over Indian goods (India = 100)

| Year | Total factor inputs | FOB price | Total factor productivity |
|------|---------------------|-----------|---------------------------|
| 1680 | 206 | 200 | 206 |
| 1770 | 270 | 200 | 270 |
| 1790 | 357 | 147 | 357 |
| 1820 | 150 | 35  | 150 |

Source: S. Broadberry, and B. Gupta (2009), 'Lancashire, India, and Shifting Competitive Advantage in Cotton Textiles, 1700–1850: The Neglected Role of Factor Prices', *Economic History Review*, 62 (2), Table 9.

The free trade policy imposed by the colonial state on India encouraged the growth of the cloth trade but did not protect domestic industry as in many other countries, including Germany and the United States. Might the Indian textile industry have survived with a protectionist policy? The magnitude of the price difference between British and Indian textiles was so large that it is difficult to conceptualize a high enough rate of tariff that could have protected the hand-spinning sector. What if tariff rates of 20–40 per cent, as adopted by many European countries and the United States, had been imposed? This might have prolonged the demise of some sectors of the handloom industry. Tariffs, however, might have had a positive impact on the nascent modern textile mills, which developed from the 1860s despite the absence of any kind of state support.

This discussion leaves two big questions unanswered. First, why did any Indian artisan producer of textiles survive at all? Artisans supplied nearly a quarter or more of the cotton cloth market as late as 1942, and employed well over two million full-time workers. Studies on artisanal weaving point at the diversity of consumption norms in India, and the fact that, in certain types of clothing, Indian consumers continued to buy handmade goods even when machine-made alternatives were available.[22] Second, why did a mill industry develop in India that competed directly with Manchester? The Indian merchants involved in the raw cotton trade had made large profits during the American Civil War. When these profits collapsed at the end of the war, they invested in modern cotton textile firms and began to produce yarn and cloth for local markets. The textile machinery producers in Britain were only too willing to sell to Indian entrepreneurs. Indian entry into modern industry was facilitated by profits made in the cotton trade, domestic availability of raw cotton, low wages, and the easy terms on which Indians could buy machines and hire foremen abroad.[23] Indian machine-made goods made inroads into the domestic market for textiles at the cost of both imports and traditional products. Imports per capita had risen from 1 yard in 1840 to 7 yards in 1880, but the increase slowed down and by 1930 the number had declined to 5 yards.

*Divergence*

The conventional narrative has been that something special happened with the Industrial Revolution in Britain. The economy of Britain moved from a Malthusian equilibrium to modern economic growth, while most other countries fell behind. India was another example of retaining extensive growth until the middle of the twentieth century.

The timing of the Great Divergence has generated a large literature. The California School and the world historians, however, propose a different view. They claim that colonization was a primary determinant of the Great Divergence. This literature sees 1800 as the starting point of the divergence between Europe and Asia. In the eighteenth century, living standards in the rest of the world were on a par with the developed parts of Europe, such as Britain (Pomeranz on China, and Parthasarathi on India; see the contribution by Pomeranz and Parthasarathi in this volume).[24] Others argue that the divergence began before colonization and may be explained in terms of a large high productivity urban sector in Northwest Europe.[25] New research shows that Britain was the first country to move out of the Malthusian trap, and much earlier than the advent of the Industrial Revolution.[26] High mortality due to war and disease in the expanding urban sectors shifted the economy to a low population growth regime and allowed per capita income to rise in England.[27] Per capita GDP declined or stagnated in most other parts of the world, making way for the Great Divergence.

Systematic quantitative evidence of wages and incomes puts this date in the middle of the seventeenth century for India. Broadberry and Gupta (2006) use a large data set on silver and grain wages from different parts of India. While the silver wage was one-fifth of the British level in 1600, the grain wage was over 80 per cent due to the low price of food grains in India, suggesting that the differences in living standards was not large. However, this difference widened over time, driven partly by a decline in wage in India and by a rise in Britain. Allen et al.'s (2011) estimates using welfare ratios of consumption baskets confirm this picture. While most countries were at a basic subsistence level, London wages bought much more than a barebones consumption basket.

Estimates of per capita GDP put that of India at 62 per cent of the British level in 1600 and show a decline all the way up to the middle of the nineteenth century.[28] The average Indian was worse off in 1750 compared to 1600 (Table 18.3). This evidence suggests that the Great Divergence began well before the Industrial Revolution. The widening of the divergence after 1800 was mainly driven by a rapid increase in British GDP per capita, while the Indian GDP per capita stagnated. The evidence suggests that Indian per capita income declined slowly but steadily during the golden age of the textile trade. As the textile trade declined and India turned into an exporter of agricultural commodities, the per capita GDP grew a little in the first phase of globalization but stagnated mostly in the nineteenth century and after 1914 (Table 18.4).

The timing of the decline is important in order to find explanations. There are two different explanations with very different implications for the role of colonization and

### Table 18.3  Measuring the Great Divergence

| Year | Indian grain wage as percentage of British wage | Indian GDP per capita as percentage of British GDP per capita |
|------|------------------------------------------------|---------------------------------------------------------------|
| 1600 | 21 | 62 |
| 1650 | 27 | 59 |
| 1700 | 25 | 40 |
| 1750 | 21 | 34 |
| 1800 | 14 | 28 |
| 1850 | 12 | 19 |

*Note*: Grain wage is nominal wage divided by the price of the local grain.

*Source*: S. Broadberry, and B. Gupta (2006), 'The Early Modern Great Divergence: Wages, Prices and Economic Development in Europe and Asia, 1500–1800', *Economic History Review*, 59 (1), pp. 2–31; and S. Broadberry et al. (2015), 'India and the Great Divergence: An Anglo-Indian comparison of GDP per capita, 1600–1871', *Explorations in Economic History*, 55 (1), pp. 58–75.

### Table 18.4  Economic growth in the long run

|  | National income (percentage per year) | Per capita income (percentage per year) |
|--|---------------------------------------|-----------------------------------------|
| 1860–85 | 1.8 | 1.2 |
| 1885–1900 | 1.0 | 0.5 |
| 1900–14 | 1.4 | 1.0 |
| 1914–47 | 1.1 | 0.1 |
| 1900–2000 | 2.0 | 1.0 |
| 1900–50 | 1.4 | 0.0 |

*Source*: T. Roy (2006), *The Economic History of India, 1857–1947*. New Delhi: Oxford University Press, Table 3.1.

globalization on economic development. First, if the decline in living standards occurred after 1800, we can think of colonization and integration into a global economy in a system of 'unequal exchange' as a possible explanation. Colonization of India began in the mid-eighteenth century. The world economy became increasingly integrated in the nineteenth century through colonization and technological changes in transportation. The Industrial Revolution in Britain created demand for raw material for industry. The textile industry was at the centre of the Industrial Revolution and British textile products competed with Indian textiles in the world market. In this scenario, the decline in the

Indian textile trade and the consequent decline of industrial activity in India may be an important factor in explaining the decline in per capita GDP and living standards. However, if the decline began closer to 1700, then the decline must be explained in terms of a failure to raise productivity in the largest sector, agriculture.

The first explanation in the literature uses very little quantitative evidence. Parthasarathi's work on the living standards of Indian weavers is an exception. Instead, this literature points to the thriving trade in textiles and other commodities from the Indian subcontinent in the seventeenth and the eighteenth centuries as indicative of a prosperous economy. Although the Indian economy did not fit the picture of a backward, self-sufficient village economy, the presence of a vibrant trading sector does not tell us much about the size of this urban economy. The Indian urbanization rate was at its highest at 15 per cent in 1600 and declined slowly until the nineteenth century, when the decline accelerated. In 1871, India's urban population stood at 9 per cent. Indian living standards declined during the years of a prosperous trade in textiles.[29] There is no doubt that the decline of the textile trade had some effect, but its magnitude was not large enough to explain the stagnation of per capita GDP.

How large was the textile trade? Reliable estimates relate to European trade with Asia. However, it is difficult to gain such estimates of the Indian Ocean trade carried out by Indian merchants. Om Prakash calculates the employment arising from the export trade from Bengal in the eighteenth century at less than 11 per cent. If trade by Asian traders was included, this number would be higher, but unlikely to be more than 15 per cent for India as the whole. Bengal was one of most globalized and industrialized regions with 15–18 per cent employment in industry in 1801. The share of industry for India overall was lower. In Britain, on the eve of the Industrial Revolution, the share of industrial employment in total male labour force was 24 per cent, rising to over 47 per cent in 1840 with a similar proportion of the population living in urban areas. The pre-colonial Indian economy, though a major exporter of industrial goods in the world, was not an industrial economy.

Figure 18.2 shows that the trend in per capita GDP tracks per capita agricultural output, but bears no relationship to per capita industrial output. Agricultural exports increased in the nineteenth century, when GDP per capita shows a slight positive trend or stagnation. Therefore, it is difficult to argue that the decline in textile exports had serious consequences for the economy overall. Certainly, there were regional effects, but in the aggregate rise in agricultural exports stabilized incomes. The agricultural sector employed two-thirds of the labour force and therefore it had a more significant effect on the economy.

## Agricultural Stagnation

Even as agricultural trade grew, peasant incomes on average did not. There was, however, considerable regional variation to this picture. The regions growing wheat

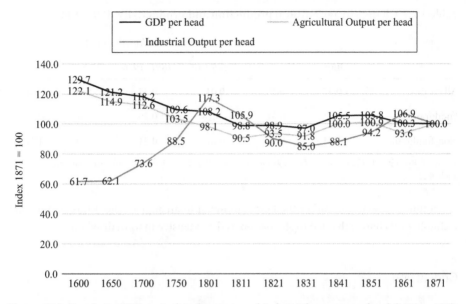

**Figure 18.2** Trends in GDP, agricultural output, and industrial output per head (1871 = 100). *Source*: Constructed from data in S. Broadberry et al. (2015), 'India and the Great Divergence: An Anglo-Indian Comparison of GDP Per Capita, 1600–1871', *Explorations in Economic History*, 55 (1), pp. 58–75.

did better than those cultivating rice. Western India did better than eastern India. The colonial government embarked on a policy of infrastructure building, and the construction of the railway network integrated markets, while the creation of the irrigation network was on a much smaller scale and had strong regional bias. Expenditure on irrigation was small compared to that for the railways. The share of capital formation in GDP remained less than a quarter than was achieved after 1947. Within this limited investment, agriculture had a small share which declined over time.[30]

Although the share of spending on irrigation was low, the colonial government built one of the largest irrigation networks in the world. Large areas were covered in some regions, but only 20 per cent of the total cultivated land was irrigated. Agricultural output increased at the extensive margin as expansion of land under cultivation came through increasing provision of water and irrigation. Overall, there was a difference in productivity growth between food and non-food agricultural products, which may suggest that rising agricultural productivity in cash crops fitted well with the objectives of colonial trade (Table 18.5).

However, there is little evidence that most irrigation was directed to non-food cash crops, which were the main exportable, at the expense of food grains. Yield per acre in wheat increased on irrigated land. Wheat exports rose too. Falling productivity in food grains was driven by falling agricultural productivity in rice. The failure to raise agricultural productivity led to stagnation under colonial rule. This is not due to increasing share of

**Table 18.5  Change in agricultural production and productivity, 1891–1946**

| | Output | Acreage | Yield/acre | Growth in yield per acre | | |
|---|---|---|---|---|---|---|
| | | | | 1891–1916 | 1916–21 | 1921–46 |
| All crops | 0.37 | 0.40 | 0.01 | 0.47 | −0.36 | −0.02 |
| Foodgrains | 0.11 | 0.31 | −0.18 | 0.29 | −0.63 | −0.44 |
| Non-foodgrains | 1.31 | 0.42 | 0.67 | 0.81 | 0.34 | 1.16 |

*Source:* T. Roy (2006), *The Economic History of India, 1857-1947.* New Delhi: Oxford University Press, Table 4.2.

agricultural exports, but rather the failure to invest in an appropriate infrastructure and technological change that led to stagnation as the extensive margin dried up.

## Conclusion

This chapter has traced the transformation of the South Asian economy from 1600s to the end of British colonial rule. It traces the rise and fall of the textile export trade and its political implications. India lost its status as an exporter of industrial goods after 1800 and became an exporter of food and raw materials to the industrial economy of Britain. This transformation had little to do with India's colonial status and subordination to British trade policy. The main reason for the shift in Indian advantage in the cotton textile market came from the superior and more productive technology of the Industrial Revolution.

In the long run, average levels of living were depressed in India. As India began to export increasing quantities of primary products, per capita GDP did not decline further. Instead it rose at a very slow rate in the nineteenth century and then stagnated in the twentieth century. The neglect of agricultural investment by the colonial government and the consequent failure to raise agricultural productivity account for the lack of intensive growth in the Indian economy. India's integration into the global economy from the nineteenth century had little consequences for actual economic growth.

## Notes

1. A. Greif (2006), *Institutions and the Path to the Modern Economy: Lessons from Medieval trade.* Cambridge: Cambridge University Press.
2. U. Dasgupta (2001), *The World of the Indian Ocean Merchant, 1500-1800.* New Delhi: Oxford University Press.
3. K. N. Chaudhuri (1978), *The Trading World of Asia and the English East India Company, 1660-1760.* Cambridge, Cambridge University Press; S. Chaudhury (1995), *From Prosperity to Decline: Eighteenth Century Bengal.* New Delhi: Manohar.
4. C. A. Bayly (1983), *Rulers, Townsmen and Bazaars: North Indian Society in the Age of British Expansion, 1770-1870.* Cambridge: Cambridge University Press; D. Washbrook

(2007), 'India in the early modern world economy: Modes of production, reproduction and exchange', *Journal of Global History*, 2 (1), 87–111.

5. L. Subramanian (1987), 'Banias and the British: The role of indigenous credit in the process of imperial expansion in western India in the second half of the eighteenth century', *Modern Asian Studies*, 21 (3), 473–510; T. Roy (2013), 'Rethinking the origins of British India: State formation and military-fiscal undertakings in an eighteenth-century world region', *Modern Asian Studies*, 47 (4), 1125–56; C. Markovits (2017), 'The Indian economy and the British Empire in the Company period: Some additional reflections around an essay by David Washbrook', *Modern Asian Studies*, 51 (2), 375–98.

6. C. A. Bayly (2003), *The Birth of the Modern World, 1780-1914*. London: Wiley-Blackwell.

7. P. T. Hoffman (2015), *Why Did Europe Conquer the World?*. Princeton: Princeton University Press.

8. M. Oak and A. V. Swamy (2012), 'Myopia or strategic behavior? Indian regimes and the East India Company in late eighteenth century India', *Explorations in Economic History*, 49 (3), 352–66.

9. R. Guha (1982), *A Rule of Property for Bengal: An Essay on the Idea of Permanent Settlement*. New Delhi: Orient Longman.

10. T. Roy (2013), *An Economic History of Early Modern India*. London: Routledge.

11. Most of British investment was in the land-abundant colonies of North America and Australia.

12. For a discussion, see Dan Bogart and Latika Chaudhary (2016), 'Railways in colonial India: An economic achievement?', in Latika Chaudhary, Bishnupriya Gupta, Tirthankar Roy, and Anand V. Swamy (eds), *A New Economic History of Colonial India*. Abingdon and London: Routledge, 140–60.

13. See T. Roy (1999), *Traditional Industry in the Economy of Colonial India*. Cambridge: Cambridge University Press.

14. H. W. Singer (1989), 'Terms of trade and economic development', in *Economic Development*. London: Palgrave Macmillan, 323–8.

15. J. A. Frankel and D. Romer (1999), 'Does trade cause growth?', *American Economic Review*, 91 (5), 379–99.

16. K. J. Mitchener and M. Weidenmier (2008), 'Trade and empire', *Economic Journal*, 118 (533), 1805–34.

17. L. Pascali (2017), 'The wind of change: Maritime technology, trade and economic development', *American Economic Review*, 107 (9), 2821-54.

18. M. J. Twomey (1983), 'Employment in nineteenth century Indian textiles', *Explorations in Economic History*, 20 (1), 37–57.

19. A. K. Bagchi (1976), 'De-industrialization in India in the nineteenth century: Some theoretical implications', *Journal of Development Studies*, 12 (2), 135–64. I. Ray (2011), *Bengal Industries and the British Industrial Revolution*. London and New York: Routledge.

20. D. Clingingsmith, and J. G. Williamson (2008), 'Deindustrialization in 18th and 19th century India: Mughal decline, climate shocks and British industrial ascent', *Explorations in Economic History*, 45 (3), 209–34.

21. S. Broadberry and B. Gupta (2009), 'Lancashire, India, and shifting competitive advantage in cotton textiles, 1700-1850: The neglected role of factor prices', *Economic History Review*, 62 (2), 279–305.

22. Roy (1999), *Traditional Industry*; D. E. Haynes (2012), *Small Town Capitalism in Western India: Artisans, Merchants and the Making of the Informal Economy, 1870–1960*. Cambridge: Cambridge University Press.

23. For more detailed discussion, see B. Gupta (2015), 'The rise of modern industry in colonial India', in L. Chaudhary, B. Gupta, T. Roy, and A. V. Swamy (eds), *A New Economic History of Colonial India*. London: Routledge.

24. K. Pomeranz (2000), *The Great Divergence: China, Europe, and the Making of the Modern World Economy*. Princeton: Princeton University Press; Parthasarathi, 'Rethinking wages and competitiveness in the eighteenth century', 158, 79–109.

25. S. Broadberry and B. Gupta (2006), 'The Early Modern Great Divergence: Wages, Prices and Economic Development in Europe and Asia, 1500–1800', *Economic History Review*, 59 (1), 2–31; R. C. Allen, J. P. Bassino, D. Ma, C. Moll-Murata and J. L. Van Zanden (2011), 'Wages, Prices, and Living Standards in China, 1738–1925: In Comparison with Europe, Japan, and India', *Economic History Review*, 64 (supplement 1), 8–38.

26. S. Broadberry, B. M. Campbell, A. Klein, M. Overton, and B. Van Leeuwen (2015), *British Economic Growth, 1270–1870*. Cambridge: Cambridge University Press.

27. N. Voigtländer, and H. J. Voth (2012), 'The three horsemen of riches: Plague, war, and urbanization in early modern Europe', *Review of Economic Studies*, 80 (2), 774–811.

28. Broadberry, et al. (2015), 'India and the great divergence: An Anglo-Indian comparison of GDP per capita, 1600-1871', *Explorations in Economic History*, 55 (1), 58–75.

29. Broadberry and Gupta (2006), 'The early modern Great Divergence'; and Broadberry, et al. (2015), 'India and the Great Divergence'.

30. B. Roy (1996), *An analysis of Long-Term Growth of National Income and Capital Formation in India (1850–51 to 1950–51)*. Calcutta: Firma KLM Pvt. Ltd.

# CHAPTER 19
## CHANGING DESTINIES IN THE ECONOMY OF SOUTHEAST ASIA
### J. Thomas Lindblad

Southeast Asia is an important player in today's world economy. The region, embracing the ten member states of the ASEAN (Association of South East Asian Nations), counts 625 million inhabitants, 8.3 per cent of the world total. Total GDP nears US$2.5 trillion or 3.3 per cent of world GDP. Per capita GDP varies enormously across the member states, presently averaging about US$4,000 at nominal prices, which corresponds to more than US$10,000 if measured at purchasing power parity.[1] Yet, for centuries this region remained spectacularly underpopulated, and when colonial rule came to an end, virtually all the newly independent nation states faced grave problems of economic development. A true metamorphosis has taken place within living memory. Was this anticipated or delayed by earlier changes in the region's economic destiny? Or, to put it differently, could the economic success in much, but not all, of the region have been predicted by observers in the colonial period, let alone in pre-colonial times? The time frame of my exploration stretches from the sixteenth century up to the mid-twentieth century.

Three key variables need to be surveyed to adequately assess the region's long-run economic development. The first one is economic growth, whether or not associated with per capita gain, whereas the second one refers to the underlying economic structure. Both have been prominently at play during the dramatic changes in the post-war era. Sustained high growth rates qualified four ASEAN member states (Singapore, Malaysia, Thailand, and Indonesia) to be included among the prestigious HPAEs (highly performing Asian economies) as designated by the World Bank in 1993. A decisive shift from agriculture to manufacturing occurred in five of the large economies (Indonesia, Thailand, Malaysia, the Philippines, and Vietnam) between the late 1960s and early 1990s.

The third key variable concerns the openness to world markets. The region is literally located at major crossroads in the world economy. Four major economies exhibit an exceptionally high ratio of foreign trade to GDP – Singapore, Malaysia, Thailand, and Vietnam – while others, notably Indonesia and the Philippines, remain more strongly oriented towards their own domestic markets. In earlier centuries, the main external influences came from either India or China. Then the radius was widened to include the Middle East and Europe, and eventually the Americas. The strong external impetus had far-reaching repercussions for both economic growth and economic structure. Did openness generate sustained growth and encourage an economic structure conducive to such growth?

In his authoritative account of the *longue durée* in Southeast Asian history, Anthony Reid identifies a succession of distinct phases of development.[2] The 'Age of Commerce', applying the label Reid himself coined in an earlier seminal study to identify the period in Southeast Asian history from 1480 to 1630, came to fruition in an aggregation of societies that more often than not succeeded in evading state formation. This is all the more remarkable as it goes contrary to expectation from experience elsewhere, where the formation of strong states preceded economic expansion or even formed a prerequisite for such a change of economic fortune. Was Southeast Asia with its 'Age of Commerce' of one and a half century the exception that proves the rule?

The subsequent Western colonialism put an indelible mark on the entire region except for Thailand (Siam until 1930). The outcome was a process of formation of states, but not nations. To what extent did colonial rule during the nineteenth and early twentieth centuries prepare the region for the challenges of economic development after independence? Addressing this issue acknowledges the need to study post-colonial economic development in relationship to the colonial legacy. In a path-breaking study, Anne Booth adopts a comparative perspective, arguing that Japanese colonialism in East Asia laid stronger foundations for rapid development after independence than did Western colonial rule in Southeast Asia.[3]

As said, this contribution focuses on the first two phases of Reid's classification, only touching on the third phase, the current post-war situation, in passing. Most attention is given to economic matters, on occasion in juxtaposition with political trends, and for reasons of space leaving aside social change and related issues.

## Society without state

Southeast Asia covers a land area of 4.5 million square kilometres. Still, by the beginning of the seventeenth century, the entire region counted less than twenty-five million inhabitants and even by 1800 total population was estimated to be no more than thirty-four million. Reid ascribes this peculiar feature of historical demography to a climate and geography that encouraged collection of forest produce and maritime trading rather than labour-intensive agricultural production.[4] With the possible exception of Central and East Java and Luzon, population concentrations were simply too low to support centres of power and authority.

The half millennium or so preceding the 'Age of Commerce' (1480–1630) saw an extreme fragmentation of polities based on charters between rulers and the surrounding population. By the mid-fourteenth century, there were twenty-three kingdoms in the broad mainland belt from Burma to Vietnam, and numerous more or less autonomous units in the 'empty' area of the Malay Peninsula and the western part of the Indonesian archipelago. Of the region's three famous ancient 'empires', Srivijaya with its center in South Sumatra had practically collapsed already, whereas Mataram and Majapahit in Java effectively covered territories of ever diminishing size.[5] Although some recentralization took place on the mainland between the mid-fourteenth and the mid-sixteenth centuries, the 'state-light' domain, an expression borrowed again from Reid, remained characteristic of the region with its bewildering array of amorphous 'states and non-states, large and small', often with unclear and porous borders.[6]

The long sixteenth century, the period from 1480 to 1630, was one of a dramatic expansion of foreign trade and shipping. The products in highest demand were spices from Maluku (Moluccas), supplemented by a wide range of forest products such as woods and resins, even ivory, rhinoceros horns, and birds' nests. Towards the end of this period of expansion, the range of tradeable goods had come to include also cane sugar and cotton. The traders included Chinese, Indians, Arabs, and a variegation of indigenous peoples from all parts of the region. The Europeans were the last to be added to the long list of participants in the region's booming trade.

A web of shipping connections evolved with nodal points. Melaka, dating from around 1400, profited from its strategic location at the main road of access by sea to the region and effectively shouldered the legacy of the defunct Srivijaya 'empire'. Similarly, Demak and other ports along the Pasisir, Java's north coast, rose to prominence in the vacuum left by the fading Majapahit 'empire'. Other thriving ports in the expanding Muslim Malay sphere included Brunei in northwestern Borneo while Hoi An in the Chinese sphere of influence on Borneo played a crucial part in maintaining shipping links with East Asia. Cities of impressive size arose. At the peak of the commercial expansion in 1630, Reid identified ten cities with an estimated population in excess of 100,000 people, five on the mainland (Pegu, Ayutthaya, Hanoi, Hue, and Melaka) and five in the Indonesian archipelago (Aceh, Banten, Batavia, Mataram, and Makassar).[7]

Trading in Southeast Asia during the 'Age of Commerce' was initially largely conducted within the region itself, even if the traders often originated from other regions. The global or interregional dimension, as opposed to the intra-regional one, was gradually strengthened. Spices from Maluku had entered Europe through Middle Eastern intermediaries already since late medieval times, and this branch of trade received a powerful boost when the Portuguese established direct shipping links with Europe around 1500. Imports of Indian textiles played an increasing part in the trade with South Asia, rising threefold in value between the early sixteenth and the first half of the seventeenth centuries. During the concluding decades of the sixteenth century, the important bullion trade was added to exchanges with other parts of the world. The influx of American silver from Acapulco through the region's eastward gateway at Manila rose fourfold between the 1580s and the 1620s.[8]

Pepper became the most spectacular of success stories. The total volume of exports of pepper from Southeast Asia doubled between the 1530s and 1560s, from 1,300 tonnes to 2,700 tonnes on average per year, climbing to a peak at 3,800 tonnes in the 1620s that was sustained into the 1640s. An increasing proportion of total exports was destined for the European market, where the Southeast Asian product soon surpassed Indian pepper in popularity. The share of Europe in total Southeast Asian pepper exports rose from one-quarter in the 1530s to about one-half in the 1560s and oscillated around 40 per cent in the 1590s and the 1620s (Figure 19.1). Meanwhile the total annual value – based on prices in Southeast Asian ports – rose fourfold from less than 80,000 Spanish dollars (real) in the 1530s to 340,000 in the 1590s, eventually reaching a peak level of 600,000

**Figure 19.1** Average annual volume of pepper exports from Southeast Asia, 1530–1649 (metric tons).
*Source:* A. Reid (2015), *A History of Southeast Asia: Critical Crossroads*. Chichester: Wiley Blackwell, 78.

Spanish dollars in the 1640s. The latter figure was twice as high as the total value of exports of the region's second-ranking spice product, cloves from Maluku in particular. It is worth noting that the pepper exports were far more voluminous than the exports of cloves, which reflects a lower price for pepper, 0.15 Spanish dollars per kilogram in the 1620s against 0.80 Spanish dollars for cloves.[9]

The pepper trade was exceptionally profitable. This is best illustrated by trends in pepper exports during the aftermath of the 'Age of Commerce'. There was a huge divergence in the value of the shipments of pepper, depending on where they were priced. The total value of imports of Southeast Asian pepper, measured at the international market in Amsterdam in the 1630s, was 4.3 times as high as the value of exports measured at the point of departure. This 'multiplier' (markup) in the transfer from one market to the next even climbed to 6.4 in the 1660s and still averaged at 4.7 times in the final decade of the seventeenth century (Figure 19.2). The discrepancy between Southeast Asian and European value was even more pronounced in the case of cloves, where the European value from the 1650s to the 1690s represented a multiple of ten or more compared to the value in Southeast Asia.[10] The key to high profits in European trade with Southeast Asia lay in imperfect information about market conditions. Exporters in Southeast Asia did not have the slightest idea of how much their spices were worth in Amsterdam.

Three events stand out as landmarks in the history of European participation in the expansion of Southeast Asia in this period. The first is the conquest of Melaka by the Portuguese in 1511, which opened up the direct spice trade between Southeast Asia and Europe. The second is the foundation of Manila by the Spaniards in 1571 that exposed Southeast Asia to the bullion trade. The third is the establishment of the Dutch East

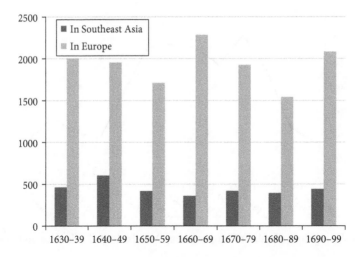

**Figure 19.2** Average annual value of pepper exports in Southeast Asia and in Europe, 1630–99 (in thousand Spanish dollars).
*Source:* A. Reid (2015), *A History of Southeast Asia: Critical Crossroads*. Chichester: Wiley Blackwell, 147.

India Company, VOC (Vereenigde Oost-Indische Compagnie) in 1602, arguably the world's first multinational. European involvement in Southeast Asian trade began in the 'Age of Commerce' and part of it survived beyond the peak in the region's expansion. The Dutch took over from the Portuguese, whereas the Spaniards remained largely confined to the Philippines.

There has been a lively discussion among historians about the role of European traders during the 'Age of Commerce' and its aftermath. Were they merely aloof observers from the sideline or did they outrank their Asian rivals? The debate has been moving back and forth between these two positions for some time, but current scholarship seems to favour the externalist view above the autonomous one. The European traders had an impact disproportionate to their numbers because of their control of long-distance trading, naval supremacy, and ready access to bullion.[11] Commercial success was secured through competition and cooperative ventures with both migrant Asian and indigenous competitors.

## State-light power

The eclipse of the 'Age of Commerce' was signalled by several seemingly unrelated events: exports of silver from Japan were banned in 1635, the fall of the Ming dynasty in China in 1644 severely disrupted Chinese shipping, and the conquest of Melaka by the VOC in 1641 secured the Dutch monopoly in the spice trade. Just as Southeast Asia had benefited more than others from the booming 'long sixteenth century', the region was especially hard hit by the seventeenth-century depression in the world

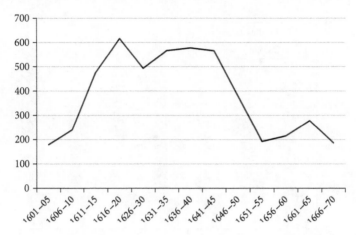

**Figure 19.3** Average annual value of cargo entering Manila, 1601–70 (in thousand Spanish dollars).
*Source:* A. Reid (1993), *Southeast Asia in the Age of Commerce, 1450–1680, Vol. II. Expansion and Crisis.* New Haven: Yale University Press, 289.

economy. Economic setbacks were aggravated by military conflict and adverse physical circumstances, such as earthquakes, possibly also tsunamis, and disturbances in the climate somehow occasioned by the 'Little Ice Age' in Europe and the northern part of Asia.[12]

Although the spice trade remained potentially highly profitable, Southeast Asia was losing its comparative advantage due the rigidly enforced Dutch monopoly as well as declining demand among consumers in Europe. The overall downward trend in the economic tide is well borne out by estimates of the value of cargo entered in the port of Manila. The high annual average at nearly 600,000 Spanish dollars prevailing for the period 1610–50 declined to one-third of its former level in the 1650s and 1660s (Figure 19.3).

The VOC emerged as the winner from the competitive strife in regional trading during the seventeenth century. By 1660 the Dutch-owned business enterprise with its diverse international labour force stood above competition in leading branches of trade. The success can be ascribed to the synergy between selective trading monopolies, the exercise of territorial power, and access to a global network. Among its rivals, the VOC was unique in combining commercial advantage with political and military operations resembling those of an autonomous state. From about 1680 onwards, the VOC's suzerainty over the decaying Mataram 'empire' was undisputed. The VOC came to function as one participant among many in the fragmented multi-state system of the archipelago, albeit one with military superiority.[13]

In the eighteenth century, the trade of the VOC grew increasingly oriented towards intra-Asian trade as opposed to trade with Europe. Total annual turnover in trading in Asia exceeded thirty million guilders in the early 1710s and reached a peak at nearly thirty-nine million in the mid-eighteenth century. The Indonesian archipelago usually accounted for more than one-half of the total, but almost all of the other half accrued from possessions outside Southeast Asia. By the early 1770s, a decline had set in with a total turnover around twenty million guilders, two-thirds of which originated from the archipelago (Figure 19.4). The final downfall in the late eighteenth century was conditioned by heavy losses during the Fourth Anglo-Dutch War (1780–4), revolution and political upheaval in Europe during the 1790s, widespread corruption and private trading by employees, and possibly also systematic errors in accounting practices.[14]

The VOC interfered in an unprecedented way in the regional economy of Southeast Asia, in particular in the island world. The company reinforced or opened up profitable avenues of exploiting the region's natural resources and comparative advantages, primarily to its own gain, although local elites also shared in the spoils. In the process, the VOC became an active participant in the slave trade of the Indian Ocean and the eastern Indonesian islands. Through the juxtaposition of its commercial and political or military operations, the company had a deforming impact on the development of indigenous statecraft, especially in Java. Differently from merchant communities of other ethnic origin, however, the Dutch bequeathed a state under construction to the region. The powerful alien state in Java was based on territorialization through taxation, applying devices inherited from the company's Portuguese predecessors.[15] The VOC reaped the benefits from local fragmentation of authority. A trend in the opposite direction became

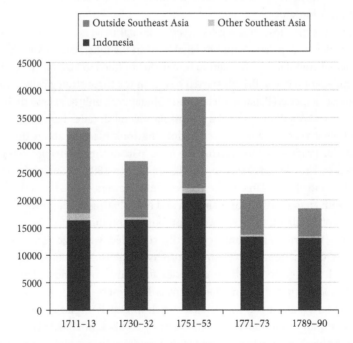

**Figure 19.4** Average annual turnover of VOC trade in Asia, 1711–90 (in thousand Dutch dollars).
*Source:* E. M. Jacobs (2006), *Merchant in Asia: The Trade of the Dutch East India Company during the Eighteenth Century.* Leiden: CNWS Publications, 306.

visible in the mainland, where a consolidation occurred of three integrated territories under new dynasties: Kon-baung in Burma from 1752, Chakri in Thailand from 1782, and Nguyen in Vietnam from 1802. This reinforced an existing cleavage between the mainland and the archipelago, the latter here also including the Malay Peninsula. The island world was more susceptible to external influences, especially Western colonialism, and this was to become all the more important during the next phase of development.

## State without nation

Towards the end of the eighteenth century, colonialism in Southeast Asia was virtually confined to the old and highly indigenized Spanish possession of the Philippines and the tiny Portuguese enclave in East Timor, not counting the quasi-state functions performed by the VOC in Java. Scarcely more than one century later, the entire region except Thailand had been subjugated to effective colonial rule. From being one of the least colonized regions of the world, Southeast Asia became a region where colonial power had profound repercussions for the development of society. The discontinuity with the pre-colonial past was especially strong in the archipelago and on the peninsula. Our concern here is with the economic impact of colonialism, leaving it to political historians to address such intriguing issues as the continuity between colonial constructions and post-colonial nation states.

The region became host to several Western colonial powers. The Dutch claim to the entire Indonesian archipelago found its legal basis in the inheritance from the dissolved VOC, but actual colonial state formation remained confined to Java for the better part of the nineteenth century. The British started out from the three strategically located ports of the Straits Settlements (Penang, Melaka, and Singapore), only to extend their authority over the nine Malay sultanates of the peninsula several decades later. The conquest of Burma and what then became French Indochina took place at about the same time and in a similar gradual fashion during the latter part of the nineteenth century. Spain was replaced by the United States in the Philippines in 1898, whereas the Portuguese continued to control East Timor. The metropolitan powers erected a range of colonial states, each with characteristics of their own and only sharing the common feature (with the exception of Thailand) that they were not founded on the conception of a nation.[16]

The Dutch historiography has repeatedly struggled with the issue whether the extension of Dutch colonial power to all corners of the Indonesian archipelago in the late nineteenth and early twentieth centuries fitted into or differed from prevailing patterns of modern imperialism. A consensus has emerged that the only exception from the standard pattern was the belated switch in Dutch imperialism from reluctant to aggressive expansion following the conquest of Lombok in 1894.[17] The international historiography has been more concerned with differences in colonial administration and the resulting endowment with regard to post-colonial development. The British were known for indirect colonial rule, notably through the Malay sultans on the peninsula. This contrasted with both the highly centralized control of French Indochina and the

Dutch tendency to far-reaching intervention, often in conjunction with local elites. The American administrators of the Philippines were the only colonial rulers in the region bent on preparing their subjects for independence. Differences in the style of colonial rule were reflected in budgetary and welfare policies with important consequences for standards of living, a matter to which we shall return later.[18]

From the early nineteenth century, the region's population began to grow more rapidly. Total population rose almost threefold during the nineteenth century and more than doubled between 1900 and 1950 (Figure 19.5). The proportion of the total population accounted by colonial Indonesia rose to a stable level of some 45 per cent, whereas second-ranking French Indochina lagged behind neighbours with its share in the total falling from 27 per cent in 1800 to 16 per cent in 1930. Meanwhile, Burma was surpassed by the Philippines in the third position. The demographic transition finally caught up with Southeast Asia, but it is hazardous to make inferences from the acceleration in population growth to the development of standards of living over time; some of the increase may even be ascribed to better statistics.[19]

Colonialism radically altered economic relations with other parts of the world. Seeking to revitalize the commercial supremacy of the VOC, the Dutch colonial authorities in Java embarked on a state-run exploitation of the island's fertile soils, dispatching export crops to the staple market in Amsterdam. In effect, this was a reversal of the preceding trend of the VOC to emphasize intra-Asian trade at the expense of

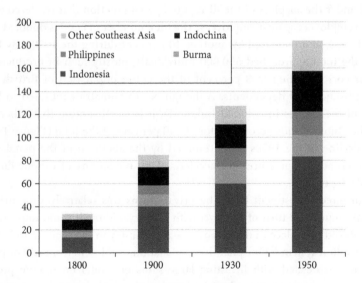

**Figure 19.5** Population of Southeast Asia, 1800–1950 (millions).
*Sources*: R. E. Elson (1997), *The End of the Peasantry in Southeast Asia: A Social and Economic History of Peasant Livelihood, 1800–1990s*. Basingstoke: Macmillan, 76–7; H. Gooszen (2000), *A Demographic History of the Indonesian Archipelago*. Singapore: Institute of Southeast Asian Studies, 43; J. Touwen (2001), *Extremes in the Archipelago: Trade and Economic Development in the Outer Islands of Indonesia, 1900–1942*. Leiden: KITLV Press, 330; A. Reid (2015), *A History of Southeast Asia: Critical Crossroads*. Chichester: Wiley Blackwell, 263.

trade with Europe. The cultivation system in Java in the period 1830–70, with coffee, sugar, and indigo as its foremost products, proved extraordinarily profitable. At least 6 per cent of Java's GDP was siphoned off on occasion, contributing as much as 4 per cent of total Dutch GDP and one-third of the public budget.[20] The cultivation system was abandoned eventually, because the state-run estates in Java had been an anomaly in the pervasive movement towards exploitation of natural resources by private capital in Southeast Asia.

The local economy provided land and labour wherever population densities were high enough to permit a release of cheap, unskilled workers from food production, which was notably the situation in Java and Luzon, but scarcely elsewhere. Private firms supplied investment capital, technology, and management and relied when necessary on coolies shipped in from poor regions far away, such as South India, South China, and Central Java. A twin system of labour mobilization emerged in the region, one operating in symbiosis with the local economy, the other consisting of enclave economies with little interaction with the surrounding society. Both systems found large-scale application in colonial Indonesia, the former one in Java and the latter one in the Outer Islands.[21] In British Malaya, however, preference was given to coolie labour relying on Indian immigrants.

The plantation belt of Deli on Sumatra's east coast (now North Sumatra) grew famous for its highly profitable cultivation of tobacco and rubber, but also notorious for scandals about abuse of labour. The system of coolie labour was devised and first tried out under the auspices of the ill-reputed penal sanction that rendered excessive powers to employers against employees. The total number of coolies doubled between 1910 and 1920, and increased by another 40 per cent during the 1920s. By the peak in 1929, the total approached 550,000 individuals, mostly men in productive ages, a number corresponding to 8 per cent of the entire population of British Malaya, including women and dependents. Although North Sumatra continued to have the majority of the coolies in colonial Indonesia, it is worth noting that other regions among the Outer Islands accounted for 30–40 per cent of the total (Figure 19.6). The system's decline in the 1930s was prompted by the abolition of the penal sanction due to international pressure and accelerated by reductions of output during the worldwide depression.

Foreign direct investment (FDI) by private firms was relatively slow in entering the region around the turn of the twentieth century, although some important fresh investments did take place in the Javanese sugar industry in the shadow and aftermath of the cultivation system.[22] One plausible explanation could stem from real or perceived uncertainties associated with investing large sums of capital on remote production sites, where protection by the colonial administration had not yet been secured. The extension of effective colonial rule over large territories in the Indonesian Outer Islands, and also in Malaya and Indochina, combined with booming markets for Southeast Asian exports to trigger massive new investment. By 1914, total FDI in the region amounted to US$1,100 million, of which US$675 million (60 per cent) was invested in Indonesia alone. The estimated total for the late 1930s was two and a half times that level and might

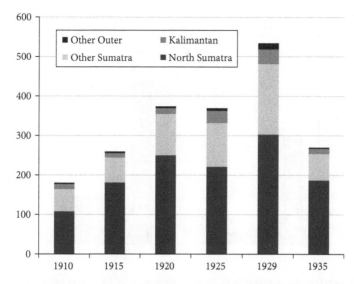

**Figure 19.6** Coolie labour in colonial Indonesia, 1910–35 (thousands of workers).
*Sources:* J. T. Lindblad (1999), 'Coolies in Deli: Labour Conditions in Western Enterprises in East Sumatra, 1910–1938', in V. J. H. Houben, J. T. Lindblad et al., *Coolie Labour in Colonial Indonesia: A Study of Labour Relations in the Outer Islands, c. 1900–1940*. Wiesbaden: Harrassowitz, 72–3; idem (1999), 'New Destinations: Conditions of Coolie Labour Outside East Sumatra, 1910–1938', in ibid., 101–7.

even have been slightly higher in 1930 before the effects of economic depression were felt. The distribution across the colonies was largely unchanged with Dutch Indonesia up front accounting for more than one-half of the regional total, followed by British Malaya, the Philippines, and French Indochina, in that order (Figure 19.7). The sole non-colony, Thailand, ranked last on both counts, which lends support to the idea that colonial rule and FDI were intimately connected.

Liberalism with respect to investment and trade was vigorously celebrated by the Dutch, the British, and the Americans, less so by the French. Nevertheless, there was a strong bias in FDI patterns in favour of investors from the colonial mother country. Dutch firms accounted for 70 per cent of FDI in colonial Indonesia, British investors held similar stakes in Malaya, and American firms were good for more than one-half of the total in the Philippines, whereas Indochina appeared as the most extreme case, with a virtual monopoly enjoyed by French companies.[23] Familiarity with legal regulations, language, and culture obviously hid behind preferences among investors for colonial targets, but direct contacts with colonial administrations were most probably important as well. Colonialism in Southeast Asia implied at least a partial reorientation in economic relations towards the outside world away from Asia and in favour of the Western metropolitan countries.

The colonial relationship also surfaced in foreign trade. The trend of the VOC in the eighteenth century to trade more in Asia, and less with Europe, was reversed by the Dutch cultivation system in Java. When foreign trade, just as foreign investment, was

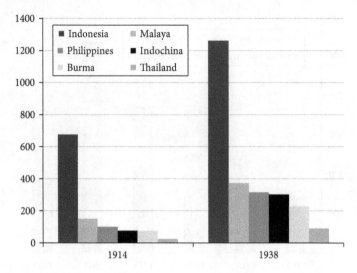

**Figure 19.7** Foreign direct investment in Southeast Asia in 1914 and 1938 (in million US$). *Source:* J. T. Lindblad (1998), *Foreign Investment in Southeast Asia in the Twentieth Century.* Basingstoke: Macmillan, 14.

liberalized in the Dutch colony after the cultivation system ended, nearly one-half of imports entering the colony came from the colony, whereas the share of the Dutch in the opposite flow of trade was as high as 60 per cent. Thirty years later, the Dutch proportion in the trade of colonial Indonesia was down at one-third. Another three decades later, by the late 1930s, only one-fifth of Indonesia's foreign trade was with the Netherlands. The delinking of mutual trade between colony and metropolitan mother country proceeded even further in the British colonies of Malaya and Burma, where the share of the United Kingdom in total trade scarcely exceeded 15 per cent. In Indochina, by contrast, one-half of the foreign trade was conducted with France. The strongest trading relationship with the mother country in the late 1930s was found in the Philippines, with the United States buying more than 80 per cent of exports and supplying 70 per cent of imports.[24]

Total exports from Southeast Asia started to increase dramatically from about 1905 onwards, and the expansion continued unabatedly up to the very eve of the economic depression of the 1930s. By the late 1930s, total exports from the entire region were estimated at US$1.6 billion, of which two-thirds originated in colonial Indonesia and British Malaya alone.[25] The expansion of exports was only in part accompanied by an increase in imports, since per capita incomes were lagging behind and failed to make a larger contribution to aggregate demand in the domestic economy. The result was a very substantial surplus in the balance of trade in all the region's colonies as well as in independent Thailand.[26] In colonial Indonesia, to cite but one example, 38 per cent of export earnings on average in the period 1900–38 were not spent on imports, a figure that also reflected the growing disparity between Java, where the surplus percentage was 25 per cent, and the Outer Islands, where it exceeded 50 per cent.[27]

Some time ago, C. P. Kindleberger aptly explained the region's trade-induced expansion as follows: 'demand was right abroad and supply was right at home.'[28] In the early twentieth century, Southeast Asia could offer a wide range of exportable products, which at that time were in high and rapidly rising demand in the world market. Java became one of the largest suppliers of cane sugar in the world, together with Taiwan and Cuba. The Outer Islands of Indonesia and the Malay Peninsula emerged as two of the world's leading exporters of tin and natural rubber, later supplemented by palm oil. Together with Burma, colonial Indonesia became the region's main oil producer. Tobacco, coffee, tea, and copra all occupied prominent positions in the wide range of exports from the archipelago; colonial Indonesia even enjoyed a virtual world monopoly in the small-scale but literally vital trade in cinchona, at the time crucial in combatting malaria. By 1929, exports per capita ranged from US$4–13 in Indochina and the Philippines to as much as US$126 in British Malaya. This statistic amounted to only US$10 in the Indonesian archipelago due to the colony's very large population.[29]

The key to success in international trade was, as British Malaya and colonial Indonesia demonstrate, not just a question of having a favourable resource endowment that enabled goods in high demand to be offered on the world market. It was also a matter of building up a capacity to raise output targets in response to market signals. In the event, export volumes were rapidly enlarged in colonial Indonesia and British Malaya during the long boom in prices of primary products from about 1905 to the mid-1920s, but also by way of compensation for the general fall in prices in the second half of the 1920s and during the 1930s. Only at the nadir of the worldwide depression, when prices for primary products had reached rock-bottom levels, did export producers in Southeast Asia revert to curtailing output, notably in rubber, tin, and sugar.[30]

Export production was organized in one of two ways. There was the Western colonial model, based on FDI, imported or locally mobilized labour and the overt or tacit support by colonial governments. In addition, an Asian model of export expansion took shape involving Chinese intermediaries in finance and trade and indigenous smallholder producers in cash crop agriculture. Indigenous entrepreneurship was particularly important in the rubber industry of Sumatra and Kalimantan and the Malay Peninsula, and in the copra trade of Sulawesi. By the late 1930s, smallholders supplied about one-half of the total exports of rubber and almost all exports of copra from colonial Indonesia and British Malaya.[31] The parallel modes of export expansion in Southeast Asia in the late-colonial era testify to the region's dynamic potential, decidedly in anticipation of what was to come to fruition after independence.

The pre-war export expansion was rooted in a highly traditional economic structure that above all emphasized the primary sector, including mining, at the expense of manufacturing and services. About two-thirds of the labour force in colonial Indonesia, the Philippines, and Burma were still engaged in agriculture around 1930. Even in British Malaya with its substantial trading sector, three out of five worked on the land, and in Thailand the share of agriculture in employment exceeded 80 per cent. Only an embryonic industrialization, attracting about 10 per cent of labour, was taking place in these colonies but, significantly, not in Thailand.[32] The traditional economic structure in almost the entire region on the eve of independence was without doubt a factor that forestalled the switch to modern, sustained economic growth.

Global connections intensified and foreign trade grew but actual income gains for the region's colonies remained unimpressive. The richest colonies, Singapore and the Malayan Peninsula, registered a growth rate of GDP per capita of only about 2.4 per cent on average per year between 1913 and 1938. British Malaya was more or less on par with the Philippines, but the long-term growth rate in the latter colony was lower still. Despite having witnessed a spectacular trade expansion, colonial Indonesia figured in the ranking between Malaya and Thailand, with a growth rate of scarcely more than 1 per cent per year. Burma appears to have been the least fortunate in terms of reaping benefit from Western colonialism (Figure 19.8).[33]

The Japanese occupation in the 1940s, revolution, and upheaval of Dutch decolonization severely depressed per capita incomes in all colonies except Malaya (including Singapore) to below the level of the late 1930s. Yet, even discounting the devastating effects on society and economy in the 1940s, it remains a fact that the rewards for the region from a protracted expansion of foreign trade were deeply disappointing. Colonialism offered stability, especially for foreign investors, and also ample commercial opportunities, but it did not encourage structural change necessary for future growth. Interestingly, however, the situation was no better in the only Southeast Asian country escaping colonial rule: Thailand.

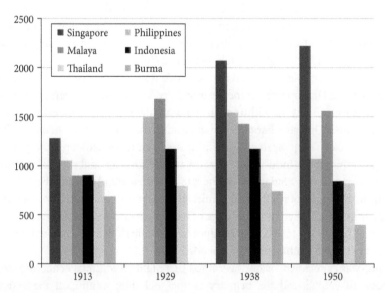

**Figure 19.8** Per capita GDP in Southeast Asia, 1913–50 (in 1990 US$).
*Sources:* A. Booth (2007), *Colonial Legacies: Economic and Social Development in East and Southeast Asia.* Honolulu: University of Hawai'i Press, 22; idem (2015), 'A Century of Growth, Crisis, War and Recovery, 1870–1970', in I. Coxhead (ed), *Routledge Handbook of Southeast Asian Economics.* Abingdon and New York: Routledge, 43–59, Table 3.4; A. Reid (2015), *A History of Southeast Asia: Critical Crossroads.* Chichester: Wiley Blackwell, 321.
*Note*: Per capita GDP expressed in 1990 Geary-Khamis dollars.

## Conclusion: Change and continuity

Income disparities in Southeast Asia today are probably larger than in any other major region of the world. In terms of GDP per capita, adjusted for differences in purchasing power, Singapore ranks on par with Luxemburg, Thailand with Brazil, and Indonesia with Egypt, while Cambodia lags behind at the level of Uzbekistan.[34] Nevertheless, economic development since about 1950 has been truly astounding in the region at large, considering also that lags in development have more often than not been caused by prolonged warfare and political strife. The financial crisis that struck in part, yet not all, of the region in the late 1990s turned out to be a relatively short-term dip, which even equipped the region to better withstand the adverse effects of the more recent Great Recession.[35] With the benefit of hindsight, could any observer of the situation in earlier centuries have foreseen the dramatic change in the region's economic destiny since the mid-twentieth century?

The most conspicuous historical discontinuity is found in the vein of state formation. Full-fledged nation states, loosely bound together in the ASEAN context, where first largely stateless societies and then colonial states lacking national identity prevailed. Recent state formation by definition rested on political decolonization, accompanied by a full or partial economic decolonization, and was reinforced by surging population growth. The ASEAN now has a population 20 per cent above that of the European Union.

A further important discontinuity is in economic structure. The excessive focus on trading, coupled with some cash crop cultivation prior to colonialism, gave way to an almost exclusive concentration on food agriculture and deliveries of unprocessed primary products to the world market. Neither was particularly conducive to modern economic growth based on high value-added production, at first in manufacturing, and later in services. At the moment, Singapore is the sole ASEAN member state to have joined the world's rank of post-industrial economies.

A third discontinuity worth noting concerns the process of economic growth itself. The pace of increase in GDP and standards of living has quickened beyond recognition, although one must not forget that much still needs to be done with respect to unequal income distributions. The acceleration in growth began at different points in time: in the 1950s for Singapore, Malaysia, and Thailand; in the late 1960s for Indonesia; in the 1990s for Vietnam and the Philippines, the last at independence ahead of all its neighbours in the region except Singapore and Malaysia. Time will tell whether this process is repeated also in Laos, Cambodia, and Myanmar.[36]

There are also continuities discernible over time that strike the eye. Openness to the world economy to varying degrees has been a constant factor for centuries in the region's economic life, owing to its strategic geographical location of resource endowments as well as a strong receptiveness to influences from the outside. The strength of the market forces in trading, both intra-regional and interregional, more than compensated for the lack of support by strong states in triggering the 'Age of Commerce'. Colonialism altered the trading relations, enhancing the exclusiveness of mutual trade with the metropole at the expense of the wider global connections. Yet, this tendency was reversed during the late-colonial period. Post-colonial developments have seen a revitalization of genuinely global trade in most, but not all, countries in the region.

A second important continuity may be observed in the spirit of entrepreneurship, both indigenous and in conjunction with foreign participants, traders, and investors alike. The most obvious manifestation was again the 'Age of Commerce', when the European trading companies jumped on the bandwagon towards the end of the boom. It is likely that Western intrusion in the region's economy had a stultifying impact on the region's economic development both in the eighteenth century and under the conditions of colonial rule in the nineteenth and twentieth centuries.

The discontinuities and continuities in the economic past of Southeast Asia cannot fail but to underscore the essentially dynamic potential of this region, even if circumstances have not always been conducive for a full realization of the possibilities. This appears to be the main lesson to be learned from surveying the changing destinies of an exciting region.

## Notes

1. Statistics for 2014 or 2015 from the website of the World Trade Organization (www.wto.org). For a critical discussion of the concept of purchasing power parity, see A. Deaton and A. Heston (2010), 'Understanding PPPs and PPP-based National Account', *American Economic Journal: Macroeconomics*, 2(4), 1–35. I was alerted to this reference by Patrick O'Brien.

2. A. Reid (2015), *A History of Southeast Asia: Critical Crossroads*. Chichester: Wiley Blackwell, 16, 214, 390.

3. A. Booth (2007), *Colonial Legacies: Economic and Social Development in East and Southeast Asia*. Honolulu: University of Hawai'i Press, 196.

4. Reid, *A History of Southeast Asia*, 6–8. The population figure for 1800 is based on R. E. Elson (1997), *The End of the Peasantry in Southeast Asia: A Social and Economic History of Peasant Livelihood, 1800-1990s*. Basingstoke: Macmillan, 76–7; and A. Reid (1988), *Southeast Asia in the Age of Commerce 1450-1680, Vol. I. The Lands below the Winds*. New Haven: Yale University Press, 13–14.

5. V. Lieberman (2003), *Strange Parallels: Southeast Asia in Global Context, c. 800-1830, Vol. I. Integration on the Mainland*. Cambridge: Cambridge University Press, 21–66; Idem (2009), *Strange Parallels: Southeast Asia in Global Context, c. 800-1830*, Vol. II. *Mainland Mirrors: Europe, Japan, China, South Asia and the Islands*. Cambridge: Cambridge University Press, 58–60, 768. The ancient kingdoms were not empires in the common sense of turning into cohesive systems with a centralized authority.

6. Reid, *A History of Southeast Asia*, 27–9.

7. A. Reid (1993), *Southeast Asia in the Age of Commerce, 1450-1680, Vol. II. Expansion and Crisis*. New Haven: Yale University Press, 13–24, 60, 76; Idem, *A History of Southeast Asia*, 62–3.

8. Reid, *Southeast Asia in the Age of Commerce, Vol. II*, 27, 30.

9. Reid, *A History of Southeast Asia*, 78.

10. Reid, *A History of Southeast Asia*, 147.

11. Lieberman, *Strange Parallels*, Vol. I, 6–15; Idem, *Strange Parallels*, Vol. II, 823–4. The modern debate about the significance of European trading in Asia was sparked off in 1955 with the

English translation of J. C. van Leur's Ph.D. dissertation in Dutch from 1934. J. C. van Leur (1955), *Indonesian Trade and Society: Essays in Asian Social and Economic History*. The Hague: Van Hoeve.

12. Reid, *Southeast Asia in the Age of Commerce*, Vol. II, 286–98; Idem, *A History of Southeast Asia*, 143–51. It is tempting, yet hazardous, to link the decline in Southeast Asia in the seventeenth century to the 'Great Divergence' debate.

13. Lieberman, *Strange Parallels*, Vol. II, 841–4.

14. E. M. Jacobs (2006), *Merchant in Asia: The Trade of the Dutch East India Company during the Eighteenth Century*. Leiden: CNWS Publications, 290–4. See also J. P. de Korte (2000), *The Annual Accounting in the Dutch East India Company (VOC)*. Amsterdam: NEHA.

15. Lieberman, *Strange Parallels*, Vol. II, 862–3. See also M. van Rossum (2015), *Kleurrijke tragiek: De geschiedenis van slavernij in Azië onder de VOC* [Colourful Tragedy: The History of Slavery in Asia under the VOC]. Hilversum: Verloren. The continuity between Portuguese and VOC taxation procedures was pointed out to me by Catia Antunes.

16. This section deals only in passing with Burma (administered as it was from India and at the time not recognized to be part of Southeast Asia), and Thailand (that was not subjected to colonial control).

17. E. B. Locher-Scholten (1994), 'Dutch expansion in the Indonesian archipelago around 1900 and the imperialism debate', *Journal of Southeast Asian Studies*, 25 (1), 91–111. Reports on the debates in the Dutch-language journal *BMGN*, 86 (1971) and the *BMGN Low Countries Historical Review*, 128 (2010).

18. J. Gommans (2015), 'Conclusion: Globalizing empire: The Dutch case', in C. Antunes and J. Gommans (eds), *Exploring the Dutch Empire: Agents, Networks and Institutions, 1600–2000*. London: Bloomsbury, 270–2; Booth, *Colonial Legacies*, 67–87.

19. Population statistics from before 1900 are proverbially weak. The figure for 1800 is based on approximations for Thailand, , and British Malaya, and almost certainly too low. In the case of colonial Indonesia, improvement of statistics may explain a more than fivefold increase for Java between 1800 and 1900 and a threefold increase for the Outer Islands between 1900 and 1950.

20. J. L. van Zanden and D. Marks (2012), *An Economic History of Indonesia, 1800–2010*. London and New York: Routledge, 50–1.

21. On the late-colonial mode of production in the Outer Islands, see J. Touwen (2001), *Extremes in the Archipelago: Trade and Economic Development in the Outer Islands of Indonesia, 1900-1942*. Leiden: KITLV Press, 101–61.

22. G. R. Knight (2013), *Commodities and Colonialism: The Story of Big Sugar in Indonesia, 1880-1942*. Leiden and Boston: Brill, 97–135.

23. J. T. Lindblad (1998), *Foreign Investment in Southeast Asia in the Twentieth Century*. Basingstoke: Macmillan, 18–19.

24. H. Dick, et al. (2002), *The Emergence of a National Economy: An Economic History of Indonesia, 1800-2000*. Crows Nest, NSW: Allen & Unwin, 128–9; Booth, *Colonial Legacies*, 91, 177.

25. Lindblad, *Foreign Investment*, 17.

26. Booth, *Colonial Legacies*, 105–7.

27. Dick, et al., *The Emergence of a National Economy*, 130.

28. C. P. Kindleberger (1962), *Foreign Trade and the National Economy*. New Haven: Yale University Press, 211.

29. Booth, *Colonial Legacies*, 90.

30. Dick, et al., *The Emergence of a National Economy*, 124–7, 155; van Zanden, and Marks, *An Economic History of Indonesia*, 96–100.

31. Touwen, *Extremes in the Archipelago*, 163–223; A. Booth (2014), 'Trade and growth in the colonial and post-colonial periods', in A. Schrikker and J. Touwen (eds), *Promises and Predicaments: Trade and Entrepreneurship in Colonial and Independent Indonesia in the 19th and 20th Centuries*. Singapore: NUS Press, 24–7. On Chinese capital in the economy of late-colonial Indonesia, see A. Claver (2014), *Dutch Commerce and Chinese Merchants in Java: Colonial Relationships in Trade and Finance, 1800–1942*. Leiden and Boston: Brill.

32. Booth, *Colonial Legacies*, 30. The distinction between agriculture and other pursuits is not always clear-cut since many rural dwellers did some non-agricultural work on the side.

33. Per capita GDP in dollars at 1990 price levels according to adjustment by the Geary-Khamis procedure. Original data in A. Maddison (2003), *The World Economy: Historical Statistics*. Paris: OECD, 180–1, as corrected or supplemented by Booth and Reid in the sources cited. Regrettably, their figures do not offer corresponding information for Indochina. For Singapore apart from British Malaya, see I. Sugimoto (2011), *Economic Growth of Singapore in the Twentieth Century*. Singapore: World Scientific Publishing, 185.

34. Based on most recent statistical data from databank.worldbank.org.

35. See further, H. Hill (2013), 'Southeast Asian macroeconomic management: Pragmatic orthodoxy?', *Masyarakat Indonesia*, 39 (2), 459–80.

36. My concern in this contribution is with general characteristics and trends in Southeast Asia at large. By implication, little attention can be given to the true outlier, Brunei, which on account of its huge oil reserves enjoys per capita incomes at the level of Norway and therefore is more comparable with the emirates in the Middle East. Issues of poverty alleviation and economic development are likely to play an all-important role in Timor Leste, scheduled to become the eleventh member state of the ASEAN.

# GLOSSARY
*compiled by Karolina Hutková*

**Abolitionism** Historical movement in Western Europe and America demanding the end of slavery.

**Anthropocene** is a proposed current geological age, starting in the eighteenth century when human activities began to have an important influence and impact on the Earth's climate, environment and ecosystem.

**Assets-Backed Securities (ABS)** Also called securitized product or structured credit. ABS are securities backed by a pool of assets, such as leases, credit card debt, royalties, or receivables. They are an alternative to investing in corporate debt.

**Balance of Payments** (BOP) statistical statement of net flows of all financial transaction between residents of a country and the world in a particular time period. These transactions consist of imports and exports of goods, services, and capital, and transfer payments such as foreign aid and remittances.

**Black Death** Pandemic of pneumonic plague that swept Eurasia. In Europe it peaked in 1347–51 and according to estimates killed 30 to 60 per cent of the European population.

**Bill of Exchange** An instrument used primarily in foreign trade. It is a written order that binds one party to pay a fixed sum of money to another party at a fixed time or on demand.

**Bretton Woods System** System for monetary and exchange rate management established in 1944 by the Bretton Woods Agreement. The Agreement was signed by forty-five, including the United States, Canada, Australia, Japan, and several Western European countries. The Agreement established the US dollar as reserve currency, fixed the US dollar to gold and compelled signatories of the Agreement to peg their currencies to the US dollar. The Agreement also established the International Monetary Fund (IMF) and the World Bank (WB) group. The key role of the IMF was to bridge temporary imbalances of payment.

**California School** The work and scholarly interventions of global historians such as Kenneth Pomeranz and Roy Bin Wong originally based at the University of California, Irvine and UCLA focusing on the Great Divergence between Western Europe and China.

**Clearing Bank** A 'bank for banks', it uses a central clearing house to transfer credits and checks between banks. The role of a clearing house is to facilitate exchange.

**Colbertism** Form of mercantilism pursued by Jean-Baptiste Colbert (1619–83), French minister of finance under Louis XIV. The core principle of Colbertism was state intervention into economy with the aim to accumulate gold. The goals of the economic policies were to achieve a positive balance of payments, impose protective tariffs, support to domestic industry, create systems of controls and inspection, and increase taxation.

**Columbian Exchange** The process of transfer of plants, animals, diseases, populations, and technologies between the Old World and the Americas in the fifteenth and sixteenth centuries.

**Commodity Chain** Network of labour and production processes whose end result is a finished commodity.

**Corn Laws** Tariffs and restrictions on imports and exports of food and grain in place in the United Kingdom and repealed in 1846.

**Cosmology** System of beliefs about the nature of the universe internal to a certain culture or religion. Modern physical cosmology is a branch of physics that studies the origin and evolution of the universe.

# Glossary

**Credit Default Swaps (CDS)** Most widely used credit derivative, it is used to transfer risk associated with investing into a bond from one party to another without transferring this bond. CDS is a financial swap agreement that forms an insurance against default risk.

**Developmental State** Type of state that takes an active role in development planning to facilitate the transformation from agrarian to modern manufacturing economies, typical for Asia after the Second World War. The legitimacy of the developmental state stems from achieving economic growth and improvement of living standard. The state is also committed to solving problems that arise as the outcome of social and economic restructuring.

**(Niebor-) Domar Model** Hypothesis explaining the causes of agricultural serfdom and slavery. It assumes that land and labour are the only factors of production, land is of uniform quality, location is ubiquitous, and marginal productivity of labour is constant. The hypothesis asserts that free land, free labour, and non-working landowners (i.e. large-scale agriculture) cannot all exist simultaneously. Only two can exist at one time and the combination depends on political factors.

**Dutch Disease** Negative economic impacts associated with large inflows of foreign currency. Foreign currency inflows lead to the appreciation of domestic currency which makes domestic products less competitive on exports markets. Dutch disease is often connected to discovery of natural resources.

**Dutch East India Company (VOC)** Dutch chartered monopoly company founded in 1602. It is normally considered the first listed public company. The Dutch government granted the company the monopoly on trade between Cape of Good Hope and the Straits of Magellan. By the eighteenth century the VOC became an important colonial power controlling the Indonesian archipelagos. High level of debts and corruption led the Dutch government in 1799 to revoke the VOC's charter and to take over the VOC's debts and possessions.

**Enclosure** Process of enclosing English open fields and common land to create units of privately owned land. Enclosure was legislated by the Enclosure Acts between 1604 and 1914.

**English East India Company (EEIC)** English Joint-stock monopoly company incorporated by royal charter in 1600. Initially it started as trading body but became an agent of British imperialism. After defeating the Indian powers at the Battle of Plassey (1757) it took control over Bengal and gradually increased its territorial possessions in India. The EEIC's trading monopoly was removed by the 1833 Government of India Act; however the Company continued to have administrative and political control of India until 1857.

**Euromarkets** Markets for transactions in dollars taking place outside the United States, free of American regulations.

**Export-led Industrialization** Also known as 'export-promotion industrialization', economic and trade polices focusing on promoting exports based on a country's comparative advantage. In general, export-led industrialization relies on the reduction of tariff barriers, floating exchange rates, and subsidies to exporters. This strategy was implemented in post-Second-World-War Japan, South Korea, Taiwan, Hong Kong, and Singapore.

**Factor Endowments** The amounts of land, labour, capital, and level of entrepreneurship a country possesses.

**Factor Prices** The price at which means of production – land, labour, and capital – are sold.

**Foreign Direct Investment (FDI)** Investment made by an individual or company to acquire 10 per cent or more of shares or voting power in enterprises operating outside of the economy of the investor.

**Foreign Security** Security, that is, shares, stocks, bonds, debentures issued in a currency other than the home country of issuer.

**Ghost Acres** Term popularized by Kenneth Pomeranz. It refers to the agricultural land of the Americas that enabled Europe to overcome the Malthusian trap of diminishing marginal returns to land. The Americas supplied Europe with commodities and foodstuffs such as sugar, timber, and cotton used both as industrial inputs and final consumer products.

**Global Value Chain (GVC)** Series of activities performed by firms and workers in the production, distribution, and sale of a product or service. Different stages of the processes of production, distribution, and sale are normally located across several countries.

**Glorious Revolution** English political change of 1688 in which the English Parliament overthrew King James II and offered the Crown to William III of Orange and his wife Mary II. The Revolution led to fundamental redesigning of governmental and fiscal institutions, constrained the power of the monarch and gave controlling powers to Parliament.

**Gold Standard** Monetary system in which participating countries agree to fix the prices of their domestic currencies to a fixed quantity of gold.

**Great Divergence** Term popularized by Kenneth Pomeranz, referring to the economic divergence between the West and the rest of the world that coincided with the Industrial Revolution.

**Gross Domestic Product (GDP)** GDP is used for measuring the size of a country's economy. It is the value of final goods and services produced within a country in a specific period of time, normally a year.

**Guild** Professional body of artisans or merchants organizing and regulating the practice of a craft or trade. In early modern Europe guilds were common and often had political power.

**Holocene** Current geological epoch, starting approximately 12,000 years ago.

**Horizontal Integration** Process of acquisition or merger of companies operating at the same stage of production in the same or different industries.

**Import-Substitution Industrialization** Economic and trade policy whose objective is to replace imports with domestically produced goods. It relies on a set of policies: active industrial policy with subsidies for strategic sectors; protective barriers to trade; overvalued currency to help manufacturers import capital goods; and restriction on foreign direct investment. This development strategy was pursued particularly in Latin America in the 1950s and 1960s as well as in several Asian and African countries.

**Indentured Labour** Indentured servants or labourers are employed by a contract to work for a specified time for an employer. Indenture contracts were typically entered into in order to meet a legal obligation, such as debts bondage, or to pay for a service – this was a typical way for European workers to finance a passage to America.

**Industrious Revolution** Concept first proposed by the Japanese demographic historian Akira Hayami and popularized by the Dutch/American economic historian Jan de Vries. It is a process of reallocation of household resources characterized by increased demand for market-supplied goods in the period 1600–1800. Since wages stagnated or even declined during this period, households needed to supply more labour to the market. This was usually female or children labour. Consequently also the supply of market goods increased.

**Joint-Stock Company** A type of a business company that is owned by shareholders through stock. This type of business entity emerged in early modern Europe to support long-distance trade. Early modern joint-stock companies were given monopolies on trade with specific world regions. The best-known joint-stock companies were the English East India Company and the Dutch East India Company.

**Laisser-Faire Policies** Policy of minimum government intervention. It is based on the assumption of 'natural' self-regulation of markets and faith that unregulated individual activity will achieve the best results for society as a whole.

**Malthusian Theory** Theory of population proposed by the English cleric and scholar Thomas Robert Malthus (1766–1834). According to Malthus human populations grow at an exponential rate while food production grows at an arithmetic rate. Population growth is limited by 'preventive' checks such as the postponement of marriage or celibacy, and by 'positive' checks such as war and famine.

**Mercantilism** An early modern doctrine of political. Mercantilism never had clearly defined policies and therefore is interpreted in different ways. In the most popular sense, mercantilism was a state policy focused on achieving a positive balance of payments on trade. Mercantilism often advocated import-substitution policies.

**Mortgage-Backed Securities (MBS)** Type of asset-backed security secured by a mortgage or collection of mortgages.

**Old Regime** Or Ancien Regime – political and social order of Europe from the late Middle Ages to the French Revolution based on the power of absolute monarchy and on relatively fixed social hierarchies.

**Open Access Social Orders** Social systems with open entry into social and political organizations. In such system, social order is sustained through political and social competition.

**Political Economy** Discipline of the social sciences that studies both political and economic factors that shapes society, state, and markets.

**Poor Laws** Body of legislation governing poor relief in England and Wales. They were developed in the sixteenth century and reformed regularly over the following centuries. The Poor Laws provision was administered through parishes. From the seventeenth century workhouses, places offering employment and accommodation to the destitute, became an important part of the system.

**Prebisch-Singer Thesis** Thesis that posits that over the long period the price of primary commodities declines relative to the price of manufactured goods. This is caused by the low elasticity of demand for primary commodities (demand for them does not increase with income). It implies that the terms of trade for countries specialized in exports of primary commodities deteriorate over time.

**Price Elasticity of Demand** Percentage change in demand for a product after a change in the price of this product. If the quantity of demanded product considerably changes in response to its price change, the product is price elastic.

**Primary Commodities** Raw or unprocessed materials, according to OECD definition: food and live animals, beverages and tobacco, and crude materials.

**Proto-industry** Pre-modern system of rural manufacturing widespread especially in European textile production. Primary production units were households, production was organized by merchants who provided raw materials and sold final goods on national and international markets.

**Putting-out** System of production in which merchant-entrepreneurs provide ('put out') material to rural households to produce goods taking advantage of low wages in rural areas. This system of subcontracting was particularly common in the pre-modern European textile industry.

**Schumpeterian Growth** Economic growth driven by innovations which are the outcome of creative destruction. 'Creative destruction', a term coined by Joseph Schumpeter, is a process of industrial transformation. It identifies product and process innovation mechanisms by which new replaces old and outdated practices, products, and so forth.

**Serfdom** Legal and economic system in which tenant farmers are bound to land by their landlord, typical of medieval Europe.

**Smithian Economic Growth** Growth that results from increasing density of markets.

**Stock** Type of security that is based on the fractional ownership of the corporation. Stocks are of two types: common and preferred. The holder of common stock is entitled to vote on corporate decisions. The holder of preferred stock does not have this right but is entitled to a certain level of dividend payments before any dividends can be issued to other shareholders.

**Structural Adjustment (SAPs)** Set of economic polices introduced as a condition to qualify for IMF and WB loans. The goal of SAPs was to reduce fiscal imbalances of borrowing countries and make their economies more market oriented. SAPs put emphasis on free market policies of privatization, fiscal austerity, elimination of trade barriers, and deregulation.

**Tacit Knowledge** The opposite to formal, codified or explicit knowledge. Tacit knowledge is knowledge embedded in a person and can be acquired only through personal experience and social contact.

**Terms of Trade** The ratio between the index of export prices and the index of import prices. It is used as a measure of country's economic health. If country's terms of trade are improving it means that it can buy more imports for every unit of exports.

**Transaction Costs** Costs incurred in market exchange and in overcoming market imperfections. They are search and information costs, bargaining and decision costs, and policing and enforcement costs. High transaction costs can prevent market exchange.

**Triangular Trade** Trading system operating between West Africa, the Caribbean and Europe exchanging slaves, primary commodities and manufactured goods.

**Useful and Reliable Knowledge** Knowledge of natural phenomena linked to technology and technology advancement. It can be seen also as a pool of best-practice knowledge

**Vertical Integration** Process in which firm acquires further stages of the same production path, such as when a manufacturer acquires its supplier and/or distributor.

**'Wimbledon Effect'** British financial institutions and the City of London's dependence on foreign banks.

**World-Systems Theory** Or World-System Analysis, is a macro-scale approach to the study of global and world history first developed by the sociologist Immanuel Wallerstein. It emphasizes the emergence of a world economic system and analyses the power structures and relations between different world areas.

# INDEX

# Index

# Index

# Index

Washbrook, David   322
Watson, Andrew   70, 71
Weber, Max   1, 20, 38, 55, 85
Weingast, B. R.   83
Western imperialism   31, 75, 287, 289, 291
West Indies
     developing trade to   109
     wealth of   111, 117 n.46
whale oil   168
White Lotus (1796–1804)   288
Williams, Eric   28, 113
Williamson, Jeffrey G.   7, 145, 283 n.11, 328
windmills development   70–1
women
     education and labour participation   86
     and fertility in China   85
Wong, R. Bin   32, 38
workhouse system   177
World Bank   238, 253, 264, 337

world economy and global environment
     4–7, 157
     Anthropocene   169–71
     biological exchanges (1492–1800)   158–62
     Industrial Revolution   165–8
     plantation system of America   163–5
World Systems School   54
world-systems theory   218
world trade. *See* global trade
Wrigley, E. A.   22, 28, 175
Wu Chengming   31

Yangzi Delta   21, 22–3, 32, 208
yellow fever   163

Zacatecas   274
Zahedieh, Nuala   107, 108, 113
zamindars   323
Zanden, Jan Luiten van   40
Zhang Zhidong   291
Zheng Yangwen   121